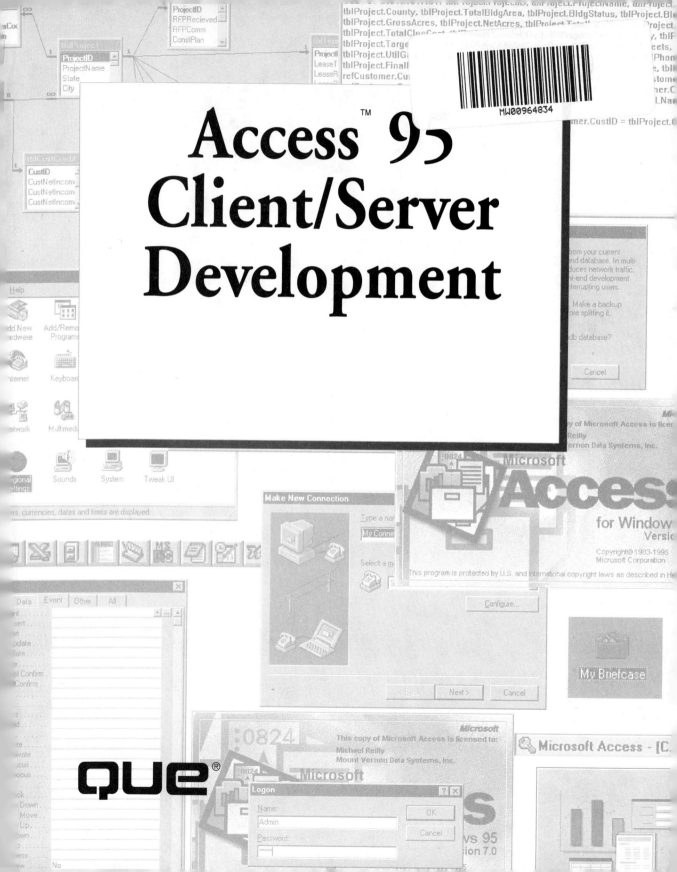

Access 95™
Client/Server
Development

que®

Access^{TM} 95 Client/Server Development

Written by

Michelle A. Poolet
Michael Reilly

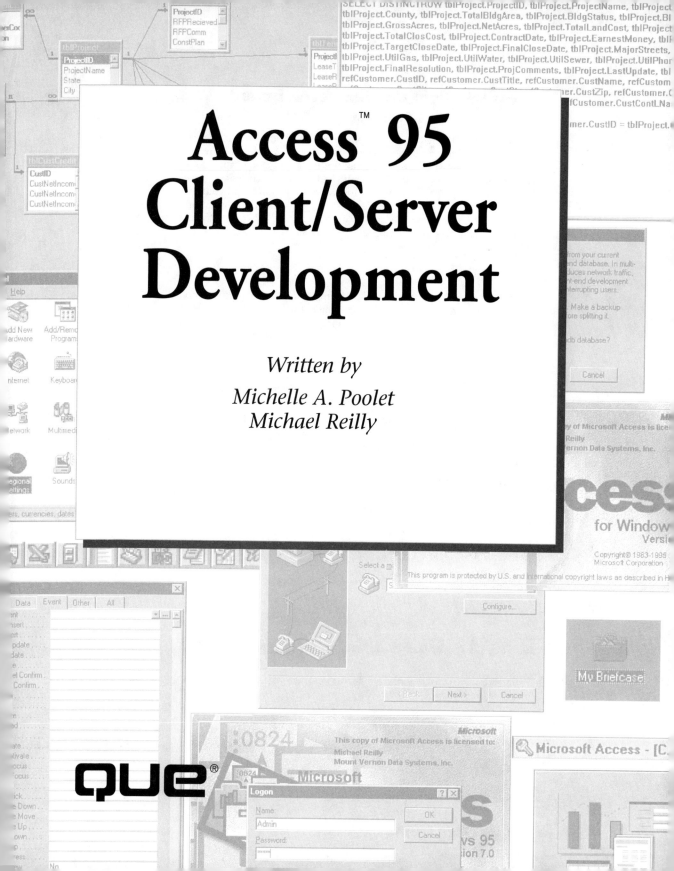

Access 95 Client/Server Development

Copyright© 1996 by Que® Corporation.

Library of Congress Catalog No.: 96-67560

ISBN: 0-7897-0366-1

98 97 96   6 5 4 3 2 1

Interpretation of the printing code: the rightmost double-digit number is the year of the book's printing; the rightmost single-digit number, the number of the book's printing. For example, a printing code of 96-1 shows that the first printing of the book occurred in 1996.

Screen reproductions in this book were created by using Collage Plus from Inner Media, Inc., Hollis, NH.

Composed in *Stone Serif* and *MCPdigital* by Que Corporation

Credits

President
Roland Elgey

Publisher
Joseph B. Wikert

Editorial Services Director
Elizabeth Keaffaber

Managing Editor
Sandy Doell

Director of Marketing
Barry Pruett

Publishing Manager
Fred Sloane

Acquisitions Editor
Al Valvano

Product Director
Robin Drake

Production Editor
Don Eamon

Assistant Product Marketing Manager
Kim Margolius

Technical Editor
Mark Robinson

Technical Specialist
Nadeem Muhammed

Acquisitions Coordinator
Bethany A. Echlin

Operations Coordinator
Patricia J. Brooks

Editorial Assistant
Andrea Duvall

Book Designers
Ruth Harvey
Kim Scott

Cover Designer
Barbara Kordesh

Production Team
Stephen Adams
Kim Cofer
Anne Dickerson
Chad Dressler
DiMonique Ford
Jessica Ford
Trey Frank
Amy Gornik
Jason Hand
Sonja Hart
Aleata Howard
Clint Lahnen
Bob LaRoche
Michelle Lee
Julie Quinn
Laura Robbins
Bobbi Satterfield
Kelly Warner
Todd Wente
Paul Wilson
Jody York

Indexer
C. Small

*To my mom, **Yvonne Poolet Williams**, who might not have understood what I was doing but who always was there, nevertheless. Way to go, Mom!*

*To my parents, **Philip and Margaret Reilly**, who have always encouraged me to write, and who have supported us in so many ways while we were starting our own business. And to my partner and co-author, **Michelle Poolet**, without whom this book would not have been possible.*

About the Authors

Michelle A. Poolet, M.C.I.S., University Of Denver, is a cofounder and President of Mount Vernon Data Systems, Inc., a computer consulting and database applications development company. She has 29 years of experience in data management, analysis, and processing on computer systems ranging from mainframes to PCs. She has worked in the fields of natural resources, medical and health care, the aerospace sciences, and academe. For three years Ms. Poolet was a member of the technical support and software development team of a prominent database management system vendor. She has, at various times in the past, held the position of Operations Manager, Telecommunications Division; Graduate Program Advisor, Telecommunications and Computer Information Systems Division; and Director, Personal Computer Skills Division for the University College, University of Denver, Denver, Colorado. She has developed and currently teaches courses in database theory, design, and programming for the Women In Computer Science Program and for the Computer Information Systems Division at the University College. She authored the SQL Handbook for database programming (*Get By in SQL*), which is used in those courses. She jointly authored a book for Boyd & Fraser Publishers, *The Acumen Series: MS-Access V2.0*, and has served as technical editor for many books published by Macmillan Publishers. Ms. Poolet is a member of the Advisory Council, Women In Computer Science Division, and a member of the Dean's Advisory Council, University College, University of Denver.

Michael Reilly has 24 years of experience in computer data processing, including extensive experience on DEC's VAX series 780/785, SEL's 32/75, the CDC 3600 and Xerox 9300. He has been involved with personal computers since 1984. His background includes programming in FORTRAN, and developing applications in Microsoft Access, Oracle, and Progress. He has worked on the VMS, UNIX, DOS, Windows, and Windows NT operating systems. Mike has held positions in management, research, software design and development, scientific data processing, computer sales and installation, training and support, and technical writing. In 1990, he cofounded Mount Vernon Data Systems, Inc., a consulting company that specializes in client/server database applications. He is a Microsoft Certified Trainer for Windows NT, and has coauthored two books on Microsoft Access. Mike has an M.A. in Physics, from Queens' College, Cambridge University. You can reach him on CompuServe, at **72421,1336**, or via the Internet, at **72421.1336@compuserve.com**.

Acknowledgments

To our project manager, **Al Valvano**, who was great to work with even when he was bugging us for the next chapter, we wish to acknowledge a great debt. Thank you, Al.

To our development editor, **Robin Drake**, who gave us tremendous moral support when we needed it, thank you!

To our copy and production editor, **Don Eamon**, who negotiated dangerous territory during the author review period, good work!

To the **Microsoft Access Development team**, which brought to the desktop computer the best little database management system in the business; don't stop now! Keep up the good work!

We'd Like to Hear from You!

As part of our continuing effort to produce books of the highest possible quality, Que would like to hear your comments. To stay competitive, we *really* want you, as a computer book reader and user, to let us know what you like or dislike most about this book or other Que products.

You can mail comments, ideas, or suggestions for improving future editions to the address below, or send us a fax at (317) 581-4663. For the online inclined, Macmillan Computer Publishing now has a forum on CompuServe (type **GO QUEBOOKS** at any prompt) through which our staff and authors are available for questions and comments. The address of our Internet site is **http://www.mcp.com** (World Wide Web).

In addition to exploring our forum, please feel free to contact me personally to discuss your opinions of this book. You can reach me on CompuServe at **74671, 3710**, or through the Internet at **avalvano@que.mcp.com**.

Thanks in advance—your comments will help us to continue publishing the best books available on computer topics in today's market.

Al Valvano
Acquisitions Editor
Que Corporation
201 W. 103rd Street
Indianapolis, Indiana 46290
USA

Contents at a Glance

Client/Server Concepts

Designing and Prototyping

Building the Application

Completing the Process

Upgrading the Application

Administering the App

Appendixes

Contents

6 Establishing the Ground Rules   153

7 Using Access as a Prototyping Tool   175

13 Building the Run-Time Application   339

IV Completing the Process   365

14 Communicating with Other Applications   367

15 Creating Help Files   399

16 Tuning the Access 95 Application — **457**

V Upgrading the Application   489

VI Administering the Application 547

19 System Administration 549

20 Replication with Access 95 573

VII Appendixes   637

A Tables for the REA Sample Database   639

B The WinHelp V4 Macros   661

Index   667

Introduction

Welcome to *Access 95 Client/Server Development*, a book about one of the most exciting and dynamic technologies in the computer database industry today. With databases moving from a traditional support role (a static repository for corporate data) to a more interactive, everyday part of company operations, it becomes necessary to understand more about how to exploit the power of the database. Client/server architecture, a technique that has been around for several years, is an excellent vehicle on which to base this exploitation, in that the client/server model seeks to split the data processing load and to place the data and software applications where they are most useful. By combining the two concepts, databases and client/server architecture, you have an end result that is greater than the sum of its parts. In this book we present the component pieces that make up the whole, and also give ideas on how to use this integrated technology.

This book is not a keystroke book. The chapters are structured to address areas of functionality or operation. Within each area the topic is explained in a generic sense, drawing on theory when appropriate. Then we look at how the topic is implemented in the realm of Microsoft Access for Windows 95 and, in the later chapters, Microsoft SQL Server. We also strive to present the business perspective—that is, how to exploit the technology and increase productivity, thereby (hopefully) gaining some competitive advantage for your company.

How This Book Is Organized

This book is grouped into seven parts. Each part organizes the chapters into groupings of related chapters. Each section builds on chapters that come before, so you can progress through the book in a logical manner, based on your individual skill level. The parts of this book are shown in the following sections.

Part I: Client/Server Concepts

Part I covers background information, Chapters 1 through 4. This part of the book sets the stage for what is to follow.

In Chapter 1, "Client/Server, What Is It?" we cover the concept of a client/server architecture, what it is and how it is applied to database structures and business models.

In Chapter 2, "The Front Office/BackOffice Concept," we explore more in depth the two-layer concept of client/server architecture, and demonstrate how readily Access 95 lends itself to this model.

In Chapter 3, "The Application Development Environment," we examine the hardware and operating system requirements to implement a client/server solution.

In Chapter 4, "Getting By in SQL '92—Structured Query Language," we work through Structured Query Language, the programming language used for all major relational database management system intercommunication.

Part II: Designing and Prototyping the Application

This part covers client/server software design techniques, Chapters 5 through 9. In this part of the book we get busy building the prototype for the client/server application, and we do it in Access 95.

Chapter 5, "Client/Server Database Application Design Fundamentals," goes through application design fundamentals, so that you will have a good idea of what you are going to do and why, before you actually start coding.

In Chapter 6, "Establishing the Ground Rules," we establish the basics concerning relationships between database entities and the various types of entities we will enforce.

Finally, in Chapters 7, "Using Access as a Prototyping Tool," and 8, "Adding Functionality to Your Prototype," we get into some application-building.

Chapter 9, "Navigation: How to Get from Here to There," concentrates mainly on navigation issues within the application.

Part III: Building the Application

Managing and securing the client/server application, and then creating/distributing a run-time application are covered, respectively, in Chapters 11, 12, and 13.

Like Chapter 9, Chapter 10, "Making the Right Connections," also concentrates on navigation issues, but this chapter explores these issues as they apply outside the application.

Chapter 11, "Managing Transactions," covers transactions, what they are, and how to implement them in the Access 95 environment. We also discuss concurrency control and record locking in Access, and the ramifications of moving to a back-end server system with a different transaction/concurrency model.

In Chapter 12, "Securing the Access 95 Application," we explore the Access 95 security model in depth.

Now that you have an application ready to roll, how will you distribute it? Whether you are considering internal distribution to your corporate end users or external distribution as shrink-wrapped software, Chapter 13, "Building the Run-Time Application," walks you through the process of creating a run-time version of your application.

Part IV: Completing the Process

This part covers inter-application communications, and includes Chapter 14, "Communicating with Other Applications." Part of the power of client/server technology is the ability to access data, database and non-database, wherever it happens to reside, from a common user interface. Access 95 and the other products of the Microsoft Office suite share the capability to "talk" to each other, and seamlessly transfer data from one application to another, or send it across the Internet via electronic mail. In Chapter 14, you see just how this is done.

Chapter 15, "Creating Help Files," covers authoring on-line help. One subject area that the authors have found has little documented support is on-line help. No application claiming to be Windows-compliant can have on-line help. So, taking the problem in hand, the authors researched and put together a comprehensive demonstration of how to build on-line help, using only the toolkit provided with WinHelp 4, the 32-bit Microsoft Help compiler.

Chapter 16, "Tuning the Access 95 Application," is all about Access 95 performance and tuning.

Part V: Upgrading the Application

This part covers transitioning the Access 95 back end to Microsoft SQL Server (versions 4.2 and 6.5), Chapters 17 and 18.

In Chapter 17, "Transitioning to Another Back-End DBMS," we discuss the reasons why you would want to port the homogeneous Access 95 application to a more powerful, more robust server back end—in effect, converting the application from a file server format to a client/server format.

In Chapter 18, "Upsizing Techniques," we follow through with three separate techniques on how to effect the transition.

Part VI: Administering the Application

Two chapters in this part, 19 and 21, cover more performance and tuning. The chapters on performance and tuning are distributed throughout the book, where they will be more relevant and useful.

Chapter 19, "System Administration," is more about system administration in the server environment, and tips and techniques to avoid problems before they happen.

Chapter 20, "Replication with Access 95," goes into depth on database replication, the Access 95 way. Replication from both Windows 95 and Windows NT is explained and demonstrated, with appropriate cautions for its use and warnings against misuse.

Chapter 21, "Client/Server Performance and Tuning," concentrates on performance and tuning in the full client/server environment, including a primer on network administration.

Factors affecting the human part of the client/server equation are covered in Chapter 22, "The Human Factor." Too often, the human factor is ignored in application development. This chapter explores the dynamics of workgroup computing, the special needs required by telecommuters, and how to introduce an emerging application to the end-user community.

Part VII: Appendixes

Appendix A, "Tables for the REA Sample Database," is the set of tables that comprise the REA database, in case you do not have ready access to a CD-ROM drive and want to follow along as we develop the REA application.

Appendix B, "The WinHelp V4 Macros," is a comprehensive listing of the WinHelp 4 macros, which you can use to enhance your on-line help systems.

About the CD-ROM

The accompanying CD-ROM contains code and database files that we have used throughout the book. The disk also contains demo software and guided tours of CASE tools (LogicWorks' ERWin & BPWin, the Chen & Associates ER Workbench, and S-Designor by PowerSoft/Sybase), Help authoring software (SolutionSoft's Help Breeze, WinWare's Visual Help, and Blue Sky Software's RoboHelp), and utility packages (Black Moshannon System's *SPEED* Ferret and All Seas' Octopus).

Access 95, when used either as a stand-alone system or as the client end of a client/server application, is an exciting product. It puts the fun back in database application development, with its support of declarative referential integrity and business constraints. The powerful Visual Basic for Applications is the alternative programming language for Access 95, and the combination of Visual Basic for Applications, Structured Query Language, and Open Database Connectivity to a broad range of back-end servers gives you unparalleled power and flexibility. As database application developers, we have spent many fruitful hours with this product, since its introduction three years ago. We hope you get as much benefit and satisfaction out of Microsoft Access as we have.

Who Should Read This Book?

Access 95 has many faces. It's a desktop database management system that can be used by people who have no prior knowledge of database design or programming. With Access 95 and assistance from its Wizards, the beginner can build applications that get things done.

Access 95 also is a powerful object/relational database environment that offers to advanced users and application developers a rich environment for developing file/server and client/server applications.

The core of Access 95 is the Jet database engine, which is highly programmable and supports Open Database Connectivity. This engine provides a very powerful and flexible platform for applications that integrate other software packages and are able to communicate through electronic mail and across the Internet.

Access 95 Client/Server Development is aimed at a wide range of readers, from technical managers to database application designers to programmers, and all in between. Certain portions of this book may appeal to specific sections of this population, obviously, but we were careful to try to keep it interesting throughout. The book assumes that the reader is an information systems professional in some capacity, and that the primary reason for reading this book is to become acquainted with client/server systems.

Some readers will have experience with database systems at the mainframe level and may be contemplating downsizing to a client/server solution. Other readers will have developed or worked with desktop database management systems and are ready to upsize to a client/server application running on the local area network. And still others may already have a client/server system in place that isn't working too well, and are looking for ways to make it better.

Throughout this book, you will find explanations of concepts that start from the theoretical and progress to show how these concepts are implemented by the software. You then judge for yourself if the software is doing an adequate job of carrying out the intent of the theory. The purpose of this approach is to give you as much background as possible in each subject area, and not limit you to a single-vendor interpretation. Therefore, this book may readily appeal to designers and technical managers, who need to know more than the immediate software environment to make things happen correctly.

This book is built around the development of a client/server application, with a lot of code examples and programming techniques and tips. Therefore, it should give value to database programmers who have not yet ventured into client/server applications programming.

This book, however, isn't just a book about technology. It also points out how, when, and where the technology can be used to exploit a situation and give the competitive edge to the reader. Therefore, it should be useful to management. It will certainly give management personnel a view into client/server applications development, and how uncertain the time line or the bottom line can be.

Mostly, this book is written for database developers, those people to whom entity modeling and data normalization are the bread and butter of life. We tried to pack every page with information and tips on the capabilities and limitations of the title software, Access 95, and what it can do for you in a development environment. We hope we've succeeded in making this a useful and interesting volume to which you can refer as the need arises.

This book assumes that you have at least a handshaking acquaintance with Access, perhaps from a previous version of the product. Although every attempt was made to carefully explain procedures used in the book, you are expected to know what to do when given a directive such as, "open a form in design mode." You are not expected to have a working knowledge of Microsoft SQL Server, although if you are contemplating a client/server application with Access 95 on one side and Microsoft SQL Server (or some other SQL-compliant server database management system) on the other, it may benefit the reader to become familiar with the environments in which you will be working.

Database Developers

Relational database developers (and those in training) will feel right at home with this book. Although the Microsoft terminology is not classically relational, we made every effort to bridge the gap between the two and still make the material understandable. As a database developer, certain chapters will be of immediate interest to you:

- Chapter 4, "Getting By in SQL '92—Structured Query Language," which highlights the changes between the old standard, SQL '86-'89, and the new SQL '92.
- Chapter 5, "Client/Server Database Application Design Fundamentals," which gives directions on how best to design in the Access 95 environment.
- Chapter 6, "Establishing the Ground Rules," spells out the implementation of the four database integrities in the Access 95 environment.

Technical Managers

Programmers tend to get mired down with the many technical details involved in developing an application, such as how to write the most optimal piece of code. Although it's certainly impressive to have an intimate relationship with a development environment, this often stands in the way of an accurate assessment or comparison of the environment with other products available to do the same task.

Technical managers must make the decision as to which development product and which toolkit or workbench will be used within an organization and whether these environments are effective and will pass the test of time. Based on internal research and testing, a new development product is chosen for evaluation. Then, based on performance during the evaluation period, the new product is either chosen as a corporate standard or rejected.

To assist with this decision-making process and the evaluation of Access 95 as a client/server development tool, technical managers may find of special interest the following sections in the book:

- Chapter 1, "Client/Server, What Is It?" which presents the overall view of client/server technology and development, and how Access 95 fits into the picture.
- Chapter 22, "The Human Factor," which delves into the human component of client/server and workgroup computing.

Project Team Leaders

All development groups, regardless of size, usually have some sort of project or technical leader who is responsible for overseeing design discussions and making final technical decisions. To be able to provide sufficient input as a project leader, you must be familiar with virtually all major features of the product you are working with. This book is of great value in determining which features of Access 95 can be used to produce the desired result in a manner suitable to your needs.

After reading this book, all project managers should have an understanding of what efforts are required to develop an entire application, using Access 95 and a counterpart back-end server. We consistently tried to point out how to get the job done in an efficient, effective manner, so that "version 1" makes it out the door on time. To jump-start the process, project leaders may want to check out the following chapters:

- Chapter 2, "The Front Office/BackOffice Concept," to get an idea of the scope of the client/server project.
- Chapter 5, "Client/Server Database Application Design Fundamentals," to get an idea of the standards that should be set during team development of a client/server application.
- Chapter 15, "Creating Help Files," to better evaluate the Microsoft WinHelp 4 compiler and Workbench.
- Chapter 17, "Transitioning to Another Back-End DBMS," to understand the reasons why you will eventually need to upgrade the server portion of your Access 95 application to a more robust, non-Access database management system.

Database Programmers

Database programmers must get the design implemented, make sure that the application does everything that everyone wants it to do, and get it done on time (and within budget). This never-ending challenge certainly can be aided by the rich set of tools provided in the Access 95 environment. Here's some suggested reading, just to get you started:

- Chapter 4, "Getting By in SQL '92—Structured Query Language," to brush up on your SQL programming skills for those ODBC calls.
- Chapter 7, "Using Access as a Prototyping Tool," to get you started in the Access 95 environment.
- Chapter 8, "Adding Functionality to Your Prototype," to extend the static prototype into a fully operational application.
- Chapter 10, "Making the Right Connections," how and when to link to non-Access data sources.
- Chapter 11, "Managing Transactions," on transaction management and concurrency control.
- Chapter 13, "Building the Run-Time Application," on how to build a run-time version of the application for distribution purposes.

Power Users

Power users are the gems of the user community. These are the folks who, with some prompting as formal training, can easily become system administrators, database administrators, or even database programmers. They are inquisitive, self-motivated, and agile of mind. This is not to say that they don't cause serious consternation to a tightly run, well-organized IS department! Their constant efforts to break out of the mold, to do things "just a little bit better," have caused many sleepless nights for IS managers.

Power users, you may want to read the whole book thoroughly, and, to get you started:

- Chapter 1, "Client/Server, What Is It?" to get a full understanding of what the client/server paradigm is.
- Chapter 2, "The Front Office/BackOffice Concept," to get you started on designing proper client/server (or at least file/server) applications.
- Chapter 22, "The Human Factor," to help you understand some of the issues that developers face during the construction of a new application, and why your colleagues in the user community sometimes behave so strangely.

System and Security Administrators

To these people falls the job of making sure that the physical and operating systems layer of IS is functional and secure. Here is a suggested reading list to get you started:

- Chapter 3, "The 95 Application Development Environment," a checklist of the physical and operating system components for a well-functioning client/server environment.
- Chapter 12, "Securing the Access 95 Application," for a full discussion of the Access 95 security model.
- Chapter 16, "Tuning the Access 95 Application," performance and tuning in the Access 95 environment.
- Chapter 19, "System Administration," system administration and security procedures in the Microsoft SQL Server environment.
- Chapter 21, "Client/Server Performance and Tuning," performance and tuning in the full client/server environment.

Database Administrators

Database administrators are responsible for the care and feeding of the database management system. Often, the responsibility of table, view, index, and constraint creation falls to the database administrator, in that the database administrator is in a better situation to have a good handle on the physical implementation issues than anyone else on the application development team.

As a database administrator, you may want to get started on the following chapters:

- Chapter 6, "Establishing the Ground Rules," for a discussion on the data types supported by Access 95.
- Chapter 7, "Using Access as a Prototyping Tool," for a discussion on how to build the tables and relationships and how to use declarative integrity in the Access 95 environment.
- Chapter 16, "Tuning the Access 95 Application," performance and tuning for the Access 95 database.
- Chapter 19, "System Administration," for database administration issues when you have ported to a second database management system on the back end.

■ Chapter 20, "Replication with Access 95," for issues regarding database replication and distribution.

Before You Begin

There are no warnings that we need give you before you begin to read this book. However, we would like to give you a word of advice. Don't get part way through this book and decide that—because of the ease of use of the products involved—you can go out and intelligently bid a client/server project! Please take the time to read (at least skim) through the entire volume. There are a lot of traps and gotchas to beware. Some tasks that seem relatively straightforward will, in fact, be much more time-consuming than you originally thought. So please, do take the time to review this book in its entirety.

Access 95 Does Windows

Microsoft Windows 95 and Windows NT (both Workstation and Server) are 32-bit operating systems that supply a graphical user interface (GUI) for ease of use and programmability. Access 95 is a 32-bit application, and, therefore, must run on one of these operating systems. Additionally, Access 95 joins in a client/server architecture with server database management systems that most likely will be running in a Windows NT Server, NetWare, or UNIX environment.

GUIs offer a more sophisticated and user-friendly environment than a command-driven interface such as DOS. Windows works in an intuitive fashion, allowing you to easily switch tasks and share information between applications. Windows also offers task-switching, virtual-memory management, drag-and-drop functionality, and standard conventions for common operations. Although overwhelmingly embraced by computer users everywhere, developers traditionally have been faced with the added burden of building applications in the extremely complex Windows environment.

To ease the burden of Windows application development, Microsoft has enhanced the Access 95 product with an incredibly rich set of tools and assists. This book assumes that the reader is familiar with completing user-oriented tasks in Windows, such as opening, closing, moving, and resizing windows. Before developing in Windows, you first must have a thorough understanding of how Windows programs "look and feel." There are books on how to design Windows interfaces, but actual hands-on experience is much more valuable.

Access 95 makes developing robust Windows database applications a rapid and enjoyable process. Database application development used to require a roomful of highly skilled designers and programmers, with extensive mappings of the data in storage hung on the walls. Access 95 has turned this around, so that a single database programmer—using the Access 95 toolkit—can produce a working prototype in a matter of days, and a production system in just a few weeks.

Features of Access 95

Access 95 contains a broad and ambitious set of features ranging from its form de-signer to transparent support of all the popular database formats. This book covers the following features of Access 95:

- The Jet, the core or engine, the heart of the Access 95 database management system, which manages data in storage and works with other database compo-nents to respond to user queries.

- The Query Engine, which parses and optimizes user queries, supports the most current standard of Structured Query Language (SQL), and calculates (using cost-analysis algorithms) the most effective way to resolve a query.

- The Open Data Connectivity (ODBC) interface and the ISAM interface, which allow Access applications to use non-native data as though it were stored in an Access 95 database.

- The Graphical User Interface, complete with Wizards, which allows all levels of users and developers to create sophisticated applications through the Menu Manager, the form design capability, and the report builder.

- The Visual Basic for Applications interface to the Access 95 Data Access Objects (DAO), which allows database programmers to manipulate the highly powerful Jet database engine and produce highly flexible and sophisticated applications.

- The WinHelp 4 compiler and Workbench, which are distributed on the Access 95 Developers' Toolkit along with the dynamic-link libraries needed to create a run-time version of an Access 95 application.

Conventions Used in This Book

A common set of terms and naming conventions is recommended throughout this book to maximize the clarity of the information. Every environment, whether a pro-gramming environment or a pool hall, has a set of terms and commonly accepted jargon. These terms enhance communication between participants in a particular environment. Imagine what it would be like telling someone to break the racked balls with the cue stick without having defined these common terms for a game of billiards. Throughout this book, the following terms are used repeatedly:

- **Database**—A repository of stored data, generally thought of as a shared resource.

- **Database management system**—The set of interwoven programs that man-age the stored data, respond to queries from end users, and provide one or more programmable interfaces for application development.

- **Table**—Analogous to a file in the non-database world. Microsoft repeatedly and consistently uses the term, "file," when it is referring to a relational table.

- **Attribute**—Analogous to a field in the non-database world. Microsoft repeat-edly and consistently uses the term, "field," when it refers to a relational attribute.

- **Client**—One-third of the client/server architecture; the front end, the portion that comprises the client interface. It usually is graphical in design and resides on the client computer, the machine operated by the end user.
- **Server**—One-third of the client/server architecture; the back end, the portion that usually is a database management system (can be Access 95 or some other vendor's database product), and resides on a network server. The client and the server communicate through the network (the last third of the client/server architecture), and all three work together to get a job done.

Examples Used in the Book

A number of examples discussed in this book grow as the book progresses, providing an approach geared more toward hands-on application development, as opposed to writing limited mini-demos. This approach saves the time that otherwise would be required to set up a new example for each feature of Access 95 being discussed. If you don't understand a particular example, find where the example was introduced.

Why Access 95 Is for You

If you're skeptical about Access 95 or just want to see what features it has that its competitors don't, do yourself a favor and read this book. Access 95 sets a standard for desktop database management systems by which all others will be compared. No other database management system available today provides the ease of use, power, speed, and flexibility available with Access 95, nor does any other desktop database management system adhere to the relational model as well as Access 95 does. Access 95 fills a long-awaited gap in the database world, bringing to the desktop the power, flexibility, and relational functionality usually found only in server database management systems.

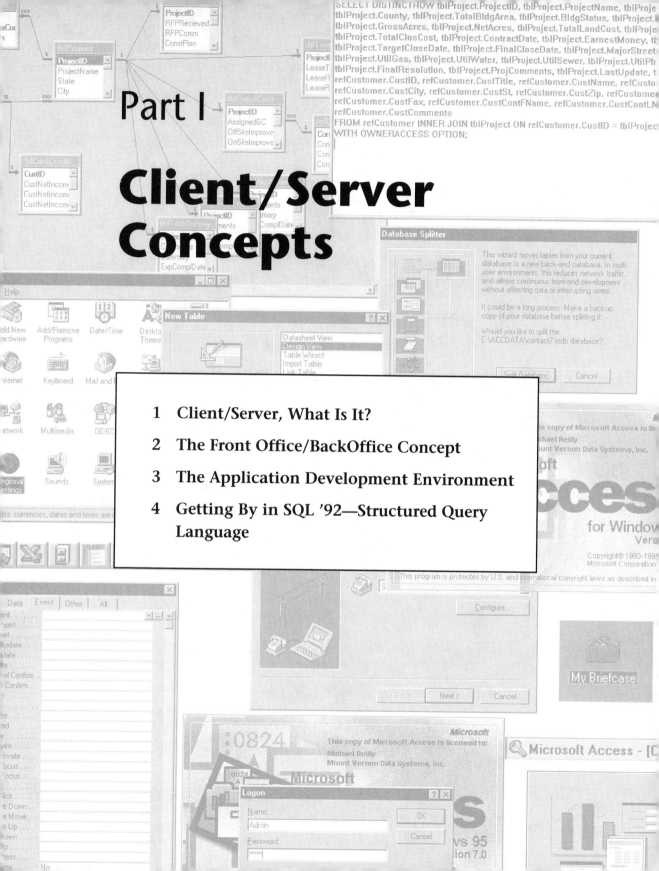

Part I

Client/Server
Concepts

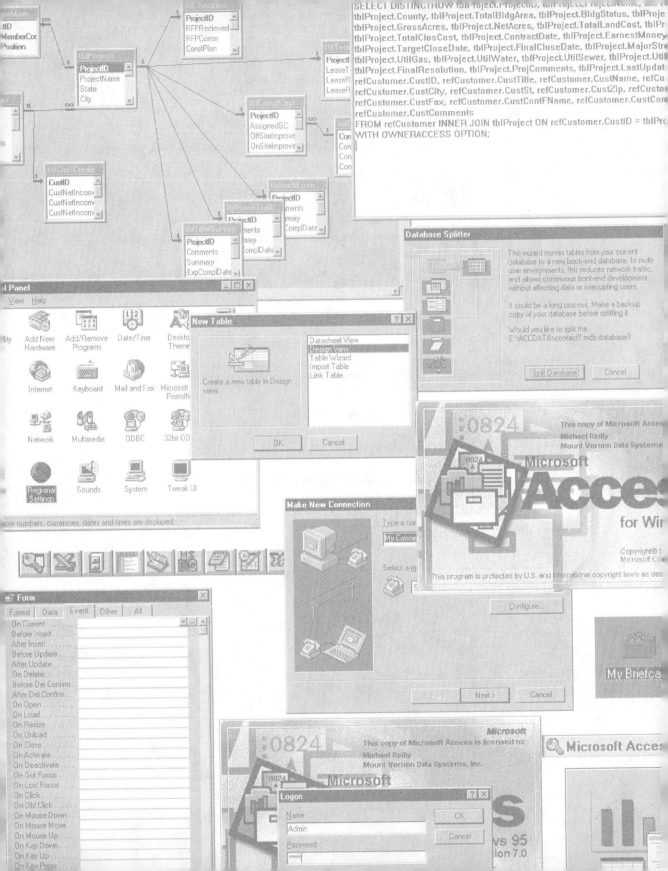

CHAPTER 1

Client/Server, What Is It?

Client/server is an adjective, a modifier—a way of doing things in computing. *Client/server architecture* is a model for distributing information system tasks; *client/server computing* is a method of implementing the model.

The client/server methodology has evolved over the past few years, and traditionally has been avaliable only to shops that were equipped with expensive and high-powered hardware/software combinations, which were staffed with professionals who had high levels of expertise in integrating dissimilar platforms—hardware and software—across unwieldy networks. This situation changed in the last year or so; we have seen the introduction of products that are built to support the client/server model.

We now have database management systems that are architected primarily as server systems, to answer multiple questions coming from many directions. We can purchase off-the-shelf "workbench software" to quickly craft highly functional client applications that query these dedicated servers. We can easily afford the hardware to put all this in place, and the new generation of operating systems that are fully network capable make the client/server paradigm not only fiscally realizable but also manageable.

In this chapter we will cover the following material:

- What the technical and business benefits of client/server computing are.
- How client/server computing supports today's business processes.
- How Access 95 fits into the picture of client/server computing.
- What's new in A95?
- A brief discussion of the internals of the MS-Access architecture.
- Requirements to run Access 95.

A Brief History of Computing Models

Back in the "good old days" of mainframes, the computing model was a *host* and *dumb terminal*. A group of video terminals with keyboards attached, which had little or no built-in intelligence, were connected to a large central computer. The central computer—the *mainframe*—sat in a large specially configured room, surrounded by air conditioning and devoted attendants in white lab coats. In response to the attentions of the "white-coats," the central computer did everything—it actually *was* the computing environment. The mainframe processed all the data, managed all the reads and writes to disk, routed all printout first to the printer buffers and then to the printers, and manipulated all the images on the attached terminals for data entry and display. Computer users initiated a request for data or for printout from the dumb terminal, but the central computer did it all, did it well, and did it fast.

The mainframe, however, had a few drawbacks. It required a small army of computer programmers to develop the instructions that would allow work to be done. The mainframe required high levels of expertise to understand its file system, discouraging ordinary people from trying to explore the data buried in its depths. The people who attended to the needs of the mainframe and the people who programmed instructions for the mainframe were highly skilled and well trained. As so often happens in a situation like this, these people developed their own community, which centered around the needs of the mainframe, and often failed to adequately respond to the needs of the business that owned the mainframe.

The Desktop Computing Modelprogram

As a business grows and changes, it must have more information, at an ever-increasing speed. The need for a faster, more responsive computing environment drove the development of tiny, self-contained computing units (desktop *personal computers*) that could be placed on a person's desk. This miniature mainframe also could do it all—data entry, data manipulation, and data reporting—from the comfort of a person's own office, with no interaction with the community of people who attended the mainframe. Software programs such as VisiCalc and Lotus 1-2-3 made statistical evaluations and "what-if" analysis possible in a fraction of the time it could be done on the mainframe. Applications packages such as WordStar and WordPerfect allowed office workers, with minimal training, to produce beautifully prepared documents. Ordinary office staffers began to understand that they could take control of the data and the presentation of the data, beyond anything the mainframe could do for them. Moreover, they could *investigate* the data.

In order to get information back from a highly defined, tightly structured computing environment, you must know the right questions to ask. In strategic planning for business, however, often the question is not well-formulated. Strategic planning requires the ability to "browse" the data, combining and recombining data items in seemingly illogical order, in an effort to garner new information. Mainframe methodology wasn't set up to support this kind of activity. Desktop computing—despite the limited amount of data that often was input into these tiny dynamos—enabled strategists to get a handle on what they needed to know.

However, desktop computing also had a few drawbacks. Each desktop computer became an "island of information." All computer users had their own ways of storing and presenting the data. Some used spreadsheet software to store data, others used word-processing documents, and still others used desktop database-management systems. With no controlling group to set standards for software, a plethora of types of packages evolved. It soon became the norm to find Lotus 1-2-3 and Microsoft Excel in use in the same department of a company. Some of these "islands of information" actually were very valuable, but additional technical constraints made sharing data between the desktop computers and the mainframe virtually impossible.

The Local Area Network (LAN) Model

Enter the era of the local area network. The LAN used physical wiring and layers of software to build connections between all these "islands of information" on the individual desktops. The idea was to link all the personal computers and allow the PC users to share files and to share peripheral equipment like printers and scanners. Eventually, the LAN was extended to include the mainframe, and (with lots of software assist and translation routines) finally data could be ported back and forth between the desktop computers and the mainframe.

The first LAN introduced its own type of computing model—*file-server computing*. All computers on a LAN are known as *nodes*, and the first LANs were either peer-to-peer or hierarchical in design. In a *peer-to-peer LAN*, one node could request a service from another node, such as "Send me a copy of that file on your disk," or "Print this for me on the printer to which you are attached." In a well-behaved peer-to-peer LAN, these services would be provided to the asker. The peer-to-peer LAN (see fig. 1.1) allowed each node to act as a server (a provider of file or print services to the rest of the network) whenever its services were needed, but actual data processing, file management, document handling, and screen painting all were handled by the individual desktop computer.

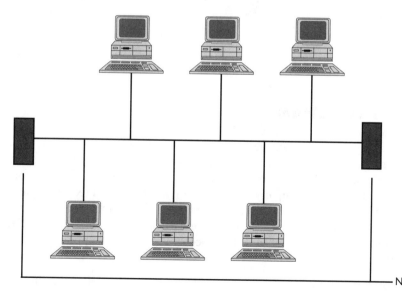

Fig. 1.1

The peer-to-peer computing model. Each computer is a "node" that can share files and printer services with all the other computers on the network.

Network nodes

The hierarchical LAN (see fig. 1.2) was configured a little differently, with a single server node that provided many services to all the other nodes, which inherited the differentiating name, *client*. Each client node can ask the server for a copy of a file stored on the server's hard disk, ask the server to print a document, ask the server to fax out a message, and on and on. The server node provided all system services, such as file management and document transfer, but the client nodes did all the actual data processing and screen presentation. It is at this point that the division of labor we have come to call "client/server" began.

Fig. 1.2

The hierarchical local area network, with a central controlling computer (the server) that directs communications between the client computers (client nodes) and provides file, print, and database services to all on the network.

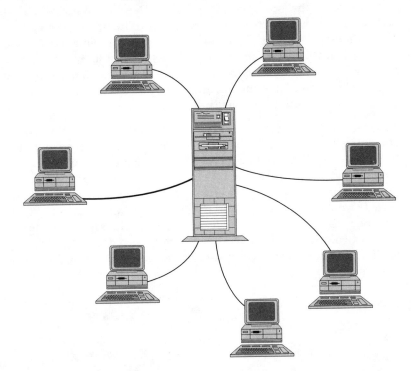

The Client/Server Model

The driving idea behind client/server computing is to split the work load and distribute it to all the components in a computing environment. There are many ways to configure a client/server environment but basically, it revolves around the concept of load balancing. The optimal client/server environment will be different for each company or each department of a company, depending on the needs and requirements of the business. The ideal is to have the server node(s) handle file management, control document transfer, perform some of the data processing (where appropriate) and have the client nodes do the other part of the data processing, handle data presentation, and screen painting.

A typical client/server computing environment is comprised of the following three major components:

- **The client**—The *client* is the (desktop) computer(s) that is requesting services of the server computer. Typically, the client machine is responsible for interpreting commands entered at the keyboard, mouse, or other input device, processing these commands, and (if additional processing is needed that it cannot provide) routing them to the appropriate device on the network. The client is responsible for painting the screen and controlling the personalization of the user's environment. It handles the presentation of data and commands that are sent from any of the server computers on the network.

- **The server**—The *server* is the computer that acts as a service provider to all the rest of the computers on a network. Typically, the server machine is responsible for system-level tasks: routing print requests to the appropriate printer, routing database queries to the correct database, returning files and applications to the client nodes on request, and acting as a communications hub for the fax modem.

- **The network** (and any "middleware") that connects client and server—without a network, client/server could not exist. The physical network—the wires and connectors—by themselves are only a beginning. Stacked on the physical wiring are layer upon layer of software that comprise the network operating system and communications protocols. Additionally, some client/server environments that require extremely fast response and/or need to handle high levels of activity—an OLTP (online transaction processing) database, for example—might have third-party "middleware" that manages the stream of commands and queries flooding against the server.

Client/server computing began as a departmental *IS* (information system) solution and now is moving into the enterprise arena, cutting across departmental and divisional boundaries, providing services for the entire corporation. In the process, it evolved in several directions, each to support a specific type of task. One form of client/server configuration is built to support high-volume transaction update environments (*OLTP*), another form is built to support *online analytical processing* (OLAP) or more commonly known as *data warehousing*. We explore each design in more detail in Chapter 5, "Client/Server Database Application Design Fundamentals."

The client/server division of labor traditionally has located the data (and its maintenance) on the server, while the user interface and all presentation schemes were placed on the client. With the maturing of the client/server paradigm and its capability to shadow the business processes, business rules and regulations are being encoded into the client/server structure. Companies have quickly adapted the technique of formalizing and standardizing business rules through their client/server applications. Historically, the business rules were stored either at the client in the user interface, or at the server in the database. This is the standard two-layer model of client/server computing. Lately, a new scheme has emerged that advocates storing business rules in a third layer, separate from both client and server. The result is the three-tiered client/server model, which, with the two-layer model, is explored in greater detail in Chapter 5, "Client/Server Database Application Design Fundamentals."

Tip

The authors' best reference for a complete discussion of client/server everything: *Essential Client/Server Survival Guide*. Robert Orfali, Dan Harkey, Jeri Edwards. Van Nostrand Reinhold, 1994.

Benefits of Client/Server Computing

In today's competitive business climate, every company from the industrial giants to the single-person corporation has to operate more efficiently than ever before. For some, this means downsizing; for others, efficient means business process reengineering. Client/server technology has made reengineering possible in many corporations. Actually, it is difficult to separate cause and effect. Introducing client/server concepts often requires a radical rethinking of the business processes. Effective reengineering, where the authority and responsibility are placed in the hands of the employees, requires that these employees have the necessary information, which is best achieved by client/server information systems.

Technical Benefits

The most obvious benefit of client/server computing in business is the capability to have many people accessing the same information simultaneously. It is important to realize that each person is not looking at a copy of the data, but at the same original data set. When changes are made by one person, these changes can quickly be seen by other users. Implicit in this concept is the requirement that one, and only one, place exists where the data is stored. Customer addresses, for example, may be stored in a centralized database, which is accessible to everyone who deals with the client—even indirectly. When a client places an order and the salesperson updates the client address information, shipping and accounting do not need to be notified—they automatically get the new address on both the shipping label and the invoice the next time they are generated.

Client/server technology allows *cross-platform computing* with the capability to combine data from disparate environments. In our example, the customer orders may be stored in a SQL Server database that runs on a Windows NT Server machine. Orders are actually entered by the sales staff, running an Access 95 application on Windows 95. The accounting department may be running an Oracle Financials system on a UNIX machine, which also is updated as part of the order entry process by the Access 95 application.

Fault-tolerant computing is easier to implement in a client/server environment. In a multi-server environment, with database replication, the user may not even notice if the main server is not operating. In the days when everyone was connected to a mainframe by dumb terminals, a system crash stopped all work until the mainframe was brought back up. The level of redundancy required to prevent this situation was partly responsible for the high cost of mainframe systems. Over-engineering was required to ensure that the parts did not fail. In a client/server environment this redundancy is achieved by installing several servers, which together cost a magnitude less than the mainframe, and spread the work load among them—with contingency plans for when problems occur. When the server is a high-end Windows NT system, RAID fault-tolerant disk subsystems can provide even more robustness to the operation.

RAID

RAID, or Redundant Array of Inexpensive Disks, is a scheme that can best be described as trying to change a flat tire on a car while driving down the highway at 90 miles an hour. Data is "striped" across multiple hard disks. The standard model for data storage places a file in multiple logically contiguous blocks or pages on a single hard disk, as many as are needed to contain the file. When striping is used, the logically contiguous blocks are scattered across multiple physical disks in an order known to the RAID controller. A file is broken into its component bytes, and the bytes are striped across the multiple disks. The RAID software then builds a "parity byte" for each *n* number of data bytes on disk, and staggers the storage of the parity bytes throughout the striped disks. In this way, when a hard disk fails, the RAID software and controller can rebuild the data from that disk on the "hot swap" hard disk that is always held in a ready state, poised to take over when one of the regular disks fails. Cool technique.

Business Advantages

The day-to-day benefit to a business that uses client/server computing is the increased productivity generated by better access to information. Resource sharing keeps cost down, and relatively inexpensive servers in the $10,000 to $30,000 range can replace the ultra-expensive mainframes.

Taking a longer-term view, client/server technology enables process reengineering, which may be needed for the survival of the company. Whether the goal is to eliminate the costs of centralized mainframe computing or to empower employees by providing them with information, the solution is likely a client/server-based system.

Today's business cycle for new product introduction is around 18 months. In this fast-moving world, two- or three-year design cycles for software development are totally out of place. Client/server technology allows rapid prototyping and development, and the quick deployment of new and improved applications, without major disruptions to the computing environment. A client/server application, for example, may be built with Access 95 as both the front end (client) and back end (server). As the volume of data grows, the back end may be upsized to a SQL Server database. The users will see no difference in their desktop interface because it is still an Access 95 application, but now it has regained the speed it had before the amount of data grew so large. If one department needs to retrieve only a limited subset of the data very quickly for a specific use, the database programmers can write a new front-end application, optimized just for this use by using Visual Basic, PowerBuilder, or another application development tool.

The rapid and economical development of client/server applications allows the company to respond to the changing conditions of the business.

Client/Server: The Model for Today's Business

Client/server technology has evolved hand-in-hand with successful businesses. If you need ammunition to convince your boss, your shareholders, your employees, or your customers that you should move toward the client/server model, consider this perspective. The industrial revolution brought us the Adam Smith model of centralized management with unskilled workers who were told just enough to do their jobs—nothing more. All decisions were made at or near the top and trickled down, as shown in figure 1.3. Sounds like mainframes surrounded by dumb terminals, doesn't it?

Fig. 1.3

The traditional organizational chart—the main-frame-and-dumb-terminal model, within which communication flows from the top down.

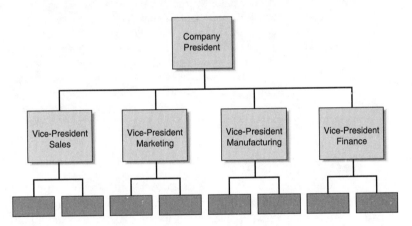

Then came the enlightened era, when employee empowerment was the rage. These "empowered" employees were uncomfortable because they had to make decisions in dealing with the customer but did not know how their contribution fit with the corporate goals. The analogy in this case is the spread of the personal computer on desktops, with all users going their own way.

Next came the management concept (or, perhaps, management "fad") of teams (represented by fig. 1.4), with the hope that the team would produce more than the sum of the individual talents—not unlike peer-to-peer networking, with shared resources available to every node.

Now, companies are reengineering around corporate values and company-wide goals that everyone understands. The strategic decisions are made by the leaders of the corporation; there is one set of rules, one common purpose, just as in client/server technology, which has the one common set of data that everyone can access. The daily decision-making is distributed to the employees of the corporation, in the same way as a client application makes some of its own decisions, and then goes to the corporate data repository when it needs more information, as shown in figure 1.5.

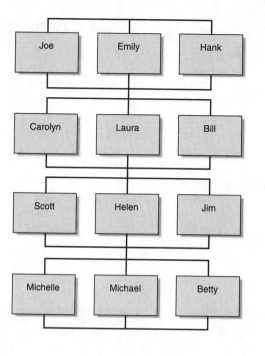

Fig. 1.4

Peer-to-peer—the "team" organizational model, within which communication flows to support the interaction between the team members.

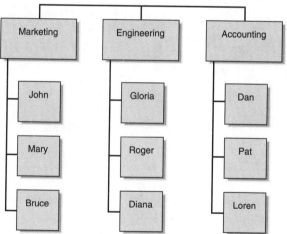

Fig. 1.5

The new organization— the client/server model, where communication flows across traditional boundaries (note the topmost line, connecting all users and departments) on an as-needed basis.

Client/server is the model on which business runs in the Information Age. It isn't being imposed on businesses by the computer community. The computer community has adopted the client/server model because it too must evolve to keep up with and reflect the needs of the business world.

Access 95 and Client/Server Computing

Microsoft Access 95 is a database management system that is at home on the desktop as much as it is on the back-end server (see fig. 1.6). Access 95 is composed of the database engine—Jet 3—which handles all the server tasks, such as file management and query resolution, and a front-end toolkit for building database client applications. Access 95 can be configured so that it is both an application to run on the client machines and a database that resides on the server. It can coordinate a local (client) database or databases with a server database(s). Because Access 95 supports the *Open Database Connectivity* model (*ODBC*), it can act as a front-end application to other Microsoft database management systems. It can, in support of ODBC, even act as a front-end application to back-end non-Microsoft database management systems.

Fig. 1.6

The Access 95 splash screen in the Windows 95 operating environment, your gateway to client/ server computing.

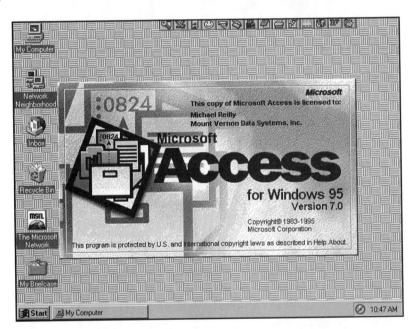

But why Access? A plethora of desktop and server database management systems are available, so you might select Access as your key development workbench for the following reasons:

- In all its renditions since its introduction three years ago, Access appeals to a wide range of users and developers, from novices to system integrators, because of the depth of its inherent capabilities and relative ease-of-use.

- Access 95 is a product that gives a tremendous amount of assistance to novice users (who often cannot even define what a database is), and allows them to build applications that get work done.

- Access 95 uses a powerful relational engine (the Jet) that is an industry leader in ODBC support and inter-database, inter-application connectivity.

- Access 95 has a rich workbench of tools for forms and reports development.

- Access 95 supports two industry-wide standard programming languages—the procedural programming language Visual Basic for Applications (for those who like lots of program code), and the non-procedural Structured Query Language— SQL (for those of you who just want to get the job done!).

- Access 95 is the database management system that provides closest adherence to the ANSI SQL-92 Standard, the database access language standard that is supported by nearly every vendor in the computer industry.

- Access 95 has the strongest support for the relational model of all desktop database management systems and arguably, of the server database management systems as well (good news for you database designers).

- It supports the updateable dynaset, view definition in the form of optimized compiled queries, a fully integrated data dictionary, full referential integrity— including cascading both updates and deletes (which previously had to be done in code).

- It exposes an exceedingly rich event model that allows for manipulation of nearly every property at run time, for maximum program control.

- Access supports a robust security model that allows full discretionary allocation of permissions throughout an application.

- Access was one of the first database management systems to support Object Linking and Embedding (OLE) technology, which allows inter-application communication and integration with other programs.

- Since version 2, Access has been empowered with the *Rushmore* technology, which enables the Jet engine to resolve complex queries with extreme quickness.

- Access 95 supports the full range of use, from single-user to file-server to client/ server environments, which means that you can scale your application across multiple hardware platforms and software operating systems, using the same front-end tools.

- Access 95 has a supplementary package—the Microsoft Access Developer's Toolkit, available at separate cost—that allows developers to compile run-time copies of their applications and develop full Help subsystems to complement, for distribution, either internally or externally—with no royalty strings attached.

The Access Advantage

Access 95 is a full-featured database application development package that can be used by a wide range of people. Computer users who need to put together quick databases for limited use can, with the assistance of the Wizards, build reasonably respectable and very functional applications without having to write code. Experienced developers can use Access 95 as a rapid-application development tool to put together prototype applications and databases and demonstrate proof-of-concept. All levels of database developers and database programmers can use the Access 95 environment to build databases and database applications, which in turn can be used in a multiuser, multi-programming client/server environment.

Wizards

An Access 95 Wizard is an encoded routine that steps you through building database objects and/or does so in a fraction of the time it takes you to do it yourself. Unlike the Cue Cards (used in earlier versions of Access and the entire Microsoft Office suite) that give you step-by-step directions on how to do something, the Wizards literally take over the keyboard, only stopping long enough to prompt the user for occasional input.

Strong Database Capabilities. Access 95 also is a powerful database engine that can multi-thread queries and provide concurrent access to multiple tables, either its own tables or those of another database management system. Access supports both pessimistic and optimistic locking, which can be modified at the programming level, and generally locks at the page level, which allows for fast and flexible modifications to the stored data (see Chapter 11, "Managing Transactions," for a full discussion on locking in the Access 95 environment).

Working from Multiple Sources. Access can integrate, present, and update data from diverse data sources. A form or report can, all at the same time, show data from a SQL Server database, an Oracle database, a dBASE file, and an Access internal reference table. The user who is looking at the data may not be aware that the data is being compiled from multiple data sources, with each source on a different computer.

Cost Efficiency of a Run-Time Environment. In this time of tightened budgets and cost cutting, Access 95 is a cost-effective product. Obviously, in the standard development environment, each developer needs a full copy of Access 95 in order to build the databases and assemble the applications. However, it is unnecessary to put a full copy of Access 95 on the desktop of each user. To create a run-time environment, on both client and server machines, you need only compile the data and application databases by using the Microsoft Access Developers' Toolkit (ADT), create an installation set (an Installation Wizard exists to step you through this task), and install where needed. Applications compiled with the ADT can be legally distributed with no further royalties owed to Microsoft. For the cost of a single copy of Access 95 and the Microsoft Access Developers' Toolkit for Windows 95, you can deliver professional-quality database applications to your organization or to your clients. Whether you are a corporate developer in search of cost-cutting measures or a consultant who wants to persuade a client to deploy your application, this approach can result in significant savings to all involved.

The run-time software takes up far less disk space than a full installation of Access 95, which may be a factor on client workstations. Because the run-time version of Access 95 does not include all the features of the development system, it will run in eight megabytes of memory. An additional benefit is that the run-time version can be configured so that the users can not look at or change the design of the tables, forms, and reports. You also can do the same with applications that are intended to run under a full version of Access 95, but the run-time software makes it easier to remove the menu options and capabilities that may allow a user to inadvertently damage the database.

Built-In Security. Access 95 has built-in security so that different users can be allowed varying degrees of access to data. Some users may need to view and edit data with no restrictions, others may be allowed only to read and modify certain tables, and yet another group may have read-only permissions. From the developer's perspective, the ability to control permissions means that it is unnecessary to develop different custom client applications for the various user groups. Figure 1.7 shows the main security screen for Access 95.

Fig. 1.7

The security options dialog box in Access 95, from which you can set user and group permissions.

Disadvantages of Using MS-Access

No system is perfect; no tool will do everything for everyone. This is as true in software packages as anywhere in the world. A software package, like a country, is defined by its boundaries. As a developer, you will push Access or any other product to its limits to extract the most value from your investment in learning that product. So it is important that you are aware of the major limitations of Access 95 before you begin to use it as a development tool. Although the following list may seem a bit alarming, forewarned is forearmed. With the knowledge you gain from the following list, you can move forward with your development projects, avoiding the pitfalls listed here, and plan appropriately:

- **No backward compatibility**—On its own, Access 95 cannot provide backward compatibility to previous versions of Access. It would be nice to be able to upgrade the server database to Access 95 and connect into it with older Access client applications but at the time of writing, backward compatibility was not an option. Out of the box, Access 95 will readily recognize and link to Access 2 databases, but Access 2 does not recognize Access 95 database files.

- **Access 95 cannot run in a 16-bit environment**—You need either a Windows 95 or a Windows NT operating environment in which to run the application. Don't try to bring down a copy of Access 95 from your 32-bit network apps server onto your 16-bit Windows or Windows for Workgroups machine. It just won't work.

- **No Support for distributed databases**—Although Access 95 has the new replication facility, it isn't a true distribution function. Access 95 manages its replicated databases through a manual synchronization, unlike the true distributed database scheme, which synchronizes through the use of a two-phase commit. *Two-phase commit* is a technique of synchronizing changes to stored databases by broadcasting the commits (instructions to commit changes to the physical database) throughout the group of databases participating in the distributed system.

- **Access doesn't offer a completely object-oriented programming environment**—Visual Basic for Applications 4, the programming language of Access 95, is an object-oriented programming language but, according to the purists, it falls short of being a true and full object-oriented environment. However, in the experience of the authors, Visual Basic for Applications 4 seems more than adequate for the task.

- **Access does not provide a programming workgroup environment**— One problem that the authors ran into is how to coordinate more than one developer who is working on the same .MDB file. Because all the objects for an application (forms, reports, program code, macros, and queries) are contained within a single file, coordinating development changes being made to an application when there are multiple programmers can be tricky. A high level of organization is a must for developers in this environment. Third-party packages are available that appear to do a reasonable job of controlling revisions and changes to data objects within an .MDB file. The authors have developed their own scheme, which works most of the time!

> **Tip**
>
> See REVISION.MDB on the companion CD-ROM.

- **Access 95 lacks a global change function that can search out and change data object names**—This lack can be especially frustrating if your client decides midway through a development effort that he has customers, not clients. Fortunately, some third-party packages are available to perform this task.

> **Tip**
>
> See the demo version of "*SPEED* Ferret" on this book's companion CD-ROM.

- **Access 95 has optional and discretionary security**—After security is turned on, a user must log on to the database. Passwords are optional. Security conforms to the discretionary model. Access 95 does have a concept of ownership; the creator of an object owns that object and must give other users permission to access or update that object. Data access permissions can be either read-only or full, and are assigned at the discretion of the security administrator. However, Access 95 alone does not provide the C2 level of security as defined by the U.S. Department of Defense. Access 95 has an encryption facility, but lacks an audit function for tracking accesses to the database.

C2-Level Security

C2 database security, as defined by the U.S. Department of Defense, requires an operating system or operating environment to meet the following standards:

- *Provide authentication*—Mandatory logon and password are required for access to the database.

- *Provide discretionary access control*—Access to certain objects is restricted to those users who have the appropriate security clearance.

- *Provide object reuse protection*—After an object is deleted or closed other users would have no way of accessing the deleted data or reading the contents of freed memory.

- *Provide auditing*—Each user's activities can be tracked, and access (or attempted access) to any protected object can be monitored.

- **Access does not provide access to the metadata repository, the data dictionary**—For those database designer/developers who are used to being able to access the full data dictionary, the Access 95 environment will be a disappointment. While it is possible to get very compete reports generated from the database documentor, portions of the data dictionary are virtually off-limits.

- **Access 95 does not have charge-back auditing built-in**—At the time of writing, the authors are aware of no third-party packages that can perform this function.

- **To back up an Access 95 database, the database must be off-line**—No access to the database, not even an attachment from other database applications, can happen during the backup.

- **No batch scheduler**—Access 95 is primarily designed as an interactive, event-driven environment, and as such provides no out-of-the-box support for batch program scheduling. The programming interface (Visual Basic 4) does, however, have a set of time and date functions, which makes possible program launch at predetermined times.

When Not to Use Access

Access 95 may not be the best tool for the following tasks:

- **Supporting very high levels of OLTP** (on-line transaction processing)— Access 95 was built as a general-purpose database management system. It was not optimized for high levels of on-line transaction processing.

- **Supporting extensive OLAP** (on-line analytical processing) **development**— Access 95 lacks the tools and architectural extensions necessary to enable true data warehousing.

- **Providing 7 by 24** (7 days a week, 24 hours a day) **service**—In order to back up, compact, or repair an Access 95 database, you first must bring it down. Database backups should be done as often as is appropriate for the value of the data. Compacting is necessary from time to time to recover the space made available when data or objects are deleted from the database. A database repair is needed from time to time to reestablish the internal pointers by which Access 95 functions.

What's New in Access 95 for Client/Server Development?

You've heard people say, "Third time's the charm." This may be the case with Access. This third iteration of a product that has revolutionized the desktop database world certainly is a keeper! If you are familiar with Access, if you used a previous version, then you may find some of your "wish-list" present in this not-exhaustive list of modifications and enhancements for Access 95. It really appears as though the Access development team listened to the feedback from users and incorporated the requested changes in this release.

Creating a Database with Wizards. Previous versions of Access included Wizards that helped the user to build tables, forms, reports, and queries. Access 95 takes the Wizards a step further, adding more Wizards that are capable of creating an entire database (see fig. 1.8). The list of available databases is limited, and it certainly will not produce a client-server application that meets corporate specifications right out of the box. Still, the videotape collection or Little League membership databases that it can generate are useful examples for a study in correct database architecture. These Wizards also are forerunners of more powerful Wizards, which in the future will be able to develop far more powerful applications.

Fig. 1.8

The Database Wizard, with which you can build predefined databases.

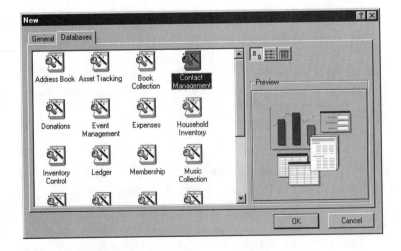

Intelligent Table Modifications. Table modification no longer must be handled in Design Mode. The database developer can, while viewing the table in Datasheet mode, add and delete columns. Although this may not be a feature that you would want to pass along to the user community at large, for the database developer/designer the ability to see a table with data in it and make adjustments and minor modifications is a real plus.

Normalizing Data with the Table Analyzer. Among the more powerful tools (from the database designer/developer's viewpoint) provided with Access 95 is the Table Analyzer Wizard. The primary purpose of this Wizard—as defined by Microsoft—is to convert flat files (spreadsheet files, files from contact managers, and so on) into a set of relational tables and give the novice user the ability to harness the power of the relational model without understanding relational theory. The Table Analyzer Wizard (see fig. 1.9) will not modify any database table without explicit permission from the user.

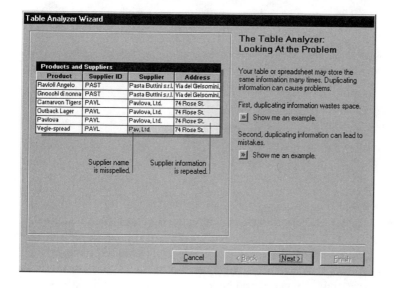

Fig. 1.9

The Table Analyzer Wizard, which analyzes the populated tables in your database and re-organizes them into logical groupings.

As any database designer/developer knows, data normalization is no trivial task. Usually, this process is accompanied by hours of intense scrutiny of the data items and their meanings, hair-pulling sessions where business rules and procedures are defined and redefined, and integration back and forth with entity-relationship models that may or may not be a true representation of the business environment. Therefore, I doubt that any serious database designer/developer would rely on the Table Analyzer Wizard to do data normalization! However, the authors have found that the Table Analyzer Wizard is a valuable check on what are believed to be fully normalized tables. It is also a reminder about those few tables we may have "constructively denormalized" for performance reasons! You can learn more about this topic in Chapter 6, "Establishing the Ground Rules."

Data Modeling

Data normalization and entity-relationship modeling are two techniques used by the database designer to develop clear, functional, and efficient database designs. Either technique can be used alone, although the authors strongly recommend using the two in tandem, and neither technique should be used without a full and coherent understanding of the business processes involved in the organization for which the database is being designed.

Data normalization, also known as *logical data modeling* or *the logical database design*, is a method of organizing data items into logical groupings based on the relationship of one data item to another. Algorithms and methods exist that are used to test the validity of these intra-data-item relationships, but the meaning and purpose of each data item must be clearly understood by the database designer. These logical groupings then become tables in a relational or object-oriented database. This technique is referred to as a *bottom-up design methodology*.

Entity-relationship modeling (*ERM*), also known as *conceptual modeling* or *the conceptual database design*, is a method of graphically representing the proposed database and the entities that will comprise the proposed database. The entities—customers, vendors, and product inventory—are related to each other in certain ways that are represented on the ERM: customers buy product and vendors supply product. The entities of the ERM translate to tables of a relational or object-oriented database. The ERM relationships also translate into the database, in a slightly different form from the entities. This technique is referred to as *top-down design methodology*.

For further reading on database design techniques, the authors recommend the following books:

- *Modern Database Management*, Fourth Edition; McFadden & Hoffer; Benjamin/Cummings Publishing Co., Inc., 1994.

- *Database Systems for Management*, Second Edition; Courtney & Paradice; Irwin, 1992.

Performance Analyzer. The Performance Analyzer Wizard (see fig. 1.10) is a cool tool that evaluates the table relationships and indexing schemes that you applied to the database in question. This Wizard generates a list of three types of optimizations: Recommendations, Suggestions, and Ideas. The Performance Analyzer Wizard is fully interactive in that you can take advantage of all or part of the Wizard's plan, or you can completely ignore it, whichever would be most appropriate for the situation. For more information on the Performance Analyzer Wizard, see Chapter 16, "Tuning the Access 95 Application."

Locating Data Is Easier. *Filter By Selection* is what Microsoft calls the capability to select a single data value in a datasheet or on a form, click the Filter By Selection icon on the top toolbar, and return a dataset restricted to that value. This feature makes finding subsets of information incredibly easy in Access 95. In figure 1.11, the cursor was placed in the city text box and the Filter By Selection icon was clicked. The results show all contacts in the city of Denver (note `Record 25 of 25 (Filtered)` at the bottom of the screen).

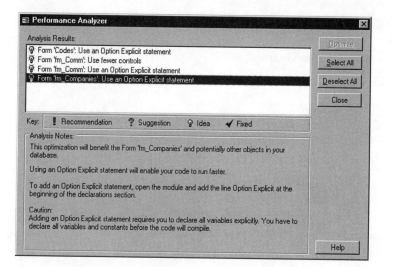

Fig. 1.10

The Performance Analyzer Wizard, which has found less-than-optimal conditions on a form and tendered some suggestions for improving performance and appearance.

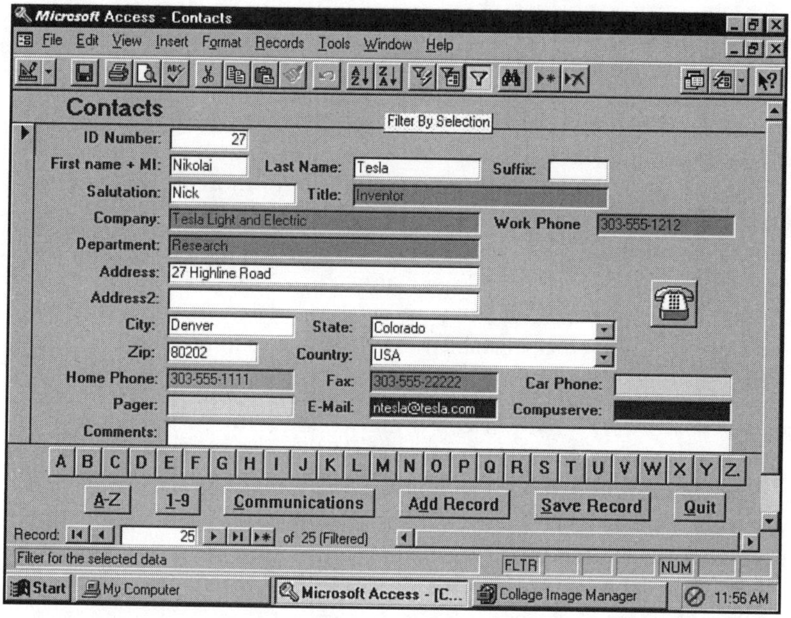

Fig. 1.11

The Contacts database, Filter By Selection, showing the restricted set of 25 contacts from the city of Denver.

Filter By Form applies Boolean logic to the Filter By Selection. Where Filter By Selection limits the search to a single criteria, the Filter By Form allows users to "and" and "or" the criteria together. This capability is an extremely powerful feature of Access 95 that can be grossly abused by novice users. Figure 1.12 demonstrates how easy it is to use the Filter By Form functionality of Access 95 to select more than one value on which to search.

Fig. 1.12

The Contacts database, Filter By Form, which allows the user to select from multiple lists of values generated from stored data, to restrict the output set of data.

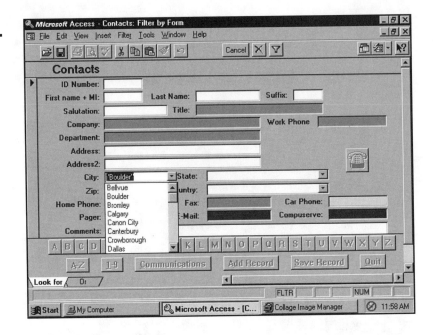

The *Simple Query Wizard* is fun and fast for power users, designers, and developers who understand table relationships, but will disappoint the truly novice users. The Simple Query Wizard walks you through building a query from one or more tables by using an intelligence technique Microsoft refers to as *background joins*, but the hook is that the table relationships have to be predefined, or the user gets dumped into the Relationship Design Window. Once you are in the Relationship Design Window, you have no option but to know relational theory and your database design. You can find more information about this in Chapters 6, "Establishing the Ground Rules," and 7, "Using Access as a Prototyping Tool."

Spell-Checking and Auto-Correcting. If you're an Access veteran, you may remember wishing that you had the spell-checker and auto-correct features of Microsoft Word to use in your applications. How often did you build links between Word and Access in the Word mail merge facility and find, much to your dismay, that the output (maybe a thousand form letters?) had misspellings. No more. With Access 95 spell-check and auto-correct are firmly in place, and it uses the same dictionary used throughout the Office 95 suite of products.

True Output Support to Microsoft Word and Microsoft Excel. Again, the veterans remember the frustration of not being able to output subreports to Word or Excel. What convolutions we went through to get decent information to the user community, and what we told our management to try to explain this deficiency! Even the Access 2 database documentor reports could not be output to Word. This shortcoming has been rectified in Access 95, and to sweeten the pie, Access 95 now supports BIFF, the Binary Interchange File Format, so cutting and pasting data from Access 95 to Excel transfers not only the data but also the data formatting. By the way, this feature works with either Office 4 or Office 95.

Improved Form Design. The new and improved forms design mode will be a life-saver for novice users and just plain fun for database developers! An immense amount of integration and consistency now exists with the other Microsoft Office products. The *Format Painter* (see fig. 1.13) is here from Word; many of the text manipulation and color options (including the AutoFormat feature from PowerPoint) are on the upper toolbar. One nice design feature is that you can build custom autoformats from your favorite form layout, and then apply it as simply and easily as the Pick-A-Look Wizard in PowerPoint.

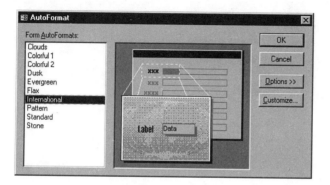

Fig. 1.13

Autoformat of a form, using the Format Painter from Microsoft Word to select a background and text presentation options.

Pivot Tables. As long as you have Excel 7, you can create *pivot tables* within Access 95. A pivot table is an invaluable assist in developing decision support system applications, in that it allows the user to manipulate into summary form large amounts of data, swapping row and column headings, revealing the data in a different light from the way it normally is stored and viewed.

Attaching to Excel Spreadsheets. The Access 95 package includes a new, enhanced ISAM driver that allows linking to an Excel spreadsheet and treats it as any other external data source (in the same manner it treats Paradox, dBASE, and other data sources).

Caution

Although in theory you can make updates in the two documents at the same time, with both documents open you may want to consider some use rules. In tests the authors made, updating cells in a 16-bit version of Excel did reflect in the Access 95 datasheet, and updating cells in the Access 95 datasheet did indeed reflect in the Excel spreadsheet, but it nearly brought a Pentium 90 with 32M of memory to its knees. Closing the Excel spreadsheet boosted performance a hundredfold. Because most shops will be heterogeneous environments, look carefully at how you mix and match the 16-bit applications with the 32-bit Access 95.

Visual Basic for Applications. Microsoft has announced its intention of adding *Visual Basic for Applications* (*VBA*) to all the Microsoft Office products. VBA is consistent with Access Basic, and offers new features for the Windows 95 operating system, including an Integrated Development Environment (IDE), easier object handling, and code behind forms and reports. VBA is a superset of Access Basic, which means that every Access Basic keyword, construct, function, and statement is supported in VBA. Now, Access developers can take advantage of new constructs and language elements in Visual Basic for Applications (see fig. 1.14), such as the Windows 95 Registry commands.

Fig. 1.14

The new Visual Basic for Applications code interface, which supports color-coded syntax features.

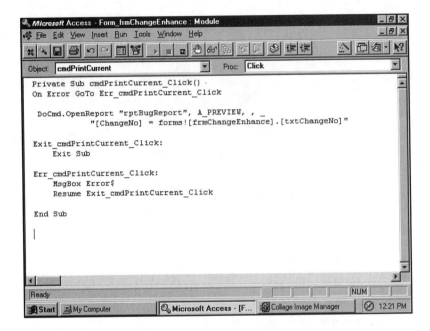

Now that Access Basic is integrated with Visual Basic for Applications, the programming interface resembles Visual Basic, with an improved editor and enhanced debugger. The editor now has color-coded syntax, a line continuation character, multipane code viewing, and line-by-line syntax checking. The debugger has breakpoints, watch variables, a call stack window, and an object browser for examining the object models of OLE automation servers.

Menu Builder. One of Access 95's new add-ons is a Menu Builder, a Wizard that walks you through creating menus for your applications. You should have a good idea of what you want in each menu selection before you begin, but you can always return to the Menu Builder to make modifications and adjustments (see fig. 1.15).

Switchboard Manager. The final touch to a professional-looking application is the *switchboard*, the term used in Access 95 to define the hierarchical menuing system used for navigating around an application. In Access 2 you did your own; Access 95 has a Switchboard Manager, which is incredibly easy to use and that produces a truly good-looking switchboard. The functionality is basic and options are restricted. Novice users will adapt it quickly, advanced designers will use it for quick prototyping and simple applications. The way in which the switchboard works is at first a little disconcerting. You build and modify the switchboard options out of the switchboard manager only, as shown in the following figure. You can open the switchboard (as listed in the forms container of the database window) in form design mode, after it's built, but the switchboard options are nowhere to be seen! You can modify the design elements of the switchboard itself, changing the colors, the lettering, even adding artwork to personalize it, and these changes are incorporated into the switchboard at run time.

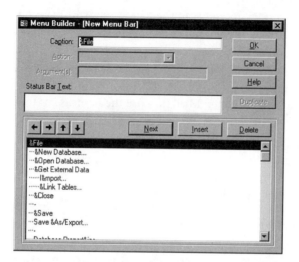

Fig. 1.15

The Menu Builder add-on, with ampersands (&) used to indicate the menu hot-keys.

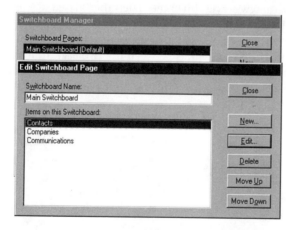

Fig. 1.16

Building the Main Switchboard page with the Switchboard Manager, adding buttons to navigate directly to the Contacts form, the Companies form, and the Communications forms.

Database Replication. Access 95, used in conjunction with Windows 95 and the Briefcase feature, supports limited versioning. The manual indicates that Access 95 supports replication, but replication implies the capability to define a distributed database environment or automated reconciliation of conflicting information (or both), and Access 95 doesn't do either. It does store a version number of each record in the database. This is the new system data type referred to as the *GUID*, the *Global Unique Identifier*, which is attached to each record in every table of the database. Each time a record is updated, the version number increases by one. When a copy of the database is tucked into the Briefcase—for example, for work on the road or at home—the likelihood of the two copies getting out of sync is very high.

Access 95 and the Briefcase synchronize the two copies by using the highest version number on modified records. All conflicts are resolved simply—the highest version number record becomes the "master" copy, and the conflict record is recorded in a conflict table. Because Access 95 doesn't scan the data values within each updated record, be prepared to manually resolve some of the synchronized changes.

Now for the good news—for some database developers Access 95 replication can be very useful in an internal development situation. The internal database developer can synchronize changes and modifications to a server or client application by using the replication feature, as long as the target .MDB files use the Briefcase or the Access Developers Toolkit Replication Manager for Windows NT.

Import/Export Wizard. Access veterans can find importing and linking under File, Get External Data—a change from the previous versions. The Wizard is helpful in stepping you through the layout of the data that you are importing, rather than forcing you to manually configure the new table. The Help system, including the Answer Wizard, contains exhaustive information on the pros and cons of importing versus linking, and Cue Card assist to get you started.

Application Splitter Wizard. Not sure how to split an Access 95 database into its client and server components? The Application Splitter Wizard walks you through splitting out the tables into a new server .MDB file. Then the Wizard deletes the tables from the original .MDB file, which becomes your new client .MDB, and attaches the server .MDB to the client .MDB (see fig. 1.17). Unfortunately, it doesn't create a module in the client .MDB that refreshes the links between the two each time the database application is run—an action that is extremely necessary for the most basic of client/server applications. We cover how to perform this task in Chapter 2, "Front Office/BackOffice Concept."

Fig. 1.17

The Database Splitter Wizard's first dialog box, with warnings, guides the user through the process of separating an application into its data and user-interface components.

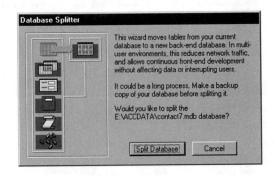

Answer Wizard. Microsoft's venture into natural-language processing is not bad for a first release. This is a Help system with character and it's a great assist for non-database or nonrelational designers who are getting accustomed to the Access nomenclature. Just for grins, when I typed the infamous, **What is the capital of Arkansas?** line, I got back a list of topics that included, "How do I capitalize names of days when I'm entering data," "Tell me about examples of input masks," and the **Ucase** and **Lcase** functions in the Programming and Language Reference section, (see fig. 1.18).

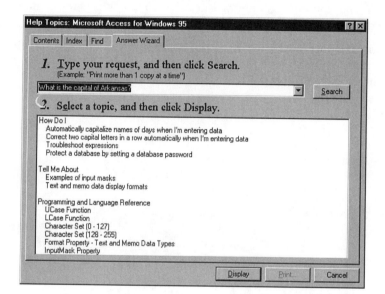

Fig. 1.18

The Answer Wizard, giving fairly reasonable answers to an unreasonable question.

Access 95 Internal Architecture

Access 95 is composed of several major components, some of which are:

- The database engine, the Jet, which handles all the server tasks, such as file management and query resolution
- The Visual Basic for Applications programming interface
- The Access graphical workbench, which includes the forms designer, the Menu Builder, and the report writer
- The Access 95 file management system
- The Access 95 security subsystem
- The Access 95 help subsystem

The Jet Engine

The heart of Access 95 is the Jet database engine. The Jet is a sophisticated multiuser engine that offers many features of a back-end server database management system to the desktop environment. As in the Jet 2, the Jet 3 has built-in support for referential integrity, table-level validation and enforcement of business rules, support for inner and outer joins, and cascading updates and deletes. The Rushmore technology enables fast searches on indexed fields. The Jet database engine also can be controlled from within Visual Basic for Applications or from any other application that makes use of the published APIs (Application Programming Interfaces) to manipulate the engine and the database directly.

The Jet 3 is composed of a set of .DLL, or dynamic-link library, files—the Jet DLL, the Data Access Objects DLLs, and the external ISAM DLLs. Figure 1.19 shows how the Jet database engine architecture fits together.

Fig. 1. 19

The Jet 3 engine and the components that comprise the Access 95 environment, showing interrelationships between the Jet and various data stores, both native ISAM and ODBC.

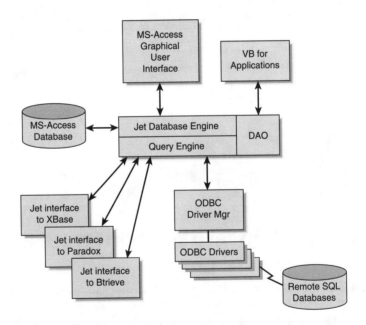

Unlike the Jet 2, the Jet 3 engine is full 32-bit multithreading. Since Access 2, the Jet engine has had the use of Microsoft's Rushmore technology, the super-fast query optimizer and retrieval mechanism that works only on indexed columns of a table. The Jet 3 now can support 32-bit ODBC drivers, giving (theoretically) better response from external data sources and non-Jet databases. The multi-threading essentially means that the Jet can now service more than one query at a time, providing faster, more accurate response to the client applications.

As in the Jet 2, the Jet 3 provides data management services, data storage, and fast data retrieval. It also provides for the full suite of data integrities—primary, referential, domain, and business (or user)—which we explore in Chapter 6, "Establishing the

Ground Rules." The Jet 3 allows unlimited levels of cascading updates and deletes, table-level or application-level data validation, inner and outer joins, and subquery and union operations. Although Visual Basic 4 is the native programming language for the Jet, it fully supports an extended version of SQL-92 (Structured Query Language, the American National Standards Institute 1992 Standard).

The programming interface to the Jet uses the Data Access Objects Data Link Library (DAO DLL). The DAO is an object-based data access language that is composed of a rich set of high-level objects that define the entire database environment and greatly ease the task of database programming.

Working with the .MDB File

Unlike most desktop databases, Access 95 keeps all the components of a database in one file. This file uses the extension, .MDB. If you choose this as the default mode of operation, a database file will include the data and also all the code, tables, indices, forms, reports, and macros. There are ways to separate code into libraries, and the data and tables into a different .MDB file. The plus here is that the developer doesn't have to track multiple versions of numerous program files, as in so many application development environments. The minus is that now, the developer has to track multiple versions of the .MDB file, and must figure out a method for cooperative development—but that's another chapter.

Access 95 doesn't reclaim pages within the .MDB file as data or objects are deleted, and it can grow quite large as code is added, edited, and moved around. Occasionally, the file must be compacted, or compressed, to squeeze out this "dead space." A compact utility is supplied to perform compacting, but you cannot compact an active .MDB file; you have to close it first. It's always a good idea (for developers in particular) to compact the database file(s) before distribution.

Access 95 System Requirements

What does it take to move up to Access 95? Remember, however, it's always better to exceed the requirements than to just meet them, especially if you are planning a long-term investment and/or you are intending to do serious database development. By heeding the following set of minimum specifications, the authors believe you will be able to use the current versions of the software:

- A personal computer (desktop or laptop) with an 80486DX or higher processor
- Microsoft Windows 95 operating system or Microsoft Windows NT Workstation or Server 3.51 or higher (Access 95 is not compatible with previous versions of Windows, such as 3.X, or Windows NT below 3.51)
- 12M of memory for use on Windows 95; 16M of memory for use on Windows NT
- Hard disk space requirements: 14M compact installation, 32M typical installation, 42M for maximum installation

- One 3-1/2" floppy drive or a CD-ROM drive, depending on which format of media your installation kit contains
- SVGA, 256-color video adapter recommended, VGA minimum
- Microsoft mouse or compatible pointing device

From Here...

In this chapter we introduced the concept of client/server computing and briefly covered how Access 95 fits into the client/server picture. From here, jump to the following chapters to find out more about the following:

- Chapter 2, "The Front Office/BackOffice Concept," if you are ready to upgrade from Access 2 to Access 95.
- Chapter 3, "The Application Development Environment," if you need assistance in choosing the underlying platforms for your client/server application.
- Chapter 4, "Getting By in SQL '92—Structured Query Language," gives more information on the SQL programming language, and how SQL-92 differs from its predecessors.
- Chapter 5, "Client/Server Database Application Design Fundamentals," shows you how to design and plan your client/server application.
- Chapter 6, "Establishing the Ground Rules," covers table design and layout.
- Chapter 7, "Using Access as a Prototyping Tool," tells you how to build a quick prototype by using Access 95.
- Chapter 12, "Securing the Access 95 Application," answers questions you may have about the Access 95 security model.
- Chapter 14, "Communicating with Other Applications," discusses the general issues of inter-application communications.
- Chapter 20, "Replication with Access 95," for an in-depth discussion on how to replicate Access 95 databases in both Windows 95 and Windows NT.
- Chapter 21, "Client/Server Performance and Tuning," explains the care and tuning of the client/server environment.

CHAPTER 2

The Front Office/ BackOffice Concept

Microsoft designated the combined package of its desktop applications for word processing, spreadsheet, and presentation graphics in Microsoft Office. This package is sometimes referred to as the *Front Office suite* to distinguish it from the *BackOffice* software. BackOffice is composed of Windows NT Server, SQL Server, SMS (Systems Management Server), SNA Server, and eventually also will include Microsoft Exchange Server. These industrial-strength programs are aimed at the developer of solutions for corporate computing, and they are used to support the Front Office products. Access is packaged in the Professional edition of Office, which reflects its capability to produce small database applications for desktop use, or to bridge to the BackOffice suite itself. Access can be used as the client or desktop component to a more powerful solution based on Microsoft SQL Server or some other back-end database management system. The Access capability to connect to many other databases makes it the ideal client development platform.

In this chapter we discuss the differentiation between the front-end, or client interface, and the back-end, or data store. These concepts are basic to file/server and client/server architecture. In this chapter, we will include the following:

- A discussion of the application .MDB file, what it is, and how it contributes to the client/server environment

- A discussion of the data .MDB file, what it is, and how it is accessed by the application .MDB

- How to upgrade an existing Access 2 database to Access 95, and then how to debug the upgraded database

- How to split a database application into front end and back end, with some help from the Database Splitter Wizard

- A discussion on local tables and remote tables, and when you should use each table

- Information on the links to attached databases, and how to refresh them if broken

Application versus Data

Designing a database application with client/server concepts can be reduced to the simple principle that the data belongs on the server, and the application belongs on the client. As you will see later, it isn't quite this easy as you start to introduce business rules, validation, and so on, but this basic concept is a good starting point from which to begin. The data on the server is available to everyone who has permission to connect to the server and to access the data. Everyone looks at one copy of the data, and updates by one user are quickly reflected on the screens of other users.

The application .MDB, on the client computer, is the user interface, and it almost always is graphical in design. This application includes the data entry forms, reports, and screens for viewing and analyzing the data. The application .MDB should contain either no or very few tables, a situation that we will discuss in following sections of this chapter.

The following discussion refers to using Access for both the client and the server component in a client/server application. Most of the comments made here apply to any combination of client and server software, such as Access 95 client to Microsoft SQL Server, or Visual Basic client to Oracle server. Note, however, that the file extension .MDB is unique to Access and Access 95.

The Application .MDB

In a client/server architecture, the application .MDB file (the client software) contains the queries, forms, reports, macros, and modules or code—but generally contains no tables of data. Rather, it uses attached tables from the data .MDB file (the server software). Because this file contains little or no data, it should not occupy much disk space on the client nodes. It will not expand over time as a result of data insertions and deletions, and it requires no compacting and defragmenting, as does the server .MDB.

In the process of developing an application, you may be faced with varying or even conflicting needs from different user groups within the organization. In this case, consider building more than one client application to satisfy the needs of your diverse user community. Each client application will use data from the same server database. You may build, for example, a client application for the data entry staff that contains only data entry forms and simple reports for checking the data input. For the management group, you can build another application that uses forms and reports to display and analyze the data but omits the data entry forms. There are multiple advantages to this approach, which are shown in the following list:

- Each user sees only the forms and reports that he or she needs. The user interface is simplified when the menu choices are limited only to what is relevant to the task.

- Security concerns are simplified because management reports and views of sensitive data are not available to the ordinary user.

- When one application is distributed to all users, you need to set permissions on queries, forms, and reports in order to restrict access to confidential data. By providing customized applications, you ensure that users without the required authority cannot run a confidential report because the report is not included in the application installed on their computers.

- Each application is smaller because it contains only what users need to do their jobs. The smaller application uses less memory, loads faster, and provides better response time.

- When one group needs a new form or report, an update to the one application can be distributed to only that group, rather than to all users. This limited distribution simplifies the upgrade process, especially in a large company.

- Changes made for one group will not adversely impact other groups.

- Design compromises that previously were necessary to satisfy different user requirements are no longer imposed on the database and on the developer. Each application can be optimized for a specific user group.

A few disadvantages to this methodology exist, of course; you never get something for nothing when developing. These disadvantages are shown in the following list:

- If a change that affects all the users must be made, it may be necessary to make the same change in several applications instead of just one. Because Access lacks a global change function for the objects that comprise these applications, this can be a tedious task unless you enlist the help of a third-party utility, such as SPEED Ferret (see this book's companion CD-ROM for a demo version).

- You must keep track of which users have which application. Fortunately, this process can be automated with tools such as SMS (Systems Management Services) or a home-grown Access 95 database (which serves a similar purpose).

- Development records-keeping is complicated because you're doing multiple-application development with differing timelines and deliverables. You can use a third-party package to help you track your development and build efforts, or you can adapt the "Revisions" database (included on this book's companion CD-ROM) to your needs.

- Maintenance and support becomes complicated; you are supporting and enhancing multiple applications, and responding to different groups with differing requirements and urgencies. The "Revisions" database on the companion CD-ROM contains the beginnings of a help desk application, with functions for tracking change/enhancement requests and bug reports.

The Data .MDB

The data .MDB file contains only data tables, table object properties, and relationships. It should contain no forms, reports, or queries unless they are needed specifically for systems-level operations or bulk data loading. If, as the system administrator, you need to modify the *reference tables* (static lists of information used to standardize data entry) you can do so by opening them in datasheet mode. If it really is more convenient to use data entry forms for reference data maintenance, and so on, you can build your own maintenance application and attach to the tables on the server. For ease of maintenance and enhanced performance, the server .MDB file should remain as unburdened as possible by client application objects.

When data records are deleted from an Access database, the space that they occupied isn't immediately reclaimed to use by the database management system. The data .MDB file grows as new records are added to the database, and will fail to shrink as records are deleted from the database. Occasionally, the database administrator must *compact the database* in order to reclaim this unused space. Unfortunately, with Access 95 there is no such thing as an on-line compacting feature or *database backup*; the database must be taken down to complete either task. During this time, no one has access to the data.

On the positive side, with only one data file to compact and back up on a regular basis, the workload is lessened, synchronization among multiple data files is a non-issue, and the data can be safely stored off-site, if appropriate. These reasons are why it's of prime importance to establish—and stick to—a regular schedule of database backups. It isn't necessary to back up the client application files on a frequent basis. These files can be treated like any other application software, where—if anything happens to corrupt the program—a simple reinstall has the end user up and running in minimum time.

Ultimately, backup strategy is at the discretion of the enterprise and should be stated in a formal policy of operations. Unfortunately, too many companies don't have formal policies developed. Therefore, the survivalist mentality says, "Get the DATA files backed up regularly; the user-interface programs we can always reinstall!"

Upgrading an Application to Access 95

Before you can consider upgrading any Access application to Access 95 you must ensure that everyone who uses the application, including the server computer, is running on a 32-bit operating system, either Windows 95 or Windows NT. You cannot mix and match Access 2 and Access 95 very successfully. You cannot attach Access 2 client applications to an Access 95 server database and hope to take advantage of Access 95's multithreading capability and enhanced concurrency model. It just doesn't work this way.

Converting an existing application from Access 2 to Access 95 is a procedure that needs some consideration and preplanning. You should perform a design and performance inventory of the application as it currently stands under version 2. Do any design problems need fixing? Do any performance problems need to be resolved that will not be addressed by Access 95? Better to work out the problems in a known environment (Access 2) than to convert to an unknown environment and risk complicating an already unsatisfactory situation with your database and applications.

Always make a full database backup before starting on the conversion process, and test to make sure that it was a good backup. Include a lot of time in your conversion plan to debug the converted database. Although the automated conversion routine is quite good, some substantial changes were made to the internal architecture between Access 2 and Access 95, so it will require some manual intervention to almost all conversion operations.

After the database is converted, it cannot be undone, and it is not backwardly compatible. You cannot convert a data .MDB file to Access 95, and then try to connect to it with an Access 2 client, as we mentioned previously—they're not compatible in that order. You can convert the client application to Access 95, however, and then connect to the old Access 2 database. After all copies of the client applications are converted—which implies that everyone on a client node has upgraded to a 32-bit operating system, either Windows 95 or Windows NT Workstation—you then can convert the server .MDB to Access 95. ALL client machines must be running a 32-bit operating system BEFORE the server database can be migrated to Access 95. This should impose minimum inconvenience on the users of the database and allow you to plan your migration in a more coherent way.

Preparing the Access 2 Database

Besides the authors' guidelines about steps to take before conversion listed in the preceding section, there are a few additional details that you want to tend to before conversion to make the operation run as smoothly as possible. These suggestions apply to any Access 2 application, whether client or server:

1. Start Access 2 as an administrator.

> **Tip**
>
> If you've never set security on Access 2 and never log on with a password, you are actually logging on as an administrator. We explain more about this situation in Chapter 12, "Securing the Access 95 Application."

2. Open the database.

3. Check the security settings to ensure that you have the necessary permissions to change objects.

4. Unless you are sure that you compiled all the code behind forms and code in modules, open a module in Design mode, select Run, Compile All Modules to compile all the code, or Compile Loaded Modules to compile just that code within the open module. If you encounter any compile errors, fix them before converting to Access 95.

5. Save your work (File, Save), close the module design window, and close the database.

6. Compact the database (Tools, Database Utilities, Compact Database). You may want to compact it into another MDB file, which you then will convert to Access 95. The original Access 2 you can retain as a backup copy.

7. Exit Access.

Now you are ready to begin the conversion process. The Access 95 manual contains a section that outlines the differences between version 2 and Access 95, some of which were covered in Chapter 1, and others which are described in the following list. The conversion routines will catch most of these differences and perform the transformation, but some items will need manual intervention by the developer. Searching for these items can be greatly simplified if you have a third-party program such as *SPEED* Ferret, a global search utility. You can find a demo copy of *SPEED* Ferret on the CD-ROM that accompanies this book.

Our conversion example is a database named "Revisions" that we use to keep track of revisions, updates, bug fixes, product version builds, and so on for products under development. The Access 2 .MDB is supplied on this book's companion CD-ROM, so that you can try the conversion process. When you do so, you will find that some problems exist that will require manual intervention.

Be aware of the following situations, and be prepared to do some manual intervention, either before or after conversion:

- Before you convert a database, make sure that all code is fully compiled in Access 1, 1.1, or 2, whichever version is relevant for the application.

- If you use add-ins or library databases created in previous versions of Access, you also need to convert them to Access 95 before you can use them.

- Before using a library in Access 95, you must establish a reference to the library database from each application that uses it. Unlike Access 2, where library references were stored in the appropriate .INI file, Access 95 stores references in the Windows 95 Registry.

- If your application makes calls into 16-bit DLLs they will not work after conversion. Modify your code (either before or after conversion) to call the equivalent 32-bit DLLs.

- If you use Visual Basic code that makes calls into a custom 16-bit DLL, it too will fail after conversion. The developer of the custom DLL must either provide a 32-bit compatibility layer for the DLL or recompile the DLL source code with a 32-bit compiler.

- If you have code that passes a value to a DLL function that doesn't accept a **Null** value for the argument, you first must explicitly set the variable to the empty string, ("").

- You cannot use circular references between libraries in Access 95. Previous implementations of Access allowed these circular references (you called procedures in library A, which called procedures in library B, which called procedures in library A), but this technique is not supported by Visual Basic for Applications.

- If you named a module the same name as a form or a report in the same .MDB file, during conversion Access 95 will attempt to resolve the naming conflict by changing the name of the module. Of course, the change will not ripple through the entire application, and you have to manually intervene to resolve the problem and get your converted application functional again.

- If you give a procedure the same name as a module, after the conversion you have to check and make sure that all references to the procedure are fully qualified (Navigation.Navigation("FirstForm", "NextForm")).

- If you give a procedure the same name as a control on a form, after the conversion you have to check to make sure that all references to the procedure are fully qualified with the name of the module it resides in—Actions.Close().

- If you gave two controls effectively the same name (the two names differ only by a space or a special character), you must be prepared to check and adjust after conversion. For example, [Last_Name], [Last Name], and [Last+Name] are all treated as the same under Access 95.

- If you have used the **CopyObject** action, naming the current database as the destination database argument, the copied object will not show up immediately. You have to close and reopen the database to view or use the copied object.

- If your application imports Excel Version 2.0 or Lotus 1-2-3 Release 1.0 spreadsheets, you will lose this functionality following conversion. Access 95 supports only Excel 3 and later, and Lotus 1-2-3 Release 2.0 and later.

- If you use the **TransferText** action to export a query, and the query contains two fields that have the same name, the action will fail. You must rename one of the fields.

- If you use a SQL statement to delimit data for export in the **TransferText** or **TransferSpreadsheet** actions, you have to make modifications after conversion. Access 95 doesn't support SQL statements in either action. Create a query and specify the name of the query in the **TableName** action argument.

- If, in your code, you assigned a string that contains a percent sign to a numeric data type, you see an error message.

- The DoCmd statement of previous versions of Access was replaced with a **DoCmd** object, and now you carry out actions by invoking methods of the object. Following conversion, be prepared to check that every instance of **DoCmd** now has a dot operator (**.**), not a space, between the **DoCmd** and the action. In Access 2, you write **DoCmd OpenForm "Switchboard"**. In Access 95, convert this statement to **DoCmd.OpenForm** "Switchboard".

- If you use the **hWnd** property in your code to pass a window handle of a form or report to a Windows routine, pass the value directly; do not assign the value to a variable. The hWnd property was an **Integer** data type in past versions; in Access 95 it is a **long** data type.

- The DAO **Category** property is no longer supported for **Form**, **Report**, and **Control** objects in Access 95.

■ If you use the **Parent** property of a control on a form or a report, under previous versions of Access the name of the form or report that contained the control was returned. In Access 95, the **Form** or **Report** object is returned. To retain the same functionality as you had in previous versions of Access, use the following format:

```
Forms!Categories!CategoryID.Parent.Name
```

This code returns the name of the Categories form; it does not return the Categories **Form** object.

■ In previous versions of Access, there was no distinction between wizards and libraries, so global wizard code was always available to the current database. Access 95 no longer treats the two elements as the same, so you must establish a reference from your application to the wizard database that contains the procedures you are using.

■ The AutoDialer functionality has been moved to Utility.MDA. A reference between the current database and Utility.MDA is automatically added during conversion.

■ If you use error-handling code to respond to OLE Automation server errors, be prepared to modify your code. Access 95 is both an OLE server and container, so the Visual Basic code returns more explicit error information.

■ If you used the dot operator (**.**) in previous versions of Access to reference **Recordset**, **Dynaset**, **Table**, or **Snapshot** objects, you have to modify the code to use the exclamation point (!) operator. Or, for the short term, you can establish a reference to the Microsoft DAO 2.5/3.0 Compatibility Library (open a Module in Design mode, select Tools, References).

■ The Visual Basic functions **EOF**, **FreeFile**, **LOF**, **FileAttr**, **Loc**, and **Seek** can no longer be used in expressions that are not user-defined **Sub** or **Function** procedures. If you must use one of these functions outside of a procedure, you must call the function from within a user-defined function that you call from the expression.

■ Line numbers greater than 65,529 in Visual Basic code are no longer supported.

■ The Next Procedure and Previous Procedure buttons that were part of the Module toolbar in previous versions of Access are no longer available. Custom toolbars that include these will convert, but the buttons do not operate.

■ If you use the **SendKeys** statement or action to choose commands from menus, you may have to modify the code because of the new layouts of Access 95.

■ Access 95 and the Jet 7 engine create indexes on either side of a relationship during conversion. If you have complex table interrelationships in Access 2, the conversion may put you over the limit of 32 indexes per table. If conversion fails because of this condition, go back to the V2 database, delete some relationships, and reconvert.

■ In previous versions of Access, you could use an expression to refer to the value of a control on a read-only form that was bound to an empty record source.

The **Null** returned was an acceptable condition. In Access 95 this isn't the case. For read-only forms in Access 95, make sure that the record source does not return a **Null** value.

Upgrading Databases from Version 2 to Version 7

The steps to convert a database are straightforward. In fact, Access 95 converts the database for you.

1. Start Access 95. You see a screen that asks if you want to create a new database or open an existing database (see fig. 2.1). The databases that you opened most recently are shown in a window. Assuming that you haven't previously opened this database in Access 95, it will not be in the list of databases.

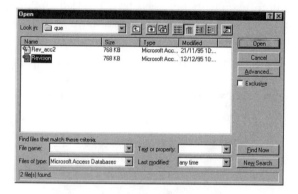

Fig. 2.1

The database file selection screen.

2. Click on the More Files option to open the Windows 95 file selection window. Find the database that you want to convert, highlight it, and then click Open. Access offers two choices—you can open this database as an Access 2 database, or convert it (see fig. 2.2). If you open it as a version 2 database, you can use the forms, reports, and macros, but you will not be able to modify the design in any way.

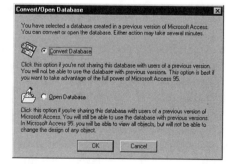

Fig. 2.2

Choosing whether to open or convert the Access 2 database.

3. Choose the Convert Database option and choose OK. Access 95 asks for a file name for the converted database. It doesn't allow you to use the old name for

the converted database, unless you choose to place the Access 95 database in a target directory that is different from the one in which the Access 2 database resides. In either case it *does* allow you to select the name of an existing file and to write over this file.

4. Select a destination file or type a file name, and then click Save.

Access 95 now begins the database conversion. As it does so it compiles, or attempts to compile, all the code in the procedures and modules.

Don't be surprised when code that compiled without errors in Access 2 doesn't compile properly with Access 95 (see fig. 2.3). The conversion process does an excellent job of making small changes in the code to reflect the difference between the two versions, but in a few cases, it cannot make the required changes. If a problem exists with the compilation, it informs you with a message box. The Help option in the message box actually is more relevant to performance optimization than to compile errors, but it is still worth looking at.

If you try this conversion by using the REVISION.MDB file on the companion CD-ROM, you encounter the previously described error message. As you close the error message dialog box, the conversion will be complete, and you will be at the database window.

Fig. 2.3

Compile errors that occur during database conversion are normal because of the differences beteween the two versions.

For anyone accustomed to Access 2, the appearance of the database window is a major change. The tabs are now arranged horizontally rather than vertically to conform to the Windows 95 paradigm. It may take some time to get used to the new look. To help the process along, click View, Details. The window (assuming that you make it wide enough) shows the date and time the database object was created, and the date and time when it was last modified.

Highlight an object, such as a table, then click the secondary mouse button. (For right handers, who usually click with the left mouse button, this means click the right mouse button. We use the term, *secondary*, to be politically correct—it applies equally well to left- or right-handed users, and may vary depending on how you configure your mouse. The highlighting procedure also works for trackballs and other pointing devices where the buttons may be arranged one above the other rather than side-by-side.) This action pops up a list of options, one of which is Properties. When you select this option, information about the object is displayed, including the owner, and a description that you can edit.

Debugging the Upgrade

If *compile errors* occur, you have to fix them manually, but they are relatively easy to track down. From the database window, select the Forms or Reports tab, and then open any form or report in Design mode—it doesn't matter which because you do not yet know where the problem is. You simply need a form or report open to use as a vehicle to reading code. Click View, Code, and then click Run, Compile All Modules. The compile operation stops at the line that contains the first error (see fig. 2.4). As you fix each error, you can restart the compile process, and move to the next error. When the error occurs in a form other than the currently open form, Access automatically opens the other form and the associated code window to show the error. If you have a large number of errors to debug, you may want to get into the habit of closing all new forms that are opened, or you may end up with a large number of forms open at the same time.

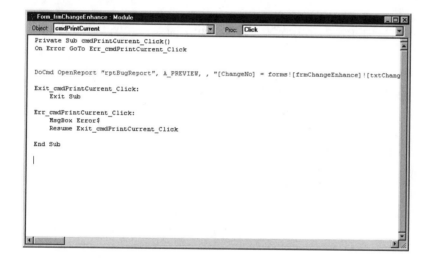

Fig. 2.4

This compile problem was caused by a syntax error due to a change in the DoCmd statement.

In the example REVISION.MDB, the first error, which is a syntax error, comes in the following example:

```
DoCmd OpenReport "rptBugReport", A_PREVIEW, ,
➥"[ChangeNo] = forms![frmChangeEnhance]![txtChangeNo]"
```

Notice that this line is shown in red on the Visual Basic for Applications editor screen. The problem here is that the **DoCmd OpenReport**, which worked in Access 2, must be changed to **DoCmd.OpenReport** in Access 95. The **DoCmd** statement from Access 2 has been replaced by a **DoCmd** object in Access 95. Therefore, you must use the dot operator to invoke a method for the object. After this change is made, the code changes from red to the normal black. Now the Run, Compile All Modules can be used again. Repeat the process until all the compile errors have been corrected.

Tip

If you use add-ins or libraries created in a previous version of Access, you must convert them before you can use them with applications written for Access 95.

When Access 95 converts an Access 2 database, it automatically adds a reference to the Microsoft DAO 2.5/3.0 Compatibility Library. This reference allows you to continue to use older versions of DAO objects, properties, and methods in your application. New applications created in Access 95 do not include this reference unless you add it manually. This is something that you may not want to do, or you may be risking future compatibility when support for the older versions of DAO objects is finally dropped (which inevitably will happen at some time in the future). To make sure that your applications will run with future versions of Access, use only the DAO 3.0 Object Library, if possible.

To convert your application to use the 3.0 Compatibility Library only, follow these steps:

1. Make changes to your code to conform to Access 95.
2. Open a code window in a module or a procedure attached to a form.
3. Click Tools, References to open the references window.
4. Deselect the Microsoft DAO 2.5/3.0 Compatibility Library.
5. Select the Microsoft 3.0 Object Library.
6. Close the References window.
7. Click Run, Compile all Modules.

If there are no compile errors, then your application doesn't need the 2.5/3.0 Compatibility Library. An additional benefit is that you no longer need to distribute the Compatibility Library with your application, as you would with a converted application that still used older methods and properties.

Splitting the Application

A client/server application needs to be in two parts, with the client interface objects stored in one file and the data objects stored on a separate file. If your application isn't already split, now is a good time to do so. Doing so, shown in the following steps, is easy:

1. Create a new database (which will become the data .MDB).
2. Copy the tables from your application .MDB over to the new database.
3. Delete the tables from your application .MDB.
4. Attach the application .MDB to the data .MDB.

Using the Database Splitter

Access 95 includes a Wizard that splits a database. You can, of course, do it yourself but the wizard goes through the same steps that you would, and does it much faster, so let it do the work. As always, you make a backup copy of the database before running this procedure. To use the Database Splitter Wizard, take the following steps:

1. Open the database.

2. Click Tools, Add-Ins, Database Splitter.

3. When prompted, provide a name for the database that will contain the tables.

The Database Splitter Wizard splits the database that you had initially opened, putting all of the tables into a new database (the one for which you provided the name). Then it attaches the tables in the newly named database back to the original database. The original database becomes the application .MDB, and it does not contain any data tables.

Local Tables versus Remote Tables

We said previously that the client application should not contain much, if any, data. One hallmark of a good developer is knowing when to modify the rules, because no rule holds under all conditions. The following two exceptions to this rule can improve performance and have little impact on the size of the application.

The first exception is when you have data that never changes. Many developers like to provide assistance for the users in the form of combo boxes or list boxes that contain *static data*. A good example of static data is the state code table. By providing this table, the developer can ensure that only valid state codes are entered. If the combo box is designed properly, the user can see both the code and the name of the state, thereby eliminating confusion (is "MA" Maine, or is it Maryland or Massachusetts?). The state codes and state names are static information that you can store in a reference table. According to the rules, tables should be stored on the server. However, a new state is rarely added. Do you really want to go to the server, generating unnecessary network traffic, for such a minor piece of data, or is it better to include the small reference table in the application .MBD file, so that the data is available locally? Although the user may know the state codes, or may not even need to reference the list of state codes, every time the form is opened the reference table on the server is accessed!

The second exception is similar to the first, but carries the idea of local storage of *reference data* a step further. This exception involves data that is relatively static, with only occasional changes. Examples of this type of data are the names of departments within your company, the internal phone list, or job titles. Changes to tables that contain this type of data may happen once a week or once a year—on an infrequent basis.

To minimize network traffic and offer better responsiveness in the client application, you may want to store these tables on both the client and the server computers.

All changes to the data would first be on the server copy, of course. Then you write code that runs when the user starts the application—called from the *autoexec macro*, or in the run-time startup parameters, for example. The code would copy the data from the server table to the replicated table on each client computer, which synchronizes them. Then all calls from the client application to this data would be made to the local copy of the data.

In the worst case, if the synchronization routine failed, or a client node does not attach to the network, the user still has the previous day's data to work with—which probably will be adequate. If you want to make the code more sophisticated, you might want to copy the data from the server only on a specific day of the week. Alternatively, you could keep track internally of when the data was last updated, and update it once a week or once a month. If the first update is done on the day when the software was installed on the user's computer, it may work out that all users update their systems on a different day. This method avoids a major bottleneck on the network first light on Monday morning, while everyone copied the data. Of course, on Monday morning, no one may realize that the system was slower than usual.

The important point to remember is that any data stored locally is either a copy of a master data set held on the server or data that never changes. Access to this reference data stored on a client computer must be read-only, with no exceptions to this rule. If a user is allowed to make changes to a local copy of the reference data, the changes are lost when the next update happens. This data loss and lack of synchronization is precisely what client/server technology is designed to avoid.

If you are going to split a database, but keep the smaller reference tables in the client application, you have two ways to do so. The first way is to allow Access 95 to split the application for you, and then use the File, Get External Data, Import option to bring the reference tables back to the application database. The second way is to perform the split manually, as shown in the following steps:

1. Make two copies of the original database file. One copy becomes the application .MDB file, the other will be the data .MDB file, so name them appropriately.
2. Open the data .MDB file in Access 95.
3. Delete all the queries, forms, reports, modules, and macros.
4. Delete all tables that you want to appear only in the application .MDB.
5. Close the data .MDB file.
6. Compact the data database.
7. Open the application .MDB file.
8. Delete all the data tables, except the reference tables that you want to keep in the client application.
9. Use the File, Get External Data, Link Tables to connect to the tables from the .MDB file that contains the data tables.
10. Close the application .MDB file.
11. Compact the database.

Refreshing the Links

When you use the Database Splitter, you simply get two .MDB files that contain the same objects that were present before the split, shared between the two. The tables from the server .MDB are by default attached to the application .MDB during the split process, and the relationships are inherited by the application .MDB. This works until the location of the server .MDB is changed. The Database Splitter doesn't supply functionality that checks that the attachment links are good, nor does it allow you to identify the new location of the server .MDB and reestablish these links.

The authors use the following two pieces of code to do just these things. The first set of procedures will, upon application startup, check the current links to make sure they're good. If the links are invalid, the user is prompted with a dialog box that allows him or her to search the directories to find the server .MDB file. The code in Listing 2.1 is included on this book's companion CD-ROM, in the CODE directory, as file 02code01.txt. It also can be found in SOLUTIONS.MDB, which ships with every copy of Access 95.

Listing 2.1   02code01.txt—The "RefreshTableLinks" Routine, Which Checks for Valid Links to Attached Tables on Application Startup

```
'in the declarations section:
'-----------------------------------------------------------------
'                    RefreshTableLinks
'-----------------------------------------------------------------
'    refresh the links to the data tables if they aren't available.
'-----------------------------------------------------------------
Option Explicit          ' Req. variables declared before being used.
Option Compare Database ' Use database order for string comparisons.

Declare Function GetOpenFileName Lib "comdlg32.dll" Alias
➥"GetOpenFileNameA" (pOpenfilename As OPENFILENAME) As Boolean
Declare Function GetSaveFileName Lib "comdlg32.dll" Alias
➥"GetSaveFileNameA" (pOpenfilename As OPENFILENAME) As Boolean

Type MSA_OPENFILENAME
' Filter string used for the File Open dialog filters.
' Use MSA_CreateFilterString() to create this.
' Default = All Files, *.*
    strFilter As String
' Initial Filter to display.
' Default = 1.
    lngFilterIndex As Long
' Initial directory for the dialog to open in.
' Default = Current working directory.
    strInitialDir As String
' Initial file name to populate the dialog with.
' Default = "".
    strInitialFile As String
    strDialogTitle As String
' Default extension to append to file if user didn't specify one.
```

(continues)

Listing 2.1   Continued

```
' Default = System Values (Open File, Save File).
    strDefaultExtension As String
' Flags (see constant list) to be used.
' Default = no flags.
    lngFlags As Long
' Full path of file picked.  On OpenFile, if the user picks a
' nonexistent file, only the text in the "File Name" box
' is returned.
    strFullPathReturned As String
' File name of file picked.
    strFileNameReturned As String
' Offset in full path (strFullPathReturned) where the file name
' (strFileNameReturned) begins.
    intFileOffset As Integer
' Offset in full path (strFullPathReturned) where file ext. begins.
    intFileExtension As Integer
End Type

Const ALLFILES = "All Files"

Type OPENFILENAME
    lStructSize As Long
    hWndOwner As Long
    hInstance As Long
    lpstrFilter As String
    lpstrCustomFilter As Long
    nMaxCustrFilter As Long
    NFilterIndex As Long
    lpstrFile As String
    nMaxFile As Long
    lpstrFileTitle As String
    nMaxFileTitle As Long
    lpstrInitialDir As String
    lpstrTitle As String
    Flags As Long
    nFileOffset As Integer
    nFileExtension As Integer
    lpstrDefExt As String
    lCustrData As Long
    lpfnHook As Long
    lpTemplateName As Long
End Type

Const OFN_ALLOWMULTISELECT = &H200
Const OFN_CREATEPROMPT = &H2000
Const OFN_EXPLORER = &H80000
Const OFN_FILEMUSTEXIST = &H1000
Const OFN_HIDEREADONLY = &H4
Const OFN_NOCHANGEDIR = &H8
Const OFN_NODEREFERENCELINKS = &H100000
Const OFN_NONETWORKBUTTON = &H20000
Const OFN_NOREADONLYRETURN = &H8000
Const OFN_NOVALIDATE = &H100
Const OFN_OVERWRITEPROMPT = &H2
```

```
Const OFN_PATHMUSTEXIST = &H800
Const OFN_READONLY = &H1
Const OFN_SHOWHELP = &H10


'procedure CheckLinks
Public Function CheckLinks() As Boolean
'-------------------------------------------------------------------
' Check links to REA_Data database; returns true if links are OK.
'-------------------------------------------------------------------
    Dim dbs As DATABASE, rst As Recordset
    Set dbs = CurrentDb()

' Open linked table to see if connection information is correct.
    On Error Resume Next
    Set rst = dbs.OpenRecordset("refContractor")

' If there's no error, return True.
    If Err = 0 Then
        CheckLinks = True
    Else
        CheckLinks = False
    End If

End Function



'Procedure FindREAData
Function FindREAData(strSearchPath) As String
'-------------------------------------------------------------------
' Displays the open file dialog box for the user to locate
' the REA_data database. Returns the full path to REA_data.
'-------------------------------------------------------------------
    Dim msaof As MSA_OPENFILENAME

' Set options for the dialog box.
    msaof.strDialogTitle = "Where Is REA_data?"
    msaof.strInitialDir = strSearchPath
    msaof.strFilter = MSA_CreateFilterString("Databases", "*.mdb")

' Call the Open File dialog routine.
    MSA_GetOpenFileName msaof

' Return the path and file name.
    FindREAData = Trim(msaof.strFullPathReturned)

End Function



'procedure MSA_ConvertFilterString
Function MSA_ConvertFilterString(strFilterIn As String) As String
'-------------------------------------------------------------------
' Creates a filter string from a bar ("¦") separated string.
```

(continues)

Listing 2.1 Continued

```
' The string should be pairs of filter|extension strings, i.e.
'   "Access Databases|*.mdb|All Files|*.*"
' If no extensions exists for the last filter pair, *.* is added.
' This code will ignore any empty strings, i.e. "||" pairs.
' Returns "" if the strings passed in are empty.
'-------------------------------------------------------------------
    Dim strFilter As String
    Dim intNum As Integer, intPos As Integer, intLastPos As Integer

    strFilter = ""
    intNum = 0
    intPos = 1
    intLastPos = 1

    ' Add strings as long as we find bars.
    ' Ignore any empty strings (not allowed).
    Do
        intPos = InStr(intLastPos, strFilterIn, "|")
        If (intPos > intLastPos) Then
            strFilter = strFilter & Mid$(strFilterIn, intLastPos, _
                         intPos - intLastPos) & Chr$(0)
            intNum = intNum + 1
            intLastPos = intPos + 1
        ElseIf (intPos = intLastPos) Then
            intLastPos = intPos + 1
        End If
    Loop Until (intPos = 0)

    ' Get last string if it exists (assuming strFilterIn was not
    ' bar terminated).
    intPos = Len(strFilterIn)
    If (intPos >= intLastPos) Then
        strFilter = strFilter & Mid$(strFilterIn, intLastPos, _
                     intPos - intLastPos + 1) & Chr$(0)
        intNum = intNum + 1
    End If

    ' Add *.* if there's no extension for the last string.
    If intNum Mod 2 = 1 Then
        strFilter = strFilter & "*.*" & Chr$(0)
    End If

    ' Add terminating NULL if we have any filter.
    If strFilter <> "" Then
        strFilter = strFilter & Chr$(0)
    End If

    MSA_ConvertFilterString = strFilter

End Function
```

```
'procedure MSA_CreateFilterString
Function MSA_CreateFilterString(ParamArray varFilt()As Variant) _
        As String
'----------------------------------------------------------------
' Creates a filter string from the passed in arguments.
' Returns "" if no args are passed in.
' Expects an even number of args (filter name, extension), but
' if an odd number is passed in, it appends *.*
'----------------------------------------------------------------
    Dim strFilter As String
    Dim intRet As Integer
    Dim intNum As Integer

    intNum = UBound(varFilt)
    If (intNum <> -1) Then
        For intRet = 0 To intNum
            strFilter = strFilter & varFilt(intRet) & Chr$(0)
        Next
        If intNum Mod 2 = 0 Then
            strFilter = strFilter & "*.*" & Chr$(0)
        End If

        strFilter = strFilter & Chr$(0)
    Else
        strFilter = ""
    End If

    MSA_CreateFilterString = strFilter

End Function




'procedure MSA_GetOpenFileName
Private Function MSA_GetOpenFileName(msaof As MSA_OPENFILENAME) _
            As Integer
'----------------------------------------------------------------
' Opens the file open dialog.
'----------------------------------------------------------------
    Dim of As OPENFILENAME
    Dim intRet As Integer

    MSAOF_to_OF msaof, of
    intRet = GetOpenFileName(of)
    If intRet Then
        OF_to_MSAOF of, msaof
    End If
    MSA_GetOpenFileName = intRet

End Function




'procedure MSA_GetSaveFileName
Private Function MSA_GetSaveFileName(msaof As MSA_OPENFILENAME) _
            As Integer
```

(continues)

Listing 2.1   Continued

```
'------------------------------------------------------------
' Opens the file save dialog.
'------------------------------------------------------------
    Dim of As OPENFILENAME
    Dim intRet As Integer

    MSAOF_to_OF msaof, of
    of.Flags = of.Flags Or OFN_HIDEREADONLY
    intRet = GetSaveFileName(of)
    If intRet Then
        OF_to_MSAOF of, msaof
    End If
    MSA_GetSaveFileName = intRet

End Function



'procedure MSA_SimpleGetOpenFileName
Function MSA_SimpleGetOpenFileName() As String
'------------------------------------------------------------
' Opens the file open dialog with default values.
'------------------------------------------------------------
    Dim msaof As MSA_OPENFILENAME
    Dim intRet As Integer
    Dim strRet As String

    intRet = MSA_GetOpenFileName(msaof)
    If intRet Then
        strRet = msaof.strFullPathReturned
    End If

    MSA_SimpleGetOpenFileName = strRet

End Function



'procedure MSA_SimpleGetSaveFileName
Function MSA_SimpleGetSaveFileName() As String
'------------------------------------------------------------
' Opens the file save dialog with default values.
'------------------------------------------------------------
    Dim msaof As MSA_OPENFILENAME
    Dim intRet As Integer
    Dim strRet As String

    intRet = MSA_GetSaveFileName(msaof)
    If intRet Then
        strRet = msaof.strFullPathReturned
    End If

    MSA_SimpleGetSaveFileName = strRet

End Function
```

```
'procedure MSAOF_to_OF
Private Sub MSAOF_to_OF(msaof As MSA_OPENFILENAME,
➥of As OPENFILENAME)
'------------------------------------------------------------------
' This sub converts from the friendly MSAccess structure to the
' win32 structure.
'------------------------------------------------------------------
    Dim strFile As String * 512

    ' Initialize some parts of the structure.
    of.hWndOwner = Application.hWndAccessApp
    of.hInstance = 0
    of.lpstrCustomFilter = 0
    of.nMaxCustrFilter = 0
    of.lpfnHook = 0
    of.lpTemplateName = 0
    of.lCustrData = 0

    If msaof.strFilter = "" Then
        of.lpstrFilter = MSA_CreateFilterString(ALLFILES)
    Else
        of.lpstrFilter = msaof.strFilter
    End If
    of.NFilterIndex = msaof.lngFilterIndex

    of.lpstrFile = msaof.strInitialFile _
                & String$(512 - Len(msaof.strInitialFile), 0)
    of.nMaxFile = 511

    of.lpstrFileTitle = String$(512, 0)
    of.nMaxFileTitle = 511

    of.lpstrTitle = msaof.strDialogTitle
    of.lpstrInitialDir = msaof.strInitialDir
    of.lpstrDefExt = msaof.strDefaultExtension
    of.Flags = msaof.lngFlags
    of.lStructSize = Len(of)

End Sub



'procedure OF_to_MSAOF
Private Sub OF_to_MSAOF(of As OPENFILENAME, msaof As
➥MSA_OPENFILENAME)
'------------------------------------------------------------------
' This sub converts from the win32 structure to the friendly
' MSAccess structure.
'------------------------------------------------------------------
    msaof.strFullPathReturned = Left$(of.lpstrFile, _
        InStr(of.lpstrFile, Chr$(0)))
    msaof.strFileNameReturned = of.lpstrFileTitle
    msaof.intFileOffset = of.nFileOffset
    msaof.intFileExtension = of.nFileExtension

End Sub
```

(continues)

Listing 2.1 Continued

```
'procedure RefreshLinks
Private Function RefreshLinks(strFileName As String) As Boolean
'-----------------------------------------------------------------
' Refresh links to supplied database. Return True if successful.
'-----------------------------------------------------------------
    Dim dbs As DATABASE
    Dim intCount As Integer
    Dim tdf As TableDef

    ' Loop through all tables in the database.
    Set dbs = CurrentDb()
    For intCount = 0 To dbs.TableDefs.Count - 1
        Set tdf = dbs.TableDefs(intCount)

' If the table has a connect string, it's a linked table.
        If Len(tdf.Connect) > 0 Then
            tdf.Connect = ";DATABASE=" & strFileName
            Err = 0
            On Error Resume Next
            tdf.RefreshLink          ' Relink the table.
            If Err <> 0 Then
                RefreshLinks = False
                Exit Function
            End If
        End If
    Next intCount

    RefreshLinks = True        ' Relinking complete.

End Function



'procedure RelinkTables
Public Function RelinkTables() As Boolean
'-----------------------------------------------------------------
' Tries to refresh the links to the REA_Data database.
' Returns True if successful.
'-----------------------------------------------------------------
    Const conMaxTables = 8
    Const conNonExistentTable = 3011
    Const conNotREA_Data = 3078
    Const conNwindNotFound = 3024
    Const conAccessDenied = 3051
    Const conReadOnlyDatabase = 3027
    Const conAppTitle = "REA Database"

    Dim strAccDir As String
    Dim strSearchPath As String
    Dim strFileName As String
    Dim intError As Integer
    Dim strError As String
```

```
        ' Get name of directory where Msaccess.exe is located.
        strAccDir = SysCmd(acSysCmdAccessDir)

        ' Get the default sample client database path.
        If Dir(strAccDir & "REA_APP\.") = "" Then
            strSearchPath = strAccDir
        Else
            strSearchPath = strAccDir & "REA_APP\"
        End If

        ' Look for the READata database.
        If (Dir(strSearchPath & "REA_data.mdb") <> "") Then
            strFileName = strSearchPath & "REA_data.mdb"
        Else
            ' Can't find REA_data, so display the File Open dialog.
    MsgBox "Can't find linked tables in the REA_data database. " _
            & "You must locate REA_data in order to use " _
            & conAppTitle & ".", vbExclamation
        strFileName = FindREAData(strSearchPath)
        If strFileName = "" Then
          strError = "Sorry, you must locate REA_data to open " _
                & conAppTitle & "."
          GoTo Exit_Failed
        End If
    End If

        ' Fix the links.
        If RefreshLinks(strFileName) Then     ' It worked!
            RelinkTables = True
            Exit Function
        End If

        ' If it failed, display an error.
        Select Case Err
        Case conNonExistentTable, conNotREA_Data
            strError = "File '" & strFileName & "' does not contain " _
                & "the required REA_data tables."
        Case Err = conNwindNotFound
            strError = "You can't run " & conAppTitle & " until you " _
                & "locate the REA_data database."
        Case Err = conAccessDenied
            strError = "Couldn't open " & strFileName & " because " _
                & "it is read-only or located on a read-only share."
        Case Err = conReadOnlyDatabase
            strError = "Can't reattach tables because " & conAppTitle _
                & " is read-only or is located on a read-only share."
        Case Else
            strError = Err.Description
        End Select

Exit_Failed:
    MsgBox strError, vbCritical
    RelinkTables = False

End Function
```

In a development environment, you occasionally need to detach from one set of tables and reattach to another, especially during testing, and doing this through menu selections can be a tedious task. This `Detach()` function can be called from a macro and quickly run out of the macro container. To implement this function for your own applications, just replace the table names in the code with the table names from your application. The piece of code in Listing 2.2 is simply an assist for quickly detaching attached tables, and is included on the companion CD-ROM, in the CODE directory, as file 02code02.txt.

Listing 2.2   02code02.txt—The User-Defined *DetachTables()* Function, Which Helps to Quickly Detach Attached Tables

```
'in the declarations section:
Option Compare Database

'procedure Function Detach()
Function Detach()
' -------------------------------------------------------------------
' Detach the tables from this client application
' -------------------------------------------------------------------
' updated 6/22/95 MAPoolet
' -------------------------------------------------------------------
On Error GoTo errDetach

    DoCmd.SelectObject A_TABLE, "refContractor", True
    SendKeys "{DEL}" & "{ENTER}", True
    DoCmd.SelectObject A_TABLE, "refCustomer", True
    SendKeys "{DEL}" & "{ENTER}", True
    DoCmd.SelectObject A_TABLE, "refState", True
    SendKeys "{DEL}" & "{ENTER}", True
    DoCmd.SelectObject A_TABLE, "refTeam", True
    SendKeys "{DEL}" & "{ENTER}", True
    DoCmd.SelectObject A_TABLE, "tblArchEnvironWetland", True
    SendKeys "{DEL}" & "{ENTER}", True
    DoCmd.SelectObject A_TABLE, "tblChecklist", True
    SendKeys "{DEL}" & "{ENTER}", True
    DoCmd.SelectObject A_TABLE, "tblConstCost", True
    SendKeys "{DEL}" & "{ENTER}", True
    DoCmd.SelectObject A_TABLE, "tblCustCredit", True
    SendKeys "{DEL}" & "{ENTER}", True
    DoCmd.SelectObject A_TABLE, "tblMessage", True
    SendKeys "{DEL}" & "{ENTER}", True
    DoCmd.SelectObject A_TABLE, "tblProject", True
    SendKeys "{DEL}" & "{ENTER}", True
    DoCmd.SelectObject A_TABLE, "tblRoadTrafficUtilDrain", True
    SendKeys "{DEL}" & "{ENTER}", True
    DoCmd.SelectObject A_TABLE, "tblTeamMember", True
    SendKeys "{DEL}" & "{ENTER}", True
    DoCmd.SelectObject A_TABLE, "tblTerms", True
    SendKeys "{DEL}" & "{ENTER}", True
    DoCmd.SelectObject A_TABLE, "tblTitleSurvey", True
    SendKeys "{DEL}" & "{ENTER}", True

    Exit Function
```

```
errDetach:
'Function was called from tools menu, therefore error is expected.
    If Err = 2489 Then Exit Function
    MsgBox "Error: " & Err & ": " & Error
  Exit Function

End Function
```

From Here...

This chapter explored the Front Office/BackOffice concept, what elements are contained in each, and how to separate an application to conform to this basic client/server design. From here, you can explore further by going to the following chapters:

- Chapter 3, "The Application Development Environment," covers the front-end and back-end hardware and software platforms.

- Chapter 5, "Client/Server Database Application Design Fundamentals," discusses client/server design methodology.

- Chapter 13, "Building the Run-Time Application," illustrates how to assemble the pieces for a run-time installation.

- Chapter 14, "Communicating with Other Applications," discusses inter-application communications.

CHAPTER 3

The Application Development Environment

When you are developing applications, you constantly must be aware of the hardware and operating systems on which the applications will run. In most cases, the user has a less powerful computer than the one you used to develop the application, and you must allow for this difference. The problem becomes more complicated when developing client/server applications because you need to consider both the client and the server environments, and the way in which the two environments interact.

This chapter covers the following areas:

- Client/server hardware options, and what makes for a good choice to support your needs
- Choosing an operating environment for the client side from the many products available
- Choosing an operating environment for the server side that will provide for your needs
- Some network concepts necessary for survival in the client/server environment
- Some different application development techniques
- Tips and hints on how to track development projects
- Test data composition and worth

Client/Server Hardware

If you already have a user community with personal computers on their desks and a mainframe or minicomputer on which the server database resides, you probably already have few options regarding hardware choice. However, you can make some relatively inexpensive upgrades that improve performance, such as adding more memory to the client computers. Remember that, in addition to the computers at either end, the network is an integral part of the hardware configuration of a client/server system, and it frequently is the source of performance problems.

The Client Hardware Platform

The client hardware platform for most users will be an IBM-compatible personal computer with a CPU based on the Intel 80x86 architecture. Desktop workstations are now available with DEC Alpha or RISC CPUs, and the Power PC may have a place in some companies. These workstations offer more power than is really necessary for a client computer. They are more suitable as replacements for UNIX-based workstations or servers. A suitable client computer, assuming Windows 95 as the client operating system, includes the following hardware (see fig. 3.1):

- A 486DX4-100, 486DX4-120, or Pentium CPU
- 16 Megabytes of memory
- 500 Megabytes or more of Enhanced IDE hard disk
- A fast network interface card
- SuperVGA Monitor and accelerated video card

Fig. 3.1

The components necessary for the client hardware.

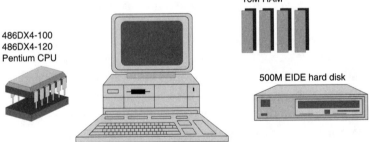

CPU. In theory, it's possible to run Windows 95 and associated applications on an 80386DX-based computer. This is a minimum configuration and will not provide satisfactory responsiveness for most users. A 386-based computer certainly cannot offer the productivity that a business needs. We recommend at least a Pentium system, preferably a 90 MHz or better. If your users are already equipped with 80486-based computers, you may have to work with what is available. But when you are purchasing computers, you will find that the Pentium 90 or 100 MHz CPU is now considered entry-level. Many computer manufacturers no longer offer 486 systems, preferring to market a range of Pentium systems. The 90 or 100 MHz Pentium desktop machines offer good performance, although the 120, 150, and 166 MHz versions may be a better long-term investment. They have a longer useful life before the users begin demanding more processing power to keep up with the latest software.

Memory. The absolute minimum memory required to run Access 95 is 12M (mega-bytes), and 16M could be considered adequate. Windows 95 will, in theory, run in 4M, but it will not run applications effectively with such a small amount of memory. You should regard 16M as the lower limit for any business computer. Even for client computers, an increase to 16 megabytes is worth serious consideration. Access really benefits from having a large amount of available memory, and the users will be de-lighted with the increased responsiveness of the database applications.

If your users are in the habit of keeping several applications open at the same time, which is quite easy and natural with Windows 95, the extra installed memory greatly reduces the time needed to swap between applications. A Pentium-based system should have at least 16M of memory. Don't spend the money for a Pentium unless it has an adequate amount of RAM to allow the system to reach its full potential.

If you purchase systems with 8M of memory, make sure that memory expansion slots are available. If all the memory slots are full, you will have to remove the existing memory when you are ready to upgrade. Plan ahead, and you can expand, rather than replace, your system components.

Hard Disk. Most personal computer owners believe that there is no such thing as too much hard-disk space on a computer, and with 1.2G (gigabyte) drives costing less than $250, there are few excuses for being constrained by a small hard disk. Of course, a large disk doesn't encourage users to clean out their directories periodically, and network administrators may not like this idea. Data files should be stored on the server, so that it can be shared, secured, and backed up as necessary. The client work-stations need to store only the applications, and therefore don't need extremely large hard disks. No matter what your company's internal policy, it's hard to justify a large hard disk, based on the size of a client application written in Access. In the worst case, each computer would need only a minimal installation of Access. If you choose to compile and distribute the application using the Microsoft Access Developers Toolkit, you will find that the client application files take up less than ten megabytes, and maybe less than six.

IDE drives are the best choice for the client systems. If the computer was built after 1994, it should have enhanced IDE (EIDE) capabilities. It may have hard-disk connec-tors on the motherboard, rather than requiring a separate controller card. The BIOS on a new computer should be able to handle hard disks larger than 528M (mega-bytes), the old IDE limit. The newer Enhanced IDE drives offer throughput speeds comparable to SCSI drives, but at lower cost, and are simpler to install.

Network Interface Card. Fast network connections are critical to client/server appli-cations. It isn't our intention to discuss networking here, other than to say that the network administrator and the database developer must work together to provide the best possible throughput. In the client computers, 10BaseT cards may be adequate. However, if the budget allows, consider the newer 100BaseT cards, which offer much better data transfer rates, but that probably will require a PCI slot to be available in each client computer. Fiber-optic cable is extremely fast and offers additional security, because it is hard to tap and generates no electromagnetic signal that can be picked up from outside the building. Fiber optics also is not susceptible to noise from other cables, which is a great benefit if your walls and ceiling spaces are already full of power and network cabling. The best arrangement is a combination of the two—"fiber backbone" to the local hub, and 10baseT (or 100baseT) to the individual computers.

Monitor and Video Card. A color monitor isn't absolutely required, but certainly is recommended for the client computers. If developers know that all the users have color monitors, the developers can employ color to provide a more intuitive user interface with visual cues. Given the price of good monitors today, and the productivity benefits, there is no reason why anyone should have to work with a monochrome monitor. Your main concern as a developer is which screen resolution to use. Many people prefer to work at 640×480, or standard VGA resolution. On a 14- or 15-inch monitor, VGA resolution gives an acceptable size for icons and text on the screen. SuperVGA, with a resolution of 800×600, works well on 17-inch monitors, but does produce tiny icons and text on smaller monitors. Currently, 15-inch monitors offer the best combination of features and price.

It is possible that your user community includes a mix of resolutions, which makes client application design more complicated. If you design for VGA, your forms will appear to have a lot of wasted space when shown on a SuperVGA screen. If you try to standardize on SuperVGA, which allows you to "load up" a database screen, you run into problems if laptop or notebook computer users load your application on their machines. Only the high-end, expensive notebook computers offer 800×600 resolution screens, and on an 11-inch screen, the icons and text are very hard to see.

Applications written in Visual Basic can use a third-party software package that automatically adjusts the size of the forms to match the screen resolution. Hopefully, a similar product will be available for Access 95 but, as this book goes to press, the authors have not found one.

The Server Hardware Platform

The choice of server hardware platform probably will be dictated by the choice of the back-end database. Access 95 can connect to any back-end database management system that supports ODBC; the decision to deploy an Access client application doesn't limit what type of back-end database software you can run. In many cases, the back-end database is defined by what is already in place. Introduction of a client/server application allows more people to use the available data, and may extend the useful life of the legacy hardware and software.

The following discussion is intended for the reader who has some flexibility about the choice of server hardware. For someone who has some years of experience with personal computers, this may not be new information. However, anyone who is downsizing from a mainframe or even a minicomputer may find this discussion useful.

If you have a choice of server hardware and software, you may want to look at a system that can run Microsoft Windows NT. As we discussed for the client systems, you can run Access 95 on Windows NT, which allows you to prototype the back-end database in Access. As the volume of data and the number of users increase, you can port, or "upsize," the Access database to Microsoft SQL Server or a similar industrial-strength database. An obvious advantage to using a server platform that runs Windows NT is that you can install hardware that is similar to the client computers. Maintenance costs and the need to stock spare parts are reduced, and all computers can be supplied by the same vendor.

There are many other hardware choices that make suitable servers. The DEC Alpha CPU is an interesting possibility. This machine supports Windows NT and Open VMS, which are converging as the result of an agreement between DEC and Microsoft. This agreement means that clusters of Windows NT machines soon will be feasible. Another reasonably priced Windows NT option is the MIPS RISC chip, around which NEC and others are building servers. If you need a UNIX server, the range of options is limited mainly by the flavor of UNIX that you want to run.

Note

If you are planning a Windows NT installation, make sure that you have the latest copy of Microsoft's Hardware Compatibility List. You can find this list on Microsoft's Technet CD, on the Microsoft forum on CompuServe (GO **MICROSOFT**), on Microsoft's Web page (**http://www.microsoft.com**) or Microsoft's FTP site, or on its download BBS, at (206) 936-6735.

If you use hardware on this list, then you should have no problems with Windows NT system compatibility. However, if your choice of hardware is not on this list, be aware that Microsoft's support staff cannot assist you if you have problems.

A suitable server machine, assuming Windows NT as the server operating system, includes the following hardware components (see fig. 3.2):

- A Pentium or Pentium Pro CPU
- 32M or more of memory
- 2G (gigabytes) or more of SCSI-II hard disk
- A SCSI CD-ROM drive for software installation
- Tape or optical backup
- An uninterruptible power supply (UPS)
- One or more fast network interface cards
- VGA monitor and video card

Fig. 3.2

*The hardware components
for the server.*

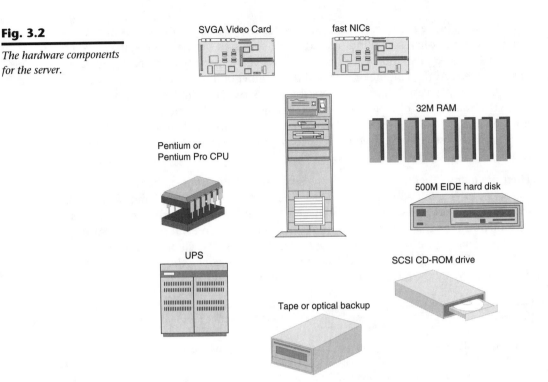

CPU. At the minimum, the server should be a Pentium system, and preferably 120 MHz or better. A 133 MHz system may be a good choice because it runs the system bus at 66.67 MHz, rather than at the 60 MHz bus speed of its slightly slower sibling. You see the benefit in moving data, rather than in computing horsepower. The old 60 and 66 MHz Pentiums do not meet today's computing standards and should be avoided for server systems, unless that era of machine is all you have available.

The new Intel Pentium Pro (P6? 80686?) may be *the* server chip for the rest of this decade—well, at least until next year. Its design optimizes 32-bit operating systems, which is what your server will be running. The P6 isn't as efficient as a Pentium when running 16-bit code, but it should have no problem with full 32-bit programs.

Modern operating systems support symmetric multi-processing—you can run multiple CPUs in one computer. Symmetric multi-processing means that the operating system code and the applications code can be equally distributed across all available CPUs. The "out-of-the-box" version of Windows NT Server supports four CPUs. To add more than four CPUs, you need to obtain a customized version of Windows NT Server from the manufacturer of your computer. If your back-end database software supports multithreading, as in SQL Server 6.0, for example, the performance improvements from multiple CPUs can be substantial.

Memory. Windows NT Server and Novell NetWare may in theory run in 16M of RAM, but not much room will be left over for applications, including your database.

For example, Microsoft recommends 32M of RAM if you plan to run SQL Server. If you then intend to add additional capability, such as Microsoft's SMS (Systems Management Server) and a mail application like Microsoft Exchange, you need 48M of RAM, and 64M would be even better. Windows NT dynamically allocates any available memory for caching, so your investment in extra memory will be used for system software, applications or caching, and will not lay idle. Of course, if you really need super-fast response times, you can follow the example of Lloyd's of London. This company has its 512M of RAM on its server, and they simply load the entire database into memory. Whatever you do, do not be tempted to cut corners on server memory. Attempting to economize here causes far more problems than trying to save a little money on the workstation configurations.

Hard Disks. It is easier to stay with IDE hard disks on the client machines, but on the server, the disks should use the SCSI-II interface, and if possible, fast-SCSI and/or Wide-SCSI. Although the raw numbers for throughput may look the same for EIDE and SCSI, those numbers are for benchmark tests. When you begin to move real data through the controller to the disk, SCSI is a far better drive for server systems. The intelligence built into the SCSI controller allows it to return control to the CPU faster because the controller takes over the responsibility for ensuring that the data is written to the disk. If you intend to add a fault-tolerant disk subsystem, SCSI is the logical choice because it can support multiple disk drives. In Chapter 19, "System Administration," we discuss how a fault-tolerant disk array can provide extra security for your data.

CD-ROM. The server doesn't need a multimedia configuration but it does need a CD-ROM drive for installing software. Windows NT isn't even available in the United States on floppy disks, it comes only on CD-ROM. Anyone who has had a software installation fail knows that it is always the last floppy disk, never the first, that cannot be read. The CD-ROM is a far more reliable medium for software distribution. Even Windows 95 takes more floppy disks than most people want to mess with, and so the CD-ROM version is preferable. Novell NetWare and UNIX systems also are distributed on CD-ROM. The CD-ROM drive should use a SCSI interface. The older CD-ROM drives with proprietary interface cards may not be supported by today's operating systems. The newer CD-ROM drives that use the Enhanced IDE interface are less expensive, but are just now being supported by most 32-bit operating systems.

Backup Hardware. A tape or optical-storage backup is standard equipment on any server. Many options are available, with more hitting the market. No matter what you choose, do not fall into a very common trap. Many system administrators religiously make backups of their systems, following standardized procedures to make sure that all of the data is captured, but they never test the backup; they never attempt to restore some data! Then one day, the system crashes or a file becomes corrupted, and they learn the hard way that their backups are not readable because a tape head is out of alignment. No matter the reason, the result may be a useless set of backup tapes. You should occasionally restore a few files from the backup tape or optical cartridge. Pick a few files from the start, middle, and end of the backup media for your test restore.

We also advise to test the restore capability by using a drive other than the one that made the backup, if one is available. Suppose that a tape drive did have a head alignment problem. It may read tapes that it has written with no problems but if your entire server is destroyed, could you use the tapes on another drive to rebuild the server and the data on a new computer?

UPS. Either the *uninterruptible power supply* (UPS) or *standby power supply* (SPS) equipment is quite reasonable in price. The difference between these two power supply systems is that the true UPS *supplies* power to the computer continuously from its battery, generating alternating current at the correct voltage. Simultaneously, the battery recharges from the building electrical supply. When the building electricity goes out, the battery doesn't charge but continues to supply power to the computer with no interruption, up to the limit of its battery capacity. Because the power to the computer is generated within the UPS from the battery, it doesn't have the spikes and voltage fluctuations found in the building's power supply.

A standby power supply, however, does not usually supply power to the computer. During a power failure, the SPS takes over supplying power within a few milliseconds. The changeover happens fast enough that the so-called "power supply" inside the computer continues to provide the 12 and 5 volt power with no interruption. The UPS is preferred for servers because no changeover period occurs, during which voltage can drop. Also, the UPS is constantly providing power, so you know that it is working. The standby power supply may fail, unnoticed until it is needed.

If you are using Windows NT, for just a few hundred dollars, you can equip this server with a UPS that interfaces with the operating system. In a situation where the power outage is lengthy, the system can be shut down in an orderly manner, following a prescribed set of steps. The size of the UPS system must be matched to the size of the server. A server with a large amount of memory and several large hard disks requires more power than a desktop computer, and probably should be in the 600-800 KVA range.

Tip

The users will find that a smaller 280-400 KVA UPS or SPS will see them through the occasional power outage (up to 15 minutes). It eliminates data loss, for example, caused by someone tripping over the power cord. It isn't essential that the clients are protected in this way, but it is cheap insurance against data loss or corruption if the power fails while someone is entering or updating a record.

Network Interface Cards. The network card in the server should be the fastest available. The newer PCI network cards offer an increase in throughput, and a 100BaseT card should be used if the rest of the network supports the newer standards for data transfer rates. If your operating system supports it, put more than one network card in the server. This can be helpful when you have a heterogeneous environment. You can bind one protocol to the first card to talk to your mainframe, and a different protocol to the second card to communicate with your Windows for Workgroups clients. This setup splits the network traffic and reduces contention for network resources.

Monitor and Video Card. This is one area in which you can save a little on the cost of the server. Assuming that it is a database server, the computer will not be used for day-to-day network management or any kind of development. So, a standard VGA monitor is sufficient, unless you want to run the client applications on this machine, and you designed them for SuperVGA screens. The server will not be required to display complex graphics, so 16 or 256 colors should suffice. A video accelerator probably isn't needed on this computer; a standard video card with one megabyte of video RAM is enough. If you want fast response, definitely use an accelerated PCI-bus video card, but you still only need one megabyte of video RAM. Adding more RAM to a video card doesn't affect the speed, it only increases the number of colors available at a given resolution.

Caution

Do not run screen savers on the database server. These applications consume CPU cycles like there's no tomorrow, and they really drag down the performance of the system. If you want to save energy, turn off the monitor when it is not needed, or even better, use one of the newer energy-saving monitors that powers itself down when not in use.

Fault Tolerance

The server will contain data critical to the success of your company. You must protect the data itself, and the users must be able to gain access to the data when needed. Fortunately, the cost of providing fault tolerance has decreased in the same way as other components of the system.

For important data, disk storage should be fault tolerant. Hardware redundancy is often ensured by *disk mirroring*, which simply means that you have two hard disks, preferably identical, that are images of each other. Everything written to the first disk also is copied to the second disk. If the first disk fails, the system administrator can shift control to the second disk (automatically, if your hardware is sophisticated enough), and then swap out the failed disk. A variation on this theme is known as *disk duplexing*. The data is mirrored on two separate physical disks, but each disk has its own controller. If either the primary disk or the primary controller fails, the data still can be retrieved and updated by using the secondary controller and disk.

One popular fault-tolerance approach requires that you install a *RAID* (Redundant Array of Inexpensive Disks) system. You can implement RAID in hardware or through software. There are various levels of RAID, from 0 to 10. RAID level 0 is not recommended for database applications. RAID 0 implements disk striping. It breaks the data into blocks (in Windows NT, these blocks are 64K in size), and then spreads the blocks across all of the disks in the array. The benefit is increased performance because multiple disk writes and reads happen almost simultaneously, using multiple read/write heads. The problem is that if one disk fails, all the data is lost. So, RAID 0 offers no fault tolerance. You may want to use RAID 0 for a read-only database where very fast access is the main concern, but it's too risky for transaction processing.

RAID level 1 is disk mirroring, and does provide fault tolerance. Essentially, it is a real-time disk backup. If a disk fails, the downtime is minimal as the second disk is "promoted" and the first disk can be replaced. Of course, no mirroring takes place until the replacement disk is brought on-line. The downside to disk mirroring is that it effectively uses only 50 percent of the total disk capacity. The other 50 percent is used only for the mirror copy of the data.

RAID 5 is the most popular approach to disk fault tolerance. It uses disk striping, but it also adds parity checking. In level 5, the parity information is spread across all of the disks. If a disk fails, the information that it contained can be rebuilt from the data and parity information on the remaining disks. You need at least three disks for RAID 5. It's more economical in its use of disk space than Level 1, because the parity information reduces the available disk space by one. So if you used five disks in the array, four contains data and one stores the parity information. The net loss of disk space is one-fifth, or 20 percent. If, however, a disk fails, the system must reconstruct the data as needed until the disk is replaced, and a program run to regenerate the data on that disk. The result of this setup is a slowdown in performance. There also is a performance hit, and a demand on system memory, when writing the data because the parity information needs to be generated.

Extending the concept of RAID 5, RAID 10 is similar to RAID 5 but uses disk mirroring in addition to the striping with parity. Expensive, yes, but in mission-critical applications, RAID 10 is worth the cost.

The advantages of hardware RAID are shown in the following list:

■ Disk controller logic bypasses the Windows NT Server driver software, and can offer high performance

■ Some systems allow hot-swapping, the capability to replace a failed disk drive without shutting down the system.

The disadvantages of hardware RAID are the following:

■ Usually expensive—the individual disks are not expensive, but the total package is.

■ May lock you in to only one vendor.

As mentioned previously, the RAID approach also can be implemented through software by using an operating system such as Windows NT Server, which offers extensive support for RAID. Note that this capability is a feature of the Server version of Windows NT and is not available in the Workstation version.

Choosing a Client Environment

If you decide to use Access 95 as your client application development platform, you cannot install it on anything other than Windows 95 or Windows NT.

Windows 95

Despite all the marketing hoopla, Windows 95 really is a major step forward in desktop operating systems. If you do not believe this, then perhaps you will accept that it removed some problems that plagued DOS, such as the 640K (kilobyte) limit, and the "Out of system resource" problem that affected Windows 3.1. Even on systems with 16 megabytes of RAM, Windows could not load several large applications at the same time. Memory wasn't the problem—it was running into the limits of the 64K resource heaps. Although this problem hasn't completely gone away in Windows 95, it is much reduced. Now it's possible to open Access and Excel at the same time. Access is a resource-intensive application and, therefore, benefits more than most applications from the improved resource management.

Management may be wary of moving to Windows 95 so soon after the initial release, but it does seem remarkably stable for a V1.0 product. Microsoft, not known for getting it right the first time, made sure that the product was thoroughly beta tested by over a million users before it was officially launched. For systems-support personnel who must deal with loading device drivers into high memory, GPFs (General Protection Faults) in Windows 3.1, and "out of resource" complaints from users, Windows 95 may be the move to make.

Another point to consider is that many employees have home computers, and many may be running Windows 95. Why not take advantage of their comfort level with Windows 95, rather than making them learn Windows 3.1 on company time?

To take advantage of the new versions of Microsoft Excel, Word, PowerPoint, Schedule+, and so on, you eventually will need to switch to Windows 95. Microsoft has announced that it will not issue upgrades to the Windows 3.1 versions of its software. Windows 95 and 32-bit applications are the upgrade path.

Windows 3.1x

If your company is currently running Windows 3.1 and is postponing the change to Windows 95, you must use Access 2.0 as the client software until the desktop systems move to Windows 95. Although this book was written for developers who are using Access 95, much of its content applies equally well to Access version 2.0. If you must stay with Windows 3.1, you may at least want to consider upgrading to Windows for Workgroups 3.11 for your client computers because it offers improved performance with 32-bit file access. Its capability to load some network drivers into extended memory also can be a real benefit.

Remember that Access version 2.0 client databases cannot connect to Access 95's version 7.0 back-end databases. If your server database software is Access, you have to keep it as version 2.0 until all your clients upgrade to Access 95. Of course, you still can use SQL Server and other powerful back-end database management systems. The authors would like to see Microsoft offer an ODBC driver for Access 2.0 that can allow it to connect to Access 95 databases, just as it connects to any other ODBC-compliant database. Then, you would be able to use a Windows 3.1/Access 2.0 client with an Access 95 back end—a nice combination for the small office that isn't ready to assume the added cost and maintenance responsibilities that the SQL back-end databases require.

Windows NT

Although Access 95 is officially titled Microsoft Access for Windows 95, it also works well on Windows NT. After all, Windows NT is a 32-bit application that runs in its own address space, not in the Windows 16-bit VDM. Some companies are bypassing Windows 95 and installing Windows NT Workstation as the corporate desktop operating system. Do not be put off by horror stories of the hardware requirements of Windows NT; NT Workstation runs quite well in 16 megabytes, all that really is needed for good performance with Access 95. In a setting where security is important and where the clients must access confidential or sensitive data, it makes sense to look at a secure, robust operating system such as Windows NT Workstation. It makes even more sense where the server environment is Windows NT Server. If the clients use Windows NT Workstation as the operating system, security and account administration can be handled by using the domain model.

Starting with version 4.0, due to ship in June 1996, Microsoft will offer the Windows 95 user interface for Windows NT, combining the ease of use for new users with the power of an enterprise operating system.

OS/2

IBM's OS/2 is a 32-bit operating system, but Access 95 isn't supported on OS/2. When OS/2 runs Windows applications, it actually runs Windows 3.1 code. As discussed in the preceding section, Access 95 will not run on Windows 3.1 and, therefore, it doesn't run under OS/2. There probably will be a version of OS/2 that runs Windows 95 32-bit applications but until then, you are limited to Access 2.0 clients if your desktop computers run OS/2.

UNIX

UNIX isn't a realistic choice as a desktop operating system unless some specific reason exists for choosing it, such as the need to run a specific software product that is available only for UNIX. Neither Solaris nor UnixWare has a large installed base in the business world for client desktops, and applications for them are few. We hardly need to add that the only way to run an Access client on UNIX would be to use a Windows emulator, which would have to support Windows 95.

Choosing a Server Environment

The choice of server operating system is more open than the choice of client operating system, which is limited to environments where Access 95 can run. The choice of server operating system is closely tied to the choice of server database. If you want to use Microsoft SQL Server, your server must be able to run Windows NT Server. If you want an Oracle back-end database, your choices expand to include Novell NetWare and UNIX. But remember that no matter which operating system you choose, you still have to connect to it with your client operating system.

Windows 95

You can use Windows 95 on the server, but doing so limits the choice of back-end databases. There are not too many options available yet that run on Windows 95. The industrial-strength databases really need a more robust operating system, such as Windows NT or UNIX. The only situation in which you can have a Windows 95 server is if you are prototyping on a development system and running Access 95 as the back end, or if you were accessing data stored in legacy Paradox, dBASE, or Btrieve databases. Windows NT makes a much better server environment than Windows 95.

Windows NT

Obviously, the connectivity between Windows 95 and Windows NT Server is easy to configure. Microsoft designed the two products to work together, and issues such as security were developed with integration in mind. If you need C2 level security, you can achieve it with Windows NT Server provided that you also use Windows NT Workstation as your client operating system. Windows 95 emphasizes ease-of-use, not tight security, and a mixed environment does not qualify for the C2 level.

Windows NT Server offers software RAID capability. Windows NT has remarkable flexibility in that it can build a RAID array from disks of different sizes, and even mix SCSI, IDE, and ESDI disks, although this situation is not really optimum. From within a Windows NT Server, you can set up disk mirroring or duplexing, and various levels of RAID fault tolerance.

Novell NetWare

Novell NetWare has the largest server installed base. NetWare is an efficient file server, and it makes a good database server for some applications. Most of the major DBMS vendors offer a NetWare product. However, NetWare was designed as a file-and-print server, not as an application server. In an attempt to broaden the appeal of NetWare and make it a generalized computing platform, Novell introduced the concept of *NLMs*, or NetWare Loadable Modules, in version 3.1 with the idea that programmers can write code to provide new system services. The NLM is actually loaded—as its name implies—as if it is part of the operating system kernel. However, this approach hasn't really caught on with programmers who are used to coding more conventional executable files.

NLMs also introduce a new set of problems. As mentioned previously, they become part of the operating system, which means that they operate in Ring 0, which usually is reserved for operating system code. The code in Ring 0 is not memory-protected, so an error in an application can crash the operating system. NetWare 4 does offer the option of running the NLM outside of Ring 0, which affords memory protection at the expense of performance. A badly behaved application still can bring down all the Ring 3 applications, but NetWare continues to run.

NetWare doesn't offer preemptive multitasking. A badly behaved or out-of-control application running under NetWare can take over the entire system and not release control, choking out other applications so that they cannot run. Most other 32-bit operating systems—including Windows NT, OS/2, and UNIX—do provide preemptive multitasking.

Because NetWare offers no support for virtual-memory services, it cannot page code to and from memory. This limits the number of applications that can run on any NetWare server. NetWare places the burden on the developer of handling potential memory conflicts.

When Novell acquired USL (UNIX Systems Laboratories) it appeared as though it would position NetWare as a file and print server, and UnixWare as a robust applications server. However, the subsequent sale of USL means that Novell must again look at developing tools for NetWare if it wants to make it a viable choice as an application server.

Windows 95 has better connectivity to Novell NetWare products than previous Microsoft desktop operating systems. If you decide on a NetWare-based back-end DBMS, keep in mind that Windows 95 offers interoperability only with NetWare 2.15 and above, including bindery-based NetWare 3.x and NetWare 4.x. It does not as yet support Novell's Directory Services introduced in NetWare 4.1, so this version of NetWare has to run the bindery emulation. Windows 95 actually allows you to select one of three clients for use with Novell. One client is supplied by Microsoft, the other two are from Novell. The choice of clients is determined by your NetWare configuration. You can use the Microsoft Client for NetWare unless you are using NetWare Directory Services, 3270 emulators with DOS TSRs, or NetWare IP (Internet Protocol). The two Novell clients are NETX and VLM. NETX works with NetWare up to version 3.11. With 3.12 or 4.x, it works only when the server is configured for the 802.3 protocol. You must install the NetWare DOS Requester software in order to run VLM.

UNIX

UNIX is an excellent platform for DBMS software. It has a wide array of features and tools available, and it is a mature product—it has been around for quite a while. A large pool of programmers and system managers are familiar with the variations of UNIX. It is often the platform on which new ideas appear first, because of its traditional connections with universities and research establishments. However, that may not be regarded as a plus in the business world. In fact, the continuously evolving free-form nature of UNIX may be more of a liability for commercial applications.

UNIX is a 32-bit operating system and does offer preemptive multitasking. It is extremely scaleable; UNIX variants are available for Intel 386 computers at the low end to massive supercomputers at the high end, and everything between. Unfortunately, one application will not run on all these different forms of UNIX. Every major hardware vendor has a proprietary version of UNIX; DEC has Ultrix, IBM has AIX, and so on. Then those who consider "proprietary UNIX" to be an oxymoron have developed LINUX, and don't forget BSD, reborn as Free BSD after USL tried to beat the competition with lawsuits rather than technology. Any application must be at least recompiled, and possibly partly modified to be able to run on different flavors of UNIX.

There have been and continue to be regular attempts to produce a "standard" version of UNIX, but with so many creative minds constantly tinkering with UNIX extensions, this probably never will happen. Each programmer believes that his or her contribution is the best way to do things—after all, this is primary the motivation for producing extensions to UNIX. The differences between the UNIX variations were introduced for performance on a specific platform or to optimize it for a particular type of application software. A standard UNIX would have to trim out much of the enhanced functionality, which is unacceptable to most people.

Part of the attraction of UNIX is that it is almost a universal operating system. You can do almost anything on a UNIX platform. The downside is that it isn't optimized for specific uses and, therefore, cannot compete with a system such as PICK or Teradata, which combine the operating system and DBMS in tightly integrated code. Microsoft's SQL Server uses much of the functionality of Windows NT to provide multithreading and multi-processing capabilities, rather than coding them into the DBMS. If any application was as tightly integrated into the UNIX operating system, porting it to other variations would be a major task.

OS/2

OS/2 can make a good server operating system. It is 32 bit, offers multithreading capabilities, and has a large installed base. OS/2 has at least as many software products for client, server, and middleware as UNIX but with a more consistent interface. Because of the larger customer base, the software available for OS/2 usually is priced closer to comparable Windows products rather then priced higher, like a UNIX product.

OS/2 uses HPFS as its file system which, unlike Windows NT's NTFS, is not a recoverable file system with transaction logging. For mission-critical data, the file system may represent a potential point of failure, which might not be acceptable.

Perhaps the biggest drawback to selecting OS/2 as an operating system is not technical, but rather because of its uncertain future. As this book is being written, industry observers are predicting the demise of OS/2 before the end of 1996. Of course, for every predictor, another believes it will continue and grow.

Mixing Operating Environments

Our advice on mixed environments—don't do it if you don't have to!

OK, so you may have to deal with a situation where the installed DBMS is Oracle on a UNIX machine, and you have to connect Windows 3.1 users to it via a Novell network. But first consider if other alternatives exist. The promise of client/server technology is that, in theory, you can construct a system *à la carte*, picking and choosing from a large list as though you were in a Chinese restaurant. The reality: unless you know exactly what you want, it's better to go with the "family special for six," and avoid the risk of totally incompatible choices. When things go wrong, it's often difficult to deduce which component is causing the problem, and getting vendor support without finger-pointing is not easy.

There are real advantages to a homogeneous operating environment. The hardware for client and server is similar, making support and maintenance simpler. For the administrator, the similarities in the software allow greater productivity and a shorter learning curve. For the user, the integration of the client and server operating systems can show benefits, such as having one user logon for access to the whole system rather than multiple passwords for different tasks.

In the preceding example, changing the user environment is probably out of the question. And the investment in the database is such that you cannot change it in the near term. One way to simplify the administration may be to replace the network software with Windows NT Server. The network administration can be handled from a Windows NT Server, without the worry of the interoperability issues of three different operating systems.

When we advise against mixed environments, we do not consider a combination of Windows NT, Windows 3.1, or Windows 95 to be mixed. These operating systems are complementary and are designed to work together under a common network protocol. It is possible, especially with Windows for Workgroups, to administer the network and the attached computers centrally. With the appropriate software installed, you can even administer a Windows NT server from a Windows for Workgroups machine. It is true that the user interface for Windows 95 looks new, but anyone familiar with Windows 3.1 or Windows NT can learn to use it quickly, and it really isn't a radical change. As mentioned previously, the Windows 95 interface will be available for Windows NT, probably by the time this book is published.

Getting on the Network

Windows 95 networking probably is new to most system administrators, and because it is the most obvious client platform for Access 95, the system administrators will need to integrate it into the existing network. It is a realistic plan to install a Windows 95 peer-to-peer network on top of a NetWare network; just remember that Windows 95 uses share-level security, which is not supported on NetWare clients, so you need to set up user-level security to restrict access to all resources that connect to NetWare clients. Windows 95 has a passthrough security model that allows NetWare to validate users, so if you set up the passwords correctly, the users only have to log on at their Windows 95 computers. You also can share printers between the two operating systems (technically, you are connecting to NetWare print queues, but the end result is the same).

If you are connecting to a NetWare network, you must ensure that Microsoft's IPX/SPX compatible protocol is loaded on the client Windows 95 systems, along with the Microsoft Client for NetWare. If you need to connect to UNIX systems, check that the TCP/IP protocol is installed. If your server is a Windows NT system, use NetBEUI or TCP/IP.

> **Tip**
>
> For a more detailed discussion of networking with Windows 95, look at *Windows 95 for Network Administrators*; Behrman, *et. al.*; New Riders Press, Indianapolis 1995.

Know the Target Environment: What Are You Planning?

Even if you plan to do your prototyping in an Access environment, you still need to consider your long-term plans, and which back-end server database is most likely to be your upgrade target. Your program design must accommodate the eventual target back end. The hardware you choose must support the new, more powerful and resource-intensive database management system—or at least have the capability to integrate into the new hardware that will accompany it. Your operating system software on both client-side and back end also must be able to support the new server software, or to integrate into the new server's operating system. The network you choose must support the change, or must be upgradable to accommodate the eventual reality. All these points must be considered as you prepare your new prototype and take it to production. You must design into the new application the capability to scale upward to bigger and more powerful hardware and software.

Application Development Techniques

Traditional system and application design methodologies don't work too well in the new client/server paradigm. Two assumptions that traditional methodologies make are: the application can be completely designed before any code is ever written, and business requirements will not change through the development life cycle. Neither of these assumptions is true.

The client/server environment is based so entirely on technology and business rules that both must be tightly integrated into the design or the development effort will fail. The technology is a culprit, a bugaboo to client/server application development—it refuses to stabilize or even to evolve at a reasonable pace! New hardware components, new software, improved techniques, and better tools continually flood the market, enabling the creation of applications that can do just about anything, but that challenge even the most competent application developer.

To compound this problem, we have the changing business scene. Client/server solutions focus tightly on the business, in an effort to be extremely responsive to business requirements. The constant need to know more, to know better, to manage the data more efficiently, and to analyze the data more effectively drive the client/server applications developer to use these new tools and techniques. The challenge to deliver better, more efficient, more effective client/server applications is an effort that will not soon dissipate.

Structured Methodology

If your introduction to programming was during the heyday of FORTRAN or COBOL, you probably are used to structured programming and structured development techniques. Structured application development was heavily influenced by structured programming techniques, and both were quite rigid in their assumptions—one point of entry, one point of exit.

The traditional development life cycle took a long time, and applications were built to last for many decades. Each step in the design process was completed and reviewed before the next step began. First, several rounds of business systems analysis and needs assessment were done. A conceptual design or designs followed, and these designs were thoroughly tested to ensure feasibility and workability. The conceptual design was followed by logical design and more testing. At some point, many months or years into the life cycle, pencil was put to paper (or fingers to keyboard) and the code started to flow. However, even program development was a slow, lengthy, and deliberate process. Data entry screens (non-GUI, nonevent-driven) were developed and reports were added to the list of things to do and test. Stub testing and stress testing were done constantly. The application was a carefully crafted piece of art that would outlive, in some cases, the people who created it.

Near the point of program completion the application was "rolled out" in a carefully planned, deliberately controlled operation. User involvement, which up to now was not a large part of the process, suddenly became a major part of the life cycle. User acceptance then hinged on a first impression of a completed or nearly completed product. Too often, it was influenced by how the software was introduced, not by its features or functionality.

Although we discussed this formal application development technique as though it is a thing of the past, it is alive and well and still very operational. There are many reasons to follow the traditional methodologies. One reason is the extensive testing that is involved at every step of the process. Another reason is the high confidence level that is developed in an application after having spent so many months or years in the planning stage.

Rapid Application Development (RAD)

In today's fast-paced world, however, time has a way of running out on projects that simply take too long to come to fruition. The authors have personal knowledge of one project that was seven years in the design phase. Even for the relatively static environment within which this project became someone's career, time did not stand still!

Never fear; the development life cycle is not dead. Remember, the intent of the life cycle is to plan, execute, and control activities for an applications development project. Traditional methods simply need to be moderated to accommodate the new client/server reality.

RAD, *Rapid Application Development*, is one methodology that evolved to meet the demand for speed in the development process. In today's frenzied business environment, the life cycle of a product, a service, or an idea may be no more than 18 months. Multi-year development cycles are no longer acceptable. You don't want to have forgotten the question by the time the answer arrives! Applications must be developed to meet changing business needs and, as the business needs change on a near-daily basis, the development must be fast. As we discussed in Chapter 1, the introduction of client/server technology often coincides with business process reengineering. Change is becoming the standard way of life in the business world, and the Information Services department should be leading the way.

The idea of Rapid Application Development is partly based on the old 80/20 rule; 80 percent of the benefit is produced from 20 percent of the time and effort. The remaining 20 percent of the benefit requires the other 80 percent of the time and effort, but if you step away from the problem and think about it, is the last 20 percent really needed to solve the business problem, or is it "window dressing" (this may not be a good choice of words—maybe it is the "icing on the cake") to make the application look good? Is the other 20 percent of the application meant for a small subset of users? Wouldn't it be better to develop an application specifically for them? There is always more than one way to resolve business problems in an efficient, effective manner.

In Chapter 1, we said that client/server technology follows the current business model. It also may be said that RAD follows the current computer technology. The traditional structured approach to applications development was used with computers that, after they were installed, were used for decades, processing jobs in batch mode, one after another. Today's computers—the ones that support client/server architecture—are based on multithreading and parallel processing, where a task is broken into component parts, which are then processed simultaneously (or effectively so) and, therefore, the total task is completed much faster. These same computers then are obsolete in three years. A similar approach is used in the development of an application by using RAD techniques.

RAD makes extensive use of *prototyping*. Prototyping is an engineering discipline that has migrated into the information systems realm. The concept of a prototype is to build a small-scale, working model of a product, or of one or more of the components of the product. In a RAD project, this means breaking down the client/server system into its component pieces and prototyping each component. You can learn more about prototyping in Chapter 5, "Client/Server Database Application Design Fundamentals."

Many steps in a RAD project can be carried out concurrently, which shortens the overall design and development time. Each part of the process has its own feedback loop built in, so you should never again hear the comment, "Nice job, but it isn't what we wanted," when you deliver a program. The business systems analysis and needs assessment is nearly continuous, and allows for user input so that the design can be modified as the development progresses. RAD is an iterative process; RAD is a process, not an event.

Prototype presentation begins early in the process. Reviewers, who should come from the user community, volunteer comments and suggestions to the tune of, "It would be really nice if we can add this feature." The design evolves, the user community has full involvement at an early stage, and the developer has guaranteed employment for lifetime.

Incidentally, it isn't unusual to develop an application in six months, from inception to production, using today's RAD tools and platforms. It also isn't unusual to throw away that application in a year, supplanting it with an enhanced version that offers additional functionality and more features.

Following the early stages of business requirements analysis and needs assessment, the first raw prototype forms, and perhaps a report or two, are presented to the reviewers. There is no code behind the forms—the forms are not connected to tables and store no data. The purpose here is to ensure that all the data elements are on the correct screen, in the right order, and that the forms are intuitive and easy to use.

As the requirements analysis proceeds and needs are solidly defined, tables design starts—both logical and physical design. These tables are connected to the prototype forms, rendering the forms functional. The testing and user feedback continues. Error checking, navigation and movement from one form to another, and menus to tie the application together are added.

Concurrently, security constraints, checking and upgrading hardware, and final definition of the business rules come together. These elements are added, one-by-one, until the needs of the user community are met. The important point is that the users, or at least a representative group, are involved in the process from the beginning and remain involved. They take ownership at an early stage of the application development, and this is what you want.

Remember that in RAD, an application is never really "finished." Rather, you deliver a version of the application, because something else always must be done as business needs change, or as the users become aware of new avenues to explore to exploit the power of their computers.

Tracking Application Changes

Client/server development involves at least two applications and with the three-tier model, it becomes more complex. If you plan to provide different front-end applications for various user groups, then you will have even more pieces of software to track. Because the development process is iterative, you will receive feedback and enhancement requests from the users. Keeping track of which request or bug fix was implemented—sometimes in more than one place—can be extremely time-consuming. Good organization is a must.

Your first task, design a couple of forms. These forms can be either paper or electronic. Either way, the intent of this design phase is that the users should have a way to document what they want or need as the application(s) evolve.

The first form should be a Bug Report Form and should include fields where the user can supply information that you will need in tracking down the problem. This form should contain the following information:

- User name and contact information—Phone, e-mail, and so on
- Hardware configuration—Memory, CPU type and speed, screen resolution, and so on
- Operating system and version number
- Other software running at the time of the failure
- The version of the application software that failed
- Failure symptoms

If you want to automate the process—because your users may not be familiar with operating systems and hardware specifications—then you may want to have them print a report from the Microsoft Diagnostics program to accompany their problem report. The diagnostic printout contains most of the information in the preceding list. The second form is the Change/Enhancement Request Form. This form is a "wish-list" and is much simpler. All you really need is the following:

- User name and contact information—Phone, e-mail, and so on
- The version of the application software under discussion
- The desired change
- A cost justification for the change, or at least a reason for the change

After these forms are returned, you should have a way of keeping track of them. On the companion CD-ROM that accompanies this book, you will find a simple Revisions database. This database allows you to track user feedback and also track which, when, and why database objects were modified. As supplied, it is a single-user, stand-alone database meant for the developer, but you can exploit this application in a multitude of ways.

First, customize some of the data entry screens to be more useful to the way in which you work. Then, use the Splitter Wizard to break Revisions into two databases. Distribute the client section to your users, and keep the data .MDB on the server, or even on your own development system. What a concept—a small client/server application that tracks changes to the corporate client/server environment!

To extend this concept further, you can take the revisions data entry forms that you customized and add them to the applications used by your own people. Add a menu entry just for Bug Reports and Change/Enhancement Requests. Then, from these applications you can attach to the Revisions data .MDB—multiple data sources from the Access 95 client environment. During test phases and after your client/server application has been installed, the users can report problems from within the applications by selecting your special menu option.

The Revisions Database Example

Revisions (RevAcc95.MDB) is a small Access 2 database that was converted to Access 95 in Chapter 2, "The Front Office/BackOffice Concept." Both versions are included on the accompanying CD-ROM. In Chapter 2, we mentioned how you might modify and expand it for your own use. In this section, we look at the major functional areas of Revisions.

The Product Build screen is used to record and track the components that go into a version release of a product (see fig. 3.3). There is a field for indicating whether this is a client or a server product release because different component sets will be included in each product. The subform is frmBuildSub in the forms container.

Fig. 3.3

The Product Build screen, frmBuild, which is used to track the components that make up a versioned release.

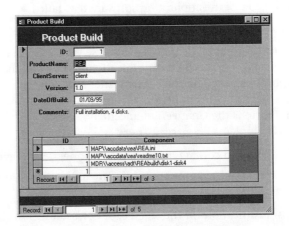

The Change/Enhancement Request Log screen is used to record and track bug reports and user-requested changes and enhancements (see fig. 3.4). The form contains two option groups. The upper group allows you to filter and view just resolved logs, or just unresolved logs, or all logs. The lower group allows you to indicate whether a log is a bug, a change request, or a no action log. (You see a European-style date here because one of the authors uses this format and the other does not, but Windows shows the correct date in either format.)

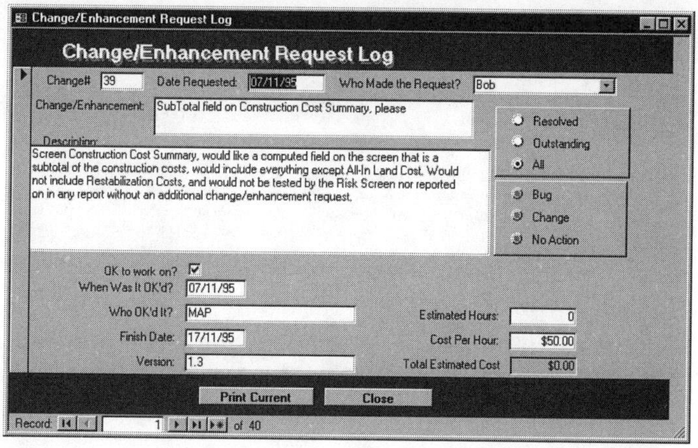

Fig. 3.4

The Change/Enhancement Request Log screen, frmChangeEnhance, which is used to track user change requests and bug reports.

The Document Tracker screen uses Object Linking and Embedding (see fig. 3.5). If you don't have Microsoft Word, Excel, and Visio installed on your computer when you view this screen, you may have problems seeing the documents. By switching to the table container, you can see that when you view tblDocTracker in design mode, the field Document is an OLE object. The screen is only a way of organizing design documents and project notes into an electronic folder for the non-Windows 95 crowd.

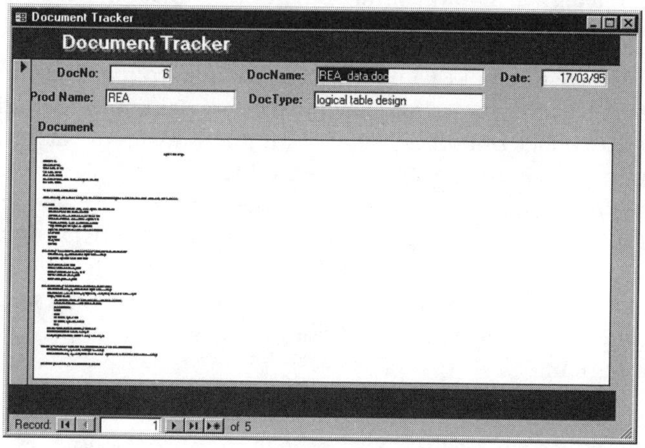

Fig. 3.5

The Document Tracker screen, frmDocTracker, which is used to track project and design documents.

The query, qryMAPChanges (see fig. 3.6), is one of many that are built on tblRevisions, the core and purpose of this little database. This screen, and others like it, is where a developer will daily track all modifications to database objects that belong to a product under development. New objects, as they are created, are entered. If an object is dropped from a product, the entries are not deleted out of tblRevisions; rather, an entry is made that indicates the object is obsolete. The table tblRevisions is an historical record of the development of database products.

Fig. 3.6

Query qryMAPChanges is one of the datasheets that is used to keep track of modifications to database objects.

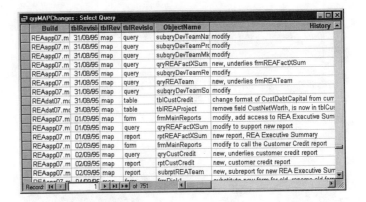

Working with Test Data

No matter how much a developer invents data to test an application, there is no substitute for using actual production data. There are several problems with "synthetic" data, which are described in the following list:

- It is limited in scope and may not test the limits of the system.
- It may not reflect the real values that will be input.
- It may be too complete (which may sound odd, but we explain in a moment what we mean).

As a developer, you may have to produce a new report, working from a single instance of a report generated by a legacy system. You may have no way of knowing if this data is a typical example, with average or normal values, or if it is a ringer—an atypical record that contains extreme values, or even incorrect values. In the design meetings with the users, try to define the data type of each field, the limits of the data that each field can contain, and the normal or average values. A good set of test data contains both normal and extreme values to test the capability of the system to handle any values that may be input. Although you may not see overflow-error messages, it's annoying to the user when a field on a form is physically too small to display a number or a name without scrolling.

How can data be "too complete?" One problem with fake test data is that all the data fields probably will be supplied with values, even though they may be no more than guesses. In the real world, users skip fields during data entry and leave blanks (or Nulls) where critical data is expected. These missing values can cause computed values to return errors, such as "divide by zero" conditions. They can cause forms and reports to behave erratically and, if used in code behind forms—such as branching logic—can disrupt the flow of the application.

If you acquire some real test data and find that the users consistently omit certain values, it may be a clue that either a design flaw or a business process problem exists. It is possible that the field(s) in question are out of sync with the way in which information is gathered. This problem may warrant a rethink and redesign of the data entry forms.

One of the benefits of RAD development is that it addresses the test-data problem of traditional software development by exposing the user community to an increasingly robust application.

Composition

Try to obtain test data from more than one user or, where appropriate, from more than one department. If you can obtain this kind of "real-world" test data, then compare the data for discrepancies. For example, one department might enter percentages as 10 percent, but another group might use 0.10 for the same data field, especially if it is using Microsoft Excel. A salesperson who deals with Canadian clients may find that the ZIP code field doesn't work for Canadian postal codes. If you are developing a client application to attach to an existing server database, the test data ideally should be a representative subset of the existing production data. Applications created for businesses that cross international boundaries may run into complications, such as date-and-time entries, currency formats, and so on. Fortunately, Windows 95 and Windows NT handle many of these variations for you, displaying the data in the correct format. Nevertheless, you should be aware of these differences and allow for the variations. For example, using a date field allows Access to handle the variations, whereas placing separate month and date fields on a form raises questions about which comes first. Internationalization of applications is a complex topic, and the subject of many articles in programming journals.

Client Participation

By now, it should be obvious that the users need to be involved in the design of the application. Because the development of an application is an interactive process, their input is needed and valuable during both the prototyping and testing phases. Look upon this participation as an opportunity. The managers who commissioned your work may have provided copies of the current forms, with the idea that they can be automated. Perhaps the users can suggest ways to improve the process if is not limited by these forms. Having to re-create forms and reports exactly, down to line spacing and font, is a real pain for a developer, and not an efficient use of time. Work with them to find ways to improve what they do, and perhaps they will be more willing to abandon the old paper forms in favor of the newer on-line methods.

If the end users will cooperate, employ them for usability testing. Have them enter some test data into a prototype of the application. Besides making obvious any problems with data formats, missing data fields, and so on you will gain valuable feedback on how they plan to use the application after it's in production, and how their idea of workflow differs from yours. Sit with the users while they enter data. Watch for erratic movement in and around the screens—data entry should be a smooth progression from start to finish.

If you plan to develop for heterogeneous hardware platforms, also plan to include testers and reviewers from each faction. The techniques and code that work well on one platform may not function at all on another. The key purposes of usability testing are to build applications that are willingly used by people and to avoid ugly surprises when the application goes into full production!

Elicit user feedback on output reports. Beware of the situation in which you were given only a brief description of the desired output from someone who has a very high-level view of the organization. Although everyone in the company shares the same set of data, it doesn't follow that everyone will want the same view of the data! Managers and executives are more interested in summary reports and statistical displays. The front-line staffers, the employees who deal directly with the customers and handle data entry, have a significantly different perspective. And remember, you cannot report on what you don't have stored.

From Here...

In this chapter, we discussed the hardware and software environments in which you will be developing your client/server applications. From here, jump to these chapters to find out more about the following:

- Chapter 5, "Client/Server Database Application Design Fundamentals," discusses how to get started on the application design.
- Chapter 7, "Using Access as a Prototyping Tool," shows how to begin building a prototype application.
- Chapter 12, "Securing the Access 95 Application," discusses how to secure your application so that it can be used on a network with control over who can make changes to the data.
- Chapter 13, "Building the Run-Time Application," teaches how to build and distribute a runtime version of the application for your client systems.
- Chapter 14, "Communicating with Other Applications," shows how to connect to other applications that are running in the same environment.
- Chapter 16, "Tuning the Access 95 Application," explains how to tune the application for peak performance in the client and server environments, and across your network.
- Chapter 19, "System Administration," details how to administer the entire system: hardware, software, and applications.
- Chapter 22, "The Human Factor," shows how preparing the users and introducing the software correctly can make all the difference in the acceptance (or otherwise) of the project.

CHAPTER 4

Getting By in SQL '92—Structured Query Language

SQL—Structured Query Language—is the *de facto* query language of all relational database management systems and is one of the two programming languages supported by Access 95. SQL (pronounced "see-quell") is a set-level language; that is, it works on sets of rows that have some common value or characteristic. This method of operation is the opposite of the way in which Visual Basic handles data, which is one row at a time.

We address SQL in this book for several reasons. First, we stated at the beginning of this chapter that SQL is the *de facto* query language of relational database management systems. SQL data manipulation language statements are even supported by most nonrelational database management systems on the market. Also, SQL is so easy to learn that it can be used as a query tool by non-programmers with only minimal instruction. Furthermore, SQL is a concise, declarative language that returns sets of data and, in a client/server environment, it is more efficient and causes less load on the network than a traditional row-by-row programming language. Finally, Access 95 uses SQL extensively. Access 95 queries are compiled SQL code. Access 95 passthrough queries usually work better and run faster when using RunSQL statements rather than the Visual Basic counterparts. SQL is a query language standard in client/server environments, and as a database professional who is exploring the client/server world, you need to know something about it.

Types of SQL

SQL is a non-procedural, *fourth-generation language* (4GL). No SQL instruction exists that opens a file or defines the layout of an input record, as you find in traditional, *third-generation procedural programming languages* (3GLs). When writing SQL code, you state what you want to do (retrieve records, modify records, set security, build a table, and so on), and you let the database management system figure out how to do the job.

SQL, in one of its manifestations, is an interactive programming language that you can use to write *ad-hoc queries* directly against a relational database management system. With the appropriate permissions, you can use *Interactive SQL* to manipulate data stored in the database, to create and alter tables, to establish security and integrity rules, to create indexes and triggers, and to remove objects from the database environment, all in real time. For regular reports or maintenance tasks, you can bundle multiple lines of Interactive SQL code into a "SQL Script" and run the script as you would run a 3GL program. The SQL statements are interpreted as they execute, usually getting minimum benefit from the database management system's query optimizer. Output from an Interactive SQL session goes to the screen or, by redirection, to a printer or system file.

A second type of SQL is *Static SQL*, which is SQL used in a batch manner, embedded in a third-generation host language program (such as COBOL, FORTRAN, C, or even Visual Basic). A Static SQL program (or COBOL with embedded SQL, depending on your point of view) is first run through a SQL preprocessor, which evaluates the lines of embedded SQL code and optimizes them for execution. The preprocessed SQL code and the host language code are then compiled together, linked into the system libraries, and transformed into a set of executable code that can be run from any batch program scheduler.

The third type of SQL, *Dynamic SQL*, is SQL code that is generated by an application at runtime, in response to user input. This is equivalent to passing variables to third-generation language code. Obviously, because the SQL search criteria are not fully known at the time the code is run, you can expect only partial optimization from any vendor version of Dynamic SQL. You can use any of the three flavors of SQL in Access 95.

Each of the three types of SQL has three types of instruction: data definition language, data manipulation language, and data control language.

Generations of Programming Languages

Programming languages are grouped into "generations," depending on how much assistance the programming language gives to the programmer and how far removed from the electronic circuitry the programmed instruction is. The higher the GL rating, the more abstracted from the hardware is the programming language.

First-generation language (1GL) programming actually isn't; it's just a way of referring to machine code, which we humans represent as a sequence of 0s and 1s, or low voltage/high voltage in an electric signal. Machine code is the language a computer's central processing unit can understand, and the instructions contained in the code get executed by the CPU.

Second-generation programming languages (2GLs) do little to shield the programmer from working directly with the computer's hardware. Although it may be true that 2GLs have verbs and statements that the programmer can use to represent sets of binary instructions, writers of 2GL code are limited in the kind of applications they can produce in a timely fashion. The 2GL program is assembled at runtime—the program instructions are translated into machine code as they execute. Assembler language is a 2GL, and there are multiple flavors of Assembler—one for each type and model of computer processor architecture.

Third-generation languages (3GLs) were developed to facilitate writing applications for business and scientific research. 3GL programming puts some distance between the programmer and the processor, which gives the programmer a chance to concentrate on the business or scientific processes that need coding. 3GL code is compiled—the source code written by the programmer is translated by the compiler program (which also was written by a team of programmers)—and linked with system libraries, which allows the compiled program to incorporate system functions into itself, into a run-time executable (machine code). Carefully written 3GL application source code can be ported from processor platform to processor platform by recompiling and linking with platform-specific compilers. COBOL, FORTRAN, PL/1, C, Pascal, and Basic are all third-generation languages.

Fourth-generation languages (4GLs) reach yet another level of abstraction that can benefit the computer programmer. 4GLs are most often associated with database management systems, and many of the functions that the programmer had to code in a 3GL (open file, input file format, print destination and layout, sorting routines, and control breaks) are handled by the 4GL. A 4GL programmer writes code instructions about what to do, not about how to do it. For this reason, 4GLs are known as "non-procedural languages." SQL and QUEL are fourth-generation languages.

Fifth-generation languages (5GLs) are those used in Artificial Intelligence research and development. These languages attempt to programmatically trace the human thought process and to define patterns of logic. Prolog is a fifth-generation language.

Origins of SQL

The concept of Structured Query Language (and relational database architecture) was born in the early 1970s at the IBM San Jose Research Facility, under the guidance of E. F. Codd, who later was recognized as the father of the relational model of database architecture. SQL, as it is known today, was one of several relational languages developed at the facility. In 1974, D. D. Chamberlain, *et.al.*, implemented a prototype language, SEQUEL-XRM and the rest, as they say, is history.

Commercial implementation of SQL began about 1979, when Oracle Corporation announced to the world that the Oracle RDBMS would run on multiple hardware platforms, would look the same to end users on each of the many operating systems to which it was ported, and used as its database programming language its own version of Structured Query Language. Relational Technology Inc. quickly followed suit by adding a SQL interface to its Ingres RDBMS. In 1981 IBM introduced a SQL product (SQL/DS) for its DOS/VSE environment; in 1982 it unveiled the same for its VM/CMS operating system; in 1983 it introduced DB2, its first SQL database. Data General Corporation introduced SQL/DS in 1982, and Sybase brought Sybase SQL to market in 1986. SQL has been and continues to be a commercial success, and nearly every database management system—regardless of its internal architecture—supports some level of SQL programming.

The SQL Standard

To say that a single *SQL standard* exists is wishful thinking. Early commercialization led to diversity in the proprietary versions of the language that were introduced with each database management system. To counter this trend toward 101 different dialects of SQL, the American National Standards Institute (ANSI) chartered its Database Committee in 1982 to develop a set of standards for SQL. Since then, the SQL Standards Committee has worked to define, refine, and extend the official and authorized version of Structured Query Language. In today's atmosphere of standards, open systems, and cooperative processing, database management system vendors who moved into the client/server arena are careful to model their version of SQL so that it is consistent with the ANSI standard.

> **Note**
>
> The American National Standards Organization (ANSI) is a part of the International Standards Organization (ISO). ANSI has been charged with establishing standards for programming languages for many years, since the early days of COBOL. Standards and recommendations made by ANSI usually inherit the ISO seal of approval.

The First SQL Standard, released in 1986, was based almost entirely on an "average" of IBM's dialects of SQL. It is only fair to point out that in their initial implementations, the three different IBM SQLs differed slightly from each other—and the '86 SQL Standard was different from all three! It also was different from all other vendor implementations of the language at the time it was published.

The '86 SQL Standard provided support for the definition, manipulation, and control of data in a relational database. This standard contained data definition statements (create table, create view), data manipulation statements (select, insert, update, delete), and data control statements (commit, rollback). It also provided for a security language (grant and revoke) and the beginnings of data integrity constraints (NULL and unique).

The 1986 SQL Standard was a minimal standard; it left many database functions undefined and open to interpretation by the vendor community. The 1989 SQL Standard attempted to more clearly define the '86 Standard, to solidify influence where the '86 Standard was incomplete (such as embedded SQL), and to address new concepts and techniques (like referential integrity and triggered actions). The '86 and '89 SQL Standards together are commonly called the SQL-1 Standard.

The 1992 SQL Standard (the SQL-2 Standard) encompasses almost all of the 1989 Standard, and is nearly five times the size of the original (1986) Standard. A lot of new territory was covered by the '92 Standard, with extensions to the original SQL that support an interesting array of concepts, such as three-valued logic, case statements, users, schemas, and sessions.

The development of SQL standards will not stop with the 1992 Standard. Already the ANSI SQL Committee is at work on a new standard (SQL-3), which may be released (all or in part) as early as 1997.

> **Tip**
>
> For a complete treatment of the 1992 SQL Standard and a good handbook of the SQL language, the authors suggest *SQL Instant Reference* by Martin Gruber, Sybex 1993.

SQL Syntax

Structured Query Language is a large language, and in no way will the authors try to present in this chapter a comprehensive treatment of the subject. Rather, this is more of a "getting by" in SQL 92, with some Access 95 extensions included. The authors have found that Access 95 is not a stickler for its own dialect of SQL; it supports ANSI SQL as it is presented in this chapter. The examples that follow each SQL statement use data types consistent with Access 95.

First, however, a few rules on SQL vocabulary. Access doesn't often use these terms in the product information it releases for external consumption. The authors suspect that this is quite intentional, that this is part of Microsoft's marketing to the unsophisticated end-user. After all, it is quite daunting to open a Help file and see references to attributes and domains, when all you want to do is insert a column into a table!

Relation is a table or a file, the database object that has physical presence on a hard disk and that acts as a container for attributes and tuples.

Attribute is a column or field in a relation. It has a name property and a data type property, or can be assigned to a domain, depending on the specific database environment. Integrity constraints and validation rules can be attached to an attribute. The number of attributes in a relation is known as the *ordinality* of the relation.

A *tuple* is a row or a record of the relation. All tuples of a relation are same-type, that is, they have the same set of attributes. The number of tuples in a relation is known as the *cardinality* of the relation.

Primary key is an attribute whose domain is a set of unique values, such that each tuple in the relation can be identified singly and uniquely. A primary key can be either a single attribute or two (or more) attributes whose values are concatenated to form a unique string.

Candidate key is an attribute that has all the qualifications to be a primary key.

Foreign key, also referred to as a *secondary key*, is a non-unique attribute in one table and a primary key in another table. The domain of the foreign key is the same as or is a subset of the domain of its primary key occurrence. Tables are joined by comparing values between the primary key occurrence and the foreign key occurrence and, in the case of the equijoin, rows are output where the two values are equal.

Data Definition Language

Data definition language is the part of SQL that deals with setting up the database environment—the create, alter, and drop statements. We cover the two most often-used entities, tables and views, and one not supported by the '92 Standard—the index.

A *relational table* is a two-dimensional object, composed of rows and columns, that acts as a container for the data in the database. At the physical level this table is a file stored on disk, with records and fields. However, the relational table—the logical model—cannot support repeating groups or array fields, unlike other file types consistent with older database architectures. In this logical model the records of the physical file become rows in the relational table, and the fields of the physical file become columns in the relational table. To avoid confusion when talking about tables and table design, the relational table also is referred to as a *base table*. We adhere to this convention and use the term base table in the rest of this chapter when referring to a relational table that was created by using the *create table* command.

A *view* is a *virtual table* that can be built from all or part of a base table, or from multiple base tables. A view has no physical presence except for an entry in the *data dictionary* (or *metadata repository*, as it is also known). A view is defined by using the *create view* statement. Once defined, it can be used like a table to retrieve or modify data (there may be some restrictions to data modification via views, however). At runtime, the definition of the view is retrieved from the data dictionary, reconstructed in memory, and populated with data, as required from the base tables from which it was created. Therefore, a view has a certain amount of overhead associated with it. Access 95 uses views, but calls them queries and compiles the queries with optimization, therefore making the use of the view (query) as efficient as possible.

An *index* is an ordered list of column values, either single-column or multi-column, which is used to enhance data retrieval or to guarantee uniqueness in the list. Each index entry is composed of two parts—one part is the value and the second part is a pointer to the database row that contains the value. Indexes are not defined in the SQL Standard because, according to Codd's 12 Rules of Relationality, a relational database doesn't need anything beyond the eight relational operators and the table itself to manage the data.

A *domain* is an object that can be used in place of data types when defining an attribute in a relation. A domain is composed of a data type, a default value, and appropriate constraints. Access 95 doesn't support the concept of domains.

An *assertion* is an integrity check, a set of rules or constraints placed upon all or part of a database but not necessarily attached to any single relation, although the integrity rule may reference one or more relations. Access 95 doesn't support creating assertions.

> **Tip**
>
> Although not strictly enforced by every dialect of SQL, it's good programming practice to end each SQL statement with a semicolon.

Create Table Statement

```
CREATE TABLE tablename (column_1 datatype, column_2 datatype, ...);
```

The SQL-2 standard code to create a table in the current database is:

```
CREATE TABLE customer (cust_code      text(12)   NOT NULL UNIQUE,
                       cust_name      text(30)   NOT NULL,
                       cust_phone     text(10)   NOT NULL,
                       cust_streetaddr text(30),
                       cust_city      text(30),
                       cust_state     text(2),
                       cust_zip       text(10),
                       date_first_contact date,
                       num_employees  integer );
```

As previously mentioned, variations of SQL are the norm, and the standard, as written, may need to be modified for a specific database platform. Normally, within Access 95 all table create statements are generated and executed when you save the table design you build in the New Table graphical user interface. However, you can write code to create tables by using the SQL interface in Query Design Mode.

To create a table in Access 95 you need to change the statement as follows:

```
CREATE TABLE customer (cust_code        text(12)
              CONSTRAINT ruleCustomerPKey PRIMARY KEY,
                      cust_name        text(30),
                      cust_phone       text(15),
                      cust_streetaddr  text(30),
                      cust_city        text(30),
                      cust_state       text(2),
                      cust_zip         text(10),
                      date_first_contact date,
                      num_employees    integer)
```

The primary key column—instead of being implied by the statement "not null unique"—is declared as a PRIMARY KEY constraint, or rule. This declaration causes not only a table to be created, but also a unique index on the cust_code column.

Access 95, contrary to the SQL-2 standard, does not let you declare a column as "not null" in the CREATE TABLE statement; it must be done in the CREATE INDEX statement (see below).

NULL is a representation of missing data. A data item can be set to NULL if the value is relevant but unknown, if the value is not relevant, or if you don't know whether or not the value is relevant. This is known as *multi-valued logic*. The three-valued logic Null has the potential to create havoc and unexpected results, if used incorrectly.

NOT NULL, when used in the create table statement, indicates that the associated column cannot be Null.

UNIQUE, when used as a modifier for a column in a table, ensures that each value in the set of values for this column will be different from all other values in the set. When a column is labeled UNIQUE, one instance of data in the column can be Null.

NOT NULL UNIQUE, when used in the create table statement, creates a candidate key from the column it modifies. A candidate key is a column that meets the criteria for primary key.

Create View Statement

```
CREATE VIEW viewname (column_1 datatype, column_2 datatype, ...)
    AS (select statement);
```

The SQL-2 code to create a view of a table(s) in the current database is:

```
CREATE VIEW cust_phonelist
AS
SELECT cust_code, cust_name, cust_phone
FROM customer);
```

Access 95 doesn't use the term, "VIEW," but rather uses the term, "QUERY." When you create a query in Access 95, you actually are creating a relational view, whose definition and run-time execution plan are stored within Access 95. Like table creation, all view-creation statements are generated and executed when you save or run the query that you created in Query Design Mode. However, you can use the SQL interface in Query Design Mode directly to create relational views.

To create a view in Access 95, you need only leave off the CREATE VIEW ... AS portion of the preceding command, and, when prompted, save it as an Access 95 query.

Create Index Statement

```
CREATE INDEX indexname
    ON tablename (column_1 [asc¦desc], column_2 [asc¦desc], ...);
```

Create an index on a table of the current database:

A single-column index:

```
CREATE INDEX idx_custname
    ON customer (cust_name asc);
```

A multi-column index:

```
CREATE INDEX idx_custzipname
    ON customer (cust_zip, cust_name);
```

To create a unique index that qualifies the column as a candidate key:

```
CREATE UNIQUE INDEX indexname
    ON tablename (column [asc ¦ desc]);
```

To create a unique index in the Access 95 environment:

```
CREATE UNIQUE INDEX uix_custcode
    ON customer (cust_code) WITH DISALLOW NULL;
```

The additional statement, "WITH DISALLOW NULL," is as close to the "NOT NULL" of the SQL-2 standard CREATE TABLE statement, which we discussed previously in this section, as Access 95 allows.

Tip

The asc or desc, when used as a modifier to a SQL statement, means you can select ascending or descending sort order for the values in the object you're creating. Ascending is the default sort order. The square brackets [ ] indicate an optional parameter. If you leave off the asc or desc modifier, your object will be ordered in the default manner.

Create Domain Statement

```
CREATE DOMAIN domain_name
    AS datatype
    [ DEFAULT default_value ]
    [ CHECK constraint_definition ];
```

The SQL-2 code to create a domain for customer codes is:
```
CREATE DOMAIN CustomerCode
        AS text(12)
        CHECK (value > 0);
```

The CREATE DOMAIN statement is not universally supported as such. In some database environments it may appear as a CREATE RULE statement, or be implemented by triggers or stored procedures. In others it may be implemented (in part) by the data type defined for a column. It also could be part of the declarative integrity statements for table creation, where the DEFAULT constraint is supported.

Access 95 doesn't support the CREATE DOMAIN statement directly, but rather gives you the opportunity to define the domain for each column by using the New Table Design graphical interface. Here, you can define the default value for a column by using the default property. You can restrict the domain values and send the end user a warning message when the restriction is violated by using the validation rule and validation text properties, respectively. The field size and field format properties further define the data type selected for each column and, as such, help define the domain of the column.

Create Assertion Statement

```
CREATE ASSERTION constraint_name
    CHECK predicate statement... ;
```

The SQL-2 code to create an integrity check to make sure that the customer phone number is filled in is:

```
CREATE ASSERTION rule_1
    CHECK (cust_phone is not null);
```

Like the CREATE DOMAIN statement, CREATE ASSERTION isn't universally supported. Some database environments may support a CREATE RULE statement that extends beyond mere domain definition and creates assertions, or integrity checks. Triggers or stored procedures can easily support assertions.

Access 95 doesn't support the CREATE ASSERTION statement directly. Using the graphical interface in Table Design Mode, you might allow zero-length strings, or disallow nulls, or code a validation rule that would initiate an integrity check. To establish or maintain referential integrity checks, you would use the Relationship Window (Tools, Relationships). Chapter 6, "Establishing the Ground Rules," goes into depth on table relationships, what they are, and how to establish them in Access 95.

Alter Table Statement

```
:ALTER TABLE tablename
    ADD [COLUMN] columnname
  ¦ ALTER [COLUMN] columnname
  ¦ DROP [COLUMN] columnname;
```

The SQL-92 code (and the Access 95 code) to add a column to an existing table in the current database is:

```
ALTER TABLE customer
    ADD COLUMN country text(20);
```

The SQL-92 code to alter an existing column, creating or changing a default value is:

```
ALTER TABLE customer
    ALTER COLUMN country default='USA';
```

Access 95 doesn't support the ALTER TABLE...ALTER COLUMN construct. To modify a column in a table using SQL code, first drop the column, and then re-create it with the new parameters. If data is stored in the column that you do not want to lose, use the Table Design Mode graphical interface to make modifications to the column properties.

The SQL-92 code (and the Access 95 code) to drop a column from an existing table is:

```
ALTER TABLE customer
    DROP COLUMN country;
```

Alter Domain Statement

```
ALTER DOMAIN domain_name
    SET DEFAULT default_value
  ¦ DROP DEFAULT
  ¦ ADD constraint_definition
  ¦ DROP constraint_definition;
```

Alter the domain for customer codes:

```
ALTER DOMAIN CustomerCode
AS text(12)
    DROP check ( value > 0 );
```

Alter View, Index, or Assertion

There is no official *alter view, alter index,* or *alter assertion* statement. To modify the structure of a view or an index, first drop it, then re-create it.

Drop Table Statement

```
DROP TABLE tablename;
```

The SQL-92 code (and the Access 95 code) to delete the table customer from the current database is:

```
DROP TABLE customer;
```

Drop View Statement

```
DROP VIEW viewname;
```

The SQL-92 code to delete the view cust_phonelist from the current database is:

```
DROP VIEW cust_phonelist;
```

In Access 95, to drop a view (query), simply delete the query entry from the query list in the database container.

Drop Index Statement

```
DROP INDEX indexname;
```

The SQL-92 code (and the Access 95 code) to delete the index, idx_custname, from the current database is:

```
DROP INDEX idx_custname;
```

Drop Domain Statement

```
DROP DOMAIN domain_name;
```

The SQL-92 code to delete the domain CustomerCode from the current database is:

```
DROP DOMAIN CustomerCode;
```

As Access 95 does not directly support the CREATE DOMAIN construct; simply reverse whatever procedure(s) you used to establish domain constraints.

Drop Assertion Statement

```
DROP ASSERTION assertion_name;
```

The SQL-92 code to delete an assertion from the current database is:

```
DROP ASSERTION rule_1;
```

Because Access 95 doesn't directly support the CREATE ASSERTION construct, simply reverse whatever procedure(s) you used to establish these assertions (integrity checks).

Data Manipulation Language

Data manipulation language is the part of SQL that deals with retrieving and modifying data from the database—the select, insert, update, and delete statements. It also covers the techniques of joining two or more tables, horizontally or vertically, and nesting one query inside another. All of these techniques enable the programmer to extract data with greater precision in fewer steps.

SQL has *closure*. Every SQL operation starts with one or more tables as the source of data, creates multiple tables in memory as it is working through the request, and outputs a "table of results" which it presents to the user.

Data Retrieval Statements

Data retrieval statements retrieve and display data from the database. The SELECT statement is the only ANSI SQL statement that falls into this category, although Access adds the SELECT INTO as a proprietary extension.

The *select statement* retrieves, orders, and displays data from the database. A select statement can use one or many tables or views, or combinations of the two.

A *predicate* is the portion of a SQL statement that evaluates to true, false, or (when NULLs are allowed) unknown. This portion of the SQL statement (usually the WHERE clause) contains comparison operators and test values for assessing stored data.

The *sort by* operator is a way of sorting the retrieved data. It only modifies the arrangement of data in the output table of results; it does nothing to the order of the stored data. There is a practical limit (usually seven columns) by which you can sort in a single SQL statement.

Grouping in SQL is a way to get summary data. The normal SQL query returns a detail report; you can get summary data by incorporating the *group by* into the SQL statement.

Select Statement. The generic Select statement is:

```
SELECT [DISTINCT] column_1, column_2, ...
    FROM table_1, table_2, ... ;
```

The SQL-92 code (and the Access 95 code) to select all columns, all rows from a table is:

```
SELECT * FROM customer;
```

The SQL-92 code (and the Access 95 code) to select a single column, all rows from a table is:

```
SELECT cust_name
    FROM customer;
```

The SQL-92 code (and the Access 95 code) to select a list of unique values from the table is:

```
SELECT DISTINCT cust_zip
    FROM customer;
```

The SQL-92 code (and the Access 95 code) to select multiple columns, all rows from a table is:

```
SELECT cust_name, cust_phone
    FROM customer;
```

The Access Select statement gives a few additional options:

```
SELECT [ALL¦DISTINCT¦DISTINCTROW¦TOP n [PERCENT]]
➥column1, column2, ...
    FROM table_1, table_2, ... ;
```

Select the first five customers we sold to:

```
SELECT TOP 5 cust_name
      FROM customer;
            ORDER BY date_first_contact DESC;
```

The *DISTINCT* modifier in the SELECT clause is the SQL Standard; Access has, in addition, a *DISTINCTROW* modifier. Use DISTINCT when you want to omit records from the table of results that have duplicates in the set of columns requested in your query. Use DISTINCTROW when you want to omit records from the table of results where the entire record is a duplicate, not just the set of requested columns.

The ORDER BY sorts the output, either in ASCending or DESCending order. We explain more about this in a following part of this chapter. The *ALL* operator is the equivalent to the * operator in the SQL-92 SELECT statement. As a matter of fact, the following two statements are equivalents:

```
SELECT * FROM customer;
```

```
SELECT ALL * FROM customer;
```

The TOP n operator (PERCENT is optional) returns the first n number of records. If no sorting is used in the SELECT statement, the first n random records are returned. If the records are sorted (use the ORDER BY clause, which we cover later), the top or bottom-most n records are returned.

Predicate Logic. Limit the selection to a specific number of rows based on some criteria:

```
SELECT column_1, column_2, ...
    FROM table_1, table_2, ...
    WHERE predicate statement ... ;
```

The SQL-92 code (and the Access 95 code) to select all columns, one row is:

```
SELECT * FROM customer
    WHERE cust_code LIKE 'T01223';
```

The SQL-92 code (and the Access 95 code) to select a subset of columns and a subset of rows from the customer table is:

```
SELECT cust_name, cust_streetaddr
    FROM customer
        WHERE cust_city LIKE 'Denver';
```

For a description of predicate operators, see table 4.1.

Table 4.1   Predicate Operators

Description	Operator
Matches the following pattern	like
Equal to	=
Not equal to	< >
Greater than	>
Greater than or equal to	>=
Less than	<
Less than or equal to	<=
Include in the list	in
Range of values	between ... and ...
Not applicable or missing	NULL
Reverse the above operators	not

The SQL-92 code (and the Access 95 code) to find the missing value is:

```
SELECT cust_phone
    FROM customer
        WHERE cust_phone IS NULL;
```

The SQL-92 code (and the Access 95 code) to search for a *range of values* is:

```
SELECT cust_name, cust_phone
    FROM customer
        WHERE cust_zip BETWEEN '80000' AND '89999';
```

The SQL-92 code (and the Access 95 code) to search for multiple criteria (use the AND operator) is:

```
SELECT cust_name, cust_phone
    FROM customer
        WHERE cust_name LIKE '%Alvarez%'
        AND cust_city LIKE 'Pueblo';
```

The *wild-card character* is used with the *LIKE operator* to extend the latitude of the search. The SQL Standard wild card to match a single character is the underscore (_). To match a string of characters, use the percent sign (%). Not every database management system subscribes to the standard. Access uses the question mark (?) to match a single character and an asterisk (*) for full string searches.

String matches, even with the LIKE operator, are exact matches, and case-sensitivity is an issue. If you have a situation in which you're searching for all occurrences of the string, "Mountain," but this string may be stored in the database as "Mountain," "mountain," or "MOUNTAIN," use the OR operator and specify all three capitalizations.

The SQL-92 code (and the Access 95 code) to use the *OR operator* is:

```
SELECT cust_name, cust_phone
    FROM customer
        WHERE cust_name LIKE '%Alvarez%'
        OR cust_city LIKE 'Grand Junction';
```

Precedence of Operations

Using the AND and OR operators in SQL works in the same way as in any other programming language—if you AND two statements together, you get all rows returned that meet both criteria (the intersection of the selection criteria). If you OR two statements together, you get all rows that meet either criteria, the selection criteria appended. Other rules for using AND and OR in SQL:

- AND and OR operators can be used in the same WHERE clause.

- The AND condition is evaluated before the OR condition.

- Use parentheses to establish precedence, as in the following example:

```
SELECT cust_name, cust_phone
    FROM customer
        WHERE (cust_name LIKE '%Alvarez%'
            AND cust_city LIKE 'Pueblo')
        OR cust_city LIKE 'Grand Junction';
```

The SQL-92 code (and the Access 95 code) for the restricted *IN operator* is:

```
SELECT cust_name, cust_phone
    FROM customer
        WHERE cust_zip IN ('80202', '80207', '80013');
```

Tip

The *restricted IN operator* is a functional equivalent to multiple OR operators.

The SQL-92 code (and the Access 95 code) for the NOT operator is:

```
SELECT cust_name, cust_phone
    FROM customer
        WHERE cust_zip NOT IN ('80202', '80207', '80013');
```

SQL Aggregates. One rule of relational table design: don't store computed values in the database; rather, calculate them as needed. To calculate a single value from a set of values:

```
SELECT aggregate (column_1)
    FROM table_1, table_2, ...
        WHERE predicate statement ... ;
```

The SQL-92 code (and the Access 95 code) to get the *average* value (works on number data types, returns a number) is:

```
SELECT AVG (num_employees)
    FROM customer;
```

The SQL-92 code (and the Access 95 code) to get the *maximum* value (works on any data type, returns same data type) is:

```
SELECT MAX (date_first_contact)
    FROM customer;
```

The SQL-92 code (and the Access 95 code) to get the *minimum* value (works on any data type, returns same data type) is:

```
SELECT MIN (date_first_contact)
    FROM customer;
```

The SQL-92 code (and the Access 95 code) to get the *sum* of values (works on number data types, returns a number) is:

```
SELECT SUM (num_employees)
    FROM customer;
```

The SQL-92 code (and the Access 95 code) to get the *count* of values (works on any data type, returns a number) is:

```
SELECT COUNT (num_employees)
    FROM customer;
```

The SQL-92 code (and the Access 95 code) to get the count of distinct values (works on any data type, returns a number) is:

```
SELECT COUNT (distinct cust_zip)
    FROM customer;
```

The SQL-92 code (and the Access 95 code) to get the count of rows (works on any data type, returns a number) is:

```
SELECT COUNT (*)
    FROM customer;
```

The *COUNT of values* and *COUNT of rows* may differ, depending on whether or not the value that is being counted contains NULLs. COUNT of values do not count any instance of the value that is Null. COUNT of rows counts all rows returned by the query, regardless of the presence of NULLs.

Sort the Output. Order the output of a query by using the ORDER BY construct, as in the following:

```
SELECT column_1, column_2, ...
   FROM table_1, table_2, ...
        WHERE predicate statement ...
             ORDER BY a_column_that_has_been_selected [ASC ¦ DESC];
```

The SQL-92 code (and the Access 95 code) to sort the output from this query so that the table of results is ordered by cust_name, A-Z, is:

```
SELECT cust_code, cust_name, cust_phone
   FROM customer
        WHERE cust_zip BETWEEN '80000' AND '89999'
             ORDER BY cust_name ASC;
```

Order the output on a column that is in the SELECT clause. The number of columns that you can order by is restricted by the individual database management system, but usually is about seven. Remember that this action arranges the rows in the output only; it does nothing to the stored data.

Group By. Create a summary report by grouping on some criteria, using the *GROUP BY* construct:

```
SELECT column_1, aggregate(column_2), aggregate(column_3), ...
   FROM table_1, table_2 ...
   WHERE predicate statement ...
   GROUP BY column_1
   HAVING predicate statement ... ;
```

The SQL-92 code (and the Access 95 code) to show how many customers we have in each zip code is:

```
SELECT cust_zip, COUNT (cust_code)
   FROM customer
        GROUP BY cust_zip
             HAVING cust_zip BETWEEN '80000' AND '89999';
```

Tip

The HAVING clause is a predicate and, like the WHERE clause, which filters rows retrieved by a SELECT before the grouping, it filters the results following a grouping.

Select Into. The SELECT INTO statement is specific to Access SQL; it is not included in the SQL-2 standard. This statement enables you to dynamically create a new table and populate it with the rows and columns selected from the table in the FROM clause. The SELECT INTO accepts the full range of valid operators: GROUP BY, JOIN, UNION, subqueries:

```
SELECT column_1, column_2, column_3, ... INTO new_table
   FROM table_1, table_2, ...
   WHERE predicate statement ...
        GROUP BY column_1
             HAVING predicate statement ...
        ORDER BY column_1;
```

Create an Old_Customer table to hold customer records from customers who were first contacted over five years ago:

```
SELECT * INTO old_customer
      FROM customer
            WHERE date_first_contact < #01/01/91#;
```

Complex Operations

A *join* is a procedure for linking related data in two or more tables. The values of the primary key in one table are compared to the values of a related foreign key in a second table, and where a match exists to the type of join requested (equals, not equals, greater than, less than), an output row is produced.

A *subquery* is one query nested within another; therefore, the alternate name, "nested query." No theoretical limit exists to the number of subqueries in a SQL statement but most database management systems have set a realistic limit of around seven.

A *union* vertically combines two sets of columns from two tables, creating a third table of results that contains all rows of both input tables. Theoretically, the two sets of columns must be "union-compatible," that is, they must have the same data type in the corresponding columns.

We need to introduce two more tables, the Order table and the Order_Line table, to demonstrate the complex operations. The database file, Customr7.mdb, which is included on the companion CD-ROM, contains both these tables and also a "SQL Scratchpad," which you can use to test these queries.

```
CREATE TABLE orders (order_num    text(16),
                  CONSTRAINT ruleOrderPKey PRIMARY KEY,
cust_code       text(12),
                    order_date      datetime,
                    order_status    text(24),
                    instructions    memo);

CREATE TABLE order_line  (order_num text(16) not null,
                  CONSTRAINT ruleOrderLinePKey PRIMARY KEY,
                    order_line_num      integer,
                    product_num         text(12),
                    order_quantity      integer,
                    order_line_status   text(24),
                    order_line_ship_date datetime);
```

Joins. There are three types of joins:

- the *equijoin*, which bases the join on an equality condition (=, >, >=, <, <=) to evaluate output rows.
- the *natural join*, which is the same as the equijoin but automatically eliminates one of the duplicate columns on which the tables were joined.
- the *outer join*, which includes in the output table of results the rows that do not have matches.

To complicate the situation, two ways exist to write a join, the '86-'89 standard (SQL-1) and the '92 standard (SQL-2). The '86-'89 standard puts the join statement in the WHERE clause; the '92 standard places this statement in the FROM clause. The '92 standard is more robust, more flexible, and supports non-equijoins in a way not possible with the '86-'89 standard. Access 95 supports the '92 standard as its native format, but it is backwardly compatible to the '86-'89. So, you can write a simple join in the WHERE clause, if you are more familiar with the technique.

In this situation, you must be wary. If you are developing client/server applications that will remain homogeneous—that is, both client and server portions will be Microsoft Access, either version 2 or 7—you can use the '92 join standard. If, however, you will use SQL passthrough or ODBC calls to a heterogeneous environment—back-end databases that do not yet support the '92 join standard—you are better off writing the joins according to the '86-'89 standard.

The '86-'89 standard (SQL-1):

```
SELECT table1.column1, table2.column2, table2.column3
   FROM table1, table2
        WHERE table1.join_column = table2.join_column
              AND other predicate statements... ;
```

The '92 standard (SQL-2):

```
SELECT table1.column_1, table2.column_2, table2.column_3
FROM table1 CROSS¦INNER¦LEFT OUTER¦RIGHT OUTER¦FULL OUTER¦UNION
➥JOIN table2
        ON table1.join_column = table2. join_column
        WHERE predicate statement ... ;
```

A Quick Word About What Kind of Results Each of These Join Types Produce

The CROSS JOIN is the Cartesian Product of the rows of both tables, all combinations of rows are used. If table_1 has N rows and table_2 has M rows, then the output table of results will contain $N*M$ rows. If you extract data from two tables without issuing a JOIN statement in Access 95, the effective result is the same as the CROSS JOIN.

The INNER JOIN is the equality condition, where the value in column_1 equals (=) the value in column_2. This is the '86-'89 standard join. Access 95 supports the INNER JOIN construct.

The LEFT OUTER JOIN output includes all rows in table_1, whether or not a match exists in table_2. NULLs are used to pad out the missing information from table_2 in the table of results. Access 95 supports the LEFT OUTER JOIN construct.

The RIGHT OUTER JOIN output includes all rows in table_2, whether or not a match exists in table_1. NULLs are used to pad out the missing information from table_1 in the table of results. Access 95 supports the RIGHT OUTER JOIN construct.

The FULL OUTER JOIN output includes all rows from both tables, regardless of a match or not. Again, NULLs are used to pad out the missing information from either table in the table of results.

(continues)

(continued)

The UNION JOIN output is the opposite of the INNER JOIN. The output includes only the rows from each table for which no match was found! NULLs are used to pad out the missing information in the table of results. Don't confuse the UNION JOIN with the UNION operator, which appears in a following section of this chapter.

Join the Customer table and the Order table to see who has placed orders recently:

The '86-'89 standard (SQL-1):

```
SELECT  customer.cust_code, customer.cust_name,
    orders.order_date, orders.order_num
        FROM customer, orders
            WHERE customer.cust_code = orders.cust_code
            AND orders.order_date >= #2/01/96#;
```

The '92 standard (SQL-2):

```
SELECT customer.cust_code, customer.cust_name,
    order.order_date, order.order_num
        FROM customer INNER JOIN order
            ON customer.cust_code = order.cust_code
            WHERE order.order_date >= #2/01/96#;
```

Please do not let the presence of the pound sign (#) surrounding the date in the last line of each of the two preceding queries concern you. This nomenclature is specific to Access only; the normal technique is to surround a date value, like a text string, with single quotes, as in the following example:

```
Select customer.cust_code, customer.cust_name,
    order.order_date, order.order_num
        from customer inner join order
            on customer.cust_code = order.cust_code
            where order.order_date >= '2/01/96';
```

However, for consistency with the Access environment, all examples that use a date as part of the selection criteria from this point forward will be written with the pound signs (#).

Tip

Tables are joined or linked on a common attribute, one present in both tables and one that has the same format and length in both tables, but not necessarily the same attribute name.

Use *table aliases* to simplify writing joins.

The '86-'89 standard (SQL-1) with table aliases:

```
SELECT c.cust_code, c.cust_name, o.order_date, o.order_num
    FROM customer c, orders o
        WHERE c.cust_code = o.cust_code
        AND o.order_date >= #2/01/96#;
```

The '92 standard (SQL-2) with table aliases:

```
SELECT C.cust_code, C.cust_name, O.order_date, O.order_num
    FROM customer AS C INNER JOIN orders AS O
    ON C.cust_code = O.cust_code
        WHERE O.order_date >= #2/01/96#;
```

A table alias can be used as an abbreviation for the table name in most database management systems. The alias usually is one to three text characters in length. A table-name modifier to an attribute is technically required only when more than one attribute of the joined set has the same name. Therefore, the table name modifier and the table alias are used to avert confusion, or when referencing the same table twice in one SQL query (self-join). Generated Access code always uses the full name of the table as a column modifier, although it will recognize table aliases when they are used.

Write a *three-table join* to see who has ordered what:

The '86-'89 standard (SQL-1) three-table join with table aliases:

```
SELECT c.cust_code, c.cust_name, o1.order_date, o2.product_num
    FROM customer c, orders o1, order_line o2
        WHERE c.cust_code = o1.cust_code
            AND o1.order_num = o2.order_num
            AND o1.order_date >= #2/01/96#;
```

The '92 standard (SQL-2) three-table join with table aliases:

```
SELECT C.cust_code, C.cust_name, O1.order_date, O2.product_num
    FROM ((customer AS C INNER JOIN orders AS O1
    ON C.cust_code = O1.cust_code)
        INNER JOIN order_line AS O2
        ON O1.order_num = O2.order_num)
            WHERE O1.order_date >= #2/01/96#;
```

Do an outer join on the Customer table and the Order table to see who has not placed orders recently:

Not supported in the '86-'89 standard.

The '92 standard (SQL-2):

```
SELECT C.cust_code, C.cust_name, O.order_date, O.order_num
    FROM customer AS C LEFT OUTER JOIN orders AS O
    ON C.cust_code = O.cust_code
        WHERE O.order_date >= #2/01/96#;
```

Subqueries. As mentioned previously, a subquery is one query that is nested or embedded inside another. Use this technique *when you want to display information from only one table*, but have to reference data in another table to determine the output. You can use a subquery to check values against a lookup table (the *evaluation subquery*), compare values against other values (the *correlated subquery*), and check for existence (the *qualified subquery*).

Usually, a subquery statement is evaluated from the inside out—that is, the innermost query is evaluated first, and the results are then used to limit and evaluate the next-outer-level query. There is the case, however, where the inner query results are dependent on the outer query findings (the correlated subquery). Most statements that can be written with a subquery also can be written with a join, although the inverse is not necessarily true. Writing subqueries is a matter of personal preference, but in some database management system environments, a subquery uses fewer resources than an equivalent join statement.

The evaluation subquery:

```
SELECT column_1, column_2
    FROM table_1
    WHERE column_1 [NOT] IN
        (SELECT column_1
         FROM table_2);
    WHERE predicate statement limiting the search to a single value);
```

Has Ski Heaven placed an order this year?

```
SELECT cust_code, cust_name, cust_phone
    FROM customer
        WHERE cust_name LIKE "Ski Heaven"
        AND cust_code IN
        (SELECT cust_code FROM orders
            WHERE order_date > #2/01/96#);
```

SQL evaluates the innermost query first. If the inner query evaluates to true, a single value is returned to the next-outer query and used to limit the processing of the entire query. Subqueries that can return only a single value are also known as *scalar subqueries.*

Which customers have not placed an order yet this year?

```
SELECT cust_code, cust_name, cust_phone
    FROM customer
        WHERE cust_code NOT IN
        (SELECT cust_code FROM orders
            WHERE order_date > #01/01/96#);
```

An evaluation subquery also can return a list of values from the inner query, which is then used as the input to the outer query. Subqueries that can return one or more columns, multiple rows also are referred to as *table subqueries.*

The correlated subquery:

```
SELECT column_1, column_2
    FROM table_1
    WHERE column_1 = ¦ IN ¦ NOT IN ¦ ANY ¦ SOME ¦ ALL
        (SELECT column_1
            FROM table_2
                WHERE predicate or selection criteria);
```

Which customers have placed more than three orders so far this year?

```
SELECT * from customer
    WHERE cust_code IN
    (SELECT cust_code FROM orders
        WHERE order_date > #01/01/96#
            GROUP BY cust_code HAVING COUNT(cust_code) >= 3 );
```

A correlated subquery is quite different from an evaluation subquery. In the evaluation subquery, the inner query is processed one time and the results are used to evaluate the entire outer query. In a correlated subquery, processing of the inner query is dependent on data from the outer query. This would be the case if the inner query computed values based on data from the outer query, and the same table is used for both. The inner query would need to be evaluated independently for each row of the outer query—a set of values from the outer query is fed to the inner query, which then makes its evaluation *on this set of values only*, and returns the results to the outer query, *for each row of the outer query*. Subqueries that can return only a single row with many columns are also known as *row subqueries*.

The qualified subquery:

```
SELECT column_1, column_2
    FROM table_1
    WHERE EXISTS ¦ NOT EXISTS
        (SELECT * ¦ column_1, column_2, ...
            FROM table_2
                WHERE predicate statement ... );
```

Is Mountain Market one of our customers who has ordered this year?

```
SELECT cust_code, cust_name, cust_phone
    FROM customer
    WHERE EXISTS
    (SELECT cust_code FROM orders
        WHERE cust_name LIKE 'Mountain Market'
        AND order_date > #01/01/96#);
```

The qualified subquery uses the *EXISTS* or *NOT EXISTS* predicate to compare values in the outer query against the existence of rows in the inner query. If one row is returned, the comparison is true, else it is false. The qualified subquery is, in fact, a form of correlated subquery because it correlates the existence (or nonexistence) of data in the inner query to events in the outer query.

Unions. The *UNION operation* merges the output of two select queries by appending the data and displaying it in an output table of results. The controlling factor is that the two input tables must have compatible corresponding columns. All the SQL Standards insist that the columns of each of the two queries that comprise the UNION must be data-type-compatible in the order specified. This is the "union compatibility" that we previously discussed.

Of course, Access 95 relaxes this constraint. The field length and data types of the corresponding columns do not have to be union compatible. Be aware, however, that this feature is specific to Access and is supported neither by the SQL Standard nor most other SQL databases. SQL passthrough queries using a UNION operator with Access 95 extensions will not work.

```
SELECT column_1, column_2, ...
   FROM table_1
   WHERE predicate statement for table_1 only
UNION [ALL]
SELECT column_1, column_2
   FROM table_2
   WHERE predicate statement for table_2 only
ORDER BY column_1, ...;
```

Show all records from both the Customer and the Old_Customer tables in the same table:

```
SELECT cust_code, cust_name, cust_phone
     FROM Customer
UNION
SELECT cust_code, cust_name, cust_phone
     FROM Old_Customer
ORDER BY cust_name;
```

Ordinarily, the UNION operation doesn't return duplicate rows. However, if you need this or if you want to speed up the query processing, use the ALL modifier with the UNION operator. This causes all rows to be returned, duplicate or not.

The ORDER BY clause can be used with a UNION; using the ORDER BY will sort the output of the entire operation. It is the last clause of the query, and references the column names in the *first* SELECT statement. Generally, column names for the output table of results are inherited from the first SELECT statement.

There is a shorthand way to write this query if you want to select all columns from the tables involved. This technique, shown in the following example, is supported by the '92 Standard and by Access 95:

```
TABLE table_1 UNION [ALL] TABLE table_2;
```

The preceding example is equivalent to the following statement:

```
SELECT * FROM table_1
UNION [ALL]
SELECT * FROM table_2;
```

Data Modification Language

Data modification language statements are used to change the contents of the database.

The *insert statement* is used to add rows to a table in the database. When a row is being added, all or some of the attributes can be included.

The *update statement* is used to modify an attribute in an existing row of a table.

The *delete statement* is used to delete entire rows out of a table.

Insert Statement. Add a row to a table:

```
INSERT INTO table_1 [ (column_1, column_2, ...) ]
   VALUES ('value_1', 'value_2' ...)
   ¦ select statement;
```

One row at a time:

```
INSERT INTO customer (cust_code, cust_name, cust_phone,
                      date_first_contract, num_employees,
                      cust_streetaddr, cust_city,cust_state, cust_zip)
        VALUES ('T90001', 'Mountain Market', '3037692000',
                '6/01/95', 18, null, null, null, null);
```

A few values in one row:

```
INSERT INTO customer (cust_code, cust_name, cust_phone)
        VALUES      ('T90002', 'Ski Heaven', '3035491919');
```

Bulk data loading:

```
INSERT INTO customer
SELECT cust_code, cust_name, cust_phone,
       cust_streetaddr, cust_city, cust_state, cust_zip,
       date_first_contract, num_employees
FROM customer_master
       WHERE date_first_contact >= #1/01/95#;
```

Notice that the order of the columns in the first example ("One row at a time") state-ment is not the order in which they were created. Also, notice that the data values to be inserted correspond to the columns as listed in the INSERT clause.

The list of columns in the INSERT clause is theoretically optional. If you choose to omit it, you must declare the values that you're inserting in the order in which the columns of the table were created.

If you know only a few attribute values at the time you insert the row, you can follow the second example and insert only those values. The other attributes in the row will default to NULLs or to the designated default value, if there is one.

Tip

ANSI Standard SQL quotes dates—that is, uses single quotes to surround a date value. Since its inception, Access has used the # symbol to designate a date in a query. To use the previous example in an Access environment, the WHERE clause would read:

```
WHERE date_first_contact >= #1/01/95#;
```

Update Statement. Update an attribute in an existing row of a table:

```
UPDATE table_1
   SET column_1 = value_1, column_2 = value_2, ... ¦ subquery
   WHERE predicate statement ... ;
```

Change existing values:

```
UPDATE customer
SET num_employees = 19,
    cust_phone = '3037692100'
WHERE cust_code = 'T90001';
```

Add to an existing row:

```
UPDATE customer
SET cust_streetaddr = '1404 15th Street',
    cust_city = 'Denver',
    cust_state = "CO",
    cust_zip = '80202'
WHERE cust_code = 'T90001';
```

Do a global find and replace:

```
UPDATE customer
SET date_first_contact = #9/01/95#
WHERE cust_code between 'T90000' AND 'T99999';
```

Tip

In the predicate of the UPDATE statement, the LIKE operator is not used. Use the more restrictive and operationally precise operators (=, < >, >, <).

Access does not support subqueries in the SET clause but does allow joins in the UPDATE clause. This is an Access proprietary feature and is not supported by any of the SQL Standards:

```
UPDATE table_1 INNER JOIN¦LEFT OUTER JOIN¦RIGHT OUTER JOIN table_2
   ON table_1.join_column = table_2.join_column
   SET table_1.column_1 = value_1,
       table_2.column_1 = value_1,
       ...
   WHERE predicate statement ... ;
```

Update the order line status of the Order Line table; set it equal to the status of the Order:

```
UPDATE order_line INNER JOIN orders
ON order_line.order_num = orders.order_num
SET order_line.order_line_status = orders.order_status
WHERE orders.order_num = order_line.order_num;
```

SQL Arithmetic. Do a bit of arithmetic on the imaginary table, Salary_Info:
Global Add:

```
UPDATE salary_info
SET annual_bonus = annual_bonus + 100;
```

Global Subtract:

```
UPDATE salary_info
SET annual_bonus = annual_bonus - 50;
```

Global Multiply:

```
SELECT employee_num, salary, commission
    FROM salary_info
    WHERE commission > 0.5 * salary;
```

Global Divide:

```
SELECT employee_num, salary, commission
    FROM salary_info
    WHERE commission > 0.5 * salary
        ORDER BY commission/salary desc;
```

Tip

You can make any of the preceding examples target-specific by adding a WHERE clause and the appropriate selection criteria.

In the order of operations, evaluation is from left to right, multiplication and division first, then addition, and finally subtraction. Use parentheses to clarify your intent.

These arithmetic operators can be used in SELECT statements, and in WHERE, ORDER BY, and HAVING clauses.

Delete Statement. Delete a row from a table:

```
DELETE FROM table_1
    WHERE predicate statement ...
    ¦ subquery ;
```

One row at a time:

```
DELETE FROM customer
    WHERE cust_code LIKE 'T90001';
```

Several rows at a time:

```
DELETE FROM customer
    WHERE cust_city LIKE 'Montrose';
```

All the rows in a table:

```
DELETE FROM customer;
```

Access allows multiple table reference in the DELETE, and allows the use of the JOIN in the FROM clause of the DELETE. This feature is Access proprietary and is not supported by any of the SQL Standards:

```
DELETE
FROM table_1 INNER JOIN¦LEFT OUTER JOIN¦RIGHT OUTER JOIN table_2
    ON table_1.join_column = table_2.join_column
        SET table_1.column_1 = value_1, table_2.column_1 = value_1, ...
    WHERE predicate statement ...
    ¦ subquery ;
```

Delete from the Customer table those customers who have not ordered since the beginning of the year:

```
DELETE FROM customer
    WHERE customer.cust_code NOT IN
        (SELECT cust_code FROM order WHERE order_date < #1/0/196#;
```

Data Control Language

Data control language is that part of SQL that deals with transaction control. A *transaction* is defined as a logical unit of work, a set of SQL statements that succeed or fail as a group. In this respect, a business transaction can differ greatly from a database transaction, which tends to look at each SQL statement as a transaction in and of itself. To retain business data integrity—both the debit from the savings account and the credit to the checking account are part of a transfer of funds transaction at the bank—it's highly advisable to define business transactions by using the following commands.

Transaction Control

During a transaction, the database progresses from a state of consistency to a state of inconsistency and back to a state of consistency, as exemplified by our preceding bank example. The purpose of *transaction control* is to avoid the situation where part of a transaction (the debit from savings) is applied to the database and part (the credit to checking) is not. This action is accomplished in Interactive SQL by the following two commands.

Commit Statement.

```
COMMIT [WORK];
```

The SQL-92 code to commit a transaction is:

```
COMMIT;
```

Access 95 doesn't support the SQL COMMIT statement. Rather, it uses the Visual Basic **BeginTrans/CommitTrans** method. We cover this in depth in Chapter 11, "Managing Transactions." The COMMIT statement (the WORK part is optional) makes changes that were a part of the modification statements preceding the COMMIT a permanent part of the database. All modification statements since the last COMMIT are considered part of this transaction.

The SQL Standard implies that the COMMIT forces a physical write to disk, but how this action is handled varies from vendor to vendor of the individual database management systems. However, after the COMMIT is issued, the changes eventually become permanent, even in the event of a system crash.

Rollback Statement.

```
ROLLBACK [WORK];
```

The SQL-92 code to roll back or undo a transaction is:

```
ROLLBACK;
```

The ROLLBACK statement is the fail-safe; it is used if, for some reason, the COMMIT cannot go to completion. The ROLLBACK undoes all modifications made by the preceding transaction, returning the database to a state of consistency, as it was before the transaction began making modifications.

Again, Access 95 doesn't support the SQL ROLLBACK statement. Rather, it uses the Visual Basic **Rollback** method. See Chapter 11, "Managing Transactions," for more on the **Rollback** method.

> **Tip**
>
> Transactions are generally set up in static or embedded SQL, with a host language statement, such as "Begin Transaction" or "End Transaction." In Access the host language is Visual Basic, and the statements that define the extents of a transaction are the methods, **workspace.BeginTrans** and **workspace.CommitTrans** or **workspace.Rollback**.

Data Security Language

Data security language is the part of SQL that deals with assigning permissions to users of the database. SQL security is discretionary—the owner (the creator) of a database object (table, view) must grant permission to others to use the object.

The statements presented here are SQL standard, '86, '89, and '92. Access 95 doesn't support an interactive Data Security Language. To set and maintain security, use the graphical interface provided with Access. Refer to Chapter 12, "Securing the Access 95 Application," for a complete discussion of the Access security model.

Grant Statement

```
GRANT select ¦ update ¦ insert ¦ delete ¦ all ON table ¦ view
    TO user_1, user_2, ... ¦ public
        [WITH GRANT OPTION];
```

The following example allows users mary, tom, joe, joy, and the entire warehouse workgroup or domain to have read access to the customer table. They, in turn, can grant permission to anyone else (WITH GRANT OPTION), but only for the select operation.

```
GRANT select ON customer
    TO mary, tom, joe, joy, warehouse
        WITH GRANT OPTION;
```

The "all" option in the GRANT clause gives the receiver all the permissions—select, update, insert, and delete—to the object specified.

The "public" option in the TO clause is a shorthand. It gives anyone who has access to the database qualified access to the object specified.

Revoke Statement

```
REVOKE select ¦ update ¦ insert ¦ delete ¦ all ON table ¦ view
    FROM user_1, user_2, ... ¦ public
```

The following example shows that user joe has had all privileges on the customer table revoked.

```
REVOKE all ON customer
      FROM joe;
```

Access 95 Extensions and Exceptions

In this chapter, the authors have attempted to point out the major areas where Access is either fully compliant with the '92 SQL Standard (and, therefore, ahead of most of the other database management systems), or where Access 95 has extensions that are totally proprietary (UNION operations). To summarize, we present the following table of differences between Access SQL and the '92 SQL Standard.

Table 4.2   Access SQL and ANSI SQL-92 Compared

Feature	Access SQL Support	'92 SQL Standard	Comments
Joins in FROM clause	yes	yes	Access doesn't support CROSS, FULL OUTER, and UNION joins
Joins in the UPDATE and DELETE statements	yes	no	Access proprietary feature
Multiple tables declared in DELETE statement	yes	no	Access proprietary feature
SELECT DISTINCTROW	yes	no	Access proprietary feature
SELECT TOP *n*	yes	no	Access proprietary feature
SELECT INTO	yes	no	Access proprietary feature
CREATE VIEW	no	yes	An Access saved query is equal to a view
CREATE DOMAIN	no	yes	No Access equivalent
CREATE ASSERTION	no	yes	No Access equivalent
Subqueries in the SET clause of an UPDATE	no	yes	No Access equivalent
Security (GRANT, REVOKE) security subsystem	no	yes	Handled by the Access
Transaction control (COMMIT, ROLLBACK)	no	yes	Visual Basic methods BeginTrans, CommitTrans, Rollback
Case statement	no	yes	Visual Basic Select Case statement
'92 Standard datatypes	no	yes	Access supports most of the '92 Standard datatypes
'92 Standard wild-card characters	no	yes	Access uses ? and * instead of the SQL Standard and %

From Here...

Structured Query Language is a powerful programming language that you can use to exploit the power of Access 95 and its relational capabilities. For additional examples of how to use SQL, jump to the following chapters:

- Chapter 6, "Establishing the Ground Rules," covers validation and business rules.
- Chapter 8, "Adding Functionality to Your Prototype," explains procedures and code-behind-forms.
- Chapters 9, "Navigation: How to Get from Here to There," and 10, "Using Resources Wisely," covers more procedures and code-behind-forms.
- Chapter 11, "Managing Transactions," explains transaction control code.
- Chapter 12, "Securing the Access 95 Application," for an explanation of the Access security model.
- Chapter 14, "Communicating with Other Applications," begins the discussion of ODBC-SQL.

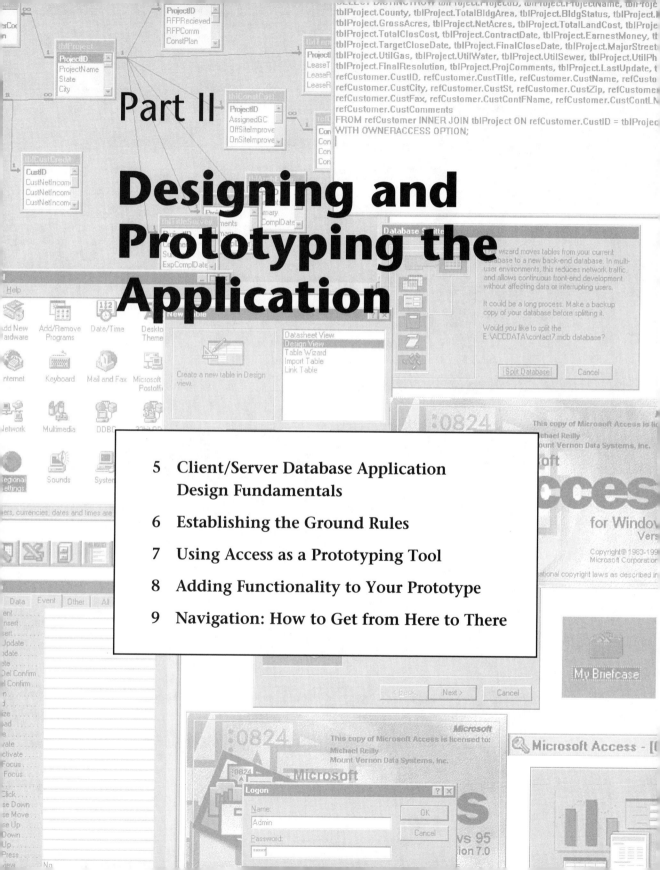

Part II

Designing and Prototyping the Application

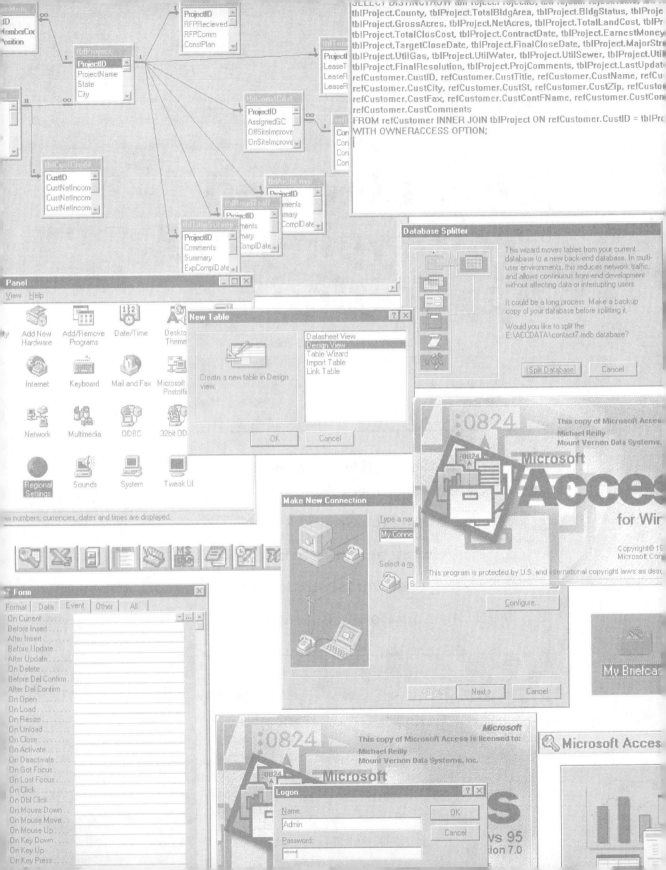

CHAPTER 5

Client/Server Database Application Design Fundamentals

As we mentioned in Chapter 1, "Client/Server, What Is It?" client/server architecture is a model for distributing information system tasks, and client/server computing is a method of implementing this model. Or, in other words, client/server computing is a way of splitting the workload and putting the hardware and software muscle where it's needed most—that's the theory, at least.

In the database arena, client/server computing takes on a slightly different perspective. Generally, in client/server computing the server is tasked with file management, document-transfer control, and some of the data processing (where appropriate). In the database client/server environment, the server still handles file and data management through the direction of the database engine, which lives on the server. Additionally, the database engine does the following few extra things when it receives a request:

- Optimizes and services queries that are sent to it by the client nodes
- Manages concurrency issues (several users or programs all trying to update the same record at the same time)
- Ensures transaction integrity (either all of a transaction or none of a transaction is posted to the physical database, but nothing in between)
- Checks security rules as they were defined on the database security subsystem
- Enforces the various integrities that it is capable of enforcing—entity, referential, domain, and user or business (the most common)
- Returns to the requesting client node only the set of data for which it asked, and no more

In this chapter we cover the following:

- Comparisons of and contrasts between the three computing paradigms: application/server, file/server, and client/server.
- On-line Transaction Processing (OLTP), what it is, and how it differs from OLAP.
- On-line Analytical Processing (OLAP), the new buzzword in database systems.
- Client and server architecture sizes, fat or thin?

- The need to plan your move to the client/server paradigm, and the need to assess skill requirements.

- The Hungarian naming convention, and how it helps you get a handle on organizing the development effort.

Computing Paradigms: Application/Server, File/Server, and Client/Server

A gradation exists in desktop computing models, which starts with the single-user mode and increases in complexity. Once single users make the decision to connect and share resources, you have moved into an *application/server* or a *file/server* environment. From application/server to file/server, there is a fairly distinct dividing line, but from file/server to client/server, no clear-cut difference exists, as many would have you believe. This is partly because file/server-client/server differentiation is not solely determined by hardware configuration, nor is it solely determined by the type of software products involved. The real criteria is where the action takes place—where is the query being processed? Let's take a closer look at each of these computing paradigms.

The Application/Server Model

In the example shown in figure 5.1, the single copy of data and the single copy of the database management system are stored on the server computer. When Kevin needs to update the data, he connects to the server's disk drive where the database is stored and downloads a copy of the database management system from the server. This operation uses CPU cycles on both computers and generates high network traffic for a few seconds. He then makes changes to the data. The database engine on Kevin's machine manages the modifications and stores the data back to the server's hard disk. Then Kevin generates a report to the network printer, again using the server's CPU cycles, shuts down the database management system, and disconnects from the remote disk drive.

In summary, in the application/server model, access to the stored data is not transparent to the user. Kevin had to overtly navigate through the network complex, find the stored data and the database management system, copy the program, and then run it locally. The only real use for the application/server is in the diskless workstation model, where Kevin's system has no hard disk and, possibly, not even a floppy disk. This arrangement is popular with IS departments because they only need to update one copy of the application, and can "meter" the number of copies made, to stay within the limits of the number of licenses. It works better with applications such as word processors or spreadsheets that are contained in one executable file. With an application such as Access, which is constantly requesting different DLLs (think of these as libraries of subroutines), the network traffic is high.

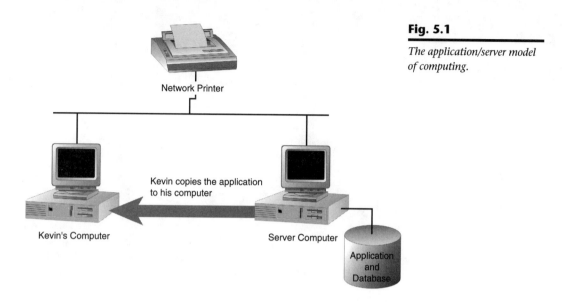

Fig. 5.1

The application/server model of computing.

Network Printer

Kevin copies the application
to his computer

Kevin's Computer

Server Computer

Application
and
Database

The File/Server Model

In the file/server database environment the query is processed at the client node. The file/server paradigm makes possible the single-copy-of-data, multiple-user model, although most data crunching is done on the client machines.

In the example shown in figure 5.2, the single copy of the corporate data resides once again on the server's hard disk. Every office person has a copy of the database engine and the database application on his or her computer. When Kevin needs to retrieve or update data, he starts his own copy of the database application, which runs his copy of the database engine. The application is "intelligent" in that it knows it needs to link to the database tables that are on the server's disk drive so that it can function properly. After the link is made, when Kevin wants to retrieve a subset of data from the database, his application sends a request to the file server for the appropriate pages of data. The file server, in turn, ships the data set to his computer, where it is massaged, manipulated, and output. Processing of the data takes place on Kevin's machine, not on the server. If Kevin needs to make a change to the data, his changes are posted to the physical copy of the database, on the server. Kevin still is using the network to extend his sphere of influence, but he is using mostly his own CPU cycles to process the data.

In summary, in the file/server model, access to the stored data is transparent to the user. Kevin only had to start up his copy of the database application; the application found the stored database, requested downloads of data from the server, crunched the data locally, managed printouts locally, and posted changes to the database on the server's hard drive—all without using a lot of the server's CPU cycles.

II

Designing and Prototyping

Fig. 5.2

The file/server model of computing.

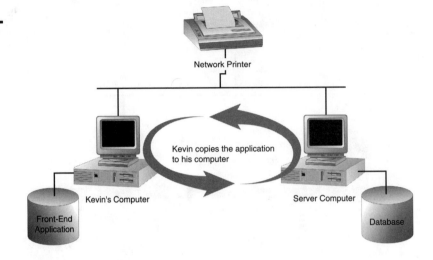

The Client/Server Model

In the *client/server database environment*, the query is processed by the server. The client/server paradigm extends the single-copy-of-data, multiple-user model by moving a substantial portion of the data crunching from the client machines to the server machine.

In the example shown in figure 5.3, the single copy of the corporate data resides on the server computer. In a pure client/server environment, only the server computer has a copy of the server database engine. Everyone else has a client application, which, depending on the type of client application we're discussing, may or may not have a copy of a database engine included. When Kevin needs to retrieve or update data, he starts up his own copy of the database application. This application also is "intelligent," in that it knows where the data is stored. Kevin's application sends requests for information to the server database management system. The server database management system receives and processes the requests right on the server computer, and sends back only the results to Kevin's machine. Updates are posted only by the database management system on the server.

In summary, in the client/server model, access to the stored data is transparent to the user. Kevin only had to start up his copy of the database application; the application sent requests for information or requests for change to the server database on the server's hard drive. The server database was responsible for processing the requests, sifting through the data, and returning to the client application only the requested information.

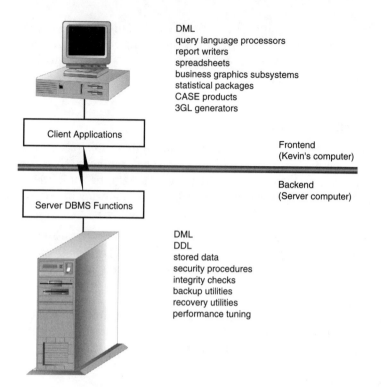

DML
query language processors
report writers
spreadsheets
business graphics subsystems
statistical packages
CASE products
3GL generators

Client Applications

Frontend
(Kevin's computer)

Backend
(Server computer)

Server DBMS Functions

DML
DDL
stored data
security procedures
integrity checks
backup utilities
recovery utilities
performance tuning

Fig. 5.3

The client/server model of computing.

II

Designing and Prototyping

The Right Model for You

The dividing line between file/server and client/server can be extremely thin. In the preceding example, it would have been possible, by coding a badly formulated query, to force the standard client/server setup into a file/server mode, where all the data must be processed on the client computer, thereby circumventing all the benefits usually associated with client/server computing.

Think of it in this way: the theory categorizes architecture and provides a basis for comparison; the implementation of the theory provides for a rich spectrum of usability, flexibility, and productivity. The theory tends to pigeonhole, proclaiming that, to be considered thus-and-so, a product must do this-and-that. In reality, products such as Access are being introduced that are difficult to categorize, in that they provide a continuum of capabilities, rather than function only within the bounds of a fixed category. They are hybrid products.

Depending on your business needs, you can start with an application/server database model, move quickly to the file/server model, and eventually—as the company and the business problems grow in sophistication—move to the client/server model. If you selected products to implement your application/server solution that do not scale easily—they do not support either the file/server or the client/server requirements—you will have to change product vendors (and migrate your data) in order to move forward.

OLTP versus OLAP

Access provides what we call the *continuum model* (a model that supports a single-user environment), and will quickly scale up to the file/server environment (Access, with its built-in capabilities and architecture, encourages users to skip the application/server model), and finally to the client/server model, all without being forced to switch workbenches, programming languages, and people skill sets.

A continuum also is the categorization of databased information systems, and at the two ends of the spectrum are *on-line transaction processing* (OLTP) and *on-line analytical processing* (OLAP). On-line transaction processing is the conventional data gathering and reporting scheme; on-line analytical processing underlies the executive information systems, decision support systems, and massive data warehousing models that are emerging in this decade. No single database can effectively be both OLTP and OLAP at the same time. Some critical decisions must be made up-front concerning the purpose of each database that will be used by the corporation.

OLTP Considerations

On-line transaction processing is the more conventional and mature of the two technologies. This is the traditional data collection, data storage, and data retrieval environment. As the data (sales information, inventory reduction, banking transactions, or airline reservations) is being generated, it is captured and stored. This type of environment is best serviced by OLTP.

Perhaps the most important characteristic of an OLTP system is the database table design. In OLTP, you must be able to capture data quickly, and you want to store it only one time—get it once, get it right, and get it fast. If your tables aren't properly normalized, if an item of data is stored more than one time (discounting primary and foreign keys), then you run the risk of compromising the integrity and accuracy of the data. The OLTP database shouldn't be burdened with having to synchronize multiple copies of John Doe's mailing address, nor should it have to accumulate and store counts, sums, and totals. Aggregate data, in an OLTP environment, should be calculated on an as-needed basis.

Two-Layer versus Three-Layer OLTP Models. How the OLTP application will be partitioned, whether a *two-layer* or a *three-layer model*, is a choice that must be made near the beginning of the application development life cycle. As we briefly mentioned in Chapter 1, the two-layer model, or two-tier model, as it is also known, is the classic client/server model, with stored data on the database server, the user interface on the client nodes, and the business and integrity rules scattered between the two. Figure 5.4 shows a conceptual illustration of the two-tier client/server model of computing.

The three-layer, or three-tier, model (see fig. 5.5) separates the business and integrity rules from both client and server portions, and places them in a third tier, known as the *business process server*. At the time of this writing, three-tiered client/server architecture is an emerging technology with a rather hefty price tag. A limited number of products are available with which three-tiered architecture can be implemented and, to our knowledge, none of them currently work with Access 95. By the time you read this book, however, this situation may have changed.

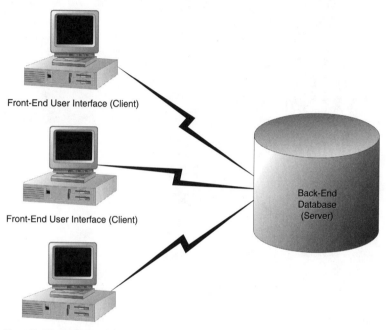

Fig. 5.4

The typical two-tiered client/server architecture, with business and integrity rules split between client and server modules.

Front-End User Interface (Client)

Front-End User Interface (Client)

Back-End Database (Server)

Front-End User Interface (Client)

II

Designing and Prototyping

Integrity Constraints, Business Rules, and Validation Checks. For the current Access 95 environment, you have to design your application around the two-tiered model. Where you locate your integrity constraints, business rules, and validation checks depends on three options: whether or not the rule should be inherited by all applications, whether or not you can embed the rule in one or another of the modules, and personal preference.

If an integrity constraint is stored at the table level—if it is a property of the table itself—and the table is an Access table, then that integrity constraint will be inherited by all applications that use the table or queries built on the table. If, for example, table Customer has the Required property for field cust_name set to Yes, any form that includes the cust_name column from table, Customer, either by direct reference or through a query, inherits the Required property. Validation checks (Validation Rule property) and the simple business rules that can be stored at the table level will function the same as integrity constraints.

Fig. 5.5

The three-tiered client/server architecture, with the business process server in the middle.

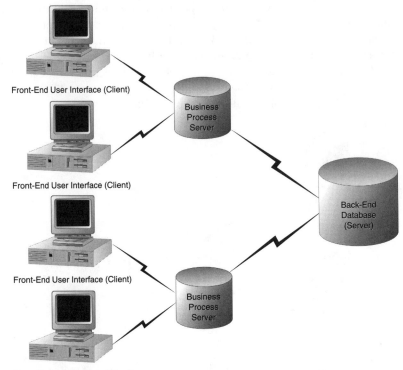

Front-End User Interface (Client)

Front-End User Interface (Client)

Front-End User Interface (Client)

Front-End User Interface (Client)

If the tables are non-Access (if the server database is Microsoft SQL Server, Sybase System 10, Oracle, and so on), then inheritance is not an issue—it doesn't happen. The capability to store (or not to store) integrity constraints, validation checks, and business rules on any of these database management systems varies from product to product. These properties also will most likely not be stored as table attributes or properties. Most back-end database management systems tend to enforce integrity, validation, and business rules by using stored procedures or triggered assertions.

If you are starting development in a homogeneous Access environment, using Access for both front-end client application and back-end server, and you plan to scale the server portion to a non-Access database management system, keep to a minimum the rules that are embedded as table properties. Make sure that the rules that are encoded at the table level in Access will translate to the new server environment. You'll have to know up front where you are going (which server database management system you will be porting to) and how soon you'll be making the port to effectively judge just how much coding you should commit to the Access tables.

Security. In an OLTP environment, *security* should be as simple as possible. It should provide the minimum limitations and restrictions as required by company policy, to avoid unnecessary overhead, which could interfere with high levels of OLTP activity. The Access 95 security model is covered in Chapter 12, "Securing the Access 95 Application."

Concurrency. Obviously, *concurrency* will be a big issue in any OLTP environment. The OLTP environment is, by definition, a highly updated one. The homogeneous Access 95 environment, with page-locking and the capability to implement either pessimistic or optimistic locking methods, provides a great deal of flexibility to the developer. When the server is a non-Access product, concurrency becomes the responsibility of the back-end database management system. Again, you must know your target server environment(s).

Performance. Performance will be a major issue in the OLTP environment. As the level of transactions and updates increase, so will the amount of time taken to perform the validity, integrity, business rule, and security checks. If immediate checking of user input at data-entry time is a priority, then these rules should be coded at the application level. However, the better design and maintenance scheme is to store the rules and check the data at the server.

It won't take long for any server to bog down as the levels of transaction updates increase. Rule checking creates an enormous overhead that is compounded by concurrency situations. Some relief can be bought by supplementing the hardware configuration for the server computer, or by distributing—either horizontally, vertically, or full replication—the database, but that also can carry a significant overhead. True relief will be achieved when mainstream database products support three-tier architecture.

OLAP/Data Warehousing Considerations

On-line analytical processing is the newer of the two technologies; it is more commonly known as *data warehousing*. The first wave of data warehousing seems to have established a beachhead in information systems technology, and the second wave is just beginning. Products designed from the bottom up to support data warehousing seem to be able to produce robust, effective methods of researching terabytes of data in storage.

OLAP, or data warehousing, was born of the convergence of three technologies: *symmetric multi-processing* (SMP) hardware and databases that could exploit it, *data transformation* and *metadata tools* for loading the data warehouses, and *multi-dimensional end-user tools* for exploiting the data in the warehouse.

OLAP technology is not necessarily consistent with relational technology. Although the OLAP database is often thought of only as a repository of historical operational data or as a decision support system—which was the way the concept was first sold to the user market—it actually is quite a different architecture. OLAP is structured to support human investigation. OLAP software represents data not in tables and columns, as the OLTP design does, but in *dimensions* and *measures*. Dimensions, or the way people want to see data, are the "bys," by region, by salesperson, by product, and so on. Measures, or numeric variables, are the units of product sold, the dollars produced in a day. People quickly turn data into information by manipulating the dimensions and units.

OLAP allows the developer to give users intuitive access to their own data, creating an atmosphere of user self-sufficiency. OLAP software is geared to allow users to follow a train of thought by offering fast response to complex queries across huge data stores. OLTP applications are based on the premise that users know the kind of information they want from their database. This is an untrue assumption for two reasons—much of a person's work is in response to requests from other people and no one ever asks the same question twice, and the stored data always contains surprises, good and otherwise, that demand follow-up.

Data stored in the OLAP environment differs significantly from data stored in the OLTP environment. Operational, or OLTP, data needs to be "cleaned" and "transformed" (denormalized and aggregated) when it is ported to an OLAP database. Operational data is not the only data source for a data warehouse. Non-database, non-tabular data—spreadsheets, publication layouts, scanned images, documents, video and sound clips—can be and often are included as part of the data warehouse. The volume of data in a typical data warehouse usually is measured in the hundreds-of-gigabytes to the multi-terabyte range.

OLAP storage systems can be classified into two types, *multi-dimensional databases* (MDDs) and *metadata pointer structure*. The following sections discuss both types.

Multi-Dimensional Databases (MDDs). The multi-dimensional database is effectively a multi-dimensional array (see fig. 5.6) that can be broken down into header blocks and data blocks, with pointers from the header blocks into the appropriate data blocks. The header blocks are composed of dimension names (region) and member names (North, South, Central). Various sophisticated indexing schemes are used to quickly retrieve the data from the data blocks.

The Metadata Pointer Structure. The metadata pointer structure creates the illusion that a user is querying against a multi-dimensional database. It actually is composed of a *metadata layer* (which redefines the relational tables and columns as a set of dimensions, members, and measures), and a set of pointers into the relational tables—essentially a data warehouse "mapping" to the relational design. This concept is illustrated in figure 5.7. This scheme will most likely be implemented by Microsoft, as the corporation moves into the data warehouse arena. For the moment, however, Microsoft products—including Access 95—are not the ideal solution for true large data warehouse development.

The statement the authors have just made should not stop an adventurous developer from seeing how far s(he) can push the Access 95 technology. Small-volume decision support systems and executive information systems that integrate other front-office applications and documents are achievable using Access 95, and reasonable response can be achieved by scaling up the back-end database with a server database management system such as Microsoft SQL Server. There are a few topics that require some consideration, however, as are discussed in the following sections.

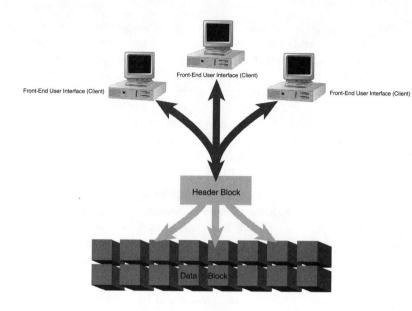

Fig. 5.6

The multi-dimensional database (MDD) data warehouse.

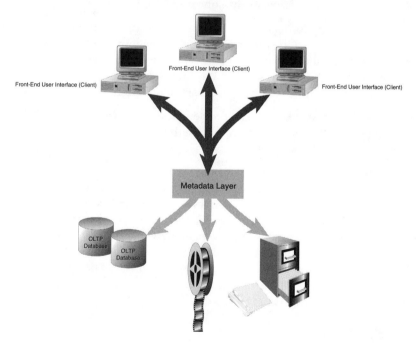

Fig. 5.7

The metadata pointer structure data warehouse.

II

Designing and Prototyping

Data Updates. The true data warehouse is a *read-only* entity. Data updates are from the operational (OLTP) database and other data sources and, as the data in these data sources are updated, they are periodically "transformed" and piped into the data warehouse—appended to existing data. The most pressing reason to avoid an end user-updatable data warehouse—especially in the Microsoft environment—is the lack of reliable tools for synchronizing these changes. Previously, we mentioned that the highly normalized data from the OLTP database is denormalized and aggregated before it is placed into the data warehouse. The accompanying implication is data item duplication within the warehouse, and synchronizing the multiple occurrences of, for example, Debra Doe's mailing address, is not a trivial task.

Additionally, data updates in a data warehouse have a different purpose from updates in an OLTP system. The historical dimension of the data warehouse is of prime importance and must not be destroyed. Through this historical component, trends can be uncovered and future marketing plans made. A badly managed and wrongly updated data warehouse may lead you to conclude that 60 percent of senior citizens in Miami have ordered winter hats with fur-lined ear flaps!

The read-only data warehouse resolves, completely and partially, two issues that cause much overhead in OLTP systems—respectively, concurrency and security.

Concurrency. In a read-only environment, where there is no chance of an update happening, there should be no locking protocol overhead. The only reason to lock, either shared-or-exclusive, pessimistic or optimistic, is in case the user who is reading the record decides to make a change to the data. With no changes happening, no locking is needed. Concurrency in a read-only data warehouse is a nonissue.

Security. Security is partially resolved in a read-only environment. No one has update, insert, or delete authority. Now, the only security issue that remains is who should be allowed to read which parts of the data warehouse.

Performance. Performance will be a major issue in the OLAP environment. Because the questions are never known ahead of time, *query optimization* will suffer. Because of the complexity of the queries themselves, volumes of data (or indexes) must be scanned before the result is produced. One of the consistently underestimated portions of the data warehouse planning stage is server and network capacity. If you are tempted to simulate a data warehouse environment by using Microsoft products, be exceedingly generous on your estimates of server requirements and network bandwidth.

Client Symmetry

How you plan to deploy your application, what your near-term plans are, dictates how you design the two portions of your application. When do you encode integrities and validation rules in the client portion of your application, and when do you encode them in the server end? The sizing of client capability versus server capability—how much code is embedded in each—is a continuum, and the exact architecture must follow the specific need of each individual installation.

Fat Client/Thin Server

The *fat client/thin server* design is best used for the database file/server model, when all screen formatting, the majority of rule checking, and most of the data processing will be at the client node. This situation is the typical homogeneous Access 95 environment, with an .MDB file at both client and server end.

Client computers require a robust hardware configuration. The network needs to be broad and fast. Processing will be handled primarily on the client machines. However, unlike system file/server setups that transfer the entire document file from the server to the client, the database file/server scheme delivers to the client only the pages of the database file that the client requests.

Even in a fat client/thin server environment, there usually are some rules, especially integrity rules and validation checks, that are embedded in the tables. As we mentioned previously, these rules will be inherited by all database objects (forms, reports, and queries) that are built on those tables and columns.

Versatility (different rules for different front-end applications that all access the same set of data) is not compromised in a fat client/thin server environment. The few rules embedded at the table level and inherited by the application forms can be overridden by an additional set of rules, established at the form level.

Thin Client/Fat Server

The ultimate *thin client/fat server* model is the mainframe-dumb terminal paradigm. The mainframe is a very fat server and the dumb terminals are positively skinny!

The thin client/fat server design and its variations are used for the database client/server model, when most of the data processing is handled at the server node. The very fat server also will do almost all of the rules checking and, in an extreme case, may even perform some of the client screen formatting. The thin client/fat server design is an atypical, heterogeneous Access 95 /back-end SQL database environment.

Thin client computers need only a minimal hardware configuration. The network needs to be broad and fast, especially if the server is doing any significant portion of client screen formatting. The server computer(s) needs to be especially robust because it will attempt to simulate a mainframe environment.

Versatility (different rules for different front-end applications that all access the same set of data) is compromised in a thin client/fat server environment. The server controls all integrity constraints, all validation checks, all business rules, and applies them uniformly to all applications that access the same data set.

The best solution is to strike a balance between client load and server load—aim for the middle of the client/server sizing continuum, which places the power where it is logically needed—screen formatting at the client node, query processing at the server node—and gives the maximum amount of flexibility to the application.

Planning Your Client/Server Application

To successfully deploy a client/server application, you must plan, plan, and plan. If you currently use a conventional methodology scheme for application and system development and are trying to adapt it to the client/server paradigm, chances that it just won't work are high. Conventional methodologies assume two beliefs—that an application can be completely designed before any code is written, and the business requirements will not change (or will change very little) over the project life cycle. Both assumptions are highly inaccurate in a client/server environment.

Because of the number of components involved in a client/server application, you must design and test, design and test, eliciting feedback at multiple stages of application development. The second assumption, that business requirements will not change, is just not realistic in today's fast-moving corporate world. The very reason so many companies elect to make the move to a client/server paradigm is because they need the information systems technology to support their business model, and that business model is in a state of change consistent with market demand.

Adapting Traditional Methodologies to the Client/Server Environment

It isn't a realistic route to abandon using development methodologies altogether. Creating applications in a random manner, driven by chaos, is a sure ticket to failure. Rather, the methodologies can be adapted to a client/server environment, and the authors suggest the following outline of a methodology presented by Francis Wang of Client/Server Connection, in the December 1995 issue of *Data Management Review*.

A client/server application is composed of at least six components—the user interface (the client application), the business rules, the data itself, the system architecture, the integration of the various system components, and the project management.

The user interface is, in today's market, an event-driven graphical user interface (GUI) that must be Windows- or Macintosh-compliant, depending on the client platform for which the application is being written. Today's end users are more sophisticated than any in the history of computing. They tend to be highly opinionated, they demand ease-of-use, they expect instantaneous gratification, they want to learn how to use a new application in three to five minutes, and they never expect to have to open the manual. Additionally, they are unwilling to wait on system response time. Beyond these demands, they are easy to please. This is your target audience—design accordingly.

The business rules in today's corporation are constantly in a state of change. It is not unusual to have the business rules modified several times over the life of a project, and you must be ready to accommodate this level of dynamic flux. The business rules need to be encoded within the application, at the server (database) level and at the client (user interface) for the two-tiered architecture, or in the business process server of the three-tiered model.

For this discussion, the *security model* is considered part of the business rules. Depending on the level of security the development effort mandates, the security model could be broken out and treated as a seventh component.

The data itself needs to be thoroughly understood. Data coming from various sources—legacy databases, non-SQL databases, relational OLTP databases—often are incomplete and inconsistent. These data sources must be reconciled and synchronized. If the design is for an operational OLTP system, the data needs to be fully normalized. If this is an OLAP development effort, the data must be structured into dimensions and measures in a format that is consistent with the needs of those who will use the data warehouse.

The *system architecture* must be identified early in the project life cycle. The architecture must support the intent of the application and database. For example, if the database needs to be geographically distributed to support a nationwide inventory control and sales system, then the architecture must be consistent with this goal. The challenge here is not so much in identifying an appropriate solution to the current problem—an endless assortment of products is available that can be used as components to the solution. The challenge is to design into the system architecture the flexibility to change and expand, accommodating requirements that no one ever thought about when the system was being built.

System integration—making the various system components, each from a different vendor, work together as a single solution with a common goal—is often overlooked in the early part of the project. The key concept for a client/server environment is that the network is the backbone of the application. It is crucial that the multiple hardware platforms, software environments, and network standards all work together seamlessly. Of course, system integration cannot precede the decision on system architecture, but it should be a deciding factor in the system architecture chosen for the project. The various parts that comprise a client/server application must have a high level of interoperability, or the application will be rejected by the user community for performance reasons.

The *project management* issues are profound in a client/server development effort. The development life cycle usually is extremely short; in the beginning the products and tools used are largely unfamiliar to the developers; the end users demand an extremely high level of usability. The challenge to the project management team is to develop the application on time and under budget, and to deliver a program to the end-user community that results in high levels of end-user satisfaction.

The *client/server design methodology* itself is a simple one in concept but rather complex in practice: define, design, prototype, and implement all six (or all seven if you count security) components concurrently. Table 5.1 should help you keep track of what should be happening and when it should happen.

Table 5.1   The New Client/Server Design Methodology Scheme

Component	Definition Phase	Planning Phase	Prototype Phase	Implementation
User Interface	gather user requirements	adopt the user interface standard	prototype user interface	build user interface modules
Business Rules	gather business requirements	develop business objects, events, and processes	prototype business rules	implement business rules
Security (optional)	gather security requirements	develop security model	prototype security model	build security modules
Data	gather data requirements	develop conceptual data model	develop and prototype logical data model	develop physical data model (create tables)
Systems Architecture	define system architecture	plan and configure system	prototype system architecture	deliver system architecture
System Integration	gather system requirements	plan system integration strategy	prototype system integration	test system integration
Project Management	define project charter	develop project plan	manage and review development of prototypes	manage development, testing, and migration efforts

The new client/server methodology is quite technical and specific, unlike the traditional methodologies, which tend to be general, high-level, and "one size fits all." The client/server methodology needs to echo the architecture of the project. The methodology for building a data warehouse will differ from the methodology for developing a distributed branch-office automation system, which will differ from the methodology for implementing a centralized high-volume transaction processing system. The success of a client/server project depends on the development of a sound technical infrastructure.

Using the Rapid Application Development (RAD) Technique

A delivery technique that is consistent with this new client/server methodology is RAD—*rapid application development*, and controlled or versioned prototypes. Rapid application development is not a new concept; it has been used in a myriad of situations for years. The common pitfall of RAD is the tendency to ignore high-level planning and design, to jump directly into code writing, and to press the prototype into production, only to have it fail nine times out of ten. This is why RAD should be coupled with versioned releases.

Each component listed in Table 5.1 (with the exception of project management) can be prototyped in a RAD environment and rolled out in a controlled versioning. This technique does much to assist the product development team. The earliest version, 1.0, introduces the product(s) to the user community long before the product(s) will be put into production. Including the user community in the development of a product guarantees user feedback and goes far toward total user acceptance when the new application is brought on-line.

In summary, this client/server methodology espouses breaking a client/server application into its component parts, and defining, planning, prototyping, and implementing each of the components concurrently.

Adopting Naming Standards

Naming standards, when developing applications, can mean the difference between on-time deliveries and chaos—or worse. The lack of consistent naming standards can take a normally straightforward job, such as making a few simple modifications to an existing program, and turn it into a nightmare.

Prepare for the Future

There are some peculiarities about the naming conventions in Access. For example, Access allows spaces and special characters in object names. There must have been all kinds of business reasons and marketing justifications for doing so, but this decision has complicated the life of the Access developer tremendously. Not only is it nearly impossible to figure out how many sets of double quotes you need in an encoded *where* clause to account for embedded spaces in the object name, you now are faced with the task of renaming objects if you plan to upsize to a non-Access back-end database. No other SQL/ODBC database supports spaces or the type of special characters in object names that Access does, and of course, a change made in an object name doesn't propagate throughout Access without the assistance of one of several third-party packages!

Sorting in the Database Container. Imagine an application with thirty-five tables, a hundred or so queries, a hundred forms, fifty reports—your normal-sized enterprise client/server application. Maintenance is a real issue if your naming convention doesn't lend itself to easy organization and identification of related reports and forms when listed in the database container. Even in a small Access application, when trying to identify the control source for a form, how do you tell a table from a query if the name of the object doesn't give you a clue?

Access Default Naming Conventions. Access 95 default naming conventions for forms and reports is slightly improved over Access 2. The problem still exists of the text box on a form, which inherits the name of the control source, which causes confusion in code-behind-forms—are you trying to reference the form object or the control source of the form object? The labels attached to the text boxes now get real names in Access 95. Rather than being assigned names like "field101," the label gets the control source name of its associated text box, with a "Label" appended as a suffix.

The Hungarian Naming Convention

If you are a programmer, you probably have established a code-writing naming convention of your own, so that you can keep track of what things are and what you meant to do on code written six months ago. If two or more of you are working on the same application, then the need to have an established naming convention grows in proportion to the size and complexity of the application itself. If you are just starting to write code, you may want to adopt a naming convention, and stick with it.

With this need in mind, the authors want to present a compilation of the most-commonly used naming convention scheme in the Access/Visual Basic arena—*Hungarian notation*. Hungarian notation was developed by Charles Simonyi as part of his doctoral thesis, and, as Simonyi was an early developer of Access, the naming scheme was quickly adapted throughout much of Microsoft Corporation. You still can find examples of Simonyi's naming scheme in the system-level tables of Access.

Essentially, the Hungarian naming convention attaches to the front of an object or variable name a prefix or "tag," all in lowercase. This prefix describes not only the kind of object or variable being named, but also what it is used for. For example, in the previous chapter we cited examples from the Customer database; in the database itself, which is included on this book's companion CD-ROM, you can see the authors' own version of the Hungarian notation.

> **Note**
>
> At this point, the authors must admit that they do not adhere strictly to the Hungarian notation in all its convolutions. We have adapted a simplified subset of the notation rules to our work, which can be seen in the examples and code that accompanies this book.

Since Simonyi introduced his scheme, there have been multiple variations and adaptations made by other programmers to products other than Access. Among the more popular schemes is the Leszynski/Reddick method, which was introduced in the February 1993 issue of *Smart Access*, and revised in later editions. The Leszynski/Reddick method uses a four-part naming convention and two levels of names—general and specific—also referred to as Level 1 and Level 2.

> **Tip**
>
> How much or how little of any of the subsequent conventions is used that we will present is a matter of personal preference. The important point to remember is to find a naming convention that works and stick to it.

The *Leszynski/Reddick nomenclature method* uses no spaces or special characters, not even the underscore (_) that is so popular in other database environments. If an object name is more than one word (a "real" speech word, not a computer word) in length, the words are run together—the first letter of each word is capitalized and all other letters of the word are lowercase. Leszynski/Reddick gives each object a four-part name, composed of a prefix, a tag, a base name, and a qualifier, and it goes together like the following syntax example:

> [prefix]tagBaseName[Qualifier]

Here, the prefix and tag (see Table 5.2) are lowercase, so that each object or variable starts with three, four, or five lowercase letters, and then the object's name is in mixed case. Finally, the qualifier, which also is in mixed case.

For example, the object tblCustomer has a tag of "tbl" and a base name of "Customer."

Leszynski/Reddick also sorts object names into two types—Level 1 and Level 2. The Level 1 is a general method of identification (see Table 5.3); Level 2 provides a much higher level of description for each object (see Tables 5.4, 5.5, and 5.6).

Table 5.2 Leszynski/Reddick Naming Convention for Database Object Prefixes

Prefix	Example	Description
zz	zzqryCustPhonelist	Unused objects that you may want to keep around for future use or reference.
zt	ztfrmCustomer	Temporary objects; all objects created in Access are considered persistent, so this "temporary" is under user control.
zs	zsUtility	System objects.
_	_rptCustomer	Objects under development; these will sort at the top of the list while under development. Remove the _ (underscore) when the object is ready for production; it will sort regularly.

Table 5.3   Leszynski/Reddick Level 1 Naming Convention for Database Objects

Object	Tag	Qualifier	Example
table	tbl		tblCustomer
query	qry		qryCustomerPhonelist
form	frm		frmCustomer
subform	frm	Sub	frmCustomerSub
report	rpt		rptCustomer
subreport	rpt	Sub	rptCustomerSub
macro	mcr		mcrAlphaButtons
module	bas		basNavigate

Table 5.4   Leszynski/Reddick Level 2 Naming Convention for Database Objects

Object	Tag	Example
base table	tbl	tblCustomer
lookup table	tlkp	tlkpStates
select query	qry or qsel	qryCustomerPhonelist
append query	qapp	qappNewInventory
crosstab query	qxtb	qxtbYTDSales
DDL query	qddl	qddlCreateTable
delete query	qdel	qdelOldCustomer
form filter query	qflt	qfltOrderByCustomer
lookup query	qlkp	qlkpFindProduct
make table query	qmak	qmakNewTable
SQL passthru query	qsql	qsqlGetProduct
totals query	qtot	qtotAllSales
union query	quni	quniCustUnionOldCust
update query	qupd	qupdCustDiscount
form	frm	frmCustomer
dialog form	fdlg	fdlgWhereIsTheData
menu form	fmnu	fmnuMenuHelp
message form	fmsg	fmsgWarningMessage
subform	fsub	fsubCustomer
report	rpt	rptCustomer

Object	Tag	Example
subreport	rsub	rsubCustomer
macro	mcr	mcrAlphaButtons
form macro	mfrm	mfrmCustomer
menu macro	mmnu	mmnuMenuFile
report macro	mrpt	mrptCustomer
module	bas	basNavigate

Table 5.5 Leszynski/Reddick Naming Convention for Database Form and Report Control Objects

Object	Tag	Example
chart or graph	cht	chtSalesByRegion
check box	chk	chkYesOrNo
combo box	cbo	cboStates
command button	cmd	cmdClose
object frame	fra	fraEmployeePhoto
label	lbl	lblFirstName
line	lin	lineSeparator
list box	lst	lstChooseInsuranceCarrier
option button	opt	optInsuranceCo
option group	grp	grpPostalCarrier
page break	brk	brkPage1
rectangle or shape	shp	shpChoicePanel
subform or subreport	sub	subCustomer
text box	txt	txtCustomer
toggle button	tgl	tglOffOn

Table 5.6 Leszynski/Reddick Naming Convention for Access Basic Variables

Variable Type	Tag	Example
container	con	Dim conMyTab as Container
control	ctl	Dim ctlListBox as Control
currency	cur	Dim curPayment as Currency
database	db	Dim dbMyDB as Database

(continues)

II

Designing and Prototyping

Table 5.6   Continued

Variable Type	Tag	Example
document	doc	Dim docReport as Document
double	dbl	Dim dblResult as Double
dynaset	dyn	Dim dynAnswerSet as Dynaset
Y/N or T/F flag	f	Dim fEndRec as Integer
field	fld	Dim fldName as Field
form	frm	Dim frmMain as Form
group	gru	Dim gruUsers as Group
index	idx	Dim idxZipCode as Index
integer	int	Dim intGetNum as Integer
long	lng	Dim lgnGetNum as Long
object	obj	Dim objPicture as Object
parameter	prm	Dim prmGetNum as Parameter
property	prp	Dim prpColor as Property
querydef	qdf or qrd	Dim qdfPeoplePhones as Querydef
recordset	rec or rst	Dim recPeoplePhones as Recordset
relation	rel	Dim relPhones as Relation
report	rpt	Dim rptPhoneList as Report
single	sng	Dim sngGetNum as Single
snapshot	snp	Dim snpMyDB as Snapshot
string	str	Dim strFormName as String
table	tbl	Dim tblCustomer as Table
tabledef	tdf or tbd	Dim tdfCustomer as Tabledef
user-defined type	typ	Dim typLongitude as Longitude
user	usr	Dim usrMAP as User
variant	var	Dim varDateDone as Variant
workspace	wrk or wsp	Dim wrkFirst as Workspace
yes/no	ysn	Dim ysnDone as Integer

From Here...

In this chapter, we covered the basic concepts of client/server architecture and design methodology. You saw how Access 95 is suited for some purposes, yet is not suited for others. To follow the development of a decision support system, refer to the following chapters:

- Chapter 6, "Establishing the Ground Rules," covers the table architecture.
- Chapter 7, "Using Access as a Prototyping Tool," teaches the beginnings of the application.
- Chapter 8, "Adding Functionality to Your Prototype," explains advanced procedures and code-behind-forms.
- Chapter 9, "Navigation: How to Get from Here to There," gives you tips on how to get around an application.

II

Designing and Prototyping

CHAPTER 6

Establishing the Ground Rules

Single-user databases often do not give much consideration to *data integrity*. The user knows the application and the data, and can spot data errors. The risk of data corruption is minimal, given that only one person is reading from or writing to the database at any time. But when a database serves multiple users, data integrity becomes an issue. As the number of users increases, the probability that two users may want to access the same record at the same time also increases. Both may even want to update the same record, and not necessarily with the same information. To prevent this type of conflict, you must put rules in place to prevent *lost updates*.

As the developer, you also must define rules that establish and protect the *relationships* between the data. For example, your application must not permit a user to delete a customer record when the customer has outstanding orders. If you do not enforce this rule, it becomes possible for the database to contain orders with no customer billing or shipping information. These *orphan records* result when a break occurs in the *referential integrity* of the data.

A client/server application needs these rules to protect the integrity of the data, to aid the user in entering correct values, and to ensure that the data follows the business rules of the company. When you begin to design a client/server application, you must plan where to enforce these rules. Is the server the best place to enforce the rules, or should the data be checked at the client application, before it is sent to the server? In the three-tiered model, you find that much of the rule making happens in the middle level.

In this chapter we investigate the following:

- Primary integrity, what it is and how it can be preserved
- Relationships and referential integrity
- Data types and domain integrity
- Validation rules, business rules, and other embedded properties

Understanding Data Integrity

Data integrity comes in two flavors—physical and logical. *Physical data integrity* refers to the physical safety of the data, after it is placed under the care of the file manager module of the database management system. For example, when a single user desktop database has problems, the impact is local, even if it is a disaster for the one user. A client/server application—or a mainframe database, which contains critical corporate data—must not fail. The selling point of the client/server application is to take the separate, unconnected and often redundant databases from the desktops, the mini-computers, and the mainframes, and then make all of this data available and consistent. The consistency comes from having one copy, and only one copy, of the data available to all. When a customer record must be changed, only one update action is necessary for everyone to see the new data.

Of course, this approach is a double-edged sword. If this one copy is damaged, no one will be able to retrieve the correct information. The impact of this damage can be enormous and, therefore, the effort devoted to prevention of data integrity problems should reflect the potential for disaster. One of the main functions of a database management system is to ensure that—after the data is placed in storage—under its care, the data will not be accidentally modified or corrupted.

One way solution developers can support physical data integrity is to ensure solid logic by using the four *database integrities*—entity (or primary), referential, domain, and business (or user)—in the table and application design.

Understanding the Relational Terminology

The relational model uses some terminology that is inconsistent with the terminology used by Access. The designers of Access have opted to retain terminology from the nonrelational paradigm, which isn't altogether surprising because Access, and Access 95, is not a fully relational database management system. The user interface and the design interface—the portion of the application development toolkit that is used to build the user interfaces—simulates the relational model. Access is a hybrid beast—one parent relational, one parent object-oriented. Access inherited the best of both worlds, melding the two technologies into an extremely powerful and capable database management system. In preparation for further discussion, we are going to define the *relational terminology*, so that you can be comfortable in the relational environment, and we will map the relational terminology to the terminology that Access uses.

- Entity, something that exists and can be differentiated from other objects. An entity can be composed of other entities, and can contain even more entities. An entity also can have characteristics, or attributes, that describe the appearance or dimensions of the entity. In a database environment, an entity is something that can be programmed, like an object. The Access equivalent of an entity is the object.

- Attribute, a singular value that represents some characteristic or dimension of an entity. The Access equivalent is the field.

- *Domain*, the set or range of values that are legal for any given attribute. Access enforces this concept with the use of Validation Rules in Table Design mode.

- *Row* or *tuple* (rhymes with "couple"), is a collection of attributes, all of which describe a single entity. The Access equivalent is the *record*.

- *Table* or *relation*, a collection of same-type rows. The Access equivalent is the file.

- *Primary key*, an attribute or attributes whose occurrences form a set of unique values, so that each row in a table can be distinctly identified. Access uses the same term.

- *Composite primary key*, a primary key formed by the concatenation of two or more attributes. Access doesn't really have an equivalent; the manual only indicates that two or more fields can be used to build the primary key.

- *Candidate key*, an attribute in a table that qualifies, within the constraints of the current domain definition, a primary key. Access doesn't really address this concept.

- *Foreign key*, an attribute in one table that is related to an attribute in a second table. The attribute in the first table also is the primary key of the second table. This scheme creates an implicit relationship between the two tables. Access uses the same concept and terminology.

- *Null*, the concept of a value either not present or unknown. Access uses the concept of Null in a more robust implementation than many database management systems.

Entity Integrity (Primary Integrity)

Entity integrity—also referred to as *primary integrity*—needs to be enforced, so that every row in every table can be directly accessed by end-user queries. The relational model, and relational databases, expose data to the user; they don't hide it as some other database architectures tend to do. Therefore, every row in a database must be directly accessible to user queries (assuming, of course, the proper security clearance). The following two corollaries exist to the rule of entity integrity:

- No primary key shall be Null.
- No change can be made that would render the primary key Null.

Access 95 supports the concept of entity integrity, the first of the four integrities, when a primary key is designated for a table. At design time, Access encourages the creator of the table to assign a primary key. However, the user has the option of ignoring this suggestion, thereby making entity-integrity support optional for non-replicated databases. With the replicated database, however, Access 95 must implement at least a system-level entity integrity, so it assigns to each row of each table a Global User Identifier (GUID). Using the GUID, Access 95 then can compare replicated rows in a table for changes, and then reconcile the various copies. However, it still is possible in a replicated database not to have user-level entity integrity in place.

SSN as the Primary Key

As a rule, do not use Social Security Number for an ID field. The exception is where salary or other reportable income will be paid out to the individual and where you must file a tax statement on the transaction. Usually, using the Social Security Number as an identifier is an invasion of personal privacy. Careless and indiscriminate use of the Social Security Number allows agencies—government and otherwise—to accumulate data about you, and most of the time, it is false or misleading.

Another reason for not using the Social Security Number as an identifier is that it is not a unique set of numbers. In the 1930s, duplicate SSN numbers were issued.

A reminder: The Social Security Number is relevant only in the United States. It is not a given that every country has some equivalent identifying number that it assigns to its citizens, and for countries that do, the formats vary wildly.

If you insist on using the Social Security Number as a primary key identifier in your application, you must be prepared to cope with individuals like the authors who refuse to give out their SSNs to anyone who does not have a legal need for it.

Relationships and Referential Integrity

The relational database, as the name implies, is all about establishing *relationships* between tables. First, attributes are grouped according to function and meaning (normalized) and are assigned to tables. Then you can imply relationships between these tables; this is what makes the relational database so powerful.

In a nonrelational database, if you have a relationship between two tables—or files, as they would be called in that environment—you have to specifically define the relationship and any characteristics of that relationship during database creation (or database modification). At the physical level these relationships are stored as pointers. In some nonrelational architectures, the relationship would have a name and properties which then determine how a record in the first file of the relationship is handled if an associated record in the second file is deleted. The up side of this setup is the performance speed associated with any pointer-driven structure; one down side is that if the relationship is not predefined, then an association between these two files cannot be dynamically constructed.

In a fully relational database these relationships are implied, not stored, and need not be predefined. At any time, a dynamic relationship can be declared and data retrieved from the join of the two (or more) tables. The lack of a pointer structure means that no additional file maintenance is needed beyond the files that contain the relational tables. Performance suffers because the dynamic construction (in memory) of these implied relationships can never match the pointer-driven retrievals of the nonrelational database.

Access 95, always the diplomat, has implemented both techniques. In the Relationships Window you redefine the relationships between tables, and assign to each relationship certain properties: cascade update and cascade delete, whether or not to enforce referential integrity, and the default join type—the EquiJoin, the Left Outer Join, or the Right Outer Join. In the Query Design Window you can dynamically join multiple tables that do not have a predefined relationship build in the Relationships Window.

The second of the four integrities is *referential integrity*. Referential integrity is needed only when there is a relationship, and the timing of the enforcement ensures that the domain of a foreign key must fall within the domain of its associated primary key.

To repeat, an attribute in table one (where it serves as a foreign key) is essentially the same attribute in table two, where it is a primary key. The two attributes have the same definition (data type and length) but not necessarily the same attribute name, such as EmployeeNumber and EmpNo. These two attributes share the same domain (set of permitted values). Referential integrity says that all this is fine, provided the foreign key doesn't have a value missing from the set of real values of the primary key. If a foreign key value isn't present in the set of real data values for the primary key, then you have the condition known as *orphan rows*, or *orphan records*. Usually, this situation is not desirable, as you will discover in following paragraphs.

Let's talk about this concept of referential integrity and orphan records on a more real level. For an example, look at a simplified order entry system for a catalog mail-order company. There will be a table named Customer and a second table named Item that contains a list of the catalog items. These two tables are connected in a M:N relationship by an Order table, which links the customer and the items ordered. In its simplest form, each row in the Order table may contain only an order number, a customer number, and an item number.

When an order is placed, you must first enter the customer information into the Customer table, if it is not already on record. After the customer information is recorded, you can enter the order information into the Order table. If this order contains two or more items, you'll have multiple rows in the Order table.

If the order is canceled, then you might delete it out of the Order table. If the customer has not ordered in years, you may delete that customer record. If the item is no longer available, you may delete it from the Items table. All these deletions are perfectly valid to the database, even if they may not make sense from a business point of view.

What do you think is the best way to handle a customer who is canceling an order? Should you delete just the order information and retain the customer on file, or should you also delete the customer? What if you chose the second option, and the customer had another, earlier order that had not yet been shipped?

In the Customer table, CustID is the primary key and in the Order table, CustID is a foreign key. Remember what was said about foreign key values—they must have a counterpart in the primary key value list. If you chose the second option (deleting both order and customer information), and that customer had another outstanding order, you will leave a row in the Order table with a CustID that didn't exist in the Customer table—an orphan record, which is a clear violation of referential integrity.

After the customer information is removed from the Customer table, there is no way to determine where to ship the outstanding order. This situation is not good for a business, and you can guarantee an angry customer and, most likely, lost sales. Bad timing can make the situation even worse: if the order was shipped but the invoice was not yet processed—and no customer record exists to supply a billing address because it was deleted. The result: a happy customer who has the goods but not the bill; unhappy boss because you shipped the goods but may never collect payment.

You can avoid all of these problems if your application includes some business rules and supports referential integrity, where appropriate. You need to identify the entities, establish the business rules that govern the entities, create relationships between the entities (where appropriate), and enforce referential integrity where needed—and that's only the beginning!

Relationships fall into three basic categories: one-to-one, one-to-many, and many-to-many. Let's investigate each kind of relationship.

One-to-One Relationships

The *one-to-one (1:1) relationship*, as illustrated in figure 6.1, relates a row in one table (table A) with a single row in a second table (table B). Say it again: for each row in table A, there can be zero or one related row in table B. The 1:1 relationship, inverted, allows each row in Table B to have at most a single related row in Table A.

Fig. 6.1

The patient to medical profile one-to-one relationship.

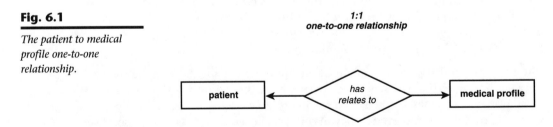

The patient:medical profile 1:1 relationship is read left-to-right.
The medical patient:profile 1:1 relationship is read right-to-left.

Why would you want to break up data that is so intimately related into two or more tables? Before the relational model, all these attributes probably would have been stored in the same file, as part of the same record. In the relational model, you can choose to do either. You can lump together all the attributes into the same table and restrict access to certain columns through the use of SQL views. As an alternative you can break out attributes that are functionally differentiated, store them in separate tables, and—when needed—combine the multiple groups of data attributes with a SQL join operation.

The following list describes a few good reasons for separating attributes into multiple tables that have a 1:1 relationship:

- **Protecting sensitive data**—In security, the first line of defense is, if the user community doesn't know it exists, it may be safe. By "hiding" from general view certain sets of attributes, the attributes that contain sensitive and/or potentially damaging data, the risk of unauthorized read or copy operations is greatly reduced. When the sensitive data is in a separate table, it's easy to assign or deny permissions on the table.

- **Reducing I/O by reducing table width**—A very wide table, a table with a few hundred columns, may exceed the physical block size determined by the operating system. When this situation occurs, each row retrieved into memory requires multiple disk input/output (I/O) operations. As you will see in Chapter 16, "Tuning the Access 95 Application," disk I/O is the single most-expensive operation in a computing environment, and certain types of queries require an inordinate number of disk I/O operations. By grouping the attributes into two or more tables, a single disk I/O can bring several rows into memory, rather than just part of a row.

- **Page lock table overflow reduction**—Many database management systems, including Access 95, use locks to handle concurrency conflicts (two or more users trying to modify the same row at the same time). Access 95, like so many other database management systems, locks at the page level—a page being both analogous to a physical block, and the unit of data that is moved back and forth from the physical disk to main memory. The page lock buffer usually is stored in memory. If multiple page locks are required for each row retrieved from the hard disk, several things will happen:

    - The database administrator has to increase the size of the lock table, thereby reducing the amount of memory available for other tasks.

    - The lock table fills up and generates an overflow message, possibly aborting queries in progress.

    - The lock table fills up and doesn't generate an overflow message, leaving the database administrator to wonder why database performance is so bad.

    - A combination of the above.

II

Designing and Prototyping

■ **Distributing data and using vertical partitioning**—A distributed database environment is an extension of the client/server architecture. A distributed database environment has multiple database servers, and some of these servers will contain the same (replicated) tables that are being continuously synchronized with each other by the distributed database management system. Other tables in a distributed database will be partitioned, either horizontally (rows number 1 through 10,000 of the Employee table live on the Alpha server and rows 10,001 through 20,000 live on the Beta server) or vertically (EmployeeNo, EmployeeName, and JobCategory of the Employee table are stored on the Gamma server; EmployeeNo, EmpHomeAddress, and EmpHomePhone are stored on the Delta server). In a fully distributed database the data is placed as close as possible to the action. Non-system-level table partitioning is a technique that is used to distribute load and enhance database management system performance, provided that the partitioning is consistent with the way in which the data is used.

In a 1:1 or 1:M relationship (we'll talk about 1:M relationships in a moment), usually one table acts as the "master" table. The other table of the relationship assumes the role of "detail" table. The detail table holds detail data about an entity, while the master table traditionally holds more general or high-level information about the same entity.

Deleting a row or rows in the detail table will not adversely impact the data integrity of the entity involved, but the inverse is not true. If data is deleted from the master table, then associated records in the detail table are left with no master, and no way to figure out where they belong.

To avoid a situation like this in Access 95, enable Referential Integrity:

1. Start Access 95. Create a new database using the Database Wizard. Click the Database tab and select the Students and Classes database. Accept all Wizard defaults.

2. Close the switchboard screen and select the Table List in the Database Container; it doesn't matter which table is highlighted.

3. Select Tools, Relationships from the top menu to open the Relationships Window.

4. Select a relationship and open its properties box by double-clicking the line that connects the two tables. The topmost of the three check box selections, Enforce Referential Integrity, when turned on, will not let you delete a row in the master table as long as an associated row exists in the detail table (see fig. 6.2).

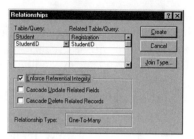

Fig. 6.2

The Relationships dialog box, which shows the Enforce Referential Integrity option enabled for this one-to-many relationship.

One-to-Many Relationships

The one-to-many (1:M) relationship relates a row in one table (table A) with multiple rows in a second table (table B). Say it again: for each row in table A there can be zero, one, or many related rows in table B. The 1:M relationship, inverted to an M:1, allows one or more rows in Table B to have a single related row in Table A. Figure 6.3 illustrates this relationship.

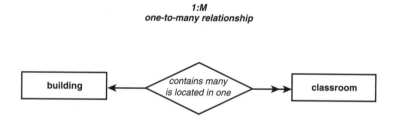

Fig. 6.3

The building to classroom one-to-many relationship.

The one-to-many relationship is the most common relationship that you will create when building relational databases. The 1:M relationship is the most common in life and in business, and the relational database management system is a reflection of corporate reality.

Typical examples of the 1:M relationship include multiple orders per customer, the names of songs on a CD or record, multiple sections of a course, and multiple treatments for a patient admitted to a hospital.

Reference Tables. Reference tables are a special case of the 1:M relationship. A reference table is a static (or nearly so) list of values used throughout one or more databases and tend to standardize data entry. This is especially true in the Access 95 environment, where data from multiple databases can be accessed from a single user application, and a reference table can be used as the source for a combo box or list box. The reference table has a 1:M relationship with the table using it. A common example is the State table, a list of state codes and corresponding state names, a table that measures 2 columns by 50 rows, which is used by the Customer table to fill in the state code information for the customer address. Table State is related to table Customer in a 1:M relationship.

Dependent and Independent Relationships. Technically, there are two types of 1:M relationships—dependent and independent. The dependent 1:M relationship states that the existence of detail rows in the many-table is dependent on the presence of a related master row in the one-table. All the 1:M examples we have given so far are dependent 1:M relationships. If no particular instance of a master row existed (a customer from our previous discussion of customers and orders), there would be no related detail rows (orders for this customer).

The independent 1:M relationship is a little different. The detail rows in the many-table would exist on their own, even if no corresponding master row existed in the one-table. Children can have one parent, two parents, or no parent. This is a very real case of orphan rows and, in this business model, an orphan row (in the database) is permissible.

To illustrate the independent 1:M relationship, we need to expand our customer-order-item example to include the vendor of the items. The Vendor table and the Item table are linked in an independent 1:M relationship (Vendor# is a foreign key in the Item table). One week after a vendor delivers a large shipment to the warehouse, the vendor goes bankrupt. Even if your business rules mandate that you must remove this vendor record from the Vendor table, you do not want the corresponding entries in the Item table removed because they reflect what you have in inventory. As a result of real-world dynamics, the master row in the Vendor table must be removed, but the detail rows in the Item table must remain behind. This is a case of valid orphan rows.

One-to-one relationships also can be classified as dependent (most normal case) and independent (rare case). One-to-one and one-to-many relationships are similar and can be managed by using the same Access 95 functions found in the Relationships Window.

Cascading Changes to the Primary Key. Access 95 enforces another referential property that is extremely useful and that will save you much code-writing. This property is the Cascade action, the second and third of the three check-box selections in the Relationships Window.

There are times—as in the case of a dependent 1:1 or 1:M relationship—when you need to delete a master row and all the associated detail rows from the detail table. Since version 2, Access handles this, as long as the Cascade Delete Related Fields option is turned on (see fig. 6.4). The delete action removes all detail rows first, and then the master so that, at no time are orphan rows left in the detail table.

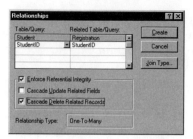

Fig. 6.4

The Relationships properties dialog box, with the Cascade Delete Related Fields option enabled.

The other cascade action, Cascade Update Related Fields, will ripple through a change in the value of the primary key from the master row to all associated detail rows. The timing on this action is tricky, far more so than the timing of Cascade Delete, because—in order to avoid the orphan row condition—the action must create a near-duplicate set of rows, master and detail, with the only difference being the primary key value. Then the Cascade Update action must delete the original primary key value set of rows, detail rows first. This procedure is necessary to ensure that the integrity of the data values—master and detail rows both and together—is retained, even if the Cascade Update action is interrupted by system failure.

One note on cascading changes to primary key values: primary keys and primary key values should be chosen so that they require little if any maintenance after they are established. If this means making the primary key "non-intelligent," or a surrogate—a simple counter field, rather than one that contains embedded information—then this would be the more appropriate way to go. Although Access 95 (and Access 2) supports Cascade Updates between tables that have defined relationships, ensuring that a primary key value modification has cascaded throughout a database of several hundred tables is a monumental make-work task. If you must have an intelligent primary key, the embedded information should be historical information that needs no modification after it is established.

In the case of the dependent 1:1 or 1:M relationship, where it is efficient to retain detail rows, even after the corresponding master row has been deleted, disable the Enforce Referential Integrity option from within the Relationships properties box.

If your data is not managed by the Access 95 Jet, you may have to write code to program in the referential integrity, cascade updates, and cascade deletes. Some of the major DBMSs support stored procedures or triggers, code that is executed as a result of an action taken in the user interface—an action such as a Delete Record. Check the user documentation of the target server RDBMS to determine how (and if) you will be able to support referential integrity after conversion from the back-end Access 95 environment.

Many-to-Many Relationships

The many-to-many (M:N) relationship (see fig. 6.5) relates many rows in one table (table A) with many rows in a second table (table B). Say it again: for each row in table

II

Designing and Prototyping

A there can be zero, one, or many related rows in table B, and for each row in table B there can be zero, one, or many related rows in table A. The M:N relationship is really a pair of 1:M relationships, one in either direction.

Fig. 6.5

The students-to-courses many-to-many relationship.

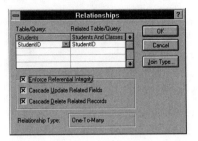

Why is the shorthand for a many-to-many relationship M:N and not M:M? Database theorists like to be precise and perfectly clear—if what they say is mostly incomprehensible. To indicate that a relationship is M:M may imply that the number of entities on either side of the colon would have to be the same, which is not true. In an M:N relationship, there might be 2 of M and 5 of N—two parents and five children. Therefore, the M:N nomenclature.

The many-to-many relationship is a little more complex to manage. Many desktop databases do not handle M:N relationships well, even to the point where the documentation suggests that this kind of relationship is not common. In fact, it happens all the time! The classic example is the student registration database. A student will register for several courses, and each course will have many registered students. When a student drops the course, you do not delete the student information from the database. Nor do you remove the course from the course listing. You actually remove the *connection* between a particular student and a specific course.

The many-to-many relationship is represented by a third table, known as an *associative table* or, in Access, a *junction table*. This associative table is the connection between the two tables in the M:N relationship. In our registration example, these tables are the Student table and the Course table. The associative table that connects these two tables can be named Registration. It would have, as its primary key, the concatenation of the primary keys of the two tables that are in the M:N relationship—Student and Course. The two parts of the concatenated primary key also will act as foreign keys. Additional associative attributes that describe the relationship can be added, if appropriate. In our registration example, associative attributes would be semester and year, credit or non-credit.

Now, let's review the steps to creating an associative table. This was already done in the Access 95 example, with the Students and Classes table, but not very well.

You would never build a table with space in the name, would you? Moreover, the following example uses an autonumber counter as the primary key. You can omit this and instead use a concatenated key:

1. Following the example built for you in the Students and Classes database we created earlier in this chapter, construct the two tables that anchor the ends of the M:N relationship (Student and Course).

2. Create a third table, the associative table (Registration) that represents the M:N relationship itself.

3. Copy each of the primary keys of the end-tables (Student and Course) into the associative table (Registration), and then concatenate them into a single primary key.

4. Add attributes to the associative table that describe the relationship, such as SemesterYear (text data type, typical values might be Fall 1996 and Spr 1996), CreditNon (text or yes/no data type), and Payment (text data, typical values might be prepayment or deferred payment).

The preceding four steps will establish an implied M:N relationship in any relational database management system environment. In Access you can formally declare the relationship by using the Relationships Window. We mentioned a few paragraphs ago that the M:N relationship is a pair of 1:M, and the following steps show you how to build the M:N relationship:

1. Add the three tables, the two ends and the associative table, to the Relationships Window, and physically line them up, end-table—associative table—end-table, Student-Registration-Course.

2. Highlight the primary key attribute of the left end-table (Student), and—holding down the mouse button—move the cursor to the right, over the corresponding foreign key attribute of the associative table (Registration). Release the mouse key. The Relationships dialog box is opened for additional description.

3. Usually, for each part of the M:N relationship, you'll want to enable Enforce Referential Integrity and leave it at Join Type One, the equijoin. For our Registration example, you would not want to enable the Cascade Delete action, because, even if a student drops out of school, you still will want the registration information for historical and count purposes (this is another example of an independent 1:M relationship). You may want to enable the Cascade Update action, in case a student number has to be modified. Save the results.

4. Repeat the last two steps, relating the right end-table (Course) with the associative table (Registration) in a 1:M relationship. Assign the same relationship properties, using the same logic for Cascade Update and Cascade Delete. Click Save. Figure 6.6 shows what the finished relationship model should look like.

II

Designing and Prototyping

Fig. 6.6

The M:N relationship between Student and Course, connected by the Registration junction (associative) table.

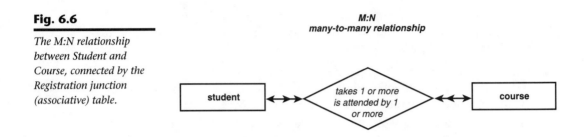

M:N
many-to-many relationship

The student:course M:N relationship is read left-to-right.
The course:student M:N relationship is read right-to-left.

The pair of 1:M relationships you just created, when coupled with the three tables (Student, Registration, and Course), form an explicit M:N relationship.

One thing to remember, if you are handling data integrity (cascade updates, cascade deletes) programmatically, with a non-Access server database management system, coding stored procedures and triggers, make sure that you delete all of the appropriate rows in the associative table. The same consideration about leaving orphan records in the detail table of a dependent 1:M relationship applies to each side of the M:N relationship if, in fact, both sides of the M:N relationship are dependent. If the 1:M relationship on either side of the M:N is independent, leave the rows in the associative table in place.

Domain Integrity and Data Types

The *domain* of an attribute is the set of values that an attribute can legally have, according to the current business rules in place and according to the definition and purpose of the attribute. The domain of student last name, for example, may be any combination of letters in the English alphabet, mixed upper- and lowercase, up to a total of twenty characters. The domain of U.S. postal code is five digits, values 0 to 9, followed by a dash, followed by four more digits, also 0 through 9. The domain of OrderShipDate, however, must be a date value greater than or equal to OrderPlacedDate.

Domains can be mistakenly thought of as data types, but they are a far more stringent qualifier than just data types. For example, Social Security numbers and telephone numbers can be defined as the same data type (usually text), but they are totally different domains.

In Chapter 4, "Getting By in SQL '92—Structured Query Language," we looked at the SQL-92 **create domain** statement, which is not directly supported by Access 95. Under the SQL-92 standard, domains can be created as database objects and can be attached as properties to an attribute of a table. The domain definition contains a data type, a clause that specifies a default value (if appropriate), constraints that restrict the allowable values for this attribute, and a collating—or sort—sequence for the data values.

Domains in Access 95

There is no direct code support for the domain in Access 95, but by using a combination of attribute properties in the table design window, you can simulate domain integrity. The data type and field size combined restrict the kind of character set input; the default value property automatically infills a default value at data entry time; the validation rule (with accompanying validation text property, as shown in fig. 6.7) further restricts the set of allowable values.

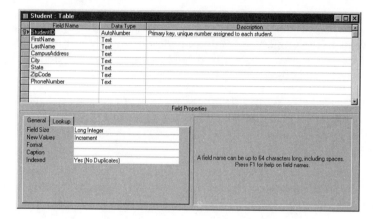

Fig. 6.7

The Table design window, with properties for the LastName field, Students table, Student Registration database.

Data Types Supported by Access 95

Let's look at the various data types supported by Access 95 and how they can assist in implementing at least a minimum level of domain integrity. Be forewarned, if you plan to migrate your Access 95 prototype back end to a server database management system, don't expect it to support either the properties-of-an-attribute feature of Access 95 or the **create domain** command of SQL-92.

Most server database management systems have a set of data types that are mostly consistent with SQL-92 standards, but may not directly support the Access 95 data type set. You may be able to implement default values and constraints by way of stored procedures and triggers, but you need to check your server database user's guide to confirm this possibility. If your intended server database management system cannot provide these features, prepare to implement them programmatically, either by Access form object properties or by Visual Basic event procedures in the Access 95 user interface.

It seems that a topic like data types should be simple or, at least, straightforward. However, here you're dealing with the entire Access 95 package, so data types become complex. The Jet database engine recognizes four overlapping sets of data types, so the data type that you select for a purpose depends on where you are in the Access package.

There is one set of data types for table design and another for query design. Visual Basic has its own set of data types (some are quite inconsistent with the rest of Access), and finally, the Jet has its own set that it recognizes. In the general data type categories discussed in the following sections, the authors present all four sets *and* also the SQL-92 equivalent—if there is one—in table format, to make comparisons a little easier.

GUID and System Counters. The Access-specific data types may go a long way toward enforcing domain integrity in an Access environment, but once outside this environment, these data types may not be recognized. This is the case with the AutoNumber data type, which is an upgrade of the Counter data type of Access 1.*x* and 2.

The *AutoNumber*, when used as the data type for the primary key of the master table, ensures that each value of the primary key is unique without any input from the data entry operator. The value is system-assigned, and can be either a set of sequential numbers or a set of random numbers, which is never repeated.

The main reason to use the AutoNumber data type with the primary key of a table is to ensure entity integrity. The AutoNumber value is assigned and maintained by the system and cannot be modified by a user program, thereby making sure that the primary key will never be Null.

When you choose to assign a primary key (or any attribute in a table) a data type of AutoNumber, you inherit the domain of AutoNumber: in the standard 4-byte version, all numbers between 1 and 2,147,647.

The *ReplicationID*, or *GUID*, is an extension of the AutoNumber. A 16-byte GUID is assigned to each row of every replicated table in a database. The GUID is strictly under system control and out of range of program development, as it needs to be. Access 95 uses this value to compare changes to replicated rows of data and, based on the version number—the more changes to a row of data, the higher the version number— resolves conflicts when it encounters them. We delve more deeply into replication in Chapter 11, "Managing Transactions."

Table 6.1 correlates the system counter data types across the four overlapping modes that comprise the Access 95 development interface. The last column is the SQL-92 equivalent data type.

Table 6.1   GUID and System Counter Data Types

Table Design Mode	Query Design Mode	Visual Basic	Access 95 Jet SQL	SQL-92 Standard
AutoNumber (long integer—4 bytes)	Not supported	Long Integer (4 bytes)	Counter or AutoIncrement	Integer
AutoNumber (ReplicationID— 16 bytes)	Not supported	Not supported	GUID	float(16)

Text and Numbers. The text and number data types will constrain an attribute to either a given set of characters or a limited value range, respectively, thereby enforcing a minimal level of domain integrity.

The *text data type* usually is accompanied by a field length designation, such as text(20) or char(10). In every database environment, if no field length designator is defined, some default value exists, such as the text(50) default in Access 95. Although the text data type will allow any letter (upper- or lowercase), number, or special character supported by the Extended ASCII character set, the field length limits the actual length of the text string. Therefore, by limiting the Zip Code field to a text(5), you can enforce input of the American 5-digit postal code rather than the 5+4 code. By adding an input mask property to this field (for example, **00000;;_**), you can limit input in each of the five positions to a digit between 0 and 9.

Number data types can help enforce domain integrity by limiting the range of values a field can contain. Access 95 input masks work only on text and date data types, so you cannot use a number data type as a way to further constrain the range limits imposed by the data type. You can use the Validation Rule property, however, to set some value restrictions within the data type itself. For example, a byte data type, by definition, will limit the input to a set of values between 0 and 255. Additionally, you can set the Validation Rule property to >250, which restricts values input to the set between 251 and 255.

Table 6.2 correlates the text and number data types across the four overlapping modes that comprise the Access 95 development interface. The last column shows the SQL-92 equivalent data type.

Table 6.2   Text and Number Data Types

Table Design Mode	Query Design Mode	Visual Basic	Access 95 Jet SQL	SQL-92 Standard
Text (length)	Text String (length)	String (fixed length) or String (variable length— type declaration is $)	Character or Alphanumeric, Char, Character, String, VarChar	(length), or Char, Character Varying, VarChar,
Number (byte)	Byte	Byte	Byte or Integer1	SmallInt
Number (integer)	Integer	Integer (type declaration is %)	Short or Integer2, SmallInt	Smallint, Integer
Number (long integer)	Long Integer	Long (type declaration is &)	Long or INT, Integer, Integer4	Integer, Int

(continues)

II

Designing and Prototyping

Table 6.2 Continued				
Table Design Mode	**Query Design Mode**	**Visual Basic**	**Access 95 Jet SQL**	**SQL-92 Standard**
Number (Single)	Single	Single (type declaration is !)	Single or Float4, IEEESingle, Real	Float or Real
Number (Double)	Double	Double (type declaration is #)	Double or Float, Float8, IEEEDouble, Number, Numeric	Double precision
Currency	Currency	Currency (type declaration is @)	Currency or Money	Double precision

Access 95's data types are described in the following list:

- The *Byte* or Number (field type=byte) is a 1-byte data type that will hold positive numbers, ranging from 0 to 255.

- The *Integer* or Number (field type=integer) is a 2-byte data type that will hold numbers that range from –32,768 to 32,767.

- The *Long Integer* or Number (field type=long integer) is a 4-byte data type that will hold numbers, ranging from –2,147,483,648 to 2,147,483,647.

- The *Single* or Number (field type=single) is a 4-byte data type that stores single-precision floating-point numbers, ranging in value from –3.402823E38 to –1.401298E–45 for negative values, 0, and from 1.401298E–45 to 3.402823E38 for positive values.

- The *Double* or Number (field type=double) is an 8-byte data type that stores double-precision floating-point numbers, ranging in value from –1.79769313486232E308 to –4.94065645841247E–324 for negative values, 0, and 4.94065645841247E–324 to 1.79769313486232E308 for positive values.

- The *Currency* is an 8-byte data type that stores and formats money amounts, and also performs an extremely accurate fixed-point calculation. The data type stores numbers, with up to 15 digits to the left of the decimal point and 4 digits to the right.

Memo Data Types. The Access 95 *memo data type* may not contribute to the enforcement of domain integrity, but it does allow the end user to write an abbreviated version of the great American novel and store it in the database!

The memo data type allows long strings, up to 64,000 characters of all kinds. There are even OLE Custom Controls that come bundled with the Access 95 Developers Toolkit and Visual Basic 4 that can turn an ordinary memo field into a mini-Rich Text word processor! If your Access application includes the capability to create custom messages or document templates through a forms interface, being able to input the message or template in Rich Text Format is a very nice feature.

Table 6.3 correlates the memo data type across the four overlapping modes that comprise the Access 95 development interface. The last column is the SQL-92 equivalent data type.

Table 6.3 Memo Data Type				
Table Design	**Query Design**	**Visual Basic**	**Access 95 Jet SQL**	**SQL-92 Standard**
Memo	Memo	String	LongText or LongChar, Memo, Note	Character

OLE Data Types. The Access 95 *OLE data type* also does not contribute to the enforcement of domain integrity, but it does allow for a huge increase in capability for the desktop database management system.

OLE (Object Linking and Embedding) data types vary from true binary objects (video clips, sound bites, still graphics, and so on) to text and word-processing documents to spreadsheets to engineering drawings—virtually any kind of non-tabular data that can be reduced to digital form. OLE data types can be stored within the database (embedded), or the database can contain a pointer to the object (linked), which is stored in its native file format elsewhere on the hard disk assembly. Because all non-tabular objects can be stored as OLE data types, no domain integrity enforcement is available.

Table 6.4 correlates the OLE data type across the four overlapping modes that comprise the Access 95 development interface. The last column is the SQL-92 equivalent data type.

Table 6.4 OLE Data Type				
Table Design	**Query Design**	**Visual Basic**	**Access 95 Jet SQL**	**SQL-92 Standard**
OLE Object	OLE Object	String	LongBinary or General, OLEObject	Bit(length) or Bit Varying (length)

Business Integrity (User Integrity)

The fourth integrity, *business integrity*, also known as *user integrity*, is an expression of the belief that a database is the reflection of corporate reality and, as such, must operate under the same set of business rules that govern the corporation.

Business integrity has no direct support from Access. The SQL-92 standard includes a CREATE ASSERTION statement, which directly supports encoding business rules at the

II

Designing and Prototyping

table level. In Access, the techniques used to enforce entity, referential, and domain integrity are combined as needed with other properties, both at the table and at the form level, to provide a level of integrity that enforces the business rules.

At the table level, in Table Design Mode, by choosing the format property or the input mask, or both, the database developer can stringently restrict the domain of an attribute. This restriction may be part of a business rule, to limit the type and amount of data allowed in a particular field. By using these properties, which normally provide domain integrity, we actually are enforcing the business rules.

The Validation Rule Property

It is the *Validation Rule property* that most closely represents enforcement for the business rules. The Validation Rule property allows the developer to specify rules, requirements, and constraints on data entered into this field. By reducing the business rules to code, they can be enforced automatically, each time data is entered into the database by way of an object protected by this kind of Validation Rule.

The Validation Rule property is found in Table Design Mode, in the lower portion of the table design window, to enforce field validation rules. It also is found in the property sheet for a table, which enables the creation of record validation rules. Validation Rules established at the table level are inherited by each form or report that is built on the table or on a query derived from the table.

The property sheet for each control on a form contains an entry for a Validation Rule, which will apply locally, only to data entered through this form. Finally, Validation Rules can be created in Visual Basic by using the Data Access Objects **ValidationRule** property.

The maximum length of the code that can be attached to an Access 95 Validation Rule property box is 255 characters. The **ValidationRule** property in Visual Basic is a string expression. The Validation Rule property is proprietary to the Access Jet, and as such, probably will not be supported by non-Access database management systems.

Business Rules

As stated in the preceding section, a database is a reflection of corporate reality and, therefore, must operate under the same set of business rules that govern the corporation. When a company first engages in creating a database to support the organization, there usually is more time and dollars spent in defining the business situation and how it operates than is actually spent in developing the database and all the front-end applications that will access the stored data.

A *business rule*, from the database perspective, is an explicit statement, stipulating a condition that must exist in a business environment for information extracted to be consistent with business policy. More simply, a business rule is embedded code that describes (and enforces) data requirements to business users. Without these business rules in place, the database—as a support and as added value to the corporation—will fail.

Converting Data Types Specific to Access 95

There are some data types that are specific to Access, which may be difficult to convert, or may not convert at all when moving the data database from Access 95 to another database environment.

Table 6.5 correlates the following miscellaneous data type across the four overlapping modes that comprise the Access 95 development interface. The last column is the SQL-92 equivalent data type.

Table 6.5 Other Data Types

Table Design	Query Design	Visual Basic	Access 95 Jet SQL	SQL-92 Standard
Date/Time	Date/Time	Date	DateTime or Date, Time, TimeStamp	Date, Time, Timestamp, Interval
Yes/No	Yes/No	Boolean	Boolean, Bit, Logical, Logical1, YesNo	Bit
Not supported	Binary	Not supported	Binary or VarBinary	Bit(length), Bit Varying(length)
Not supported	Value	Variant	Value	not supported
Not supported	Not supported	User-Defined	User-Defined	Not supported
Lookup	Not supported	Not supported		Not supported

The Date/Time is an 8-byte data type that stores date and time information. In Access 95, the valid dates are January 1, 100 to December 31, 9999. Date and time data types historically have had compatibility issues in different database management systems. However, in the Access 95 environment, if the non-Access server database cannot comprehend the Access date/time data types or functions, the server simply moves all data to the client machine and lets the Jet database engine handle the processing locally.

The Boolean data type is used to represent any expression that can evaluate to either True (nonzero) or False (zero). Keywords True and False can be used to represent the values –1 and 0, respectively. The property sheet settings for the Boolean data type are: Yes/No, True/False, and On/Off, each pair of which evaluates to –1 or 0, respectively. Most database management systems support some form of Boolean data type.

The Binary data type is not used by Access 95. Rather it is supported by the Query facility and the Jet when attaching to tables controlled by database management systems that do support the Binary data type. It is included in table 6.5 for completeness.

II

Designing and Prototyping

The Variant data type can store any kind of Visual Basic variable—numeric, string, date/time—basically, anything except fixed-length string and user-defined data types. The Variant data type also can contain the special values, Null, Empty, Error, and Nothing. This is the default data type for variables whose data type isn't explicitly declared. There is no type declaration character for the variant. As long as the variant variables are kept local—that is, in the client Access environment—no compatibility problems should arise with non-Access database management systems.

The Lookup is a very special (and Access 95-specific) "data type" that is included in the table design window. This feature allows database developers to define combo or list boxes for text fields at the table level rather than at the form level. The row source for these lookups can be another table, or it can be an embedded list. The embedded list version of the Lookup will stay local, so back-end conversion is not an issue. The table reference version of the Lookup will try to access a table from the server, so some modifications may be needed.

From Here...

In this chapter, we talked about the four database integrities and how important they are. We discussed entity integrity and how to enforce it in Access 95. We covered referential integrity and the three relationships that depend on referential integrity. We investigated domain integrity and how to enforce it through the various data types supported by Access 95. And finally, we discussed business, or user, integrity and how to enforce it, at least in part by validation rules and default values encoded at the table level. For more information, see the following chapters:

- Chapter 7, "Using Access as a Prototyping Tool," presents more discussion on how to build tables and implement relationships between tables.

- Chapter 8, "Adding Functionality to Your Prototype," covers advanced procedures and code-behind-forms.

- Chapter 11, "Managing Transactions," discusses replication.

- Chapter 18, "Upsizing Techniques," discusses upsizing to non-Access databases.

- Chapter 22, "The Human Factor," covers more ground rules on database design.

CHAPTER 7

Using Access as a Prototyping Tool

Access 95 is a great *prototyping tool*. The Jet database engine is powerful enough to offer many of the features of a server database, and it supports both the SQL '92 Standard and Visual Basic for Applications, which is a powerful object-oriented programming language. In this chapter we cover the following areas:

- Creating an Access 95 database
- Building a table and assigning properties, validation rules, and so on to the columns of the table
- The pros and cons of using the table properties versus coding these properties into the client-end application
- Reference tables, what they are and how they should be positioned in the client/server environment
- The database documentor and the OLE connection to Microsoft Word
- The Relationships Window and how to use it
- Entity-Relationship Modeling, inside Access and beyond

Pluses and Minuses of Prototyping in Access

Access can be used to prototype the entire client/server application, both the user interface—the client application—and the server application. Some of the benefits of using Access as a prototyping tool include the following:

- The capability to develop prototypes quickly (rapid application development)
- The capability to develop prototypes in a desktop environment without needing server access
- A wide choice of migration paths to the server database management system
- The availability of a rich toolkit to help in upsizing the prototype
- Possible performance gains by converting the client application to Visual Basic code

■ The capability to evolve the user interface (the client application) during the prototyping phase, responding to end-user concerns

■ The constancy of the user interface during and after server conversion

Preserving Functionality

Perhaps the biggest drawback to prototyping in Access is that, when you do connect to a non-Access server database, it may not be able to offer all the functionality that you had built into your prototype. You need to be aware of the limitations of both Access and the target server database software.

When you choose Access as the prototyping tool, the client software for your finished production application probably will remain an Access application. Unless there are significant performance problems that can be directly attributed to the Access code and techniques of accessing data, it doesn't make much sense to convert the client application to anything else. The users will contribute to the evolution of the front end during the development phase. Then, they will see the same set of forms and reports during and after the conversion to the server database. If the conversion is handled properly, the only difference noticed by the users should be a few changes in how some parts of the application work and a general decrease in response time.

As we just mentioned, when performance is an issue (and when is performance not an issue?), portions of the client application can be re-written in Visual Basic for Applications. The data entry screens are always a good candidate for conversion to Visual Basic, because here you need tight code and fast response. Data entry staffers will perform a certain set of activities repeatedly. They will deal with a set of predefined screens for data input and retrieval. Integrity checks and validation rules will be stored on the server database management system, offloading that task from their client environment, which will give them the perception of better response time. Generally, data entry staff doesn't need the flexibility and capability offered by the Access 95 run-time environment.

For the portion of the client application that belongs to the managers and the decision makers, you may want to leave it as pure Access 95 run time. The managers and decision makers will take the time to learn how to exploit the Access interface and the added features that you build into the application.

For certain server database management systems, you can find software tools to assist with the conversion, or "upsizing," as Microsoft calls it. On the Developer Net CD-ROM (DevNet), you can find an upsizing tool for use with Microsoft SQL Server. This toolkit provides advice on how to structure your Access application for a successful port to SQL Server, and includes some additional tools to help with the conversion.

Database Definitions and Documentation

One reason that Access is so popular for both prototyping and building applications is that you can easily *create tables*. The table design screen is laid out a little like a spreadsheet, and the data items, data types, and descriptions are easy to enter.

Additional column properties, such as field size, field format, input masks, label captions, default values, and validation rules are only a mouse click away.

Building tables by using the Access 95 GUI is easier—and to many users, far more intuitive—than writing a string of SQL "create table" statements, which is how you have to build tables in most relational database management systems. Figure 7.1 shows the graphical interface used to create and modify tables. After the tables are constructed in Access 95, several ways are available to transfer them to a server database, at the appropriate time. We look more closely at how to do this in Chapter 18, "Upsizing Techniques."

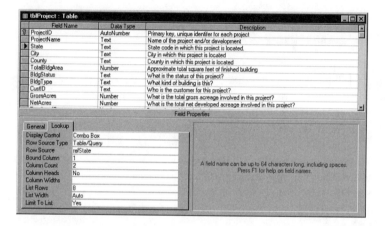

Fig. 7.1

Access Table Design Mode, showing column (field) properties, with the lookup property on the background tab.

You need to use care when creating tables in Access 95, and you need to become acquainted with the capabilities of your target server database. Some column properties that you can assign in Access 95 don't carry forward to the server database. Input masks, default values, some validation rules, validation statements, support for zero-length strings, and even Null support may not transfer directly to the target database. If you will be assembling the user interface—the client portion of the application—while connected to Access 95 tables, these field properties are inherited by (and copied over to) any form or report built on these tables. After the Access 95 back end is replaced with a server database management system and the tables are no longer Microsoft Access tables, this inheritance feature ceases to exist.

Access 95 has the new *lookup property*, which is the second tab in the field properties section of the Table Design Window. This feature is totally an Access 95 proprietary function and will not be supported by any other relational database management system. However, if—as mentioned previously—you plan to create all or part of the client interface while attached to Microsoft Access, you can save time and maintain consistency by using this "lookup" feature at the table level.

If this prototype application will be upsized in the near future, you may want to be judicious in the time spent implementing these properties at the table level, and instead invest the time implementing them in the form of stored procedures or triggers on your target server database. You may even choose to implement some of these properties in the forms and reports of the client application.

On the other hand, if you will use this Access 95 server .MDB for a lengthy period, or if you have not yet decided to which server software you will port, you may want to invest the time and effort now to establish these rules at the table level. Doing so now ensures that the rules are applied and that they can be documented and re-coded, if needed, when the upsizing finally takes place.

Each of these properties is discussed in turn, both in this chapter and also in subsequent chapters.

Building a Sample Database

To illustrate the prototyping capability of Access 95, we will build a database, insert some tables, and establish the relationships. This database will be used and enhanced in following chapters. If you are new to Access 95, you can follow along as we build it now. If you have some experience with building Access 95 databases, you can skip this section and rejoin us when we get to the section, "Entity Models," later in this chapter. The database itself is on this book's companion CD-ROM, so you can copy onto to your hard disk for modification. Please read the following description of the database application so that you are acquainted with both its scope and its purpose, and what it is supposed to do.

The REA Database

This database and application is for a real-estate investment company, Real Estate of America, Inc., which we shall shorten to REA or REA, Inc. REA purchases land—suitable building sites—and then constructs buildings that either will be sold or leased. The process of buying and building on land is a complex subject because many factors can influence the outcome, and all of these factors are time-dependent upon each other. The land must be secured, all contracts and deeds signed, all transfer of ownership completed before construction can commence. Meanwhile, engineering drawings of the building(s) are being developed, and potential renters, buyers, and/or investors (as appropriate), are lined up.

After the land is secured, all the necessary construction permits and approvals must be obtained, and all the contracts must be signed before the work can begin. When the work is underway, the problems of staying on schedule, expected occupancy dates, and late penalties must be dealt with. There is quite an element of risk that must be managed in order to ensure a profitable project. This database is designed to track the process, and ensure that no contracts are signed until all the requirements are met.

Many people are involved in a project. The customer must be identified and persuaded that REA can meet their needs for residential, office, or warehouse buildings. The land officers must find suitable land for building, and arrangements must be made to purchase it. General contractors must be contacted and their bids evaluated before awarding contracts for the construction project. Field engineers and consultants must be assigned to each project at the appropriate time. REA project coordinators must keep on top of what's happening with each project at all times.

Each step in the process requires input from different people within the company. A team is assigned to each project, with a team leader or coordinator who oversees the project from beginning to end. Obviously, each team member must have access to the stored data. The data is updated at each step in the process and passed along to the next member. Because of time constraints, many tasks are happening simultaneously. This model is not a classic workflow where the project is handed off by each person in the chain, never to be seen again. Rather, you are looking at a situation where the project may be worked on by multiple team members at the same time, and where one team member may release a project only to have it come back around. This application is ideal for client/server technology, where several people need access to the same data, to enable them to work on interlinked, mutually dependent parts of a project.

This process is even more complicated because the customer will not sign unless the price is right (of course), which cannot be completely determined until the costs of the land and the building are known. In the ideal situation, the tenant signs the lease and REA signs the land purchase documents immediately following, with construction to start the next day. This situation rarely happens.

One situation that REA would like to alleviate altogether is buying the land long before the tenant commits to the lease, which effectively forces them to keep the land in inventory. Another situation that REA wants to totally eliminate is not being able to secure the land after the tenant commits. Either situation can result in serious financial losses, so timing is critical to minimizing the impact.

Other losses can occur when the general contractor fails to complete the building in time for the tenant to move in and REA has failed to bind the general contractor to a penalty clause. You probably can imagine many other scenarios in which REA can lose money on a deal like this. Imagine trying to track dozens of deals and potential deals by using a manual system, paper forms, and individual non-networked computers. Scary thought, isn't it?

The point of this database application is to reduce the exposure to risks, minimize the chance of errors, and thereby free up the company team members to work on more deals. To achieve this end, REA needs to have one copy of the project data for consistency that, for efficiency, it makes available to everyone.

REA already has a network in place, and everyone is using Microsoft Windows for Workgroups as their client operating system. We plan to prototype the client and server parts of the application in Access. Then, as the volume of data grows, we will add a Windows NT Server to the network, running Microsoft SQL Server, and migrate the server component. The desktop client application will remain the same when the server portion is upgraded.

II

Designing and Prototyping

REA has also asked for a messaging system to be incorporated into the application. This setup differs from their e-mail system. It is a way for team members to attach notes and annotations to specific projects and specific items within the projects, and to pass these notes to other team members in an efficient manner. This messaging system replaces the sticky notes and pieces of paper that used to be attached to project folders back in the days of paper forms.

Creating the New Database

Let's start by creating a database for REA, Inc. This is a simple process that doesn't involve pre-allocating hard-disk space or writing code. Figure 7.2 shows the New Data-base dialog box, from which you can build a database from scratch or invoke the assis-tance of the Database Wizard.

Fig. 7.2

The New Database dialog. The front tab (General) for a blank database and the rear tab, which contains 22 database templates from which you can start when building your own.

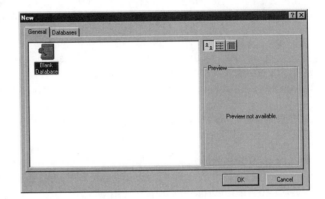

When you *create a database* in Access 95, you are realy establishing a "data space" and setting up the system tables—the data dictionary—for your application. The *database administrator* (the systems-oriented individual who is responsible for the care and feeding of a database management system) usually takes care of this task in a main-frame or server-based environment. And, in this kind of an environment, there are many "create database" options that can be invoked or not, as needed. In the desktop environment, anyone—from a database administrator to a database designer to an applications programmer to an end-user—can create a database. Access 95 does have a relatively rich set of database properties, but because it was developed for use by a wide range of people with an even wider range of expertise, the default set of proper-ties will work fairly well for a high number of situations.

In Access, open a new database, and then take the following steps:

1. From the File menu, select the New Database option.
2. Select the Blank Database icon in the New dialog box, and click OK.
3. When prompted for a file name and directory, type REA_DATA in the File Name box and create the .MDB file in an appropriate directory on your hard disk. Access builds a blank database and opens it in the Database Window.

4. Select <u>T</u>ools, <u>O</u>ptions to view the database Options dialog box, as shown in figure 7.3.

5. Click the Advanced tab. Set Default record locking to E<u>d</u>ited Records, which is what you always want in a client/server application.

6. The Default Open Mode should be set to <u>S</u>hared. Again, this is the normal mode for a client/server application.

7. The OLE/DDE Timeout is set to 30 seconds by default. If you plan to use these inter-application communication methods, you may find that this parameter is too short by half, and a setting of 60 seconds may work better.

8. Select the other tabs to view the many database operational parameters. For now, leave the default settings. The rule in our shop when creating a database is to make sure that default database open is shared mode, and that default record locking is edited record. All else, we leave as is until we need to change it.

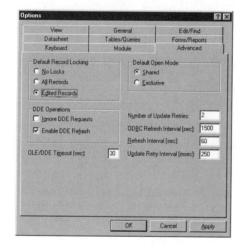

Fig. 7.3

The Database Options dialog box contains the database operational parameters.

II

Designing and Prototyping

Building the Tables

Now it's time to add a table to the database. We will walk through the creation of one table. The others (there are 16 tables in all), you can copy from the CD-ROM, using the Microsoft Access import function and importing them into this database or, if you don't have access to a CD-ROM drive, you can build each table from the specifications listed in Appendix A, "Tables for the REA Sample Database."

The table we will add is tblProject, the "main" or central table of this application. TblProject contains core information about each building project undertaken by REA, Inc. The Project table is comprised of twenty-nine or so columns, or fields, as they are called in Access terminology. Each field has between five and eleven properties, depending on the data type of the field. The properties do not have to be set in the field definition; they can be declared in the forms or reports that are built on the table. However, if they are established at the table level, then any form or report that is built on the table (or on a query built on the table) "inherits" the property.

To create the tblProject table, take the following steps:

1. Click <u>N</u>ew to add a new table to the database. Notice that you have a few new choices in the Table Design dialog box that were introduced with Access 95 (see fig. 7.4). The Datasheet view is new, as are the Import Table and Link Table options. The last two options were found under the File menu in Access 2; in Access 95 you can find them in two places, here in the New Table dialog box and also under the <u>F</u>ile, <u>G</u>et External Data menu selection.

Fig. 7.4

The New Table dialog box, showing the five options available; three are new to Access 95—Datasheet View, Import Table, and Link Table.

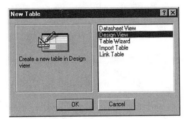

2. Select the Design View option and click OK.

3. If prompted, save the table and name it tblProject.

4. Input the ProjectID as an AutoNumber field as shown. Indicate in the Description column that this is the primary key of the table. Highlight the ProjectID line by clicking in the left margin of the window, and then click the Primary Key button (designated by a "key" icon) on the top toolbar. You should see a key appear in the left margin of the ProjectID line, which indicates that ProjectID is the primary key field for this table.

5. Input the remaining fields as listed in Table 7.1.

Table 7.1   The tblProject Fields

Field Name	Data Type	Description	Field Properties*	Lookup
ProjectID	AutoNumber (Long)	Primary key, unique identifier for each project.	NewValues= Increment Caption= Project# Indexed= Yes (No Duplicates)	
ProjectName	Text(50)	Name of project and/or development.	Caption= Project Name Required=Yes Indexed=Yes (Duplicates OK)	

Field Name	Data Type	Description	Field Properties*	Lookup
State	Text(2)	State code in which this project is located.		Display Control= Combo Box Row Source Type= Table/Query Row Source= refStates Bound Column=1 Column Count=2 Limit To List=Yes
City	Text(30)	City in which this project is located.		
County	Text(30)	County in which this project is located.		
TotalBldgArea	Number (Single)	Approximate total square feet of finished building.	Caption= Total Square Footage	
BldgStatus	Text(20)	What is status of this project?	Caption= Building Status	Display Control= Combo Box Row Source Type= Value List Row Source=; planning stage;under construction; construction complete;closed Limit To List=Yes
BldgType	Text(30)	What kind of building is this?	Caption= Building Type	Display Control= Combo Box Row Source Type= Value List Row Source=; single-family home;multi family home;retail bldg;office bldg;warehouse Limit To List=No

(continues)

Table 7.1 Continued

Field Name	Data Type	Description	Field Properties*	Lookup
CustID		Who is customer for this project?	Indexed= Yes (Duplicates OK)	Display Control= Combo Box Row Source Type= Table/Query Row Source= refCustomer Bound Column=1 Column Count=2 Limit To List=Yes
GrossAcres	Number (Single)	What is total gross acreage involved in this project?	Caption= Gross Acres	
NetAcres	Number (Single)	What is total net developed acreage involved in this project?	Caption= Net Acres	
TotalLandCost	Number (Single)	Base price paid for the land.	Format= Currency Decimal Places=2 Caption= Total Land Costs	
Acquisition Cost	Number (Single)	Total acquisition costs other than base land and closing costs.	Format= Currency Decimal Places=2 Caption= Acquisition Costs	
TotalClosCost	Number (Single)	Total closing costs for the sale to new owner.	Format= Currency Decimal places=2 Caption= Total Closing Costs	
ContractDate	Date/Time	Date the contract was signed.	Format= Short Date Caption= Contract Date	

Field Name	Data Type	Description	Field Properties*	Lookup
EarnestMoney	Number (Single)	How much earnest money was put down on project?	Format= Currency Decimal Places=2 Caption= Earnest Money	
InspectExpire	Date/Time	Expiration date of inspection period.	Format= Short Date Caption= Inspection Expiration Date	
TargetClose Date	Date/Time	Target closing date.	Format= Short Date Caption= Target Closing Date	
FinalCloseDate	Date/Time	Final closing date, the date the purchase is completed, or project is finished.	Format= Short Date Caption= Final Closing Date	
MajorStreets	Text(60)	Major cross streets closest to project.	Caption= Major Cross Streets	
UtilElectric	Text(60)	Electric company servicing project.	Caption= Electric Company	
UtilGas	Text(60)	Gas company servicing project.	Caption= Gas Company	
UtilWater	Text(60)	Water company servicing project.	Caption= Water Company	
UtilSewer	Text(60)	Sewer company servicing project.	Caption= Sewer Company	
UtilPhone	Text(60)	Phone company servicing project.	Caption= Phone Company	

(continues)

II

Designing and Prototyping

Table 7.1 Continued

Field Name	Data Type	Description	Field Properties*	Lookup
Final Resolution	Text(60)	Final outcome of this project.	Caption= Final Resolution	
ProjComments	Memo	Additional comments or notes regarding this project.		
LastUpdate	Date/Time	Date last change made to this record. Takes the timestamp from the system clock.	Format= General Date Default= Date( )	
ByWhom	Text(12)	Last user who made change to this record. Logon id of person who made the change.	Form Property Default= Currentuser( )	

* The entries in the Field Properties column are those where the value varies from the Access 95 default.

Figure 7.5 shows tblProject in Table Design mode.

Notice that the field names have no embedded spaces, although Access allows this feature. The authors advise using a variation of the Hungarian notation naming convention for field names (see Chapter 5, "Client/Server Database Application Design Fundamentals," for a full discussion of Hungarian notation) for the following reasons:

> Embedded spaces and/or special characters, with a few exceptions—notably the underscore (_)—will be rejected by almost every server database management system to which these tables might be upsized. This means that you have to change field names at the table level, which profoundly impacts the client application.

> The mixed case of Hungarian notation is easy to read and converts readily in the server environment to either mixed case or all uppercase. Your best bet, if migrating soon, is to know the naming conventions and restrictions of your server database management system and to follow them in Access.

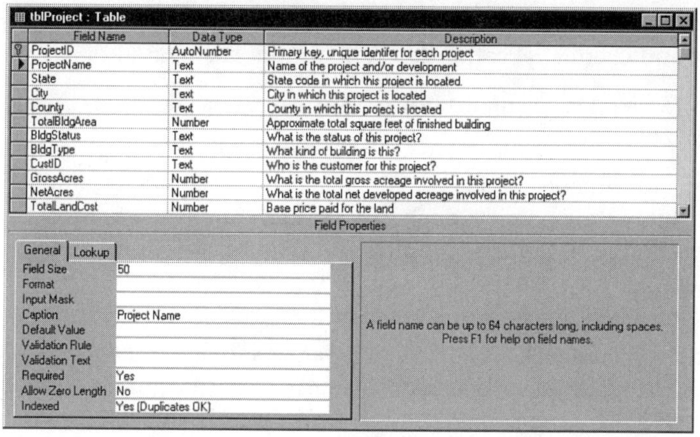

Fig. 7.5

The Project table in design mode, showing the General field properties of the ProjectName column.

Take just a moment to fill in the descriptions for each field, for two reasons—it's a good idea to define each field, what it is, and how it will be used. This action alleviates any confusion on the part of any database programmer or end user, and the text entered as a description will be inherited (copied over) as the status bar text of a form, wherever that field is used—giving you built-in, on-screen assist for the data entry forms.

AutoNumber Data Types

The Access 2 Counter data type has become the Access 95 AutoNumber data type.

We chose to use an AutoNumber data type for the ProjectID because each project must have a primary key value, a number that can uniquely identify each project stored in the REA database and that can link the assorted rows from many tables into a coherent unity. There really is no other data item in the Project table that would be a good candidate for the primary key, so we are making one by using the AutoNumber. In this case, the ProjectID will carry no value, so the AutoNumber data type will work well.

You would not want to use the AutoNumber data type for every design situation. For example, if you were setting up a student registration database, you would use a Student ID number, which already is assigned to each student, as the primary key in the Student table and as part of the primary key in the Registration table. There are many situations where predetermined and preassigned identifiers for the major entity—the major theme of a table—are the best candidates for the primary key position.

Note that you may need to modify an AutoNumber data type if you port the Access 95 back-end database to another database management system. Not all DBMSs support the automatic incrementing of a field at the system level, so you may have to add your own program code to take care of assigning a new number to each record.

General Field Properties. Let's look at each of the field properties, and then explore how your prototype and client application can benefit from using them.

The Field Properties, General tab contains the following options:

- **Field Size**—For text data types, the field size is the maximum length of the character string; for number data types, how long and what kind of number (byte, integer, long integer, single, double, replication id). Access 95 stores data in a minimum compressed mode, stripping off leading zeros (from number fields) and trailing blanks (from text fields), so this value is only an indication of the maximum size character string or number allowed.

- **New Values** (AutoNumber only)—How new values should be generated as records are added to the table; choices are incrementally (previous number plus one) or randomly generated. When you define a replicated database, the AutoNumber (long integer, 4 bytes) automatically converts to a ReplicationID (16 bytes) and switches from incremental to random, to ensure that new records entered in different replicated databases each will have a unique value. Of course, if you attach your Access client application to a non-Access back-end, the AutoNumber concept may not be supported (Microsoft SQL Server 6 has a comparable Global ID), and Access 95 replication is a nonissue (Microsoft SQL Server supports the distributed database model).

- **Format**—How should the value be presented? This property affects how data is displayed, not how it is stored. Each time a field is used in the application, regardless of how many times or in how many reports or forms it appears, the format is inherited unless it is programmatically overridden in the form or report. For Date/Time data types, the presentation selection allows a full timestamp (General Date), a formal date with day-of-the-week (Long Date), a medium and short date format, and long, medium, and short time formats. For Number data types, the choices are (9,999.99), general (display as entered), currency ($9,999.99), fixed (9999.99), percent (multiply by 100 and append the % symbol), and scientific (standard scientific notation). Access 95 has a set of formats that are fairly consistent with the universe of database formats, so you should find that most Access 95 formats are supported by your non-Access database management system.

- **Decimal Places** (Number only)—How many places to the right of the decimal point should be presented? This option allows user override of the default number of decimal positions allocated with each number field size.

- **Input Mask**—A pattern to assist in data entry. Typical input mask patterns are Social Security number, telephone number, and ZIP+4 number. Access 95 allows a full range of user-defined input masks. This property may not be supported by many non-Access databases.

- **Caption**—The label for this field when it is inserted into a form or a report. If no caption is declared, the field name is used. Effectively, this allows for an *internal field name* (the assigned field name), and an *external field name* (the caption name that appears on the data entry form). Systems staff—database administrators and database designers/developers—historically tend to assign cryptic names to columns (fields) of a table, and can continue to do so in Access 95. The end-user community tends to look for more coherent, understandable field names, and they can have them if the caption property is used for this purpose. After the tables are moved to a non-Access back-end, the caption property most likely will cease to exist.

- **Default Value**—This value is automatically entered into a field when a new record is added in data entry mode for either the form or the data sheet. This selection can be a tremendous time-saver for data entry and a way of enforcing business rules and standards (if implemented). This property will not propagate to non-Access databases, but you can code validation rules in the forms of the client application.

- **Validation Rule**—A Validation Rule is an expression that limits or restricts the set of values that can be entered into a field. Access 95 employs this vehicle to enforce domain integrity. Validation rules are any valid expression, such as the contents of a SQL WHERE clause or a **DLookup** statement, and are checked after update of a field, before focus is relinquished. This is another property that will not propagate to non-Access databases.

- **Validation Text**—This is the error message that accompanies a violation of a validation rule. It appears in the message area at the bottom of the screen.

- **Required**—Is data entry required for this field? If no, Nulls are allowed. If yes, Access 95 waits until you try to save the new record before insisting that you enter a value for this field (Nulls are not allowed in field ...). This property should be carried forward to a non-Access database, as exemplified by the SQL **create table** extension, **not Null**.

- **Allow Zero Length**—This is a string that contains no characters, indicated in Visual Basic by the "" (no space between the double quotes). Combining Required=No and AllowZeroLength=Yes gives you the opportunity to differentiate between a field value that doesn't exist (ZeroLengthString), and one in which you can indicate that you don't know if it exists or not (Null). For example, EmployeeSpouseName is Null if the EmployeeMaritalStatus field is "married"; EmployeeSpouseName would be a zero length string if "single" was placed as the value of EmployeeMaritalStatus field. Zero length strings are not widely supported, and are not part of the SQL '92 standard.

- **Indexed**—Create an index on this field? This flag causes the Jet engine to create the appropriate indexes when the table design is saved. All indexes created in Access 95 should be created during the upsizing to a non-Access back-end.

Lookup Properties. The Lookup tab brings the definition of list and combo boxes from the form level back to the table level (see fig. 7.6). As we mentioned previously in this chapter, the *Lookup property* and the way it is implemented is proprietary to Access and probably will not propagate to a non-Access back end. However, because Lookups are underlaid by embedded lists or reference tables that can be kept local to the client application, they can be implemented successfully, regardless of your upgrade plans.

Fig. 7.6

*The Project table in design
mode, with the Lookup
Field Properties tab
selected.*

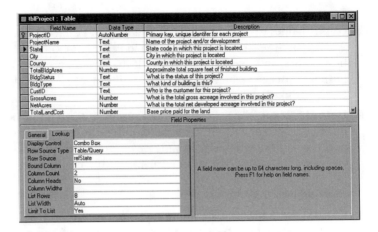

The Display Control property has three options, Text Box, List Box, and Combo Box, which are described in the following list:

- The *Text Box* is, of course, the standard form control through which data is displayed from the table to the user.

- The *List Box* is a form control that lists a set of choices for a field value. The list is always present on-screen and greatly facilitates data entry by allowing selection with a mouse click or a single keyboard character. The limitation of a list box is that the user cannot enter a value that is not in the list.

- The *Combo Box* is a List Box that stays rolled up, so it uses less form "real estate." Data entry is done in two ways—by typing a character or two of the selection, which causes the combo box to fall open and the nearest match to be highlighted or by using the mouse to open the combo box and highlight the selection. You can program a combo box to accept values not in the list, and with a bit of additional programming (and a row source type of Table/Query), you can dynamically update the list.

The Lookup tab field properties for the Text Box are restricted to Display Control. The following list describes the properties for both List Box and Combo Box:

- **Row Source Type**—The type of source for the data, either a Table/Query, a Value List, or a Field List.

- **Row Source**—The contents depend on the Row Source Type property. If Row Source Type is Table/Query, this data comes from a table, from a query, or from a SQL statement that references a table or query. If Row Source Type is Value List, this is a list of items separated by semi-colons (;). If Row Source Type is Field List, the data comes from a list of field names that were taken from a table, a query, or a SQL statement referencing a table or query.

The semicolon at the beginning of the list of values was the way in version 2 (and still is a way in version 7) to introduce a blank value in the combo box drop-down list. If you fail to include this in the list of values, then when you're using the form, if you tab into the combo box control and Limit to List is turned on, you cannot get out without selecting a value—whether or not you wanted to. Cool, huh?

- **Bound Column**—The column of the table to which this control is bound or linked, and which is updated when a value is selected from the list or combo box.

- **Column Count**—The number of columns to display in the list box or combo box.

- **Column Heads**—Should the first row of the list/combo box be column headings?

- **Column Widths**—How wide should the columns be in a multi-column list or combo box? Indicate a width for each column, separated by a semi-colon(;).

The Lookup tab field properties for just Combo Box are described in the following list:

- **List Rows**—The maximum number of rows displayed when the combo box is opened. If the number of selections exceeds the number of rows, then a vertical scroll bar automatically appears.

- **List Width**—The width of the combo box, all columns. The combo box of multiple rows can be attached to a single-field display, so that when the combo box is closed, only the single field value is displayed. When the combo box is dropped down, the multiple fields are displayed, the better to aid value selection.

- **Limit to List**—Allow values other than the values in the combo box list? If yes, only values from the list can be selected; otherwise, the user can input a different value.

Setting Up the Other Tables. The other tables of the REA database are described in the following sections. The purpose of each table is given, how it relates to the other tables in the database, and how the relationship should be expressed in the Relationships Window, which are covered in later sections of this chapter. The full layout of each of these tables can be found in Appendix A, "Tables for the REA Sample Database," and on the companion CD-ROM.

The Construction Costs Table. The Construction Costs table contains cost information for the general construction sections of a project. The Construction Costs are dependent for its existence on an associated Project—without a project there can be no construction costs—and it is related to the Project table in a 1:1 relationship. In the Relationships Window, these two tables are connected as: 1:1, Enforce Referential Integrity is turned on, Cascade Update Related Fields and Cascade Delete Related Fields is turned on, and Join Type 2 (left outer) is selected.

The Terms & Assumptions Table. The Terms & Assumptions table contains information regarding the terms and lease/purchase assumptions that are made on a project between REA, Inc., and its customer. Terms & Assumptions are dependent on an associated Project for their existence and are related to the Project table in a 1:1 relationship. In the Relationships Window, these two tables are connected as 1:1, Enforce Referential Integrity on, Cascade Update Related Fields and Cascade Delete Related Fields on, and Join Type 2 (left outer).

The Checklist Table. The Checklist table is a checklist for a project. This table contains time-related and order-sensitive information. The Checklist is dependent on an associated Project for its existence, and is related to the Project table in a 1:1 relationship. In the Relationships Window, these two tables are connected as 1:1, Enforce Referential Integrity on, Cascade Update Related Fields and Cascade Delete Related Fields on, and Join Type 2 (left outer).

The Messages Table. The Messages table is a set of slots where users can leave messages for each other. In this application, it is not tied into the corporate mail system. The Messages table does not appear in the Relationships Window.

The Customer Table. The Customer table is a reference table, a list of customers and information about each. The Customer table has a 1:M relationship with the Project table; a customer can be involved in one or more projects. This relationship is independent—both the Customer records and the Project records can exist without each other. In the Relationships Window, these two tables are connected as 1:M, refCustomer to tblProject, Enforce Referential Integrity on, Cascade Update Related Fields on, Cascade Delete Related Fields off, and Join Type 1 (equijoin).

The Customer Credit Table. The Customer Credit table contains sensitive information, regarding the credit history of a specific customer. Between Customer and Customer Credit, a dependent relationship exists—without a customer there would be no customer credit report—and in this application, a 1:1 relationship exists between the Customer table and the Customer Credit table. In the Relationships Window, these two tables are connected as 1:1, Enforce Referential Integrity on, Cascade Update Related Fields on, Cascade Delete Related Fields on, and Join Type 2 (left outer).

The Contractor Table. The Contractor table is a reference table, a list of contractors (general contractor, roofing contractor, architectural contractor, and so on), and also information about each contractor. The Contractor table has a 1:M relationship with the Construction Costs table; a contractor can be involved in one or more projects. This relationship is independent—both the Contractor records and the Construction Costs records can exist without each other. In the Relationships Window, these two tables are connected as 1:M, refContractor to tblConstCost, Enforce Referential Integrity on, Cascade Update Related Fields on, Cascade Delete Related Fields off, and Join Type 1 (equijoin).

The States Table. The States table is a reference table comprised of state codes and corresponding state names. The States table has an implied 1:M relationship with any table that contains an address (city, state, ZIP), or otherwise needs to decode the state code. The States table doesn't appear in the Relationships Window.

The Team Table. The Team table is a reference table comprised of a list of team members and phone numbers. Team members, in this context, are defined as employees of REA. This reference list is a list of all employees who could be assigned to a project team. In the conceptual model, the Team table has a 1:M relationship with the Team Member table; a person in the Team list can be involved in one or more project teams. However, due to operational constraints inherent with many-to-many relationships, the Team table does not appear in the Relationships Window:

```
(refTeam ------>>  tblTeamMembers <<------ tblProject)
```

The Team Member Table. The Team Member table includes the people who are assigned to a project team, occupying positions like project manager, land agent, attorney, and so on. The Team Member table has a M:1 relationship with the Project table; there are one or more team members for each project. This relationship is dependent—the Team Member records cannot exist without an associated Project record. In the
Relationships Window, these two tables are connected as 1:M, tblProject to tblTeamMembers, Enforce Referential Integrity on, Cascade Update on, Cascade Delete on, and Join Type 2 (left outer).

The Archaeology, Environmental, and Wetlands Table. This table is a place to record issues that deal with archaeological findings, environmental issues, wetlands penetration, and even endangered species threats for each project. A 1:1 relationship exists between the Archaeology, Environment, and Wetlands table and the Project table. The rows in this table are dependent for their existence on an associated Project—without a project there would be no issues about archaeology, environment, or wetlands—and is related to the Project table in a 1:1 relationship. In the Relationships Window, these two tables are connected as 1:1, Enforce Referential Integrity on, Cascade Update and Cascade Delete on, and Join Type 2 (left outer).

The Road & Traffic, Utilities & Drainage Table. This table is a place where you can record information about roads and traffic patterns, utilities, and drainage issues for each project. A 1:1 relationship exists between the Road & Traffic, Utilities & Drainage table and the Project table. The rows in this table are dependent on an associated Project for their existence—without a project, there are no issues concerning roads and traffic or utilities and drainage—and is related to the Project table in a 1:1 relationship. In the Relationships Window, these two tables are connected as 1:1, Enforce Referential Integrity on, Cascade Update and Cascade Delete on, and Join Type 2 (left outer).

The Title & Survey Table. In this table, you can record information regarding the title and survey for each project. A 1:1 relationship exists between the Title & Survey table and the Project table. The rows in this table are dependent for their existence on an associated Project—without a project, there would be no issues about title and survey—and are related to the Project table in a 1:1 relationship. In the Relationships Window, these two tables are connected as 1:1, Enforce Referential Integrity on, Cascade Update and Cascade Delete on, and Join Type 2 (left outer).

Reference Tables. Several tables in the REA database were given the prefix designation "ref" rather than "tbl"—for example, refContractor. The idea of a *reference table* is that, for most of the user community, it is a read-only table, and addition to or modification of the data is strictly controlled. In this example, a business rule was established that everyone will work with a contractor that is selected from a list of company-approved contractors. To be placed on this list of contractors, a contractor must meet quality and price standards and have a record of completing work on time. Only a few senior individuals within REA have the authority to update this list and to add or remove contractors. The ordinary user sees the information in the contractor table on a read-only basis, set with the Access security options.

Reference tables whose contents tend to be modified occasionally or frequently should be placed on the server rather than on the client. If a reference table, such as refContractor, is stored centrally on the server, everyone has immediate access to the latest modifications. If this table was stored on the client computers, it would need to be replicated on a regular schedule. The people with update authority to refCustomer also are clients in our client/server environment, so we would have to replicate changes from their computers, reconcile differences, and then replicate the refContractor table back out to all of the client computers. Although this updating process is technically possible, from an administrative and business point of view, it's simpler to keep this reference table on the server.

Placement of Reference Tables. Most of the tables for your application will be placed in this server MDB file. There may be a few tables, as we mentioned previously, which are better placed in the client .MBD file. Static data reference tables such as refStates, which is just a listing of state names and the corresponding two-letter state codes and whose contents doesn't often change, are good candidates for client residence. Storing this table locally means less network traffic and quicker response in the combo boxes on the client forms.

The criteria for deciding where to place a reference table—on the server or on the client—are described in the following list:

- **Size**—The refStates table adds very little to the size of the client application, while refContractors can contain several hundred records each with a dozen fields, and can take considerably more space.

- **Frequency of data modification**—The refStates table changes only rarely, but refContractors is modified frequently, sometimes on a daily basis.

- **Number of accesses per day**—The refStates table may be used quite often as the various components of a deal are put together, but refContractor may be accessed only once or twice per deal. It makes sense to keep local (and handy) the reference data that will be used most often.

- **Number of users involved in the replication process**—If you had to replicate to all the users in the corporate community modifications to a reference table every day, you would generate more network traffic, perhaps even an unacceptable volume of increase in network traffic.

The Database Documentor

As was mentioned in Chapter 1, "Client/Server, What Is It?" Access doesn't have a directly accessible *data dictionary* that you can examine and modify. In most server database environments, the database administrator or data dictionary administrator has direct control over the data dictionary (also known as the *metadata repository*), which is where the table layouts, rules, relationships, security information, audit trail data, and so on, are stored. Developers often will print out parts of the data dictionary as a reference, particularly when converting from one database management system to another.

Access does offer a way to print the definitions of database objects, and the Access 95 facility is improved over previous versions of Access. From the top menu, select Tools, Analyze, and Documentor to get the dialog box shown in figure 7.7.

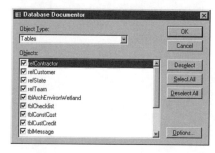

Fig. 7.7

The Access 95 Database Documentor dialog box, with table objects displayed for selection.

You can choose to display various levels of detail for each object, whether it is a table, a query, a form, or other object (click the Options command button). The most detailed level display provides enough information to allow you to totally rebuild a database from scratch, if necessary (see fig. 7.8).

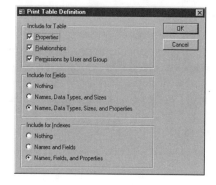

Fig. 7.8

The Database Documentor Options screen, which allows for varying levels of detail in the printed database report.

Readers familiar with Access 2 may recall that the database definitions could be printed directly from Access, but could not be exported, for example, to a Word file because all the detail information was contained in sub-reports. Access 2 had a real problem with sub-reports—they simply didn't export to Word or Excel. This lack is corrected in Access 95. The Print Preview window has an icon for Office Links, which allows you to output the definitions to Word as an .RTF file. In fact, it automatically opens Word so that you can either edit the file or save it to your hard disk for later reference (see fig. 7.9).

Fig. 7.9

The Word Office Link, showing the report generated by Access.

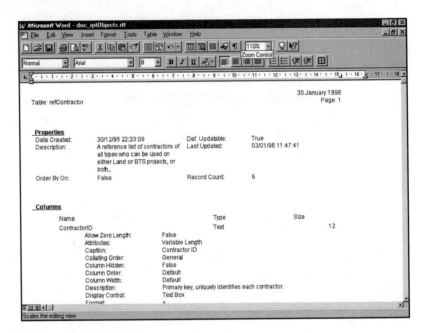

Other Documentation Tools

Many third-party vendor tools are available that can be readily purchased to assist in the task of documenting an Access application. Some products not only produce a listing of table objects, they provide cross-reference information on which fields of a table are used in which forms, reports, modules, and so on. Some products check for consistency in naming and data type, while others flag unused fields. At the time of this writing, the authors find that many of the third-party vendors have not yet finished porting their tools to Access 95.

Entity Models

The *entity model* is a visual or graphical layout of the database tables and the relationships between them. Access doesn't include entity modeling tools, although third party packages—*CASE tools*—are available that do just that. Access can show the tables and relationships after the tables have been built, and it allows you to construct, remove, or modify relationships in a graphical display.

In the purest theoretical relational model, the relationships—one-to-one, one-to-many, and many-to-many—are implied, not declared, by defining primary keys in each table and positioning foreign keys in related tables. Then, by writing a SQL join statement (see Chapter 4, "Getting By in SQL '92—Structured Query Language"), the implied relationship dynamically becomes reality.

In the implementation of the theory, the relationships can be declared, or defined, before any query is executed, and these relationships are kept on file in the data dictionary. This foreknowledge—coupled with operational statistics also kept on file, such as how many columns per table, how many rows per table, which columns are indexed and which are not, and so on—allows the database engine to more quickly return results from a query.

Therefore, for operational and performance reasons, when you can predefine a relationship, you want to do so. This doesn't hinder you from dynamically defining other relationships on an as-needed basis; they just don't run as fast as their predefined cousins.

Using the Relationships Window

We looked at the *Relationships Window* when we discussed the types of data relationships in Chapter 6, "Establishing the Ground Rules." When you open the Relationships Window, you see something that looks like the start of an entity relationship model. It doesn't show as much detail as a comparable display from an entity modeling program, but it is sufficient for a quick look to ensure that the relationships are correct. Particularly, you can easily see if any extra, unwanted relationships somehow have been created.

Establishing predefined relationships between tables—besides providing better query performance—gives Access a chance to enforce referential integrity. If no relationships were built between a pair of tables, it would be very easy to delete a master record and leave related orphan records in another table because Access cannot enforce referential integrity unless it knows that a relationship exists.

Many people who put together Access applications just build queries that combine tables and let the software handle the relationships. This attack works only if the names of the related keys in the two tables are identical and if the two fields are the same data type. This implied relationship is not optimized, which makes the query optimization less complete. If the relationship is predefined, any query that uses it can be precompiled and fully optimized. As a designer, you should know and understand the relationships between the tables in your database and define them with as much care as you define the fields within the tables.

So how do you build relationships within Access? For the following example, we use the REA database that you just built:

II

Designing and Prototyping

1. Open the database.

2. Select the Tables tab, if it isn't already selected.

3. On the top menu choose Tools, Relationships. The Relationships Window opens. Maximize it to give yourself room to work.

4. On the top menu, choose Relationships, Show Table to open the Show Table dialog box (see fig. 7.10).

Fig. 7.10

The Show Table dialog box of the Relationships Window, showing the list of tables in the REA database.

5. Double-click tblProject, and then tblConstCost, to add them to the workspace, as demonstrated in figure 7.11.

Fig. 7.11

The Relationships Window, with tblProject and tblConstCost ready to connect.

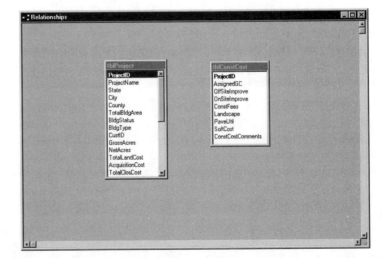

6. Close the Show Table dialog box.

7. Make sure that the ProjectID field is visible in both tables.

8. Click the ProjectID field once in the tblProject table to select it.

9. Drag the ProjectID field from the tblProject table and drop it on the ProjectID field in the tblConstCost table.

This action builds the link between the two tables. The Relationships dialog box opens (see fig. 7.12). Notice that Access already deduced that this relationship is one-to-one. The table from which you dragged ProjectID appears in the left column, and the table on which you dropped ProjectID appears in the right column. You can select, drag, and drop more than one key field if you have, for example, a concatenated primary key (a primary key composed of two or more fields), or you can add the additional parts of the concatenated key directly in the Relationships dialog box.

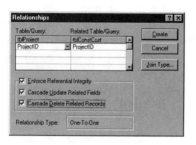

Fig. 7.12

The Relationships dialog box, showing the ProjectID fields from tblProject and tblConstCost in a one-to-one relationship.

10. Click the check box to turn on the Enforce Referential Integrity option.

   The two check boxes below the Enforce Referential Integrity option are now available. These are the Cascade Update and Cascade Delete options that we previously discussed.

11. Click the check box to turn on Cascade Update Related Fields.

12. Click the next check box to turn on Cascade Delete Related Fields.

   This is a *dependent relationship*—each row in tblConstCost depends for its existence on the related row in tblProject. Therefore, should the ProjectID value change for a row in tblProject, you want this change to ripple down to the associated construction costs, which are represented by a row in tblConstCost. This is the Cascade Update feature. Likewise, if a project row is deleted in tblProject, you want to remove the associated row in tblConstCost—this is the Cascade Delete feature. Dependent relationships nearly always implement Cascade Update and Cascade Delete.

13. Click Join Type to look at the list of available joins (see fig. 7.13).

14. Select join type 2, and then click OK.

   The Join Type 2 (left outer join) shows all the records from tblProject and any associated records from tblConstCost. Again, because this is a dependent relationship, most of the time you want to show rows from the "master" table, tblProject, whether or not an associated row exists in tblConstCost. In the odd case where you want to do something different, you can override the join type 2 in the Query Design Window.

II

Designing and Prototyping

Join Type <u>1</u> (the equijoin) gives you a list of rows from tblProject, but only the rows that have associated rows in tblConstCosts. As the dialog box states, only include rows where the joined fields from both tables are equal. This generally is the type of join selected when two tables are in an independent relationship, as exemplified by refCustomer and tblProject.

Join Type <u>3</u> is the right outer join. This join produces a list of all rows from tblConstCost and associated rows in tblProject, which is an inverse dependency situation.

It isn't the number of the join type that signifies anything, but the way in which the tables are selected that determines how the join will be expressed. It pays to read the text in this dialog box because Access uses the actual table names to describe what it will do. This information makes it easy to figure out which type of join you need. For consistency, you should drag the key field from your master table in a one-to-one relationship, or from the "one" side table in a one-to-many relationship, and drop it on the secondary or "many" table.

Fig. 7.13

The Join Properties dialog box.

15. Close the Join Properties dialog box (click OK), and then click <u>C</u>reate to add the relationship to your database.

    Notice how the 1:1 relationship is shown by an arrow that points from tblProject to tblConstCost (see fig. 7.14). The 1 at each end of the table indicates that this is a one-to-one relationship.

16. Double-click the arrow if you want to open the Relationships dialog box again.

    Alternatively, you can click the arrow once to select it, and then click the secondary mouse button to bring up the shortcut menu. One of the menu options is Edit the Relationship.

17. Repeat the procedures for adding tables to the Relationships Window and creating the relationships. Use the information contained in the early part of this chapter, under Database Definitions, which describes each table and its relationship to the other tables in the database, and figure 7.15, to guide you.

18. Close the Relationships Window when you finish creating the relationships.

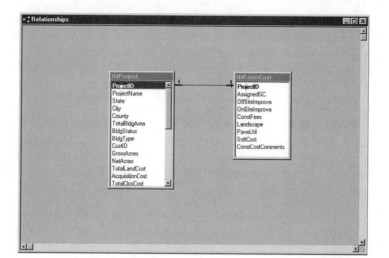

Fig. 7.14

The tblProject and tblConstCost tables, in a 1:1 relationship.

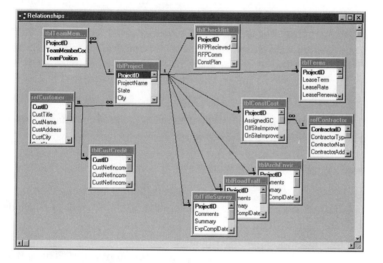

Fig. 7.15

The REA database, as seen through the Relationships Window.

II

Designing and Prototyping

Other Modeling Tools

True entity modeling tools work differently from the procedures we have used in this chapter. With an entity modeling tool, or CASE tool, as they are also known, you use the tool to build a model—including all the tables and columns and relationships, and the CASE tool then generates the tables in a target database.

The upside of this CASE technique is that you are first building a model, not a database, so you can graphically view the layout at any time—unlike Access, where you must have the tables built before you can see them in the Relationships Window.

Additionally, you can minimize the CASE model—look at just the tables without the added distraction of the column list—more easily than you can achieve a comparable view in Access. Design changes are simple in a CASE tool, and the CASE tool tends to track naming conventions and data type assignments and to keep the design consistent—a real benefit when you're designing a large (several hundred table) database.

The downside of the CASE technique is that you may not be able to assign properties specific to a particular database management system, so you may still need to do some table design, even after the CASE tool generates the target database. Also, of course, each CASE tool restricts the design to its particular methodology—so, if you don't like the way in which one CASE tool manages relationships, your only option is to investigate another CASE tool.

The final deciding factor on which CASE tool to use to assist your database design efforts rests with which suite of database management systems the tool supports. The purpose of a full CASE tool is to not only give you a graphical environment in which to lay out your conceptual view of the database, but also to then create the tables, rules, and relationships embedded in the CASE design in the target database. If a CASE tool doesn't support the database management system for which you're designing, you're just wasting time using this tool. Additionally, the authors recommend that if you decide to use the assist of a CASE tool, that you select one that supports not only Access (and Access 95), but also the server database management system. We further discuss why this is so important when we get into the chapter on upsizing to the server database.

On this book's companion CD-ROM, you will find samples of three popular CASE tools that are available for the desktop environment, all of which support Access. At the time of this writing, only one company has an Access 95/SQL Server 6 version available, but all are working on upgrades, which will be available "soon."

The first CASE tool is ERWin, Entity Relationship for Windows, from Logic Works, Inc. ERWin uses the IDEF1X data modeling standard (methodology), which is the data modeling standard for the U.S. Air Force. If you are familiar with various methodologies and have used more than one, you will quickly become accustomed to ERWin's way of doing things. As it says in the ERWin/Quickstart documentation, "This database definition language specifies both the graphical and syntactical methods for describing the structure of databases in a vendor-independent manner." It has a companion product, BPWin, which is used to develop data flow diagrams and business process models. Together, the two products provide a comprehensive environment in which to design both the database and the processes that drive the database. The ERWin/QuickStart and the BPWin/QuickStart, which are both included on the CD-ROM, are enough to give you an idea of how these products work.

The second CASE tool, Personal DB-Designer from Chen & Associates, uses the famous Chen entity-relationship methodology, which was one of the original methodologies developed. This tool also is database-specific, not generic, and is designed to coordinate tightly with Access. It also is the least expensive of the three, by a magnitude of price.

The third CASE tool, S-Designor from Powersoft Corporation, uses a modified Martin Information Engineering notation to support its conceptual model to physical implementation scheme. The support for client/server architecture, corporate workgroups, and the segmented model/submodel makes it a viable candidate for very large project design.

From Here...

In this chapter we talked about how to start building a prototype application. We looked at the database documentor provided by Access 95 and other third-party packages that provide enhanced database documentation. We discussed entity relationship models and how they are represented in the Access 95 Relationships Window. We briefly looked at several popular CASE tools available for the desktop environment. For more information, go to the following chapters:

- Chapter 8, "Adding Functionality to Your Prototype," covers how to turn your prototype into a full-fledged application.
- Chapter 9, "Navigation: How to Get from Here to There," explains how to design navigational paths through your application.
- Chapter 11, "Managing Transactions," for a discussion on transaction management.
- Chapter 13, "Building the Run-Time Application," explains how to compile your application and build an installation set.
- Chapter 15, "Creating Help Files," covers how to build, compile, and integrate interactive help files into your application.
- Chapter 22, "The Human Factor," covers the human element in the client/server environment.

II

Designing and Prototyping

CHAPTER 8

Adding Functionality to Your Prototype

End users will do one of three basic operations with an application: enter data by using some kind of data entry mechanism, selectively search for and isolate data online, or retrieve data via on-line or printed reports.

If you followed this book on a chapter-by-chapter basis, you have some tables defined in the REA database. Now you must provide a way for the users to access the data in these tables.

In this chapter we cover the following areas:

- The three basic operations, and how they are performed in an Access 95 environment
- Linking to the tables stored in an Access 95 back-end .MDB
- Planning and building forms with the Form Wizard, templates, and master forms
- Building reports
- Working with macros, particularly the Autoexec and Autokeys macros
- Introduction to modules and programming (why you should write code)
- Global functions
- Code behind forms
- Introduction to Visual Basic for Applications
- Error trapping

Operational Issues

Data is loaded into a database in one of two ways—data entry forms or bulk data load utilities. Data entry forms generally allow one record at a time to be added to the database. Bulk data load utilities are programs that can transfer data in electronic form (it doesn't have to be a database format) into a table.

Forms are the main *data entry mechanism* for the run-time Access application. There is *bulk data loading* capability available in Access 95 but it's built into only the full development version. If this functionality is something that you, as the application developer, determine the end-user community must have, then you need to program access to this functionality from the application itself.

Selective searching and isolating data on-line can be handled in several ways. The data entry forms can be used to view data already stored in the database, with the added value of allowing modifications and changes to the data. For those instances where data modification should not be a user option, a read-only version of the data entry form can be created. For more versatility and flexibility, read-only forms (referred to as *on-line reports* by the authors)—which differ markedly from the data entry forms—can be created and given to the user community. Filter by selection (single search criteria) and filter by form (multiple search criteria) are readily supported by the Access 95 development environment, and can give the end-user community as much or as little capability to query the database as you, the developer, deem wise and suitable.

Data retrieval by on-line or printed reports is an extension of the selective search and isolation of data. Access 95 gives you the capability to generate printed reports from your on-line forms simply by converting a form object to a report object. However, the appearance on paper of a raw conversion from on-line form to printed report may not be suitable for your needs—such as shades of black and gray as the report writer converts screen colors to monochrome suitable for printing. You may want to spend a few minutes reformatting the appearance of the report-converted-from-a-form-object, or just create the reports from scratch (or with the use of the Report Wizard, which is covered later in this chapter).

The end-user community expects to be able to do other things in this event-driven environment. They will want to be able to do the following:

- Choose which form or report to access and manipulate
- Select the order in which they view the data or perform update tasks
- Route printed reports to different printers

All these functions are available, either through built-in support from the Access 95 environment, or through good event-driven application design.

Some application functionality can be automated with *macros*, a sequence of instructions that are executed as a group for a given action, such as clicking a command button. For other actions, you have to use code (global modules and event procedures). You should place all of this added functionality in the client application when you are building your prototype in Access.

> **Note**
>
> If you were using a development workbench that supported the multi-tier model—client layer, business rules layer, server layer—the functionality we are discussing would be split between the client application and the business rules server.

The Client Application

What we have effectively said is that you need to create another database—another .MDB file—which will become your client application. After this file is created, you then need to connect it to the server .MDB file that contains the tables. To do this, follow these steps:

1. Start Access 95 and create a New Database, using the Blank Database option.
2. Name the new database REA_APP.MDB, and click the Create command button.
3. At the Tables tab in the Database window, click the New button.
4. In the New Table dialog box, select the Link Table option from the list, and then click OK.
5. In the Link dialog box, highlight the REA_DATA database. Click Link.
6. In the Link Tables dialog box, click Select All, then click OK (see fig. 8.1).

Fig. 8.1

The Link Tables dialog box, listing the tables in REA_DATA.MDB.

The second way to link tables is to use options in the top menu, as in the following steps:

1. Select File, Get External Data, Link Tables.
2. In the Link dialog box, highlight the REA_DATA database. Click Link.
3. In the Link Tables dialog box, click Select All, and then click OK.

Using either technique links the tables from the server database to the client database. You can tell when a table is attached or linked by its appearance when you open the client database. The arrow to the left of the icon that represents each table name is the link indicator, as seen in figure 8.2.

II

Designing and Prototyping

Fig. 8.2

The table list, showing tables that are linked into this database.

> **Tip**
>
> Under certain circumstances you may want to embed a copy of certain tables into the client .MDB. To do this you use the same technique for linking tables, except that you choose the Import Table option rather than the Link option. In Chapter 14, "Communicating with Other Applications," we talk more about the differences between linking and embedding, and the pros and cons of each technique. For this example application, however, all tables will reside in the server .MDB.

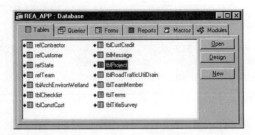

Managing the Relationships

When you link to a set of Access 95 tables, you can no longer modify the table relationships that were established in the server .MDB. Unlike Access 2, which allows you to delete or modify characteristics of a relationship in a set of linked tables (it did indicate that the relationships you were modifying were inherited), Access 95 now forces you to go to the source, to the server .MDB, to modify these relationships.

From the main menu, select Tools, Relationships and go to the Relationships window. As shown in figure 8.3, you can see that the relationships established in the server .MDB are fully intact. Now, try to delete one of the relationships. You see a message that says you cannot delete a relationship inherited from a linked database. When you click a relationship line and bring up the Relationships dialog box, you cannot alter any of the properties of the relationship—again, unlike Access 2. To make changes in the relationships, you must open the server database.

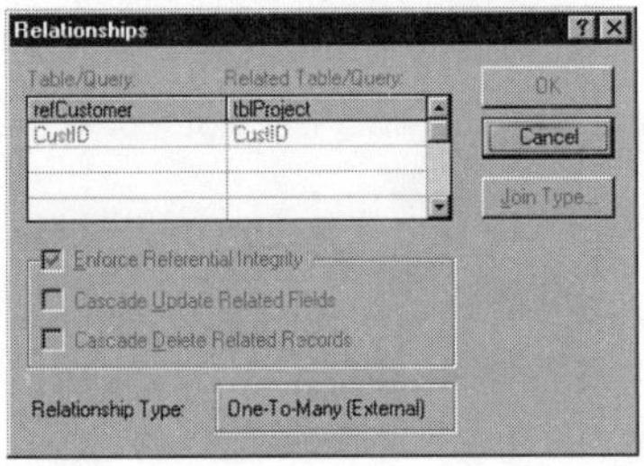

Fig. 8.3

The Access 95 relationship dialog box, showing the inherited relationship properties dimmed out.

> **Tip**
>
> After modifying a relationship in an .MDB file that is linked to a client .MDB, first detach and then reattach the tables from the client .MDB. This technique ensures that the links are properly refreshed and that all changes in the server database are recognized by the client application.

Setting Table Properties

Now, look at the linked table properties. In the table list of the database container, highlight tblProject and open in design view. You have to respond to a message box that states this is an attached table and, therefore, some properties cannot be modified. Click Yes. Select the ProjectName field, and then browse through the Field Properties box in the lower half of the screen.

Most of these field properties cannot be modified, but a few can. The Format, the Input Mask, and the Caption—the parameters that control how the data is displayed but don't affect how the data is stored—can be modified in the client database. It's not wise to enable changes to the other properties that govern data storage, such as field length, in the client database because there may be a discrepancy with the server database, which would lead to lost data or database corruption.

Even if you are considering using Access as your back-end server, you may want to plan accordingly when assigning formats, input masks, or default values at the table level. The input mask, for example, entered as a field property in the table design window is a kind of default mode of operation. If your database application will have to accommodate international data, such as postal codes or phone numbers, you want to add code behind forms to dynamically adjust the input mask, depending on the value of country.

Suppose that you are writing a customer tracking application for a multinational company. You do not want the postal code hardwired to the United States ZIP code format. This format is totally inadequate for Canadian postal codes, and certainly would not work for European codes. You can better handle this situation by having the text boxes on the data entry form arranged so that the value of country is specified first for each record input. Then you write code behind the country text box object so that, as the user exits from that text box (AfterUpdate method), the input mask for that record is set to a mask appropriate for that country.

The authors' normal practice is as follows: if the user selects USA for the country, then the State Code text box shows only the 50 states, plus DC and Puerto Rico. If the user selects Canada, then the State Code text box shows a list of Canadian provinces. Similar code attached to the OnCurrent property of the form dynamically adjusts the input mask for telephone numbers and postal codes, depending on the value of country. As always, you must know your users and know the business rules when designing a database and constructing the application to make it truly useable.

The code in Listing 8.1 (file 08CODE01.TXT, which you can find on the companion CD-ROM), switches the data-entry input masks for telephone number and Zip code, depending on whether or not "USA" is chosen as the country code.

Listing 8.1   08code01.txt—Change Data Entry Input Masks, Depending on Which Country Code Is Chosen

```
Sub comboDeptCountryCode_AfterUpdate ()
'-----------------------------------------------------------------
'    switch telephone & zip code input masks, depending on which country
'    is selected in the first field of the form
'    comboDeptCountryCode and comboCountryCode are form objects
'    this code is attached to the Form properties, On Load event
'-----------------------------------------------------------------

    comboDeptCountryCode = UCase$(comboDeptCountryCode)
    forms![frmRegistration].Refresh
    If (comboCountryCode = "USA") Then
      [txtUserCode].InputMask = "!\(999) 000\-0000;;_"
      [txtContactPhone].InputMask = "!\(999) 000\-0000;;_"
      [txtContactFax].InputMask = "!\(999) 000\-0000;;_"
    ElseIf (comboCountryCode = "CAN") Then
      [txtUserCode].InputMask = "!\(999) 000\-0000;;_"
      [txtContactPhone].InputMask = "!\(999) 000\-0000;;_"
      [txtContactFax].InputMask = "!\(999) 000\-0000;;_"
    Else
      [txtUserCode].InputMask = "!CCCCCCCCCCCCCCCCCCCC;;_"
      [txtContactPhone].InputMask = "!CCCCCCCCCCCCCCCCCCCC;;_"
      [txtContactFax].InputMask = "!CCCCCCCCCCCCCCCCCCCC;;_"
    End If
End Sub
```

Planning the Forms

Now that you have started development on your client application, what do you put in it? It's a good idea to step back for a moment and decide which functions you need to add to your database application. If you are familiar with or have used other desktop database software, then you have some concept of how these client applications are put together. Take a piece of paper (or open a session of Windows Notepad) and list the functions you need to add to your client application. Include at the outset data entry, data viewing, printing reports, and navigation.

The first logical step may be to start building forms for entering data into the tables. In the older desktop database environments that predate Access, the standard data entry scheme was to map each table to a separate data entry form. There were a couple of reasons for this logic: each table was stored as a separate file on the hard disk (so logically, this step made sense), and relating (or joining) two tables in the older, non-relational databases was a non-trivial task that resulted in (generally) non-updateable sets of data returned.

Data Entry Forms

In a relational database it isn't mandatory that the data entry forms follow exactly the structure of the tables. The ability to easily combine data from multiple tables is the whole point of using a relational database. Data entry forms created in an Access environment can be built on updateable queries that join two or more tables.

However, just because you are using relational technology, you cannot totally ignore the table design and build data entry forms any old way. Remember, the purpose of data entry is data capture. You want to get the data and "get it once, get it right, get it fast." A logical correspondence should exist between the database tables and the order and layout of the forms used by the data entry staff. This indicates that the design of the data capture portion of your application has been planned and well thought out. If a serious discrepancy exists between the table layout and the data entry form layout, such that data entry becomes a difficult and tedious task with slow response, there may be a fundamental problem with the design of the database that requires revisiting and redesign.

When your clients include people who spend a great deal of time entering data, they need responsiveness in the application. The simpler the form—and the query upon which the form is based—the quicker the records can be updated. Your data entry forms should update only one or two tables each, although they may use reference tables behind the combo and list boxes to assist the data entry effort. But will all of your forms be data entry forms?

Forms for Viewing Data

Forms used to view the stored data—or even analyze it—may draw on multiple tables, depending on the need. Remember, data is rarely viewed in the same way it is entered into the system; the purpose of a relational database management system is to allow the user to extract information from stored data. Forms used to view data are generally built on queries that combine many tables, and because of the increased complexity of the underlying query, it may be impossible to update the data on the form. For this reason, view forms may have to be read-only.

Forms used to view the data may be used company-wide. Everyone in the company will have an opinion about the stored data, and the opinions will rarely be the same. For this reason and others (security, performance, and data integrity are tops in our opinion), it is wise corporate policy to limit the ability to modify *the single copy of the stored data* to a specific group of people.

Multiple Forms for Various Users

Another strategy in designing applications company-wide is to develop different client interfaces for different groups within the organization. Again, no rule exists that says everyone in the company must have the same client application, just as not everyone in the company needs to have access to all the data in the database. It is reasonable to have one client interface for the data entry staff, another for the marketing staff, a third for management, and so on—all of which tap into the corporate database.

II

Designing and Prototyping

Building Forms

The placement of items on a form should be designed with the user of the form in mind. While this sounds as though we are stating the obvious, the authors have seen too many cases where the form (data entry or view form) simply echoes the order of the fields in the underlying table. This echoing works only if the table was built to reflect the way in which the user works. It doesn't work if, over time, fields have been added to the database as a result of input from several user groups with different priorities. Also, most databases realistically evolve with the changing requirements of the company, thereby growing more and more complex.

Another temptation to avoid is to make the input form look just like the output reports, with data entry boxes rather than data values. Again, investigation will probably show that the people entering the data and the people viewing the reports are in different positions in the organization, have different priorities, and see the data from completely different perspectives.

Using the Form Wizard

As anyone who has used the *Form Wizard* knows, it produces very basic forms. Certainly, it is a starting point for the beginning developer and is useful for generating quick forms that the system administrator can use for updating reference tables or doing system maintenance.

If you are unfamiliar with the Form Wizard, try it out. If you are familiar with it from Access 2.0, you will see a few changes, all for the better. For example, the Autoform: Columnar option (shown as a selection in fig. 8.4) now produces a form where the fields are arranged in multiple columns if necessary, so that all fields can be viewed at once, rather than as one long list, as they were in Access 2.0. (If you are not acquainted with the Access 2.0 Form Wizard, it used to generate some very long forms, which made moving around the form awkward and necessitated quite a bit of fix-up before the Autoform was reasonably useable.)

Fig. 8.4

The new Autoform: Columnar option, which produces a form with multiple, snaking newspaper-style columns for viewing and entering data.

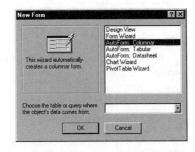

Another nice feature in Access 95 is automatic inclusion of combo boxes. Because Access 2.0 had no way to designate a lookup as a field property in table design, you had to create combo boxes after the Form Wizard was done. This creation involved deleting the plain text box and replacing it with a combo box, binding it to a field in an underlying table or keying in a list of choices, and rearranging the cursor tab order on the form. Now, when a field has a lookup property specified at the table level, the Form Wizard automatically makes this field a combo box.

Tip

A new feature in Access 95 allows you to convert a text box to a combo box without first deleting then adding, as explained in the text.

Open a form in Design mode, select any text box, and click Format, Change To for the list of options.

To demonstrate, build a form for the tblProject table by taking these steps:

1. In the database window, click the Forms tab, and then click New.

2. In the New Form dialog box, choose Autoform: Columnar from the list.

3. Select the tblProject table for this form.

4. Click OK.

   Access builds the form. Note the combo boxes on the form.

5. If you want to save the form, use the File, Save As option, and name it frmProject1. Your form should resemble figure 8.5.

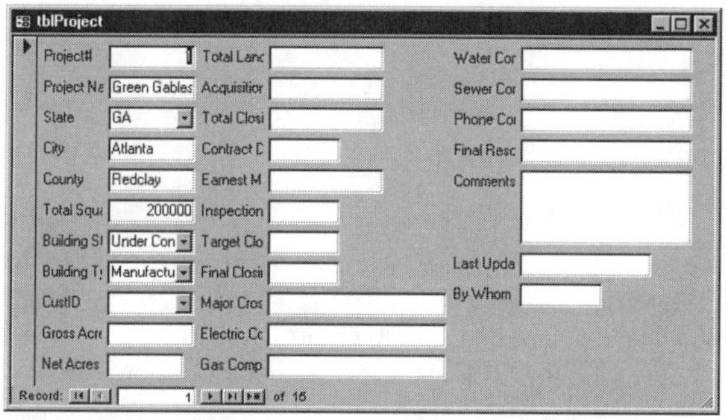

Fig. 8.5

The form built by the Form Wizard is basic, but it gets the job done.

Designing a Master Form

For a business application, where there will be a series of forms that should all have the same "look and feel," a better approach than the Form Wizard is to start with a blank form, and then add elements common to the entire series of forms. Use this form as a master form, and make a copy of it each time you begin work on a new form.

Tip

To quickly copy a database object, including a form, in the database container, from the object list, highlight the object you want to copy and, from the top menu, click Edit, Copy, and then Edit, Paste, and give the copy a new name.

In a business application, when the users switch from one form to another, the common elements (titles, headers, command buttons) should not jump around (or "wiggle") on-screen. This consistency looks more professional than a series of forms where buttons shift, the header size varies, and the colors change for no good reason. Ideally, the user should be able to scan through the entire series of forms by clicking on a "next" button without having to move the mouse on-screen. Making the form appearance consistent from the beginning is far easier than attempting to align design elements and objects after the fact.

You may want to include the following items on this master form (see fig. 8.6):

- A corporate identifier, such as a name or company logo
- The name of the application, such as Sales Contacts
- A place holder for the name of each form
- The name of the user group for which this application was built
- The Page *n* of *m* indicators for multipage forms
- "Forward" and "back" or "next" and "previous" buttons for moving between forms
- Command buttons for adding, saving, and deleting records
- A "close" button to shut down the form
- Any necessary copyright or legal notices

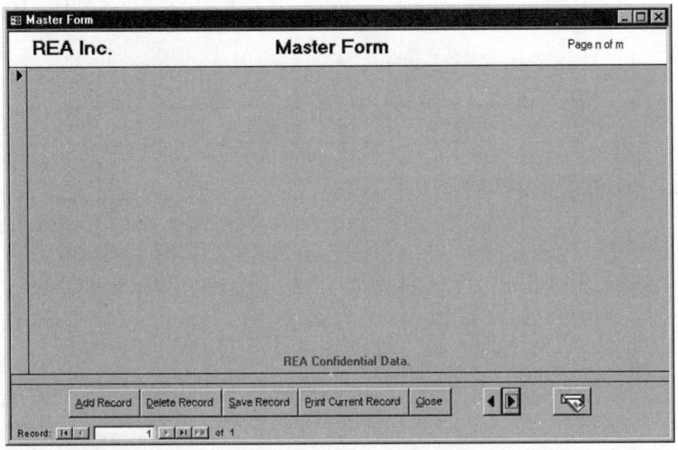

Fig. 8.6

The Master Form can be copied for a consistent look throughout the application.

> **Tip**
>
> A prime reason to put an explicit Save command button on each form is to avoid unexpected loss of data. Access usually is good about saving changes to data, but in a shared environment—a client/server environment—you can get unexpected results if the database tables aren't updated before a secondary form is opened. See Chapter 9, "Navigation: How to Get from Here to There," where we discuss navigation in greater detail.

Creating a Form from a Template

Access 95 allows you to specify a form for use as a template. To find this option, click on Tools, Options, choose the Forms/Reports tab, and type the name of the form you want to use as a template in the Form Template text box. However, when building a new form with the Access 95 form template, you get only the section properties (size of header, detail, and footer), and the control properties of the form itself. It doesn't bring over any controls or data fields from the template form. So if you want to copy controls, bitmaps, or data fields from the template form to the new form, you have to copy and paste the objects on the new form by hand. The authors feel that using the master form concept is a more complete solution to consistency in a suite of business forms.

Forms Based on Queries

Now, you build a slightly more complex form. This time, create a query and use it as the basis for the form. You have to use a query when you combine data from two or more tables to present on a form.

> **Tip**
>
> For business solutions, you should always base your forms on queries rather than tables. As discussed in Chapter 12, "Securing the Access 95 Application," you can lock users out of the table design but you still can allow them to run queries against these tables. It's easier to add security to your application if you use queries in the initial form and report design.

If you are adding security to your client application, you can take steps now that will save time later. From the database container, select Tools, Options from the top menu. This action opens the Options dialog box for this database. Select the Tables/Queries tab. In the Run Permissions section, make sure that the Owner's option is selected, and then save this selection by clicking OK (see fig. 8.7). Chapter 12, "Securing the Access 95 Application," explains this action in greater detail.

Fig. 8.7

The Options dialog box, with Run Permissions (Owner's) selected for Tables/Queries.

Creating a Query. Access 95 has introduced a new feature, the Simple Query Wizard, for building simple queries. The authors suggest that you BYOQ—*build your own query*—and forget about using this Wizard. See the associated caution for reasons. We will walk you through creating a new query, however, by using the Simple Query Wizard. If you have neither the computer configuration mentioned in the caution nor lots and lots of patience, please do not attempt the following exercise.

Caution

You may have trouble running the Simple Query Wizard under Windows 95 if you have other programs open. Even on a 80486 with 16M of RAM, the authors had to shut down background tasks and schedulers to eliminate out-of-memory errors, even though the Resource Meter showed all resources at over 90 percent availability. On a 20M 80486 laptop, using the Simple Query Wizard was such a lengthy procedure that the authors abandoned the attempt and resorted to building the query in plain design mode. However, the authors had no trouble running the Simple Query Wizard on a Pentium P90 with 32M of RAM, running Windows NT!

---

1. Select the Queries tab in the database window, and then click New. The New Query dialog box opens.

2. Select the Simple Query Wizard from the list and click OK (see fig. 8.8).

3. Select table tblProject, and then select all of the fields by clicking the right-pointing double arrow (see fig. 8.9).

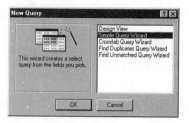

Fig. 8.8

Choose the Simple Query Wizard to help you build a new query.

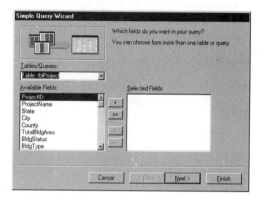

Fig. 8.9

Choose table(s) for the query from the drop-down list. Choose field(s) for the query by clicking the right-pointing arrow to move field names from left-hand column to column on the right.

4. Immediately select table refCustomer, and then select all of the fields by clicking the right-pointing double arrow. Click Next.

5. Select the detail option (show every field of every record), and then click Next.

6. Save the query as **qryProjCustWiz**, and select the Modify Query Design option. Click Finish. The query opens in design view (see fig. 8.10). Notice that the relationship between the two tables, tblProject and refCustomer—which is inherited from the server database—is shown in the query design window.

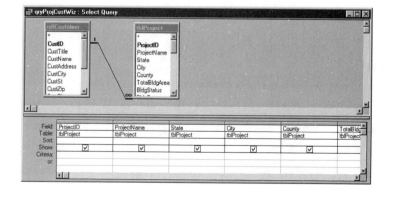

Fig. 8.10

QryProjCustWiz in design view.

7. Click View, SQL from the menu, or click the selector (down arrow) on the leftmost button of the Query Design Toolbar and select the SQL View option.

You see a lengthy SQL statement that lists every field in both tables and the join of the two tables, as shown in figure 8.11.

Fig. 8.11

This window shows the
SQL statement generated
by Access 95.

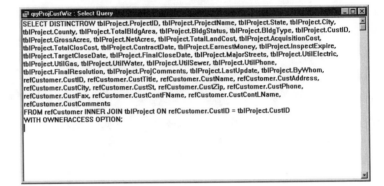

```
qryProjCustWiz : Select Query

SELECT DISTINCTROW tblProject.ProjectID, tblProject.ProjectName, tblProject.State, tblProject.City,
tblProject.County, tblProject.TotalBldgArea, tblProject.BldgStatus, tblProject.BldgType, tblProject.CustID,
tblProject.GrossAcres, tblProject.NetAcres, tblProject.TotalLandCost, tblProject.AcquisitionCost,
tblProject.TotalClosCost, tblProject.ContractDate, tblProject.EarnestMoney, tblProject.InspectExpire,
tblProject.TargetCloseDate, tblProject.FinalCloseDate, tblProject.MajorStreets, tblProject.UtilElectric,
tblProject.UtilGas, tblProject.UtilWater, tblProject.UtilSewer, tblProject.UtilPhone,
tblProject.FinalResolution, tblProject.ProjComments, tblProject.LastUpdate, tblProject.ByWhom,
refCustomer.CustID, refCustomer.CustTitle, refCustomer.CustName, refCustomer.CustAddress,
refCustomer.CustCity, refCustomer.CustSt, refCustomer.CustZip, refCustomer.CustPhone,
refCustomer.CustFax, refCustomer.CustContFName, refCustomer.CustContLName,
refCustomer.CustComments
FROM refCustomer INNER JOIN tblProject ON refCustomer.CustID = tblProject.CustID
WITH OWNERACCESS OPTION;
```

8. Click the View icon again to get to the Datasheet View, to see the data.

9. Click the View icon a third time to return to Design Mode.

10. Close the query.

It's a good idea to check the SQL code for queries that you build. If you are familiar with SQL, you're probably used to writing joins in the SQL '86-'89 style, so consider this a chance to gain further insight into what Access 95 does in the SQL '92 style. If you are new to SQL programming, it's a good way to begin learning how a query is built with SQL '92. You almost certainly will be using SQL with any other server database, so this is a chance to begin your learning curve. (See Chapter 4, "Getting By in SQL '92—Structured Query Language," for a full treatment of the SQL programming language.)

A quicker, easier, less memory-intensive way is available to build a query—the same technique you used if you built queries in Access 2.0. If you ran into the out-of-memory problems in the preceding section, you are forced to use this method. To use this technique, take the following steps:

1. From the Database container, with the Queries tab selected, click New.

2. At the New Query dialog box, select Design View from the list and click OK.

3. From the Show Table list box, select table tblProject and click Add (see fig. 8.12).

4. Again, from the Show Table list box, select table RefCustomer and click Add.

5. Click Close to close the Show Table list box.

6. Click the asterisk at the top of the tblProject list box. The asterisk (*) means that you want all the fields in this table.

7. Drag the asterisk down to the first (leftmost) cell of the lower window and drop it in the Field row of the first column (see fig. 8.13).

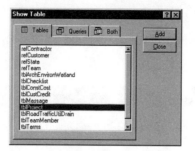

Fig. 8.12

Here, you select tables that you want in the query.

Asterisk ──

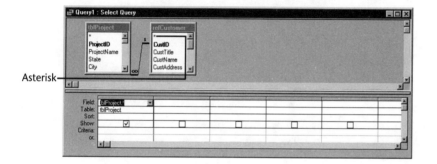

Fig. 8.13

The query design window, with tblProject selected.

8. Double-click the asterisk at the top of the refCustomer list box. Double-clicking has the same effect as the drag-and-drop selection method you just used for tblProject.

9. From the menu, select File, Save As/Export, and save this query as **qryProjCust**.

10. From the menu, select View, SQL.

    Notice that this query is shorter than the previous one, which was built with the Simple Query Wizard (see fig. 8.14). Rather than a long list of field names, the SQL statement now uses the asterisk to signify that you want all the fields in both tables. This query will be interpreted and processed faster than the previous query created by the Query Wizard.

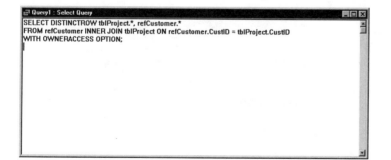

Fig. 8.14

This statement is much shorter than the previous SQL statement.

11. From the menu, select File, Close to close the query.

Congratulations, you just did a better job of query building than the Simple Query Wizard, and it took less time!

Adding a SQL Button to the Toolbar

Clicking the View button on the toolbar alternates between Design mode and Datasheet mode. To view any other mode (including SQL mode), you have to drop down the list of options attached to this button. To make it easy to check the SQL code, you can add a SQL button to the Query Design toolbar by taking these steps:

1. Make sure that you are in Query Design view and from the menu, select View, Toolbars.

2. Select Customize.

3. Select the Query Design category from the list.

4. Drag the SQL button up to the toolbar at the top of the screen and drop it next to the Run button or the View button—for quick changing between view modes.

5. Repeat this process for the Query Datasheet toolbar (turn it on at the first Customize Toolbars dialog box), so you can easily move from either design mode or Datasheet mode to SQL mode.

Building a Query-Based Form. Now that you have created the query, you can start building the form. Actually, you will build two forms and connect them. The first form contains information about Projects and Customers. The second form is the master form, which we previously created in this chapter.

You build the first form by taking the following steps:

1. From the Database container, select the Forms tab, and then click New.

2. Select the query that you just built, qryProjCust, as the basis for the new form.

3. Highlight the Form Wizard, and then click OK.

4. Select all the fields from the Project table, and from the refCustomers table, select only the Customer Name. Click Next (see fig. 8.15).

Fig. 8.15

Use this screen to select from a list of fields those you want to place on your form.

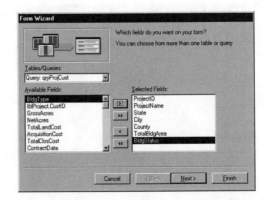

5. Specify that you want to view your data by tblProject. Click <u>N</u>ext.

6. Select the <u>C</u>olumnar layout, click <u>N</u>ext.

7. Select the Standard format. (OK, select any format you want; it's your form, so have some fun!) Click <u>N</u>ext.

8. Name the form **frmProjCust**, and choose the option, <u>O</u>pen the Form to View or Enter Information. Click <u>F</u>inish to see the results (see fig. 8.16).

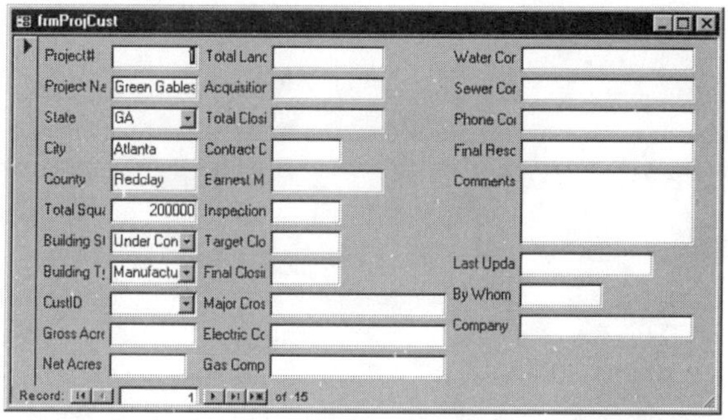

Fig. 8.16

The frmProjCust, as designed by the Forms Wizard.

Combining the New Form with the Master Form. Well, now you have the basic form, which isn't too inspiring, but at least it has the fields from the tables tblProject and refCustomer that you wanted. However, it doesn't have the headers, footers, and control objects from the master form, which we discussed in a previous part of this chapter. How do you combine this new form, which has the fields we want, with the master form? The easiest way to do so is to take the following steps:

1. Copy the fields on your new form by drawing a box around all of them and clicking <u>E</u>dit, <u>C</u>opy from the menu (or pressing Ctrl+C, or using the <u>E</u>dit, Select <u>A</u>ll option from the top menu (see fig. 8.17).

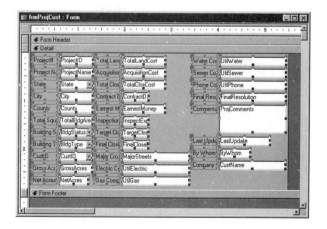

Fig. 8.17

The frmProjCust in design mode, with all fields selected and ready for copying to another form.

2. Close the frmProjCust form.

3. Open the Master Form in Design View.

4. Position the cursor in the detail section of the form, and use <u>E</u>dit, <u>P</u>aste (or Ctrl+V) to drop the copied fields onto the Master Form.

5. Save the form as **frmProjCust**, overwriting the original form, frmProjCust (see fig. 8.18).

Fig. 8.18

The fields from frmProjCust, copied over onto the Master form.

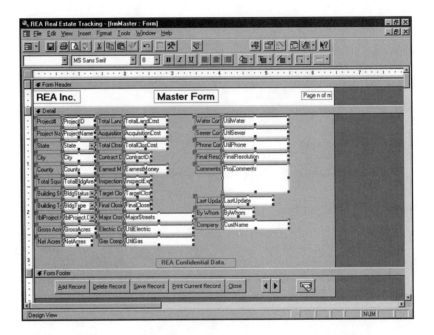

6. Using the Form properties box, modify the record source for the form, to qryProjCust.

7. Change the label at the top of the form (Format tab, Caption) from Master Form to **Projects**.

8. On the form itself, at the top right, change the Page n of m to Page **1** of **3**.

9. Save the form with these changes, switch to Form View, and look at your work (see fig. 8.19).

The form contains the data fields that you need, but the layout could use some work. If you are new to Access, experiment with the formatting, alignment, and palette tools to make the form more pleasing to the eye and easier to use. Check the tab order so that the cursor moves from text box to text box in a logical manner. Remember, the data-entry personnel who will use these forms must live with them, day in and day out. They need forms that enhance productivity. The example shown in figure 8.20 is only one possible "look and feel" for the form.

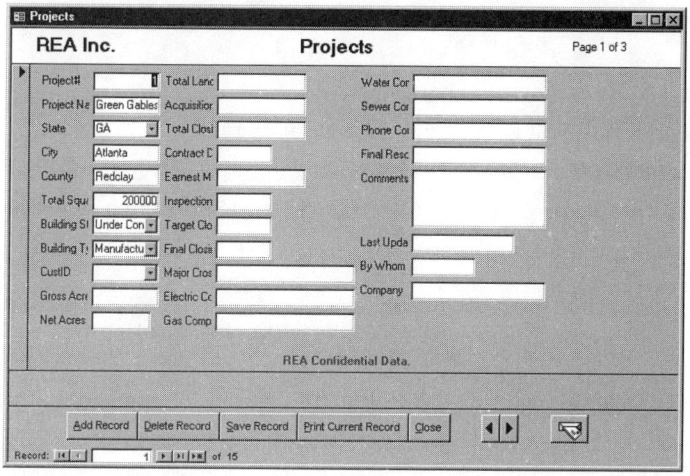

Fig. 8.19

The modified frmProjCust incorporated into the Master Form in Form View, with changes as listed.

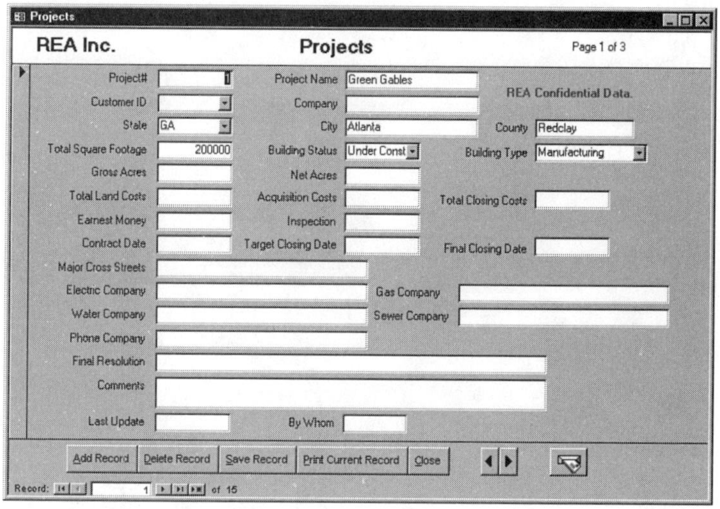

Fig. 8.20

Experiment with the form layout to produce a useable, visually appealing form.

Building a Form with Drag-and-Drop. For the Customers form, try a different approach. Here, you build the underlying query, make a copy of the master form, and then add the required data fields by taking the following steps:

1. Build a new query, using the table refCustomer, and select all of the fields. Name this query **qryCustomer**.

2. In the database window, select the Forms tab, highlight the Master Form, and then click the secondary mouse button to pop up the shortcut menu for this form.

3. Click Copy to place a copy of the form on the Windows Clipboard.

4. Click the secondary mouse button anywhere in the database window.

II

Designing and Prototyping

5. Click Paste; when you see the dialog box that asks for a form name, type **frmCustomer**.

6. Open the form, frmCustomer, in Design View.

7. Change the Master Form label on the header to **Customers**.

8. Change Page n of m in the header to page **2** of **3**.

9. Open the form's properties box and change the Record Source to **qryCustomer**.

10. Change the form caption to **Customers**, and then close the properties box.

11. Click the Field List icon on the top menu.

12. Select all the fields, either one-at-a-time or in groups, and drag them down on to the form.

13. Position the fields to produce a useable form (use figure 8.21 as a guide, if you like).

14. Close the Field List.

15. Save the form.

16. Switch to the Form View to see how the form looks on-screen.

Fig. 8.21

The finished frmCustomer, in Form View.

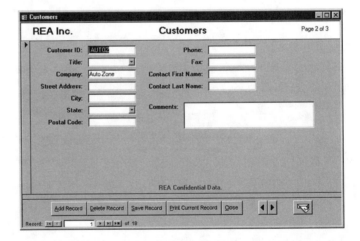

Notice that some of the properties haven't changed from the Master form. In the header is the Customers label; the label caption is still lblMasterForm (click the All or the Format tab in the properties box to see this). If you want, you can change these label names to match the form. Note that when you use the Wizard to build a form, a text box is given the same name as the control source (such as Phone), and the accompanying label is given the control source plus Label (as in Phone Label).

However, if you drag the fields on to a form, as we just did, the text boxes inherit the control source name, but the accompanying label names change to Label160, Label189, and so on. This is a little different from Access 2.0, where under either circumstance (Form Wizard or manual drag-and-drop), text boxes were given the control source name and labels were given the name Text*nn*, where *nn* is an automatically incrementing number. The authors hope that Microsoft fixes this behavior differentiation in the first maintenance release of Access 95. While they are at it, they should go for making the labels Hungarian notation, with no space, as in lblPhone. See Chapter 5, "Client/Server Database Application Design Fundamentals," for more information on the Hungarian naming convention.

The authors suggest that you manually rename each of the text boxes by using a consistent naming scheme, such as appending "txt" to the beginning of the Name property. The text box, CustPhone, then becomes txtCustPhone under this scheme. We have seen problems arise when writing code because of confusion on the part of the program or the programmer, as to whether CustPhone refers to the text box CustPhone or to the data field CustPhone in the underlying table or query. Although this is a bit of extra effort when initially building the forms, it helps later on by preventing hours of debugging code. The authors want to add to their wish list: Microsoft could add this differential naming of text boxes to the form-building function.

Synchronizing Related Forms

In two situations, you need to keep forms synchronized. In the first situation, you have more than one form open on-screen. If the second form is a subform, keeping both forms synchronized is easy—Access can do it for you if you use the Form Wizard to create the form/subform. The Form Wizard automatically builds the connection between a form and a subform, if one of the following two cases exist:

- If the relationship between the two tables is predefined (if there is a relationship defined in the Relationships window of the data .MDB)

- If no previously defined relationship exists, but if each of the two tables contains a column with the same field name and data type

If you manually added a subform to a main form by dragging it from the database window and dropping it on the main form, then you have to supply the names of the connecting fields.

We discuss how to move from the Projects form to the Customers form, and keep both forms synchronized, in Chapter 9, "Navigation: How to Get from Here to There," where we cover form navigation.

Creating Sample Reports with the Report Wizard

Every business thrives (or suffocates) on printed reports. The report writer embedded in Access 95 is powerful, and with some patience you can produce very useful, informative, and professional-looking reports.

Unlike the forms, reports—by their very nature—tend to be more varied in appearance and layout. Some reports must be printed on paper oriented in landscape mode, and others need to be printed in portrait orientation. Some reports need to look like spreadsheets, while others need to resemble print-shop documents. Therefore, rather than set up a Master Report, as we did a Master Form, the authors suggest that you use the Report Wizard to generate reports for you, and that you write down the production options you used with the Report Wizard for the next report that you will design, so that you maintain some semblance of a standard.

Now, you generate a report of Projects and Customers, and group it by state and city. In the process you can calculate the square footage and the percent of total square footage by project under construction.

Use the following steps to generate a report:

1. Select the Reports tab in the database container, and then click New.

2. From the New Report dialog box, select Report Wizard from the list (see fig. 8.22) and use query qryProjCust as the basis for this report. Click OK. It may take a few minutes for the Report Wizard to activate.

Fig. 8.22

The New Report dialog box, with the Report Wizard selected.

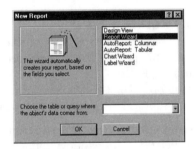

3. From the first Report Wizard screen (see fig. 8.23), select the following from the Available Fields list: ProjectID, ProjectName, State, City, TotalBldgArea, tblProject.CustID, CustName, CustPhone, and CustFax. Move each field from the Available Fields list to the Selected Fields list by highlighting the field and clicking the single right-facing arrow. Click Next.

Fig. 8.23

The first Report Wizard screen, giving you a chance to choose a table or query as the report source and the field list for inclusion (or not) in the report body.

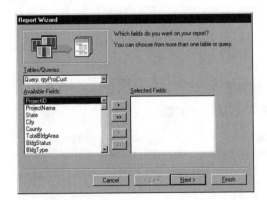

4. You want to view your data by project, which should be highlighted. If it isn't highlighted, do so now. You also can take a moment to look at the difference between the "by customer" and "by project" layouts, and even explore the "more information" that the Wizard gives. When you're through, come back to this screen, and click Next.

5. You will want to group by two criteria, state and city, in that order. In the leftmost box, highlight State, and move it to the rightmost box by clicking the right-facing single arrow button. Do the same with City, so that the right box shows, from the top down, an entry for State, an indented entry for City, and an indented entry for the rest of the fields on your report. To check out the Grouping Options here, go ahead, but keep the Grouping Intervals Normal. When you're through, come back to this screen and click Next.

6. You will want to sort the detail lines on this report by Project Name, so use the top combo box to select ProjectName (keep the sort setting to ascending—the icon to the right of the combo box should read A-Z). You'll do some summaries on the data, so click the Summary Options command button. The Summary Options screen appears (see fig. 8.24).

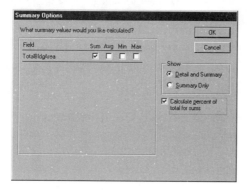

Fig. 8.24

The Summary Options screen of the Report Wizard—a new feature of the Access 95 Report Wizard.

7. The Report Wizard determined that the only detail field suitable for statistical evaluation is TotalBldgArea. Now, choose to Sum the values and to Calculate the percent of total for sums. Show Detail and Summary should remain selected. Click OK. When you return to the Summary Information screen, click Next.

8. Now you need to choose a layout for the report. Here, a landscape orientation works best, and keep the selection, Adjust Field Width So All Fields Fit On A Page, checked. You can choose any layout that suits you—the authors will choose Align Left 1. Click Next.

9. The style is as personal as the layout, so choose your favorite (or the corporate standard). To maintain corporate consistency, you may want to keep a record (on paper or in Notepad) of the options you chose for layout and format. The authors are going with the Corporate format. Click Next.

10. The title of this report is Projects and Customers. Choose to Preview the Report and then click Finish. You now can preview your finished report.

11. To maintain the naming convention we have established, go back to Design view (close the Print Preview screen) and choose File, Save As. Save the new report Within the Current Database As, and give it the new name, **rptProjectCustomer**. Click OK.

12. The next time you have access to the report list in the database container, delete the entry, Projects and Customers. Although this is a lovely convenience that Microsoft has introduced in the Report Wizard—giving the report object the same name as the report title—it's neither efficient nor effective. The authors discussed the reasons for adopting specific naming conventions in Chapter 5, "Client/Server Database Application Design Fundamentals." We heartily suggest you discard this Access 95 affectation and stick to a naming convention that doesn't include embedded spaces or special characters.

The finished report from the Report Wizard needs a little adjusting. As a standard, you can make some of the following kinds of modifications:

- Select a smaller point size for headers (report, page, and group)—these elements tend to be generated at 11 to 14 point, which takes up valuable real estate on your printed forms. The detail lines, which is what users really want to see, are generated at 8 or 10 point, depending on the font you choose.

- Adjust the width of the page or the printer margins so that every other page is not a blank page. This adjustment may mean shifting or resizing lines and text boxes.

- For better viewing, make all column headers and detail text boxes right-aligned or center-aligned.

- If you want the report title on every page, move the information out of the Report Header into the Page Header.

- If you want the date on which the report was generated to appear at the top rather than at the bottom of the page, move the date out of the Page Footer into the Page Header.

- If the column headers are extraordinarily long, stack them. Widen the entire set of column headers for consistency. For headers you want to stack, place the cursor at the dividing point in the string of words and press Ctrl+Enter to force a page break within a label.

- Make sure that the number and date fields are properly formatted and aligned, not only in the detail lines of the report but also in the footers—group, page, and report.

- Add page breaks as needed. In this example a Force New Page on State Header, Before Section produces a nicely segregated report that is easy to read.

- Add a page break on the Report Footer, Before Section, to isolate report totals on a separate page from the rest of the data. Your report should resemble figure 8.25.

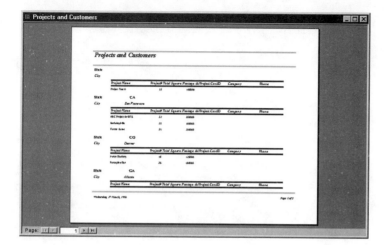

II

Designing and Prototyping

Fig. 8.25

The finished Projects and Customers report.

Working with Macros

The first iteration of your prototype contains some tables, forms, and reports. Each form or report may have to be opened individually from the database window, and closed by using the standard menu bar. The next step is to provide a method for the users to move between forms, and a front-end menu system so that they can go directly to the place where they need to work. You also need to add some intelligence to the system to trap errors in the data, allow the users to open related forms, add new records, and so on.

Macros are just a stored series of instructions and mouse movements that can be called and run when required. If you find that you, or your users, are performing the same steps frequently, it may by more efficient to write a macro. If you have used word-processing software or spreadsheet software, then you may be familiar with macros. It's a surprise to many people new to Access that you cannot record a macro, as you can in Word or Excel, but in these other applications, only relatively simple macros—sequences of keystrokes—can be recorded. The more complex Access macros, with branching logic and tests for conditions, must be written by using the built-in macro language.

Constructing an Access macro is a little more complex than recording a macro. The *macro design screen* allows you to construct a macro step-by-step, selecting options from a list, and adding small segments of code where necessary. Many actions available in the macro are unavailable from the menus and so, could not be recorded even if Access had a macro record function available. In an application such as Word, macros are often used to automate keystrokes. In Access, macros usually are employed to extend the functionality of the application. Another difference in Access is that the macros are stored in groups, as shown by figure 8.26, so you can cluster several associated macros for ease of maintenance.

Fig. 8.26

A group of Access macros.

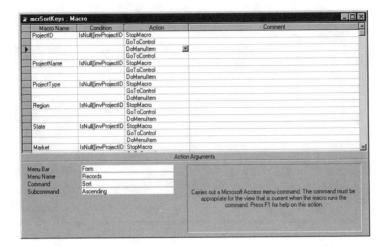

When You *Must* Use Macros

In Access 2.0, the only macro that you really needed was the Autoexec macro. This macro was replaced to some degree by the startup options in Access 95. There are a few instances in Access 95 where a macro is the only way to invoke a special functionality for which you're looking. These instances are described in the following list:

- The Autoexec macro, when you need to do something on application startup that isn't supported by the Access 95 startup options

- The Autokeys macro, when you need to assign actions to key combinations in your application

- Customized menus for the Access 95 run-time environment

- Customized toolbars for the Access 95 run-time environment

The most obvious example of macro use in applications is in building a customized menu bar by using the Menu Builder Wizard. The Wizard builds a series of macros that are used to construct the custom menu for the application. When you use this Wizard, just let Access build the macros. It's an enormous waste of time to try to better the Wizard by writing your own code.

You will have to use a macro to perform some action when the user clicks a button on a toolbar that you added to, or modified for, the run-time environment. You cannot attach a coded procedure to a toolbar button, but you can attach a macro.

Tip

For the situations when you simply must attach code to a toolbar button, here's how you do it. First, create a macro that contains one command—RunCode—and have this command call your Visual Basic procedure. Then attach this macro to the button. Clicking the button activates the macro that then calls the procedure.

The following sections discuss the two special-purpose macros that you may want to use as standards in your applications—Autokeys and Autoexec.

The Autokeys Macro

Access allows you to assign actions to key combinations by using a key-assignment macro, which must be named Autokeys. For example, you can use a Ctrl+P combination to print the current record. Because this action is assigned to the key in the macro, it works no matter where you are in the application—it is global to the application. You can assign actions to specific keystrokes for any control on a single form if you need this level of control, but the Autokeys macro is an efficient way of making a key combination universally available.

The Autoexec Macro

The Autoexec macro in Access 2.0 was the way in which you presented the application as the user opened it. Normally, you load a form—often a menu or switchboard form—and hide the database so that the user cannot access it. The Autoexec macro can contain code to make sure that the user has registered the application before allowing them to proceed, or it may display a legal or corporate policy notice on-screen for a few seconds.

With Access 95, Microsoft introduced the Startup options, which you can use to set up the presentation of the application and provide the user community with the ability (or lack of ability) to do some customizing to their own version of the application (see fig. 8.27). However, you still may need to use the Autoexec macro—and in a client/server application, you must use it—to perform additional tasks at startup. At application initiation the Access 95 Startup options take effect first, and then the Autoexec macro is run.

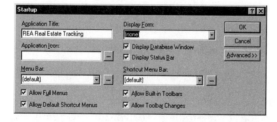

Fig. 8.27

The Access 95 Startup dialog box.

Which kinds of tasks might you include in an Autoexec macro? In a client/server environment, the following three possibilities quickly come to mind:

- Have the client application copy an updated version of a reference table from the server over to its own hard disk.

- Open a different form, depending on the user name. You hide the database window and open the normal switchboard form for most users, but if you log on as the administrator, you may decide to show the database window, and you may opt to open a form that you use to add new end users to the system.

■ Check to see if the server tables are attached, and handle the errors that occur if they are not. We address this topic in greater detail in Chapter 19, "System Administration."

There is a progression in a developer's skill set that involves macros and modules. Real beginners with Access use neither macros nor modules. Instead, they use the Wizards to put command buttons on forms, but they don't know where the code is stored. As soon as a need arises to do something not covered by the Wizards, the neophyte will build a simple macro. For a time, the applications are full of macros, with no modules. Then the macros become limiting, and the only solution is to learn how to write code, in modules or code-behind-forms. Soon, the applications produced by this developer will contain modules, and no macros (except for the previously mentioned Autoexec, Autokeys, and menu macros).

> **Tip**
>
> If you want to get the benefit of the Autoexec macro but you need to add more complex code, you can write the code as a *function*. Your Autoexec macro needs to contain only one instruction, the RunCode and the name of your startup function.

Why Write Code?

With macros and wizards you can produce some neat applications in Access. So why would you want to write code? There are several reasons why—for example, to handle the following situations:

■ Errors

■ Create your own functions

■ Pass arguments to code

■ Make your application easier to maintain

Error Handling

When a macro fails for any reason, it halts the program and displays a code window so that you can learn more about the problem. For your user community, you can turn off the capability to look at the code after an error happens by using the Startup options. This change, however, doesn't solve the problem and may only complicate the debug situation. If you write your own code and include error-handling routines, you can control what happens. You can send the user an error message that specifies exactly where the problem occurred. This may not do much to calm the frayed nerves of the user, but it does help you track the cause of the problem. If you can, train your end-user community to write down the text of the message or to keep it on-screen while they call you. Explain to them that the more specific they can be about what happened, the faster you can fix it.

You also can make sure that even if the code fails, the user is not left with an application that is hung, requiring a computer reboot—which is possible with aborted macro code. It's never a good idea to turn off or reboot the computer during an Access session, either run-time or full development copy, because doing so can leave the database in an unknown state, which can cause data corruption. This problem is exacerbated when the user is connected to an Access server, because the client database engine is manipulating data directly on the server. If your server database is non-Access, it probably will not allow partial or incomplete transactions, which is what you initiate by aborting your client session, which provides a measure of safety for the data. Access is fairly good at preventing data-integrity problems, if you handle errors smoothly.

Creating Your Own Functions

Access has a range of built in *functions* that perform financial, statistical, and mathematical calculations. If these functions do not meet your specific needs, you can create functions and call them when they are needed.

Passing Arguments to Your Code

Macros can have *arguments* specified within the macro. An argument is a value used during the execution of a piece of code. These values, stored within the body of the macro, are code that the macro uses when it runs and cannot be changed dynamically. If you use Visual Basic code, you can supply the arguments at the time the code runs by way of a dialog box to the user. This capability gives your programs much more flexibility than the hard-coded values in a macro. Additionally, you can assign the value of these arguments to code variables, which isn't possible in a macro. Using code opens up all kinds of possibilities.

Making Your Application Easier to Maintain

A *macro* or a set of macros is a separate object that is stored in the database. The *modules*, or Visual Basic code, can be stored as separate database objects in their own container or can be stored (attached) to a form or report object. It is often easier, especially with short pieces of code, to build them directly into the form or report (*code-behind-forms*). When you do so, you know exactly what the code is for and how it is called. An additional benefit to code-behind-forms is that, if you copy the form or report to another database, the code by default goes with the form. If you use macros or modules, you also need to remember to copy them over, which means keeping track of which macros and modules are referenced by which forms or reports.

Other Reasons for Using Code

Other reasons exist for using code rather than macros, such as the capability to create database objects or use OLE automation to interact with other Windows-based applications. See Chapter 14, "Communicating with Other Applications," for more information on this topic.

Converting Macros to Code

One new function introduced in Access 95 is the capability to *convert macros to code.* If you have a group of macros, the Wizard converts each macro within the group to a function within a module. All problems encountered during the conversion show up highlighted in red, so you can quickly check to see whether or not the conversion worked. This feature is great for programmers who are making the transition from building macros to writing code. You can convert your macros, and then examine the code to learn how to write your own modules and functions.

The steps to do the conversion, shown in the following list, are not intuitive:

1. From the macro container, highlight the macro you want to convert.

2. Select File, Save As/Export.

3. In the Save As dialog box, select the Save as Visual Basic Module option, and then click OK (see fig. 8.28).

4. When the Convert Macro dialog box appears, make sure that the Add Error Handling to Generated Functions and Include Macro Comments are turned on, and then click Convert.

5. You are notified when the conversion is completed.

Fig. 8.28

The File, Save As dialog box, which contains the option to convert a macro to a module.

Using Global Functions

When code is stored in a module, it becomes by default a *global function* and is available to any form or report within the application. If you copied a form or report that depended on this global function to another database, you also have to remember to copy the module, just as you do with a macro. A global function is useful when the same code is used in many places. You could use command buttons, for example, to move from one form to another in the application. You could build the same code behind each navigation button on each form, but an alternative to this time-consuming and hard-to-maintain technique is to create a function to handle navigation between forms. In this case, you have to supply some arguments to the function—such as the name of the form you are moving *from* and the name of the form you are moving *to.*

One drawback with global functions is that they must be available at all times because they are global and can, therefore, be called from any form or report, or even from another function. The global function must be registered in memory every time the application is loaded.

Writing Code Behind Forms

Code behind forms is perhaps the most radical change for a traditional programmer. Any *control* on a form can have code associated with it. A control is a graphical object, such as a text box, command button, combo box, or object frame. To get to the code you first must open the form, then select the control, and open the properties box. Select the events tab. An *event* is an action, such as a mouse click, key press, or change in the data in the control. Code can be associated with any event, which is why this kind of code is referred to as an *event procedure*. Each control on a form—and the form itself—has a list of events that it recognizes, as shown in figure 8.29.

Fig. 8.29

The Form properties box with the Event tab selected, showing the various events recognized by a form.

When you click the box with the *ellipsis* (...) to the right of the event, you are taken to the Visual Basic code window and the code for this event. From here, you can view and modify code for the other events on this form or report. You also can get to the code by clicking the View, Code option on the menu. Using this option takes you to the start of the code listings. If you think of the code as a series of pages in a book, View, Code takes you to the first page of the code book, and allows you move to other pages. Going to the code from a control on a form or report takes you directly to the page in the book for the control, but it also gives you the opportunity to access the other pages of code.

> **Tip**
>
> If you change the name of a control on a form, all code behind the object seems to "disappear." This action occurs because the code is bound to a control that, after the rename, seemingly no longer exists.
>
> Go to the code window, look under Object:General, and there you find your code. Copy the code onto the Clipboard, omitting the first and last line (you get new first and last lines in your new function or subroutine), and then rename the subroutine or function to match the new control name. You now have your code back and operational.

Introduction to Visual Basic for Applications

The programming language for Access 95 is Visual Basic for Applications. It replaces Access Basic, which was used in previous versions of Access. Actually, the differences aren't that great, and mainly, they add both flexibility and compatibility with the programming language used in other Microsoft Office software. As a Microsoft applications developer, you will sooner or later have to work with Visual Basic for Applications, if you haven't already done so. The plus to Visual Basic for Applications is the capability to code for multiple software packages and, more important, the capability to code across the boundaries of these packages and integrate the software functions to produce extremely powerful applications.

Visual Basic for Applications is an *event-driven programming language*. Every object in Access responds to a set of events. Coded *procedures* are associated with events. The code is run every time the event is recognized by Access. Unlike traditional programming, there is no sequence of events and no predetermined flow through the code.

When you wrote a program in FORTRAN or COBOL, the program started at the first line of code and ran to completion, with calls to subroutines along the way. The programmer decided the order in which the code ran and, therefore, controlled the results for the end user. The end user followed along, supplying data in a strict order, as required by the program.

In event-driven programs, the order of the events is decided by the users: they can click a control, select a menu item, or enter data into a box on a form in any order. Although this capability gives enormous flexibility to the user, it requires more thought and planning on the part of the programmer.

Suppose that you are asked to write a simple application to print a mailing label. In a traditional programming language, the program asks the user to input the name and address, and then prints the label. The program then either terminates or re-queries the user for another name and address. In an event-driven environment, you build a form. Your form has a box in which users type the name and address, and a command button that users click to print the label. There is also a command button that closes the form.

Now, what happens if the user clicks the Print button before entering the data? Does the event-driven application print a blank label? It should contain error-trapping, which asks the user to enter data to print, and not print a label until the application has the data. So, the sequence of events that happens when the user clicks the Print button depends on the condition of another object on the form—whether or not it contains data. Similarly, when the user clicks the Close button, do you program the form to simply close? A user-friendly application (to use an overworked expression) then looks to see if a name and address were entered and not printed, warns of the condition, and then asks if the user really wants to close the form. Again, the code behind this button employs branching logic, which depends on the value in another field. The interrelationships in event-driven programming can quickly become complex, even on an apparently simple form.

As a developer, you don't have to turn over control entirely to the user. In the mailing label example, by simply adding some code-behind-forms, you can make the Print button invisible (appear dimmed out), until the name and address information is entered into the text box. The drawback to this approach is that the form could seem to be overly nervous, with buttons appearing and disappearing. If your forms are laid out logically (from the user's point of view), the code behind the form can perform the necessary checks and balances unobtrusively and with minimum impact on the workflow.

Error Trapping: Be Kind to Your End User

As we mentioned previously, one benefit of using modules and code behind forms is that you can trap errors. The first statement in your code for every function or subroutine should be the OnError GoTo .... When an error is encountered, give the user an error message that indicates where in the program the problem happened. If you just leave the error message as `MsgBox Error$`, then only a system-level message from Access 95 displays on-screen, which may not be very informative to the user.

Include the Resume code (`Resume Exit …`) so that even if the action fails, control is returned to the user rather than locking up the application. A typical code setup looks like the following example, which you can find in the Contact7 database on the frmContacts form, behind a button labeled Communications, which you can find on this book's companion CD-ROM:

Listing 8.2   08code02.txt—Typical Example of the Use of Resume Code

```
Private Sub Communications_Click()
'------------------------------------------------------------
' An example of how to use the resume code feature
'------------------------------------------------------------
On Error GoTo Err_Communications_Click

    DoCmd.OpenForm "frmComm", , , "[IDNumber] =
    ➥Forms![frmContacts]![txtIDNumber]"
```

(continues)

Listing 8.2 Continued

```
Exit_Communications_Click:
    Exit Sub

Err_Communications_Click:
    MsgBox "Error in moving to communications form",0,"Error"
    Resume Exit_Communications_Click

End Sub
```

The preceding code opens the frmComm form at the same record that currently is shown on the frmContacts form. If an error occurs, the user sees the message shown in the MsgBox line. After reading the error message and clicking OK, the user is returned to the starting form. The second, associated form, is never opened. Were the error-handling code not in place, the user would need to see a dialog box stating that Run time error 438 has occurred, which isn't very helpful in tracking the cause of the problem.

Note

When you use the Wizard to convert macros to modules, Access 95 includes the error-handling and resume code. It leaves the generic error message, Msgbox Error$, in place because it has no way of knowing what an appropriate error message will look like, so go ahead and modify the error messages in the newly converted module.

From Here...

In this chapter we reviewed the Forms Wizard and how it changed from Access 2.0 to Access 95. Then we investigated beyond the Forms Wizard and explored the concepts of master forms and template forms. And finally, we checked out the Access 95 report writer. In all, in this chapter we covered the following:

- The three basic operations and how they are performed in an Access 95 environment
- Linking to the tables stored in an Access 95 back end .MDB
- Inherited relationships
- What to include in a client application
- Building a form, both with and without the Form Wizard
- The Access 95 form template
- Building and using a master form

- Synchronizing related forms
- The Access 95 Switchboard Manager
- Introduction to macros
- The Autoexec and Autokeys macros
- Introduction to modules and programming
- Global functions
- Code behind forms
- Introduction to Visual Basic for Applications
- Error trapping

For more information on these topics, jump to the following chapters:

- Chapter 4, "Getting By in SQL '92—Structured Query Language," gives a thorough treatment of the SQL programming language.
- Chapter 5, "Client/Server Database Application Design Fundamentals," gives more information on the Hungarian naming convention.
- Chapter 9, "Navigation: How to Get from Here to There," gives you information on how to design navigational paths through your application.
- Chapter 12, "Securing the Access 95 Application," discusses the Access 95 security model.
- Chapter 14, "Communicating with Other Applications," discusses inter-application communication and the differences between linking and embedding.
- Chapter 19, "System Administration," explains how you can check for live links to the server database.
- Chapter 22, "The Human Factor," discusses the human element in the client/server environment.

II

Designing and Prototyping

CHAPTER 9

Navigation: How to Get from Here to There

Navigation through an application—especially a large, complex application—is a subject worthy of its own book. Much has been written on this subject, mostly found under the topic headings, "client interface," "user interface," and "end-user computing." Depending on your point of view and the standards in place in your organization (or on both), you may have some preconceived notions of how the user community may (or may not) move through an application. We also have opinions on this topic, which we present in this chapter.

In this chapter, we cover the following:

- Why it is important to allow free-flowing access through an event-driven program
- Vertical and horizontal navigation within an application
- What to do when you reach the end of a form
- Direct navigation versus branching logic
- Developing custom menus and toolbars for your application
- Using the Menu Builder
- Building switchboards and front-end menus for entry point control
- The Access 95 Switchboard Manager

Event-Driven Programming

Event-driven programming means giving program control to the end user. The user decides how to use a form, either by entering data, searching for data, or performing other actions. If you move back a level from the forms and reports to the entry point of the program—the Switchboard (see fig. 9.1)—the user is faced with more decisions on how to use the application. When you build a front-end menu or use the *Switchboard Manager* to develop a front-end menu, you can give the user multiple entry points to the program environment.

Fig. 9.1

The REA Main Switch-board, which is the entry point for everyone using this application.

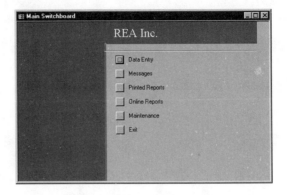

People in the same company work differently, even when using the same tool. Every person has a different task, agenda, and time frame, so each develops a specific way of using the tool. Software applications are today's business tools, so you must design these tools for maximum use, flexibility, and efficiency. If you have a group of heads-down data-entry personnel who spend all day moving between one or two forms on the screen (order entry clerks, for example, at a mail-order company), they will have a much different set of requirements for the software "tool" than the upper-level decision makers, who use the decision support screens and capabilities built into the software. Your task, as a developer, is to provide applications that meet the requirements of both groups, and all others between these two groups, while retaining the flexibility, integrity, and performance features that make your software a pleasure to use.

In our real estate company example, just as in the real world, no single person works through a project from beginning to end. It takes a *workgroup* to complete a project, and all members of the workgroup have a responsibility to record project information on their parts of the process. Each project team member needs to be able to jump in at the appropriate point in the process, which requires the application to have multiple points of entry. The second requirement, based on the concept that nobody in today's business world has the luxury of working on only one project at a time, is the ability to move quickly between projects within the database.

Movement within Your Application

When your users start your application, they probably will see a menu, a selection of choices for further action, possibly designed by using the Switchboard Manager. From here, they will select an option and then will be taken directly to the form or report that they want to use.

While looking at, for example, construction cost information on a building project, users may want to move to another form—lease terms—on the same building project. Perhaps the users then want to drill down from a summary form to more detailed information on an underlying form for the same project, or perhaps look at the same information on the same form, for several different projects. Your users will not expect to have to return to the top menu each time they want to select a different form. Rather, they expect to be able to navigate through the various forms in a logical sequence, jump to a different form, or select a new project record, all without leaving the form they are currently using. A manager who is looking at a potential trouble spot on a summary form doesn't expect to use menus to navigate a circuitous path to the underlying data. Rather, the manager expects to use a single mouse click to go directly to the data in question.

Vertical Navigation

The authors define *vertical navigation* as the ability to *"drill down"* into the data, looking at more and more detailed data related to the original record with each click of the mouse, and then to return at will to the top level. At first glance, it seems the simplest way to do so is to open forms in succession until the desired level of detail was reached, and then close the forms again to return to the starting point.

In most environments, including Access 95, problems arise when this approach is used. The first resource to be exhausted is computer memory. If you open a second form without first closing the current form, it obviously will require more memory to hold both forms in memory than takes to hold one. Assuming that the client computers do not have unlimited memory (a valid assumption in today's workplace), at some point the application starts swapping out data from memory to the Windows page file, using the virtual memory capability in an attempt to accommodate the user's request for more open forms. As you already know, disk I/O is the slowest and most expensive computer operation, and using virtual memory considerably impacts the performance of your Windows applications. Eventually, you may reach a point where the application can open no more forms and generate an error message to the unfortunate and unsuspecting end user.

One solution is to close each form as you open the next, so that one form at a time is open in memory. A variation on this theme, which generates a smoother transition from form to form, is to open the second form and immediately close the first. For a brief moment, two forms are in memory but in the experience of the authors, this approach works well even on systems with limited memory. The downside (we are always dealing with trade-offs when designing software, or anything else for that matter) is that it takes longer on the return trip to navigate back through the forms to the starting point, because you have to reopen each form on the trip back. If all the forms were open—stacked one behind the other—you would only have to close the currently visible form to expose the one directly behind it. Of course, if this form was swapped out to disk (virtual memory), it may not appear as quickly as your users expect. So, maybe the downside of opening the form again is not so bad after all.

II

Designing and Prototyping

> **Caution**
>
> Be very careful about using the open-second-form-and-immediately-close-first-form technique
> in a true file server environment, where the client application is stored on a server, and portions
> of the graphical interfaces—as needed—are requested by the client terminal. Continually open-
> ing and closing graphical forms as the authors suggest creates undue stress and load on the
> network and the network administration staff, and application performance will be unaccept-
> able. The authors' technique works best in a client/server environment, where the graphical
> forms are stored locally and only a copy of the raw data needs to be shipped across the net-
> work—like the homogeneous Access environment.

But wait, there's more. If you opened one form after another, and then closed them again to back up, you inadvertently constrained the end users in what they can do in the application! The only way the end users can return to the starting point is to re-trace their steps.

If you implemented the technique suggested by the authors, because the end user has only one form open, he or she can open any other form and can choose a different route back to the starting point. Now, users have the freedom to move from any form to any other form, choosing their own path through the application. All you, as the developer, have to do is make sure that each occurrence of a form displays the appropriate project information, which is done by linking the forms together by way of project number.

In some situations, it is appropriate to use pop-up forms, small secondary forms that "pop up" over a main form to show detail data or related data. The rule in a mixed hardware environment with restricted computer memory (as of this writing, using the current version of Access 95, we're talking 16M of RAM for the run-time applications)—you should have no more than three forms (one main and two pop-up forms) open at any one time.

If you want to really tailor your application to your user community (and be regarded a hero), consider the following technique. If you keep track of which form the user started from, you can return him or her to that form at any time. Suppose that a team member has started entering data on a new project by using the Project form (see fig. 9.2), and then input some financial information on the Financials form. As he closes the Financials form, he is automatically returned to the Project form, where he starts to record data on the next project. Shortly thereafter, the project coordinator looks at the Risk Advisory screen, and notes a problem with the financial data. She clicks on the problem item, and the Financials form opens with the details. Now when she closes the Financials form, she returns not to the Project form or to the main menu, but to the Risk Advisory screen.

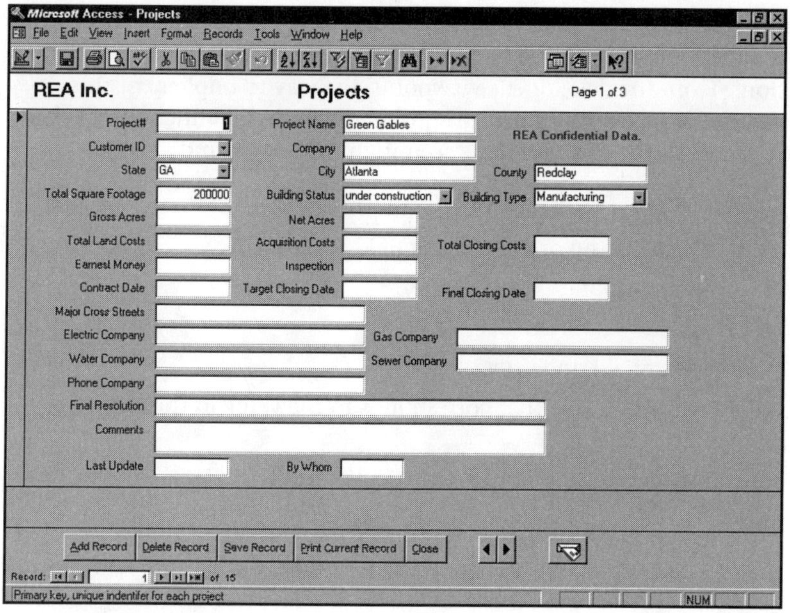

Fig. 9.2

The vertical and horizontal navigation buttons at the bottom of the screen allow movement from project to project or screen to screen within one project.

This flexibility in navigation makes an application extremely useable—and lack of this kind of flexibility renders the application cumbersome and unwieldy. We discuss this kind of navigation in greater detail in the code examples that follow in this chapter.

Horizontal Navigation

By *horizontal navigation*, we mean the ability to move from one record to another, while remaining on the same form. Most of the forms you build will use the navigation buttons at the lower left corner of the screen to move from one record to another. Generally, this setup works fine but consider how you should handle vertical navigation. If you use the Command Button Wizard to build a command button that opens a second form from the first form, the second form can show one of two things. It can show all the records in the database, or it can show only the records that relate to the record on the first form.

In the first case, where the second form can show all records in the database, you don't know which data relates to the record on the first form. You have lost data synchronization between the two forms.

In the second case, where the second form can show only records that relate to the record in the first form, the only data available on the second form is a filtered subset of the database. Although you now have data synchronization, you cannot change to a different record on the second form; you must return to the first form to see other records in the database.

From the end user's point of view, the ideal situation is to be able to move from record to record on the same form, and from form to form on different records—all with no restrictions. From the developer's viewpoint, the way to implement this scheme is to build global navigation functions. After you write the function, you can attach it where needed, so the end user can "seemingly" move around at will.

A navigation function should perform the following steps:

1. Find the value of the linking or connecting field on Form 1.
2. Store this value in a temporary local register.
3. Open Form 2.
4. Go to the connecting field on Form 2.
5. Find the record with the value that corresponds to the value in the temporary local register.
6. Move the cursor to the first data input field on the form.
7. Close Form 1.

The result of this sequence of operations is that the user now is at Form 2 with the correct record showing and can move freely to other records. Form 1 was closed and that area of memory currently occupied by Form 1 has been released.

The actual code to do something like this is shown in Listing 9.1, which you can find on the companion CD-ROM.

Listing 9.1 09CODE01.TXT—By Implementing the Logic Described in the Preceding Text, You Can Offer Your Users Highly Flexible Navigation Options in Your Applications

```
Function navigate(FromForm, ToForm, FirstField, ToLink, CurVal)
' ------------------------------------------------------------
' Enhanced navigation: move to the next form and carry the system
' variable OpenArgs forward, so we can always end up where we
' started from.
' ------------------------------------------------------------
' Attach to OnClick property of the horizontal navigation buttons
' Do not use Option Explicit in declarations,
' or define OrigForm as string
' ------------------------------------------------------------
On Error GoTo Err_Navigate
'   define the variables used in this procedure
 Dim MyForm As Form
 Set MyForm = Screen.ActiveForm
 Origform = MyForm.OpenArgs
'   make a note, is this call originating from Risk Assessment screen?
 If Origform <> "frmRiskEval" Then
 Origform = FromForm
 End If
'   do an overt save of data on the calling form to force a write
'   to disk, open the called form while retaining the name of the
'   calling form, find the correct record, move to the appropriate
```

```
'   text box on the called form, make sure the called form is
'   maximized, close the calling form.
  DoCmd.DoMenuItem A_FORMBAR, A_FILE, A_SAVERECORD
  DoCmd.OpenForm ToForm, A_NORMAL, , , , , Origform
  DoCmd.GoToControl ToLink
  DoCmd.FindRecord CurVal
  DoCmd.GoToControl FirstField
  DoCmd.Maximize
  DoCmd.Close A_FORM, FromForm

Exit_Navigate:
 Exit Function
Err_Navigate:
 MsgBox "Error on moving between forms", 0, "Navigation Error"
 Resume Exit_Navigate
End Function
```

When You Reach the End of the Form...

What do you do when you reach the last text box or control object on a form? Usually, when the user presses the Tab key, the cursor moves from one field on the screen to the next, especially when in browse or read-only mode. When you get to the last field on-screen, however, you can choose to build in the following several actions to your application, depending on who is the intended user:

- Go back to the top of the form, staying on the same record
- Go back to the top of the form, moving to the next record
- Go back to the top of the same page in a multi-page form, staying on the same record
- Go back to the top of the same page in a multi-page form, moving to the next record
- Go to the next page of a multi-page form, staying on the same record
- Go to the next form in sequence, staying on the same record—most useful in data-entry mode

The first three options can be specified within Access 95. If you do not change the default property ("Cycle" in the properties box, form design mode, as demonstrated in fig. 9.3), you get the second option. The second and fourth options are identical for a single-page form. The fifth option actually happens automatically unless you specified that you want to return to the top of the page. The last option, to move to another form, requires some code to specify which form comes next.

Although this navigation motion is strictly a matter of preference and existing application standards that may be in force in your shop, the authors have found that most users prefer to stay on the same record as they progress through the sequence of forms. If they want to view a different record, they initiate the change by clicking a navigation button.

II

Designing and Prototyping

Fig. 9.3

The Form properties box's Other tab, showing the cycle property set to Current Record.

The authors suggest that no matter which *end-of-form cursor behavior* you decide to make standard, you do so on the Master Form so all forms are consistent. In form design mode, open the Form properties box and, under the Other tab, set the Cycle property to your choice.

Direct Navigation or Branching?

Occasionally, a logical flow through a process exists that is reflected in the database application, so that it's possible to progress from one form to the next, entering all the required data in the process. However, this may be the exception rather than the rule. Often, you find that users have a form open they want to keep open, but they also want to access other information on another form. When an employee is looking at a specific project, for example, the employee may want to know the name and phone number of the customer who is associated with this project. Figure 9.4, the Projects form, shows the Customer ID and the customer (Company) name. Wouldn't it be nice to just click on the customer name and get the remainder of the contact information? OK, let's do it.

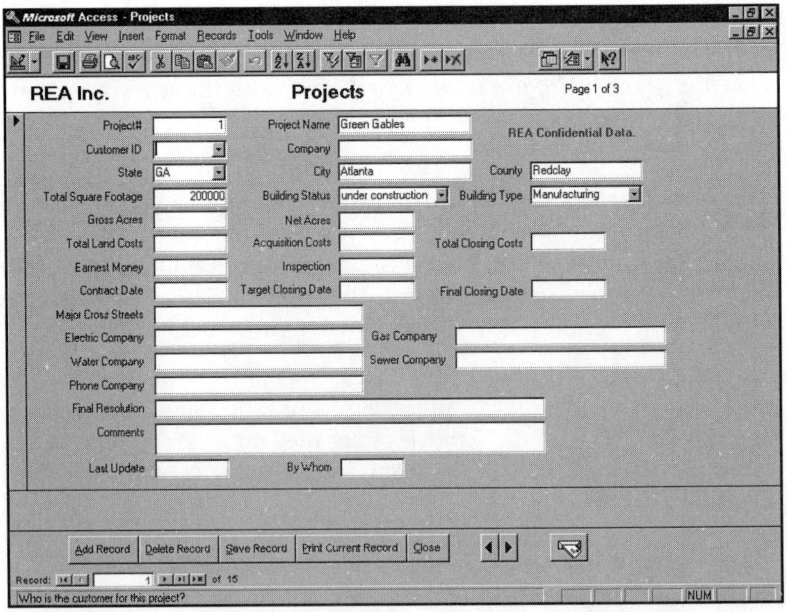

Fig. 9.4

The Projects form, showing Customer ID and customer (Company) name but with no way to get additional customer contact information.

To begin, you can rearrange the Projects form so that the customer information is presented in a better way. Right now, the Customer ID and Company name fields are on the Projects form. Notice that when you select a Customer ID in the combo box, the corresponding value for the Company name is displayed. What happens, however, when you try to assign a new customer to a project, a customer that doesn't have an assigned customer ID or accompanying information on file in the database? (See fig. 9.5 for the resulting error message!) You can type a new customer code in the Customer ID field but when you try to type the company name, you see an error message announcing that you cannot enter a value in the blank field on the "one" side of an outer join. (This error message appears on the lower left corner of the screen, in the status line, unless you try to move to another record—in which case, you see a dialog box that contains the error message.)

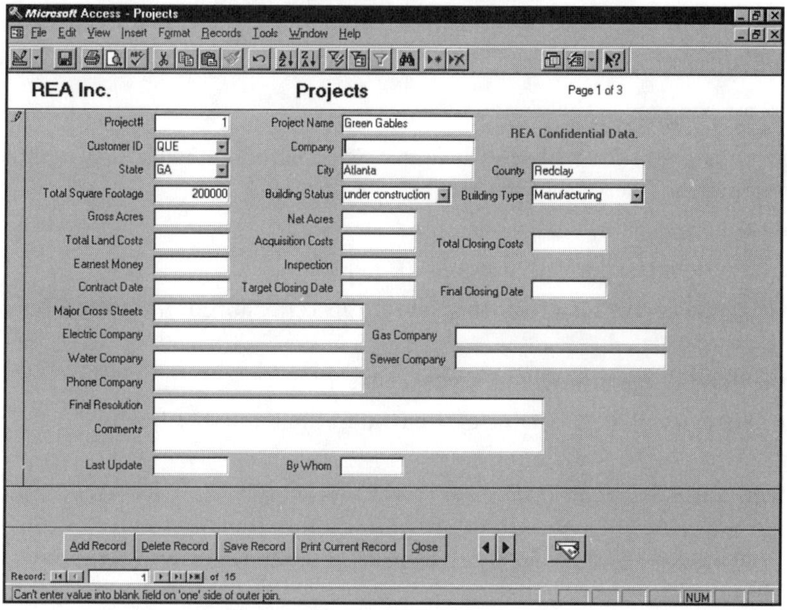

Fig. 9.5

This error message (at bottom of screen) is produced when you try to insert a customer name into this form.

The situation you just encountered is that the customer table is related to the project table in a one-to-many relationship—one customer can be associated with many projects. This Projects form contains data-entry fields for the "many" side of the relationship—so from this form, you can't add data to the "one" side of the relationship, the Customer table.

Adding Code to Open the Customer Form. One solution to this quandary is to modify the properties of the Customer Code combo box, turning on the Limit to List property (see fig. 9.6). Then, when you type a customer identifier that isn't in the list, an event occurs, which gives you the opportunity to allow the user to add to the customer list. You can write code that opens the Customers form, so that the user can enter the details of the new customer. After this is done, the user can close the Customer form and return to the Project form to continue entering data on the new project.

Fig. 9.6

The combo box comboCustID properties box, showing Limit To List equal to Yes.

Let's step through this process because it makes more sense when you actually do it.

First, we make some changes to the combo box:

1. Build a query based on the table, refCustomer. Select only the fields CustID and CustName. Save the query as **qryComboCust**.

2. Open form frmProjCust in Design View.

3. Open the Properties box for the Customer ID field.

4. Change the name of this field to **comboCustID** (this is the author's variation on Hungarian notation).

5. Change the Row Source Property to **qryComboCust**.

6. Select the Company field (the name of the field in the Properties box is CustName).

7. Change its Control Source to read **=[comboCustID].[Column](1)** (see fig. 9.7). This code sets the control source to the second column; the first column is column(0)—column count starts at zero—of the combo box and, therefore, the second column returned by the query.

Fig. 9.7

The properties box for text box CustName, with the control source set to display the customer's name as retrieved by the comboCustID control, which is on the same form.

8. Change the Enabled property to No.

9. Change the Locked property to Yes.

10. Change the Tab Stop property to No.

11. Change the background color to match the form background. This is the authors' standard way of indicating that a field on a form is not updateable.

The reason for changing the Enabled, Locked, and Tab Stop properties is that the company, or customer name, is determined by the customer ID and, therefore, should not be changed on this, the Projects form. These changes should happen on the Customers form. The authors changed the background color of the customer name field to indicate to the end user that this is a reference field for display purposes only, and cannot be updated here.

Setting Up to Enter New Customers. Now for the logic of the situation, where the end user tries to associate a new customer—who is not already listed in the database—to a project. The first step is to make sure that the end user didn't accidentally enter an incorrect customer code, then verify that this is indeed a new customer. If the end user replies yes, then we open the Customers form and allow the end user to input all information about this new customer. Finally, after data entry is complete, the end user closes the Customer form and returns to the Project form.

To set up for entering new customers, take the following steps:

1. Open the form frmProjCust in design mode, and select the Customer ID combo box.

2. Open the properties box for the field.

3. Change the Limit To List property to Yes.

4. For the Not in List Event, add an event procedure. The code shown in Listing 9.2 is on this book's companion CD-ROM.

Listing 9.2 09CODE02.TXT—This Logic Opens the Associated Customer Form and Allows Users to Enter a New Customer into the Database

```
Private Sub comboCustId_NotInList(Newdata As String,
➥Response As Integer)
On Error GoTo Err_comboCustId_NotInList

Dim strSQL As String 'Build a SQL statement which adds a new
➥entry to the table.

'  Check to confirm that this is a new customer
msgtext = "You entered " & Newdata
msgtext = msgtext & " This is not the code for an existing
➥customer in the list."
msgtext = msgtext & " Do you wish to add information for a new
➥customer to the list?"
Response = MsgBox(msgtext, 292, "Entry Not In List")
```

(continues)

Designing and Prototyping

Listing 9.2   Continued

```
'  If it is not a valid entry, end this routine
If Response = 7 Then
Exit Sub
End If
'  If it is a valid entry,add it to the table with a SQL command.
'  Turn off warning messages to the screen, run the SQL command,
'  then turn screen warning messages on
strSQL = "insert into refCustomer
➥(CustID) values ('" & Newdata & "')"
DoCmd.SetWarnings False
DoCmd.RunSQL strSQL
DoCmd.SetWarnings True
'  Now open the Customer form so the user can enter the other
'  information about this customer
[comboCustId] = " "
 DoCmd.OpenForm "frmCustomer", A_NORMAL, , , , , "frmDeProjCust"
 DoCmd.GoToControl "txtCustID"
 DoCmd.FindRecord Newdata
 DoCmd.GoToControl "txtCustName"
 DoCmd.Maximize
 Exit Sub
Exit_comboCustId_NotInList:
 Exit Sub
Err_comboCustId_NotInList:
 MsgBox Error$
 Resume Exit_comboCustId_NotInList
End Sub
```

After entering the event procedure code, switch to design mode, and try typing a new customer code into the Customer ID field. You will see the message generated by the preceding code, as shown in figure 9.8.

Fig. 9.8

The intelligent combo box Customer ID, requesting more information about the customer code just entered, which doesn't match any entry already in the customer list.

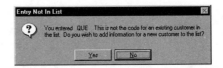

If you answer No when queried about entering a new customer to the list, then the event procedure is aborted and you return to the Projects form. Notice how the combo box pops open so that you can select an existing customer. Enter a new customer code into the Customer ID field again but this time, answer Yes. Now the Customers form pops open (see fig. 9.9) so that you can enter more information about the new customer. Go ahead, enter some information. Then close the Customer form.

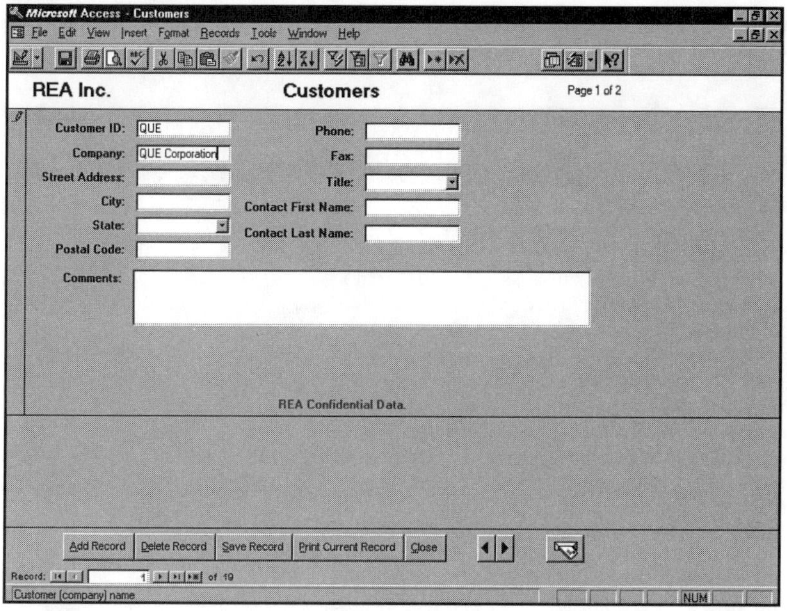

Fig. 9.9

The Customer form opens to allow new data to be added to the customer list.

Refreshing the Projects Form with the New Customer Information. Now you are back at the Projects form, but where is the new customer information that you just entered? The new customer code doesn't even show up in the combo box list. What happened?

Actually, nothing happened—that's the problem. You are still looking at the Projects form and at the associated data, as it was when you first opened that form. If you closed the Projects form and opened it again, the query that is used to populate the combo box runs again, and then shows the new customer that you just entered. (To do this, you may need to press Esc to cancel the changes that you were trying to make, before you can close the form.)

However, you really don't want to force the end user to close and reopen the form. A cleaner solution is to choose the Records menu option and select Refresh, which reruns any queries used by this form.

So, how does the refresh happen? There is no event on this form, the Projects form, that suits your needs. The Activate event is the closest, but this event will perform the refresh every time you open the form, which is unnecessary and will only generate additional network traffic. The Project form only needs to be refreshed when the Customer form closes. Perhaps you can put the code to trigger the Refresh behind the Close button on the Customers form. (You can put the code in the On Close property of the form—but because a Close button already exists, with code behind it, keep the code in one place.)

The code behind the Close button on the Customer form should resemble the following example:

Listing 9.3   09CODE03.txt—Refresh the Contents of Underlying Form When the Associated Pop-Up Form Is Closed

```
Private Sub cmdClose_Click()
'----------------------------------------------
' Refresh the contents of the underlying form
' when the associated popup form is closed
' do not use Option Explicit in declarations
' or declare CurVal as variant
'----------------------------------------------
On Error GoTo Err_cmdClose_Click
CurVal = [txtCustID]
DoCmd.Close A_FORM, "frmCustomer"
Forms![frmProjCust].Refresh
DoCmd.GoToControl "comboCustID"
Forms![frmProjCust].[comboCustId] = CurVal
DoCmd.GoToControl "comboState"
Exit Sub

Exit_cmdClose_Click:
  Exit Sub
Err_cmdClose_Click:
  MsgBox "Error closing customer form", 0, "Error"
  Resume Exit_cmdClose_Click
End Sub
```

In this code, the value of the Customer ID from the txtCustID field is stored on the Customer form in a variable named CurVal, before the form can be closed. Then we refresh the Project form, and set the value of the combo box to the stored value of the Customer ID. Finally, we position the cursor at the next field, which—in this case—is the State combo box.

Displaying Information about Existing Customers. This procedure works well for adding a new customer to the database. Now, look at another type of form, a pop-up form that displays information about existing customers. To construct this form, follow these steps:

1. Build a new form, using the Form Wizard, based on the query, qryCustomer.

2. Include the following fields: CustID, CustContFname, CustContLname, CustPhone, and CustFax.

3. Use the defaults offered, a columnar format and a standard style.

4. Give it the title, **Customer Contact**, and finish in Design View.

5. Set the following properties for the form itself:

   - Scroll bars: Neither
   - Record Selectors: No
   - Navigation Buttons: No

- Control Box: Leave as Yes for now
- Min Max Buttons: None
- Close Button: Leave as Yes for now
- Allow Edits: No
- Allow Additions: No
- Allow Deletions: No
- Data Entry: No
- Pop Up: Yes
- Modal: Yes

6. Add a command button to the form, or to the form footer, that closes the form. The quickest way to add a command button is to open the Toolbox, make sure that the Control Wizards button is selected, and then drop a command button on the form and tell the wizard to build a form button that closes the form.

7. After you create the Close button, you can set the Control Box property of the form (on the Format tab) to No.

8. Set the Close Button (also on the Format tab) to No if you want, but by default, it deactivates when you turn off the Control Box.

9. If the screen is maximized, convert to normal window sizing and resize the form so that, when seen in Form View, it measures about 2.5" by 2.5" (see fig. 9.10).

10. Close this form and name it `frmCustContact`.

Fig. 9.10

The Customer Contact pop-up form, which is activated by clicking the telephone icon to the right of the Company field.

Adding a Button to Activate the Customer Contact Form. There, you have the pop-up customer contact form built, now you need a command button on the Project form to activate it.

1. Open frmProjCust in Design View. Using the toolbox and the Command Button Wizard to save time, place a command button on the form to the right of the Customer information.

2. When the Command Button Wizard dialog box gives you the opportunity, select Form Operations, Open a Form, from the lists.

3. Specify the form you want to open: frmCustContact.

4. Choose the option to open the form and display specific data.

II

Designing and Prototyping

5. For the connecting fields, select comboCustID from form frmProjCust, and CustID from form frmCustContact.

6. Put a picture on the button such as a telephone, or some text if you prefer.

7. Name the button **cmdContact**.

8. When the button-building is finished, save the form, switch to form view mode, and try it out.

If you have no customer associated with a building project, then the entire Customer Contact pop-up form will be blank. However, business rules dictate that you should not have a building project without a customer! You can find more information about embedding business rules in your application design in Chapter 6, "Establishing the Ground Rules."

Workflow Navigation

The authors don't propose stepping you through building each of the forms for the REA application here. These forms and more are available in the REA database supplied on this book's companion CD-ROM. The authors, however, do suggest that you install the REA application, so that you can see how the flow from one form to another works. The order in which you navigate through the various components looks like figure 9.11.

Fig. 9.11

Navigation through the REA application, which follows the Switchboard layout.

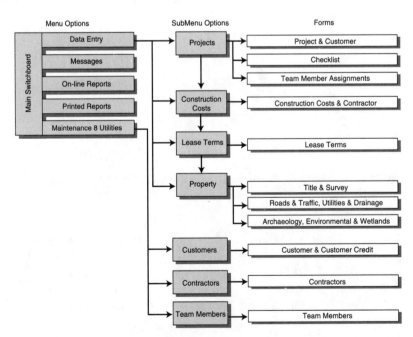

Several possible ways are available to navigate through these forms. You can start at the Project & Customer form, and work your way down through the Checklist and Team Members to Construction Costs & Contractor. Or you can have a form titled, "Project" which contains only three menu choices plus a Close button, for these three forms—a menu form, effectively. The end user could decide to move to any of these three forms but, on closing each form, would be returned to the Project form before being allowed to move on to the next. The decision of how navigation will be implemented depends on how the work is divided between the end users and on who is responsible for each part of the process.

To illustrate this concept, look at moving from the Projects & Customers form to the Checklist form. On the frmProjCust form, open the properties box for the Next Record button at the bottom of the screen. The code that goes in the On Click event for this button is:

```
=navigate("frmProjCust","frmChecklist","txtRFPRecieved",
➡"txtProjectID",[txtProjectID])
```

This code calls the navigate function, which has the following arguments:

```
Function Navigate(FromForm, ToForm, FirstField, ToLink, curval)
```

The form frmProjCust is the **FromForm**, the form from where we are starting. The form frmChecklist is the **ToForm**, the target form in this move. The text box **txtRFPRecieved** is the FirstField—the field where we want the cursor to be when the new form is opened. Text box **txtProjectID** is the name of the field on the target form that will contain one of the "connecting" values between the two forms. Finally, **[txtProjectID]** is the value contained on the current form, which is the other "connecting" value, which we will need to match in order to synchronize records between the two forms.

Please note that the first four arguments are in quotes because we are passing field names. The last value is in brackets, because we are passing the value currently in the field, not the name of the field.

On the form frmChecklist, open the properties box for the Previous Record button at the bottom of the screen. The code that goes in the On Click event for this button is shown in the following example:

```
=navigate("frmChecklist","frmProjCust","txtProjectName",
➡"txtProjectID",[txtProjectID])
```

Loosely translated, this code means "Move from frmChecklist to frmProjCust, place the cursor in the text box named txtProjectName, and synchronize the two forms on the record value present in the text box txtProjectID of the form frmChecklist."

Now you can jump back from the Checklist form to the Projects form. Note that the big benefit of using this navigation technique is that you can move between records on any form, and as you change forms, you stay on the same record. The REA application on this book's companion CD-ROM has more of this form-to-form navigation enabled.

II

Designing and Prototyping

Also, a few paragraphs ago, we discussed using the **openargs** property to track the originating form on a navigation movement. This **openargs** property is not accessible from Form Design View; it can be changed only via embedded code. When a form calls a second form by using the **openargs** property, the name of the first form can be encoded into **openargs**, and this value can be passed to the second form. If the first form is an "anchor" position, you can use **openargs** to allow the user to move from record to record on the called form, or even to move to other forms, but on exit from the called form(s), the user is returned to the calling form—the "anchor" position.

The **openargs** property isn't limited to this scenario. It can be used to transfer any information that you need to pass to a form, as the form is opened.

Menus and Toolbars

In a run-time version of an Access application, there rarely is a need to give end users the full functionality provided by the standard menus supplied with Access 95. The purpose of a run-time version (we discuss design and building of run-time applications in Chapter 13, "Building the Run-Time Application") is to provide users with access to the database as needed, as appropriate, without supplying them with tools that theoretically can corrupt the client application or, worse, the server database design.

End users will almost always need some functions and will almost never need others. For example, the user should never be able to close a form or the application from the top menu, which would leave Access open but leave only a blank screen for the user to look at. Your application should always provide command buttons on each form to do the ordinary functions such as add, edit, and save records; close the form; and print the current profile. Your application should never give users access to form or report design modes if your shop standards do not allow this level of end-user empowerment.

A good argument in favor of removing commands in the top menu that allow movement between forms is to maintain *flow-of-control*. Throughout this chapter, we discussed navigation issues and how to write code to enable navigation from form to form, record to record, without "losing your place." This can be done only by programming the navigation command buttons provided by you, the developer, on the various forms. If the user activates the top menu commands, then navigation control through the application most likely will be lost.

The authors have found that end users are most comfortable when they have the familiarity of the top menus ("Windows compliance"), in addition to the navigation command buttons. To do this and to avoid loss of control, the authors suggest creating custom menus for use with your application.

Building Custom Menus

Custom menus are reasonably easy to build and offer a level of control to the end user, without compromising the carefully planned navigational schemes that you built into your application.

You can use the *Menu Builder facility* (Tools, Add-Ins, Menu Builder) to construct drop-down menus just like the menus at the top of the Access 95 screens. In practice, you probably will end up building custom drop-down menus to enable routine tasks such as printing screens or cutting and pasting, and leave application-specific navigation to command buttons built into your forms.

Tip

If necessary, each form can have a custom drop-down menu associated with it. As an interface designer, however, you want to avoid confusing the end user with too many dissimilar menu layouts. Consistency in menu selections, consistency in form layout and command button functionality, even consistency in color cues are all important to the usability of a form and the acceptability of an application.

You may have noticed that the Access 95 top menus keep changing as you first open a form, then switch it to design mode, or even open a code window. This lack of consistency is needed to respond to the changing requirements of the various modes of operation within Access 95. This doesn't mean that all these menu choices should remain available in the client application, because rarely does a client application make available the design modes or the code window.

You can assign a custom menu to your client application, regardless of whether it will run under a full version of Access 95 or be compiled and distributed as a run-time application, just by indicating in the Tools, Startup options the name of the custom menu bar that you constructed for this application.

Using the Menu Builder

You build custom menus with the Menu Builder, which can be started in either of two ways.

Method 1:

1. At the database window, click Tools, Add-Ins, Menu Builder. Select New. The Menu Builder dialog box opens, as shown in figure 9.12.

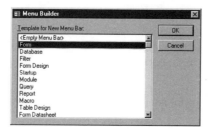

Fig. 9.12

The Menu Builder dialog box, which lists the type of custom menus you can build for your application.

2. Choose a menu to use as a template for your new menu. The Form menu is the best selection for data-entry purposes. Click OK, and the Menu Builder [New Menu Bar] dialog box opens, as shown in figure 9.13.

Fig. 9.13

The Menu Builder [New Menu Bar] dialog box with existing menu options listed, which you can modify.

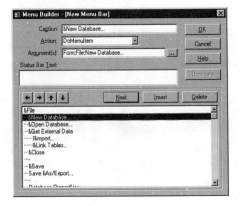

3. Delete any menu items that you do not want available to the user.

4. Save the new menu with a suitable name, such as **menuREA**.

On each form where you want this menu used, add the menu name to the Form properties box, under the Other, Menu Bar heading.

Method 2:

1. Open a form in Design View, and open the properties box.

2. Select the Other tab in the properties box.

3. Click the Menu Bar property (see fig. 9.14).

Fig. 9.14

The Form properties box, Other tab, Menu Bar property selected.

4. Click the button with the ellipsis (...) at the right of the Menu Bar property. This action opens the Menu Builder.

5. Choose a menu to use as a template for your new menu.

6. Delete any menu items that you don't want available to the user.

7. Save the new menu with a suitable name.

You can add options to the menu items if you desire. This addition is a little more complicated, and you should do so only if you think it is appropriate.

You can change the *shortcut menus* for your forms, also, from the Menu Builder. The shortcut menu is the menu that pops up on-screen when you click the secondary mouse button. Unfortunately, the Menu Builder template list doesn't include a standard Shortcut menu—a loose end in Access 95. If you decide to modify a Shortcut menu, the manual advises starting out with an empty menu bar and proceeding from there.

Creating a Global Menu Bar

You can specify a custom menu bar as the standard for all the forms and reports in your application. From the top menu, select Tools, Startup option. The Startup Dialog box opens (see fig. 9.15), which allows you to specify custom menus for both the regular menu bar and the shortcut menu bar. By inserting the name of a custom menu at this point—effectively making this property global—you then do not have to remember to add the custom menu name to every form in your application. You still retain the option of defining a custom menu bar for any specific form by placing the menu name in the properties box of the form. This setup overrides the global menu entry for that form only.

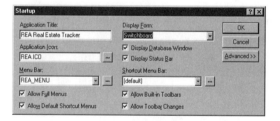

Fig. 9.15

The database Startup dialog box, where you can specify custom menus for both the regular menu bar and the shortcut menu bar (the one initiated by clicking the secondary mouse button).

Adding Custom Toolbars

Toolbars, more so than drop-down menus, are more functional to the graphically inclined end user and are an added value to the smallest and most ordinary database application. However, be judicious; do not over-do a good thing. Too many icons on a toolbar, too many icon pictures that are not intuitive, and too many toolbars can contribute to end-user confusion and decreased acceptance of your application.

As with the resident philosophy on menus, you do not want to allow all the buttons on the standard Access 95 toolbars to be visible or active. You can build a custom toolbar for the application, and then display it rather than displaying the default toolbars provided with Access.

Incidentally, if you plan to use the ADT (Access Distribution Toolkit) to distribute run-time applications rather than giving everyone in the organization a full development copy of Access 95, then—if you want the end users to have toolbars—you have to provide custom toolbars because the run-time copy of Access 95 has none.

Building a custom toolbar is straightforward. You just have to use care in your cursor movement and positioning. The following steps explain how to do so:

1. From the database container, in the top menu, select View, Toolbars, which displays the Toolbars dialog box, shown in figure 9.16. Click New.

Fig. 9.16

The Toolbars dialog box, from which you can modify existing toolbars or create custom toolbars.

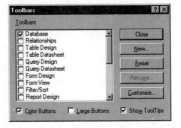

2. Give the new toolbar a name, such as **MyBar** or **REAbar** for this application, and then click OK.

3. The new toolbar name should be in the list and highlighted; click Customize.

4. Drag the buttons from the various toolbars onto your new toolbar (it shows as a very small toolbar on-screen, with only an X button on it. From the Records Toolbar, grab the buttons for New Record, Delete Record, First Record, Previous Record, Next Record, and Last Record, as shown in figure 9.17.

5. From the View Toolbar, grab the Close button and drag it to your custom toolbar.

Fig. 9.17

The Customize Toolbars dialog box.

6. From the File Toolbar, grab the Print and Print Preview buttons.

7. Click Close.

8. From the menu, select Tools, Startup, and deselect the option to allow built-in toolbars (see fig. 9.18).

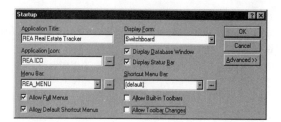

Fig. 9.18

In the Startup dialog box, disallow Access default toolbars by deselecting the Allow Built-In Toolbars option.

9. Close and then reopen the database (this step is necessary to activate the startup option, but you do not need to close Access 95). You should see your custom toolbar in place of the standard Access 95 toolbars (see fig. 9.19).

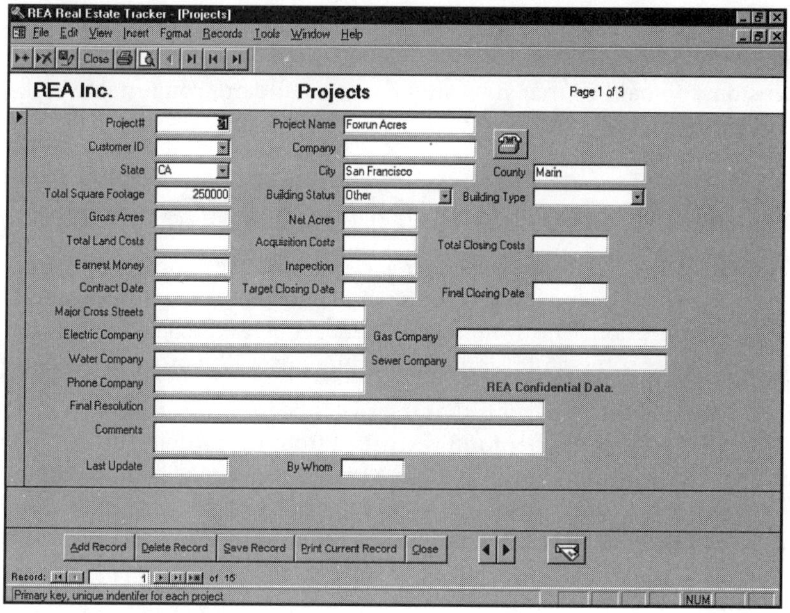

Fig. 9.19

Your custom toolbar in place of the standard toolbar normally used by Access 95.

Your custom toolbar can offer much, but not all, of the functionality of the command buttons that we placed on the master form. You use command buttons on the form in place of toolbar buttons because the command buttons on the form can be programmed to do far more complex actions than the toolbar buttons can.

When you open a form such as frmCustProj in Design View, you will see that the only toolbar buttons displayed are the buttons from the custom toolbar. Your new custom toolbar is the only toolbar available on queries, reports, and even the database window. (At this point, you will want to reactivate the built-in toolbars because you will not be able to do further development without them.)

As with custom menus, you can provide customized toolbars for different forms or reports in your database applications. Because there is no entry in the form property box to specify a toolbar, as there is with the menu bar, you need to use the ShowToolbar command in a macro or module. Attach the command to the OnOpen event of the form or report in order to activate the appropriate toolbar on opening the form (or report).

> **Tip**
>
> Don't forget to turn off the custom toolbar as you leave the form (or report), or you could end up with a screen full of assorted toolbars!

However, use this feature sparingly to avoid confusing the end user and violating the concept of standards. Plan carefully and accordingly before implementing either custom menus or custom toolbars, so that you can provide a standard, comfortable look-and-feel to your user community.

Working with the Switchboard Manager

The Switchboard Manager is new in Access 95. In Access 2.0 the developer had to build a menu (or sequence of menus) to provide a list of choices for the users when they enter the client application. The Switchboard Manager gives the developer an assist on this, and produces some professional-looking menus in the process.

A drawback of the Switchboard Manager is that the switchboard form stays open in the background, behind whatever other form was called from the switchboard. If you are programming for a low-memory environment, a better choice may be to build your own menu or switchboard forms, so that you can control which forms stay open in memory, thereby making better use of your limited resources.

A second drawback of the Switchboard Manager is that it is difficult to incorporate into a prototype application. When you build an option button and indicate that it should open a form, the Switchboard Manager requires that the name of the form be in its list, which means that that form must already exist—or at least some dummy form with this name must be in the database forms container. (Sounds reminiscent of the COBOL programming environment and stubb programs.) If you construct your own system of switchboard and menu forms, you can build the prototype menus, and then build the forms later.

The authors opted to write a short function that merely pops up a message that says this menu item is not ready, so that we could build the menu system without having all the forms in place. In this way, when the Switchboard Manager requires the name of a form that does not exist, just plug in the RunCode option.

The switchboard layout for our REA application (see fig. 9.1) is defined by the first switchboard page in Table 9.1.

Table 9.1   The REA Switchboard Layout

Switchboard Pages	Items on This Switchboard
Main Switchboard	Data Entry Switchboard Messages Printed Reports Online Reports Maintenance Switchboard Exit Application
Data Entry Switchboard	Projects Switchboard Construction Costs Lease Terms Property Switchboard Close
Projects Switchboard	Projects & Customers Checklist Team Member Assignments Close
Property Switchboard	Title & Survey Roads, Traffic, Utilities & Drainage Archaeology, Environmental & Wetlands Close
MaintenanceSwitchboard	Customers & Customer Credit Contractors Team Members Close

The Switchboard Manager design is somewhat confusing because the layout isn't exactly hierarchical. At the top level (see fig. 9.20), you must define all the levels of switchboard that will be used in the application. You can design a switchboard for the top level, and then go down a level or two and define a new switchboard at that point. So, you must plan your switchboard design carefully.

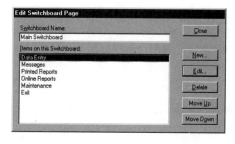

Fig. 9.20

The Edit Switchboard Page dialog box, from which you design and build the switchboards.

The authors built a switchboard by using the preceding scheme (see fig. 9.21), with some cosmetic changes, such as the label on the main switchboard form. You can modify the design even further, perhaps change the "Projects Switchboard" entry (see fig. 9.22) to appear on-screen as "Projects..." (the ellipsis indicates that more choices are available below this level, just as Access 95 does in the drop-down menus).

Fig. 9.21

The Main Switchboard, showing the top level of the hierarchy in Form View.

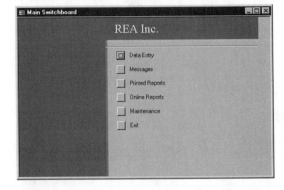

Fig. 9.22

The Data Entry Switchboard, called from the Main Switchboard.

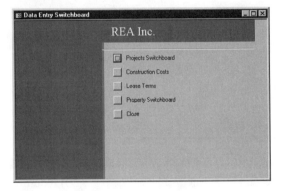

From Here...

In this chapter, we covered some of the concepts of user interface design and how to build navigation paths through an application. We discussed vertical and horizontal navigation, while developing code to assist our movement through the REA client application. We looked at instances of direct and branching logic navigation, and we developed forms and code to support both.

From here, jump to the following chapters:

- Chapter 6, "Establishing the Ground Rules," for more information on embedding business rules into your application design.
- Chapter 11, "Managing Transactions," discusses transaction management within an application.
- Chapter 13, "Building the Run-Time Application," shows how to create an installation set.

- Chapter 14, "Communicating with Other Applications," contains a general discussion of inter-application communications.
- Chapter 15, "Creating Help Files," explains how to build, compile, and integrate interactive help files into your application.
- Chapter 16, "Tuning the Access 95 Application," discusses Access 95 performance and tuning.
- Chapter 22, "The Human Factor," discusses the human element in the client/ server environment.

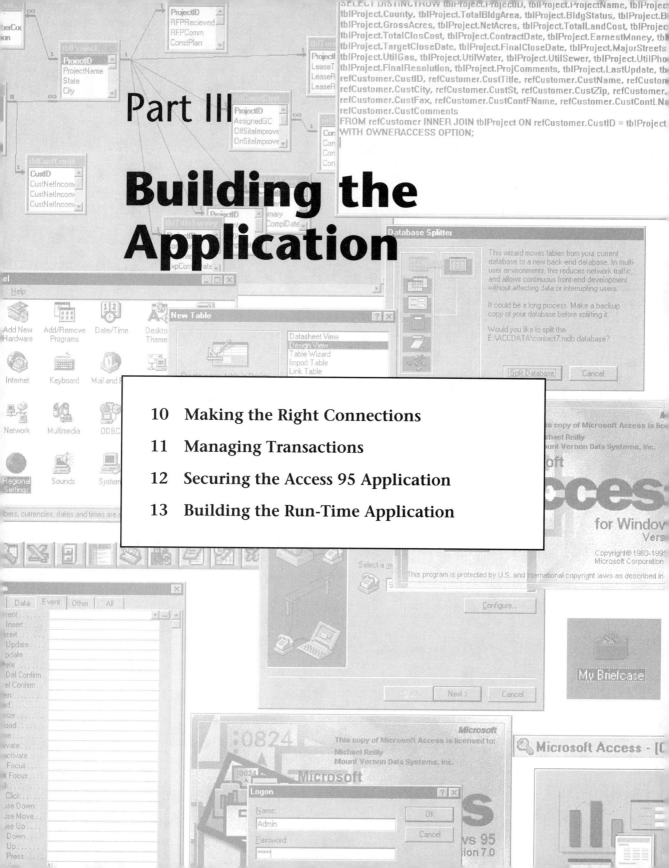

Part III

Building the Application

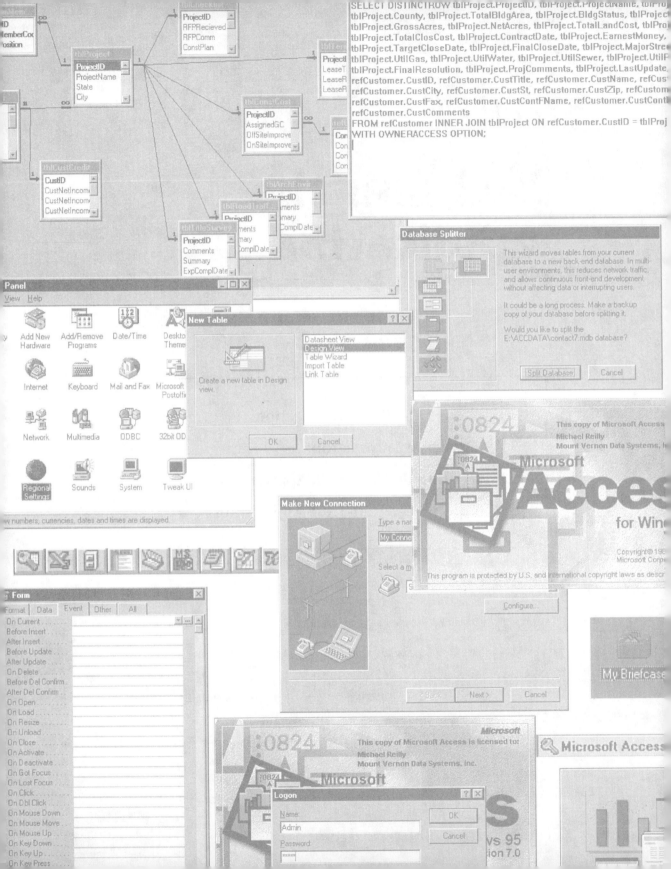

CHAPTER 10

Making the Right Connections

Access is appropriately named. It not only allows you access to the data stored within your desktop database(s), it also provides tools to allow you to connect to, retrieve, and update data stored in a wide variety of other formats. You can import data that was collected by using other applications, or you can create links to the data. The external data doesn't need to be in a database—it can be a spreadsheet, a text file, or any one of many graphics formats.

Assuming that the connection you want to make is to a server database, Access offers several ways to connect. How you design, configure, and manage these connections makes a difference in the performance of your client/server application, which may be more accurately referred to as a client-connection-server application. Because Access is capable of connecting to many different server database management systems, no one "right answer" exists when designing a connection strategy. In this chapter, we look at the different connection methods and discuss how to get the most out of these connections.

It is possible to link to tables in more than one server database, although you should do so with care because it increases the complexity of the application. When the two server databases are controlled by different database management systems—and possibly different operating systems—caution is needed. In these "heterogeneous joins" you have to be familiar with the different dialects of SQL, and you need to keep track of which dialect to use with which server table.

In this chapter, we cover the following:

- The Access programming model, what it is and how it works
- Data import, export, and linking to non-database files
- ODBC and how to build an ODBC connection
- Connecting to a server database management system
- Linking Access to server tables and views
- How to build and use pass-through SQL queries
- Server stored procedures and how they can impact your application

- Optimizing connections to the server
- Reference tables and the best place to store them
- Techniques for bringing back from the server only what you need
- Query optimization

The Access Programming Model

Access can be thought of as having three major layers or components. The top layer is what the user and the developer see. This layer is the Access interface, which offers a comprehensive toolkit for building and maintaining tables, queries, forms, reports, macros, and modules. You see this interface when you open the database in Design mode at the database window.

The middle level is the Jet Engine, which is the data management layer, or how the database management system interacts with the data by using the instructions that you provided in the user interface layer (see fig 10.1). The Jet engine in Access 95 is version 3.0. (Confused by the numbering scheme? You are not alone.) The Jet engine provides Access 95 with its flexibility in connecting to other data sources. The same Jet engine is provided with Visual Basic 4, and also can be called from within Excel. The Jet Engine is comprised of several modules, including the following:

- **Query Manager**—This module manages query objects and results, builds SQL statements and optimizes queries, and enables heterogeneous joins. Query Manager routes queries to the ISAM Manager or Remote Manager as necessary.
- **ISAM Manager**—This module handles access to ISAM drivers for external data sources, and controls the Jet ISAM.
- **Remote Manager**—This module converts queries from the Query Manager to ODBC API calls that retrieve data from ODBC databases, and then passes the results back to the Query Manager.

The lowest level is the *ODBC* connectivity layer, which Access uses to connect to other relational databases, without having to write SQL statements that are specific to each server. Briefly, the concept of ODBC is that a query written in one database environment can be passed to a different database management system, with the appropriate language translation handled by default by the ODBC driver, and the results returned, again with all necessary translation being done by the ODBC driver. The originating database management system should not need to know the language syntax of the server database management system. We discuss ODBC in more detail later in this chapter.

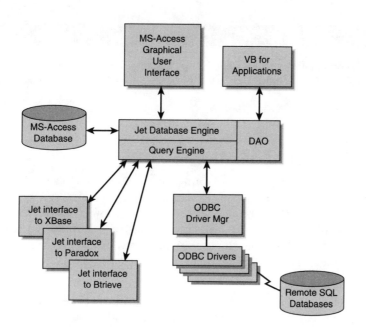

Fig. 10.1

The Jet database engine schematic, illustrating how the components fit together.

Data Import and Export

The capability of Access to exchange data with other applications opens up all kinds of possibilities. Access can bring in data from Excel or Lotus 1-2-3 files or from text files output from Microsoft Word, which then can be passed through to a server database. You can use the connectivity of Access to obtain data from a mainframe, and then pass it to a spreadsheet for analysis, or to your word processor as a mail-merge file. Use the File, Get External Data, Import option to bring in data, and the File, Save As/Export option to save the data in another format (see fig. 10.2).

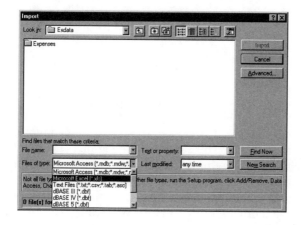

Fig. 10.2

The Import dialog box, which is where you start the process of importing non-database data into Access.

Tip

When you import a spreadsheet into a table, put the field (column) names in the first row. Access can use the first row of the spreadsheet to name the fields in a table it creates to hold the imported spreadsheet data.

Linking to Non-Database Files

When you import data into Access, you are storing a copy of the data in an Access database. Any changes made to the copy of the data stored within Access are not echoed in the original data. If you want data modifications to flow back and forth between the database and the original files, you can establish a link to the files rather than importing them. With a link, the data isn't brought into the database and isn't stored by Access, but the link shows in the Access 95 database container as an attached table.

If you link to an Excel spreadsheet, for example, an Excel icon will appear beside the link name in the table list of the database container, as shown in figure 10.3. Now, when changes are made to the Excel data through a database application interface, you see the modifications in the original Excel spreadsheets. Actually, these changes are being made within the spreadsheet by Access 95.

To drop a link to an external file, just delete the entry in the table window of the database container. You are really only deleting the link to the file; the data itself remains, safe and sound, in the external file.

Fig. 10.3

Linked Excel table shows in the Database window as an Excel table—the imported table looks like a native Access table.

When an external data file such as a spreadsheet is linked to Access, it still can be opened by its native application, although not when it is already open in Access. Similarly, if another user has the spreadsheet open in Excel, Access cannot open it for use within the database environment. This safety measure resolves the problem of whose updates will write to disk. As with most applications that use a simple single-user file management system, no record-locking mechanism is available, which can span both applications simultaneously. The Access 95 user manual claims that you can have certain files open in both applications at the same time, but this capability doesn't seem to be true with Excel 5.

Excel offers the second user a read-only copy of the open file. The authors recommend that the programmer handle this situation in the following manner. Depending on the business situation—if it's okay for users to view possibly inaccurate data (*dirty reads*)—it's no big deal. If this situation isn't okay, then get a Windows programmer to advise whether or not it's possible to turn off this feature of Excel. Access can control dirty reads within its own environment, but it cannot (out of the box) control external applications and what they may or may not do.

Caution

Take care when importing spreadsheet data that includes calculated fields. Only the current value of the calculated cell is imported; the formula that produces it is not.

If after importing the spreadsheet into an Access table, you change a data value of one of the fields that was input to a "calculated field," unlike the spreadsheet paradigm, the "calculated" change doesn't happen. Access tables may look like spreadsheets, but they lack the built-in power of a spreadsheet.

Bring in only the base cells from a spreadsheet, and rebuild the calculated fields in Access forms or reports. Remember the authors' rule on storing calculated fields in an operational database: **don't**.

Available Sources and Drivers

The list of external data sources to which Access 95 can connect includes, but may not be limited to the following:

- Other Access databases
- Microsoft Excel spreadsheets, from version 3.0 on
- Lotus 1-2-3 WKS, WK1, and WK3 spreadsheets
- dBASE III, dBASE IV, and dBASE 5.x files
- Paradox versions 3.x, 4.x, and 5.x files
- Microsoft FoxPro 2.0, 2.5, and 2.6 files
- Text files
- Databases that support the ODBC (Open Database Connectivity) model (currently at 100+ vendors and counting)

To access the external data sources, Access uses one of the installable ISAM drivers. If you don't see all of these data sources in your list of drivers, it's possible that the "typical" option was selected when Access 95 was installed on your computer. Some drivers available to Access 95 are not included in a "typical" installation. If you need the driver for a data source that isn't in your list, run the Access 95 Setup again, and choose the Add/Remove option. (You need the disks or the CD-ROM for this.) The Data Access check box is where you find the ISAM drivers, and you can then add them to your installation.

Linking versus Embedding

Depending on how much centralized control over documents and data you need in your shop, you may choose to either embed or link. To embed data within Access, and then to remove the original source document from common access is to force everyone to come to one central store for the data, and to ensure one point of data entry and modification. To embed data within Access, and then not remove the original data source risks unsynchronized data.

To link data sources to Access may be the more flexible scheme. Although it allows multiple points of data entry and modification, any view of the data—taken from either the native application or from Access—shows the same set of values. In addition, Access stores information locally about the linked tables, and the connections to them.

To link to a document or data source, the source must be on your computer, or else you must have network access to the computer on which the data source is located. Also, you must have the appropriate permissions to access the file in question.

ODBC: Open Database Connectivity

The ODBC model was developed by the SQL Access Group, which is a consortium of most of the major database software and hardware vendors in the database market. ODBC is a connectivity API (application programming interface) that was developed as a vendor-independent scheme for allowing different databases to talk to one another. ODBC allows applications to access multiple different databases ("heterogeneous data access"). Although ODBC is generally associated with Microsoft and although Microsoft worked hard to get the concept of ODBC universally adopted, it isn't a Microsoft specification.

Perhaps the impression that ODBC "belongs" to Microsoft arose from Microsoft's strong commitment, in the face of competing standards, to ODBC. Many of the major database vendors support other connectivity standards at the same time as they write and distribute their ODBC drivers. Almost every major database vendor has now written to the ODBC standard, and the list of available drivers runs into the hundreds. ODBC also shows up in applications other than databases. Microsoft Word uses ODBC to perform mail merges, and Microsoft Query (which comes with Excel) is designed to interface with ODBC data sources.

The ODBC Standard

The ODBC standard consists of the following three components:

- **Application**—The application calls the ODBC functions that send SQL statements and retrieve the results.
- **Driver**—A DLL (Dynamic Link Library) that processes ODBC calls, directs the SQL statements to the correct database, and returns the results to the

application. The driver translates the SQL request into the correct flavor of the SQL language for the target database.

■ **Driver manager**—This manager loads drivers as needed by an application.

The idea behind ODBC is that a SQL query written in the syntax of the client database management system can be translated and passed to the server database management system without the writer knowing the server language syntax. ODBC has made all the difference in application portability. If the server database management system changes, in theory you need only the ODBC driver for the new server, and the queries should still run just as they did before. In practice, this scheme works reasonably well.

For this reason, be careful that you don't limit yourself to the functionality available only in your client environment. The server database management system may provide valuable features and services that you can use, if you know about them. Become familiar with the capabilities of the server database management system so that you can use it most efficiently.

On the other hand, there may be functionality available in your client environment that cannot be supported by the back-end server. Some Access code cannot be handled via ODBC because no equivalents exist in other database management systems. You cannot send nested transactions via ODBC, for example, because most back-end servers do not support nested transactions. You can write a SQL union statement in Access 95 that appends two dissimilar recordsets, a situation that isn't supported by any other database management system. When you encounter a situation that cannot be handled with ODBC, there are alternatives, which we cover in a following section of this chapter.

Setting Up an ODBC Connection

In order to connect to an ODBC data source from your client system, you first must add the data source to the list of available sources. In the following example, we connect to a SQL Server database:

1. Open Control Panel, and then click on the 32-bit ODBC icon, as shown in figure 10.4.

> **Note**
>
> If you installed Windows 95 over a previous version of Windows or Windows for Workgroups, you may see two ODBC icons. The version you want to use here is labeled 32bit ODBC. The other is just labeled ODBC. If you do not see the icon, most likely the ODBC option wasn't selected when Access 95 was installed. Run the Access 95 Setup again to install this option. Using the Add/Remove Components feature in Setup allows you to modify the existing installation.

Fig. 10.4

The 32bit ODBC icon and the (16-bit) ODBC icon both will be in the Control Panel program group, if you install Windows 95 over an existing version of Windows.

The 32bit ODBC icon

2. Select the System DSN button from the Data Sources dialog box. The System Data Sources dialog box opens (see fig. 10.5). If you have no other data sources defined, the dialog box is empty.

Fig. 10.5

The Data Sources Dialog box, showing the available ODBC data sources (and corresponding drivers).

3. Select Add. The Add Data Source Dialog box opens, showing a list of the installed ODBC drivers (see fig. 10.6).

Fig. 10.6

The Add Data Source dialog box, from which you can add a new ODBC driver.

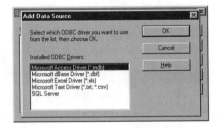

4. Select SQL Server and click OK.
5. In the ODBC SQL Server Setup dialog box shown in figure 10.7, add the following information:

Data Source name:	**PUBS**
Description:	**Publishers database**
Server:	*The name of your server*

Network Address: *The address on the network for the server database*

Network Library: *The name of the SQL Server Net-Library DLL*

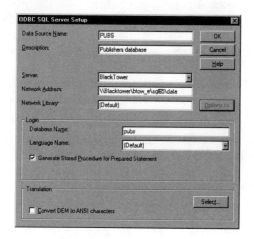

Fig. 10.7

Adding SQL Server as an ODBC source through the ODBC SQL Server Setup dialog box.

The preceding example uses the PUBS database, the sample database included with Microsoft SQL Server. Usually, you can leave the Network Address and the Network Library Address as (Default) when running SQL Server. If you have a copy of SQL Server on your computer, you can enter **local** rather than a server name. The assumption here is that you are developing on a Windows NT Server platform, not just on Windows 95, and that you can start a SQL Server session and an Access 95 session at the same time.

To connect to a server database other than Microsoft SQL Server, you need to install the ODBC driver on your computer according to the instructions provided by the software manufacturer. After the driver is installed, you can follow the preceding procedure to establish an ODBC connection to the other server database.

Connecting to the Server

Now, consider how Access 95 makes connections to a server database. The possible connection methods are the following:

- Link to the server tables
- Access the server directly, using Visual Basic for Applications code
- Use pass-through queries to run SQL statements on the server and return the results

Each approach has benefits, and each implies certain system requirements. The following sections look at each approach.

Linking to the Server Tables

Linking to server tables is the most commonly used method, is usually the most efficient, and—if you have used Access for development before—is the most familiar technique of the three. After you link the tables, they look and act just like Access tables. They show up in the database window, although the icon for a linked table differs from the icon for a local table. Access automatically makes the connection to the server when you open a linked table, or when the user opens a form or fires off a report that uses data from a linked table. If you want, you can open a linked table, just like a local table, in your Visual Basic code by using the **OpenRecordset** method.

To link to a table, you must have network access to the node on which the server database management system is located. You must have the necessary permissions from the network operating system to establish a network connection to this server. You must have permission to access tables on the server database. This permission is granted by using the security features of the remote database.

The biggest problem with linked tables, as we pointed out previously, is that Access 95 stores the paths to the tables and looks for the linked tables in the same place every time. If the tables are moved, you have to provide a mechanism for the connection to be reestablished.

> **Tip**
>
> If you are using Windows 95, Windows NT, or Windows for Workgroups, set up the connections to shared disk drives so that the connection is restored on startup. This change causes the shared remote disk to use the same local drive letter every time the computer boots up, so that Access 95 can more easily find the database tables.

Access keeps within itself a local copy of the field and index information for each linked table. This makes for faster response when you open a table, and significantly reduces network traffic. However, it also means that you must drop and relink any attached tables when you change the field definitions or the indices to keep the information synchronized. You will do this many times during prototype or rapid application development.

You can open linked tables in Design mode, although when you do you see a warning screen, telling you that these tables are linked and only certain properties are modifiable. In fact, the only properties that you *can* modify relate to how the data is formatted in the Access application. Properties that affect how the data is stored (data type and length, index type) are off-limits to modification from a linked database. You shouldn't try to duplicate the changes that you might make to a server table from an attached Access session; keep the two synchronized by dropping and relinking the server table.

The server database may (and probably will) have its own password, one that differs from your Access 95 password. Rather than requiring the user to type the password every time a connection is made, Access 95 can store the password locally, and pass it to the server as required. If this situation is acceptable in your shop—if you are not C-2 compliant—then obviously, you should have security turned on in Access, as we discuss in Chapter 12, "Securing the Access 95 Application."

If caching the password isn't an allowed option under your company's security policy, caching can be turned off. For an explanation of how to turn off caching, see Chapter 19, "System Administration." All security added in the client application will function in addition to security at the server end, which is set up according to the server security model.

With no type of security logon or password in the Access 95 application or environment, anyone who can get in to Access on a user's desk can slip through, into the server database.

Linking with ODBC

The following exercise assumes that you have a copy of Microsoft SQL Server available and that you have a logon already established to the SQL Server database named PUBS.

To see how a server database is linked in Access 95, open a new blank database, and name it **PUBS95**. You will connect from this database to the Microsoft SQL Server PUBS database.

1. Use the File, Get External Data, Link Tables menu item to open the Link Dialog box.

2. In the Link Dialog box, for Files Of Type, select ODBC databases from the list. This selection takes you to the SQL Data Sources Dialog box.

3. In the SQL Data Sources Dialog box, select PUBS (see fig. 10.8).

Fig. 10.8

The SQL Data Sources dialog box, with the PUBS database selected.

4. At the SQL Server Login screen, type your password (see fig. 10.9). This allows you to attach to the server tables (see fig. 10.10).

III

Building the Application

Fig. 10.9

The SQL Server Login dialog box, which appears when you first connect to a SQL Server data source.

Fig. 10.10

Attaching to the SQL server tables: the list of available tables from Pubs database, ready to be selected and linked to the Access client.

Linking SQL Views

Most SQL databases allow you to create *views*. You can link to server views from Access in exactly the same way as you link to a table. Access "sees" a view in the same way it "sees" a table, except that the view is a linked table with no indexes—so Access cannot store the index information locally. This is a problem only when you try to update the view (view updateability is specific to the relational philosophy supported by each specific server database management system). The solution is to create in Access an index specification on the linked view. Make the index the column or columns whose values uniquely define each row of the view. Access then can use this local index to build a *dynaset* (effectively, an updateable view) that can be used in your Access forms and reports. We discuss dynasets in more detail throughout this chapter and specifically in the section, "Limiting Dynasets."

When connecting to a Microsoft SQL Server database, you do not have to manually create indexes for linked views. During the process of linking, if you included a view in the list, Access 95 requests that you designate a column or columns to serve as a "unique record identifier"—a primary key in Access terms, and from this primary key it automatically constructs a unique index. However, because you have no chance to study the data in the view to determine the best candidate(s) for primary key, you can do one of two things. You can decline to select a unique record identifier and just press the OK button; if so, this linked view will be non-updateable. Or, you can make your best guess at a primary key candidate and later on, after you have a chance to review the data in the linked view, you can drop and relink, with a more plausible primary key.

Access 95 behaves in this way because of the inherent difference in the philosophy of views between Access and other database management systems. As you already may have noticed, Access doesn't have an object named a "view"—rather, it has queries that result in updateable dynasets. A truly relational "view" is updateable if and only if the view contains the primary key of the underlying table on which it is built. Therefore, not all views are updateable. Access 95 needs a way to manage linked data locally if it's going to be updated, and it does this through the indexing scheme, which is driven by a designated primary key.

When linking views from a server database, it's a good idea to check with the server database administrator or systems administrator to ensure that the view, as originally defined in the server environment, was meant to be updateable.

From Chapter 4, "Getting By in SQL '92—Structured Query Language," the following syntax shows how to create a unique index:

```
CREATE UNIQUE INDEX IndexName ON ViewName (ColumnName[, ColumnName, ...])
```

To delete an index, use the following syntax:

```
DROP INDEX IndexName
```

In Access, you can build the index By creating a data definition query by taking the following steps:

1. Open the Access database that contains the data tables. You cannot create an index on attached Access tables.

2. Start a new query without using a Wizard, open in Design View, do not select any tables.

3. From the top menu (see fig. 10.11), select Query, SQL Specific, Data Definition, which will cause the SQL Data Definition Query window to open.

4. Type the **create unique index** query described previously into the code window.

5. Run the query.

Fig. 10.11

Setting up to build an index by using a Data Definition Query.

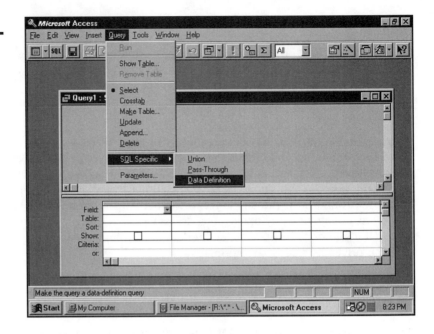

Accessing the Server Directly

To access a server directly, you can write Visual Basic code, employing the OpenDatabase method, and supplying an ODBC connection string. You can open a dynaset or retrieve a snapshot. You should be aware that this direct access method is far less efficient than using linked tables. We mentioned previously that when you link tables, the Jet database engine makes local copies of information about the linked tables. It knows which server the tables are on, and it has the field and index information available. If you access the remote tables directly, Access has to request this information from the server for each time a query is run.

Direct server access is probably best reserved for Visual Basic 4.0 applications, where tight control of the data is required, and end-user flexibility is neither required nor desirable. If you are using Access 95 to construct your client application, linking to the tables is the preferred method. If you do choose to use direct access, you still will need all previously mentioned network and server authorizations, just as if you were linking to the server table.

Using Pass-Through Queries

When you build a query in Access, it compiles and runs the query against the table or tables specified, whether they are local, remote, or a combination of the two. Some or most of the work load is handled by the Jet database engine on the client machine. In contrast, when you write a pass-through query, Access sends the query directly to the server without compiling it. The query is written in the server dialect of SQL, and may contain non-standard SQL extensions that Access cannot understand. Any attempt to compile this kind of a query locally will result in an error from the Access compiler, even though the query is perfectly legal on the server. The version of the SQL language on your server may use different syntax or semantics than Access SQL, with single versus double quote conventions being different, and differing uses of wild-card characters being just the beginning. It is the responsibility of the database programmer to know the various flavors of SQL for which s(he) is writing.

Because no compilation occurs at the client, you can use the power of the server, including stored procedures and intrinsic functions that don't even exist in Access SQL, and cannot be coded by using the code available within Access 95. You can code data definition, security and authentication, and server administration commands into pass-through queries.

You cannot assume that, just because a query runs in Access, it will run anywhere else. It may work if you are using ODBC connections, because the point of ODBC is that it translates queries into the SQL version of the target server database. But other database management systems will not support the user-defined functions that you may have built into Access, nor generally can you prompt the user for an input parameter at run time, like you can in Access.

Although using linked tables usually is the most efficient approach in this heterogeneous environment, situations exist where a pass-through action query can be faster than action queries acting on remote tables. Bulk load operations and multiple record deletes are examples where the pass-through query will run faster and should be considered when you have a large number of records to update. Running a pass-through query is faster than directly accessing the tables, and is the optimal solution for operational databases that are under heavy transaction processing load. Like the direct access method, pass-through queries do not use locally stored field and index information. Because the query is processed entirely on the server, this isn't a disadvantage for the pass-though query. There would be no benefit in having locally stored copies of the field and index information for server tables.

The biggest restriction with pass-through queries is that they return snapshots, which cannot be updated. Not only can the user not make updates, but updates made by other users will not show up until the query is run again to obtain a fresh copy of the data. A regular Access query returns an updateable dynaset, and changes made by other users show up at the specified refresh intervals.

To create a pass-through query, take these steps:

1. Create a new query by using the Design View option, but select no tables.
2. Under the Query menu, select the type of query that corresponds to the stored procedure.
3. Under the Query menu, select the SQL-Specific option, then Pass-Through.
4. Specify the ODBC connection string, the Returns Records option, Log Messages, and ODBC Timeout values (see fig. 10.12).
5. Save the query.

III

Building the Application

Fig. 10.12

Setting the ODBC properties for a pass-through query.

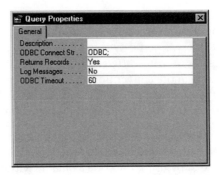

Stored Procedures

Access 95 defines a *stored procedure* as, "One or more SQL statements that can accept user-declared variables, conditional execution, and other control-flow statements, and that reside on a server." Think of stored procedures as subroutines that you can call from within a pass-through query. The stored procedure is already compiled and optimized on the server, which means that it executes at high speed. Network traffic is reduced because you only send to the server the name of the stored procedure, not the code for the entire procedure. Also, when the stored procedure resides on the server, it can be called from different client applications, with the assurance that it returns the same results each time.

Some database management systems limit your access to only the use of stored procedures, and do not allow you to directly link to, or otherwise access, the tables. Any data retrieval or update must be carried out through a stored procedure; this means that if no stored procedure exists to do what you need, you have to build one—assuming that you have permission to do so on the server—or have one built to your specifications. If the server isn't under your control, and you are just building the client application, then you either have to figure out a different way to get the data or request that a stored procedure be written to do what you need. For obvious reasons, restricting database access to a list of stored procedures is appealing to environments where centralized (and tight) control of the data and the layout of the database is of utmost importance.

You can use stored procedures to bypass the problem of trying to modify a non-updateable snapshot of the data that is returned by a pass-through query. You have to collect input from the user on the client system, and then run a pass-through query that feeds the input data to the server, calling a stored procedure to update the correct records on the server. This method requires a local table in which to store your records at the client end before they are updated on the server. Use code behind the OnUpdate and OnInsert properties of the form to run the stored procedures to modify or add records to the server database, or create a command button that allows direct posting of the records to the server.

Using Resources Wisely

There are several reasons why you should tailor the data returned from the server to the exact requirements of the application, and of the end user. Network traffic is obviously one of the main considerations. Making your application appear responsive to the user is another. Security may be a factor: if the client application only retrieves the data fields that a user needs, it is less likely that they will find a way to look at data for which they are not authorized.

Optimizing Connections

Every time that you make a connection between the client and the server, you are using resources at both the client and the server ends of the connection. Obviously, if you can limit the number of connections, you can reduce the demands on the system resources. You can use several techniques to limit connections, which improves the overall system performance. The following sections describe these techniques.

Before trying to limit connections, however, you must determine how your server will handle these connections. Some servers use connections that are resource-efficient, but that can process only one query at a time. Microsoft's SQL Server is an example of this kind of server. Other servers offer more advanced connections that can handle several partially completed queries simultaneously. In this case don't worry about connections; Access 95 uses one connection to the server and allows multiple queries across this connection. If, however, you are limited by the server to one query per connection, you need to figure out how to keep the number of connections to a minimum.

Limiting Dynasets. The Access 95 Help system offers this definition: a *dynaset-type Recordset object* is a dynamic set of records that can contain fields from one or more tables or queries in a database and may be updateable. The Recordset object represents the records in a base table or the records that result from running a query.

A dynaset that contains 100 or fewer records uses only one connection to the server. But when the dynaset grows to more than 100 records, it needs two connections—one connection is used to return the key values from the server, and the other is used to fetch the data for the records currently visible on-screen. The second connection is available for other dynasets to use when retrieving data, but the first connection is held for the exclusive use of the dynaset in returning key values. The connections aren't released until either all the key values are returned or the dynaset is closed by the application. If you design data retrieval so that the queries ask only for a few records, the number of connections are minimized.

You also can keep to a minimum the number of connections by closing connections that are no longer needed by your client application. The recommended way to do so is to place this line in the Open event procedure of a form based on the recordset:

```
Me.RecordSetClone.MoveLast
```

For another recommended way to minimize the number of connections, you can use the TOP 100 PERCENT query (if your server database supports this query—not many do!) to ensure that all the records have been returned. However, either of these two approaches results in the form opening more slowly, so they are not a good idea when you are dealing with very large recordsets.

Using Local Reference Tables. We previously mentioned that you should keep small reference tables on the client computer—obviously, retrieval performance is better. Every time a form must go to the server to fill a combo box or a list box, it requires another connection to the server, and more network traffic.

Using Fewer Server Reference Tables. At times, you really don't need to use a combo box or a list box with a reference table. Each combo or list box means more overhead, and not just for the network connections that we are discussing. Each combo or list box is effectively another window on-screen, which takes more management and more resources from the client computer to display. The form loads faster and runs better if you keep the combo and list boxes to a minimum. For example, it's easy to put in a reference list for state codes. However, what if your application is designed to allow a house-cleaning service to schedule its employees. How often do these employees cross state lines? In how many states do they really work? Two? Perhaps a 50-state lookup table is overkill for this situation. Do you even need a state field, or can you hard code it on forms and reports?

Establishing Timeouts. If your users often start an application, and then leave it standing idle while they do other work, you may want to close their connections to the server. They may have used the capability of Windows 95 to switch to another task, with your application minimized in the background. The connections are restored when they perform an action that requires a connection to the server.

By default, the time-out is set to 10 minutes (actually, it's set to 600 seconds). No convenient way exists to change this setting, other than to edit the Windows 95 Registry on each client computer. Unless you are both the system administrator and the database developer, you may not be allowed to modify the Win95 Registry. In theory (that is, according to the Access 95 manual), the setting is in the following folder in the Registry:

\Microsoft\Access\7.0\Jet\3.0\Engines\ODBC

If you start up the Registry editor, you find this entry under \MyComputer\ HKEY_LOCAL_MACHINE\SOFTWARE\. If you are not familiar with the Registry, stay out of it—you could do some serious damage!

Changing the ODBC Refresh Interval

A more reasonable value to change—one that is more accessible to you as a developer—is the ODBC refresh interval. In the database, use the menu item Tools, Options, click the Advanced tab to set the ODBC Refresh Interval. This is the default interval at which Access refreshes records that are being accessed by using ODBC. The default is 1,500 seconds, or 25 minutes, but you can change this number to anywhere from 1 to 3,600 seconds. A very low value ensures that changes made in any place on the database are shown throughout the network almost immediately, at the expense of high network traffic. A large value ensures that a timed out connection stays timed out, but also slows down the frequency at which updates to records are propagated throughout the system. A small value ensures that all changes to the data are visible to the other users almost immediately, but again, the trade-off is an increase in the network traffic. If your users mainly browse data that doesn't change frequently, a longer refresh interval may be appropriate. In a situation with heavy transaction processing, you may want to shorten the refresh interval and accept the extra load on the network.

Bringing Back Only What You Need

When you build a query, you may be in the habit of selecting all fields (*) from each of the tables, rather than choosing individual fields on an as-needed basis. Then, while you are designing a form or report, you can select the fields that you need and ignore fields that you don't need. If you need to modify the form at a later date—for example, to add an additional field or two—under this technique, that field will already be in the query, so you just drag it onto the form.

> **Tip**
>
> There is some thought that a query may run faster (although the jury is still out on this one) if the select statement contains the all-fields indicator (*) rather than if the Jet has to parse a long list of fields in the select statement. However, "faster" may just mean a quicker response in sending off the query—not necessarily in returning the data, which is what really counts.
>
> The (*) technique is probably not any faster in a networked environment because:
>
> - Queries are precompiled and optimized by Access, so it's not necessary to parse the query every time it runs.
> - Bringing back extra, unnecessary fields means additional network traffic, more I/O on the server, and overall, slower response times.

Hiding Fields Until Needed. Be especially careful about bringing back memo and OLE object fields that you don't need because they can take a large chunk of the network resources and will make the application appear slow to respond. You can use several techniques to "hide" these fields, but still make them readily available to the user.

- Move the little-used fields to a secondary form. On the main form, place a control that pops up the second form when the user needs to see the additional fields. You can restrict the data on the secondary form to only the data that relates to the current record on the main form (the Form Wizard steps you through relating the primary and the secondary form). Suppose that you scanned each employee's ID picture into the Human Resources database. Does the picture need to show up every time the employee record is accessed, or only when someone needs to jog his or her memory about which employee is the subject of the record?

- Set to No the Visible property of the controls that are bound to OLE or memo fields. Then add a command button that changes the property to Yes. In the preceding example, you might have a "frame" for the employee picture, which actually is a large, transparent command button with a wide border. When the HR Director clicks inside the "frame," the photograph appears after a slight pause while the image data is being transferred across the network.

- Place Memo and OLE fields on a second page of the form, which usually is off the bottom of the screen. Add a command button to allow the user to scroll down to the second page. The information will not be retrieved until the user moves to the second page, and will not be retrieved at all if the user moves to the next record or the next form without looking at the second page of the form.

The above techniques rely on the fact that Access doesn't retrieve the data for OLE Object and Memo fields until the data is displayed on-screen. If the user never requests the data, it isn't brought across the network. If network traffic is kept at a reasonable level, the user doesn't notice the momentary delay in retrieving the data when it is needed.

Using Snapshots. You can specify that the data returned to the client is only a non-updateable snapshot rather than an updateable dynaset. As long as the user doesn't need to update the data—and as long as you have fewer than 50 records in the recordset—the form will open faster because retrieving the snapshot is faster. To perform this technique, set the form's AllowUpdating property to No Tables. If the recordset is large or contains memo or OLE objects, you should use the dynaset, which is more efficient because it doesn't retrieve these fields until they are needed.

Automatic Query Optimization

The Access Jet has two techniques that it uses to optimize data retrieval and to give the impression of extremely fast response—splitting the workload for a client/server query and pre-fetch retrieval.

Jet Engine Optimization

The local Jet engine allows processing of as much of a query as possible on the server because it reduces network traffic by restricting the number of records returned. In most cases, the server is a more powerful computer than the client; therefore, it makes sense to use this processing power. Routine select, update, append, and delete queries can be passed to the server for processing. However, some queries cannot be handled in this way. They include the following:

- **Heterogeneous joins from multiple data sources**. The join must be performed locally because the query cannot be split across the data sources.

■ **SQL constructs that do not translate to the server DBMS**. Examples include TOP *n* or TOP *m* PERCENT queries.

The Jet attempts to split queries into components that can be handed off to the server and components that must be run locally.

Background Population

Access has a neat trick to help an application offer faster response. When you open an attached ODBC table in a datasheet view, it looks like all the data is present. Actually, Access retrieves a group of rows to fill in the visible part of the datasheet. Then, it continues to retrieve rows at intervals (100 rows every 10 seconds is the default) and dumps them into memory (*read-ahead buffers*, also known as *pre-fetch* in other database environments). Rows are retrieved even faster if the end user scrolls around the data set or if idle time is available on the computer. When the client computer runs out of memory, the data overflows into a temporary file. The location of this file is set by the TEMP variable when the client computer is started. The net result is that the query appears to have completed when records are still being transferred. Using this trick makes more sense than making the user wait until all of the data is returned. Background population is not available for Recordset objects created with Visual Basic code.

From Here...

In this chapter, we covered the programming model that Access uses, what it is, and how it works. We discussed data import and data export, and how to link to external (non-database) files. We discussed ODBC, and then we connected to an ODBC data source (the Pubs database supplied with Microsoft SQL Server). We discussed pass-through SQL queries and stored procedures and how they can impact your application. We talked about optimizing queries, optimizing connections to the server, and optimizing placement of reference tables, either on the client or on the server.

From here, jump to the following chapters to find out more about the following:

■ Chapter 11, "Managing Transactions," gives more information about transactions.

■ Chapter 12, "Securing the Access 95 Application," teaches how to secure your Access 95 application.

■ Chapter 17, "Transitioning to Another Back-End DBMS," discusses server database management systems.

■ Chapter 19, "System Administration," covers more on system administration.

■ Chapter 21, "Client/Server Performance and Tuning," discusses performance and tuning in a client/server environment.

III

Building the Application

CHAPTER 11

Managing Transactions

Transaction management is (or should be) built into every database management system. Transaction management is sometimes confused with its close cousin, *concurrency control*, which we also cover in this chapter.

The basic concept of transaction management is to ensure that a *transaction* completes entirely or not at all. *Concurrency*, on the other hand, is the assurance that two or more people will have access to the same data at the same time, without risking the integrity of the data or the business transaction.

In this chapter, we cover the following subjects:

- Transactions: what are they?
- The differing states of a transaction.
- Transaction recovery schemes and how Access 95 handles transaction management.
- Heuristics on how to size a transaction.
- Concurrency: what is it?
- Concurrency control and the three major categories of concurrency violation.
- Optimistic and pessimistic locking schemes.
- Locking through bound forms, by using macros or by writing Visual Basic code.

Understanding Transactions

A *transaction* is defined as a logical unit of work, a set of statements or commands that either succeed or fail as a group. There are at least two distinct viewpoints that define this logical unit of work. One view, which is intuitive from the end users' perspective, is the *business transaction*. The second view is the database or system transaction.

A typical business transaction may resemble Listing 11.1 (coded in interactive SQL, for demo purposes only):

Listing 11.1 11codeD1—Demo Code to Illustrate a Typical Transaction

```
/* confirm that requester has a valid checking account */
select CheckingAccountStatus
        from CheckingAccount
        where CustomerName like 'Joe Sixpack';

 /* confirm that requester has large enough balance in savings
    ➥account to cover transfer of funds */
select SavingAccountBalance
        from SavingAccount
        where CustomerName like 'Joe Sixpack';

/* credit checking account by the transfer amount requested */
update CheckingAccount
        set CheckingAccountBalance = CheckingAccountBalance + $1000
        where CustomerName like 'Joe Sixpack';

/* debit savings account by the transfer amount requested */
update SavingAccount
        set SavingAccountBalance = SavingAccountBalance - $1000
        where CustomerName like 'Joe Sixpack';
```

This business transaction is composed of five database transactions: two read operations, two update operations, and one commit operation. In any transaction processing system—which by definition, operational databases are—there must be some provision for "*transaction atomicity*," an all-or-nothing operation. In *business transaction atomicity*, if some of the updates are executed and the system goes down before all updates are completed (signaled by the SQL **commit** statement), all updates must be either undone or canceled.

To tell the database to treat these five transactions as a single unit, you designate in code the beginning and the end of the transaction. Some SQL environments have a proprietary **begin trans** statement to mark the beginning of a business transaction. Other database management systems simply infer the beginning of a transaction when the user issues a statement that would modify the database, and has no other transaction active at the time. The transaction is ended with a **commit** or **commit work** statement to save the changes, or a **rollback** statement to reject them.

At any given moment in a transaction processing environment, some updates from a single business transaction will already be written to the hard disk, some will reside in memory, and some will be in both places. Should the system crash or otherwise abnormally terminate operations, one of the following two things must happen:

- If the transaction executed some but not all of its updates and did not issue the **commit** statement, upon system restart all updates—even updates already written to the physical database—must be undone or rolled back.

- If the transaction executed all updates and did issue the **commit** statement, but for reasons not yet discussed, the modifications were not yet written to the database, upon system restart, all updates will be redone or posted to the physical database.

In a multiuser environment with multiple business transactions executing, the confusion about which update was where when the system failed can be overwhelming. Therefore, these rules of transaction management must be established and faithfully adhered to by the database management system.

Single system failure is a fact of life. It must be both expected and planned for. There are ways, by integrating into a transaction processing system certain levels of redundancy, to alleviate downtime that results from system failure. See Chapter 19, "System Administration," for a discussion on fail-safe environments.

System failure can result from the following sources:

- **Logical errors**—When a system fails due to this source, a transaction fails because of some internal condition, such as bad data, data not found, or resource limit (hard disk capacity, memory) exceeded.

- **System errors**—The operating system or environment is in an undesirable state, such as deadlock.

- **Computer failure**—Here, hardware failure resulting in loss of volatile storage (memory) is called a soft crash.

- **Disk failure**—In this case, hardware failure resulting in loss of stored data (hard disk) is called a hard crash.

States of a Transaction

The *transaction model* can be written in algorithmic form, and it can be portrayed graphically, but in either case the following conditions must be true:

- If the database was in a state of consistency before the transaction began, it must be in a state of consistency when the transaction is ended.

- If a transaction contains a set of updates, then at some time during the transaction the database will be in a state of inconsistency.

- It is the responsibility of the programmer to define (business) transactions properly, so that each (business) transaction preserves the consistency of the database.

The transaction model can be algorithmically demonstrated, as shown in Listing 11.2 (another demo code block).

Listing 11.2 11codeD2—The Algorithm That Describes the Transaction Model Spoken of in the Accompanying Text

```
T1:     read A(a1, a2, ..., an)
        a1 = a1 - x;
        write A(a1, a2, ..., an);
        read B(b1, b2, ..., bn);
        b1 = b1 + x;
        write B(b1, b2, ..., bn);
```

The *transaction state diagram* in figure 11.1 graphically demonstrates the different states of a transaction. A transaction can be in one of five states: active, partially committed, failed, aborted, or committed.

Fig. 11.1

The transaction state diagram, which shows the five different states of a transaction.

Transaction State Diagram

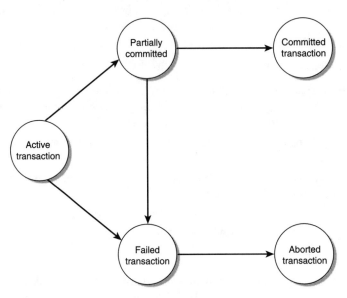

An *active transaction* is in the process of reading and updating data.

A *partially committed transaction* has executed all statements but has not yet issued the **commit**. This transaction can either succeed or fail.

A *failed transaction* has discovered that normal execution can no longer proceed. Failure can be caused by any of the reasons listed previously in this section.

An *aborted transaction* is a transaction that was rolled back. The database was restored to the stable state prior to the beginning of this transaction.

A *committed transaction* has successfully executed the **commit** statement.

Regardless of how you visualize a transaction, a transaction must be both correct and atomic. To be correct, each transaction must contain program code that preserves database consistency, which is the responsibility of the database programmer. To be atomic, all operations associated with a transaction must execute either completely or not at all, which is the responsibility of the database management system.

There is an *ACID test* for transactions. For a transaction to be sound, the following conditions must be true:

A   **Atomic**. A transaction either commits or aborts.

C   **Consistent**. A transaction must be a correct transformation of the system state. A transaction can neither violate system requirements (failure to update all pointers in a bidirectional linked list, for example), nor can it violate business requirements (failure to debit the savings account after crediting the checking account).

I   **Isolated**. A transaction must be isolated from the updates of other transactions, that is, it must be *serializable*.

D   **Durable**. The effects of a transaction—once committed to the database—will persist even beyond a system failure.

The decision to commit/rollback should always be made as soon as possible, such as if all SQL operations that are part of a given transaction are successful, the commit should follow immediately.

Transaction Recovery Schemes

There are multiple *transaction recovery schemes* that handle protecting the integrity of the data in the case of a failed transaction, the most popular of which is the *log-based scheme*. The log-based scheme is most often found as part of a server database management system, such as Microsoft SQL Server.

The essential element of the log-based recovery scheme is a transaction or *protection log file*, which should be established on a hard drive, separate from the drive(s) on which the database resides. Each time a record on the database is modified, an entry is made on the *transaction log*. The entry consists of a *transaction identifier*, an image of the record before update, and a corresponding image of the record after update. When a transaction is completed, a *commit record* that contains the transaction identifier also is written to the transaction log.

Transactions are initially buffered in memory. Then, before they are written to the hard disk, transactions are first written to the transaction log. After the write-to-log operation is complete, they are written to the physical database or, if the database has synchronous write capability, the transaction updates can be written to both transaction log and database simultaneously. This log-based scheme offers multiple insurance of transaction atomicity:

- If the database comes down before the buffered transaction begins its write to the transaction log, upon database restart it will be as though that transaction never happened (transaction in *volatile storage*—memory—is lost).

- If the database comes down before the buffered transaction is completely written to the transaction log, upon database restart that transaction will be rolled back (no commit record is found).

- If the database comes down during the write to the physical database, and the write to the transaction log was completed (including commit record), upon database restart the transaction updates will be reposted to the physical database.

III

Building the Application

How Access 95 Handles Transactions

Access 95 buffers transaction updates in memory until they are committed. No accommodation is made for transaction logging in the pure Access environment. The "window of opportunity" for atomicity failure is small, but it's still present.

Take the example of a transaction that encompasses 12 updates to three tables in an Access server database. For the sake of argument, suppose that these three tables have a one-to-many-to-many relationship; therefore, the 12 updates in this single transaction involve related data. A fault during the transaction process would compromise the business integrity of the data.

If the transaction is in progress—is an "active transaction" in the transaction state diagram—with some updates completed and others not, and Access 95 goes down, you have a condition of *atomicity retention*. The updates are being cached in memory and wouldn't be written to disk until the transaction has committed. When Access goes down, then everything in memory is lost, including the partially completed transaction. When Access comes up again, the end user has the opportunity to start the transaction again, from the beginning, with no compromise of the integrity of the database.

The problem, and "the window of opportunity," happens when Access 95 goes down following the commit, during the few milliseconds it takes to flush the updates from memory to disk. Access 95 single-threads updates to the database, thereby serializing the process, updating one page (block) of database records at a time. The chances of 12 updates to records located on three tables existing on a single page of the database is extremely slim. A more normal condition would be a minimum of three pages involved in the write operation, and possibly more. Should Access come down during the midst of the write, it's quite possible to have one or two tables updated (partially or completely), and not the third. End result—incomplete transaction, loss of transaction atomicity, and the end user facing a manual correction to the interrupted transaction.

> **Caution**
>
> If the preceding scenario is a situation that your applications and database environment cannot tolerate, then you want to seriously consider replacing the Access server portion of your database with a server database management system that supports some form of transaction management and protection.

Wrap a business transaction in code to indicate to the Access engine to treat this group of data manipulation statements as a single database transaction. The Visual Basic code to signal the start of a transaction is **BeginTrans**. In the same manner, at the end of the data manipulation statements, insert the Visual Basic statement **CommitTrans**.

A typical *batch update transaction* from locally collected data that can be periodically uploaded or "posted" to server may look like Listing 11.3 (which you can find on this book's companion CD-ROM, as 11code01.txt).

Listing 11.3 11code01.txt—Post Locally Collected Data to the Server

```
Private Sub cmdPost_Click()
'.................................................................
'  attach this code to a command button on the data entry form
'  so the user can post locally collected updates to the server
'.................................................................
Dim db as Database
Set db = CurrentDB()

On Error GoTo Err_cmdPost_Click

BeginTrans           '      begin the transaction
' copy data from the local tables into the remote tables,
' force a rollback on the server if an error occurs
' by using the dbFailOnError option
    db.Execute "insert into tblRemoteOrder select *
    ➥from tblLocalOrder", dbFailOnError
    db.Execute "insert into tblRemoteOrderDetails select *
    ➥from tblLocalOrderDetails",        dbFailOnError

' delete data in the local tables once copy is done
    db.Execute "delete from tblLocalOrder"
    db.Execute "delete from tblLocalOrderDetails"

    CommitTrans          '      commit the changes made
    Requery          '      refresh the data entry screen

Exit_cmdPost_Click:
    Exit Sub

Err_cmdPost_Click:
    MsgBox Error$
    Rollback
    Resume Exit_cmdPost_Click

End Sub
```

This code is meant to "batch" new records on orders and order details that were collected through a data entry form on the client and stored locally. When the data entry operator presses the command button, Post to the Server, this code executes. The code copies the locally stored orders and order details to the equivalent server tables. If the SQL statements are syntactically correct and if the user has the appropriate permissions, the **execute** method will not fail, not even if no update activity exists on the server. Therefore, always use the **dbFailOnError** option when using the **execute** method to run a modification query. This technique generates a trappable error and causes a rollback on all successful changes if any of the records affected are locked or cannot be modified, therefore retaining transaction atomicity.

III

Building the Application

Sizing Transactions

Calculating *transaction size* is as much an art as it is a science. In any computing environment, although—even beyond databases—there is an optimal size for each transaction, depending on the circumstances. The minimum size may be dictated by business rules (you cannot have a credit to one account without a corresponding debit to an associated account). This policy limits the minimum size of a finance transaction to two writes, with possibly two or more corresponding reads.

The maximum size of a transaction may be dictated by more system-oriented criteria, such as system stability, ability to sustain *cascading rollbacks*, size of page file, and so on. The rule, if there is such a thing, is to make the transaction large enough to be cost-effective (each **commit** statement results in a write to the protection log or to the hard disk), but not so large that a **rollback** brings the system to a standstill.

For the Access 95 environment, because Access buffers transactions in memory until commit, too small a transaction results in numerous writes to the server disk, possibly overloading the network. Too large a transaction results in resource contention on the client side, with Access 95 grabbing memory needed by other applications, or excessive use of the swap file in an effort to extend virtual memory.

In an *OLTP* (*online transaction processing*) system that uses transaction logging, database modifications are buffered until one of two things happen—a block of memory is filled or a commit is issued by a transaction, at which time the write to the transaction log will happen. In the Windows NT environment, you're looking at a block size of 4K. To ensure safe commitment of the transaction in a single write to disk, the authors suggest that you never create a transaction that will exceed the block size less 10 percent. Likewise, to prevent writes to the transaction log that contain less than a full block of data, the authors suggest that you try to create transactions that contain multiple updates to the data before you issue the commit statement.

When calculating how many records to include in such a transaction, you need to determine the record length in bytes and the operation involved. Calculate the record length by summing the length in bytes of each field in the record (refer to the specific database management system user's guide for data types and lengths). For each insert operation, there will be only an after-image of the record; for each delete operation, there will be only a before-image; and for each update operation, there will be both a before-image and an after-image. The absolute size of the transaction identifier in bytes can be found in the specific database environment documentation, but usually, 10 percent of the block size is enough to accommodate this overhead.

Concurrency Control

The first cousin to transaction management is *concurrency control*. Transaction management deals with one transaction at a time running against a database. Add multiple users, with each user trying to access the same set of data, and you will quickly need some rules and regulations to handle the conflicting requirements imposed on the database. Enter the concept of concurrency control.

There are three major categories of *concurrency violation* that exemplify the most common situations in a multiuser environment that isn't protected by strong concurrency control—the lost update, the uncommitted dependency, and the inconsistent analysis.

The Lost Update

The *lost update* is represented in figure 11.2. Two end users are updating the same record in inventory and, without some kind of concurrency protection in place, the second update overwrites the first, resulting in incorrect inventory information and one of the two customers getting a backorder notice.

The Lost Update

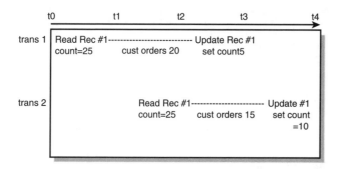

Fig. 11.2

The lost update, which illustrates how one update can be overwritten or, "lost," if no controls are in place to prevent such an occurrence.

The Uncommitted Dependency

The *uncommitted dependency* is an example of an out-of-control long transaction. Two end users are trying to fulfill customer orders for the same product. The first transaction has updated the inventory record, but for reasons unknown, this update is timed out or aborted, and rolled back. Meanwhile, the end user of the second transaction has had to try to appease a customer with backorders or alternate product selections.

The Uncommitted Dependency

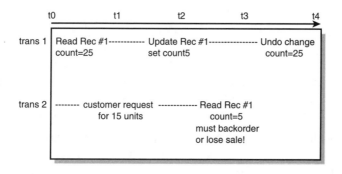

Fig. 11.3

The uncommitted dependency, which illustrates how inaccurate data can interrupt productivity in an uncontrolled update environment.

The Inconsistent Analysis

The *inconsistent analysis* is a typical situation that involves heavy transaction updating and attempts to do real-time statistical gathering (see fig. 11.4). This situation is analogous to the old saying "As soon as it's in print, it's obsolete." The first end user is attempting to gather statistics on inventory count (assumedly accurate), while the second end user is busy updating the inventory count. This situation may never be satisfactorily resolved and may require a realignment of management and end-user expectations.

Fig. 11.4

The inconsistent analysis, which illustrates one difficulty of trying to use a single data source for both update and decision support (statistics gathering).

The Inconsistent Analysis

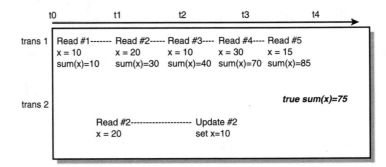

Locking Techniques

From the discussion in the previous section, you know that a transaction has to preserve database consistency. When a transaction is executed alone, it transfers the database from one consistent state to a new consistent state. However, when multiple transactions run concurrently, the consistency of the database can be compromised, even though each transaction on its own may be programmatically correct.

The database management system must be able to *schedule multiple transactions* so that the executing updates will maintain the consistency of the database. Most database management systems *serialize* the scheduling, that is, they execute the instructions from an entire transaction as an uninterrupted set.

One technique used to prevent these kinds of problems is locking. Initially, locking was a binary situation. If the lock was applied to a row, a page, a table, or the database by a transaction, then no other transaction could access the locked data. This *binary locking scheme* proved to be very restrictive, and *multi-mode locking schemes* quickly followed. Several different types of multi-mode locks are available, some of which are proprietary to specific vendors. The general types are described in the following list:

■ **No-lock**—Used for browse mode, where no update of the record(s) being browsed is intended. No-lock cannot be upgraded to an s-lock or x-lock without a reread of the record(s) involved.

■ **Shared** or **s-lock**—Used for read with intent to update, can be upgraded to an x-lock without a reread of the record if, and only if, no other transaction has an s-lock on the same record(s). All multiple transactions can hold s-locks on the same record at the same time.

- **Exclusive** or **x-lock**—Used for read plus update or update only. Only one transaction at a time can hold an x-lock on a record.

The *lock decision table* in figure 11.5 gives a graphic view of how these three different types of locks interact with each other. As demonstrated in the decision table, if transaction #1 has a record x-locked and is in the process of updating it, then transaction #2 can browse with no-lock (this condition is known as "dirty read"), but that's all it can do. It cannot read with s-lock nor read with x-lock until transaction #1 releases its x-lock on the record.

Multi-Mode Lock Decision Table

trans#1	trans#2 no-lock	s-lock	x-lock
no-lock	Y	Y	Y
s-lock	Y	Y	N
x-lock	Y	N	N

Fig. 11.5

The Multi-Mode Lock Decision Table, which demonstrates accessibility (no-lock or browse accessibility, shared-lock accessibility, or exclusive lock lack of accessibility) when two transactions try to access the same record at the same time.

An extremely expensive situation can happen in an environment that uses these locking schemes. It's known as *deadlock*, or the *deadly embrace*. Deadlock is demonstrated in figure 11.6. The figure shows two transactions, each reading a record with x-lock. Immediately after, each transaction requests (with x-lock) the record held by the other. As we can see from the multi-mode lock decision table, neither request can be honored. Both transactions end up waiting for each other until, by whatever scheme is in force, one of the transactions is rolled back while the other goes to completion.

The Deadlock Situation

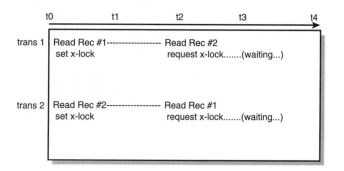

Fig. 11.6

Deadlock, which illustrates how two transactions that both are trying to access a record held by the other, can tie up each other in a deadly embrace.

III

Building the Application

As a group, the many different ways of applying locks are known as *lock-based proto-cols*. These lock-based protocols attempt to ensure *serializability of transactions* by determining the execution order of the transactions at run-time, when the first in-compatible lock mode is requested. This sets up a potential for a deadlock situation.

> **Note**
>
> There are other transaction-management schemes that use timestamps, the *timestamp-ordering protocol*. These schemes select an ordering among transactions in advance of execution, by applying timestamps during reads and during writes. These schemes have the advantage of ensuring serializability and preventing deadlock, although rollbacks of some transactions still can happen.

Different parts of the database can be locked, starting at the row level, progressing up to the page and table level, and finally to the database level. When talking about an Access 95 client/server application, the assumption is that no one other than a data-base administrator has the authority to open a database in exclusive mode, or x-lock at the database level. Use the Access 95 Security features, as explained in Chapter 12, "Securing the Access 95 Application," to ensure this condition.

Also, when Access 95 is accessing a non-Access server database, the server database handles all the locking—Access 95 usually will not perform any locking on ODBC databases. For this reason, you should always set the **RecordLocks** property of a form to No Locks or Edited Record—No Locks allow the server database the freedom to apply row or page locking (the technique most often used), and Edited Record is treated by the server as a No Lock situation. In the authors' opinion, Edited Record works best for all multiuser environments, whether they are pure Access 95 or non-Access back-end server databases. The following discussion on locking refers primarily to Access tables and to external linked tables under the control of the Microsoft Jet database engine.

Optimistic versus Pessimistic Locking

In an Access 95 environment you can control locking data either through bound forms (with macros), or with Visual Basic code. Also, to add more flexibility to your model, you can apply one of three types of locking schemes—optimistic, pessimistic, or full table.

Locking native tables in Access 95 can be performed in one of three ways: at the page level (the default), the full table(s) or query underlying a recordset, or the entire data-base. When the Jet database engine locks a record from an external non-Access-format database (dBASE, FoxPro, or Paradox), it locks the minimum amount (record, page, or file) that is lockable in the external database engine.

Locking through Bound Forms. Using bound forms is the easiest and most straight-forward way to develop multiuser applications and ensure concurrency integrity through locking. By binding the application forms to a table or query (Form, Design

View, Form properties, Data tab, Record Source), and setting the RecordLocks property to Edited Record (see figure 11.7), you can ensure that two users who try to update the same record do not overwrite each other's changes.

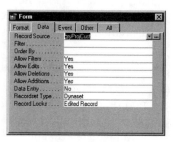

Fig. 11.7

Form frmProjCust, opened in Design View (Properties box, Data tab), showing the bound record source and the record locks set to Edited Record.

When you set RecordLocks to Edited Record, you are ensuring that, as soon as a user begins to edit any field in a record on-screen, this record and the page of the database on which the record resides are exclusively locked until the editing is finished, saved, and the user moves to the next record. Other users of the database can view the record being edited, but they can do nothing until the record is released. This scheme, known as *pessimistic locking*, ensures that only one person at a time can edit a record.

Pessimistic locking has both good and bad points. Because by default, bound forms lock at the page level, the edited record and all other records that live on that page are exclusively locked until the transaction that is performing the updating is committed or rolled back. In Access 95 the page size is 2K, or 2048 bytes, regardless of operating system. Depending on how long (how many bytes) each record is, there may be one or many records per page. If the environment is one of high-volume transactions, where records are quickly locked and unlocked, pessimistic locking is a good scheme to use. If the transaction is an interactive, user-driven transaction where "data brows-ing" is part of the operation, pessimistic locking would lock up the page of records for an unacceptably long time. Optimistic locking, which we look at in a few paragraphs, would be a better choice for this processing paradigm.

Pessimistic locking assures that the user is looking at the most current version of the data. The potential for data corruption caused by lax concurrency control is greatly minimized because no other user can modify the record while it is being edited.

Two other options are available for the RecordLocks property, No Locks and All Records. Each option has qualities that recommend their use at certain times. No Locks is the default value for form creation and reflects the scheme known as *optimis-tic locking*. Optimistic locking allows two users to edit the same record at the same time. However, when one user saves her changes, this record is briefly x-locked, for the actual database update process. When the second user tries to save his changes, he sees a message from Access that warns the record currently being edited was modified since it was last read. Then the second user can discard his changes and reread the record manually, save the current changes to the clipboard, or overwrite the first user's changes without even looking at them.

The *No Locks philosophy*, or optimistic locking, assumes the 80-20 rule, that most record retrievals in a database environment are not for update purposes, that the user requesting the data will read or print copies of the record and go on to the next. In some environments this rule may be true, in others, it may not be true. Improper use of optimistic locking, especially in a high transaction-update/interactive-transaction-processing environment, can lead to apparent data corruption that is wrongly attributed to the database engine.

The *All Records locking option* exclusively locks all records in the underlying table(s) or query while the form is open in either Form View or Datasheet View. Other users can read the data (dirty reads) but cannot modify the data until the form is closed. This option is one to use if you are backing up or exporting data through a form, or doing some other procedure that demands the immediate availability of all records involved, without interruption. You also can use the All Records locking scheme in an action query, which ensures that none of the records involved in the action query are tied up by other users while the action query is running.

For review, dirty reads are those that are allowed but the accuracy of the data is not guaranteed. One user may be allowed to view or read records that are currently being updated by a second user. The first user may think she is getting timely and up-to-date information but in a dirty read situation, this may not be true.

Also for review, *action queries* copy rows to a new, dynamically constructed table or to an existing table of the database (*make-table queries* and *append queries*, respectively), change data in existing tables (the *update query*), or delete rows from existing tables (the *delete query*). These queries all differ dramatically from the standard *select query*, which just asks questions of the database engine and returns a set of rows in response. Obviously, to retain data integrity during an action query procedure, you want to disallow everyone else from making changes to the same set of records.

Locking through Macros. If, for some reason you don't want to use the form property itself to set the record locking scheme or if you need the ability to dynamically modify the locking scheme, based on some action taken on the form, you can use macros to change the locking scheme. Locking with macros uses the default page-level scheme, just as locking with bound forms does.

The **SetValue** action is coded in the macro design window as follows:

```
Action=SetValue
Item=Forms![formname].[RecordLocks]
Expression=2      ' this is for the Edited Record option.
                  ' For the No Lock option, use the value 0,
                  ' for All Records use value 1.
```

You can further customize your multiuser environment by modifying the *global locking behavior* parameters listed on the Tools, Options, Advanced tab (see fig. 11.8). By setting the Default Record Locking on this dialog box, all forms that subsequently will be created in this database will inherit the indicated default locking scheme. *Default Open Mode* should be set to Shared for all multiuser applications, and the Number of

Update Retries can be changed according to need. The default value is 2, which (in a database with a high degree of update activity and record contention) may be too low. The Update Retry Interval is set to 250 milliseconds, or about 1/4 second. Again, depending on your specific environment, whether you are primarily an interactive or a batch transaction processing shop, this value may need adjustment.

Fig. 11.8

Global locking behavior, set in the Options dialog box, on the Advanced tab.

Locking through Visual Basic Code. Bound forms and macros certainly are the easiest ways to manipulate the various locking schemes available in Access 95, but they don't give you the flexibility that Visual Basic procedures give. When you write custom locking procedures and run them from an unbound form, you can completely tailor the locking methods and conflict handling to any situation you may encounter in your environment.

For example, you may have a batch process that runs from a form, in which you overtly define the transaction, and you only need to lock the records during the transaction processing period—not for the whole time the form is in use or even being edited. The following simple code shows examples of both pessimistic and optimistic locking.

For these examples, the authors are using Visual Basic procedures to update the phone number for a customer contact, using parameters passed to the procedure from the form. You can find the code in Listing 11.4 (11code02.txt), on the companion CD-ROM.

Listing 11.4   11code02.txt—Code Which Uses Pessimistic Locking to Update Phone Numbers

```
Function PessimisticLockPhone (OldNumber, NewNumber)
' -----------------------------------------------------------------
'   Use pessimistic locking to update phone numbers
' -----------------------------------------------------------------
```

(continues)

III

Building the Application

Listing 11.4   Continued

```
On Error GoTo Err_PessimisticLockPhone

     Dim dbCurrent as Database, wrkCurrent as Workspace
      Dim recCust as Recordset
     Dim varTime as Variant

Set wrkCurrent = DBEngine.Workspaces(0)
Set dbCurrent = wrkCurrent.Databases(0)

' Open a dynaset for the FindFirst method
Set recCust = dbCurrent.OpenRecordset("qryCustomer", dbOpenDynaset)

recCust.LockEdits = True     ' select pessimistic locking
recCust.FindFirst "CustPhone = 'OldNumber' "
wrkCurrent.BeginTrans          ' begin the transaction
recCust.Edit                 ' lock the page
recCust!CustPhone = "'NewNumber'"
recCust.Update
wrkCurrent.CommitTrans             ' write data to disk, unlock page

Exit PessimisticLockPhone:
     Exit Function

Err_PessimisticLockPhone:
     MsgBox Error$
     Rollback
     Resume Exit_PessimisticLockPhone

End Function
```

You can find the code shown in Listing 11.5 (11code03.txt) on the companion CD-ROM.

Listing 11.5   11code03.txt—Code That Uses Optimistic Locking to Update Phone Numbers

```
Function OptimisticLockPhone (OldNumber, NewNumber)
'-----------------------------------------------------------------
'   Use optimistic locking to update phone numbers
'-----------------------------------------------------------------
On Error GoTo Err_OptimisticLockPhone
     Dim dbCurrent as Database, wrkCurrent as Workspace
      Dim recCust as Recordset
     Dim varTime as Variant

Set wrkCurrent = DBEngine.Workspaces(0)
Set dbCurrent = wrkCurrent.Databases(0)

' Open a dynaset for the FindFirst method
Set recCust = dbCurrent.OpenRecordset("qryCustomer", dbOpenDynaset)

recCust.LockEdits = False     ' select optimistic locking
```

```
recCust.FindFirst "CustPhone = 'OldNumber' "
wrkCurrent.BeginTrans          ' begin the transaction
recCust.Edit
recCust!CUstPhone = "'NewNumber'"
recCust.Update                 ' lock the page
wrkCurrent.CommitTrans          ' write data to disk, unlock page

Exit_OptimisticLockPhone:
    Exit Function


Err_OptimisticLockPhone:
    MsgBox Error$
    Rollback
    Resume Exit_OptimisticLockPhone

End Function
```

In some situations, you may want to give your users the ability to test first to see if a record is locked before actually trying to start an edit session that uses this record. Without this test, a user sees an error message from the Jet engine that reads, Couldn't update, record currently locked by user *username* on machine *machinename* (#3260). This kind of error is really annoying when the data being entered is complex or requires a lot of keystrokes. Testing first keeps the user from killing the programmer.

Listing 11.6 demonstrates a cleaner means of handling this conflict condition, by setting the **LockEdits** property to True (pessimistic locking), and then using the **Edit** method to attempt a lock and trapping error code 3260 if it is returned. You can find the following code in the file, 11code04.txt, on the companion CD-ROM.

Listing 11.6   11code04.txt—Test to See If a Record Is Already Locked before Allowing Updates

```
Function IsRecordLocked (Rec as Recordset) As Boolean
'-----------------------------------------------------------------
'    Use pessimistic locking to determine if a record
'    is already locked
'    If the record is locked returns true, else false
'    Trap error code 3260 and return
'-----------------------------------------------------------------
On Error GoTo Err_IsRecordLocked

    IsRecordLocked = False

Rec.Edit                       ' try to edit the current record
Rec.MoveNext
Rec.MovePrevious
MsgBox ("The record " & Rec " is available for editing."),
➥0, "Testing Record Availability")
Exit Function                  ' no error, return false
```

(continues)

```
Listing 11.6   Continued
```

```
Exit_IsRecordLocked:
    Exit Function

Err IsRecordLocked:
    If Err = 3260 Then        ' record locked, return true
        IsRecordLocked = True
        MsgBox ("The record " & Rec " isn't available for editing.")
        ➥, 0, "Testing Record Availability")
    End If
    Resume Exit IsRecordLocked

End Function
```

Error Handling for Concurrency Conflicts

Regardless of the locking scheme you choose to implement—either pessimistic or optimistic—there are times when your users will run into *concurrency conflicts*. When using pessimistic locking, if the **Edit** method succeeds in obtaining write access to the record in question you can be sure that the update will succeed. However, there are a few situations that may arise that call for error handling.

If the current record of a recordset was changed or deleted from the base table since it was read from the corresponding dynaset, the **Edit** method will cause an error code 3197 (data has changed, operation stopped). In the following code, you can refresh the data in the recordset by using the **Move 0** method and trying again. If the record was not deleted, the second **Edit** method should work. If the record was deleted, the user sees an error code 3167.

The other common error code returned is 3260 (current record locked by another user). The solution to this problem is simply to wait and retry the **Edit** method. Unless you have a serious contention situation on a very few records, a subsequent retry should succeed in securing the record for update. You can find the following code in Listing 11.7 on the companion CD-ROM.

```
Listing 11.7   11code05.txt—Trap Error Code 3197 (Data Has Changed,
Operation Stopped) or Error Code 3260 (Current Record Locked by
Another User) before Allowing Updates
```

```
PessimisticErrorHandler:
'------------------------------------------------------------------
'    Embed in a routine to trap error codes 3197 or 3260
'    and respond accordingly
'------------------------------------------------------------------

Select Case Err.Number
Case 3197                   ' data has changed since last read
    recData.Move 0          ' refresh recordset
    Resume                  ' try another read
```

```
Case 3260                        ' record is locked
    LockCounter = LockCounter + 1    ' try to get lock two times
    If LockCounter > 2 Then
' display error message & give user the option to retry or cancel
    Choice = MsgBox(Err.Descritpion, vbCritical + vbRetryCancel)
        If Choice = vbRetry Then    ' let's try it again
        LockCounter = 1             ' reset lock counter
        Else
        Resume FailEdit            ' edit failed; go to FailEdit
        End If
    End If

    DoEvents        ' perform system events, delay random
                    ' intervals, increasing each time lock fails

    RandomCounter = LockCounter ^ 2 * Int(Rnd *3000 + 1000)

    For x = 1 to RandomCounter: Next x
    Resume                          ' try it again!


Case Else
    MsgBox ("Error " & Err.Number & ": [ccc]
            " & Err.Description, vbCritical)
    Resume FailEdit

End Select

FailEdit:               ' what to do when the edit fails
wrk.Current.Rollback    ' call rollback method & cancel transaction
...
```

When using optimistic locking, the Jet doesn't lock the page until the **Update** method is executed. Consequently, more than one person can be making changes to the same record at the same time.

If another user succeeds in committing changes to a record that you are editing before you can commit, then your **update** method will cause an error code 3197 (data has changed, operation stopped). You can refresh the data in the recordset that you are accessing by using the **Move 0** method, and then examining the changed record to determine if you should overwrite the other person's changes.

When using the **update** method, you may get an error code 3186 (couldn't save, currently locked by user *username* on machine *machinename*) or an error code 3260 (couldn't update, currently locked by user *username* on machine *machinename*). The best solution here is to wait and retry the **update** again.

Occasionally, when you use the **AddNew** method, you also may see one of the previous two error codes. When adding new records to a table, the Jet engine checks to make sure that enough room is available in the last page of the table for the new record, and then attempts to lock the page. If there is insufficient space for the new record a new page is allocated and the new record is stored on the new page.

If another user has the last page locked, a subsequent retry should succeed in securing the page for locking. You can find the code shown in Listing 11.8 on this book's companion CD-ROM.

Listing 11.8   11code06.txt—Trap Error Code 3186 (Couldn't Save...), Error Code 3197 (Data Changed, Operation Stopped) or Error Code 3260 (Current Record Locked by Another User) before Allowing Updates

```
OptimisticErrorHandler:
'------------------------------------------------------------
'    Embed in a routine to trap error codes 3186, 3197 or 3260
'    and respond accordingly
'------------------------------------------------------------

Select Case Err.Number
Case 3197                        ' data has changed since last read
   If recData.EditMode = dbEditInProgress Then
 ►' error occurred on edit
     recData.Move 0                        ' refresh recordset
     Resume                                ' try another read
   Else
     Set recCopy = recData.Clone()      ' make copy of recordset
' display changed values and let user decide on course of action
     Choice = MsgBox(" Would you like to overwrite the current
     ►record with your version?"), vbQuestion + vbOKCancel)
         If Choice = vbOK  Then    ' overwrite the current record
              Resume
         Else
              Resume FailUpdate       ' bail out and rollback
         End If
   End If


Case 3186, 3260                   ' record is locked or cannot be saved
     LockCounter = LockCounter + 1     ' try to get lock two times
     If LockCounter > 2 Then
      ' display error message and give user
      ' the option of retrying or cancelling
     Choice = MsgBox(Err.Descritpion, vbCritical + vbRetryCancel)
         If Choice = vbRetry Then    ' let's try it again
         LockCounter = 1             ' reset lock counter
         Else
         Resume FailUpdate            ' bail out and rollback
         End If
     End If

     DoEvents       ' perform system events, delay random intervals,
                    ' increasing each time lock fails

     RandomCounter = LockCounter ^ 2 * Int(Rnd *3000 + 1000)

     For x = 1 to RandomCounter: Next x
     Resume                              ' try it again!
```

```
Case Else
    MsgBox ("Error " & Err.Number & ":
    ➥" & Err.Description, vbCritical)
    Resume FailUpdate

End Select

FailUpdate:              ' what to do when the update fails
wrk.Current.Rollback     ' call the rollback method and cancel
                         ➥the transaction
...
```

From Here...

In this chapter, we covered some of the concepts of transaction management and concurrency control.

From here, you can jump to the following chapters to learn more about related topics:

- Chapter 12, "Securing the Access 95 Application," discusses security policies and procedures.
- Chapter 19, "System Administration," discusses currently available fail-safe technology.
- Chapter 22, "The Human Factor," discusses the human element in the client/ server environment.

III

Building the Application

Securing the Access 95 Application

Security in Access always seems to cause more than its share of confusion. Perhaps people who write security programs don't like to talk about what they do. If you really want to know the details about Access security, search the Microsoft TechNet and Developer Network CDs for information on Access security—it's all there.

Access 95 security is always present, which you always should keep in mind. Most people don't realize that, when they install Access and start using it without supplying a logon or password, they are actually using the default logon. You don't have to add security features to your application—you only use what is already there.

This chapter discusses the following security-related areas:

- The need for security
- The Access 95 security model
- The workgroup administrator
- Users, groups, and passwords
- Permissions and access to data
- Administrator access and responsibilities
- The Security Wizard

Why Do I Need Security?

Several reasons for implementing security in Access 95 are shown in the following list:

- To protect sensitive data on a local database
- To restrict availability of server data via an Access 95 client
- To prevent users from modifying the database structure or changing the application
- To protect intellectual property rights

Protecting Data in a Local Database

Desktop databases make it easy to collect, store, and view large amounts of information. Because it's so easy, users may not realize the value of the information, whether corporate data that may be valuable to a competitor or lists of names and addresses that may be of interest to a telemarketing company. More and more personal computers are being linked to networks. Even in a small office, a Windows 95 or Windows for Workgroups network gives everyone the ability to share data. This sharing, while great for productivity, is not so good for security. Unless some precautions are taken, anyone on the network with a copy of Access 95 can view or modify the stored data or the database structure. Actually, end users can connect to Access 95 data by using Excel, Word, or Microsoft Query.

You can take a few steps that, in addition to the security built into Access 95, will help secure the Access environment. If nothing else, these steps raise awareness about security concerns. You may want to implement some or all of the following ideas, depending on how sensitive your data is and what level of physical security is in place:

- Keep the Access 95 database on a computer that is not connected to the network
- If the computer is on the network, keep the database on a disk or partition that is not shared. (Share only the directories that need to be shared, not the entire partition.)
- Use a logon for the network software. Windows 95, Windows for Workgroups, and Novell NetWare offer this capability. Don't automate the logon process so that the user is logged in when the computer is turned on. You must be sure to require a user ID and password.
- Many newer PCs allow you to set up a system-boot password. This BIOS setting can be overridden only by draining the CMOS battery, so use it with care.
- If you want a truly secure network, use Windows NT as your network operating system.

Restricting Access to the Server Database

In Chapter 10, "Making the Right Connections," the authors mentioned that Access 95 will store a password to the server database. This feature is useful because it allows the user to seamlessly analyze data from one or more servers, without logging in manually each time a server is accessed. It also means, however, that the server security is now only as good as the security in Access 95.

Preventing Changes to the Application

After you install the client application, you don't want the end-user community changing it arbitrarily. All changes should be made through the development team, or whoever is responsible for maintaining the application. This is even more true if you plan to use the Windows 95 replication feature to pass changes to run-time copies of the application on the user computers. Any changes that they may have made will be overwritten every time you replicate a new application file.

If an exception exists to this policy, it may be if your client application is an executive information system. In this case the users may need the capability to add queries so they can look at data in new ways. The security model used in Access 95 allows you to secure the tables, while allowing the users some flexibility in other areas, such as query development.

Protecting Intellectual Property

If you are an independent developer, you will want to protect your applications, which is *intellectual property*, from being used without your knowledge and permission and without compensation. Even if you are employed by the company for whom you developed the application, you don't want an employee taking the code with them when he or she leaves, or perhaps slipping a copy to a competitor. When you use the Access 95 Distribution Toolkit to produce a run-time application, you need to secure it so that others cannot access your design simply by opening it under a full copy of Access 95.

The Access 95 Security Model

Access 95 employs user-level security. This differs from most other desktop database software, which uses share-level security. The user-level security model allows users to be authenticated, and then allows access to objects to which they have permission. Let's look at how this is done.

User-Level Security versus Share-Level Security

In the Access 95 environment, which implements *user-level security*, users log on and are authenticated when they supply valid passwords for their accounts. Each person who has a user account may belong to one or more groups. The system administrator assigns permissions on objects to users and groups. Different users and groups can have different permissions on the same object. A sales clerk, for example, can look up the price of an item, but only a manager can change this price. The clerk has Read Data permission; the manager has Update permission on the table that contains the pricing information.

Actually, the sales-clerk group, not just the sales clerk, has Read Data permission on this table. When you add a new sales person, you just make this individual a member of the sales-clerk group, and the person inherits the permissions of the group to which the new clerk belongs. You don't need to assign specific permissions to the new employees—just add them to an existing group. Adding, removing, or reassigning employees is handled by group assignments, which greatly simplifies administration.

Each person is responsible for, and has control over, his or her own password, which the system then uses to authenticate the user's identity and group affiliations.

Share-level security is the normal security method that is used in most desktop systems. A password must be assigned to a permission on an object, not to a specific user.

Under this scheme, you assign a read-only password (which the sales clerks would know) on the pricing table. A read-write password also can be assigned to the table and given to the sales manager. This scheme gets complicated fast. Suppose that you have a second table, such as customer orders, for which clerks and managers both need write permission. You can give it the same password as you give the read-only permission on the pricing table, so that sales clerks can update the orders table but not the pricing table. But now, the same password gives read-write permission on one table, and read-only on another. If you add a few more tables with differing requirements, this approach quickly becomes impossible to administer.

At this point, you may think that you can use one password for the clerks, another for the managers, and assign them where appropriate. Congratulations. You just invented a form of user-level security.

Continuing with the preceding example, suppose that accounting needs read-only authority on both pricing and orders. Neither password already assigned will work for them, and you can assign only one password to each permission. So, the managers know the read-write passwords on each table, accounting knows the read-only passwords on each table, and the sales clerks know the read-only password on pricing *and* the read-write password on orders (which must, therefore, differ from the read-write password on pricing). User-level security looks better all the time. When you build relational databases and start joining tables, share-level security becomes unworkable.

The important point to remember with user-level security is that it requires you to define both the object and the user. You do not put update permission on a table. You grant update permission on a table to a user or a group of users. When someone says, "The zip code database is read-only," he or she means that all users have been assigned read-only permission on the database.

User Authentication

When a user logs on, Access checks to see if the user is in the list of approved users in the SYSTEM.MDW file. Access also checks which groups include this user. Then, every time the user requests a table, a form, or any other object, Access checks to see if the user—or any of the groups to which the user belongs—has the required permission to access the object. If so, the request proceeds; if not, the user is denied access.

> **Tip**
>
> A user can access an object if *any* of the groups to which this user belongs has the required permission. This is the reverse of the Windows NT security model, where, if any group of which the user is a member is *denied* permission, the user cannot access the object.

Using the Workgroup Administrator

When you first installed Access 95, you were asked for some information—user name, company name, and so on. Access 95 uses this information to build a security identifier. The SYSTEM.MDW file stores this identifier. During the installation, Access 95 also adds one user, named Admin, to the list of users, which also is stored in the SYSTEM.MDW file. You can add new groups and users, and related information is stored in this default SYSTEM.MDW. You can use this same MDW file for as many different applications as you desire.

Adding a New Workgroup

When you begin to secure the application, you want to create a new SYSTEM.MDW file. You do this with the *Workgroup Administrator*, a utility program that comes with Access 95. Each new SYSTEM.MDW file is, in Microsoft terminology, a "workgroup." You definitely want to keep separate workgroup files if you are developing applications for more than one client, so that you can add the appropriate users for each client to their own application, with no intermixing of names, groups, or clients.

The SYSTEM.MDW file in Access 95 replaces the SYSTEM.MDA file in Access versions 1.x and 2.x. The SYSTEM.MDA file was the repository for security information in these versions of Access.

The Workgroup Administrator is used when you need to add a new workgroup or to change from one workgroup to another (see fig. 12.1). We will create a new workgroup, but first, a little housekeeping is needed. When you install Access 95 on Windows 95, it doesn't add the Workgroup Administrator to your Start Menu Programs. If you install on a Windows NT system, the Workgroup Administrator is included in the group that is built by the installation process. You probably will want to run this program frequently, especially if you are testing security on an application or working on more than one project. Add a shortcut to your Access 95 program group, and for the target, use the file WRKGADM.EXE, which you will find in the same directory as your Access 95 executable files.

Now, run the workgroup administrator.

Fig. 12.1

The Access 95 Workgroup Administrator dialog box, from which you can either create a new workgroup or join an existing workgroup.

Select the Create option to create a new workgroup, which brings up the subsequent dialog box, Workgroup Owner Information (see fig. 12.2).

Fig. 12.2

Establishing a new workgroup and giving it a unique workgroup name, which is case-sensitive.

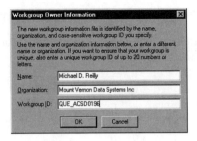

Pay careful attention to the note in the dialog box that says you should make the workgroup unique. If you do not supply your own *Workgroup ID*, it isn't hard for others to crack the security model. (The registered user name and company is filled in by default, so anyone with access to your computer can create a workgroup with a blank ID, and anyone who knows your name and company can do the same thing with little effort). Enter a Workgroup ID that will not be easily guessed. You can make it complex, with non-alphanumeric characters. The Workgroup ID is not a password, so you don't have to type it with any frequency. You will want to retain a copy of the Workgroup ID in a safe place, however—just in case. The only reason why you would need it again is if the SYSTEM.MDW file (or whatever you rename it) is deleted and could not be recovered from backup copies, and you had to re-create it. After the database is secured with this workgroup file, the only way to get back into it is with the same workgroup information, including the exact same Workgroup ID.

The best thing to do with a Workgroup ID is to write it on paper and place this paper in a safe, or in a safe-deposit box, preferably in off-site storage (in case you have to rebuild after a fire or flood).

Give the new workgroup information file a different name to distinguish it from your everyday SYSTEM.MDW file, which isn't secure (see fig. 12.3). Remember that, when you installed Access 95 it didn't ask for a workgroup ID. The default workgroup file it builds has a blank Workgroup ID, and isn't secure.

Fig. 12.3

Assigning the newly created workgroup a new workgroup information file.

Access 95 shows you the information one last time before it builds the new file (see fig. 12.4). Check it and make sure that what you wrote down is the same as what is on-screen. You might take this opportunity to make a screen capture and print it to store with your handwritten notes.

Fig. 12.4

Confirmation of the newly established workgroup information, which you may want to capture as a printed screen and put in a safe place for future reference.

From now on, you cannot get back to the workgroup ID. Nor can anyone else, which makes it very secure. No matter which name you choose, stay with the convention and use the .MDW extension. This isn't mandatory, but you will find it easier to switch between workgroups if you stay with this suggested naming standard.

If your server database is built on Access 95, consider placing the workgroup SYSTEM.MDW file in the same directory as the server MDB file for the application that you are building. If you do so, you can even leave it with the name, SYSTEM.MDW, although pros and cons exist to this action. Some disk utilities report—and offer to delete—what they think are duplicate files, and you (or an eager assistant) might do just this while cleaning up the disk on some rainy afternoon. So think through your .MDW naming schemes.

Keeping the MDW file in the same directory as the server MDB file has the advantage that, when you share the directory, everyone on the network can get to both files, and you then do not have to share the development directory.

Even if your server database isn't written in Access 95, at some point you must create a shared directory on one computer for the workgroup MDW file. As you see in Chapter 13, "Building the Run-Time Application," all the clients must connect to the same MDW file so that changes in passwords, new users, and so on are effective network-wide. In theory you can replicate the SYSTEM.MDW file to every user's computer each time you add or remove a user. But the users then would not be able to change their own passwords, or if they did, the changes would be lost at the next replication.

Switching Between Workgroups

After you define a new workgroup, you can use the Workgroup Administrator to toggle between the various workgroups. You will see the same dialog box when you start the Workgroup Administrator but this time, select the Join option. If you elect to browse for the file, the Administrator looks for other .MDW files, as illustrated in figure 12.5, which is why you should use .MDW as the file extension.

After you select the file, Access 95 confirms that you have joined the workgroup. At any time, to learn which workgroup you are in, the quickest method is to bring up the Workgroup Administrator.

Fig. 12.5

Using the Workgroup Administrator to browse for workgroup information files when joining an Access 95 workgroup.

Users, Groups, and Passwords

As we previously mentioned, when Access 95 is first installed, it only has one user account. The name of this user is Admin, and it doesn't have a password. When you start Access 95, it looks for the *Admin user*, and if no password is assigned, it loads the program. Most users who are unfamiliar with Access security assume that there is no security, and that they don't have to log on. Actually, they are logging on as the Admin user. The owner of all tables, queries, forms, reports, and code that they build is the Admin user.

Assigning an Administrator Password

The simplest step in *preventing unauthorized access to your database* is to assign a password to this Admin user. As you soon will see, this setup isn't very secure but it keeps the honest people honest. To assign an Admin password, follow these steps:

1. Start Access 95 with the appropriate SYSTEM.MDW file. Do not open a database.

2. From the top menu, select Tools, Security, User And Group Accounts (see fig. 12.6).

Fig. 12.6

Select the User And Group Accounts menu item from the Security option, Tools entry of the top menu.

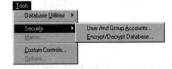

3. From the User and Group Accounts dialog box, select the Change Logon Password tab (see fig. 12.7).

4. Leave the Old Password field blank, and type a new password in both the New Password and Verify boxes. Click OK, and you have a new password.

5. Shut down Access 95, and then restart it. You will see the logon dialog box (see fig. 12.8).

6. Log in with your new password.

Fig. 12.7

The User and Group Accounts dialog box.

Fig. 12.8

The Access 95 Logon dialog box.

To remove the password, just repeat the process, give the current password when prompted for the Old Password, and leave the New Password blank. If you are a member of the Admins group you can go to the User and Group Accounts Dialog box, click the Users tab, and click the Clear Password button.

Adding Users

Most network administrators will admit that their jobs would be a great deal easier if they didn't have to deal with users, and database administrators feel much the same way. However, a client/server database needs users, so you can add some by taking the following steps:

1. Start with Access 95 running, no database open.
2. From the top menu, select Tools, Security, User and Group Accounts. The User and Group Accounts Dialog box opens at the User tab (see fig. 12.9).
3. Click New to add a user.
4. Type the Name of the new user, add a Personal ID, and then click OK. The new user is added to the system.

Now you can log on as the new user or as Admin. If you removed the Admin password, Access 95 starts without giving you the Logon dialog box, and you cannot choose the user. Realistically, there isn't much point in *assigning user accounts* if the Admin account isn't protected from illicit use.

Fig. 12.9

The User and Group Accounts dialog box, User tab selected.

If you use the database in a production mode as well as being its developer or administrator, why not set up a second account for yourself? You can assign normal user privileges to your alter ego account, and use it when you are not performing system administration tasks. Networks administrators will already be familiar with this concept. The benefits include the following:

- Lowers the risk of you inadvertently making damaging changes to the database

- Allows the developer to spot potential problems with the level of security assigned to the users, which may not be obvious when you are logged on as Admin

- Keeps the system more secure if you are called away from your desk for a few minutes (paranoid, aren't we?)

A better idea is to build yourself two accounts, a user-level and a *superuser*, which has the full suite of Admin permissions. Then demote the Admin account to something less. You shortly will see why this change is a good idea.

The personal ID that you entered is similar to the Workgroup ID. It is not the password. (In fact, your new user was added without a password. If you want to assign the user a password when you establish this user account, use the Change Logon Password option, which forces the user to change the password the next time s(he) logs on.) The personal ID is a way of making each user a unique identifier.

Working with Groups

We talked previously about how Access 95 uses groups to maintain database permissions. Log on as your underprivileged user, and you will see that you can select users, and see groups to which each belongs. But you cannot add users, delete users, or clear the password. You also cannot assign users to groups. You can change the password, but only for the current user you are logged on as.

Now, the only groups shown are Admins and Users. From where did this second group, named Users, come? When you added a new user—your underprivileged user—it was by default put in a group called Users (see fig. 12.10).

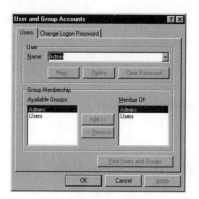

Fig. 12.10

The User and Group Accounts as seen by a user.

Now log off (shut down Access 95) and start Access 95 again, log back on as Admin when requested to do so. Notice that the name of the last user to log on is shown in the logon dialog box. Click on Tools, Security, User and Group Accounts.

> **Note**
>
> Depending on the level of security in your shop, your policies may not allow the last user logon to be displayed. So far, the authors have not found a way to turn off this feature. Windows NT has the capability to hide the last logon, so this option may eventually trickle down to Access 95.

In the User and Group Accounts dialog box, an extra tab, for Groups, is visible in the dialog box that wasn't visible to a user logon (see fig. 12.11). The New, Delete, and Clear Password buttons are available and not dimmed out (refer to fig. 12.10), and the Add and Remove buttons in the group membership section also are available. Notice that Admin is a member of the Admins and Users groups. It's somewhat confusing to have a user named Admin and a group named Admins, so make a mental note to keep them separate. Now select another user, the one you created previously, and you see that the user whom you just added is only a member of the Users group and not of the Admins group.

Fig. 12.11

The User and Group Accounts dialog box, as seen by an Administrator. It has the extra "Groups" tab, which is seen only by members of the Admins group.

III

Building the Application

Now, you can add your superuser account, and then add this user to the Admins group. And if you want, you can remove the Admin logon from the Admins group. You must perform the operations in this order because Access 95 does not allow you to delete all the users from the Admins group. At least one account must exist with Admin authority, or else you could lock yourself out of the database. You can test these operations if you choose; you will be stopped by an the error message if you try to do anything illegal or potentially harmful to yourself.

> **Tip**
>
> Access 95 doesn't allow you to delete the Admin account but you can demote this account by removing it from the Admins group. You also cannot delete the Admins or Users groups.

Adding a group is as easy as selecting the Groups tab and clicking the New button. Again, you must supply a unique identifier for the group, which remains secure. To re-create the group (in case you inadvertently deleted the SYSTEM.MDW and need to rebuild it), you have to supply that identifier.

If you find that you don't have permission to add a group, you probably logged on as Admin, and then removed Admin from the Admins group. You no longer have the required authority to add users. You must log off and log on again as a member of the Admins group. Until you do, you cannot even put Admin back in the Admins group—the loss of authority is immediate when you remove a user from a group.

When you delete a group, you don't delete the members of the group. Their accounts are modified so that they no longer are members of the deleted group, but the user accounts are still there, with all other group assignments that they have. At the least, they will be members of the Users group.

To become familiar with the security menu, add groups named Sales and Accounting. Also, add several users that you can assign to the groups.

Using Passwords

Passwords in Access 95 are case-sensitive. User names are not, but the passwords are. If you forget the administrator password on a unique SYSTEM.MDW file, you may be looking for another job because there is no way around the security once it is set. There are no back doors into Access 95.

As an Administrator, you have the power to clear the password from any account or to set up a new logon password. This power is particularly useful when someone tells you that he has forgotten his password or when an employee leaves and neglects to inform anyone of the password that (s)he was using. If you don't know the old password, first use the clear password option, and then assign a new password.

Access 95 has a new feature, the *Set Database Password option*. This feature allows you to quickly *secure a database* by assigning a password to the database itself. This security is share-level, not user-level, which means that everyone who logs on needs to know the database password, and this password is the same for everyone. Because everyone with authority to use the database uses the same password, it is less secure than user-level security, and offers the same access to everyone regardless of position within the company.

You can add user-level security after you set a database password, and then if you want, remove the database password. If user-level security was set, only users who have permission to administer the database can add or remove a database password.

You shouldn't use a database password if you plan to replicate the database. The synchronization process will fail if a database password is in place.

The Set Database Password option is visible only when a specific database is open. It doesn't appear in the menu options when no database is open.

Permissions and Access to Data

Establishing new user accounts and setting up new groups isn't the only work you must do in a user-level security model. You also must assign permissions to database objects for these various users and groups.

Assigning Permissions on Database Objects

Now that you defined your users and groups, open the database REA_APP.MDB (which is on the companion CD-ROM, directory Chapter 12). Open the Tools, Security menu. You will notice the additional items listed here, including the Set Database Password option that was mentioned in the preceding paragraphs.

Besides the User and Group Accounts, there is another option, User and Group Permissions. You use this option to *grant permissions* on the database objects to the groups in your user community. Click this option to open the User and Group Permissions dialog box, as shown in figure 12.12.

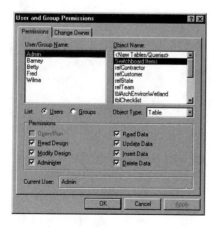

Fig. 12.12

The User and Group Permissions dialog box, from which you can modify user and group permissions to objects in the database.

III

Building the Application

At the bottom of the dialog box, Current User is listed as Admin. The Admin user currently has complete permissions for any database object (all the boxes under Permissions are checked. Now look at the user, Barney (see fig. 12.13). Barney looks as if he has no permissions at all!

Fig. 12.13

The User and Group Permissions dialog box— user Barney currently has no table permissions.

In this view we have the individual users listed. If instead we select List Groups, we see quite a different view. The Users group has permissions on the database (see fig. 12.15), and the Admin group does not (see fig. 12.14). If you browse the different objects for the two groups, you will find that this restriction applies throughout the database.

Fig. 12.14

The User and Group Permissions dialog box: the Admins group doesn't have permissions on database objects.

In fact, any member of the Users group currently has permissions to do anything they want to the database. You cannot remove any user from the Users group, Access 95 doesn't allow this. Everyone with an account in the SYSTEM.MDW file *must* be a member of the Users group. You may need to remove certain permissions from the Users group and allocate to them only those permissions needed for them to do their jobs.

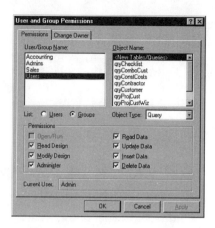

Fig. 12.15

The User and Group Permissions dialog box: the Users group has full permissions on all database objects.

To *remove permissions*, highlight all the objects in the Object Name box, and then click the permission boxes to remove all permissions. Now you can turn on the following permissions (click the Apply button after setting each group of permissions, or Access keeps reminding you to do so):

Group "Admins":

> Turn on the Administer option for all objects. This turns on all the other options.

Group "Users":

Tables	No permissions
Queries	No permissions
Forms	Open/Run
Reports	Open/Run
Macros	Open/Run
Module	None (Open/Run is set on by default and cannot be turned off)

For reasons that are unclear to the authors, every time you turn on Read Data for a table or a query, the Read Design also is turned on. One reason for this may be that Access needs to read the design so that it knows how to display and format the data. It seems, however, as if this could be accomplished without allowing the end-user community read access to the table design mode of your database. In a secure environment, you do want to turn off the Read Design permission to the database but by doing so, you also automatically turn off the Read Data permission and thereby deny the user access to data in the tables. However, there is a way around this problem.

WithOwnerAccess Option

You should include *WithOwnerAccess option* in every query you build. "WithOwnerAccess" means that when a query is run, it runs with the permissions assigned to the owner of the query, not the permissions of the user currently logged in. Assuming that the owner of the query is the developer, and a member of the Admins group, these permissions include the ability to read the table(s) on which the query is built. The user can run the query, temporarily assuming the guise of the query owner, and thereby get access to the data in the table(s). This temporary ability doesn't extend to seeing into the design of the table(s), it's limited to running only the specific query. So, it is a good idea to include the "WithOwnerAccess Option" in all the queries that you create.

Changing Ownership

If you built your superuser/developer account at the start of the development process, and used this account logon when you were developing the application, then everything you built belongs to the superuser. But, what happens if you are also doing development while logged on as Admin? The owner of some database objects will be Admin, of course, and if you remove Admin from the Admins group, this may pose a problem. The solution is to use the *Change Owner option* in the User and Group Permissions dialog box to allow you, the superuser, to *take ownership* of the objects in the database (see fig. 12.16).

Fig. 12.16

The User and Group Permissions dialog box: changing ownership of a set of database objects.

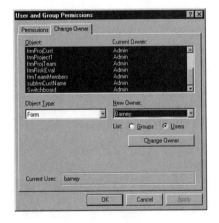

Actually, the Change Owner option enables you to take ownership of any object in the database, except for queries. A flaw seems to exist in the way Access handles queries in this module. It cannot transfer ownership of any query that includes the WithOwnerAccess option, but it can transfer ownership of queries that use the default UserAccess option. This capability suggests that the name of the owner is hard-coded into the query when it is compiled—a clear breach of security for the sake of performance. The only solution to this situation is to remove the WithOwnerAccess option from all the queries, then take ownership, and restore the WithOwnerAccess option.

As you can see, it pays to plan ahead and build your user account names and security before you commence work on the database itself. After you take ownership of the application, you can distribute it without the concern that people can copy your design. Chapter 13, "Building the Run-Time Application," looks at how you build a secure run-time application.

Administrator Access and Responsibilities

As the database administrator, you or the appointed *database security administrator* should be the only people who are allowed to add or delete users from the system. We encourage you to allow the users to change their own passwords, however, because they may be more receptive to using passwords if it is something they can control. Access security doesn't offer all the options of Windows NT, where passwords can be of a minimum length, expire in so many days, cannot be repeated, and so on. But Access security certainly beats the "password" of Windows 95, which you can sidestep by pressing the Esc key. (If you look closely at the Windows 95 login box, it does say that this is your *networking* password).

The normal way to change a password in the full development copy of Access is to select from the top menu, Tools, Security, User and Group Accounts, select Change Logon Password tab, and use the dialog box to change the password. However, in the run-time application, the end user doesn't have this menu option. Some organizations would have each end user running to the database administrator or the database security administrator every time (s)he wanted or needed to change a password. There is however, another solution: to put a button somewhere on a form—the main-menu form or switchboard—that will pop up a dialog box that will allow the user to change his or her own password.

Figures 12.17 and 12.18 illustrate a scheme that the authors used in past application development. This scheme involves a dialog box that changes, depending on the logon of the user. If the logon is that of a user, then each user should be able to change only his or her own password—for obvious reasons. But if the logon is an administrator's, the administrator should be able to change anyone's password.

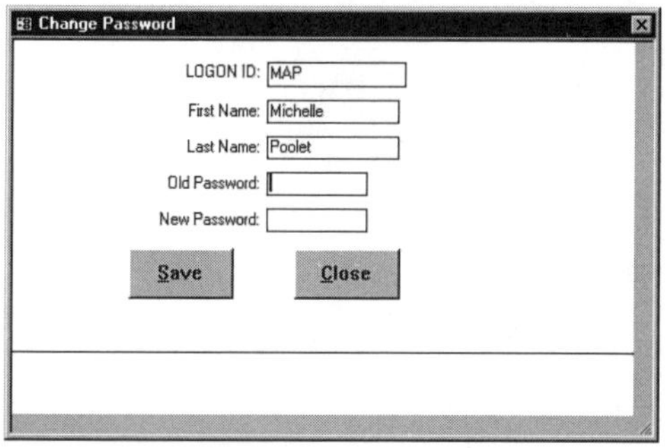

Fig. 12.17

The customized add-on Change Password dialog box: as the individual user sees it in order to change his/her own password.

In the user version of this dialog box, you are asked for the old password before it can be changed to a new one, presumably to prevent some dastardly person from slipping in and modifying the password while the owner is temporarily absent (refer to fig. 12.17). On the other hand, leaving an unattended computer is a security breach because people walking by can conceivably change data values without leaving a trace of who they were. Anyone who has dealt with security issues can tell you that physical security is the first line, and is as important as anything software-oriented.

Fig. 12.18

*The customized add-on
Change Password dialog
box: as the database
administrator sees it,
which allows him/her to
assign new passwords to
end users as needed.*

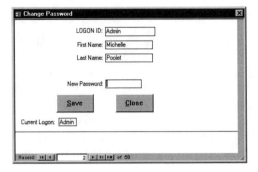

In the administrator's version of this dialog box the requirement to enter the old
password has vanished (refer to fig. 12.18). As an administrator, you only need
to assign a new password. You don't need to know a user's old password—so
we deactivate the Old Password text box when an administrator logs on. The
code in Listing 12.1 goes behind the OnOpen property of the following form,
frmAdminChangePassword, which you can find on the companion CD-ROM,
in the Code folder.

**Listing 12.1   12code01.txt—Activate or Deactivate Controls on the Change
Password Custom Form, Depending on the Identity of the Individual**

```
Private Sub Form_Open(Cancel As Integer)
'------------------------------------------------------------
' test to see who is accessing the Change Password form and
' activate or deactivate the controls accordingly
' attach to the OnOpen property of the Change Password form
'------------------------------------------------------------
On Error GoTo Err_Form_Open

    If CurrentUser() <> "Admin" Then
    [txtCurrentUser].Visible = False
    [lblCurrentUser].Visible = False
    [txtTMbrCode].Enabled = True
    [txtTMbrCode].Locked = False
    DoCmd.GoToControl "txtTMbrCode"
    DoCmd.FindRecord CurrentUser()
    DoCmd.GoToControl "txtOldPassword"
    [txtTMbrCode].Enabled = False
    [txtTMbrCode].Locked = True
    Forms![frmAdminChangePassword].NavigationButtons = No
    Else
    [txtOldPassword].Visible = No
    End If
Exit_Form_Open:
    Exit Sub

Err_Form_Open:
    MsgBox Error$
    Resume Exit_Form_Open

End Sub
```

After the new information is entered on the Change Password form, the following code (in the file, 12code02.txt, which you can find on the companion CD-ROM in the Code folder), is located behind the OnClick property of the Save button, executes:

Listing 12.2   12code02.txt—Change the Password for the User as Indicated by the Entries in the Custom Change Password Form

```
Private Sub btnSave_Click()
'-----------------------------------------------------------
' change the password for the user as indicated by the
' entries in the customer Change Password form
' attach to the OnClick property of the Save button
' which is part of the Change Password form
'-----------------------------------------------------------

On Error GoTo Err_btnSave_Click
    ' Change the password for a user account.

    If IsNull([txtOldPassword]) Then
    [txtOldPassword] = ""
    End If
    If IsNull([txtNewPassword]) Then
    [txtNewPassword] = ""
    End If

    DBEngine.Workspaces(0).Users([txtTMbrCode]).NewPassword
    ➥[txtOldPassword], [txtNewPassword]

    If CurrentUser() <> "admin" Then
    DoCmd.Close
    Else
    [txtNewPassword] = ""
    End If

Exit_btnSave_Click:
    Exit Sub

Err_btnSave_Click:
    MsgBox  "Error"
    Resume Exit_btnSave_Click

End Sub
```

The security option generally is unavailable on the top menu of a run-time client application, as was mentioned previously. As a result, you have to make a choice about how you plan to add users. If you, as the administrator, are using the full development copy of Access 95 most of the time, you can simply use the Security menu option to add new users to your environment. If, however, you normally use the run-time version of the application, you may not want to (or may not be able to, because of memory restrictions) be forced to start a full Access session just to add one user.

The authors have developed another scheme to resolve this situation, which is demonstrated by the form, frmAddNewUser. In the run-time product, place a transparent button somewhere on the opening screen, such as on top of the corporate logo. When someone clicks in this area, the program checks for the logon ID, using the CurrentUser() function. If the user is not an administrator, nothing happens. When the user is an administrator, however, we open the Add New Users dialog box (frmAddNewUser), which allows for the addition of a new user (see fig. 12.19).

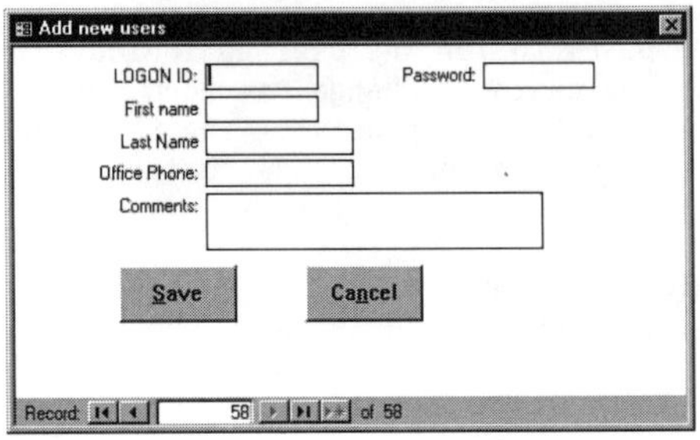

Fig. 12.19

The custom add-on Add New Users dialog box, which can be used only by a member of the Admins group.

The *Add New Users* dialog box allows for either adding or deleting a user. When the form is first opened, there are three command buttons showing at the bottom—Add New User, Delete User, and Close. When either the Add New User or Delete User button is clicked, the buttons on the form disappear and are replaced with two others, Save and Cancel. The latter version of the form is the one shown in figure 12.19.

Because security is not super-tight in this application, we autogenerate a unique User ID from two sources—the name of our company (REA) and the user's new logon ID. Also, specific to this application, while we are adding the new user, we also add them to the table of team members at the same time. You can include other features as needed, such as asking for a unique ID rather than generating it by default (which satisfies tighter security requirements), or by looking for password confirmation.

The code behind the Save button on the frmAdminAddUser form looks like the example shown in Listing 12.3 (12code03.txt).

Listing 12.3   12code03.txt—Create a New User Account and Add to the Already-Existing Group Users

```
Private Sub cbtnSave_Click()
On Error GoTo Err_btnSave_Click
'----------------------------------------------------------------
' To create a new user account and add to the group Users
' attach to the OnClick property of the Save button
'     name of new user          = [txtTMbrCode]
'     PID for new user          = REA &  [txtTMbrCode]
'     password for new user     = [txtPassword]
'----------------------------------------------------------------
```

```
    DoCmd.DoMenuItem A_FORMBAR, A_FILE, A_SAVERECORD, , A_MENU_VER20

    Dim wrk As Workspace
    Dim usrNew As User
    Dim strMsg As String
    Set wrk = DBEngine.Workspaces(0)

    If IsNull([txtTMbrCode]) Then
    MsgBox "You must supply a logon ID for this user"
    DoCmd.GoToControl "txtTMbrCode"
    GoTo Exit_btnSave_Click
    ElseIf IsNull([txtTMbrFName]) Then
    MsgBox "You must fill in a first and last name for this account"
    DoCmd.GoToControl "txtTMbrFName"
    GoTo Exit_btnSave_Click
    ElseIf IsNull([txtTMbrLName]) Then
    MsgBox "You must fill in a first and last name for this account"
    DoCmd.GoToControl "txtTMbrLName"
    GoTo Exit_btnSave_Click
    End If

    If IsNull([txtPassword]) Then
    [txtPassword] = ""
    End If

    'Create new user account and append
    Set usrNew = wrk.CreateUser([txtTMbrCode],
    ➥"REA" & [txtTMbrCode], [txtPassword])
    wrk.Users.Append usrNew

    'append the account to the built-in Users group
    usrNew.Groups.Append wrk.CreateGroup("Users")

' reset the controls so that Save User, Cancel and
' the Password text box are invisible
DoCmd.GoToControl "txtTMbrCode"
    [btnDeleteUser].Visible = True
    [btnClose].Visible = True
    [BtnSave].Visible = False
    [btnCancel].Visible = False
    [btnAddNewUser].Visible = True

    [txtPassword] = ""
    [txtPassword].Visible = False
    [lblPassword].Visible = False

Exit_btnSave_Click:
    Exit Sub

Err_btnSave_Click:
MsgBox  "Error"
    Resume Exit_btnSave_Click

End Sub
```

With these two dialog boxes, you can administer security for your user community from the client application at either your desk or theirs. From a user terminal, log in with your account name, and all your administrative privileges become available. Add a user, delete a user, and then remember to log out before leaving their terminal!

Using the Security Wizard

The *User-Level Security Wizard* offers a way to quickly secure your database. Interestingly, it also offers a quick way to unsecure it, if you want to make it available and open to all users.

Securing the Database

You will find this Wizard under the Tools menu, Security option, User-Level Security Wizard. Let's step through how this wizard works. The opening dialog box is shown in figure 12.20.

Fig. 12.20

The User-Level Security Wizard opening dialog box.

If you want to secure a database, log on as your superuser/developer, not as Admin. Start the *Security Wizard* and select all objects to be secured. Notice that the current user is shown in the Wizard dialog box. Click OK. At this point, if the user Admin still is a member of the Admins group, you see a warning screen, as shown in figure 12.21.

Fig. 12.21

The User-Level Security Wizard: the warning that advises you to remove user, Admin.

The Security Wizard will build a new, secure database, so you still will have the original database with which to work if needed (see fig. 12.22).

You may want to check that the queries in the new, secure database belong to the superuser/developer logon that you used when you secured the database. The Security Wizard actually exports all the objects into the new database, and they inherit ownership from the new database. You can do this export with the same end result, but the Security Wizard does it for you very quickly.

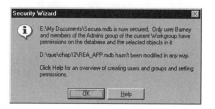

Fig. 12.22

The User-Level Security Wizard: the new database, Secure.mdb, will be built by the Security Wizard.

Remember the "change ownership" problem we discussed previously? This is another work-around to the problem of not being able to change ownership on queries when the WithOwnerAccess option is set. Using the Security Wizard actually is the best way to secure a database.

After the database is secure, you can assign permissions to the users and groups who need to access the data. By locking up the database completely, and then relaxing the security as appropriate, there is a lesser likelihood of security holes. Trying to secure a database piece-by-piece invariably leads to some objects being overlooked, thereby compromising security.

Unsecuring the Database

If you log on as Admin, and the user Admin still is a member of the Admins group, then running the Security Wizard actually removes restrictions on all the selected objects and makes the database unsecure and, therefore, open to any user. If you then remove the Admin password, users will not even have to log on to obtain unrestricted access to the data, the design, the tables, and the code.

From Here...

This chapter reviewed the Access security model, and how you use it to secure your application. You looked at adding users and groups to your security scheme, assigning permissions on objects, and granting permissions to the users. You learned how to secure an application, while still allowing the user to change passwords to keep their data secure. You then learned how to unsecure a database.

For more information on these topics, see the following chapters:

- Chapter 13, "Building the Run-Time Application," for information on how to build and distribute a secure run-time application.
- Chapter 19, "System Administration," for information about local and remote database administration.
- Chapter 22, "The Human Factor," for a discussion of the human element in the client/server environment.

Building the Run-Time Application

Access gives you the capability to build compiled *run-time applications* that can be distributed free of royalty charges to end users within your corporation, or for resale. This chapter covers the following areas:

- Look at the reasons for building a run-time application
- Discuss the tools available to build a run-time application
- Examine the features these tools offer the applications developer
- Explore how to use these tools to your best advantage
- Learn how to produce and distribute a stand-alone Access application that doesn't require a copy of Access on every desktop

Compiling Applications

Back in the dark ages of programming, you wrote a program, compiled it, loaded it, and—if you were lucky—it ran. The *compiled code* was in some machine-readable format, and (unless you were fluent in binary or hexadecimal) could not be checked for errors—you had to return to the source code to do this. As more programming tools were developed, you had a better chance that your program would run with minimal pain on the developer's part.

Then, came programming languages such as BASIC, which is interpreted at run time, rather than compiled. Efficiency of operating code was traded for ease of use, ease of programming, and ease of debugging. A complex piece of software like Access 95 now offers the capability to compile queries and modules, while retaining the ease of use of an *interpreted program*.

At times, it is appropriate to compile an Access 95 application. Some of the reasons for doing so are shown in the following list:

- To prevent users from changing the application code
- To protect your intellectual property
- To make the program smaller and easier to distribute

Microsoft gave more reasons to compile Access 95 code and added a set of tools just for this purpose. These additional reasons include the following:

- The capability to legally put a copy of your application on multiple computers without having to buy a copy of Access 95 for each user
- The opportunity to produce a shrink-wrapped software package based on Access 95

This seems like a really good deal, but how do we do it?

The Access Developer's Kit

First you need a copy of Access 95—the "full version of Access" that we have discussed throughout this book—to develop the application. You may have picked up a copy either at your local computer store or through mail order from your favorite supplier.

To create run-time copies of your application you need the Microsoft *Access Developer's Toolkit for Windows 95* (its official title). If you want to impress the people at your local user group meeting, call it the *ADT*. Some refer to it as the *ADK*, or *Access Distribution Kit*. However, if you ask for the ADT at your local computer superstore, chances are they won't have a clue about what you are saying—so, what's new? The ADT is not a high-demand item; therefore, you probably will have to order it from one of the companies that specialize in selling software to programmers. The better mail-order houses will know about it, and some may stock it or be able to obtain it at short notice. If you work for a large company, the reseller who provides the corporate software (Microsoft Office and so on) should be able to furnish a copy.

What Is the ADT?

The ADT is a set of utility programs—actually, wizards—that work with Access 95 to enable you to build compiled applications. Figure 13.1 shows the different program items that are installed in Microsoft ADT program group. Perhaps more important, the purchase of this kit entitles you to compile and distribute these applications, with no further royalty payments to Microsoft Corporation. Your users need only the compiled code to run your programs—each user doesn't need to own a copy of Access 95. If your interface is well crafted, they may not even know that the application that they are running is based on Access 95. They will think you did it all yourself. If this sounds too good to be true, keep reading!

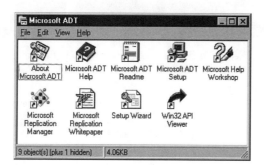

Fig. 13.1

The Access Developers Toolkit folder, showing the items installed by the ADT.

What's Included in the ADT?

The ADT includes a CD-ROM and two manuals. The ADT doesn't seem to be available on floppy disks. The assumption probably is that all developers have CD-ROM drives. Certainly, if you are running Windows 95 or Windows NT, you have no excuse for not owning one. Actually, besides the ADT CD-ROM, you also will find a CD-ROM that contains sample databases and other good stuff, such as the Microsoft Developer Network Starter Kit, a preview of the upcoming Mastering Microsoft Access CD-ROM-based self-paced course, and the *Microsoft Developer Roadmap*.

Also included in the ADT are the *Microsoft Access Language Reference* manual and the *Microsoft Office 95 Data Access Reference* manual, in printed format to supplement the Access on-line documentation.

Last, but not least, you will find the *Win32 API Declarations File and Viewer* and the *Microsoft Help Workshop*. The former is used to view and copy declarations to the Clipboard and from there into your applications. The latter is used to assist in building and compiling Windows Help files (see Chapter 15, "Creating Help Files," for more information on the Windows Help subsystem).

Requirements to run the ADT are as follows:

- A Pentium-level computer, with at least 16 to 20M of RAM
- A range of 15–30M of space on the hard disk
- A CD-ROM drive for installation
- Monitor capable of displaying VGA or SVGA graphics

What Does It Cost?

The cost of the ADT is not as much as you might think, given the potential it offers. Street price runs between $350 and $500 for this one-time (per version of Access) purchase. You can use the ADT to build applications that (hopefully) will bring in cashflow from shrink-wrapped software, or the ADT can be used to save your company IS budget for other purposes. The cost of the ADT can be recovered rapidly. In fact, if you had the Distribution Kit for Access 2, you even get a rebate on the Access 95 kit. The ADT is not software that gets discounted much—it isn't a package that anyone buys in quantity.

III

Building the Application

Caution

The Access 2.0 ADT cannot be used to build Access 95 applications, and the Access 95 ADT cannot be used to build Access 2 applications. Access 95 is a 32-bit application; Access 2 is a 16-bit application. The two distribution kits are not compatible.

What Will It Do for Your Application?

When you use the ADT to build a set of *installation disks* for your application, you can be assured that the installation program has the same professional look and feel as any piece of Windows software that you purchase off-the-shelf. The installation program will contain all the code to query the user about where to install the application (you set the default). It checks for disk space, runs any macros or preliminary programs that you may need run up front, and then performs the install. Literally, the end user only has to insert the first installation disk (or begin the CD-ROM install, if you opt to create a CD-ROM installation disk), and use the Windows 95 Add New Software option in Control Panel, and then follow the on-screen directions.

To install on a Windows NT system, use the traditional A:\SETUP or double-click the setup.exe file in File Manager. For either operating system, the installation process builds a new program group (again, the name is your choice), and installs both the program and an icon. You also can supply the icon if you have artistic skill or a good icon-builder program. The installation process looks smooth and professional. The dialog boxes look familiar to anyone who has installed Windows 95 and Microsoft Office. These dialog boxes meet all the Windows 95 standards. With the capabilities provided by the ADT, you really don't need to write your own installation program.

If you need more persuading that the ADT is a *Good Idea*, consider this: it builds *Windows 95 shortcuts* for you, and updates the *Registry*. If you feel you can do a better job of these tasks than the Microsoft programmers who wrote the ADT wizards, you are in a league by yourself. Most database developers, including the authors, have better ways to allocate their time, and will not mess with the Windows Registry if they can avoid doing so.

The ADT also assists you with integrating support for *OLE custom controls*, and adding *replication* to your software. The *Microsoft Replication Manager and Transporter*—which you can redistribute—is used to create and manage replicated systems and to add replication scheduling to applications. All this is done by way of a graphical user interface that allows you to provide the support tools for remote sites and for your road warriors.

How and Where Should the ADT Be Installed?

The ADT uses the normal Windows 95 or Windows NT installation process, essentially the same process that it builds for your application. The ADT supplements Access 95 with some of its own wizards, so the logical place to put the ADT is in the same directory structure, or at least on the same hard disk as the development copy of Access 95.

ADT also builds its own folder, although you may want to make it a subfolder of your Access 95 folder for convenience.

> **Tip**
>
> Be careful if you already have the ADT for Access 2.0 on your system. The setup program for the Access 95 ADT doesn't look for, or warn you that it will overwrite some of the old version files. Some files in the new version of the ADT have the same name as files in the older version, and these files will be overwritten if the two ADTs are installed in the same directory. Files with different names are left in the directory—the Access 95 ADT doesn't perform "cleanup" of past versions. It's a better idea to install the Access 95 ADT to its own directory, which is why the authors suggest installing it as a subfolder, under the Access 95 folder.

How Run-Time Access Differs from the Full Version

Significant differences exist between the run-time version of Access 95 and the full "developer" version of the same product. Some of these differences are helpful in securing the application; others can be problematic unless you make allowances for them. Briefly, the differences are described in the following list:

- The menus and toolbars are different. The built-in toolbars which appear in the development version of Access 95 do not appear in the run-time version, but your own custom toolbars do. The default run-time menu is very limited; any choices relating to the design of the application have been removed. If you want you can provide a set of custom menus for your application that extends the choices.

- The database window is hidden in the run-time version, so that no way exists to select and open a form from the database container. To open the application with a specific form, you must specify the form in the Startup options, and give the user a means to navigate through the application from there.

- In the run-time version an error in a macro will cause the immediate termination of the entire application, with no message to the user. Untrapped errors in Visual Basic for Applications code modules do the same thing. Avoid macros (except for the macros Access builds for the custom menus, and the Autoexec and Autokeys macros) in your run-time applications. All Visual Basic code modules used in a run-time application must have some built-in error handling.

- Because the database window is hidden in the run-time version, the user cannot drop and reattach tables. Therefore, you have to provide code that tests to ensure the server tables are available and if not, the code must then ask the user to supply the location of the file that contains the data tables. (Look in the OUTLINE.MDB file that comes with the ADT for an example of code that does this, or refer to the Solutions.MDB file in the \Access\Samples subfolder. The upper window topic is Use Multiple Databases; the lower window topic is Link Tables at Startup.)

- Online help should reflect and support your application, so you need to supply a Help file and specify the name of this help file on the properties sheet of each form and report. In the run-time application there is no online help, unless you supply it.

- In the full development version of Access 95, holding down Shift during startup bypasses the Autoexec macro and takes you directly to the database window. This technique isn't permitted in the run-time version, where holding down Shift has no effect during startup. Similarly, the Ctrl+Break combination is deactivated, so that the user cannot interrupt the execution of a module, although it still works to stop a query that is out of control and is returning far more data than expected.

Tip

Rather than having to build a run-time distribution set and install it to see what it will look like, build a shortcut to both your Access files and your application file, followed by **/runtime**, as in the following example:

```
{full_path_name}\msaccess.exe {full_path_name}\rea.mdb /runtime
```

This shortcut runs the REA database in simulated run-time mode.

Transitioning to the Run-Time Application: What You Do and Don't Need

To ensure a successful transition from a development application to a run-time application, you must do a little planning and preparation. The database itself must be ready, and you will need some additional files. The best approach is to put these files, and a copy of your database MDB file, in a new directory, which is referred to as the *Build Directory*.

What to Include in the Distribution Build Directory

Besides the MDB file, you need the following files:

- The SYSTEM.MDW file, with the security that you added in Chapter 12, "Securing the Access 95 Application"

- An icon for your application, in .ICO format

- A compiled Help file or files

- A .BMP file for the "splash" screen

- If you previously created a custom workgroup information file (SYSTEM.MDW) that is critical to the operation of the application, include it too

The SYSTEM.MDW file included in the build can be the same file that you usually use to run Access 95, unless you have a custom workgroup information file, as indicated in the fourth bullet in the preceding list. You should make a copy of it in the Build Directory, however, before bringing up Access. Because the ADT Setup Wizard runs under Access, which means that Access is running, you cannot use the SYSTEM.MDW file in the Access 95 directory for the build—definitely a chicken-and-egg situation.

> **Note**
>
> If you are creating a client installation set, and your server database is an Access 95 database, then you don't need to include either the server .MDB file or the SYSTEM.MDW in the build. Both files should be located on the server, so that all client users can access the common data.MDB and SYSTEM.MDW.

The *icon* is the small illustration that shows up when your application is added to the program group, and under Windows NT, when it is minimized. Use an icon editor to build a suitable icon from a graphics file, and store it as a .ICO format in your build directory.

The *splash screen* is the screen that pops up as the application starts. The screen serves two purposes. The first service is to provide information to the user—the name of the application, copyright notices, version numbers, and so on. The second reason is to distract the user while the application loads, and give the impression that it loads quickly. If this last comment sounds cynical, watch how other applications load. From splash screens to "tips of the day," many techniques are employed, but all with the same intent. Design your splash screen with plenty of diversion—let it load at application startup—and while the user is looking at it, the rest of the application can be loading in the background.

You should create help files specific to the application because the Access 95 development system help files are not included in the run-time and even if they were, they would not provide answers to most questions about your application. See Chapter 15, "Creating Help Files," for guidelines on building help files.

What You Don't Need to Include

You do not need to include some Access files with the application. There is no real reason, for example, to include the design wizards in a run-time application, as there is no way for the user to implement them. You don't need to include the Workgroup Administrator because the user will not be changing workgroups. Each Access-based application will be installed as a separate entity with the appropriate SYSTEM.MDW file, so the user is automatically in the right workgroup.

You don't have to include the Access executable files. The run-time versions of these files are placed on the distribution disks by the Setup Wizard. Because you will include your own application-specific Help files as described in Chapter 15, you don't need to include the Access Help files.

What You Aren't Allowed to Distribute

Some files that come with Access 95 are not covered under the royalty-free license to distribute the run-time application. These files are mainly wizards and add-in files. One important point—you cannot legally distribute the Access Help file with your application—you must build your own (see Chapter 15, "Creating Help Files," for more information on how to do this). This limitation makes sense because application users aren't concerned with running Access, they only want to know how to run the application. The documentation that comes with the ADT details which files you may distribute.

Preparation for Distribution

There are a few steps that you can take before building disks that make your application smaller, faster, and more efficient.

Set the Startup Parameters

Open the database and select Startup from the Tools menu to open the Startup Dialog Box (see fig. 13.2). Type the application name, the name of the icon file for the application, and the name of the form that should be opened on startup. You also should supply the name of your custom menu macro on this form, in the Menu Bar field. All other parameters can be left as the default.

Fig. 13.2

Setting the startup parameters for an application in the Startup dialog box.

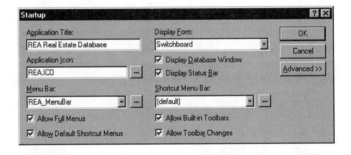

Compile All the Code

Code that isn't already compiled must be compiled each time it runs, slowing the application. The compiled code runs faster; also, now is the time to ensure that all the code works, or at least compiles. Better that you discover any code problems now than to have end users discover them after distribution.

Remove All Comments

You commented your application diligently, so that anyone can follow your exquisite logic and flashes of inspiration. Now the authors are telling you to remove the comments. (You *did* comment your code, didn't you?) Actually, remove the comments only from the copy that goes into the Build Directory, not from your working copy.

Besides denying assistance to anyone who may slip in through a hole in your security model, removing these comments reduces the size of your application. It then requires fewer disks for distribution, installs in less time, and loads and runs faster. Recompile after removing the comments, just to ensure that you did not also accidentally remove some code.

Compact Your Application

The .MDB file in Access 95 tends to grow rapidly while you are developing (space formerly occupied by deleted objects isn't immediately reclaimed), and shrinks back to a more reasonable size after it is compacted. For the reasons mentioned in the preceding paragraphs, the smaller the .MDB file, the better. Chapter 16, "Tuning the Access 95 Application," discusses other reasons why frequent database compaction is a good idea.

Building the Run-Time Application

After all the files that you will need are assembled in the Build Directory, you are ready to begin building the run-time version of your application. Start the process by clicking the Setup Wizard icon or entry in the ADT folder. This action starts Access 95, and then activates the Setup Wizard (see fig. 13.3). If you are familiar with the version 2.0 Setup Wizard, you will find this new Setup Wizard to be more helpful, although it also is far more complex.

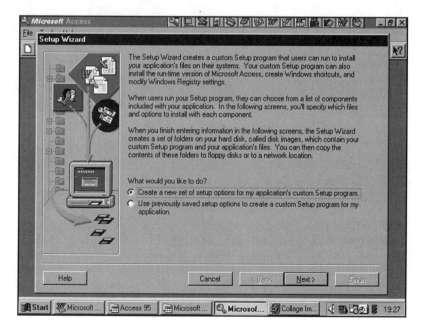

Fig. 13.3

The ADT Setup Wizard: the introductory screen with setup options to start anew or use a previously created setup template.

III

Building the Application

When the Setup Wizard starts, it offers you a choice of either creating a new set of setup options, or using a previously created set. Every time you build a new set of options, save it so that it can be reused each time you rebuild the distribution disks for that project. Also, of course, you can modify an existing option set for a new project. In Access, these stored option sets are known as *templates*.

Adding Files to the Distribution Set

Start by creating a new option set for our REA project, which we want to distribute as a run-time application to the employees of REA Corporation. You select the Create New Options button, and continue to the next screen (see fig. 13.4).

Fig. 13.4

Building the distribution file list by adding files (client.mdb and server.mdb, custom SYSTEM.MDW, icon file, help file) to the list.

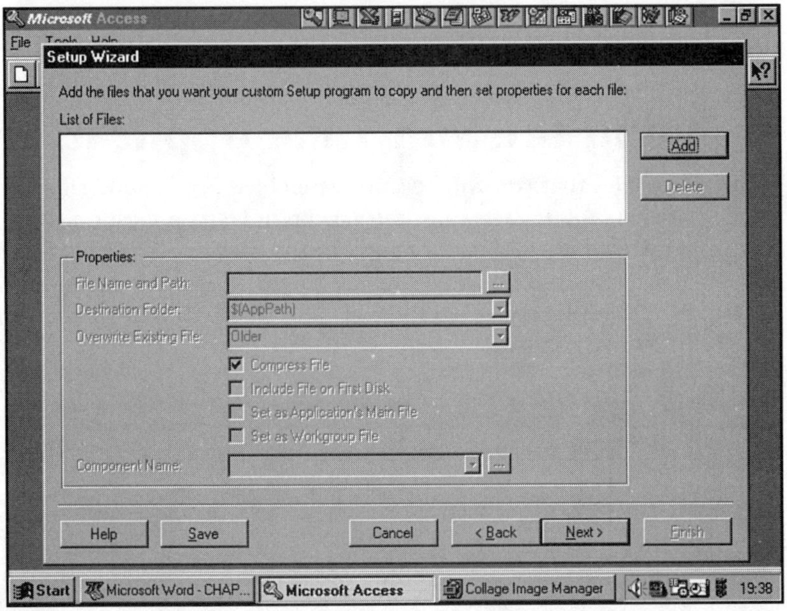

In this Setup Wizard dialog box, you specify the files that you want to include in your build. Click the Add button, and then locate the files by using the Windows 95 file-selection interface—unless you like typing folder and file names (see fig. 13.5).

Start with the MDB file for your client application, and label it as the main file by checking the Set as Application's Main File box on-screen. Note that its default destination is **$(AppPath)**. In other words, this file will be installed in the application path the user specifies. You don't have to worry about what this path might be—the installation program handles the destination dialogs. No matter what your user specifies for the install disk and directory, it is substituted for the $(AppPath) parameter. If you are using the ADT for the first time, you may be beginning to appreciate how much work and irritation it saves.

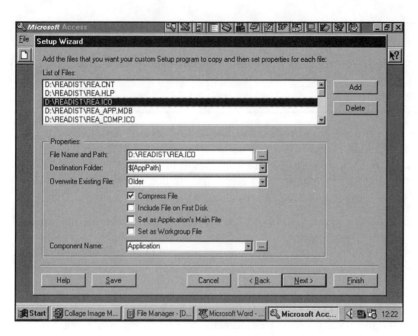

Fig. 13.5

Adding the icon file to the distribution set and indicating that it is to live in the same folder $(AppPath), where the application will eventually reside.

When your application installs, it can place files in $(AppPath), $(AppPath)*subfolder*, $(WinPath), or $(WinSysPath). The last two are of course the path to the Windows 95 folder, and the path to the system subfolder for Windows 95.

Usually, you want to set the Overwrite Existing File option to **Always**. If you do not, then a new release of your application may not install properly. The **Older** option, where a newer file replaces an old one, may work for many files, but probably will not work for your database MDB and workgroup MDW files. The date on these database files reflects the last time they were opened rather than the install date, and so the date stamp of the .MDB or .MDW file on the hard disk often will be later than the build date of the new release.

Make sure that the *Compress File* option is turned on. Access 95 files compress to a significantly smaller size, even after the database is compacted. The only files that you should leave uncompressed are README files, which the user may look for on the first disk. Leave these files uncompressed, and then the user can read them with Notepad or Wordpad.

Don't call your ReadMe file by a name with only two characters in the file extension, such as READ.ME. The compression algorithm will have trouble renaming it, so use a three-character extension, such as README.TXT. In a similar vein, you may want to use short file names that follow the DOS 8.3 naming standard (*filename.ext* is equivalent to "8-character" file name, "3-character" extension). Although Windows 95 and Windows NT can handle long file names, they both offer the capability to boot to DOS. Finally, staying with short file names lessens the risk of your application files being corrupted by some third-party disk utility.

> **Note**
>
> In the Add File dialog box of the Setup Wizard, remember that the properties shown on the lower part of this screen refer to the file that is highlighted in the upper part of the screen, and that file properties can change, depending on the needs of a specific file.

The option to force the file onto the first disk also should be used for these information or README files because this is where the user expects to find them. If this option isn't selected, the Setup Wizard shuffles the files to minimize the number of disks required for the build. If a file changes in size between builds, the assignment of files to the floppy disks in the installation set can change.

Don't try to force files onto the first disk unless they really need to be there. If you check this option for a large number of files, they all will not fit. Even if these files should fit, it is preferable to let the Wizard allocate the files to the various disks of the build.

One file should be designated as the *workgroup file*—this is your SYSTEM.MDW. Although the SYSTEM.MDW can be assigned any name, for consistency, keep the MDW extension. If you don't specify a workgroup file, the Setup Wizard builds one. This generated file does not have the security and user information that you need for your application, so make sure that you supply the proper .MDW file.

Adding the Splash Screen

The splash screen is a graphic, which can come from anywhere. You create or copy the graphic to fit the needs of the application. Remember, if you're copying copyrighted material, you must have permission from the author or artist to use his or her material in the splash screen (or anywhere else in the application). If the splash screen is original material, you can use any graphics or artwork software package to create and manipulate, and then save as a bitmapped file, with a .BMP extension.

The trick to adding the splash screen is that the graphics file must have the same name as the database .MDB file, but with a .BMP extension. Set the .BMP install path to the same path as the database file—that is, the application path. When Access starts, if it finds a .BMP file with the same name as the .MDB file, it uses this .BMP file as the splash screen. The setup of the splash screen is that simple!

Installing Components and Options

New in this version of the ADT is the capability to define your files as *components* of the application, as the Access 95 software installation itself does. In the Access V2 ADT, every file you listed was installed, and only one installation "option" existed, the Full Install. Being forced to press a button to choose the only available option often resulted in confusion on the user's part when installing the application. The Access V7 ADT adds full capability to break your custom application into components, as seen when installing programs such as Microsoft Office, Access 95, and other Windows 95 software. You can subdivide your application into components, some of which are mandatory and some of which may (or may not) be installed at the user's discretion (see fig. 13.6).

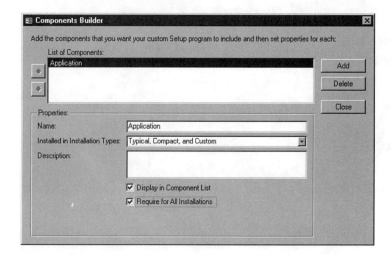

Fig. 13.6

The Components Builder dialog box, showing the list of components and installation type options: typical, compact, and custom.

Three install options are available: Typical, Compact, and Custom, and the components of your application will be assigned to one or more of these install options, as appropriate.

The *Typical install* is the norm for desktop systems with available disk space. The *Compact install* leaves out some nonessential files, and is intended for portable computers where disk space and memory usually are more limited.

The *Custom install* is for the more experienced user, and can include extra features, more documentation, additional utility routines, and the capability to deselect features not needed or wanted. You can specify whether a file is to be included in all three installation options, only in the Typical and Custom (thereby omitting it from the Compact installation), or only in the Custom Installation. The essential files, such as the database and workgroup files, can be shown here although the user has to install them if you check the Require for All Installations box. These essential files also can be left out of the list displayed to the user, if you prefer not to show files that must be installed in all cases.

If you don't set up the components and installation options here, you can do so at a later step in the Setup Wizard process, when it prompts you to do so.

Setting Up Shortcuts

The next phase of the Setup Wizard helps with building the *shortcuts* that your application will use in a Windows 95 installation (see fig. 13.7).

Fig. 13.7

Setting up a Windows 95 shortcut for your application, using the Setup Wizard shortcuts dialog box.

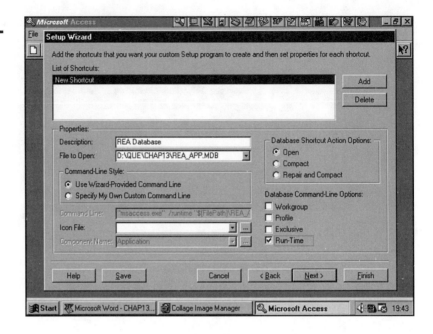

The first shortcut you want to specify is the one that brings up your application, using the run-time version of Access 95. Select the database .MDB file as the file to open, and then type the description for the shortcut. The *Database Shortcut Action Option* in this case is Open. Check the box to add the Run-Time option to the command line. This action ensures that the database file will be opened by using a run-time version of Access 95 . If you do not supply a run-time version of Access 95, the database will be opened with a full development copy of Access 95, provided that one is available. Also, check the Workgroup box so that the application will use the .MDW workgroup file for security and user rights. The alternative, the Profile option, tells Access to look at a user profile stored in the Registry for this information.

Other shortcuts which you should add are the capability to *Compact* the database, and to *Repair and Compact* the database (see fig. 13.8). The new version of the setup wizard makes it simple to include these shortcuts. With each of these options, check the Workgroup box so that the repair and compact processes are controlled by the security settings in the workgroup file.

As you move from this screen, the Setup Wizard informs you if you have not included the run-time version of Access 95 in your distribution file list, and offers to include it (see fig. 13.9). You don't have to copy the run-time executable file to your build directory.

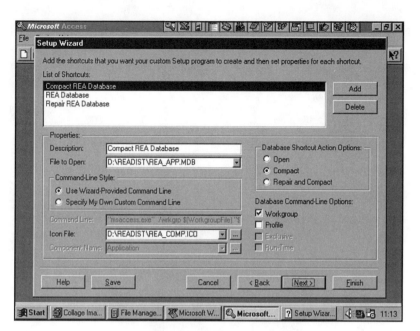

Fig. 13.8

Adding the Compact Database and Repair Database shortcuts, which makes it easier for end users to maintain their own copies of the software.

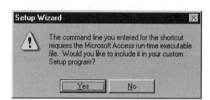

Fig. 13.9

The Setup Wizard offers to include the Access 95 run-time executable file in the custom setup, if you forgot.

Including Other Access Components

You can include and distribute some Access components with your application (see fig. 13.10). For example, you should include the ODBC Support with SQL Server if your back-end database is running on Microsoft's SQL Server. You have to include the Workgroup Manager, even if your users will not be changing workgroups. You must use a workgroup file for security information. If you try to turn off this feature, you see a warning message as you try to move out of this screen. Replication should be included if you intend to use the Windows 95 Briefcase replication facility. And of course, you will want to leave the Access Run-Time option checked. If your application generates charts and graphs, you can distribute a run-time version of Microsoft Graph 5.

Fig. 13.10

*The different components
you can distribute in an
Access 95 installation
setup.*

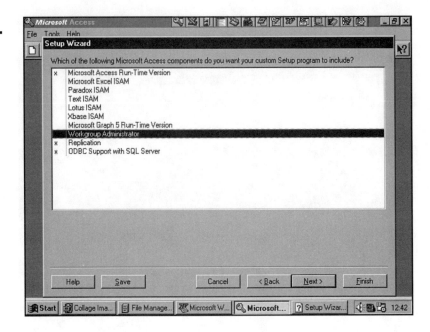

Configuring Replication

If replication is turned on, you have to set up some replication parameters (see fig. 13.11). See Chapter 20, "Replication with Access 95," for a full discussion of replication.

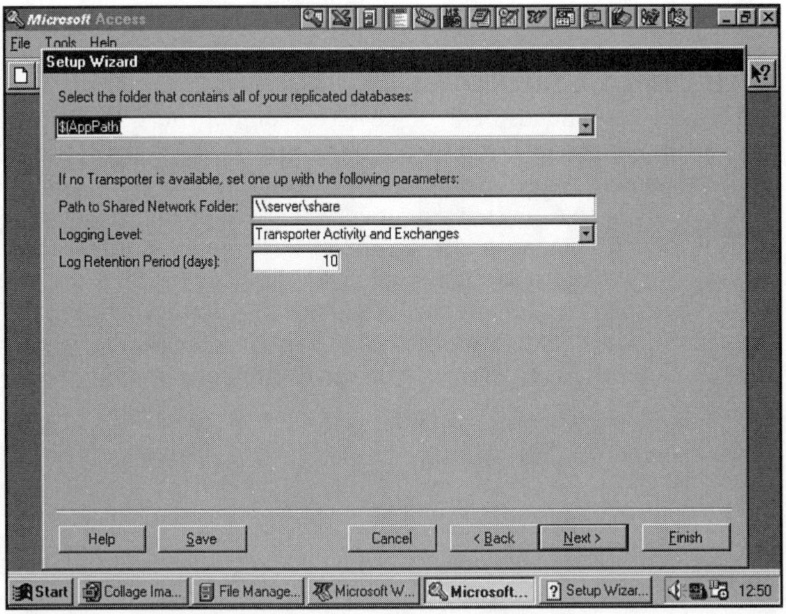

Fig. 13.11

*Configuring the replication
parameters with the Setup
Wizard.*

Configuring Components

If you did not do so previously, now you have the opportunity to configure the components of your application (see fig. 13.12). Note that when you looked at the Components list the last time—from the Add files screen—it allowed you to add components. Here, you can reorder components, but you cannot add them. By clicking the up and down arrows to the left of the topmost window, you can move the highlighted entry up or down in the list. By this stage of the build, you should have added all the necessary files and components for a proper installation, and here you can change the order and some of the properties.

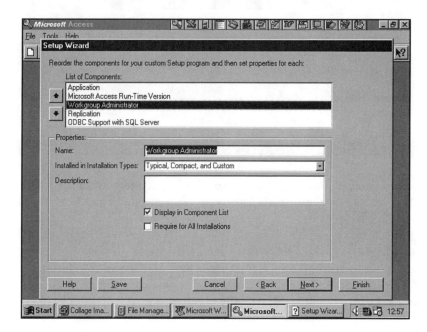

Fig. 13.12

The Components screen of the Setup Wizard, with the scrolling control to the left of the upper window that allows you to reorder the listed components.

For example, you may want to include the Replication option only in the custom setup, so that only those users who need it can install it, and those who do not need this option can omit it by selecting a Typical installation. Items such as the Workgroup Administrator and the ODBC support can be set to not even appear in the Component List when the user installs the program. You can even leave the Access run-time off the list, if you don't feel that it's necessary to let your user know that this is an Access-based application.

Identifying Your Application for the User

One new feature in the Setup Wizard is the capability to include some information about the application, the version number, and your own company information (see fig. 13.13).

Fig. 13.13

Giving a full description of your application, including company name and version number, to the Setup Wizard.

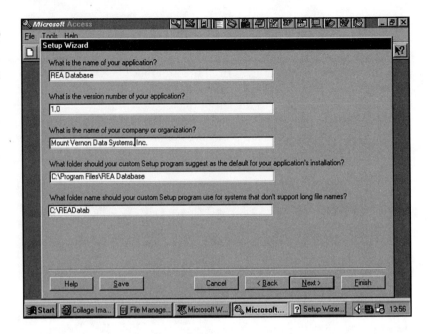

Also, on this screen you can provide the suggested installation directory for your application. The users can, of course, install it wherever they want, thanks to the capabilities in the Setup program.

Running an Executable File after Installation

Executable files include batch files, so you can write a batch file to run any cleanup routines or provide information to the user. For example, you can run a batch file after installation to pop up the README.TXT file in Notepad or Wordpad, or to offer a tutorial that you may have put together as part of a new-user training package. Just a note on the tutorials: if you choose to launch one immediately following completion of the install, give your users a command button that bails them out from any point within the tutorial. Don't force them to click backwards through several levels of forms to exit the tutorial.

Make sure that you include the batch file in your list of files for the distribution set, and check the box entitled Allow Setup to Complete, which ensures that the setup completes before the batch file is run. The user sees the dialog box, stating that the setup has completed successfully, and then the executable file will run. If you do not check this box, the file will run, but the user may not realize that the setup has, in fact, completed (see fig. 13.14).

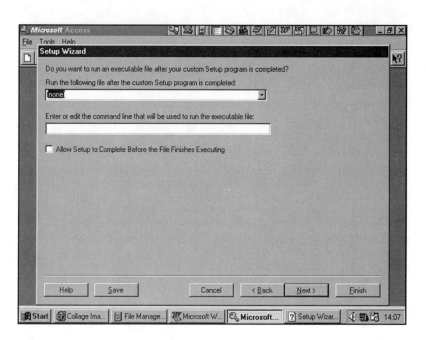

Fig. 13.14

Indicating to the Setup Wizard that you want to run an executable file (perhaps a tutorial) after setup completes.

Building the Disks

The Setup Wizard asks where it should build the distribution disks (see fig. 13.15). More precisely, it builds a series of folders, each of which contains the files that belong on one floppy disk. Consider building the subfolders under the build directory or folder, rather than under the ADT folder. (The path suggested after default installations of Access 95 and the ADT is starting to become rather long.) The only disk option in this version of the Setup Wizard is 1.44M high-density floppies, but it is unlikely that you use anything else.

Fig. 13.15

Indicating to the Setup Wizard the path to the folder where the disk images will be stored.

III

Building the Application

On the off chance that you will press installation CD-ROM disks, choose either the Network Setup or the Compressed Network Setup. Both write all the files for the installation set to a single folder, where they can be copied over to a CD-ROM for pressing.

The Wizard offers you the option of storing the compressed files. The benefit in this is, if you run the Setup Wizard again with minor changes, it runs faster because it doesn't have to compress the files for a second time. The downside to storing these compressed files (as opposed to re-creating them) is that it takes extra space on your hard drive. The best compromise may be to store these files while you are fine-tuning the distribution disk setup, but don't bother to keep them after the setup is in its final form.

Installing from a Network. You now have the choice—new in this version—of building a *network installation* folder. All of the files will be stored in this folder, in either compressed or uncompressed format. Each client user can connect to this folder on the server and install the application, without fussing about floppy disks and installation sets.

The Build Process

After all the parameter choices are made, only compressing the files and building the disk images remains (see fig. 13.16). This is an extremely CPU-intensive process that, even on a Windows NT system, takes most of the CPU cycles for some time.

Fig. 13.16

Building the disk images takes several minutes, depending on the size of the files to include in the build.

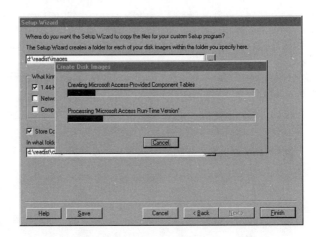

It may take between 5 and 20 minutes to build the disk images, depending on how fast your system runs and how much you have included in your build. You may want to plan the build during a lunch break, or when you have to attend to other non-computer tasks. When the build process is complete, you are notified (see fig. 13.17).

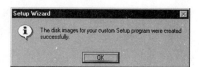

Fig. 13.17

Build process completion, with a notification that the build completed without error.

Distributing Your Application

How you decide to distribute the application depends on the kind of database that you are using for the server and the extent of the distribution. The critical question is whether the server is an Access database or whether it is a foreign database management system.

Distributing the Server Application

If the server database is not Access 95, it must be installed according to the supplier's instructions, and the required accounts built and permissions assigned so that it can be accessed by the users by way of the client Access application.

If the server is an Access 95 database, it must be copied over to the server computer. Note that the database doesn't have to be "installed" on the server. As we pointed out in Chapter 1, "Client/Server: What Is It?" Access isn't really running in true client/server mode because changes to the Access server database are handled by the client application. The database on the server is opened by the clients, not by a local copy of Access. In fact, a copy of Access doesn't even need to be present on the server computer, not even the run-time version. You don't need to create installation disks for the server database; you just need to copy it to the appropriate directory on the server.

> **Tip**
>
> Looking to the future, you can copy the network installation folder to a CD-ROM, and then distribute copies of your application by duplicating the CD-ROM. If this kind of distribution is in your plans, you may want to check into the Windows 95 Auto-install feature, which automatically runs the setup program on the CD-ROM the first time it is read.

Distributing the Client Application

Now that you have the folders that correspond to the installation disks (see fig. 13.18), you only need to copy the contents of each folder to a floppy disk, and label each disk in the set. If you have a large number of users, or plan to market the application, a commercial disk-replication service can produce labeled copies in a day or two.

Fig. 13.18

The disk image folders, each of which contains a set of files that is part of the installation set. Copy the contents of each folder to a floppy to make the set of installation disks.

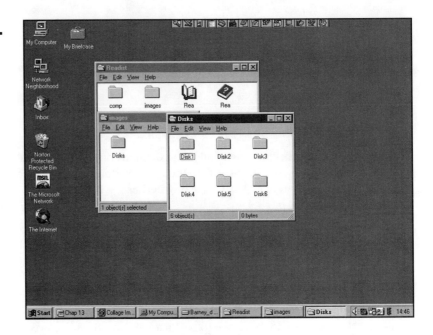

To install the application, the user inserts disk 1, and then runs the Windows 95 Add/ Remove Programs option in the Control Panel. Your application installs in the same way that any other Windows 95 application is installed—asking for target directories, and offering the choices of Typical, Compact, or Custom installation. For a Windows NT installation, the user runs SETUP.EXE from the floppy disk or double-clicks the file, setup.exe, in File Manager.

Installation via Network

If you choose an over-the-network installation, the user must connect to the folder or directory in which the files are stored, and run SETUP.EXE. Of course, this means that the folder must be shared and, in a Windows NT or a NetWare environment, the user must have the necessary permissions to run the setup program and copy files.

> **Tip**
>
> If you have an Access 2.0 application and want to offer a network install capability, create a directory on the server disk. Under this directory, create subdirectories DISK1, DISK2, and so on, one directory for each disk of the installation set. Copy the files from each floppy disk into the corresponding directory. The user then can connect to the DISK1 directory on the server and run SETUP.EXE. This method works for most Windows-based software, not just Access.

After **setup.exe** has run and the program is installed, the user no longer needs the connection to the network share that contains the distribution files. He or she only needs the connection to the server. It's a good idea to leave the distribution files shared, in the event that a user has problems and needs to reinstall, or gets a new computer. Because all the data in the database is stored on the server, the client software, the front-end application, can be reinstalled at any time, without adversely affecting the data component.

Running the Application Across the Network

Do not assume that you can install the client software once on the server, and have the users point to that directory and run from there. Many network administrators like to do this because it makes upgrading the software very easy (one copy of the application program). This setup, however, really doesn't work in an Access environment.

What will not happen if you choose this "application server" method? The installation does not install the shortcuts on each user's machine. It also does not install a group of DLLs into the Windows 95 path on each user's computer, assuming that the users have at least a copy of Windows 95 on their desktop. The application then looks in the local Windows 95 directory for these files and it doesn't find them; it generates an error message on the user's computer. DLLs normally are stored in the SYSTEM folder of the Windows directory, so that they can be used by any Windows program or application.

Any Access application that runs from an application server generates an enormous amount of network traffic—the hallmark of the file/server model of computing. An application such as Word or Excel loads most of the required software on startup, so there is a big load on the network, and then the traffic drops off. Access 95, however, is constantly needing DLLs, loading them and then unloading them from memory, as required. It must do this because the software is too big to fit in memory all at once. Additionally, Access constantly sends queries to the server database and in a file/server environment, the Access server doesn't process the query but returns the entire data set to the client database engine for processing.

You can alleviate some of this problem by adding more memory to each user's machine but the real answer is to do two things—install the client application locally on each user's computer, and migrate the data component to a true client/server database management system.

If software distribution really is a big issue in your company, consider simplifying it by adding Microsoft's Systems Management Server (SMS). This BackOffice component tracks computer configurations and installed software, and allows you to distribute software across the network to users that you designate.

Distributing a Client Upgrade

The disks created by the Setup Wizard are great for the first installation of the client software, but what about an upgrade to your application? Do you need to rebuild the installation set each time you make a change to the user interface and, therefore, "upgrade" the client application? The authors know of four ways to handle an upgrade:

III

Building the Application

- Distribute a completely new installation set of disks
- Distribute the client .MDB file only on an upgrade disk
- Do an over-the-network broadcast update of the client software
- Replicate the client .MDB file to all users who are using the Windows 95 replication

New Distribution Set. The first method is safe because you know that the application will be installed correctly, even if the user specifies a new directory for the upgrade. However, distributing a completely new installation set of disks requires associated costs in time and materials. Your time to build the distribution set is less because you saved the template, and perhaps the compressed files, but the user still must go through a reinstall, shuffling multiple disks in and out of the floppy drive. As an extra benefit of this method, you can add a batch file to run after the upgrade is complete that deletes all old files no longer needed by your application.

If you are a producer of shrink-wrapped software, this option or the following one may be your best bet for getting upgrades to your users.

Upgrade Disk. You can distribute the upgrade on a floppy disk if your .MDB file fits on one disk. The Setup Wizard has the capability to split files between disks (which, if your .MDB is large, probably is what happened in the first place to create the installation set). Even when it looks as though the .MDB file is bigger than 1.44M, you can make the file fit onto a single floppy. Use a compression utility to squeeze it down to a reasonable size. If you use a third-party utility such as PKZIP, WinZIP, or WinZIP95, you can make an executable file from the compressed file or files that you're distributing. The end user simply copies the executable file to the correct directory and runs it to uncompress the contents. The downside of this method is that you are relying on the user to get the files into the correct directory. It is true that utilities like PKZIP can store a directory path and unzip to that, but this forces the user to have the application installed in some chosen default directory.

Network Broadcast Update. If you installed over the network, it may make more sense to upgrade the same way. Even if you installed from floppy disks, upgrading over the network still is an option, especially when the application has grown and no longer fits onto a single floppy disk, even with compression. You can create a batch file that copies the upgrade to all the user computers on the network. If you prefer, you can place the upgrade on the server hard disk and let the users connect and download it. The latter method isn't recommended because it again places the responsibility for software upgrades on the users—yet, when they do not properly install the upgrade or have problems, you know who gets the panicky phone calls. The best idea is to use an administration package like SMS to send an upgrade to everyone who has a release of the product installed.

If you are a producer of "Web-able" software—software that was uploaded to a World-Wide Web or FTP site and is available to users by downloading—upgrades can be handled in the same way. If you have registration software at your Web/FTP site, which captures user e-mail addresses as they download the software, then it's an easy matter to broadcast the availability of an upgrade.

Replicating the Changes. The last option is to use the replication capabilities of your system to distribute the upgrade. You can replicate not only the data, you also can replicate modifications to the client application. This technique is a neat and tidy way to use the new features of Windows 95 to make your life easier.

Testing Your Distribution Disks

You must test the distribution disks to ensure that you haven't omitted any critical files. The initial testing can be performed on the development system. During the testing, rename your Access 95 folder so that the run-time version of the application cannot find files there. Otherwise, even if a file or DLL is missing from the installation set, the run-time finds it in this folder, and you will not realize that the file is missing from the run-time set. Ideally, final testing should be done on a computer that has never had Access 95 installed, so that you can verify that your distribution disks contain all the DLLs and other required files needed for proper operation. If you really want to be rigorous, use a computer with a brand new Windows 95 installation and no other software—then you will know for sure that your package installs all the files, and you aren't picking up a DLL some other application previously installed.

For obvious reasons, test the application on a computer configured as closely as possible to those of your intended user systems. Memory in particular is critical for any Access application. It may run on your development system with 32M of RAM, but will it work on an 8M corporate desktop system?

After you test the disks, it's time to make copies and distribute the application.

From Here...

This chapter covered how to make a set of distribution disks for your application, using the Setup Wizard supplied with the Access Developer's Toolkit. We discussed the contents of the Toolkit, licensing, and distribution policies. Then we looked at how to customize the setup so that your application includes all the necessary files, and then builds the correct shortcuts when installed.

From here, you can jump to more advanced related subjects by reading the following chapters:

- Chapter 12, "Securing the Access 95 Application," discusses the Access 95 security model.
- Chapter 15, "Creating Help Files," covers guidelines about building help files.
- Chapter 16, "Tuning the Access 95 Application," covers guidelines for performance tuning your application.
- Chapter 20, "Replication with Access 95," discusses Replication parameters.

III

Building the Application

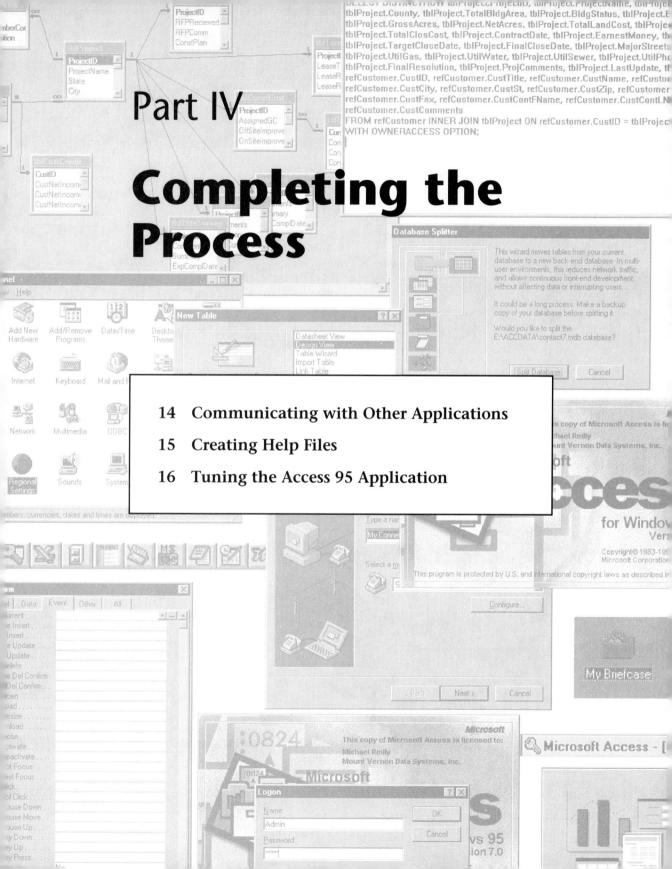

Part IV

Completing the Process

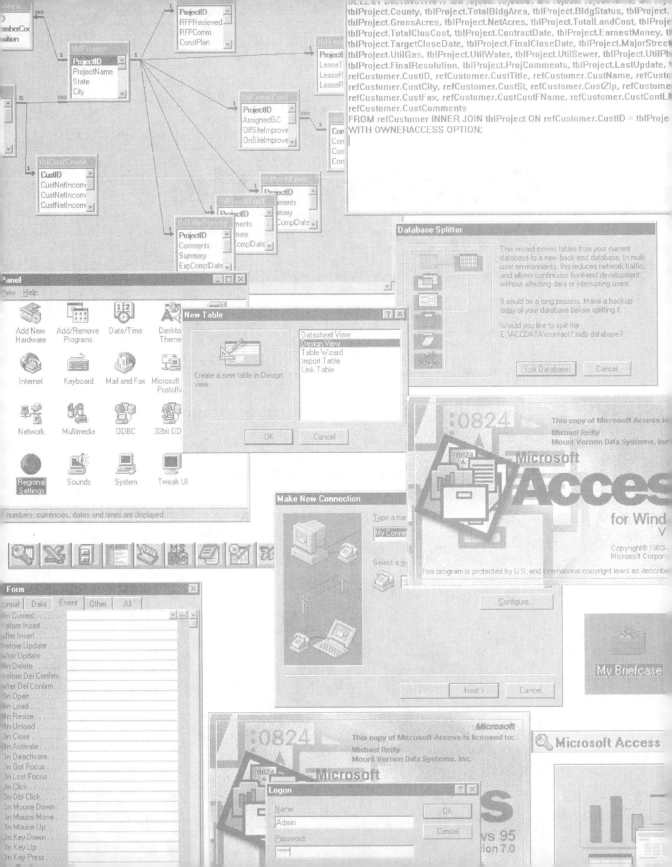

CHAPTER 14

Communicating with Other Applications

Access is a wonderful client application for making data accessible to the user. It offers a broad range of data formatting and presentation options. Often, however, just looking at the data is only the beginning. The users want to do more—incorporating the query results in a spreadsheet for analysis or generating a written report or audio-visual presentation. They may need to put together a financial analysis that can be first run in a spreadsheet program, and then incorporated into the database, as part of a group project. The ideal solution is to use the power of Access to control the selection and flow of data, and then use other software packages to present and analyze the data. You can use several methods to move data between programs for just this kind of a purpose.

Access can work with many other software packages, passing data to them or importing data from them, so that the dividing line between applications becomes blurred. The user interface is consistent between applications, the "look and feel" is the same, and data can be freely exchanged between programs. Going a step further, data from one program can be embedded within a file from a second program, while retaining links back to the originating program. In this chapter, we look at how this is done, and how it extends the usefulness of the client/server applications even further.

In this chapter we will cover the following topics:

- How Microsoft Access and other desktop applications can cooperate to jointly process data
- Object linking and embedding (OLE) and how to use it for inter-application communications
- Dynamic data exchange (DDE), what it is and when to use it
- How to integrate Access 95 and Microsoft Word
- How to integrate Access 95 and Microsoft Excel
- How to set up RAS connections for the "Road Warriors"
- Remote-control software options

Integration and Workflow

Your client/server application may represent a significant portion of the user's interaction with the computer, but unless it is comprehensive, it cannot cover all the tasks and functions that you need to perform during a typical business day—there is no reason why it should. Applications are already available that meet many users' requirements for flexibility and ease-of-use. All you have to do, as a developer, is integrate your Access application with the existing software that (probably) already lives on the user computers.

Technical Considerations

While still in the planning stage, consider the drain on system resources when your users are exchanging data between applications that are running locally. Do both (or all) of the applications have to be open at the same time during this data transfer? Even if they do not, will the users want to open both applications to ensure that the data is transferred correctly? If either answer is yes, the demand on system resources will be increased significantly.

We know that running Access 95 requires a substantial amount of memory (12 to 16M), and we know that it actually allocates for itself much of the memory available on a computer when it first starts. Computers that are already resource constrained may not be able to run multiple applications concurrently. If the user computers are fed the application programs from a network applications server, response time may be extremely slow as pieces of the application (and the data) are moved back and forth across the network. The solution, if the budget allows, is to add more memory to the client computers, and consider moving the software programs off the applications server and onto the client machines.

Alternative Clients

You don't always need to access data stored in an Access database through a customized user interface, or even through the Access software. Alternative software is available that can allow users to retrieve data from familiar platforms. *Microsoft Query*, which comes with Microsoft Office, and is embedded in both Word and Excel, is a powerful query tool, and can retrieve data from any ODBC data source, including Access and Microsoft SQL Server.

Object Linking and Embedding versus Dynamic Data Exchange

Two major technologies exist for exchanging data within Windows-based programs—*Dynamic Data Exchange* (DDE) and *Object Linking and Embedding* (OLE). Each technology offers benefits, each has drawbacks, and each requires some additional system resources. Both types of data exchange mechanism can be set up by using the applications and operating system features, or they can be implemented through Visual Basic code.

How DDE Works

Dynamic Data Exchange (DDE) allows Windows-based applications to communicate with each other. It automates cutting and pasting information between applications. DDE offers the following capabilities:

- One application can request information from another. For example, in a DDE exchange with Access, a Word macro can request data from specific fields contained in an Access table. You will see this in action later in this chapter, when we discuss the Word Mail Merge feature.

- An application can send information to another application. For example, by using DDE, Excel can send spreadsheet data to Access.

- An application can send commands to an application. For example, a Word macro can send a command to Access to open a table and provide a list of the fields in the table.

In any DDE exchange of information, the initiating application is referred to as the client, and the responding application is the server. The same terminology is used in OLE applications. Do not confuse these terms with your client/server components in the database application. In DDE and OLE, the client and server applications can be running on the same computer, or on different computers, and can switch places with each other. A familiar example of a DDE application that works between computers is the Chat program from Windows for Workgroups and Windows NT. (This application actually uses NetDDE.) A single application can be involved in several DDE exchanges at the same time and can act both as the client and as the server.

Using Access as a DDE Server

Access can act as a *DDE client* or a *DDE server* application. Access doesn't support automatic updating of links between the two applications, but it does notify the client application when a change occurs in the Access database; then the client application can request an update on the linked data from Access. The end effect is equivalent to an automatic update of the DDE links.

The following Word Basic macro uses Access as a DDE server to read the data from the Contacts table of the Contacts database, and dump it into a file named CONTACTS.TXT. You create this macro by taking the following steps:

1. From a new document in Microsoft Word, click Tools, Macro.

2. When the Macro dialog box opens, give the macro a name, and then click Create.

3. The macro inserts two statements, **SUB MAIN** and **END SUB**, on the document. Copy the code file, 14code01.txt, from this book's companion CD-ROM and paste it between the two statements. Alternatively, you can key in the code as you see it printed in Listing 14.1.

4. If necessary, modify the path to the CONTACTS.MDB file in the code. Make sure that Access 95 also is running on your computer.

5. Click the Run Macro icon on the macro toolbar. You see DDE activity as the Word Basic code is executed. Briefly, it opens the CONTACTS.MDB, selects the CONTACTS table, and exports the data to a text file titled, Contacts.txt, which appears in the same directory from which the Word Basic code is run.

Listing 14.1   14code01.txt—Use DDE and This Word Macro Code to Open CONTACTS.MDB, Read Contacts Table, and Output to a Text File Named CONTACTS.TXT

```
Sub MAIN
'-------------------------------------------------------------
' Use DDE fro Word to open the Contacts.MDB
' database, read the Contacts table, and output a text file.
' Access 95 must be running for this to work properly.
' This code works from either Word 6 or Word 7.
'-------------------------------------------------------------
code1 = DDEInitiate("MSAccess", "System")
' modify the directory and path to the Contacts.MDB if necessary
DDEExecute Code1, "[OpenDatabase E:\ACCDATA\Contacts.MDB]"

' Read the data from the Contacts table
Code2 = DDEInitiate("MSAccess", "Contacts;Table Contacts")
MyContacts$ = DDERequest$(Code2, "All")
DDETerminate Code2

' Close the database.
DDEExecute Code1, "[CloseDatabase]"
DDETerminate Code1

' Insert the data into a text file.
Open "Contacts.TXT" For Append As #1
Print #1, MyContacts$
Close #1

End Sub
```

How OLE Works

Object Linking and Embedding (OLE) is a specification that allows users to integrate data from several applications. OLE is based on the concept of the *compound document*. In this computing paradigm, the application isn't important to the user, the document is. The OLE document serves as a container or repository for other objects. In this case, an object can be another document, a part of a document, or a file. It can even be a graphic image, a sound bite, or a video clip. Any OLE object can be added to an OLE compound document, because the compound document doesn't need to *know* the details about the source of the object. As long as the application supports the OLE specification, data can be freely exchanged.

The application that contains the compound document is known as the *OLE client application*, and the application that provides the object—and is used to modify it—is known as the *OLE server application*. Access 95 can act as either an OLE client or server.

IV

Completing the Process

Access 2.0 functioned only as an OLE container or client, and not as an OLE server.

So how does this OLE concept benefit the user? In the early days of Microsoft Windows computing, the user had to start a second application, create or retrieve the object, copy it to the Clipboard, close the second application (an optional step, but necessary if resources were tight), and then paste from the Clipboard into the first application. An operation like this was even more complex with DOS-based programs, without the assistance of the Windows Clipboard. As a result, DOS-based word-processing packages were forced to support multiple graphics formats (which allowed the insertion of images into the text), or offered spreadsheet-like capabilities (to build tables within the text document).

In the newer document-centric approach that OLE supports, the user need only select the type of object required from a list displayed within the compound document application. The server application automatically opens so that the user can create the object. On closing the server application, the compound document is updated. If the object already exists and needs only to be placed within the compound document, the user needs to select the object file only by name.

When the object needs to be edited, the user only has to double-click the object in the compound document. The server application will open, and the object can be edited in place. This process is known as *in-place activation*. Some applications, such as Microsoft Paint or Paintbrush, pop up on top of the compound document. With the more sophisticated applications, such as Word or Excel, the toolbars and menus change to those of the OLE server application. When you finish editing the object, clicking anywhere outside it (on the compound document) closes the server application and restores control to the toolbars and menus of the client application, such as Word or Excel.

Combining an object into the compound document can be handled in one of two ways, either by linking or embedding. There are advantages and disadvantages to both, so look at each method, and consider the advantages and drawbacks of each.

Linking. When an object is linked into a compound document, the only item stored in the compound document is the link, or pointer, to the object in storage. The object remains in its original location, in its original format. The size of the compound document grows slightly, reflecting the addition of the links to the file. The linked object can be updated by using its native application, without having to open or change the compound document.

"A major drawback of this technique is, if the linked file is moved or deleted, the compound document cannot find the linked object when it's opened (which generates an error message in most cases).

Copying a compound document to another computer requires that you copy both the document and all linked files. If the document and linked files are in different directories, copying to another computer requires an identical corresponding directory structure on the target computer, or the link will fail.

Embedding. When an object is embedded within a compound document, a *copy* of the object is inserted into the compound document. The size of the OLE client obviously increases, roughly by the size of the document added.

When you make changes to the original object, these changes are not reflected in the embedded copy. To make changes to the copy, the compound document must be opened and the object edited from within the compound document. Editing the original document in no way affects the embedded copy.

When a compound document is copied to another computer, the embedded object also is copied. There are no problems with destination directory names because the two files are effectively one.

To illustrate the difference, you can follow these steps, using an empty Access database and a spreadsheet of your choice. The example uses a spreadsheet that contains contact information—a flat file database, in fact. These steps show the differences between linking and embedding:

1. Open or create an empty database.
2. Build a new (empty) form.
3. Select the Insert, Object option from the top menu to open the Insert Object dialog box, as shown in figure 14.1.
4. Select the Create from File option (see fig. 14.2).

Fig. 14.1

Use this dialog box to select an object type to insert into the Access form.

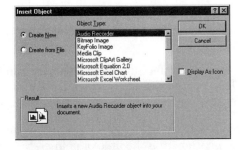

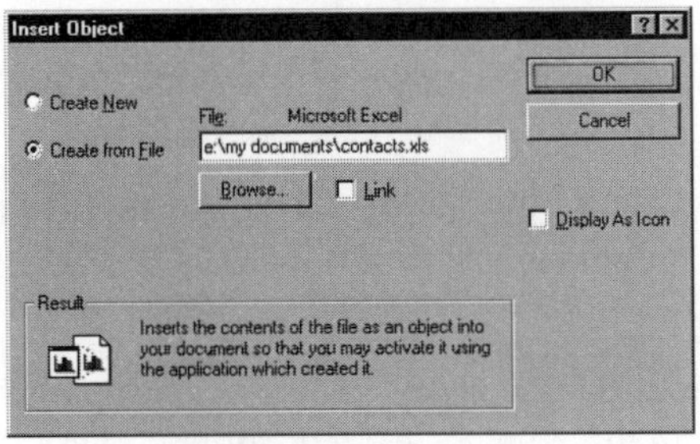

Fig. 14.2

Use this dialog box to select an existing file to insert into the Access form.

5. Using the Browse option, find and select the spreadsheet you want to place in the Access form.

6. Leave the <u>L</u>ink box unchecked, and click OK to embed the spreadsheet into the Access form. The spreadsheet becomes part of the Access form.

7. Open the properties box of the spreadsheet object. Change the properties of the embedded spreadsheet to Enabled=Yes and Locked=No.

   If you omit this step, the embedded object will not be editable or updateable.

8. Switch to Form View. Your screen should resemble figure 14.3.

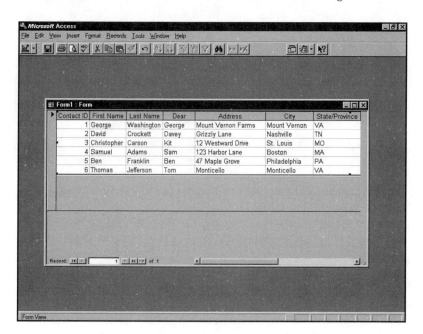

Fig. 14.3

The spreadsheet is embedded as an object in the Access form.

9. Double-click the embedded spreadsheet to open Excel. Notice in figure 14.4 that the Access toolbars changed to the Excel toolbars as the in-place activation of Excel is invoked.

10. Click anywhere outside of the spreadsheet area to restore the Access menus and toolbars.

11. Switch back to Form Design View and delete the embedded spreadsheet.

    If you close Access without deleting the spreadsheet, and if you use Excel to make changes to the data in the spreadsheet, you will not see these changes reflected in the spreadsheet next time you open Access. You would not expect to because the spreadsheet in Access is a copy of the spreadsheet you changed in Excel, and no connection exists between the copy and the original. You can even delete the original spreadsheet, and the embedded copy in Access will not be affected.

Fig. 14.4

The spreadsheet is opened for editing in Excel, with the Excel toolbars available for use.

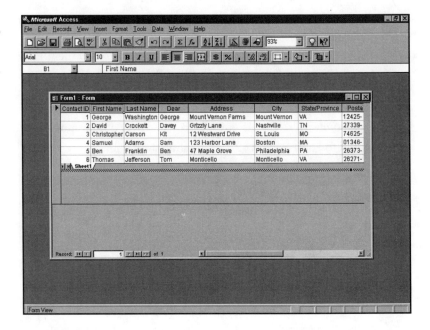

12. Repeat steps 3, 4, and 5 to find and select the spreadsheet a second time.

13. This time, click the Link option in the Insert Object dialog box to link the spreadsheet to the Access form, and then click OK.

14. Change the properties of the embedded spreadsheet object to Enabled=Yes and Locked=No.

15. Switch to Form View mode.

16. Double-click the embedded spreadsheet to open Excel, as demonstrated in figure 14.5. Arrange the Excel and Access windows so that both applications are visible. Notice that the title bar of the Excel window shows the name of the spreadsheet, in this case, Contacts.xls.

17. Make some changes to the data in the spreadsheet, and notice how these changes are reflected in the linked spreadsheet of the Access application.

18. Close the Excel window.

19. Switch the form back to Design View, and select the Edit, OLE/DDE Links option from the top menu. The Links dialog box opens (see fig. 14.6). This dialog box is the "central controller" for the links that are part of this Access application. From here, you can maintain the links and their operational characteristics (Automatic or Manual Update).

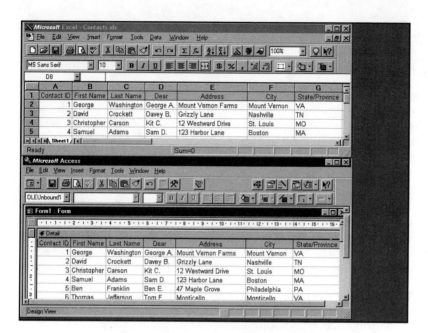

Fig. 14.5

This time, the spreadsheet is opened for editing in Excel as a separate window.

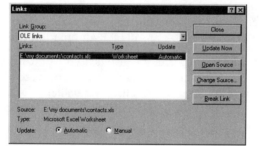

Fig. 14.6

The Links dialog box can be used to control the updating of the links.

20. Close the dialog box, save your work, and shut down Access.

21. Open Excel and make a few more changes to the data in the spreadsheet you've just linked into the Access form. Save the changes and close Excel.

22. Open Access and open the database and the form that contains the linked spreadsheet. You see the changes you just made in the spreadsheet in Excel. Notice that the form takes a little longer to appear on-screen than normal because it's updating the links.

Automatic updating of links is an option in most OLE programs and can be shut off with the Options dialog box. In this way, the user can choose to update links manually on an as-needed basis, or leave the links to be automatically updated.

23. Close Access.

OLE Automation. OLE, as previously described, works at the user interface level. Anyone running a copy of an OLE application can link or embed objects. If we go a step further, developers and programmers can use OLE Automation within their custom applications.

The OLE specification establishes how applications can *expose* or make available their objects to other applications that support OLE, macro languages, and development tools. The exposed objects are referred to as *OLE components*. OLE Automation is a development tool that allows the developer to access and manipulate another application's objects from outside the application. OLE Automation components differ from regular OLE objects because they are not visible to the user. They can be accessed only by using a programming language such as Visual Basic for Applications. The main use of these components is to automate tasks that require no user interaction. OLE automation objects are temporary; they are created using code and disappear after the code is run. Therefore, OLE automation objects cannot be linked or embedded.

Access 95 is an OLE Automation controller. Examples of other applications that expose their objects as OLE automation servers include Microsoft Word, Excel, and Project. Access can manipulate objects within these server applications. Access also includes the Object Browser, which lets you view objects within other applications, and examine their methods and properties. Any application that can function as an OLE Automation controller can start Access and manipulate its objects. Microsoft Excel, Project, Visual Basic, and Visual C++ are all OLE Automation controllers.

When an OLE server application is installed, it registers itself with the operating system. In Windows 95 or Windows NT, the OLE registration entries are placed in the Registry. The client applications open this list to find the available OLE server applications. Figure 14.7 shows a list of OLE server applications for a typical Windows 95 installation.

Fig. 14.7

This dialog box shows the available objects that can be inserted into Access. Only a partial list is visible in this window.

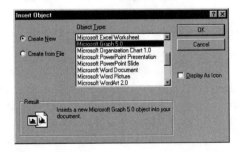

How DDE Differs from OLE

Access makes more use of OLE and OLE Automation, in part because it's easier to implement than DDE. OLE Automation is a more robust method of *interprocess communication* than DDE. In the Access environment, DDE has a maximum string length of 32K, which makes OLE the only option for transferring large blocks of data, graphics images, and most audio and video files.

If you have to exchange data with an application that doesn't support the OLE standard, then you have to use DDE. If you have to communicate between a 32-bit server application and a 16-bit client application, then DDE works where OLE may not. DDE even works in Windows NT, when the 16-bit application is running in the WOW (Windows-on-Windows) 16-bit subsystem, and the 32-bit application is running in the full Windows NT 32-bit subsystem.

If the two applications are running on different computers, then you need to use the *NetDDE* functionality built into Windows 95 and Windows NT in order to move data back and forth.

Integrating with Microsoft Office Applications

Access is available as part of the Professional edition of Microsoft Office for Windows 95, and is closely integrated with Word and Excel, which also are part of the Office suite of programs. We will use these programs as examples to illustrate how data is exchanged and managed by the various applications. Of course, you aren't limited to using Microsoft software. Other Windows-based applications offer the same or similar connectivity. But Microsoft has gone to considerable lengths to make the individual program menus as similar as possible throughout the Office suite of applications, and to other software such as Microsoft Project.

Connecting with Microsoft Word

The most common application running on desktop computers is the word processor. For many reasons, the data stored within Access must be exported to a word processor (mailing labels, form letters, and so on). Access can *output data to Word* with ease, using any one of multiple techniques.

Exporting Data from Access to Word. The simplest approach to exporting data out of Access into Word is to export from a form, using the File, Save As/Export option. The exported data can be saved as a text file, or as a Rich Text Format (RTF) file. Word can manage either of these formats. RTF output can closely resemble an Access table in Datasheet View, as shown in figure 14.8.

You also can output data into Word by selecting the Tools, Office Links, Publish It with MS-Word option from the top menu in Access. The only difference is that the Publish It option automatically starts Word, while the File, Save As option gives you a choice of whether or not to start Word after the file is exported.

Fig. 14.8

The data in this form has been exported from Access to Word, using RTF.

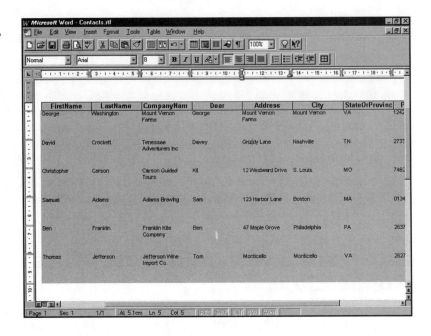

Using the Interactive Mail Merge. When a database contains sales-contact information, customer lists, and so on, the office staff will often want to use the mail-merge feature of Access or Word to generate form letters, mailing labels, or address books. Using this feature is easy to do from an Access database. The technique also works from an Access client with attached tables like you may have in a client/server environment, enabling any server data to be used for a mail merge.

First, look at how the mail merge works from within Access. This technique can be recommended only for systems with at least 16M of RAM because the process has Word and two instances of Access open at the same time. It also assumes that the users have the full development version of Access, not just a run-time application. To use the mail-merge feature from within Access, take these steps:

1. Open the database, and then highlight the table to use as the source of data for the mail merge from the list in the database window.
2. Click the drop-down box attached to the Office Links icon (the blue W) on the toolbar.
3. Select the Merge It option from the list.
4. Specify that you want to Create a new Word document. Word starts up at this point.
5. Click the Insert Merge Field button in Word (see fig. 14.9) to show which fields are available for inclusion into the merge document.
6. Select several fields and insert each of them into the document.

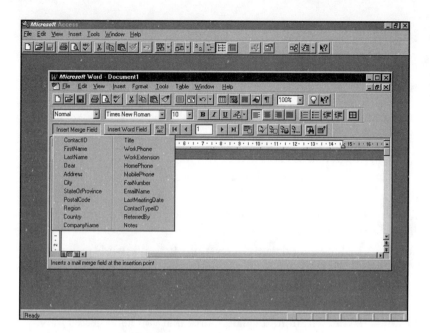

Fig. 14.9

The Insert Merge Field button opens a list of the fields in the source table or query.

7. Use spaces and line feeds to format the selected fields, and add the date, your name and address, and so on, as though you were creating a form letter.

8. Use the View Merged Data icon in the Word mail-merge screen to see the actual data in the document (see fig. 14.10). Notice on the Taskbar that there are—in addition to Word—two instances of Access running.

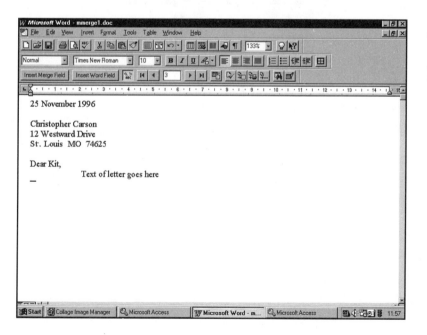

Fig. 14.10

The mail-merge document, populated with data from an Access query.

IV

Completing the Process

9. Save the document, giving it a name that you will remember.

You can use the Find Record icon in the Word mail-merge screen to locate a specific record from the data source. However, the Mail Merge Wizard is using DDE to communicate with Word, so you cannot use the querying features built into Word to select a subset of the merge data. The final mail merge will be composed of this document and an Access query that selects and sorts the data. You can use this document with different queries to customize the mail-merge process by taking these steps:

1. Build a query in Access that selects the data you want to include in the Mail Merge.

2. Save the query.

3. With the query highlighted, click the Office Links icon and select the Merge It option from the drop-down list that appears.

4. This time, select the Link your data to an existing Microsoft word Document option.

5. Select and open the Word mail-merge file that you built previously.

6. You see a message, as shown in figure 14.11, that tells you that the data source of the document is different from the data source that you had selected in Access. This is what you need, so accept the warning and click Yes.

Fig. 14.11

You have now designated a query as the data source for the mail merge, so you can ignore the warning that appears above the Mail Merge Wizard dialog box.

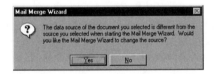

7. Confirm that the data you see in the mail merge is what you selected in the query. You can do this by clicking the Edit Data Source icon and looking at the query (see fig. 14.12).

The building of a mail-merge document can also be driven from within Word, rather than from Access. This approach works for users who do not have the full copy of Access on their systems, assuming that they do have Office 95 installed. Office 95 includes the necessary 32-bit ODBC drivers to connect Word to Access files, SQL Server databases, and Excel spreadsheets. The Office 95 applications use DDE to run Microsoft Query, when retrieving data is necessary.

To build a mail-merge file from within Word, do the following:

1. From the Word top menu select Tools, Mail Merge. The Mail Merge Helper opens, as shown in figure 14.13.

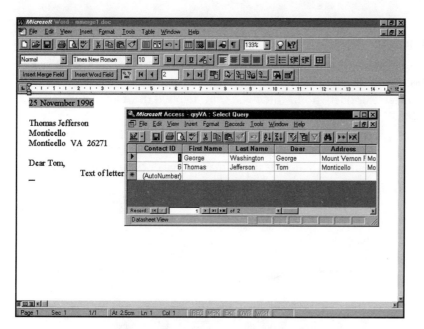

Fig. 14.12

You can view the mail-merge source query in Access, using the Edit Data Source icon in the Word mail-merge toolbar.

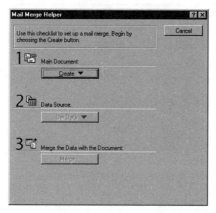

Fig. 14.13

Use the Mail Merge helper to select the data source for the mail merge.

2. Select the <u>C</u>reate button to begin creating the document. Choose the appropriate document type from the list. For this exercise, choose Form <u>L</u>etter.

3. Specify whether you want to use the Currently <u>A</u>ctive Window as your document or create a <u>N</u>ew Main Document for the mail merge. Choose the Currently <u>A</u>ctive Window.

4. Select the <u>G</u>et Data, <u>O</u>pen Data Source options to retrieve the mail-merge records from the Access database.

5. In the Open Data Source dialog box, change the Files of <u>T</u>ype option to read MS Access databases (*.mdb).

6. Select the database that will provide the records for the mail merge (choose any handy database). Click Open.

7. If you are asked to confirm the data source, select MS Access Database via DDE. Word opens Access and retrieves the list of tables and queries in this database.

8. Select the table or query from which you want to build the mail-merge records, and click OK.

9. When prompted, edit the document to include the required fields in the merge. Click the Select Merge Field icon to drop down a list of available fields. Select the fields that you want to include in the mail-merge document. Add spaces, line breaks, formatting, and so on as desired.

10. Click the View Merged Data icon to look at the results. Your screen should resemble the one shown in figure 14.14.

11. Save the mail-merge document.

Fig. 14.14

The mail merge document shows the fields that were selected for the mail merge.

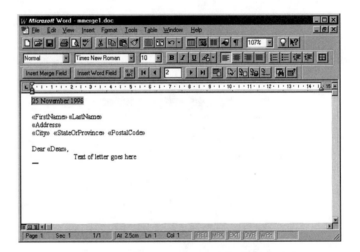

Note that Access 95 databases can be used only for mail merges with Word 7.0 (Word for Windows 95). Just as Access 2.0 cannot read Access 95 database files, Word 6.0 expects to use Access 2.0 to open the database file and, therefore, the combination of Word 6.0 and Access 95 files will not work. However, if you open an Access 2.0 database with Word 7.0, you are asked if you want to convert the database as it is opened by Access 95. You can use the Access 2.0 file in a mail merge, whether or not you convert it.

The mail merge allows you the option of connecting to Access tables or to queries. If you connect to an Access file that is the server component of an application, it will contain only tables, so you use tables as the data source for your Word mail merge. If you connect to the Access client component, you still can retrieve data from the attached Access tables. Extending this concept, you can connect to an Access client and use attached tables that are from a server database, such as Microsoft SQL Server or Oracle.

It is possible to perform a mail merge direct to SQL Server tables, but not by using the standard Mail Merge option on the Word menus. For a mail merge that involves any multi-tier database as the source, you have to use the `MailMergeOpenDataSource` statement in a Word Basic macro. For the average user, it's far easier to connect to the Access client on the desktop, assuming that the desktop computer has the resources to do so.

Exporting Reports from Access to Word. Exporting Access reports to Word could hardly be simpler. After you format the Access report the way you want it, click the Office Links icon at the top of the Report Preview screen (see fig. 14.15). The report is exported in RTF format, and Word opens automatically, as shown in figure 14.16.

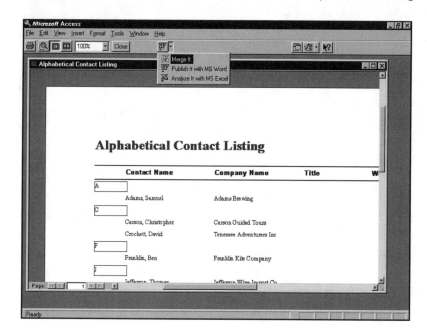

Fig. 14.15

Use the Access Office Links to export a report to Word.

Going from Word to Access. Now that you have seen how to transfer copies of the data from Access to Word, what about the inverse? Can you include Word documents in an Access table, and when would you want to do so?

You can add fields to your database table, of the OLE object data type, and store Word documents in the OLE object field. You may want to do this, for example, when designing a document management system to track relevant articles and notes while researching a book.

Fig. 14.16

The data from this report was exported to Word in RTF format.

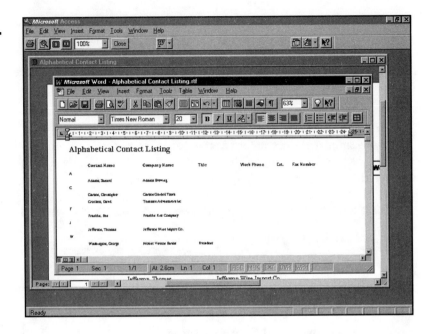

When document files are placed in the OLE object field, they can be linked or embedded. The points raised earlier in this chapter apply to your decision to link or to embed. The two approaches have the following trade-offs:

- Embedding allows in-place editing to view and change the document within Access.
- Embedding documents increases the size of the container file significantly.
- The File menu doesn't change when the document is being edited in place, which means that the Save and Print options apply to the Access form, not to the embedded document.
- Linking doesn't increase the size of the database file.
- The links must be maintained—if you move a linked document, you have to reestablish the link or you can lose track of the data.
- The linked documents are available in their original form for editing, printing, or saving as new Word (or Excel or Project) files.

Both linking and embedding large document files have drawbacks as well as benefits. It is the opinion of the authors that Access is not the best choice for a full-scale document management system. However, using linked files in Access may be a good way to keep track of a limited set of documents for a small project. This is for each person to decide on a case-by-case basis.

Importing Word Documents into Access. No direct import from a Word document, or even an RTF format file, exists to Access. To bring data from a Word file into Access, it first must be output in Word as a text file (.TXT). Data contained in a .TXT file should have a delimiter between fields such as a tab or a comma. The authors actually prefer to import this type of data into Excel first because Excel can readily parse text data into separate columns. Then, after making sure that all the data is in the correct columns, the data can be imported into Access.

The Power of Excel

Excel works closely and nicely with Access. Many people use Excel to build *flat-file databases*, and it works well in this role. So, why do you need both Access and Excel? Each application offers a set of features that the other either lacks or offers to a lesser degree. The benefits offered by Access include the following:

- Access queries offer more power and flexibility than the sorting and selecting capabilities of a spreadsheet.
- Access can link tables by using relational technology, which a spreadsheet cannot.
- Access forms can include default values and provide data validation.
- Access forms can more closely follow the business rules, turning fields on and off, depending on the data being input.

Excel has the following features that it can contribute:

- Excel has enormous capability for data analysis, "what-if" decision support, and plain old number crunching.
- Excel has more flexible chart generating features than Access.
- Excel is less resource-intensive, and is a more familiar interface to many users, than Access.

You can easily export data from Access into Excel and, therefore, it's easy to export from a server database via Access into a spreadsheet. In certain situations, data from an Excel spreadsheet needs to be imported into Access, and again, this is easy to do.

Exporting from Access to Excel. Exporting data from an Access form to an Excel spreadsheet works in the same way as exporting to a RTF file. Using the File, Save As menu option, you can save the data as an XLS file (see fig. 14.17), which is compatible with Excel versions 5 and 7.

Fig. 14.17

The data from this form was exported to Excel as an XLS format file.

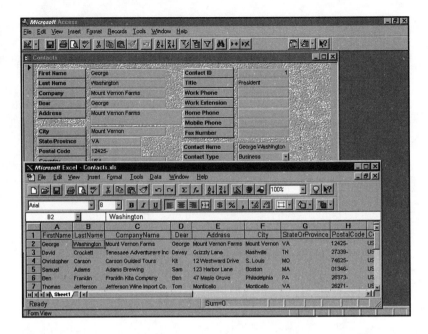

As with Word, you can export data to Excel by using either the menu commands (Tools, OfficeLinks, Analyze it With MS Excel), or by clicking the Office Links icon and choosing the Excel option. The data will be exported in XLS format, and the procedure automatically opens Excel with the exported data visible.

Exporting data from an Access report also is just as easy. Select the report, and then use the same options as described previously to export the data to a spreadsheet.

Importing from Access to Excel. Excel can use the power of the Microsoft Query add-in to extract data from external sources, such as Access databases. Use these steps to bring in data from an Access database:

1. Under the Data menu item in Excel is a Get External Data option. Select this option, which takes you to the Select Data Source dialog box, from which you can select a data source. Initially, this box is empty, as shown in figure 14.18.

> **Note**
>
> If you don't see the Get External Data option on the Data menu, you may need to rerun the Office 95 setup, and make sure that Microsoft Query is selected in the Data Access options.

2. Select Other to bring up a list of ODBC data sources, as shown in figure 14.19.

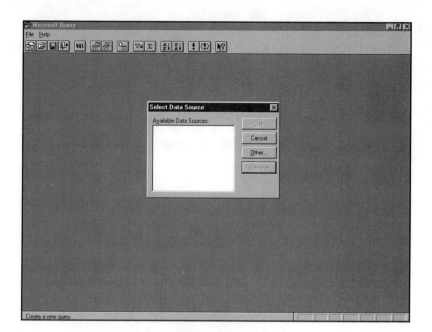

Fig. 14.18

The Excel Select Data Source dialog box that is part of Microsoft Query. This is how you select data sources to bring database tables into Excel.

IV

Completing the Process

Fig. 14.19

Part of Microsoft Query, this is the list of available ODBC data sources.

3. Select MS Access 7.0 database from the list and click OK.

4. Select a database from the standard file select dialog box. This database is added to the list of Available Data Sources, as shown in figure 14.20.

Fig. 14.20

The chosen Access database is added to the list of data sources.

5. Click Use to begin building the data selection query. The query builder window should look familiar—it's quite similar to the dialog box used in Access, as seen in figure 14.21.

Fig. 14.21

The Access database appears with a list of available tables for this query.

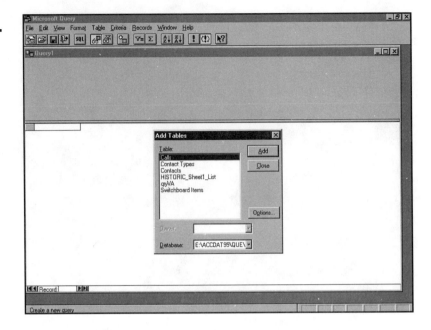

6. From the list in the dialog box, select the tables you want to use, and then Close the Add Tables dialog box.

7. Select the fields you want to see in the output data. The query now looks like figure 14.22.

Fig. 14.22

Select the output fields for this query.

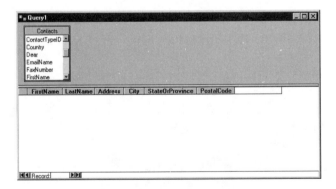

8. Click the Show/Hide Criteria icon (the eyeglasses with the database table in the background) to open the criteria window.

9. Type the search criteria.

10. Use the Query Now button (the exclamation point) to run the query with the search criteria (see fig. 14.23).

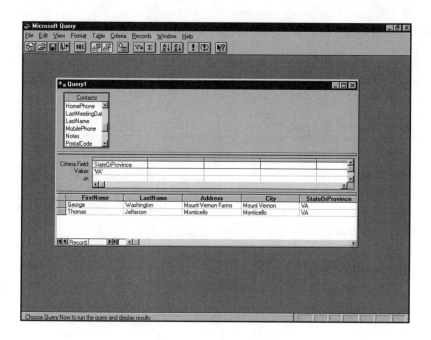

Fig. 14.23

The query window in Microsoft Query runs just like an Access query does.

11. Click File, Return Data to Microsoft Excel. The data, as selected by the query, is returned to Excel and inserted into the spreadsheet, as shown by figure 14.24.

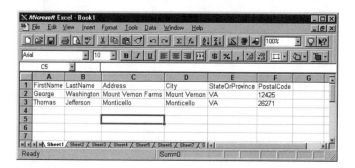

Fig. 14.24

The data selected by the query is inserted into the spreadsheet when you leave the Microsoft Query window.

Preparing Data for Import. Excel itself offers a very flexible import facility, which is ideal for preparing flat-file databases created in Excel, or text files with delimiters between data entries, for import into an Access database. The first row of the Excel spreadsheet should contain the field names. If you are importing to a new table, these names become the Access field names. If you import into an existing table, these field names should correspond exactly to the field names in the table so that Access knows where to import the data. After the data is formatted in Excel, the Access File, Get External Data option can be used to import the data.

Linking Excel and Access. Excel 95 offers some impressive new features that extend its interaction with Access to new levels. These features are among the add-ins supplied with Excel. It is now possible to automatically convert an Excel spreadsheet into an Access table. Or more precisely, Excel and Access interact to create a new table. After the table is built, the Excel data and the Access data are linked. Then, the Access Form Wizard takes over and builds a form in which to display the data.

> **Note**
>
> This task is extremely resource-intensive, which may push typical user computers beyond their current limits.

Use the following steps to perform this conversion:

1. Open the Excel spreadsheet that you want to convert.

2. Select the Data, Access Form option from the Excel menu.

3. When prompted, choose an existing database into which the data will be imported, or specify a name for a New Database (see fig. 14.25).

At this point you can tell the Wizard whether your data has a header row that contains field names. Excel then triggers the building of a new table in the selected database, and starts the Access Form Wizard to build a form for the data. You will have all the options normally offered by the Form Wizard, including which fields to include on the form. When this procedure is completed, you have a table in Access that contains the Excel data. Changes made in either application will appear in the other, even when only one application is open at a time.

Fig. 14.25

Use this dialog box to specify the destination Access database for the Excel data.

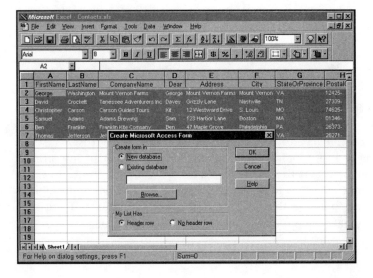

4. Make changes in each application's data and see how it's reflected in the other application. Close Excel and make changes in the Access data.

5. Close Access and open Excel. Note the changes have been made.

6. Make some changes to the Excel data. Close Excel.

7. Open Access again: note the changes also appear here.

Excel also has the capability to copy Excel data into an existing Access table or to generate or refresh an Access report. Spreadsheet software certainly has come a long way!

Using DDE and OLE with Visual Basic for Applications

It is not the purpose of this book to go into depth on Visual Basic for Applications programming of DDE and OLE. Actually, that is a book in itself. Now that you have some idea of the power of DDE and OLE automation, we suggest that you check out one of the many excellent references on the topic, and begin applying these techniques to your own applications.

Tip

If you are interested in exploring the programming possibilities of OLE, the authors recommend *Building OLE Applications with Visual Basic 4*, by Forrest Houlette, David Fullerton, Mike Groh, Steven Ellis White, and Jeff Cummins, Que Corporation, 1995.

To explore the programming possibilities of DDE, you might try *Special Edition Using Access 95*, by Roger Jennings, *et.al.*, Que Corporation, 1995.

Exporting Access Objects as Mail

A form or report in Access can be sent as a mail message. Access data isn't sent as native .MDB files; it must be converted first. The available output formats for mailing are Excel XLS files, RTF document files, or plain DOS text files. The mail option is disguised under the File menu as a Send option, and selecting this option brings up the Send dialog box, as shown in figure 14.26.

Fig. 14.26

The Send dialog box allows you to select the output format in which the data will be sent as a mail message.

You can select a profile to use for mailings. Usually, you use the default Microsoft Exchange settings, which you set up when Windows 95 was installed, but you can specify other Exchange profiles if you want, as shown in figure 14.27.

Fig. 14.27

The Choose Profile dialog box allows you to select the Microsoft Exchange profile to use when sending the Access data to the recipient.

If you want to configure a different profile, you can do that. If you opt for the default profile, you will see the Exchange screen with the Access output file shown as a mail attachment. From this screen, you may direct the mail to the intended recipient (see fig. 14.28).

Fig. 14.28

The Microsoft Exchange New Message dialog box; use this dialog box to specify the recipient for the Access data.

Dial-In Access for Road Warriors

Client/server applications present a whole new range of challenges when the client part of the application is loaded onto a portable computer and taken on the road, or when the employees who travel must have some means of accessing the corporate data back at the home office. Even employees working from home may need to connect to the server. There are several software solutions, and each offers benefits but involves some compromises.

Remote Access Services (RAS)

Microsoft has included *Remote Access Services* (RAS) in its operating system software for several years now, and it's relatively easy to configure and use. The principle of using RAS is that when the user connects by way of a telephone line, it is just as if they were another node on the network. They can connect to shared resources, use printers that are shared on the network and, of course, connect to a network computer that contains the server database. The only difference is in the speed of the connection, which in most cases is slow. It is important to note that a *RAS* connection acts just like a network connection—the client application is running on the portable computer, not on the host to which it connects.

There are some tricks that can be employed to speed up the response of the database over this slow connection, and we discuss them in Chapters 16, "Tuning the Access 95 Application," and 21, "Client/Server Performance and Tuning."

An alternative to establishing a full client/server link is to have a copy, or a replica, of the server database on the mobile computer. There are few notebook computers that can run SQL Server, so this approach works only if the server database is an Access database, or if a subset of the server database can be replicated to Access. Then the RAS connection can be used to synchronize the replica with the original data. We discuss replication further in Chapter 20, "Replication with Access 95," but for now we just mention that Access 95 uses the Briefcase replication built in to Windows 95.

Configuring RAS and Dial-Up Networking. In Windows for Workgroups and Windows NT, the remote dial-in software is known as RAS, or Remote Access Services. In Windows 95, it is found in the My Computer folder, and is known as *Dial-Up Networking*. In either case, configuration is similar, and the examples shown apply to Windows 95. To add a new connection into your server, follow these steps:

1. Open up the Dial-Up Networking Folder.

2. Click the Make New Connection icon (see fig. 14.29).

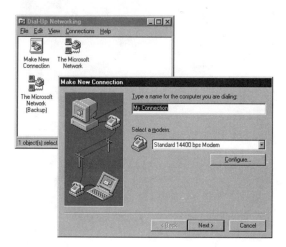

Fig. 14.29

You add a new Dial-Up connection from the Dial-Up Networking folder.

3. Type **My Connection** (or something similar) as the name of the new connection.

4. Confirm the modem selected is correct (there may be multiple choices if PCMCIA modems are issued by the company and there is no standard modem type).

5. Confirm your modem settings—connection speed, parity, and so on—and then move to the next screen.

6. Type the phone number for your server connection. Note the area code field. This is used to determine if you are placing a long-distance call.

7. Move to the next screen, which confirms that you have built a new dial-up connection entry. Click Finish to save this entry in the Dial-UP Networking folder.

Now you should configure the connection to ensure that it is set up correctly for your server. That is, the network parameters, protocols, and so on match those on the server. The following steps demonstrate how this is done:

1. Select the icon for your server connection, and then click with the secondary mouse button to bring up the pop-up menu, and select Properties. You can change any of the connection settings from here, including the phone number and the modem type.

2. Click the Server Type button to bring up the networking parameters (see fig. 14.30).

Fig. 14.30

Configuring a Dial-Up Connection: select from the networking protocols supported by Windows 95, specify to log on to the network upon connecting.

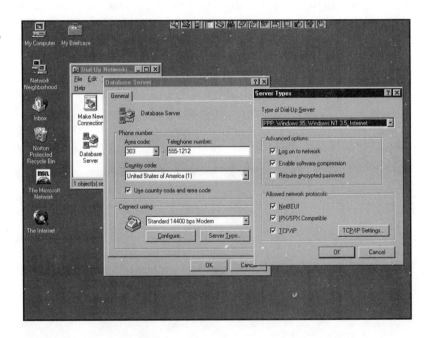

3. Select the correct networking options, and then click OK twice to exit.

The three protocols from which you can choose, as shown in figure 14.30, are *NetBEUI*, *IPX/SPX Compatible*, and *TCP/IP*. If you choose TCP/IP, you may need to configure the TCP/IP settings, including the IP address. However, Windows NT Server can assign the IP address for you, using the DHCP (Dynamic Host Configuration Protocol) feature. For more information on this feature, consult a reference such as Que's

Special Edition Using Windows NT Server 3.51. The same advice applies if you are unsure of which protocol to use. NetBEUI can connect via a NetBIOS gateway, and give you access to systems running other protocols, even when the RAS connection is using only NetBEUI into a Windows NT Server.

Other options in the Dial-Up networking configuration include connections into Netware and UNIX systems, as shown in figure 14.31.

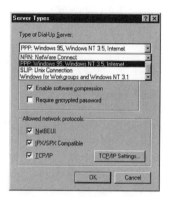

Fig. 14.31

Dial-up networking can connect to various different servers.

Configuring Call-Back Options. The server configuration for RAS dial-in is similar, with a couple of extra settings. This install will give you the ability to use a Windows 95 machine as a dial-up server. The server, assuming that you are using Windows NT Server, can be configured to dial out, to accept incoming calls, or both. Each user must be added to the list of permitted dial-in accounts—just having an account on the server isn't enough. (Under Windows 95, the function is named Dial-Up Networking, not RAS. To function as a DUN Server, you must install the Microsoft Plus! For Windows 95 Pack, which is not discussed in this book. It sets up a single connection to the Windows 95 machine and can act as a gateway to a NETBEUI or IPX/SPX network. It cannot act as an IP router, nor does it have the robust authorization capability to act as a true firewall.)

Additionally, the server can be configured for dial-back options, as shown in figure 14.32.

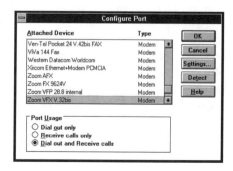

Fig. 14.32

Configuring a RAS Server: the Dial-back number can be preset to a specific number or input by the caller.

If either dial-back option is selected, the RAS Server checks that the user is in the list of valid RAS accounts, and then hangs up the connection and calls the user. The more secure option is to call a preset number—possibly the user's home or a remote office. If someone else were to dial in under this user's name, the call-back to a preset number might stymie intrusive intentions. A less-secure option is to allow the caller to specify a number at the time of initial connect that the RAS server can then use for the call-back. This option is exercised by companies with traveling sales staff. They may have to dial in from a hotel phone or from a client's office. Using the dial-back option, the call can be billed to the company, possibly even to a WATS line. Of course, there is always the problem of getting around the hotel switchboard—let's hope we see a major improvement in both the quality and pricing of hotel telephone systems in the next few years.

Remote-Control Software

Several software packages are available (*remote-control software*) that allow a remote computer to dial in and take over control of a host computer. PCAnywhere and Carbon Copy are two examples of this kind of application. In this scenario, the Access client application is running on the computer at your office, and you dial in from a remote site with your portable. The office and portable computers both must be running the same remote-control software. After the computers are connected, the screen images from the office computer are reproduced on the portable screen, and the keystrokes and mouse input from the portable are sent to the office computer. So, you can use and update the database on the server via your office computer, under remote control from your portable.

The advantages of this method are that a minimum set of data is traveling over the telephone line, and when the desktop client is a more powerful computer than your portable, you can tap into its processing power. As long as the remote-control software runs fast enough to provide screen updates at an acceptable rate, the client/server application appears to be running on the portable computer.

The disadvantages include a potential loss of security. When you use RAS to dial in to a server, the server security is handled by the system administrators, and the logon process is at least as tight as if you were a local client. Using remote-control software implies that your office computer is operational, even though you are not at the office. So anyone with physical access to the office can get into your system. There are workarounds for this, including password-protected screen savers, or using the computer key lock to disable keyboard input (if you can find the keys). Windows NT allows a user to lock the workstation, requiring a password to unlock it, but still permits network connections. Also, the dial-in process with the remote software can include password protection, although it may not be as secure as the RAS approach, which uses the full Windows NT security model.

Obviously, both the RAS and the Remote Control approach, when used to connect to the server, are effective in updating the server data—just as if the portable were another desktop client. Neither approach is as fast as a copy of the database on the portable. The combination of RAS with Briefcase replication may be the best solution for most Road Warriors.

From Here...

The days when applications were only standalone products is gone. We live in an information age when not having current, accurate, and integrated data carries a high price tag. Access 95 has undergone serious revisions since its inception to become a vehicle to support this need. Access 95's power to communicate through both Microsoft Office applications (such as Word and Excel) and external data formats places Access 95 in the forefront of database technology. Access 95 is an excellent tool that can communicate across multiple document formats; it can import files from other database applications and digest the data for you to use within Access or in your word-processing and spreadsheet applications.

The networking capability of this product demonstrates that the modern office is anywhere you need to be. Access 95, through RAS connectivity, supports the always-on-the-go Road Warriors, so they never need be out of touch. Software communications enables people-to-people communication for a better, more productive business environment.

From here, jump to the following chapters to find out more about these related issues:

- Chapter 16, "Tuning the Access 95 Application," gives an in-depth discussion of performance and tuning issues in the Access for Windows 95 environment.
- Chapter 20, "Replication with Access 95," discusses database replication, Access-style.
- Chapter 21, "Client/Server Performance and Tuning," introduces more information on performance and tuning issues.

CHAPTER 15

Creating Help Files

In the scheme of the application life cycle, it seems that *documentation* historically has been relegated to the back row. Not that documentation isn't important! Ask anyone—they'll tell you that documenting what you are planning to do, what you are doing, and what you have done is of the utmost importance. But who really does it, or wants to do it?

We all have excuses, and they are by and large, valid excuses for not performing the documentation in a timely fashion. The development of the database comes first, the constant changes are impossible to keep up with, the boss expects the application code to be completed by the end of the day, week, month... we'll do it at the end of the project.

The time to document is not when the project is nearing its end but throughout the entire life cycle of the project. Schemes and tools exist that will assist and make the task easier, but you simply have to get mentally prepared to just do it!

This chapter covers the following documentation-related areas:

- Documenting the application, where and when
- Status bar assist
- The control tips property
- The What's This button property
- The Help Compiler
- Creating context-sensitive help
- How to include the help files in your application

Documenting the Application

On-line help files are one of the easiest ways to provide end users with a quick assist, while they use your application. Today's users don't want to spend time working through tutorials or pouring over user's manuals, they just want to get the job done.

The first rule of application development in the event-driven paradigm is this: *the program must be intuitive to use.* If you follow the Windows standard for menuing and behavior, if you use templates and/or master forms for form development, as was discussed in Chapter 8, "Adding Functionality to Your Prototype," you will build a consistency of look and feel into your applications that makes it much easier to use.

The authors do not propose to present here a comprehensive treatment of the creation and implementation of on-line help; rather, only a kind of "get by" that should be more than enough to get you started. *On-line documentation* is a topic and career path in itself, with many volumes dedicated to a full treatment of the subject. Multiple commercial authoring tools are available to assist in creating help files (RoboHelp and Doc-to-Help are two of the more famous) for the Windows environment.

When we speak of on-line help, we are referring to assists, prompts, status-line text, pop-up boxes, and separate windows that give reference information, tips, and instructions. Occasionally, these mechanisms are activated when the user makes an overt call for assistance. At other times, these mechanisms activate as a triggered event when the user moves into or out of a control object on a form.

If on-line help is treated as an on-going process—as part of application development— it becomes a form of documentation for the application. This process begins at the table level, when the tables are first created, continues through the prototype stage, and carries on to the finished product.

Because you have to structure the *on-line help* to the intended user community, we should mention here the various categories of application users, which break down into the following five general groups:

- **Novice users**—These users are just learning what a computer is, and haven't really learned yet that a computer is more than an electronic typewriter.

- **Intermediate users**—These users are comfortable with application packages but draw the line at trying to single-handedly troubleshoot operating system/ network problems or hardware situations. This group breaks down into two subgroups, the intermediate timid and the intermediate robust.

  Intermediate timid users—Under direction, these users reluctantly delve into the mysteries that underlie application packages. What separates this group from the next is a lack of self-confidence.

  Intermediate robust users—Users of this intermediate level will try anything once and are super to work with, because they have not learned fear. Telephone support with this kind of person is a joy because they are generally careful and persistent and will try to precisely describe what the support call was about.

- **Power users**—These users are, with some training, ready to graduate into applications programming and systems administration. They are self-motivated and immensely curious, and they often become the unofficial, local computer-support person. This kind of user can be a boon or a pain to the information systems group, depending on the resident corporate mentality.

The generalization: organizations that truly empower the end user will embrace and exploit the skills of a power user. Organizations that are control freaks will label a power user "the problem employee."

It has come to the attention of the authors that no matter which user group a person falls into, no one reads printed documentation, except as a last resort. Novices tend to feel overwhelmed by the printed "jargon," with references to mystical functions and activities, and so extract no real value from the documentation. Intermediate users are too busy, need to get too much done in not enough time, to take a few moments to reference the documentation until they really, really need to—besides, they can always ask the power user! The power user may, in fact, be the one who resorts to printed documentation more than any of the others. Remember, the power user likes this stuff, and wants to find out more. Knowledge is a natural high to the power user, and the knowledge base is partially contained in the printed documentation.

Commenting the Table Creation

On-line help should start at table creation, with proper annotation of the Description column in Table Design View (see fig. 15.1).

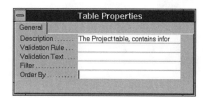

Fig. 15.1

Annotating the description in Table Design View for both table and columns.

By inserting coherent descriptions in each column, and even going so far as to describe the purpose and function of each table, you are accomplishing two things:

- You are documenting the purpose and function of each column in the table, and of the table itself, which is an invaluable assist for workgroup colleagues and maintenance programmers;

- You are filling in the status bar property of any form that will be generated from this table or a query built on this table (more about this work later).

The comments inserted into the Description column at table design time are brought forward, or *inherited*, by text boxes of a form built on this table (or a query created from this table)—specifically, the Status Bar Text property. For this reason, you want to be very discreet and coherent when inserting comments at the table level. Even though you, as the developer, are intimately acquainted with the data and its meaning, imagine yourself as a novice end user, and write the column descriptions from this point of view.

This scheme of perpetuating table-level comments works for homogeneous Access environments only. Access tables that are upsized to server database tables lose the description information in the process, thereby losing a good source of table-level documentation. Additionally, all forms built on the newly converted server table will have no commentary to populate the status bar text property of the text boxes.

Using the Status Bar Text Property

The *Status Bar Text property* is a quiescent form of on-line help (see fig. 15.2). It's a property of every bound text box on a form, in either Design, Datasheet, or View mode. The text is displayed at the bottom of the screen—in the lower left, for a length of about 50 characters, depending on the screen resolution—and is the commentary from the table design phase, which was discussed in the preceding section.

Fig. 15.2

The properties box, Status Bar Text property; the comment from the property box is displayed at the bottom of the screen when this form is run in Form View.

When users tab into or click in a text box, the status bar text switches to the commentary relevant for this bound object. The table description for the associated column to which this text box is bound was incorporated into the form when the field was added to the form, assuming that the table/query was of Access origin.

The status bar text is embedded, not linked, so changes to the description of the column in the table do not ripple through to associated fields on a form. You can delete the commentary in the table design for a column, but the status bar text for form fields already created doesn't change. You can upsize the Access table to a server database and "lose" the column descriptions, and the status bar text for form fields already built will not change.

Note

The status bar text is best used for generic information about a field, for explaining the meaning and purpose, or for giving hints on how data should be entered—for example, Enter date in MM/DD/YY format. Because the status bar text is small and inconspicuous, it is easily overlooked by some end users, so a bit of training may be needed for some of the user community.

> Status bar text is used, however, throughout the entire Microsoft Office suite of products, *so this is one way to stay consistent with the "look and feel" of other software already in use in your environment.*

Using the Control Tip Text Property

The *Control Tip Text property* is new to Access 95. You saw it before in the Microsoft Office suite of applications, where it's commonly known as *balloon help*. Now you can create balloon help for the applications you build under Access 95 (see fig. 15.3).

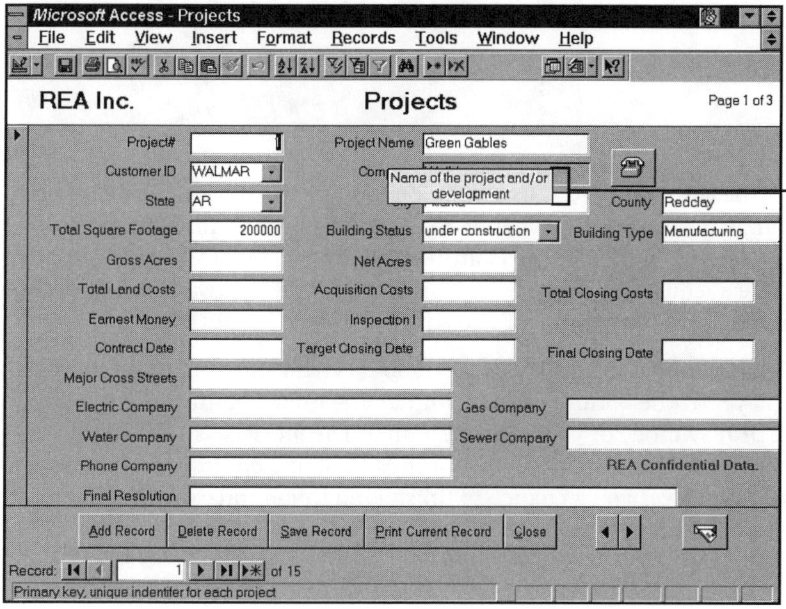

Fig. 15.3

The balloon help feature, new to Access 95 applications.

— The help balloon

The Control Tip Text property is activated simply by positioning the mouse pointer over a control on a form and leaving it there for a few seconds. Whatever you code in the property box for Control Tip Text "balloons," this code appears in a balloon message. The maximum string length for a balloon message is 255 characters. The Access 95 on-line help indicates that control tip text "balloon help" functions in the same way in either Form View or Datasheet View, but in fact this doesn't seem to be true. Balloon help works fine in single or continuous Form View, but doesn't seem to work at all in Datasheet View.

If a lesson is to be learned here, it's that all the on-line help schemes we talk about in this chapter must be tightly integrated with the development of the application. As the application specifications change, so will the on-line help. Coordinating the two is a non-trivial task, granted, but it's a task that needs to be handled with care and conscientiousness. Getting misinformation from the on-line help system is only slightly less aggravating than getting no information at all.

Fig. 15.4

Set the balloon help by using the Control Tip Text property in Design View.

For consistency, the authors suggest, if you decide to implement control tip text help, that you coordinate the on-line help messages displayed in the Status Bar Text property with the messages displayed in the Control Tip Text property. Although initially, this may seem like a redundant suggestion, you will find that the two forms of on-line help can reinforce the message that you're trying to send to the end users.

The status bar text is limited to a string of about 50-60 characters—that's the most that can be displayed at the bottom of the terminal; the exact length of the message depends on the display mode of your video terminal. The message is all there; the end is simply truncated. For longer help-message strings, enabling control tip text and repeating the message gives you a chance to finish (and to reinforce or supplement) what you were saying in the status bar.

The Access 95 on-line help indicates that you can set control tip text in one of the following three ways:

- By placing the message directly into the property box in form Design View
- By referencing a macro in the property box
- By referencing a procedure in the property box

In the first production release, however, it seems as though the Control Tip Text property box accepts only static messages, and it doesn't function correctly if given a reference to a macro or a module. The authors suspect that the eventual intent is to be able to manipulate the contents of Control Tip text in different ways, depending on your needs. So, in light of this assumption, now you should investigate why you would use one method over another.

By placing the help message directly in the property box, you are limited to 255 characters, including spaces, but you can do a direct copy or paste of the status bar text into the Control Tip Text property. The two properties are even on the same tab sheet (Other) of the properties box. This technique is the quickest and most convenient for developing control tip text on-line help. However, you have no control over word wrap or the arrangement of text—it's all done automatically and generically. The string of text may be broken at seemingly inappropriate places and each line is centered in the balloon box.

To gain control over word placement, you need to place a reference to a macro in the Control Tip Text property box—after the feature is activated. Again, you are limited to 255 characters, but you can determine how the text is arranged in the balloon box. Figure 15.5 shows the authors' concept of what a control tip text box that uses an underlying macro looks like, except that rather than a dialog box, you probably would see a balloon.

Fig. 15.5

The author's conception of what a control tip text box that uses an underlying macro may look like. Notice the controlled placement of text.

Today, without the operational control tip text feature, you still can create a help macro and attach it to controls on a form—see REA_App.mdb, mcrRiskHelp on this book's companion CD-ROM. This help macro is simple to construct and highly functional (see fig. 15.6). All help is in the form of dialog boxes, which have to be explicitly called by clicking on the green question marks strategically placed on the Risk screen (frmRiskEval). You were viewing this setup in figure 15.5.

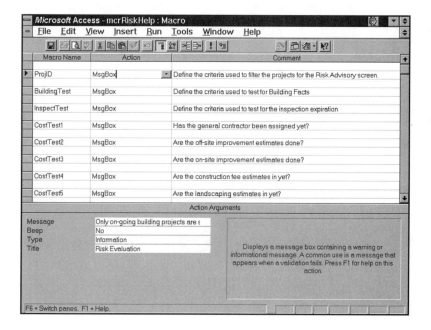

Fig. 15.6

The macro group, mcrRiskHelp, showing the many MsgBox messages that support the custom on-line help for the form, frmRiskEval.

All help dialogs are bundled together into a single macro group for ease of maintenance. Each macro is separated from the next by a blank line, in keeping with good macro-coding convention. The basic information for a single help macro looks like the entries in Table 15.1.

Table 15.1 On-Line Help Macros		
Macro Name	**Macro Action**	**Arguments**
BalloonHelp	MsgBox	**Message**—Insert your help message here. Open the zoom box (position cursor in the message line and press Shift+F2). Use a Ctrl+Enter to break the text string into multiple lines; use the space bar to position each line if left justification is not adequate.
		Beep—On or off.
		Type—This is the symbol which appears on the left side of the dialog box. You can leave it off entirely if you choose.
		Title—Placed in the title bar of the dialog box.

The last method that eventually might be implemented for control tip text is to place a reference to a procedure in the property box. Projecting into the future, the procedure call could be a local event or a global event, depending on the need. Presumably, you code some kind of message box, not unlike the macro message box described previously. The maximum flexibility and power, obviously, can be achieved by using reference calls to coded procedures, and help information can extend to strings of nearly 1,024 characters. From an Access 95 MsgBox function, you can even call the WinHelp associated with your application (see following sections in this chapter) but at some point, you must question just what you need to accomplish with balloon help.

Note the use of the "at" symbol (@) in this function. Now you can create *formatted error messages* and denote the different sections of the string by using this symbol. As shown in figure 15.7, the first section appears in bold print, the second in regular weight lettering. The word Solution is automatically placed on the dialog box, in bold weight lettering. The third section of the strMsg, which immediately follows the word "Solution," appears in regular weight.

Fig. 15.7

The new formatted text dialog box, showing the multiple formatted sections.

Just in case, however, the following example (the file, 15code01.txt, is found on this book's companion CD-ROM, in the Code folder) is the kind of message box help you can create by using event procedures. To see how it works, attach the code to a command button labeled, Press Here.

Listing 15.1   15code01.txt—An Example Message Box to Demonstrate the New Formatting Capabilities

```
Private Sub Command2_Click()
'----------------------------------------------------
' message to exemplify the multiple formatting styles
' available in an Access 95 message box
'----------------------------------------------------
Dim strMsg As String, strInput As String

' Initialize string.
    strMsg = "Number outside range.@You entered a number that is "
    & "less than 1 or greater than 10.@Press OK to enter " _
    & "the number again."
' Prompt user for input.
    strInput = InputBox("Enter a number between 1 and 10.")

' Test value of user input.
    Do While strInput < 0 Or strInput > 10
        If MsgBox(strMsg, vbOKCancel, "Error!") = vbOK Then
        strInput = InputBox("Enter a number between 1 and 10.")
    Else: GoTo exit_Command2_click
    End If
    Loop
' Display user's correct input.
    MsgBox "You entered the number " & strInput
io
exit_Command2_click:
Exit Sub
End Sub
```

Using the What's This Property

The *What's This* property has been around the Microsoft Office suite for nearly as long as balloon help. At the top of each product screen, in the toolbar near the right side, is an icon that looks like an arrow cursor with a question mark attached. Click it and your mouse cursor assumes the arrowhead/question-mark form and now, when you click anywhere on the screen, you see information about what you clicked.

This feature is known as the *What's This property*. This property can be turned on and, theoretically (at least according to the on-line help and the Access Language Reference Manual), the What's This property button displays on the title bar of a form, if the Min Max Buttons property is set to None (see fig. 15.8).

Fig. 15.8

The What's This Button property, set to Yes and the Min Max Buttons property, set to None in the form design properties box, Format tab, which is needed to implement What's This? on-line help.

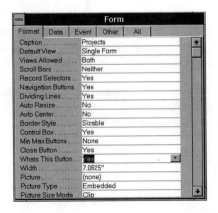

The way it's supposed to work goes like this. The user clicks on the What's This button, the Help Select mouse pointer (which is how Microsoft refers to the arrow/question-mark cursor) is enabled, and the user can click any object on the form to get more information on the object.

Of course, by implication, your application has custom Help files (WinHelp, discussed in a few pages) that are complete enough to reference every object on every form. This task is not trivial and, depending on the needs of your user community, you may or may not want to invest the time necessary to fully enable What's This help. In many ways, What's This help overlaps or repeats the help that you already coded by using status bar text help and control tip text help.

If you decide that you can successfully use the What's This help scheme, perhaps for displaying a special category of help, you need to build a set of custom help files (next section). You also need to specify the following settings in form design:

- For the form, a property named HelpFile (the Other tab of the properties box), which is the name of the compiled custom help file for your application
- Another form property, HelpContextID (located below Help File on the Other tab), which is a unique identifier for each topic in the custom help file
- For each form object that will support What's This button help, a **HelpContextID** value (Other tab of the object property box)

If you specified your custom help file for your application (in the run-time .INI file, for example—see Chapter 13, "Building the Run-Time Application"), then when the What's This button is pressed, Access calls the Windows Help routines that will load the custom help file specified by the **HelpFile** property and display the topic that is specified by the **HelpContextID** property. If no **HelpContextID** is specified for the control, the HelpContextID for the form will be displayed. If neither the form nor the control has a custom **HelpFile** designated, Access Help will display.

The **HelpFile** and **HelpContextID** properties are part of the following kinds of controls: bound object frames, charts, check boxes, combo boxes, command buttons, forms, images, labels, lines, list boxes, option buttons, option groups, rectangles, re-ports, subform/subreports, text boxes, toggle buttons, and unbound object frames.

Windows Help Files

The appearance of Windows Help (*WinHelp*) changed dramatically with Windows 95, and the new look and feel is carried over to the 32-bit environments, such as Access 95 and Visual Basic 4, that allow custom Help files to be included as part of the application package that you construct for distribution. The following list briefly outlines the changes in the 32-bit Help subsystem for Windows 95:

■ The WinHelp interface is a multi-tabbed dialog box, with tabs labeled Contents, Index, Find, and Answer Wizard (see fig. 15.9). The drop-down menus that contained Contents, Search, Index, and Cue Cards are gone.

■ The *Contents dialog box* is arranged in alphabetical, hierarchical order with many levels of index entry, represented as books (see fig. 15.9). When you double-click an index entry, the closed book opens and the sub-level book or page index expands. The first time a WinHelp file is opened, it establishes a contents database file (VBAACCSP.GID, for Access 95) in the directory where the application is stored.

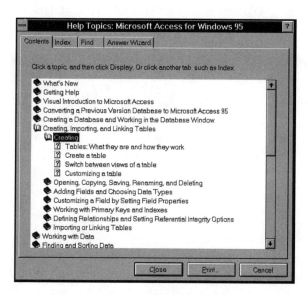

Fig. 15.9

The Windows/Access 95 Help System, the new Contents dialog box.

■ The *Answer Wizard* is a dialog box that allows search and retrieval on either keyword(s) or full phrases typed by the user, and presents the results at three distinct levels—"How Do I...," "Tell Me About...," and the Programming and Language Reference level (see fig. 15.10). This setup is a very convenient way to present the search results for differing audiences.

Fig. 15.10

The Windows/Access 95 Help System, the new Answer Wizard.

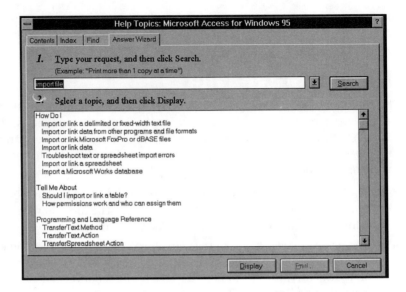

■ The *Index dialog box* is double-level, a new feature with Windows 95 (see fig. 15.11). The search interface and engine are similar to the Answer Wizard, but Topics Found is a pop-up dialog box, rather than embedded, and the topics aren't sorted into three categories, as they are in the Answer Wizard dialog.

Fig. 15.11

The Windows/Access 95 Help System, showing the new double-level Index dialog box, which organizes help topics for easier retrieval.

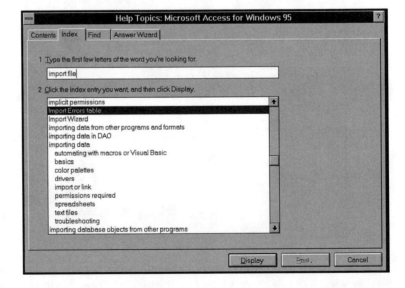

■ The *Find dialog box* is faintly reminiscent of the old Search screen in previous versions of Windows Help—only Find, in the opinion of the authors, is not as user-friendly (see fig. 15.12).

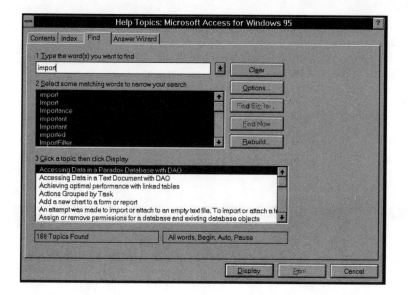

Fig. 15.12

The Windows/Access 95 Help System, the new Find dialog box.

- There now is graphics support for sixteen million colors (if you are really fussy about your presentations).
- Support for .AVI, .WAV, and .MIDI files is built-in, no additional DLLs required.
- You can now call up to nine secondary windows at the same time.
- Configurable button bars are available in secondary windows, and secondary windows are auto-sizable to match the length of the text in the topic.
- Cue Cards for performing procedures step-by-step are enhanced.

Note

When you install the Access Developers Toolkit, the Contents of the ADT Help is added to the end of the Access 95 Help file Contents. Index entries for Help file topics that are associated with components of the ADT also are merged into the Access on-line index, so you can search the on-line index for information on ADT components. (ADT topics aren't available through the Answer Wizard.)

What Goes into a Help File?

You can create Windows help files like those that are so much a staple of the Windows environment. Unfortunately, it appears that information on how to do this is missing from the Access 95 package. The manuals that come with the standard release of Access 95, *Getting Results* and *Building Applications*, don't even mention it. The ADT manuals, *Access Language Reference* and *Office 95 Data Access Reference*, both are programming reference manuals that give only definitions of **HelpFile** and **HelpContextID**.

This may sound awful, but unless you already know how to build help files, you have to refer to sources other than the packaged Access 95 products. For example, if you have the thin volume that came with the Access 2.0 ADT, the *Help Compiler Guide*, you have a very good reference for the previous Help compiler (WinHelp V3), or if you have access to third-party help authoring software, you can use the reference manuals included with them.

It's rumored that on-line help is available in a new facility included with the ADT, the Windows Help Workshop. Unfortunately, the main help file, HCW.HLP, seems to have been compiled with a help compiler that is initially incompatible with Windows NT V3.51, service pack 3!

Tip

If you are trying to initiate a help file in Windows NT File Manager by double-clicking the .HLP file, and you see error messages that refer to a needed upgrade in your Help compiler, you may be able to resolve the problem with a simple associate:

1. In File Manager, select File, Associate.

2. Browse and select the file, WINHLP32.EXE, in the Windows/System32 subdirectory. Click OK.

3. After you are back in the Associate dialog box, you should see the path and file name for WINHLP32.EXE in the Associate With text box. Press OK.

4. Double-click REAHELP.HLP in File Manager. It now should execute without error.

To create Windows Help (WinHelp), you need several types of source files, depending on how fancy you want or need to make your Help subsystem. Table 15.2 lists almost all the source files you need.

Table 15.2 Source Files for WinHelp

Type Source File	File Ext.	Description
Project File	.HPJ	(Make File) **Required**. Text file that lists the options and other files that comprise the Help subsystem. The Help compiler is run by using this file as the prime argument to create the .HLP file. Names of all .RTF topic files must be listed in this project file.
Topic File	.RTF	**Required**. The individual files that contain the topical information that is displayed in the Help subsystem—effectively, the meat of WinHelp. A small Help subsystem may need only a single .RTF file; most require several to many. The .RTF files can contain graphics, and will contain encoding

Type Source File	File Ext.	Description
		to include graphics, to jump to linked .RTF files, to designate keywords for the keyword listing, and to designate the browse sequence in the Help subsystem, once compiled. In the 32-bit version of WinHelp (V4.0), each .RTF file can contain 32,767 topics, and the number of .RTF files is limited only by available disk space.
Contents File	.CNT	**Optional**. The contents file that outlines the hierarchy of the on-line help and includes jumps into the topic files. The contents of this file display as the Table of Contents in the compiled Help file. New with WinHelp V4.
Bitmap File	.BMP	**Optional**. A single graphic image in device-independent Windows bitmap format. BMP graphics can be included in the .RTF files or can be converted to .MRB or .SHG files for display in the Help subsystem. In the 32-bit version of WinHelp (V4.0), a total of 65,535 bitmaps can be used.
Windows Metafile	.WMF	**Optional**. A single graphic image in Windows metafile format, such as is created by a drawing or engineering package. Can be used the same way as .BMP files.
Hypergraphic Bitmap	.SHG	**Optional**. A hypergraphic bitmap that contains a .BMP graphic or metafile graphic that was converted by SHED.EXE into .SHG format. Then, using the Hotspot Editor, you can embed hotspots into the .SHG bitmap, so that a user who views the image in a Help subsystem can click a spot on the image and pop up or jump to other parts of the Help subsystem that explain that portion of the image.
Multiple-Resolution	.MRB	**Optional**. Bitmap files that contain multiple versions of the same bitmap, at different screen resolutions, compiled into one file. When a user displays a Help topic that contains an .MRB graphic, the bitmap that corresponds to the current screen resolution is the graphic that displays. This compile must be done by MRBC.EXE.

Using these files may sound complicated, but the authors suggest that because you are reading this passage and are obviously not a professional WinHelp author, that you start with text-based Help files and add features and graphics as you grow more comfortable with building Help subsystems. Creating text-based WinHelp is fairly simple, and is shown in the following steps:

1. Gather information for the Help topics and plan how you want the layout to look.

2. Create the .RTF (Rich Text Format) files that contain all the text you want contained in the Help files.

3. Create the .CNT file (new with WinHelp V4) to describe the hierarchical index for the Help subsystem.

4. Add control codes that give the Help file its characteristic look and feel, such as "hot spots" and keyword searches.

5. Create the .HPJ file that gives direction on how the Help file should be compiled.

6. Compile the file or files by using the new Windows 95 Help Workbench.

7. Test and debug the Help file, using the Help Workbench.

8. Integrate into your application.

Optionally, you can add graphics and macros to your Help file to give it more pizzazz. The implementation gets fairly tricky, however, especially as you add more and more sophistication. You should start with the basics and move forward from there.

Planning Your Help

Before you start creating *topic files*, take a moment to determine what exactly this Help file you're developing is supposed to do. WinHelp V4 was reengineered to not only deliver on-line help, but also to function as a platform for multimedia and hypertext applications. For a discussion of the full capabilities of the new WinHelp V4 engine, refer to Chapter 12, of *Programming Windows 95 Unleashed*, by Sams Publishing.

However, you still need to make some decisions up front about how your Help file will work, and what functionality you plan to deliver with it. Some of the issues include the following:

■ Will this Help file be a part of an application or will it be a stand-alone program, such as a tutorial? As a part of an application, the Help file probably will contain many screen shots (.BMP files), context-sensitive help capability, browsing functionality, and it must take up minimal space in memory because this memory is shared with the parent application. As a stand-alone package the Help file opens in full-screen mode, probably contains complex graphics, and has to include a setup program for installation.

■ Will this Help file be run from the hard disk or from a CD-ROM? How the file is distributed probably will affect the type of compression used (see Compress option in a following section of this chapter for more information).

■ Are you creating this file for both 16-bit and 32-bit environments (do you have to provide backward compatibility to Access V2)? If yes, you can do it one of the following two ways:

- Distribute a copy of Win32s—the 32-bit library for Windows 3.1—with the WinHelp V4 Help file to all your Windows 3.1x and Windows for Workgroups 3.1x users.

- Compile the Help topic files under the Windows 3.1 Help compiler, creating a 16-bit WinHelp file. Then, to add back some of the functionality of WinHelp 4, provide an uncompiled version of the .CNT file (the contents file). The Help file runs on a 16-bit Windows platform as usual, but when it is run in a 32-bit environment, such as Windows 95 or Windows NT 3.51, it has the Contents functionality provided by WinHelp 4.

Creating the Help File Text

The first tool that you will need to create a Help subsystem is a word processor that supports .RTF, the Rich Text Format. The text that comprises the Help files must be written and saved as .RTF files, which is the Microsoft standard format for inter-application and interprocess communications. Microsoft Word, WordPerfect, and AmiPro support this format. You should use the word-processing software you are most familiar with to create your Help files. The authors will work through the exercises in this chapter with Microsoft Word 6, in a Windows NT 3.51 environment.

> **Caution**
>
> Do not use the Windows 95 WordPad to create Help files. WordPad doesn't save topic files in an .RTF format that is compatible with the WinHelp 4 compiler.

The general layout of Help files usually is hierarchical. This layout may start with a main file that lists the subfile contents, and then a file for each major functional area that you want to include in the Help system. Some second-level functional areas that you may consider writing help on are Menu Commands—both the upper, drop-down menu, and the Switchboard menu(s), or Policies & Procedures—both business and operational, or the Data Dictionary (which maps well to context-sensitive help), or all the above. Figure 15.13 illustrates a typical hierarchy of help files, with suggested main and subtopics.

Fig. 15.13

A suggested architecture for Help file organization.

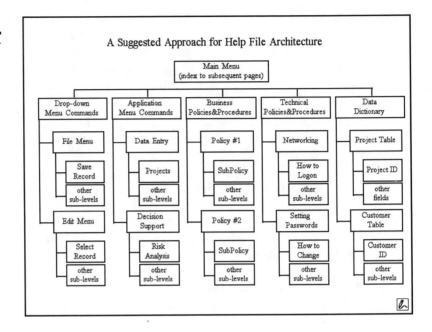

One scheme the authors used in the past to "quickly" generate a data dictionary for the help files is to use the Access Database Documentor. This technique is especially valuable under Access 95 because now the Database Documentor is capable of writing the entire report to Word. Previous versions of Access were unable to output the entire report so in the past, data dictionary capture was a combination of interapplication communications and reentering data from printed reports.

To generate a data dictionary, take the following steps:

1. From the database container, select the Tables tab.

2. Select Tools, Analyze, Documentor. This action opens the Database Documentor dialog box.

3. The combo box titled Object Type at the top of the dialog box should have Tables listed. Choose Select All, and click Options to open the Options dialog box.

4. Include for Table: Properties and Relationships. It's probably a bad idea to put Permissions and Securities in an on-line help file.

5. Include for Fields: select the last option, Names, Data Types, Sizes and Properties. This option gives you the world about each column in a table, but it's the only way to print the column description.

6. Include for Indexes: Nothing, unless you want to display indexing information in your on-line help system. The problem with publishing this kind of information is that indexing is subject to change, depending on data access and performance requirements (see Chapter 17, "Transitioning to Another Back-End DBMS," for more information on indexing). A similar argument holds true for

Permissions and Securities, that the topic is dynamic enough so that publishing accurate and timely information might not be possible.

7. Click OK twice to initiate the build of the table documentation. This process may take a few minutes, depending on the size of your database.

8. After the report is ready (you view it in print preview), choose the Output to Word icon (or choose Tools, OfficeLinks, Publish it with MS Word). Again, depending on the size of the report, this may take some time. Using this set of options, count on fitting two fields and table information on the first page and three fields (plus all properties of each field, of course) on every page thereafter. Incidentally, the document created is in Rich Text format.

Now that you have the data dictionary in Microsoft Word format, make a *copy* of it and place the copy in a directory entitled *ProgramName*Help to reformat for the help files. The authors suggest doing so because of the time that it takes to generate a data dictionary report, you always want to have a backup copy on hand.

As the database grows and tables are modified, you always can rerun the Database Documentor, selecting single tables as needed, to update the data dictionary report and the help files.

At this point you need to take time to reformat the data dictionary document. As initially generated, this document contains everything about everything—which may not be what you have in mind for a set of help files. While you're at it, build the other documents, each of which will cover a single topic that you want to include in your help subsystem. When you are done creating the documents, you can begin encoding them.

One note on building the help text files: be conservative with your fonts. The font you use to create your files also must be available on your target audience's computing systems, or all your carefully planned and laid-out files will "inherit" whatever is available. This may not result in a reasonable appearance for your end product.

Windows 95 comes with a large selection of fonts of all types—raster (bitmapped), vector, and TrueType—in a multitude of styles. For readability, however, the authors suggest you limit font selection to a 10-point sans serif (Arial TrueType or Microsoft Sans Serif are almost universally available and are a good choice for on-screen help), and restrict the variations to regular weight, bold for titles, and the occasional italic for emphasis.

Encoding the Help File Text

Each help file is broken into topics, with each topic equal to a single "page" of information—approximately, what a reader can see on a single screen. Topics don't have to be separate physical files, they all can be part of the same .RTF, but they do need to be separated by hard page breaks (Ctrl+Enter in Microsoft Word).

A topic contains the text of the help file and jumps to other related topics. Optionally, each topic also can contain a title, context strings, keyword indicators,

IV

Completing the Process

browse-sequence indicators, build tags, macros, comments, and graphics. Figure 15.14 shows a Word 6 document that contains these elements. The tool bars were customized for writing books, which probably renders the layout useless to the average reader.

Fig. 15.14

A sample help topic file in progress, with footnotes for title, context string, and keywords.

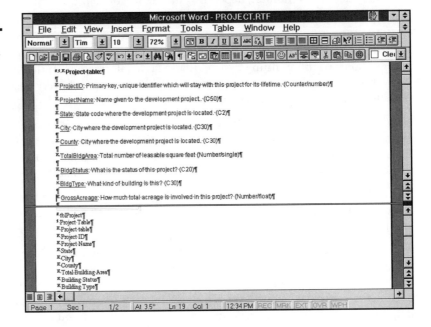

Each of these components is created by using footnotes and a specific character at the beginning of the footnote that designates the kind of property that you're building. Now, look at each of these components more closely.

Title. The title for each topic isn't strictly required but strongly recommended. The title gives an introduction to the topic and usually is formatted in bold. Titles appear in the Answer Wizard list and in the lower box of the Find dialog tab. If the title is missing, the find list will contain an entry that looks something like

```
>> Untitled Topic <<
```

—not very informative.

The footnote symbol to insert before the title—just after the start of document or after the hard page break—is the dollar sign ($). In the document, type the title—for example, in figure 15.14, Project table—you return to the beginning of the line, from the top menu select Insert, Footnote, and then choose Custom Mark, type the dollar sign ($), and click OK (see fig. 15.15). You're now in the footnote area of the page, and your footnote designator is a $. Retype the title. The authors, who are not excellent typists, are in the habit of grabbing a copy of the title (Ctrl+C to the Clipboard) just before inserting the footnote, pasting the title into the footnote (Ctrl+V), and removing the bold feature of the text (Shift+Home to highlight the text string, Ctrl+B to de-bold the text).

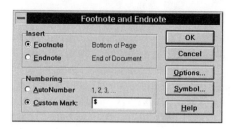

IV

Completing the Process

Fig. 15.15

The Insert Footnote dialog box with the custom footnote, the dollar sign ($), selected for insertion.

All the footnote symbols that this chapter covers can be inserted in front of the title of each topic. Any critical ordering is indicated in the appropriate property discussion. Titles can be up to 128 characters long, although you may want to shorten the title to 40 characters or so. Some display windows in the help dialog boxes tend to show only 40 or so characters.

Context Strings. A *context string*, or *topic id*, is the primary key for the Help file; each context string value uniquely identifies each topic. Within the entire Help subsystem, including all .RTF files that are part of your Help, each topic must have a unique context string. Context strings can be up to 255 characters long, can contain A-Z, a-z, 0-9, periods (.), and underline (_), but no spaces permitted.

The context string value is designated as the target, or destination, of a jump, so when you code a jump from topic A to topic B, in the jump you must include the context string for topic B. A topic can contain multiple context strings, positioned throughout the topic, so that a user can jump into a topic from some point from within or from outside the topic.

> **Note**
>
> The context string, staple object in previous versions of WinHelp, was renamed the "Topic ID" in WinHelp V4, which is the 32-bit Help system of Windows 95.

Keywords. *Keywords*, or *key phrases*—because you can include a full phrase as a keyword—are the entries that appear in both the Find and the Index dialog tabs of the Help system. The Help search engine does non-case-sensitive and partial matches to your keywords, so a search on the keyword, "find," brings up topics like "find," "Find," "find-and-replace," "Find_Click," "FindFile," and "FindCountry."

You can designate multiple keywords per topic by separating the keywords with a semicolon (;), just don't insert a space after the semicolon before typing the next keyword. The footnote designator is an uppercase K. All ANSI characters except the semicolon are accepted as keyword entries, including accented characters.

Browse Sequence. The *browse sequence values* are used to order the pages for use with the Browse Forward (>>) and Browse Back (<<) command buttons. It isn't clear to the authors, however, that these Browse Buttons are used extensively in the Windows 95 Help subsystem, although there is no reason why you cannot include them in your own custom Help files. It appears that the browse paradigm was replaced by the jump, assisted by micro-command buttons termed *chiclets*, no doubt named after the famous chewing gum. Still, in the Windows 3.11 world, Browse Buttons are widely used, and you may opt to incorporate a more traditional-looking form of Help into your application.

To incorporate the *Browse Buttons* into your Help screens, you must use the **BrowseButtons** macro, and specify its use in the CONFIG section of the .HPJ file, which we discuss in the following section. The footnote character for browse sequence is the plus (+) sign.

Browse sequence values are two-part: the first part designates the group, the second part specifies the order, and the two parts are separated by a colon (:). A group named Main may be composed of multiple topics, which translate to Help screens, and the numbers assigned to the order might increase by 10, as in the following example:

```
main:00010
main:00020
main:00030
```

Using this kind of numbering scheme allows insertion of additional topics in the browse sequence without being forced to renumber subsequent topics.

The entire browse sequence value is a character string but the order portion usually is designated as numbers. Sorting the browse sequence string is in ANSI order, not in numeric, so precede the numbers with leading zeros.

Build Tags. *Build tags* are used to keep order within the various component pieces that make up a Help file. You need to use build tags only if you plan to develop multiple versions of a Help file, and you need to include some components in one version, other components in another, and perhaps all components in a third version.

The footnote character for the build tags is the asterisk (*), and it must be the first reference mark in the list that precedes the title or the beginning of the topic. In the footnote section, you enter the name of the build in which this topic will be included, such as ALL, or TEST1, or Registered_Shareware. All alpha and the underline (_) are valid characters for a build tag, and the compiler doesn't distinguish case, so all uppercase or mixed case are only for visual enhancement in the .RTF file.

A topic can be included in multiple builds. To do so, just enter all build names into the footnote section, separated by a semicolon (:). Don't insert a space after the semicolon. If you wanted to include a topic in both the ALL build and the Registered_Shareware build, in the footnote section it will look like the following:

> * ALL;Registered_Shareware

Any topics that don't have a build tag will be included in all builds. You need to include the build tags in the BUILDTAGS section of the .HPJ file, which is discussed in the section, "The Help Project File," which follows in this chapter. In the 32-bit version of WinHelp (V4.0), a total of 16,383 build tags are allowed.

Macros. *Macros* are used in the Help subsystem to do things such as make the browse buttons appear and disappear, depending on the need to have them present, or to create "hotspots" on embedded graphics. A macro can call another macro, but you're generally restricted to using macros when entering a topic. There's no **on exit** action, wherein you can execute a macro. So, if you want a macro to make something happen or to make an object appear on a single topic screen, you probably need to code an inverse macro for every other topic of the Help subsystem.

The footnote character for a macro is the exclamation point (!), and you can specify multiple macros to execute in sequence by separating them with a semicolon (;). In the 32-bit version of WinHelp (V4.0), all limits for macro length and nesting are removed. Macro length is constrained only by the amount of local memory available when the macro is executed, so you may want to stay below the 10K limit. Some new macros (26) were added to extend functionality.

Due to the authors' lack of experience with using macros in the Help subsystem, we will not explore this option further. We have included, however, the full suite of WinHelp V4 macros in Appendix B of this book, for reference and completeness. You can find more discussion about using macros in the Access V2 *Help Compiler Guide*, which is included with the Access 2 ADT, or in Chapter 12 of *Programming Windows 95 Unleashed*, by Sams Publishing. *Designing Windows 95 Help, A Guide to Creating On-line Documents*, by Que Corporation, 1995, also covers this topic, quite comprehensively, and Chapter 11 specifically covers macros.

Comments. Document everything you do, even the on-line Help. You can document everything by using the *comments* option. The footnote character is the "at" @ symbol. All ANSI characters, including the semicolon, can be used in the comments string.

Hotspots. A *hotspot*, or *jump*, is a place on a Help file that has interactive capability. In the compiled Help file hotspot text is green in color and is underlined. When you click a hotspot, one of the following things can happen:

- You can jump to another topic in the Help file
- You can jump to another Help file

- You can bring up a pop-up window with information that defines or explains the hotspot
- You can execute a macro

Each of the four types of hotspots is created in a slightly different way. To see these differences, the following sections look at each method.

Jumps Between Topics in the Same Help File. Jumping between topics of the same file is like cross-referencing in a book; this extends the narrow, constraining hierarchical nature of the original Help file structure. To indicate a hotspot, or jump, mark the text with a double underline. Immediately following the underlined text, insert the context string of the target location, and make it hidden text. In Microsoft Word, the keystroke sequence to perform this operation is shown in the following steps:

1. Highlight the entire hotspot (jump) word and (according to the Word 6 on-line help) press Ctrl+Shift+D, or click the double-underline icon on the top toolbar. On many keyboards, the Ctrl+Shift+D key combination may not work. We suggest you customize the toolbar to add the double-underline if you plan on creating help files.

2. Move to the end of the double-underlined word and type the context string of the target to where you want to jump. Highlight the target, -id.

3. Click Format, and then Font and turn on the Hidden option of the dialog box. Click OK. The context string word disappears.

Now the only way to see your designated target context strings is to turn on the format codes. In reveal codes mode, where you display the formatting information, a jump resembles the example shown in figure 15.16.

Jumps Between Help Files. Jumping between Help files is nearly as easy as jumping between topics of the same Help file. Actually, you jump to a topic in a second Help file. The encoding is similar except after the context string, you add an "at" (@) symbol and the name of the other Help file, as shown in the first entry in figure 15.17.

Popping Up Pop-Up Windows. A *pop-up window* is a small window that contains information about or a description of the hotspot to which it is attached. A pop-up window can be associated either with text or with graphics. Creating the pop-up is much like creating a jump, except that rather than a double underline, you would use a single underline. In the 32-bit version of WinHelp (V4.0) the size limitation for a pop-up window was increased to 4,095 characters, which is a little long for a well-designed pop-up.

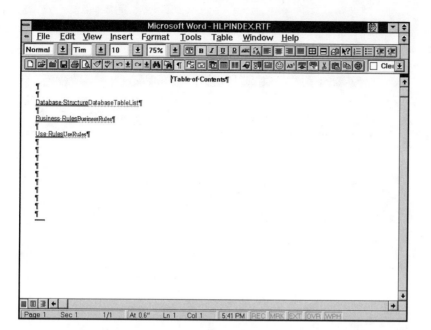

Fig. 15.16

The hidden context string is exposed by using the MS Word reveal codes (display formatting information) mode.

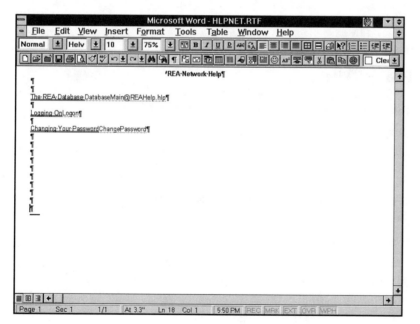

Fig. 15.17

Jumping between topics of different Help files requires only that you give the target Help file address (@REAHelp.hlp).

Like the jump, the context string follows immediately after the title, and is hidden text, as demonstrated in figure 15.18.

Fig. 15.18

An entry for a pop-up window, CCPopup, follows the title Construction Costs table. The pop-up might contain a brief description of the Construction Costs table.

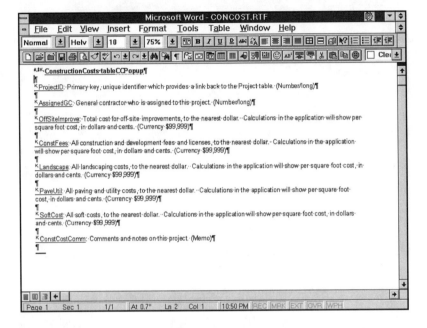

The Help Project File

When you have the topic files built and encoded, the lion's share of the job is done. You still need to build a few other source files, primarily the *.HPJ file*, also known as the *Help Project file*.

The .HPJ file tells the compiler how to assemble the Help subsystem. The .HPJ must be a text or ASCII file, so no matter which word processor you use to construct it, make sure that you save it in the proper format. The .HPJ is laid out much like an .INI file, with sections in brackets. To add comments to the .HPJ file, precede the text with a semicolon (;). These lines are ignored by the help compiler.

The .HPJ file is broken into the following sections:

- **FILES**—The topic files to be included in the build; required.
- **OPTIONS**—The various options which control the build of the Help subsystem; optional.
- **BUILDTAGS**—Lists build tags; optional.
- **CONFIG**—The registry of DLLs, macros, buttons, and menus used in the Help subsystem; required, if any are used.
- **CONFIG:WindowName**—Designates the macro(s) which are run when a window is opened.

■ **BITMAPS**—The registry of bitmapped images; required, if any are used.

■ **MAP**—Associates context string with context numbers for context-sensitive help; optional, unless context-sensitive help is required.

■ **ALIAS**—Defines aliases for a context string; optional.

■ **WINDOWS**—Defines window characteristics; required, if secondary windows are used.

■ **BAGGAGE**—External files that are to be maintained by the Help subsystem's file manager.

■ **MACROS**—Associates macros with keywords.

The order of the sections isn't important, unless an Alias section exists. The Alias section always must precede the Map section.

The FILES Section. The *FILES section* is used to list all topic files that will be used in the Help subsystem. This section is always required. The Help compiler uses the path specified by the ROOT option to locate the topic files listed. If the path is incorrect or if the topic file is not in the directory indicated, an error message is generated.

For very large Help systems, you may not want to include all the topic files in the .HPJ but you can include a reference to another ASCII text file(s) that lists the topic files. The following list shows an example of a FILES section:

```
[FILES]
arch.rtf                 ; the Archaeology & Endangered Species,
                           Environmental & Wetlands table

busrules.rtf             ; the business rules which are implied and/or
                           enforced

cheklist.rtf             ; the Checklist table

concost.rtf              ; the Construction Cost table

title.rtf                ; the Title & Survey table

userules.rtf             ; use rules for this application

#include<hlpnet.rtf>     ; index to network topics, stored in separate file
```

The OPTIONS Section. The *OPTIONS section* specifies the various options that control the creation of the Help subsystem and the kind of feedback that you can get as the build progresses. This section should be listed first in the .HPJ file so that the options can apply to the entire process.

The options that may or may not be included are as follows. There is no mandatory ordering sequence unless there is a REPLACE option. If a REPLACE option is used, it must come before the ROOT or BMROOT options. In previous versions of WinHelp, the OPTIONS section was optional. However, in WinHelp 4, there are now so many options to specify that you probably will have an OPTIONS section in all your Help files. Detailed explanations of each of the options are shown in the following list:

IV

Completing the Process

- **BMROOT**—The directory where the bitmap files are kept.
- **BUILD**—Which topics to include or exclude in the build process.
- **CHARSET**—Specifies the default character set (new).
- **CITATION**—Adds a citation to the end of all text copied or printed from the Help file (new).
- **CNT**—The name of the Contents (.CNT) file (new).
- **COMPRESS**—The type of compression to use during the build.
- **CONTENTS**—The context string of the contents topic.
- **COPYRIGHT**—Includes a unique copyright message in the Help file.
- **DBCS**—Indicates whether or not topic files will use a double-byte character set (new).
- **DEFFONT**—Specifies the default font used in WinHelp text boxes (new).
- **ERRORLOG**—Places compile errors in this designated file.
- **FORCEFONT**—Maps the font type in the topics file to a different font type in the compiled Help file.
- **FTS**—What level of information is to be included in the index file for full-text searching (new).
- **HLP**—The name of the compiled Help (.HLP) file (new).
- **ICON**—The icon to use when the Help file is minimized (old, not listed in WinHelp V4).
- **INDEX_SEPARATORS**—Indicates the characters WinHelp uses to identify first- and second-level index entries (new).
- **LANGUAGE**—The sort ordering for foreign-language versions of the Help file (old, not listed in WinHelp V4).
- **LCID**—Replaces option LANGUAGE, specifies the language of the Help file and, by implication, the sort order (new).
- **MAPFONTSIZE**—Maps the text in the topics file to a different size font in the compiled Help file.
- **MULTIKEY**—Points to an alternate or supplemental keyword table.
- **NOTES**—Should the Help compiler display notes? (new).
- **OLDKEYPHRASE**—Should I use a key-phrase file? (new).
- **OPTCDROM**—Optimizes the Help file for use on a CD-ROM (old, not listed in WinHelp V4).
- **REPLACE**—Specifies a path prefix to replace and its replacement (new).
- **REPORT**—Controls the message display on-screen during the compile and build.
- **ROOT**—The location of topic and data files.

- **TITLE**—The text displayed in the Help title bar.
- **TMPDIR**—Specifies the directory (folder) in which to place the temporary files that are created during the Help file compile step (new).
- **WARNING**—Controls the level of error message displayed to ERRORLOG during the compile and build (old, replaced by NOTES).

Following is a sample OPTIONS section, taken from the REA Help files:

```
[OPTIONS]
ROOT=x:\REA\help
TITLE=REA Help Files
COMPRESS=off
CONTENTS=MainMenu
COPYRIGHT= REA Project Tracking System V1
ERRORLOG=d:\clients\que\help\helplog.txt
ICON=e:\REA\help.ico
REPORT=on
WARNING=3
BUILD=Master
```

Option: BMROOT. The *BMROOT option* designates the directory or directories where the bitmap image files are stored. If you specify a BMROOT option, you don't need to list bitmap paths and files in the BITMAPS section. If you choose to omit the BMROOT option, the Help subsystem looks for bitmaps in the directory specified by the ROOT option. You can have any number of BMROOT statements in this section.

The syntax of BMROOT is shown in the following example:

```
BMROOT=pathname[, pathname]
```

The following entry, for example, indicates that bitmaps are stored in the \REA\Help\ BMP directory on the E drive and in the Graphics\REA\Help directory on the D drive:

```
[OPTIONS]
BMROOT=E:\REA\Help\BMP,D:\Graphics\REA\Help
```

Option: BUILD. The *BUILD option* designates which topics are included or excluded during the build process. You need to use this option only if the .RTF files have build tags encoded within them. The BUILD option uses the following syntax:

```
BUILD=expression
```

Here, *expression* is a logical statement that specifies which topics to include or exclude in the build. Like logical expressions in any programming language, they generally are evaluated from left to right. The logical expressions used are described in the following table:

Symbol	Description
( )	Parentheses, which delineates a group to be evaluated as a unit
&	AND operator
¦	OR operator
~	NOT operator
tag	Build tag

The order of operations, from left or right, uses the following precedence rules:

- Expressions within parentheses are evaluated first and as a unit
- Expressions with a logical NOT (~) are evaluated next
- Expressions with a logical AND (&) are evaluated next
- Expressions with a logical OR (¦) are evaluated last

The following table lists examples, all of which are valid BUILD expressions, use the MASTER, DEMO, and TEST build tags in the topic files:

Example	What Is Built
`BUILD = DEMO`	Topics that carry the DEMO tag or topics with no tags
`BUILD = DEMO&MASTER`	Topics that carry both DEMO and MASTER tags, or topics with no tags
`BUILD = DEMO¦MASTER`	Topics that carry the DEMO tag or the MASTER tag, or topics with no tags
`BUILD = (DEMO¦MASTER)&TEST`	Topics that carry the DEMO tag or the MASTER tag, and that also carry the TEST tag, or topics with no tags
`BUILD = ~MASTER`	Topics that do not carry the MASTER tag, or topics with no tags

Option: CHARSET. The *CHARSET option* (new) designates the default character set which will be used for the fonts in the Help file. The operating system character set determines its capability (or lack thereof) to support various international alphabets. Windows NT uses the Unicode character set; Windows 95 supports Western, Mid-East, and Far-East sets. If your .RTF writer specifies a character set, this set takes precedence over this option. Microsoft Word 6 and later specify character sets; previous versions do not.

The following line shows the syntax of CHARSET ischaracter set, where *charset-value* would be Unicode, Western, Mid-East, or Far-East:

```
CHARSET=charset-value
```

Option: CITATION. The *CITATION option* (new) appends a citation to the end of any information (except the context-sensitive pop-up windows) that is copied or printed from the Help file. The syntax of CITATION is shown on the following line:

```
CITATION=text
```

Here, *text* can be any alpha characters, numbers, and special characters, up to 2,000 bytes in length.

Option: CNT. The *CNT option* (new) identifies the name of the Contents file (.CNT) to associate with the current Help file. If the OPTIONS section doesn't contain a CNT statement, the Help compiler looks for a file name with the same name as the Help file but with a .CNT extension, and use that, instead.

The context of the CNT portion of the .HPJ file looks like the following example:

```
CNT=contents-file
```

Here, *contents-file* is any valid file name supported by the current operating system and that has the suffix .CNT.

Option: COMPRESS. The *COMPRESS option* designates the level of compression to use during the build. The compression schemes and ratios have changed from the previous version of the WinHelp compiler, and the new parameters (WinHelp V4) are presented here.

The syntax of COMPRESS is shown in the following example:

```
CITATION=compression-level
```

Here, *compression-level* can be any of (or a sum of) the levels shown in the following table:

Hex Value of Compression Level	Meaning
0x00	Compiler (Help Workshop) doesn't compress the Help file
0x01	Compiler (Help Workshop) uses best judgment to determine optimal compression for current Help file
0x02	Compiler (Help Workshop) uses Phrase compression on text
0x04	Compiler (Help Workshop) uses Hall compression on text
0x08	Compiler (Help Workshop) uses Zeck compression on text
0x10	Compiler (Help Workshop) uses RLE compression on bitmaps
0x20	Compiler (Help Workshop) uses Zeck compression on bitmaps

For the pragmatic (the authors included), here is a list of hints and tips on which compression routine to use:

- If you want maximum compression, specify 0x12 as the compression-level.
- If you specify Phrase compression, the Help Workshop creates a phrase-table (.PH) file. If the Help Workshop finds an existing phrase-table file during the compile, it deletes the file and creates a new one. You can indicate, within Help Workshop, that you want to use the old phrase-table file, but the compression is never quite as good as building a new one.
- Hall compression uses the FTSRCH.DLL file that is included with both Windows 95 and Windows NT V3.51.
- If the COMPRESS option is set to 1, the Help Workshop will choose between Hall and Phrase compression based on the size of your .RTF files. If the total size of all topic files is greater than 1M, the Help Workshop uses Hall compression.

Option: CONTENTS. The *CONTENTS option* designates the context string (or topic ID, as it's known in WinHelp V4) of the "main" topic file. This file is usually a Table of Contents or an Index. If the CONTENTS option is omitted from the .HPJ file, the Help compiler assumes that the first file it finds listed in the [FILES] section is the "main" file.

The context of the CONTENTS portion of the .HPJ file looks like the following example:

```
CONTENTS=contextString
```

The CONTEXT statement for the REA Help subsystem looks like this example:

```
[OPTIONS]
CONTENTS=MainMenu
```

Option: COPYRIGHT. The *COPYRIGHT option* (new) provides for a unique copyright message in the Help file. The maximum size of the COPYRIGHT option in the old scheme was 75 characters. This limit was raised in WinHelp V4 to 255 bytes.

The COPYRIGHT portion of the .HPJ file looks like the following example:

```
[OPTIONS]
COPYRIGHT= REA Project Tracking System V1
```

Option: DBCS. The *DBCS option* (new) specifies whether the files to be compiled will use a double-byte character set. The context of the DBCS statement looks like the following example:

```
DBCS=value
```

Here, *value* is either Yes or No. The Help Workshop compiler automatically recognizes certain language IDs (LCID) and forces the DBCS option to a setting that is consistent with the LCID.

The following LCIDs force DBCS=YES. The following language identifier values also are used with the LCID option (described in a following section):

Language Identifier	Locale
0x0411	Japan
0x0404	Taiwan
0x1004	Singapore
0x0C04	Hong Kong

The following LCIDs will force DBCS=NO:

Language Identifier	Locale
0x0409	American
0x0C09	Australian
0x0C07	Austrian
0x042D	Basque
0x080C	Belgian
0x0809	British
0x0402	Bulgarian
0x1009	Canadian
0x041A	Croatian
0x0405	Czech
0x0406	Danish
0x0413	Dutch (Standard)
0x0C01	Egyptian
0x040B	Finnish
0x040C	French (Standard)
0x0C0C	French Canadian
0x0407	German (Standard)
0x042E	Germany
0x0408	Greek
0x040E	Hungarian
0x040F	Icelandic

(continues)

(continued)

Language Identifier	Locale
0x0801	Iraq
0x1809	Ireland
0x040D	Israel
0x0410	Italian (Standard)
0x2C01	Jordan
0x3401	Kuwait
0x0426	Latvia
0x1001	Libya
0x1407	Liechtenstein
0x0427	Lithuania
0x140C	Luxembourg (French)
0x1007	Luxembourg (German)
0x042F	Macedonian
0x080A	Mexican
0x0819	Moldavia
0x0818	Moldavia
0x1801	Morocco
0x1409	New Zealand
0x0414	Norwegian (Bakmal)
0x0814	Norwegian (Nynorsk)
0x2001	Oman
0x0415	Polish
0x0416	Portuguese (Brazilian)
0x0816	Portuguese (Standard)
0x0418	Romanian
0x0419	Russian
0x0401	Saudi Arabia
0x081A	Serbian
0x041B	Slovak
0x0424	Slovenia
0x0C0A	Spanish (Modern)
0x040A	Spanish (Traditional)
0x0430	Sutu
0x041D	Swedish

Language Identifier	Locale
0x100C	Swiss (French)
0x0807	Swiss (German)
0x0810	Swiss (Italian)
0x2801	Syria
0x041E	Thailand
0x0431	Tsonga
0x041F	Turkish
0x3801	United Arab Emirates
0x0422	Ukrainian
0x0420	Urdu
0x0436	Zulu

Option: DEFFONT. The *DEFFONT option* (new) specifies the default font for the lists on the Contents, Index, and Find pages of the compile Help file, and in the Topics Found dialog box. The context of the DEFFONT statement looks like the following example:

```
DEFFONT=font-name,font-size,charset
```

In this example, *font-name* specifies the name of the font to use, *font-size* specifies the point size of the font to use, and *charset* specifies the character set (CHARSET option) to use.

Option: ERRORLOG. The *ERRORLOG option* places compile errors in a designated file for viewing. It also sends the error messages to the screen during the compile. The path that accompanies the file name can be absolute or relative to the path specified in the ROOT option.

The ERRORLOG statement looks like the following example:

```
[OPTIONS]
ERRORLOG=d:\clients\que\help\helplog.txt
```

Option: FORCEFONT. The *FORCEFONT option* maps the font type in the topics file to a different font type in the compiled Help file. When this option is used, the Help file is displayed by using only the single font specified. The font must be spelled exactly as it appears in the Windows Control Panel list. If you specify a font that the Help compiler doesn't recognize, it resorts to its default, the Helvetica font. In the 16-bit version of WinHelp, the font type names were restricted to 20 characters; in the 32-bit version, the limit was increased to 31 characters. Additionally, in the 32-bit version, you now can use Wingdings.

The FORCEFONT statement looks like the following example:

```
[OPTIONS]
FORCEFONT=Arial
```

Option: FTS. The *FTS option* (new) specifies the kind of index file to create for the full-text search feature. The FTS statement looks like the following example:

```
FTS=fts-value
```

Here, *fts-value* is one or a sum of the following values:

Hex Value	Meaning
0x01	Create an index file for full-text searching
0x02	Include untitled topics (such as context-sensitive Help topics) in the index file
0x04	Include information to support phrase searching
0x08	Include information to provide feedback on phrase searches
0x10	Include information to support similarity searches

Option: ICON. The *ICON option* is used to specify the icon that will be used when the Help file is minimized. The icon file must be in .ICO format. This is an old parameter and may not be supported by the new WinHelp V4 compiler, but it is included here for backward compatibility. The ICON statement looks like this example:

```
[OPTIONS]
ICON=e:\REA\help.ico
```

Option: HLP. The *HLP option* (new) is used to specify the name of the compiled Help file. The context of the HLP option is shown in the following line:

```
HLP=help-file
```

Here, *help-file* is a valid file name that is supported by the operating system. If the .HLP extension isn't provided, it's automatically appended. If the Help compiler cannot find an HLP statement in the .HPJ file, it gives the compiled .HLP file the same name as the project (.HPJ) file.

Option: INDEX_SEPARATORS. The *INDEX_SEPARATORS option* (new) identifies the special characters that WinHelp uses to delineate separate keyword entries. The context of the INDEX_SEPARATORS option is shown in the following example:

```
INDEX_SEPARATORS="separator1separator2"
```

In this syntax, *separator1* is the character used to separate keywords in an entry, and *separator2* is the character used to separate entries in a list. If this option is not specified, the default comma and colon values (" , : ") will be used.

Option: LANGUAGE. The *LANGUAGE option* designates the sort ordering in the Search keyword list for foreign-language versions of the Help file. As of Windows 3.11, the only language sort order supported, other than English, was Scandinavian. This is an old parameter and was supplanted by the LCID option, but is included here for backward compatibility. The LANGUAGE statement looks like this:

```
[OPTIONS]
LANGUAGE=scandinavian
```

Option: LCID. The *LCID option* (new) specifies the language of the Help file, which in turn is used to determine sort order for keywords and index listings, and which character to use for curly quotes. The context of the LCID option is shown in the following example:

```
LCID=language case-insensitive case-sensitive
```

In this syntax, the variables have the following meaning:

Parameter	Description
language	The hex value of the language on which to base sorting (see the DBCS option)
case-sensitive, case-insensitive	The bit flags for ignoring non-spacing marks and symbols in each condition

Hex Value	Meaning
0x2	Ignore non-spacing marks
0x4	Ignore punctuation
0x6	Ignore non-spacing marks and symbols

For example, the following line specifies that the language of the Help file is American English, and for both case-sensitive and case-insensitive searches, the sort order should ignore non-spacing marks and symbols.

```
LCID=0x0409 0x6 0x6
```

Option: MAPFONTSIZE. The *MAPFONTSIZE option* maps the text in the topics file to a different size font in the compiled Help file.

The MAPFONTSIZE statement uses the following syntax:

```
MAPFONTSIZE=m[-n]:p
```

Here, *m* is the size of the font used in the topic files and *p* is the size of the font intended for the Help file. All fonts—when the topic files are compiled into a Help file—change from *m* to *p*. The optional argument, *n*, allows for a range of font sizes to map to *p*. When used, all fonts in the topic files that fall into the size range *m* to *n*, inclusively, convert to size *p* in the compiled Help file.

The following two examples illustrate how the MAPFONTSIZE option can be used:

```
[OPTIONS]
MAPFONTSIZE=12:10          ; convert all 12-point fonts to 10-point
MAPFONTSIZE=18-24:16       ; convert all font sizes between 12-point and
24-point to 16-point
```

You can use as many as five MAPFONTSIZE statements in the OPTIONS section; only one font size or range of sizes can be addressed in a MAPFONTSIZE statement. If you specify a font size in a subsequent MAPFONTSIZE statement that was specified in an earlier statement, then the latter MAPFONTSIZE statement will be ignored.

Option: MULTIKEY. The *MULTIKEY option* specifies the footnote character to use for an additional keyword table.

The MULTIKEY statement looks like the following:

```
MULTIKEY=footnotecharacter
```

Here, *footnotecharacter* is a case-sensitive letter used to designate keywords in the footnote section of the topic files. If, for example, the footnotecharacter were designated as an uppercase letter L, then topics that were encoded with the footnote character, "L," would have their keywords incorporated into an additional keyword table, but the topics that were encoded with a lowercase "l" would not. This option is shown in the following example:

```
[OPTIONS]
MULTIKEY=L
```

Any alphanumeric character can be used for a keyword table except K, k, A, or a, which are reserved for the Help system standard keyword table and the ALink keyword table, respectively. You can have as many as five keyword tables in a Help subsystem, including the standard, but because of performance limitations and system constraints, the *Microsoft Help Compiler Manual* suggests that you limit the number of tables to two or three.

Option: NOTES. The *NOTES option* (new) indicates whether or not the WinHelp compiler displays notes while compiling the Help file. The context of the NOTES option is as follows:

```
NOTES=0 ¦ 1 ¦ yes ¦ no
```

Here, the value is binary, either yes or no, 1 or 0. The default is NOTES off.

Option: OLDKEYPHRASE. The *OLDKEYPHRASE option* (new) controls whether or not an existing key-phrase file should be used when compressing a Help file with phrase compression. The context of the OLDKEYPHRASE statement looks like the following:

OLDKEYPHRASE=*value*

Here, *value* is either Yes or No. If Yes, then the existing key-phrase file (.PH) will be used for phrase compression.

Option: OPTCDROM. The *OPTCDROM option* optimizes the Help file for use on a CD-ROM. This option aligns topic files on predefined block boundaries, which makes retrieval more efficient but slightly increases the size of the compiled Help file. This is an old parameter and may not be supported by the new WinHelp V4 compiler, but it's included here for backward compatibility. The OPTCDROM statement can take any of the following forms:

```
[OPTIONS]
OPTCDROM=yes
OPTCDROM=true
OPTCDROM=1
OPTCDROM=on
```

Option: REPLACE. The *REPLACE option* (new) replaces old file-path prefixes with new file-path prefixes. If you have to move a set of files that are part of a Help subsystem— like the topic or bitmap files—from one folder to another, you don't need to search and replace every instance of the old path name with the new; you just need to make the change one time in this option. The context of the REPLACE statement looks like the following:

```
REPLACE=old-prefix = new-prefix
```

Here, *old-prefix* is the old path name for a file and *new-prefix* is the new path name. The following example replaces the current path for the help directory to a path that is located on a network server:

```
[OPTIONS]
REPLACE= e:\accdat95\QUE\help = \\DBServer\REA\help
```

Option: REPORT. The *REPORT option* controls the message display to the screen during the compile and build. The context of the REPORT statement looks like the following:

```
REPORT=yes ¦ no
```

In this example, a *yes* allows the Help compiler to display progress messages on-screen during the build. The default value is set to yes. If you specified an ERRORLOG option, the compiler writes the REPORT messages to the log file. To speed up the compile process, turn off the REPORT option.

Option: ROOT. The *ROOT option* designates the location of topic and data files, which are listed in the Files section of the .HPJ file.

The context of the ROOT statement looks like the following:

```
ROOT=pathname[,pathname]
```

The *pathname* can be an absolute path, complete with drive letter, or it can be a relative path from the project directory. If the ROOT option is used, all relative paths that are specified in the Help file are relative to a path specified in the ROOT statement. If the ROOT option isn't used, then all relative paths that are specified in the Help file are relative to the directory that contains the .HPJ file.

If the .HPJ file doesn't contain a BMROOT option, then the Help compiler looks in the directories specified by the ROOT option for all bitmap files. The bitmap file names also can be listed in the BITMAPS section of the .HPJ file.

The ROOT option for the REA application looks like the following:

```
[OPTIONS]
ROOT=x:\REA\help
```

Option: TITLE. The *TITLE option* specifies the text that displays in the Help title bar, up to 50 characters in WinHelp V4.

The TITLE statement looks like the following:

```
[OPTIONS]
TITLE=REA Help Files
```

Option: TMPDIR. The *TMPDIR option* routes to a new destination all temporary files that are created as a by-product of the compile process. Usually, the compiler builds these temporary files in the current directory, and if the current directory cannot hold both the Help files and the temporary files, it aborts. The context of the TMPDIR statement looks like the following:

```
TMPDIR=folder
```

In this example, *folder* is any valid directory or folder name supported by the operating system, which has enough room to hold the temporary files that are built during the compile process.

Option: WARNING. The *WARNING option* controls the level of error message displayed to ERRORLOG during the compile and build. This is an old parameter and may not be supported by the new WinHelp V4 compiler, but it's included here for backward compatibility. The context of the WARNING statement looks like the following:

```
WARNING=level
```

The warning levels are as shown in the following table:

Level	Information Reported
1	The Help compiler reports only the most severe errors.
2	The Help compiler reports an intermediate number of errors.
3	The Help compiler reports all errors and warnings.

The BUILDTAGS Section. All build tags that you encoded in the topic files must be listed here, in the *BUILDTAGS section*. If you haven't used build tags, this section is not needed. Under the 16-bit version of WinHelp, a maximum of 30 build tags could be listed in this section, but the new 32-bit version raises the limit to 16,383.

Build tags are not case-sensitive and may not contain spaces. Only one build tag per line, but you can insert a comment on the same line, following a build tag. The specific build tag to be used for a build is specified by the BUILD option, as in the following:

```
[BUILDTAGS]
MasterBuild      ; the master set of files for all releases
TestBuild        ; the test set
```

> **Note**
>
> The Microsoft Help Workshop (described in detail in a following section of this chapter) doesn't have a facility to modify the BUILDTAG section of your .HPJ file. You have to handle the creation and modification of the BUILDTAG section by loading the .HPJ file into a text editor.

The CONFIG Section. The *CONFIG section* is the registry of all DLLs, macros, buttons, and menus used in the Help subsystem, and which macro(s) are to execute when the Help file first opens. Help macros can add either buttons (browse forward/browse back) or menus to Help subsystems.

Each line of the CONFIG section can contain up to 254 characters; you can have an unlimited number of lines. The following example is taken from the *Windows Help Compiler Guide*:

```
[CONFIG]
RegisterRoutine("bmp", "HDisplayBmp", "USSS")
RegisterRoutine("bmp", "CopyBmp", "v = USS")
CreateButton("btn_up", "&Up", "JumpContents('HOME.HLP')")
BrowseButtons()
```

This example CONFIG section performs the following actions:

- Registers the HDisplayBmp DLL, which is required to display extended bitmapped images
- Registers the CopyBmp routine, which will copy a bitmap from an embedded window
- Creates an Up button (with hot-key option) to aid in use of the Help subsystem
- Adds Browse buttons to the Help toolbar

The CONFIG:WindowName Section. The *CONFIG:WindowName section* contains the macro or macros that are run when a window is opened. The macro statements are limited to one macro per line, and if more than one macro is specified per window, they will run in the order in which they are listed. The following example closes all secondary windows when the SecWindow2 window is opened:

```
[CONFIG:SecWindow2]
CloseSecondarys()
```

The BITMAPS Section. Any bitmapped images that aren't located in the directories specified in the ROOT or BMROOT options must be listed in this section, the *BITMAPS section*. Usually, bitmap locations are designated in the BMROOT option of the OPTIONS section, so this section is not often used. In the 32-bit version of WinHelp (V4.0), a total of 65,535 bitmapped files can be listed. The following shows an example of the BITMAPS section:

```
[BITMAPS]
15fig01.bmp
15fig02.bmp
x:\REA\Help\project.bmp
```

This section is included in WinHelp V4 for backward compatibility only, and eventually will be phased out. New WinHelp files should define bitmapped images in the BMROOT portion of the OPTIONS section.

The MAP Section. The *MAP section* is required only if you want to implement context-sensitive Help in your application. Here, you associate context strings or aliases (specified in the ALIAS section) for context strings with context numbers, which are referenced in the application. The application passes the context number to the Help subsystem, and the associated topic is then displayed.

Context numbers are long integers, unsigned, greater than zero, and can be specified in either decimal or hexadecimal, using standard C-language notation for hex. A 1:1 relationship exists between a context number and its associated context strings; a context number can only be used to reference a single context string. When included in the Map section, the context strings and context numbers are separated by white space, either by using the space bar or the Tab key of the keyboard.

The following is an example of the many formats you can use to map context strings to context numbers:

```
[MAP]
tblProject              1          ; the project data entry screen and at-
                                     tributes

txtProjectID            100

txtProjectName          110

txtState                120

txtCity                 130

txtCounty               140

tblConstCost            2          ; the construction cost data entry screen
                                     and attributes

txtCCProjectID          200

txtAssignedGC           210

OffSiteImprove          220

tblChecklist            0x0001     ; the checklist data entry screen and
                                     attributes

txtCkProjectID          0x0002

txtRFPReceived          0x0003

txtRFPComm              0x0004

#define vscroll         0x010A     /* the vertical scroll bar */

#define hscroll         0x010E     /* the horizontal scroll bar */

#include <riskform.h>              ; context mapping for the Risk screen
```

You can include other files of mappings by specifying the **#include** command, or you may directly include C-language header files, which must begin with the **#define** command and are commented with the standard C-language comment line (*/* comment here */*).

If you use this section and also define aliases for the context strings, the Alias section must precede the MAP section in the .HPJ file. In the 32-bit version of WinHelp (V4.0), a total of 16,000 entries are permitted in the Map section.

The ALIAS Section. In the *ALIAS section* you can assign one or more context strings to an alias. There is an M:1 relationship between context strings and aliases; many context strings may be assigned to a single alias. A single context number can be associated only with a single context string or with a single alias. By associating multiple context strings with a single alias, you can effectively create a 1:M relationship, context number to context string, by way of the alias. In the 32-bit version of WinHelp (V4.0), a total of 4 billion aliases can be defined.

```
[ALIAS]
txtProjectID   =  ProjectID   ; map all project ids to this alias
txtCCProjectID =  ProjectID
txtCkProjectID =  ProjectID
```

The WINDOWS Section. The *WINDOWS section* defines window characteristics such as size, location, and color, and this section is optional unless a secondary window will be used. In the 32-bit version of WinHelp (V4.0), up to 255 discreet window definitions can be entered.

The general syntax of the WINDOWS statement is as follows:

```
window-name = "caption", (x-coord, y-coord, width, height), state&buttons,
(scrolling-RGB), (nonscrolling-RGB), state
```

The following table describes the different components of the WINDOWS statement:

Table 15.3 The Window Section Parameters

Parameter	Description
window-name	Name of the window that uses the defined parameters. For the main Help window, parameter value is **main**. For a secondary window, name can be any unique string, up to 8 characters. All jumps into the secondary window must use this unique name as part of the context string.
caption	Appears on the title bar of the Help window. For the main Help window, this option can be specified by the TITLE option in the OPTIONS section. The title can have up to 50 characters.
x-coord, y-coord	Placement of the upper left corner of the Help window, specified by the horizontal and vertical positions mapped to a 1024×1024 coordinate system, the upper left being location 0,0. Windows Help does an internal mapping of the 1024×1024 coordinate system onto the resolution of the video card. If a video card has an hres×vres pixel resolution, and the horizontal and vertical positions are represented by horizPos and vertPos, then the x-coordinate of the window corner is *horizPos* * (hres/1024), and the y-coordinate is *vertPos* * (vres/1024).

Parameter	Description
width, height	Width and height of the window, which are determined based on the 1024×1024 coordinate system.
state&buttons	Indicates whether or not a window will be displayed as maximized, and defines the buttons to display in the window's button bar, if any. This parameter is a sum of one or more of the following values:

Hex Value	Meaning
0x0001	Maximize the window and ignore the *x-coord, y-coord, width, height*, and *state* parameters given in the type definition
0x0004	Turn off the default buttons on the button bar (used only for the Main Help window)
0x0100	Add the Options button to the button bar
0x0200	Add the Browse buttons to the button bar
0x0400	Add the Contents button to the button bar
0x0800	Add the Index button to the button bar
0x1000	Add the Help Topics button to the button bar
0x2000	Add the Print button to the button bar
0x4000	Add the Back button to the button bar
0x8000	Add the Find button to the button bar

Parameter	Description
scrolling-RGB, nonscrolling-RGB	A trio of three-digit numbers (RRR, GGG, BBB with values from 0 to 255), which represents the background colors for the scrolling and non-scrolling regions in the window, respectively. The three digits represent the intensity of the red, green, and blue components of the color. If this option is not present, window inherits normal system colors.
state	Formerly the topmost parameter, for a secondary window type, specifies that the window, when opened, is to remain on top of all other windows (as in the Access 2 Cue Cards). For backward compatibility the value 1 can be used. For WinHelp V4, the parameter is the letter "f," followed by a number that is the sum of the following options:

Value	Meaning
1	Display the window on top of other windows
2	Automatically size the window vertically to match the length of the topic (not available for the Main Help window)

IV

Completing the Process

The following example shows the Windows section from the REA Help .HPJ file:

```
[WINDOWS]
main=" REA Help Files",(460,0,540,1023)
```

The BAGGAGE Section. The *BAGGAGE section* lists external files that are to be maintained by the Help subsystem's file manager. These files are often multimedia elements that the Help compiler stores locally, in the Help file system. This scheme is far more efficient than storing the external files under the control of the operating system because the Help subsystem doesn't have to depend on the availability of the operating system file manager when retrieving a file. In the 16-bit version of WinHelp, you can store a maximum of 1,000 bitmaps as baggage files; the 32-bit version increased this limit to 10,000.

The reference to the topic file must be exactly the same as it appears in the topic file, as baggage filenames are case-sensitive. Use the ROOT option to specify all or part of the path to the baggage files, and then specify the rest of the path (if any) relative to the ROOT path.

For example, if the ROOT entry looks like the following entry:

```
[BAGGAGE]
ROOT=x:\REA\Help
```

then the relative path to the topics directory, main topics file, which lies one below the Help directory, looks like:

```
Topics\MainFile.RTF
```

The MACROS Section. The *MACROS section* is new to WinHelp V4. This section associates macros with keywords, and the macros are executed each time a user selects the specified keyword in the Help index.

Each entry in the MACROS section is a three-liner, and the format looks like the following:

```
[MACROS]
keyword1[;keyword2;...;keywordn]
macro1[;macro2,...,macron]
title
```

Each portion of the MACRO section contains the following parameters:

Parameter	Description
keyword	Specifies keyword(s) to associate with the macro(s) on the following line. Use semicolons to separate keywords.
macro	Specifies which macro(s) to run when a keyword from preceding line is selected from the index. Separate multiple macros with semicolons.
title	Specifies the title to display in Topics Found dialog box when the selected keyword is linked to two or more Help topics. If no title is needed, leave blank. Titles are limited to 255 characters.

There are certain constraints that you must observe when using the MACRO section:

- You cannot use comments in this section; semicolons are already used to delimit keywords and macros.
- There are no limits to the number of three-line keyword macro definitions in this section; however, you can only use a keyword one time.
- You cannot include a file in the MACROS section.

The Help Compiler

The next tool that you need to create a Help subsystem is a *Windows Help compiler*. The 32-bit help compiler that is compatible with Windows 95 (but not necessarily with Windows NT 3.51, sp3) is named *HCRTF.EXE*. This compiler converts the .RTF files into a form readable by the Windows 95 Help engine, WINHLP.EXE. New to Windows 95 and Access 95 is the Help Compiler Workshop, *HCW.EXE* (which may have problems running on Windows NT 3.51, sp3).

The help compiler files usually are distributed with software that developers purchase, such as the ADT, Visual Basic 4.0, or any of the language compilers (Microsoft Visual C++, Borland C++, Symantec C++). There also is a copy of the 32-bit Help compiler on the Developers' Network Level II (DevNet) CD.

Note

It appears that Help files compiled under previous versions of the Windows Help compiler do run without recompiling under the new Microsoft Help Workshop, although they cannot take advantage of the new features of WinHelp V4. The authors tested with a limited set of help files created in Microsoft Word 6 and compiled with the unsupported Help compiler, HLPWHAT6, which is provided on the Microsoft Level II Developers' Network (DevNet) CD/October 1995.

Previous versions of the WinHelp compiler were DOS programs—you had to shell out to a DOS box to compile the Help file. The 32-bit version of WinHelp (V4) is a Windows application, named the *Microsoft Help Workshop*. The following list describes the files that should comprise the Help Workshop:

- *Microsoft Help Compiler* V4.0 (HCW.EXE and HCRTF.EXE)
- *Microsoft Hotspot Editor* V2.0 (*SHED.EXE*)
- *Microsoft Multi-Resolution Bitmap Compiler* V1.1 (*MRBC.EXE*)
- The on-line help files for the Help Compiler (HCW.HLP) and the Hotspot Editor (*SHED.HLP*)
- The Help Workshop contents files (*HCW.CNT*)
- The Help Workshop data link library (*HWDLL.DLL*, in the Windows System folder)

■ The Help Workshop link library (Microsoft Help *Workshop.lnk*, in the ADT folder)

Note

If you are using Windows NT version 3.51, you must install the Service Pack to print on-line Help topics from the Help Workshop.

The two files, HCW.EXE and HCRTF.EXE, work together to compile your Help file. You always should call HCW.EXE, the Help Workshop. In turn the Help Workshop calls HCRTF.EXE, the Help compiler, when it is needed.

Fig. 15.19

The properties box for the Help Workshop, installed under Windows NT 3.51 sp3.

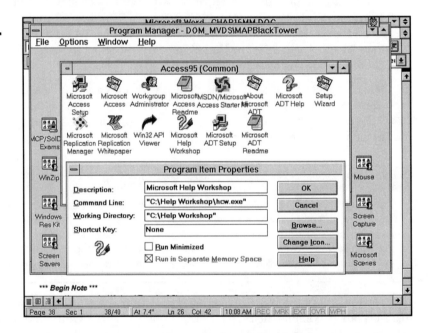

The Help Workshop not only can compile your Help file, it also can assist in building both the .HPJ and the .CNT files. By using the Project File Editor function of the Help Workshop, you get some assistance in constructing an .HPJ file and, by using the Contents File Editor, you can construct a Contents page (an Index to the Help file), with minimal pain.

Bring up the Help Workshop by double-clicking the program icon or by double-clicking the HCW.EXE file entry in File Manager (see fig. 15.20). Select File, New, and then decide whether you want to create the Help Project or the Help Contents File. You may want to start by creating the Help Project file (which acts like an outline of your Help system), build the individual topic files, the core of the Help system, and then add on the Help Contents. By doing things in this order, you can run test compiles of your Help system to check the appearance and navigational features (or both) as you are developing the text files.

Fig. 15.20

The Help Workshop main screen, with the Help Project and Help Contents file builder dialog box open.

The Help Project File Editor starts with a bare-bones set of entries for the .HPJ file (see fig. 15.21). You then add the remaining statements, based on the needs and extent of the Help file you are building. Refer to the Sections and Options previously discussed in this chapter for guidance and direction in choosing criteria for inclusion.

Fig. 15.21

The Help Project File editor, showing a starter file and requester buttons that allow you to add statements to the .HPJ file that you are building.

Note

When building the .HPJ file, don't try to edit the statements in the large window directly. Use the requester buttons to assist in adding, removing, and modifying the components of the file.

Fig. 15.22

The REA Project File under construction, showing the various options and a list of files to be compiled into the Help system.

After you finish adding all the components you think that you will need to the .HPJ file, it's time to test and run. Click the Save & Compile button in the lower right and hold your breath. Obviously, the smaller and more simple the Help file components, the better the chance for a clean compile the first time (see fig. 15.23).

Fig. 15.23

A more-or-less clean compile of the REA Help file.

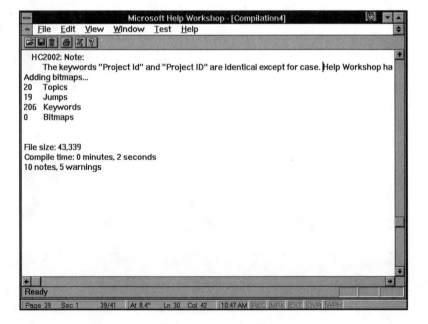

Something you may want to keep in mind while you run these compilations: each time the compile is run and a Help file is built, the Help compiler creates a temporary file of the same size in the topic file folder. Be forewarned, if your Help file is large, you may run out of space on the current hard disk or partition, and your compile will abort. You can designate a folder on another physical device or logical partition (see the TMPDIR option further back in this chapter) to store the compiler temporary file.

Now that you have a compiled Help file, you can test it by running it in debug mode. To do this, from the main Help Workshop screen click File, Help Author, and then click File, Run WinHelp. The requester that appears next asks: which Help file you want to run, where the .HPJ file for this Help file is located, and how you want the Help file to be initiated—as though it were called from an application, as though it were invoked by double-clicking a file icon, or as though it were a pop-up application (see fig. 15.24). If you just finished working with an .HPJ file in the Project File editor, this Help file will be presented in the WinHelp debug screen.

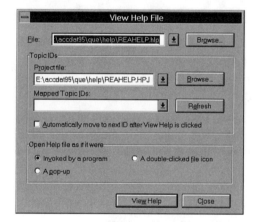

Fig. 15.24

The WinHelp debug screen, setting up to run the compiled Help file in the background.

Click the View Help button to see your Help file in action. By doing multiple iterations of your Help file and running both compiles and debug tests as it's built, you can design and develop a Help subsystem for your applications that looks every bit as professional as anything that ever came out of a shrink-wrapped box (see fig. 15.25).

Note

After debug mode is turned on, it will be on for all Help files you view. To turn off debug mode, deselect File, Help Author.

Fig. 15.25

The REA Help file, activated, using the Index search dialog box.

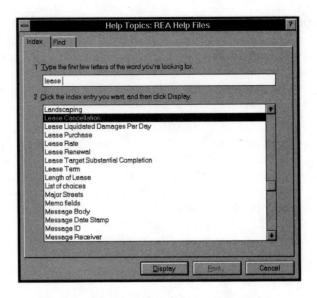

Building a Contents (.CNT) File

The *Contents file* is new to WinHelp V4. This file is the book-and-page Contents screen of the new Windows Help systems. A Contents (.CNT) file can contain the following data:

- *Headings*, also known as *books*, which contain a group of related topics. View the contents of a book by double-clicking the book icon. Books can contain other books.

- *Topics*, which include the text that appears in the Contents tab sheet, and all hotspot information for jumps.

- Commands that direct the layout and appearance of the Contents and Index.

- Name of the default WinHelp file.

- Title to display in the Help Topics dialog box.

- Names of secondary WinHelp files to include in the Index listing.

- Directions to leave out the Find tab—displaying the Find tab is the default, so you need to include this command only if you do not want the Find tab included in your Help file.

- Names and locations of other tabs to display.

The .CNT file is an ASCII file, and can be assembled in one of three ways: by using a text editor (Microsoft Word, Notepad, WordPad, WordPerfect) and saving as a DOS or text file; by using a third-party package that will help you create WinHelp applications; or by using the Microsoft Help Workshop and the Contents File editor.

To implement the last choice, from the Help Workshop screen choose File, New, and select Help Contents from the two choices presented. The new screen (see fig. 15.26) asks for the Help file name and a default Title to appear on the title bar of the Contents tab. If you press the Edit button just to the right of the top line, you can bring up a dialog box that offers a bit more assistance.

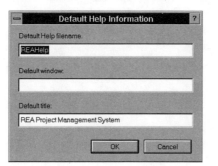

Fig. 15.26

The Contents file editor, building a new Contents (.CNT) file for REAHelp.

Add Headings—Books—by choosing the Add Above or Add Below button on the right side of the screen, and then select the Heading option and type the title name. The Books should be major divisions of your Help topics, and may correspond to the separate topic files that you built for your Help subsystem. The authors found it a bit easier to enter all the first-level books, then any second-level books, and finally on to the individual topics—pages. You'll see why in just a few paragraphs.

Fig. 15.27

Adding Headings—a Book title—to the Contents (.CNT) file in the Contents File editor.

After the books are added, you can begin adding the pages. Highlight a book entry, click the Add Below button, and answer the questions in the dialog box. The authors suggest you use a conversational, informational title, rather than a cryptic title that makes sense only to database designers and system administrators. The topic ID (the second text box shown in fig. 15.28) was formerly known as the context string (the authors have *no* idea why this terminology change was made in WinHelp V4), and is the phrase that you encoded in the footnote section of your topic files, preceded by the pound sign (#). The Help file name entry allows you to span multiple Help files, incorporating them into a single Contents list. Start with one file, compile and test it, and then add the second and the third Help file. Incorporate, compile, and test in increments, and you will have a much better chance of tracking down bugs.

Fig. 15.28

Adding a Topic—a page title—to the Contents (.CNT) file in the Contents File editor.

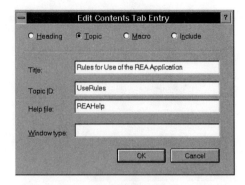

> **Note**
>
> The context string, the code embedded in the footnote section of the topic files that is preceded by a pound sign (#), is known as a *topic ID* in WinHelp V4. A search of the on-line Help for the Windows Help Workshop failed to turn up a single reference to context string. Apparently, not only has the terminology changed (for no obvious reason), but all backward references to the term "context string" have been erased.

After you enter the pages, save the file as **Helpfile.CNT** and recompile. Run in the debug window (File, Help Author, and then File, Run WinHelp), and check out your Contents page (see fig. 15.29)! Notice that when you double-click a page in the Contents list to move to the associated Help topic, four tabs now appear at the top—Contents, Index, Back, and Print. Previously, before you adding the Contents file in the compile, there were only three tabs.

Fig. 15.29

The compiled REA Help file with Contents page.

Design Tips for Your Help Files

In summary, here are few design tips compiled from various sources that you may want to consider before running off and building your award-winning WinHelp file.

- Headings (books) are containers for topics (pages). Only pages actually connect the user with the topic material.

- A page usually is a jump to the related topic material, but it also can be used to run a macro.

- A page can be used to define a jump to another Help file and to a specific window type.

- Users can print all pages in a book and also all nested books by clicking the book icon, then clicking the Print button. The authors know of no way to turn off this feature. Warn your user community about this before someone accidentally prints the entire contents of the Help file.

- Books that are nested beyond the third or fourth level may confuse or frustrate your user community, so keep the book index shallow.

Third-Party Help Tools

It appears, from research done by the authors, that no discussion of Help files is quite complete unless some space is given to the availability of third-party Help authoring tools. Although the Microsoft Help Workshop is quite nice, especially compared to its DOS-based predecessors, the authors understand that the third-party packages available are well worth investigating, especially if building Help subsystems constitutes a significant portion of your time.

The following companies have products that support WinHelp V4.0:

WinHelp Office (RoboHelp)
Blue Sky Software (California, USA)
Domestic: 1-800-677-4946 or 1-619-551-2485
Fax: 1-619-551-2486
International: 01-619-459-6365

Included on the accompanying CD-ROM is a demo disk, "Windows 95 Help—What's New?" which is compatible with Microsoft Windows, Windows NT, and Windows 95.

Help Breeze 2.0
SolutionSoft (California, USA)
Domestic: 1-408-736-1431
Fax: 1-408-736-4013

Included on the accompanying CD-ROM is a "non-working" demo of HelpBreeze 1.6, the WinHelp3-compatible version of HelpBreeze. At the time of publication HelpBreeze 2.0, which is compatible with either WinHelp3 or WinHelp4, was just starting to ship.

Visual Help Pro
WinWare, Inc. (California USA)
Domestic: 1-800-507-HELP or 1-714-586-4492
Fax: 1-714-586-9792

Included on the accompanying CD-ROM is an evaluation copy of Visual Help Pro.

Help Writer's Assistant (Professional)
Olson Software (New Zealand)
Domestic: 64-6-359-1408
Fax: 64-6-355-2775
The Internet: 100352.1315@compuserve.com

The following companies will (eventually) have products that support WinHelp V4.0:

WexTech Systems (**Doc-To-Help**)
1-202-949-9595

Software Interphase (**Windows Help Magician**)
1-401-397-2340

Building Context-Sensitive Help

When you add context-sensitive help to your applications, you give the user a chance to access the Help subsystem simply by placing the cursor on the screen object in question and pressing F1. WinHelp V4 adds to the time-honored F1 technique the other options of positioning the cursor over the object in question and choosing the What's_This option of the right mouse button, or dragging the top toolbar question mark (?) over the object.

Context-sensitive help requires that you tightly coordinate the application objects that are queried with the Help file. First, write topic text about each object, and then modify the application to call the correct topic. Modifying the application involves assigning numeric values (context numbers) to the objects in the application, then using the mapping function of the Help Workshop (or hand-coding the correlations between context strings—topic IDs—in the MAP section of the .HPJ file) to associate a context string with a numeric value. Remember, a 1:1 relationship exists between context strings and numeric values.

If you use the prefix IDH_ to context strings in your topic files that will be mapped to numeric values and, therefore, to context-sensitive help, the Help compiler can give you an assist in debugging the compile. Where it sees an IDH_ prefix, it assumes that this topic will be called directly from the application. It then can cross-check that all topics with prefix IDH_ also are mapped in the MAP section of your project (.HPJ) file. The compiler also can find IDH_ files that are listed in the MAP section but are not present in the topic files.

To map context strings to context-sensitive help, take the following steps:

1. Start the HCW compiler.
2. Open your project (.HPJ) file.
3. Click the Map button.
4. Click the Add button of the MAP dialog box.
5. Enter the context string (topic ID), the numeric value you have assigned to this context string and, for posterity's sake, a brief comment (see fig. 15.30).

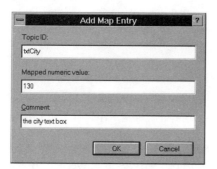

Fig. 15.30

Mapping numeric values to context strings (topic IDs).

Integrating Help into Your Applications

To integrate your WinHelp file into Access 95, you can type the name of the Help file in the File property box, Help File property, as shown in figure 15.31. Then you can enter the context number for the topic into the Context ID property of the form or control on a form, to link the control with the appropriate topic in the custom Help file.

Fig. 15.31

Linking the REA Project form with the custom Help to provide context-sensitive help.

IV

Completing the Process

Under the run-time of Access 2, you insert a line in the application .INI file, the context of which looks like the following:

```
helpfile=c:\REA\REAhelp.hlp
```

Apparently, this was changed with Access 95. The run-time option *helpfile* was renamed AppHelpFIle, and now is located in the Windows Registry. AppHelpFile is available only to applications that are running in the Access 95 run-time environment.

Also, if you are undecided about whether or not you should include a custom Help file with your application, understand that in a run-time environment, when a user presses the F1 key, Access 95 generates an error message that refers to the missing MSACCESS.HLP file.

From Here...

This chapter covered on-line help, what it is, and why you want to employ it. You started with documenting the database tables during the table creation process and moved to the functions contained within the form Design View—status bar text, control tip text, and the What's This? property. You moved on to WinHelp, and did some comparisons between WinHelp V3, which runs on Windows, Windows for Workgroups, and Windows NT below version 3.51, and the new WinHelp V4, which is meant for Windows 95 and Windows NT 3.51 and above. You looked at the new Windows Help Workshop, and went through the process of planning, creating, and encoding the Help text and using the Help Workshop to build the project (.HPJ) file and the Contents (.CNT) file. Finally, you went through how to map your topic files to an Access 95 application.

From here, you can jump to these chapters to find out more about the following:

- Chapter 8, "Adding Functionality to Your Prototype," discusses how to use templates and master forms in your application development.
- Chapter 13, "Building the Run-Time Application," gives you information about how to include a custom Help file in the run-time version of your application.
- Chapter 16, "Tuning the Access 95 Application," covers indexing and performance tuning.
- Chapter 22, "The Human Factor," discusses the human element in the client/server environment.
- Appendix B, "The WinHelp V4 Macros," for tips and hints on using macros in the Help files, and a complete listing of all WinHelp macros.

Tuning the Access 95 Application

Performance and tuning of an application, of an environment, is the portion of application development that is usually overlooked during design and programming. Usually, performance evaluation and tuning are left until after the application is installed and in use. The authors present some ideas in this chapter about how to plan for performance, how to target certain production goals, and how to twist and tweak after the application is in place. This chapter covers the following areas:

- Single-threading and multithreading, and the advantages in a multithreading environment
- Hardware upgrades and what it can do for you
- Doing some application evaluation using Access 95 wizards
- How to optimize the Access 95 environment
- How to optimize your application

Where to Look for Problems

The more complex the installation the more potential for problems. Any place where data traffic can get congested is a possible *bottleneck*. Figure 16.1, which uses the *ANSI/SPARC* three-layer model of data independence as its foundation, attempts to pinpoint some of the potential trouble spots.

Obviously, we cannot cover all the points in this graphic, but we will cover many, from the Access 95 perspective.

Fig. 16.1

Where performance problems can occur.

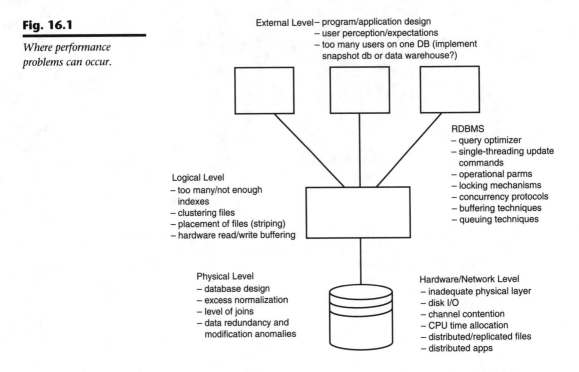

External Level– program/application design
– user perception/expectations
– too many users on one DB (implement snapshot db or data warehouse?)

RDBMS
– query optimizer
– single-threading update commands
– operational parms
– locking mechanisms
– concurrency protocols
– buffering techniques
– queuing techniques

Logical Level
– too many/not enough indexes
– clustering files
– placement of files (striping)
– hardware read/write buffering

Physical Level
– database design
– excess normalization
– level of joins
– data redundancy and modification anomalies

Hardware/Network Level
– inadequate physical layer
– disk I/O
– channel contention
– CPU time allocation
– distributed/replicated files
– distributed apps

Single-Threading versus Multithreading

A *thread* is an executable unit within a process. A thread, to a user, is a task getting done. The computer operating system, which shields the computer user from the intricacies of the hardware, divides the work to be done into *processes*. To each process it allocates memory, system resources, and at least one *thread of execution*.

A *multitasking environment*, such as Windows NT, assigns a process to each application or task currently running, and then runs each thread for a very short time before it switches to the next thread in line, and then the next, and so on. To the user, this *thread switching* (also known as *task switching*) is invisible, and it seems as though many things are happening on the computer all at the same time. In reality, the application threads are running concurrently, each thread occupying a narrow slice of time.

Most DOS-based or Windows-based applications (word processors, spreadsheets, and so on) are traditionally *single-threaded*—for your spreadsheet program, the computer processor executes only a single task before it's off to service a thread that belongs to the printer queue or to the file manager.

If an application is written so that the application process can spawn multiple threads, the computer processor will service these multiple threads, thereby giving the application a larger share of the processor's time. The result is better application performance.

The latest Jet database engine, version 3, contains the following improvements over previous versions:

- The Jet engine is multithreaded. By default, one thread performs read-ahead operations, a second thread performs write-behind operations, and a third performs cache maintenance. Now the Jet can have more than one operation pending within a given time frame or, with a multi-processor system, can do more than one thing at a time.

- A new index structure reduces the amount of index space required to store the indexes, and reduces the amount of time required to create complex indexes. To optimize the indexes for maximum performance, compact the database on a regular basis.

- Indexed pages no longer contain read locks, which has the effect of removing lock-handling overhead on read-only operations, which significantly enhances performance in a multiuser environment.

- DELETE operations now run faster. Improvements were made on the mechanism that removes data from table pages. Where it previously deleted data row-by-row, it now can remove an entire chunk of a page in a single operation.

- The Jet's read-ahead capability for sequential processing was enhanced. The page-allocation mechanism now has a higher likelihood of placing data from the same table on adjacent pages of the hard disk.

- Implicit transaction processing now is built into the Jet 3 engine. This processing allows you to take advantage of the improved transaction speed provided by optimistic locking, without being forced to use the BeginTrans and CommitTrans methods in your code. To retain full control over writing data to disk, to ensure that every update is written to disk, or to bundle multiple updates into a single transaction, you still should write explicit transactions, bounding either end with the BeginTrans and CommitTrans statements, respectively.

- Sorting is improved by the addition of a new sorting mechanism to the Jet 3. Indexing fields that are always requested in sorted order, however, still is a very good idea.

- The Jet 3 now has a dynamically configured database cache that is allocated at start-up. The size of the database cache is based on the amount of system memory available. (The database cache contains the most-recently used pages of data, and records to be updated, waiting to be written to disk.)

> **Caution**
>
> Access 95 and Windows NT 3.51 have a minor conflict situation with the two memory models. In the authors' experience, when running 16-bit applications such as Microsoft Word and Excel concurrent with the 32-bit Access 95, if Access 95 is brought up before
>
> (continues)

(continued)

the 16-bit apps, it is possible—after the applications have been running for an hour and you have used Alt-Tab to toggle between applications—to lock up the NT operating system, with total loss of cursor control, forcing the shutdown and restart of NT Server. The authors suspect this problem may be due in part to this new feature of the Jet 3, the dynamically configurable database cache. The error condition looks like Access 95 has overlain memory that was being used by Word, or Access 95 failed to register memory use and Word tromps over it. (Tech support says this doesn't happen, but trust us, it can and does!)

To alleviate this problem, bring up all the 16- or 32-bit applications that you will use, and then bring up Access 95. The authors suspect that, by populating memory ahead of time, Access 95 is constrained to a "safe" level of cache. The trash-NT Server problem happens much less frequently when using this start-up technique.

If you use a start-up group on your NT Server, and if Access 95 is in the startup, make sure that the Access 95 icon is the last to be added to the group.

The authors have noticed no corresponding problem when running Access 95 under Windows 95.

- The Jet 3 provides new-and-improved ISAM support for Excel 5.0 and 7.0, for text files, for Lotus 1-2-3 Release 3.0 spreadsheets, for Paradox 5.x, dBASE 6.x, and FoxPro 3.x files.

Hardware Upgrades or Software Speed Gains?

In the search for better database performance, you may have to make some decisions about whether to invest in new or additional hardware or to put more money into development of the software to provide speed gains. There are three areas of hardware you want to look at investing in: the server, the client, and the network.

We discussed the requirements for the server in Chapter 1, "Client/Server, What Is It?" It should be a state-of-the-art system, at least as far as the relevant components are concerned. The disk subsystem, for example, needs to be top-of-the-line for acceptable performance in a busy shop.

You have greater flexibility in choosing components for the client computers, and hardware depends on intended use. Usually, if your hardware is reasonably new—less than eighteen months at the outside—it probably is adequate. Only for special use clients (multimedia systems development, database development, and desktop publishing) do you want to consider hardware upgrades. Again, consider the specifications listed in Chapter 1.

The *network* is the core component in a client/server environment, and is often overlooked and underfunded, which can result in a real *bottleneck* in your production performance, especially if you are used to a file-server environment and now are moving to client-server applications. Depending on the number of client users, the number of servers, the number of client/server applications, and the type of network protocol involved, your requirements will vary, but the authors' rule for networks: bandwidth, bandwidth, and more bandwidth.

> **Tip**
>
> The authors suggest a pair of excellent networking resource guides. The first is Vol. 2 of the Windows NT 3.51 Resource Kit, *The Windows NT Networking Guide*. The second is *Networking Windows NT 3.51*, Second Edition, by John D. Ruley, *et al.*, John Wiley & Sons Publishers, 1995.

More Memory or Faster CPU

As we stated, you cannot run Access 2.0 in less than 8M of RAM, and Access 95 requires 16M for adequate performance. Because of the way most motherboards are configured, it usually is easier to install 16M than it is to install 12M of RAM. In terms of return on investment, an extra 8M of RAM costs around $240 (at the time of writing). This investment is rapidly repaid in enhanced performance and (assumedly) productivity. Beyond 16M, it's doubtful whether the client computers will benefit greatly by increasing memory, except for the previously listed special-need clients.

If your computers are Intel 80486-based, and will support it, consider upgrading to a faster CPU. A 100 or 120 MHz 80486 now is priced below $100. If the motherboard has a ZIF socket, the upgrade is simple. If the motherboard lacks this socket, the computer is probably too old to upgrade.

The performance benefits of the Pentium Overdrive CPUs (Pentium chips with a 32-bit data path that fit an 80486 socket) are not much greater than those seen with a fast 486 chip. The Overdrive upgrade path probably is not as cost-effective as the faster 486. It's not as easy to demonstrate the benefits of a CPU upgrade, compared to the benefits of adding memory. This difficulty of comparison may be because of the other hardware component factors—such as the bus type and the speed of the hard disk—that were matched to the original CPU. By upgrading only the CPU, you may be initiating a mismatch, thereby negating some of the enhanced-performance benefits of the faster CPU.

Adding a second CPU is an option currently reserved for the server. If your back-end server is running Microsoft SQL Server or another database management system capable of multithreading, adding a second CPU to the server computer brings significant gains in performance throughout the network.

Memory Sweet Spot

The *memory sweet spot* is a point beyond which adding memory does not bring much, if any, benefit. For applications that use Access 95 and are running on Windows 95, this range is 12-16M. For Windows NT, the sweet spot probably is closer to 24-32M.

You can test this sweet spot in the Windows NT environment by taking the following steps:

1. Edit the startup settings in the BOOT.INI file to include the /MAXMEM=*mm* parameter, which varies the amount of memory actually used. Start with 32M.

2. Cycle NT, bring up one or more of your most memory-intensive applications and run them, using Performance Monitor to evaluate and observe.

3. Adjust the value of the /MAXMEM parameter, reduce it by 20 percent, cycle NT, and repeat the stress test.

4. Repeat the /MAXMEM parameter adjustment and stress test, adjusting the amount of useable memory until your performance takes a hit. At this point, you know the needed minimum memory requirement for the applications that you are running on Windows NT.

Disk Caching: Solution or Problem?

There are *disk controllers* available that have random-access memory dedicated to caching. These controllers show very fast numbers on benchmark tests. Best use for these *caching controllers* may be on the server because the controllers obviously cost more than a standard disk controller and do not usually come with a normal desktop computer configuration. But the catch with this rationale is that, unless you need a fast response on a read-only database, the server is not really a good place to put a caching controller.

The problem with *hardware caching* is that, after the database management system or the operating system writes a block out to the disk hardware cache, it thinks that the record was written to the physical disk (in the case of the database management system, to the physical database). If the system crashes before the data in cache is written to the hard disk, the data is lost, but the database/operating system has no way of knowing that this condition exists. Data integrity can be severely compromised by the lack of synchronization between the database management system/operating system and the caching controller. With a read-only database, where fast data retrieval is the prime consideration and lost updates cannot happen, a caching controller may help. The authors advise that you investigate vendor claims carefully before investing in caching controllers for your database environment.

Modern operating systems such as Windows NT by default assign available system memory to cache disk I/O. This software cache approach offers the following benefits over (hardware) cache memory on the controller:

- The amount of memory allocated to cache is dynamically adjusted for optimum overall system performance.

- Adding memory means buying more system memory (general use), not memory specific to a caching controller.

- The amount of software cache available can exceed what may be supplied on the caching controller.

- Windows NT uses a transaction model to provide a recoverable file system (NTFS only), which can correct problems caused by power outages or component failure.

The authors' suggestion: if you have $400 to invest in your server computer, add 16M of system memory to the motherboard rather than a caching disk controller with 4 or 8M of RAM that cannot be exploited by other system processes.

Optimizing the Access System Environment

Access 95 runs under either the Windows 95 or the Windows NT operating systems, so some of the points that we discuss in this section may be more relevant to one operating system or the other.

If you are running a full development copy of Access 95 but you aren't making use of many of the wizards or add-in tools, use the *Add-In Manager* to uninstall the tools that you use the least. This action reduces the memory requirements of Access 95 and decreases the time it takes to load. To use the Add-In Manager, select Tools from the top menu, choose Add-Ins, and then the Add-In Manager. Within the Add-In Manager dialog box, select from the list of Available Add-Ins the tools that you want to remove, and then click Uninstall. These changes take effect the next time you cycle Access 95.

Occasionally check the Windows Taskbar or the Task Manager and close the applications that you are not using.

Increase the amount of RAM on your computer(s). According to Microsoft Corporation, Access 95 requires 12M of RAM to run but in the experience of the authors, even the Access 95 run-time can barely function in 12M. To develop and create distribution sets, you almost certainly will need 32M of RAM.

If you have a *RAM disk* on your computer, get rid of it!

Periodically perform *housecleaning* tasks. Get rid of files you no longer need. Compact your databases (you need to do this anyway to ensure your database statistics are updated and the pages of data that comprise the tables are positioned for fastest retrieval, so that the query optimizer works well). Defragment your hard disk. If you're on a Windows 95 machine, use the Disk Defragmenter (click the Windows Start button, select Programs, Accessories, System Tools, Disk Defragmenter) or use a third-party disk defragmenter program, such as the Norton Utilities for Windows 95. If you're using a Windows NT machine, the NTFS file system, by its very nature, tends to fragment the hard disk much less than other file management schemes.

Tip

For a full discussion on the Windows NT NTFS file system, see *Inside the Windows NT File System*, by Helen Custer, Microsoft Press, 1994.

You may have to adjust the *virtual memory settings* under Windows 95. Normally, the default value works fine. In one case, however, relocating the virtual memory file may enhance performance, which is when either of the following situations is true:

- If the disk space on the drive currently hosting the virtual memory file is severely limited
- If the speed of the drive currently hosting the virtual memory file is slow

In either case, performance is enhanced by relocating the virtual memory file to a faster, more spacious *local* disk drive. To relocate the virtual memory file in Windows 95 (or to change the amount of space allocated for the file), go to the Windows Control Panel, double-click the System icon, select the Performance tab, select Virtual Memory, select Let Me Specify My Own Virtual Memory Settings, then specify another hard disk or enter a new value in the Minimum text box.

If you're using a *single-user database* (if you have a personal-use database that you and no one else is using), install Access 95 and the database on your computer. Don't use a network server.

If your Windows *wallpaper* is a full-screen background bitmapped image, replace it with a solid color or a pattern bit map, or no wallpaper at all.

Evaluating Your Access 95 Application

Besides all the things we have mentioned so far, you can follow a checklist, of sorts, to assist in optimizing your Access 95 application. The checklist looks like the following:

- Use the Performance Analyzer and the Table Analyzer Wizards.
- Check the Access system specifications.
- Check for optimized table performance.
- Make sure your linked tables are the best that they can be (see the following section, "Linked Table Performance").
- Check for optimized external SQL database performance.
- Optimize your multiuser environment.
- Improve query performance.
- Improve filter performance.
- Improve find-and-replace performance.
- Improve form and subform performance.

- Improve list-box and combo-box performance.
- Improve report and subreport performance.
- Improve Visual Basic for Applications code performance.

The Performance Analyzer

The Access 95 *Performance Analyzer* is a wizard that checks through your database relationships and object design (forms, reports, code) and, based on the criteria listed in the preceding section, will provide recommendations, suggestions, and ideas, or a combination of the three.

A *recommendation* from the Performance Analyzer is something that you want to seriously consider following because a critical flaw was detected somewhere in the design. A *suggestion* you may also want to consider, but the criticality is much less than that of a recommendation, and the suggestion may be counter to your business requirements. An *idea* is just that, and may or may not be worth considering—it's your decision. *Notes* regarding each level of diagnosis for each object are displayed in the Analysis Notes section of the dialog box.

To get to the Performance Analyzer wizard, select Tools from the menu, choose Analyze, and then select Performance. The Performance Analyzer dialog boxes start appearing, and the first one presented allows you to choose which database object(s) you want analyzed (see fig. 16.2). If you choose the data.MDB for analysis, the Performance Analyzer has only the tables, any forms built for system or database administration purposes, and the relationships to evaluate.

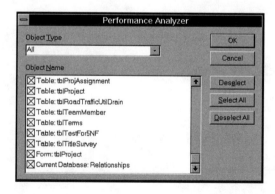

Fig. 16.2

The Performance Analyzer choice screen, where you can select the database objects to be analyzed.

Figure 16.3 shows a typical response from the Performance Analyzer. Even after the authors intentionally deleted relationships, both 1:1 and 1:M, the Performance Analyzer declined to do more than just present an idea. An idea must be handled manually; the Performance Analyzer automatically optimizes only recommendations and suggestions.

Fig. 16.3

The Performance Analyzer results, in this case showing only several ideas that might enhance application performance.

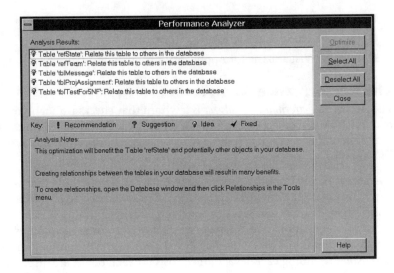

The Performance Analyzer works on more than data.MDBs. Figure 16.4 shows the results of an analysis performed on all objects of the client.MDB, REA application. In this list of results, the Performance Analyzer had a suggestion, which was to relate the table tblProject with table tblCustCredit—even though both tables are linked, and both reside in the REA_Data.MDB file. Additionally, the Performance Analyzer had some ideas regarding the modules in the client application ("Use an Option Explicit statement"), which—from a good programming standpoint—should be qualified as suggestions.

Fig. 16.4

The Performance Analyzer's suggestion regarding two tables in the REA database. It also expressed many ideas, all relating to the underlying code behind the forms and reports.

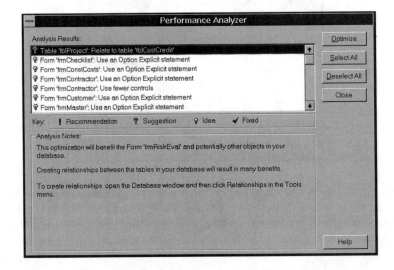

To use the auto-optimize feature of the Performance Analyzer, select the recommendation or suggestion from the list and click the Optimize button. Seemingly, there is no discussion from this point forward; the recommended or suggested action is simply taken and the bullet to the left of the highlighted result in the list (exclamation point (!) for a recommendation and question mark (?) for a suggestion changes to a check mark (✓), indicating that the "problem" is "fixed."

The authors decided to let the Performance Analyzer auto-optimize the suggestion to relate table tblProject with table tblCustCredit, and the result was interesting. As shown in figure 16.5, the extra relationship between tblProject and tblCustCredit (lower right) is redundant. TblProject, the project table, is already related to refCustomer, the customer table, in an M:1 relationship, and refCustomer is in turn related to tblCustCredit, the customer credit report, in a 1:1 relationship. The Performance Analyzer simply "completed the triangle," adding a redundant and unnecessary relationship to the REA database schema in a linked .MDB file. Additionally, the Performance Analyzer failed to enforce referential integrity, which guarantees that a CustID—the customer identifier—used in the Project table did indeed have a counterpart already listed in the Customer Credit table. Enforcing referential integrity in a 1:M relationship is a basic rule of database design in any environment. The final failing is the join type assignment, to Join Type 1, or the equijoin, which means that any query (or form or report based on such a query) that seeks to extract data from the Project table and the Customer Credit table gets only the projects for which a customer credit report is on file.

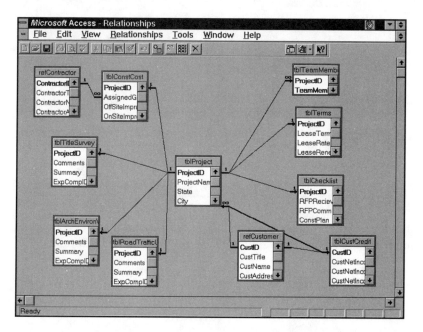

Fig. 16.5

The results of the auto-optimization of tblProject and tblCustCredit: a triangular and highly restrictive relationship.

The authors had to shut down the client.MDB, open the data.MDB, and back out of the relationship change that was made to the data.MDB. The authors suggest that you use the Performance Analyzer carefully, and consider the implications of any auto-optimizing changes recommended or suggested by the Performance Analyzer.

The Table Analyzer Wizard

The Access 95 *Table Analyzer* is a wizard that scours the tables of a database, searching for data redundancy. Data redundancy is defined as a *non-key* data item that is stored more than one time in a database. For example, customer street address, in almost every circumstance, is not a key field, neither primary key nor foreign key. If, in your production database, a customer's street address was stored more than once, this doubling is an instance of *data redundancy*.

Another way to look at the presence of data redundancy is that if you have to update a customer's street address, you have to change the street address in more than one place. When you modify the database, and the modification involves a *non-key* attribute (like the street address), you should have to modify only a single row in the entire database.

The Table Analyzer is stored under the Tools menu, Analyze option, Table selection. The opening dialog box of the Table Analyzer looks like figure 16.6.

Fig. 16.6

The introductory dialog to the Table Analyzer Wizard.

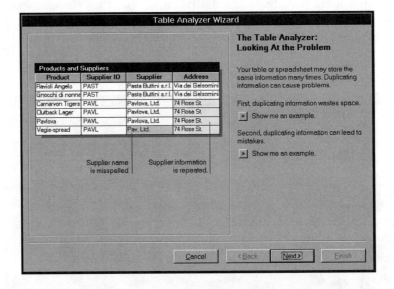

The Table Analyzer searches through a populated table, looking for instances of data redundancy, and then suggests a way to split the table to eliminate the redundancy (see fig. 16.7).

Select the table to analyze, and then choose to let the Wizard do the analysis. You see a solution, which you then can modify by dragging fields from one table to another, before saving the output of the Table Wizard's work (see fig. 16.8).

The new, split tables do not replace the original, they are created in addition to the original table. With this in mind, you have to make sure that you have room on your hard disk to hold the new tables you are creating.

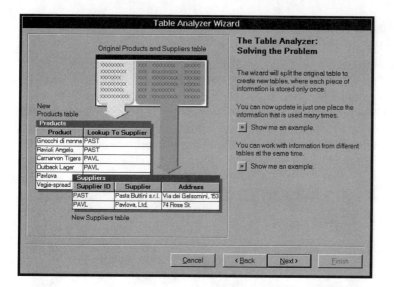

Fig. 16.7

The Table Analyzer, explaining how it will split tables.

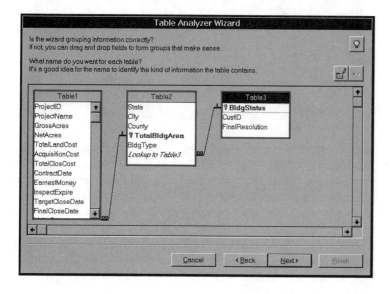

Fig. 16.8

The Table Analyzer's solution to the Project table and the perceived redundancy within.

The Table Analyzer works best on well-populated tables, so your best chance of a valid solution is to use a set of test data that is highly representative of your production data. You also want on the order of 100 rows of data per table to be analyzed, if possible.

If you choose a table that has fewer than two rows of data, the Table Analyzer gives a message that says not enough data is present to make a valid assumption. You have to do the table analysis manually. I suggest that you skip this step. If you are designing databases, you should be able to bring tables minimally into Third Normal Form without resorting to the use of the Table Analyzer. The Table Analyzer is particularly helpful in identifying violations of Fourth and Fifth Normal Form, and eliminating the multi-valued dependencies that are characteristic of each.

Figure 16.9 shows a common situation, and some of the problems that can quickly arise as a result of improper normalization. TblProjAssignment, the Project Assignment table, is shown in both design and datasheet mode. Actually, Project Assignment is an associative table that links employees, project team leaders, and projects. Its primary key is the concatenation of all three columns that comprise the relation. As illustrated, there is an obvious level of redundancy, but less obvious (and more important) are the multi-valued dependencies present within the table.

Fig. 16.9

The Project Assignment table, in design and datasheet mode, showing multi-valued dependencies that are a violation of Fifth Normal Form (5NF).

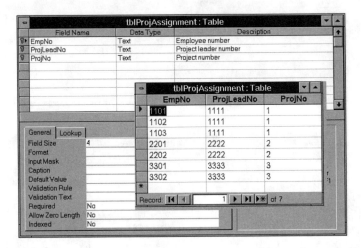

Employees are related to both Projects and Project Team Leaders; each association is a M:N relationship. An employee can be assigned to multiple projects, and a project can have one or more employees assigned to work on it. Continuing, each employee is associated with one or more project team leaders, and a project team leader is associated with one or more employees. Depending on variation in the business rules, each Project must have one and may have more than one Project Team Leader (coleaders), and a Project Team Leader may head more than one project. This is a very confusing and intricate set of relationships between the attributes of a single row in the table, and representing them as an associative table isn't the best solution.

The better approach is to decompose this small table into a pair of relations, but you want to do it carefully. Improper splitting of the tables leads to a situation known as *loss decomposition*, which means that, when you join the two split tables to extract information, you get rows in the joined table that never existed in the original! This result is the violation of 5NF because, when a relation is in 5NF, you can join it to its logical counterparts and not create extraneous and incorrect rows of data in the joined tables.

Interestingly, the Table Analyzer wouldn't touch this table. Realizing the complexity of the situation and triggering the fact that all columns were part of the primary key, it advised not to split the table.

You won the grand prize if you figured out how to decompose this table so that you avoid loss decomposition: EmpNo and ProjNo in the first relation (primary key is the concatenation of both attributes), and ProjNo and ProjLeadNo in the second relation (primary key is the concatenation of both attributes if a project can have coleaders, otherwise only ProjNo).

A similar example, but with slightly fewer constraints on the relation, is shown in figure 16.10, tblTestFor5NF, the StudentAdvisor table. In this relation you see three columns, StuNo (student number), Major (major area of study), and Advisor (student advisor for a major area of study). A student can have multiple major areas of study, and a major area of study has many students enrolled, so the relationship student to major is M:N. A major area of study has one or more advisors and, depending on the business case, an advisor may advise in one major area of study or may advise in many major areas of study. The resulting relationship, major to advisor, may be 1:M or it may be M:N. The authors' heuristic, a design for the worst case, suggests this relationship would be M:N. Finally, between student and advisor, an M:N relationship exists in that a student may have more than one advisor (as a result of the dual or treble major), and an advisor can advise more than one student.

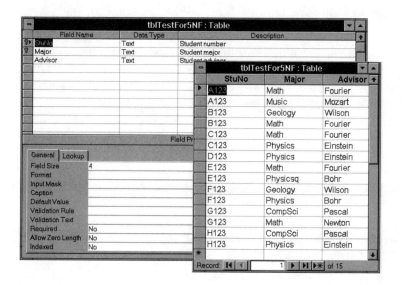

Fig. 16.10

The Student Advisor table, in design and datasheet mode, showing multi-valued dependencies that are a violation of Fifth Normal Form (5NF).

The Table Analyzer took an interesting approach to this example. As illustrated in figure 16.11, it split the Student Advisor table into two, a Student table composed of an AutoNumber primary key and the student number, and an Advisor table that contains the advisor (primary key) and the major. Using this approach, your business case is constrained to an advisor who is advising for one and only one major area of study. And, a student is allowed one and only one advisor.

Fig. 16.11

The Table Analyzer splits the Student Advisor table into a model that is inconsistent with the business rules.

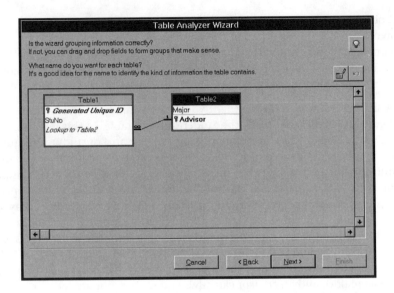

Two points the authors want to make in wrapping up this discussion are the following:

- The deeper the normal form, the more tiny tables (low ordinality) you will have in your database and the more often you will be joining to extract information. This situation actually adds additional burden to the query engine and may have a substantially adverse effect on performance and response time.

- Don't depend on the Table Analyzer to do the job. It does a fair analysis and presents a viable solution, but the solution may not fit the policies and procedures in place in your business model.

Tip

For an excellent and thorough discussion on entity-relationship modeling and data normalization, the authors suggest looking into *Modern Database Management* by Fred McFadden and Jeffrey Hoffer, Benjamin/Cummings Publishers, 1993.

Optimizing Table Performance

Any relational database management system will perform best if the tables within the database are fully normalized—if they were designed to eliminate redundant non-key data. A well-designed database—one that is correctly normalized—is a must for fast data retrieval and quick row updates. Use the Table Analyzer (described in the preceding section) to assist in detecting data redundancy and improper normalization.

Choose appropriate *data types* for the fields in a table. When defining a field, use the smallest data type and length that gets the job done. You can save space in storage and improve join performance by using correct data types. The following list shows the tips for data type selection:

- If you will be storing both text and numbers in a field, choose a text data type. You cannot store text in a number data type.

- Use the number data types for fields on which you will be performing computations. Otherwise, store non-computational numbers (Social Security numbers, phone numbers, ZIP codes, and so on) as text data types.

- If you need the capability of sorting, grouping, or indexing text data, don't declare the data as a memo or OLE data type. Neither memo nor OLE fields can be indexed, grouped, or sorted.

- Sorting sequences differ between text and number data types. Text data types sort numbers as character strings (1, 10, 100, 2, 20, 200) not as ascending or descending values.

- Many date and time formats do not sort properly if defined as text data types. Make sure that dates and time are defined with the Date/Time data type.

Refer to Chapter 6, "Establishing the Ground Rules," for a full discussion on data types.

Create *indexes* on the fields you sort by, join on, or set criteria in the **WHERE** clause of a SQL statement. Dramatic performance improvements have been made when the join columns from both tables being joined are indexed. Review the queries that underlie reports and forms, and index the fields used to join two tables. By default, primary key fields are indexed when the primary key designation is made, so you don't have to do these a second time. Also, index fields that are used to sort the output or that are used to specify criteria for the output. Searching for a record through the Find dialog box is much faster when using an indexed field. Indexing is a complicated topic with both up sides and down sides, some of which are the following:

- Each index created is another table that must be stored on the hard disk, inside the .MDB file, so your disk space requirements are greater than originally calculated.

- Each time a row of a data table is updated, added to, or diminished by deletion of a record, the related indices also must be modified. This synchronization is handled by the Access 95 database engine to ensure data integrity. However, one row of a table with 15 fields that were indexed will cause 16 change operations to the database if that row is deleted.

- The benefits of indexing on data retrieval usually outweigh the costs involved in data modification, unless little disk space is available for index storage or there is a very high level of transaction processing (addition, deletion, and modification of rows of data).

- If you're building a multi-field index, adhere to the principle of minimality—use as few fields as possible to create a viable index.

- If you have an operational database whose main function is data capture and transaction processing, index frugally. If you have a decision support database whose main function is data retrieval, or a data warehouse, index like there's no tomorrow! The two database functions, operations and decision support, are diametrically opposed. You can tune for one or tune for the other, but you can't tune for both and get a satisfactory result. Don't expect one database to be all things to all people.

Linked Table Performance

Linked tables, whether Access format or those of SQL Server, are external tables. These external tables are located in another file, occasionally on your local computer, but more often across the network on a server computer. Transferring data from these external tables can take time, so you should do some of the following things that enhance performance:

- View only the data that you need. Use filters or queries to return only the data required. In this way you limit the amount of data that is transferred across the network.

- For adding data to a linked table, create data entry forms that open in Data Entry or Add Record mode. In this way, Access doesn't have to return any data to the client computer from the linked tables, as it does if the form is opened in either Edit or ReadOnly mode.

- Avoid using functions in the criteria field of a query that involves linked tables. Especially important to avoid are the domain aggregate functions, such as Dsum. Domain aggregate functions force Access to retrieve all the data in a linked table before it can execute the query.

- Implement use rules for linked tables—don't unnecessarily page up and down through the datasheet and don't jump from beginning to end of the dataset. Linked tables return rows to the client application in sequential order, page by page, and best performance is achieved by scrolling through the rows as presented.

- Assume that others on the network are also trying to access data from these linked tables that you are viewing and/or modifying. Avoid locking records for any longer than you absolutely must. We discuss locking in the multiuser section a few pages from here.

External SQL Database Performance

If your client application connects to a back-end SQL database and you can link to the SQL tables, do so. Linked tables are considerably faster, more powerful, and more efficient to work with than tables that are opened directly.

If your client application uses the Access user interface, you probably are linking to the SQL tables. Directly opening tables on a server database can be achieved only by coding the appropriate commands in Visual Basic for Applications. If your client application has some Visual Basic code that does direct table open, then here are some things you can check for:

■ Retrieve and select only the data needed. Refer to the previous discussion on linked tables for specific situations.

■ Don't retrieve updateable result sets if you are not updating the data. Set the RecordSetType property of the form to Snapshot to bring back read-only data.

■ Cache the data on the client, especially if it will be used more than once during the course of the processing. It's far faster to retrieve a single large set of rows (multiple pages) and cache them locally than to retrieve many individual rows. By default, Access 95 forms and datasheets cache data, so you need to use this technique only if you are retrieving a dynaset created in Visual Basic. Use the CacheStart and CacheSize properties to specify the range of data within the RecordSet and use the FillCache property to quickly fill all or part of this range during program operation.

■ Don't use queries that force the client computer to process the data. When accessing data stored on an external SQL database server, use the dialect of SQL that is recognized by the server. The Access Jet processes external data only when a query is issued that is not a legal query to the external server. (Not all dialects of SQL are created equal!) Queries that contain the following conditions will cause local processing of data:

> WHERE clause restrictions on top of a query with a DISTINCT in the SELECT statement.

> WHERE clauses containing proprietary operations, such as user-defined functions that involve linked columns. Only the parts of the WHERE clause that cannot be processed remotely are processed locally.

> Joins between tables from different data sources.

> Joins over aggregates or with DISTINCT in the SELECT statement.

> Outer Joins containing syntax not supported by the server database engine.

> ORDER BY arguments, if not supported by the remote server.

> Multi-level GROUP BY arguments, such as arguments used in reports with multiple grouping levels.

> GROUP BY arguments on top of a query with a DISTINCT option.

> GROUP BY arguments containing operations that cannot be processed remotely.

> Crosstab queries that have more than one aggregate or that have an ORDER BY clause that matches the GROUP BY clause.

> TOP or TOP PERCENT in the SELECT statement.

Multiuser Performance

Most databases are meant to be used by many people, at the same time. Access supports this paradigm right out of the box, without having to rewrite any of the application code. However, you can do some things to enhance multiuser performance.

Separate the data (tables) from the other database objects and store only the data.MDB on the server. Store the client.MDB on each client computer. This separation achieves the following two purposes:

- Local management of the user interface (the client.MDB) is quick and under the control of the local computer.

- The amount of network traffic greatly diminishes when only the data must be transported between server and client computers.

Choose an appropriate record-locking strategy (see the following section).

Avoid locking conflicts by adjusting these following operational parameters found on the Tools, Options, Advanced tab screen:

- **Refresh Interval**, measured in seconds, is how long Access takes to automatically ripple through changes in records to other users on the system. These changes are seen when viewing records in datasheet or form view, or when running reports. The default setting is 60 seconds, although valid values range from 1 second to 32,766 seconds.

- **ODBC Refresh Interval**, measured in seconds, is the length of time between automatic record refreshes when you're accessing data by using ODBC. The default setting is 1,500 seconds (25 minutes), although valid values range from 1 to 32,766 seconds.

- **Number of Update Retries** is the number of times Access tries to save a changed record that is locked by another user. The default setting is 2, although valid values range from 0 through 10.

- **Update Retry Interval**, measured in milliseconds (1/1000 of a second), is the wait time between attempts to save a modified record that is locked by another user. The default setting is 250 milliseconds, although valid values range from 0 to 1,000 (1 second).

Convert the workgroup information file to Access 7 (covered in a following section).

Optimize table performance, both local and linked (covered previously), and optimize remote SQL table performance (covered previously).

Record-Locking Strategies in a Multiuser Environment

In Chapter 11, "Managing Transactions," we discussed locking protocols, how they work, and when to use certain kinds of locking procedures. Briefly, the following paragraphs describe the various types of locking strategies from which you can choose.

No Locks, or optimistic locking, doesn't lock the record being edited. Only when the change is saved (Update method) is an attempt made to lock the record. If the attempt is successful, the changes are saved to the database. If the attempt to lock the record is interrupted by another user—who also is trying to save changes to the same record—a conflict situation is created. Access gives some options, shown in the following list, on how to handle the conflict:

- Overwrite the other user's changes
- Copy your changes to the Windows Clipboard
- Discard your changes

Edited Records, or pessimistic locking, locks the record being edited and avoids the conflict situation that can happen under optimistic locking strategy. Actually, Access locks at the page level, so not only is the record that is being edited locked, every other record on the page (or block) of the database also is locked. If another user or application tries to edit one of these locked records, this user sees a special "locked record" symbol on-screen. This strategy ensures that edits on a record, once started, will finish.

The All Records lock will lock all records involved in the table(s) or query underlying the form or datasheet being edited for the entire time the form or datasheet is opened. Although this method of locking provides excellent performance for the application that holds the locks, everyone else in the multiuser environment will suffer. While the lock is held, no other application can edit or lock the same set (or subset of) records.

When Access 95 is accessing a non-Access server database, the server database handles all the locking—Access 95 usually doesn't perform any locking on ODBC databases. Therefore, you always should set the RecordLocks property of a form to No Locks or Edited Record—No Locks allows the server database the freedom needed to apply row or page locking (the technique most often used), and Edited Record is treated by the server as a No Lock situation.

Converting the System.MDA

Access 95 can use the *System.MDA* from previous versions of the product; however, it takes more memory resources to do so. To take full advantage of the enhanced security model of Access 95, and to save on memory use, convert your System.MDA (also referred to as the *workgroup information file*) to System.MDW. Refer to Chapter 12, "Securing the Access 95 Application," for an in-depth discussion of this situation.

> **Note**
>
> If you have any member of a secured workgroup who will not be upgrading to Access 95, don't upgrade the System.MDA from the previous version. The Access 95 members of this workgroup have two options—use the Workgroup Administrator to enroll in the previous version of the System.MDA or create a new user account and workgroup on the Access 95 version of the System.MDW.

To convert the System.MDA (previous version) to a *System.MDW* (Access 95), after making sure no one in your environment is using the old System.MDA, take the following steps:

1. Start Access 95 without opening a database.
2. Select Tools, Database Utilities, Convert Database.

3. In the Files of Type box select Add-in (*.mda), select the System.MDA file to be converted and click Convert. The Database To Convert From dialog box appears.

4. In the Convert Database Into box, take one of the following actions:

   - Type a new name for the Access 95 workgroup information file
   - Select a different location for the Access 95 workgroup information file, retaining the old name or selecting a new name

5. Click Save. To save the new workgroup file with the .MDW extension, select Workgroup Files (*.MDW) in the File of Type box before saving.

6. Use the Workgroup Administrator to join the converted workgroup information file (System.MDW).

One new feature of the security model in Access 95 is the capability of any user to print user and group information. If you have users whose accounts were converted from the old to the new System.MDW file, they must join the Admins group before they can take advantage of this new capability, or their accounts must be re-created in the new System.MDW file. To re-create a user account, re-enter the exact user name and personal identifier that was originally used to create the original System.MDA account.

Query Performance

A great deal can be done to make sure that full query optimization is assured in your application. First, and possibly most important, make sure that the columns that need to be indexed are. *Rushmore technology* works only on indexed columns.

Queries formed by joining two (or more) tables should have these join columns indexed, on both sides of the JOIN, in both tables. Any field used to set the selection criteria for the query (entries in the WHERE clause of the SQL statement) also should be indexed, as we previously mentioned in this chapter.

Queries that involve one Access 95 table and one ODBC table are sometimes optimized by default by the Jet engine. This situation happens if the Access table is small and both join columns are indexed. In this case, query processing is done locally but performance is greatly improved because Access asks only for the relevant records to be returned from the server, rather than the full table.

Make sure that join columns have the same or comparable data types for best performance.

When creating a query, specify only fields that you will need for the display. If you use fields to establish selection criteria but don't display them, clear the Show check box before running the query.

Avoid calculated fields or functions in sublevels of a nested query. This kind of construction creates a query so complex that it defies optimization. If it isn't possible to avoid this situation, base the form or report on the outermost query and create a calculated control for the form/report that is based on the inner query.

When using a join as input to a GROUP BY query, select the display columns and GROUP BY column(s) from only one table, if possible. If your query, for example, totals the QuantitySold column in an OrderDetails table and groups by OrderID, using a date range from the Orders table as restriction criteria, specify the SELECT and the GROUP BY for the OrderID column from the OrderDetails table, not the OrderID column from the Orders table.

For better query performance, use GROUP BY on as few columns as possible.

If a complex query includes joins, consider doing the query in two (or more) parts. Create one query that extracts the larger relevant data set from one table, then use this query as input to a second, in which you can do the join. Breaking apart queries into their component pieces and executing them serially boosts performance in an environment with restricted memory resources.

Avoid restrictive criteria on calculated fields or non-indexed columns.

If you have a JOIN query, and the join column also is used to restrict the set of rows returned (in the WHERE clause), consider using the join column from the "one" side of the relationship. The set of rows to search in the table of the "one" are smaller than the corresponding set of rows on the "many" side and, therefore, the query should run faster.

If you must sort the output of a query, first build an index on the column you are planning to ORDER BY.

If your data is relatively static—that is, if it doesn't change often, and your security model will allow it—consider using make-table queries, which create physical tables when run. Then use these output tables as the basis for your forms, reports, and *ad hoc* queries.

Avoid using *domain aggregate functions*, such as the **DLookup** function, in a query. It's better to either add the table referenced in the **DLookup** to the main query or create a subquery to find the data.

For *crosstab queries*, use fixed-column headings when possible, which can account for significant speedup in the query resolution. For tips on how to do this, search the Access Help Index for "crosstab query," select the article "Sort or limit column headings displayed in a crosstab query."

Use the BETWEEN operator, the IN operator, and the = operator on index columns when possible. The Rushmore technology can better optimize queries that use these operators.

Filter Performance

In Chapter 1, we introduced the *Filter By Form* feature, which is new to Access 95. Although this is an excellent tool to offer to your user community, if the underlying table is large or if the underlying query is complex, it may seem to take forever for the Filter By Form window to display data. You, as a designer, have some influence over what and how data is displayed in each of the text boxes when Filter By Form is used.

> **Tip**
>
> If one or more fields are continually used to set search criteria in Filter By Form, consider indexing the field(s), especially if the number of rows in the underlying table (query) is large and the field variance (number of unique values in the set of data for the field) is moderate to low. You usually will immediately notice better performance by doing so.

Usually, poor performance in Filter By Form manifests itself in one of two ways—the list takes too long to display or the list doesn't display at all. You can adjust some of this behavior by changing the options or properties settings.

To optimize performance for a single form, take the following steps:

1. Open the form in design mode, select the text box you want to control, and open the property sheet.

2. Choose the FilterLookup property (Data tab) and set the property value to reflect the kind of performance you prefer.

   • If the list takes too long to display, set the FilterLookup property to "never." The next time Filter By Form is run, the user has two choices in the list—Is Null or Is Not Null. The user is restricted to returning one of two sets of data—the set that has a value for the text box field, and the set that does not.

   • If the list takes too long to display, another setting you can use is the default, "database default," and in conjunction modify the global Options entry. (To get to the Options dialog box, select Tools from the menu, Options, the Edit/Find tab.) Clear the option that applies to the kind of field with which you are dealing. For example, if the field property that you just set to "database default" belongs to an indexed field, clear the Local Indexed Fields check box from the Options screen.

   > **Note**
   >
   > The changes made in the Options dialog box affect all Filter By Form operations throughout the database, not just for this form.

   • If the list isn't displaying field values, but only the choices, Is Null and Is Not Null, make sure that the Filter Lookup property is not set to "never."

   • If the list isn't displaying any values and if the property value is "database default" or "always," check the Options dialog box, the value for the text box labeled, Don't Display Lists Where More Than This Number of Records Read. If the number of entries in the field list exceeds this option value, the field list will not display. You can do one of two things—increase the option value so that it is longer than the longest field list or index the field. If the field is indexed, the field list is shorter because Access reads only the set of unique values.

To optimize performance for all tables, queries, and forms, take these steps:

1. From the Access top menu, select Tools, Options, Edit/Find tab, and set the Filter By Form defaults accordingly.

2. If the list of values takes too long to display in non-indexed fields only, try limiting the lists to *indexed* fields only. Clear the check boxes for Local Non-indexed Fields and ODBC Fields on the Options - Edit/Find dialog box (see fig. 16.12).

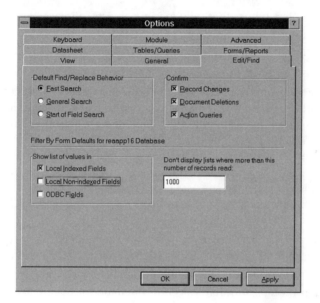

Fig. 16.12

The Options dialog box, Edit/Find tab, showing the Filter by Form defaults.

3. If the list of values takes too long to display in indexed fields, clear all three check boxes, Local Indexed Fields, Local Non-indexed Fields, and ODBC Fields. The assumption is that too many records exist in the indexes for the lists to display quickly.

4. If the lists do not display from either indexed or non-indexed fields, increase the number in the text box, Don't Display Lists Where More Than This Number of Records Read.

5. If the lists do not display from either indexed or non-indexed fields, only from the two choices, IsNull or IsNotNull, make sure that something is checked for the Show List of Values In selection.

Find-and-Replace Performance

For the fastest searches, search for whole field values on indexed fields. If you must use the wild card, don't start a string with the wild-card character (*Tom*) but rather, start the search string with a real string value (Tom*) and follow with a wild-card character to pick up all instances of the value that contain the string.

If you're always searching the same non-indexed field, seriously consider indexing it.

Form and Subform Performance

The following is a list of suggestions (but not all of these are followed by the authors) for enhancing performance on your forms and subforms:

■ Don't open forms across a network. Use the client/server paradigm.

■ Avoid overlapping controls.

■ Use bit maps and other graphic objects sparingly.

■ Convert unbound object frames that hold graphic objects to image controls.

■ Use black-and-white, not color, bit maps.

■ Close forms that are not being used (see Chapter 9, "Navigation: How to Get from Here to There," for more information on how to architect this concept).

■ If a form in your application is mainly used for data entry, set the DataEntry property of the form to yes so that the form opens with a blank record, ready to accept data. When a form opens in Edit mode, Access must load all the records from the underlying table (query) before you can get to the blank record for data entry. To accommodate both needs, set two controls, one DataEntry and one ViewRecords, on-screen. When the user is in DataEntry mode, the ViewRecords command button is visible; when the user is in ViewRecords (Edit) mode, the DataEntry command button is visible. This allows the user to switch back and forth at will.

■ Build subforms on queries rather than on base tables. Include in the query only fields from the record source that are absolutely necessary. Extra fields in the subform can substantially decrease performance.

■ Index every field in the subform that links it to the main form, and vice versa.

■ Index all fields in the subform (query) that are used to determine selection criteria.

■ If the records in the subform are read-only, set the three properties AllowEdits, AllowAdditions, and AllowDeletions to no, or set the RecordsetType property to snapshot. (Snapshots are not updateable.)

■ Consider converting subforms to list boxes or combo boxes. When Access loads a form with a subform, it actually loads two forms into memory.

List Box and Combo Box Performance

List boxes and (especially) *combo boxes* are wonderful features of the Access programming environment. These features help tremendously in setting standards for data entry and in selecting data values for record searches. However, they can stress system performance, so you can do a few things to optimize these controls, which are shown in the following list:

■ Base the list box or combo box on a saved query rather than on a SQL statement. The saved query is optimized for execution based on system statistics; the SQL statement is executed dynamically and, therefore, cannot match the optimization achieved by a saved query.

> **Tip**
>
> If you use the List Box/Combo Box Wizard to build these controls, the Wizard always creates an unbound text box and uses a SQL query as the row source. To change the RowSource property to a saved query, click the ellipsis (Build button) next to the properties box. When you're in the Query Builder window, select File, Save, and type the name of the query you are building, which will substitute as the row source. Close the Query Builder and choose Yes when Access asks if you want to update the property.

- Use only fields that are absolutely necessary in the query that is the RowSource property for the list box/combo box.
- Index the first field displayed in the list box/combo box for faster list retrieval.
- Index all fields used for criteria restriction.
- In combo boxes, if you don't need the fill-it-in-automatically-as-you-type feature, turn off the AutoExpand property.
- If you are using the *AutoExpand* feature of a combo box, the first non-hidden column in the combo box—the one the AutoExpand is matching—should be a text data type, not a number data type. To find a match in the list, Access converts number values to text, thereby incurring large overhead in processing the list.
- If possible, don't create list boxes/combo boxes from linked or remote data. If the data is static (doesn't change often), import the tables into the local client and build the list boxes/combo boxes using these. Then create code that, on startup of the application, copies down from the server or remote data source a fresh version of the "static" tables, which should give every client at least daily synchronization with changes to the data made from the server.

Report and Subreport Performance

Reports and subreport optimization reads a great deal like form and subform optimization, only not as extended.

- Don't open reports across the network. Use the client/server paradigm.
- Avoid overlapping controls.
- Use bit maps and other graphic objects sparingly.
- Convert unbound object frames that hold graphic objects to image controls.
- Use black-and-white rather than color bit maps (most of your printed reports will not take advantage of color printing anyway, so save time and space from the onset).
- Avoid sorting and grouping on expressions.
- Index fields you sort or group on.
- Build subreports on queries rather than on base tables. Include in the query only those fields from the record source that are absolutely necessary. Extra fields in the subreport can substantially decrease performance.

- Index every field in the subreport that links it to the main report, and vice versa.
- Index any field in the subreport (or query) that is used to determine selection criteria.

Visual Basic for Applications Code Performance

Writing code is as personal as writing a letter, and each person has his or her own style. The authors are making a sweeping statement here: To improve code performance, you must develop an efficient approach to writing modules. This takes years of programming on multiple systems—each with limited resources—learning from other programmers, and adding your own signature style to your program code.

Additionally, you can do a few things that, across the board, tighten up the code that you are writing for your Access applications:

- Make sure that the code in your database is compiled. Recompile code after renaming a database—renaming a database decompiles the code in that database! To compile all code, from an open Module window select Run, Compile All Modules, and then (if it's a clean compile) select File, Save All Modules.
- Always explicitly declare variables in the declarations section of each module.
- Use the most specific data type possible when declaring variables.
- Avoid the use of the variant data type as much as possible, and use it only for your local Access database (see Chapter 6, "Establishing the Ground Rules," for more information on the use of the variant data type). The variant, although more flexible, uses more memory and processor time for different functions.
- If you refer more than once to the value of a property or a control on a form, or to a data access object or its property, create a variable for it and refer to the variable rather than to the full control/object identifier.
- Use the Me construct for form references in event procedures.
- Use the IIf discriminately. Access must evaluate both branches of the IIf statement, so avoid it if either branch of the expression takes a long time to evaluate. Replace IIf with an If...Then...Else (it's usually more efficient).
- Use string functions when appropriate—the $ functions (such as Str$ function) when working with strings and the non-$ functions when working with variant or non-string data types. In this way, Access does not have to do type conversions.
- Use the integer or long data type for math when possible. Table 16.1 ranks numeric data types by calculation speed.

Table 16.1 Comparison of Number Data Types and Relative Calculation Speed	
Numeric Data Type	**Speed of Calculations**
Integer, long	Fastest
Single, double	Next-to-fastest
Currency	Next-to-slowest
Variant	Slowest

- Use dynamic arrays; reclaim memory with the Erase or ReDim statements.
- Use constants (rather than variables), when possible.
- Use bookmarks; set a bookmark rather than using the FindNext method to return to a particular record.
- Index fields on which you are likely to use the FindRecord and FindNext methods. These methods work much faster on indexed fields than on non-indexed fields.
- Organize your procedures and modules. Visual Basic loads a module into memory when a procedure stored within it is called. Therefore, by organizing into modules the procedures that are used together, you can avoid excessive disk I/O because you will have all related procedures in memory with a single read.
- Eliminate dead code and unused variables. *SPEED* Ferret, (a demo copy of this application is included on the companion CD-ROM), is an excellent tool to assist in locating unused variables.

Optimizing the Jet

The Jet 3 database engine has some *tuning parameters* that, under controlled conditions, you can modify. The default values for these parameters, however, are close to the optimal setting for most situations. Benchmark testing has shown that modifying Jet tuning parameters produces minimal performance improvement, and may result in performance degradation if the changes are not carefully monitored.

Jet tuning, by its nature, depends completely on individual circumstances, and so should be carefully tested before implementation in a production situation. The test bed should contain test data that is representative of the real production data, in quantities comparable to the production set. The routines to test should be the same as the production routines, and should be done on computers that are typical of the machines in use.

MaxBufferSize

The *MaxBufferSize* tuning parameter controls the size of the database cache, in Kbytes, that the Jet grabs on startup, although the actual size is up for discussion. The authors have sources that say two things—the maximum size can be limited and the maximum size is limited only by the amount of memory available. No matter which is the case, the MaxBufferSize is an integer value with a minimum of 18, a maximum of 4,096, and a default value of 512. The database cache stores pages from the physical database, and contains data most often or more-recently read and written.

Memory used for the Jet database cache is memory that isn't available to other applications. Once seized, the Jet doesn't release database cache memory until it is brought down.

ReadAheadPages

The *ReadAheadPages* tuning parameter control the read-ahead buffer. It is the number of 2K pages from the physical database read into memory in anticipation of sequential processing. Every time a read-record request is processed that results in an input operation from the hard disk, this number of pages will be read into the read-ahead buffer. The minimum value for ReadAheadPages is 0, the maximum value is 31, the default is 16.

Page caching can be a true advantage for sequential record processing, but it also can seriously inhibit performance for random record retrieval. Reading from and writing to the hard disk is the singularly most expensive operation on a computer, and if your ReadAheadPages is set to the maximum value (31), each time you request a record that isn't already in the database cache (the potential for this situation is high in random record processing), the Jet will not fetch a single 2K page of data, but 31 2K pages.

PageTimeout and LockedPageTimeout

The *PageTimeout* and *LockedPageTimeout* tuning parameters give the Jet an indication of the "freshness" of the data pages in the database cache. Each time a data page is read into cache, it acquires a read timestamp. Based on the value of this read timestamp, the Jet makes an educated guess as to whether or not the copy of the data in cache is valid, accurate data.

In Jet 2 both locked and unlocked pages shared the same time-out parameter. Now, each has its own setting. The values are measured in half-seconds, the minimum is zero, the maximum is two billion, and the default is five billion. For a database opened in exclusive mode (single-user), these parameters have no meaning.

IdleFrequency

The *IdleFrequency* tuning parameter determines when a page in the read-ahead buffer has outlived its usefulness. This determination is based on the number of move attempts, or record pointer resets, that were executed. If a page in the cache isn't used after *n* number of Seeks or MoveNexts, it is discarded.

If your database environment is primarily reading data, with low levels of update, increasing this parameter may show some benefit in your overall performance.

LockRetry and CommitLockRetry

The *LockRetry* and *CommitLockRetry* tuning parameters determine how many times the Jet tries to gain access to locked pages before giving the user an error message. These parameters (obviously) function only in a multiuser environment, and function only when an attempt to lock a page fails. The default value is 20, the minimum is zero, the maximum is two billion.

When you edit a record in a shared database environment, depending on the locking protocol you have chosen—optimistic or pessimistic—the Jet tries to get a lock on the page. If it fails, it doesn't notify the user immediately; rather it retries *n* number of times to lock the page before finally giving up and notifying the user. If you're using transaction processing (BeginTrans and CommitTrans methods), the Jet will try LockRetry times CommitLockRetry number of times before the user is aware that a problem exists.

If you are programming applications for the Jet by way of Visual Basic 4, then—depending on which platform your application is running, Windows 3.x or Windows 95—the tuning parameters will be located either in VB.INI or in the Windows Registry, location DbEngine.DbIniPath, respectively. For additional information on how to modify the Jet parameters for a single session, while your Visual Basic application is running, the authors suggest *Optimizing Visual Basic 4*, by Ward R. Hitt, Que Corporation, 1995.

The Jet 3 tuning parameters are accessible through the *Windows Registry*, by running the RegEdit.EXE program. (Previous versions of the Jet included the tuning parameters in the Access.INI files.) Although the default database tuning parameters will meet most needs, the odd case occurs where it may be necessary to set values for certain circumstances.

To customize these parameters, use a customized set of Registry keys, known as a *user profile*, to override the standard Registry settings. You use the **/Profile** command-line option to specify the user profile you want your application to use. To create a user profile, take these steps:

1. Start the Registry Editor and navigate to the \HKEY_LOCAL_MACHINE\ SOFTWARE\Microsoft\Access\7.0 key of the Registry.

2. Create a key named **Profiles** under the 7.0 key.

3. Under the Profiles key, create a value with the name of the profile that you want to create, and give it a string value of `Software\YourCompanyName\YourAppName\YourApp'sVersionNumber`.

4. Re-create any keys under the Microsoft Access key that you want to modify— except the Profiles key—and copy their values under your Profile key, which

now should be located at `Software\`*`YourCompanyName`*`\`*`YourAppName`*`\` *`YourApp`*`'`*`sVersionNumber`*.

5. Modify the values that you want to change.

6. Create a command-line for your application that specifies your user profile. For example: `msaccess.exe /profile "`*`YourProfileName`*`"` *`YourApplicationName`*`.mdb`. You also can use a user profile to customize the Microsoft Jet database engine settings. You can find the Jet settings in \HKEY_LOCAL_MACHINE\SOFTWARE\Microsoft\Jet\3.0.

To override any Jet 3.0 database engine default settings, take the following steps:

1. Under the `Software\`*`YourCompanyName`*`\`*`YourAppName`*`\`*`YourApp`*`'`*`sVersionNumber`* profile key, create a key named **Jet**.

2. Under the Jet key, create a key named **3.0**.

3. Add values of the appropriate name and type, and then specify the settings. You can model your values after the values in \HKEY_LOCAL_MACHINE\ SOFTWARE\Microsoft\Jet\3.0.

Note

For an assist in setting up your application environment, consider using the Setup Wizard. Besides all the other things the Setup Wizard can do, it can add to the Windows Registry keys and entries for your application.

From Here...

In this chapter we covered performance and tuning in the Access environment. Although these topics are specific to Access 95, a lot of what was covered can be used in previous versions of Access, or can be applied to non-Access database applications— especially the information about design principles.

From here, jump to the following chapters to find out more about related subjects:

■ Chapter 1, "Client/Server, What Is It?" for an introduction to the Filter By Form paradigm.

■ Chapter 6, "Establishing the Ground Rules," for a discussion on entity relationships, normalization, and data types.

■ Chapter 9, "Navigation: How to Get from Here to There," for information on forms handling.

■ Chapter 11, "Managing Transactions," for a discussion on locking.

■ Chapter 12, "Securing the Access 95 Application," for a discussion on the Access 95 security model.

Part V

Upgrading the Application

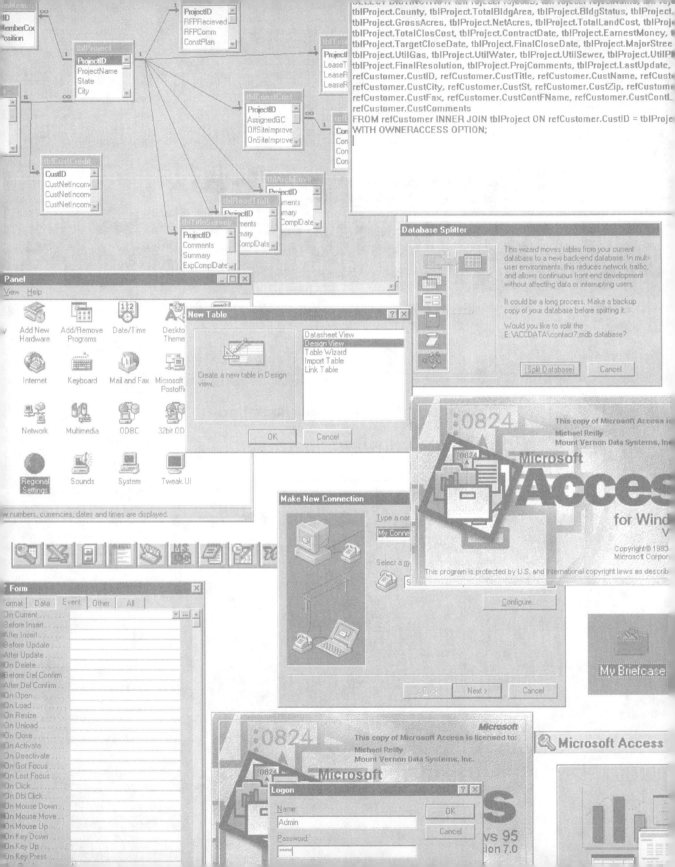

CHAPTER 17

Transitioning to Another Back-End DBMS

Eventually, it will happen—the day arrives when you must begin planning how to upsize your database environment. Unfortunately, from a horsepower perspective, it doesn't take long to outgrow the capabilities of a homogeneous Access environment. From the corporate perspective, it may take even less time because of issues such as security, workgroup productivity, scalability, and data distribution.

What are some of the benefits to moving beyond the file/server architecture, into a true client/server paradigm? In this chapter we cover the following issues:

- Scalability and the inherent benefits
- Reasons to move up to a database server back end
- Candidate database management system servers
- How and when to make the move

Scalability Requirements

Scalability has been defined as the ability to swap interchangeable parts and grow a system, without having to rewrite it, as the demand on the hardware and software increases. Access belongs to a family of software products that have a high level of interchangeability and that function well on a variety of hardware platforms of varying capacities and capabilities.

The following four components of a database environment should be scaleable:

- The application interface
- The database management system
- The operating system
- The hardware platform

The Application Interface

The *application interface* is in good part what, in this book, we have referred to as the client.MDB. The user community interacts with this part of the database and to them, *this is* the database.

Access provides an ideal environment for application interface development. The non-programming portion of Access—the Menu Builder, the Forms and Report Wizards, the query builder that generates SQL code, and the Tools Wizards—all provide an ideal environment for producing prototype applications. The prototype can grow into a real application through the use of macros and Visual Basic for Applications to control user navigation and data presentation and handling.

As the program requirements change and grow, the application interface can be expanded. Portions—especially portions that require more control over user actions, such as the heads-down data entry part—can be rewritten in Visual Basic, as time and internal Information Systems talent permits. By remaining consistent with the "look-and-feel" of Windows applications—which is easy to do when working in the Access and Visual Basic environments—the greater the chance that your end users will accept your products. The higher the user community comfort level with software that you have produced, the higher the probability of full adoption of future releases that follow the same paradigm.

The Database Management System

The database management system is both the core of database file operations and the entire package that includes user-interface toolkits, language compilers, ODBC and SQL translators, query optimizers, security administrators, replication managers, and so on. The database management system manages data—arranges for its storage and retrieval, constructs and manages indexes, and sets up and maintains transaction logging to protect updates and prevent loss of data integrity. The query optimizer reviews queries from the user community and develops a query plan. The engine executes the query plan—using all resources available—and returns the result set to the user who originated the query, balancing this task with potentially dozens of other simultaneous requests in a multiuser environment.

At the bottom of the scalability index is the single-user database management system; at the top end is the multiuser, multithreaded engine that can service hundreds or even thousands of concurrent connections. As a database engine, Access is on the low end of this spectrum. Any database opened in exclusive mode effectively renders Access a single-user system. Previous versions were single-threaded, they could do only one thing at a time; Access 95 is multithreaded and, on a single-processor machine, can still only do one thing at a time, but it can have multiple tasks in progress. On a multiple-processor computer, Access 95 can provide enhanced performance to a limited number of users, but it still is based upon a file/server model of computing.

When the Access engine begins to run out of gas, due to either an increase in the size of the user community or a change in the application requirements that cannot be handled by the file/server architecture, it can be replaced by a larger and more robust client/server database management system. The upgrade within the software family is Microsoft SQL Server, although by no means is this the only server database management system that is compatible with the Access application interface. Any client/server database management system that supports the *ODBC* (Open Database

Connectivity) standard (and there are many) can act as a back end to the Access or Visual Basic application interface.

The Operating System

The *operating system* partners with the database management system, either loosely or tightly, to manage data in storage and to get queries resolved. Although previous versions of Access are able to run on Windows (or Windows for Workgroups) 3.x; Access 95, being a 32-bit application, must run on a 32-bit operating system such as Windows 95 or Windows NT. Both the client and the server portion of the Access application can start life in a Windows 95 environment. As the demands on the application grow, the server portion can be moved over to a Windows NT machine, even to one with multiple processors for enhanced performance.

There are many similarities between Windows 95 and Windows NT; each is a *preemptive multitasking operating system*; each operating system controls which programs run for how long by allocating to each task a priority and a sliver of time in which to execute. Each is a *multithreading operating system*, which treats a program as a single process and assigns one or more *threads of execution* (*threads*) to each process. Multiple threads within the same process give all these threads access to the same memory address space, providing for fast inter-thread communication. Multithreaded operating systems, such as Windows 95 and Windows NT, are more powerful than their single-threaded counterparts.

There also are many differences between the Windows 95 and the Windows NT operating systems, but the most obvious is that Windows NT supports *symmetric multiprocessing (SMP)*—it can take advantage of multiple CPUs, if they are present. Windows 95 cannot do this, and probably never will—at least in the foreseeable future. Windows 95 isn't meant to be a server operating system; it is meant to be a second choice as a client to the Windows NT Server operating system (the first choice for the client in a heavy use corporate environment is Windows NT Workstation).

Symmetric multiprocessing treats all processors as equals, and each has equal access to the same physical memory. Windows NT schedules threads, one (or more) for each operating system or application program process, which then execute on the next available processor. A thread isn't bound to a single processor for its life; if its time slice expires and it is scheduled out, when the thread next runs, it may be assigned to a different CPU. Windows NT thus can perform dynamic load balancing, extracting the best performance from the resources available.

On a single-CPU computer the presence of multiple threads means that a user can continue to do some lengthy process while another thread is executing in background, but only one thread at a time can actually be executing (this is known as *time-slicing*). On a multiprocessor computer, several CPUs may be running several threads (one thread per processor) from the same program, simultaneously, in parallel. This can result in dramatic performance increases for applications that are capable of multithreading.

V

Upgrading the Application

Both Access 95 and Microsoft SQL Server are multithreaded, so that each can take advantage of the SMP feature of Windows NT. Each engine allows for a varying number of threads. By default, the Access 95 Jet has three internal threads (user-modifiable in the Windows Registry), assigned for background services like:

- Read-ahead for sequential processing
- Write-behind for writing commit records
- Database cache maintenance tasks
- Quiescent database detection, to determine when a change has been made to the shared-mode database

Each Access user process is assigned its own thread.

Microsoft SQL Server uses the *Symmetric Server Architecture*, which is a single-process, multithreaded architecture. SQL Server makes great use of the Windows NT native thread services; NT schedules all threads preemptively, while assigning each thread in turn to the most available CPU in a multiprocessor environment. The NT native threads handle database system chores such as page faults and asynchronous I/O. Microsoft SQL Server has a configurable parameter, *MaxWorkerThreads*, for user connections. The virtual picture is one worker thread per user connection. When the number of simultaneous users exceeds the MaxWorkerThread value, SQL Server pools the worker threads and assigns the next available thread to a waiting user connection.

This single-process, multithreading approach of Microsoft SQL Server involves little system overhead and little memory use, especially compared to the single-process-per-user model. The following example shows the type of resource savings you can expect.

The following list shows Microsoft SQL Server memory requirements for 200 user connections and MaxWorkerThread set to 100:

@user connection = 27K

@worker thread = 28 K

(200 * 27K) + (100 * 28K) = 8.2M of memory for 200 database users

Contrast this example to a process-per-user architecture, with an average memory requirement of 350K per user:

(200 * 350K) = 70M of memory for 200 database users

The Hardware Platform

Scalability in hardware is extremely vendor-dependent. Although some vendors offer computers that can be physically upgraded by adding more memory or a second CPU, it's often easier and more cost-effective to simply replace the old server or client computer with a new one.

The life of a microcomputer, whether as a client desktop or a server workstation, is still about three years, at which time it will be obsolete, at least two to four generations behind the technology development curve. To extend the useable life of a computer system, the authors suggest that when purchasing computer hardware, you make sure that the system is "balanced"—that the strength of the CPU is matched by an appropriate amount of RAM, and the capacity of the hard disk is realistic for the expectations placed on the individual machine. The biggest failing of most new computers available on the market that the authors have seen is a lack of memory included in the base package. Almost universally, within the first year, client and server systems both are undergoing brain surgery, getting additional memory implants. Start with a suitable system that meets the requirements for the next 2-1/2 to 3 years, then plan for periodic replacements.

At the time of this writing, a typical departmental office configuration may resemble the system described in Table 18.1.

Table 18.1 Typical Office Desktop Computer (Client Node) and Office Server Computer (Server Node) Configuration

Component	Client Node	Server Node
CPU	Pentium-75 or Pentium-90	Dual Pentium-166 or single/dual PentiumPro or AlphaServer or MIPS or NEC
Memory	16M	64-128M (depending on need)
I/O bus	PCI	PCI
Video bus	PCI	PCI
Hard disk	1G/IDE	multi-gigabyte SCSI or RAID-5
Floppy drive	1.44 (3.5")	1.44(3.5")
CD-ROM drive	optional, ATAPI interface	mandatory 4x, SCSI interface
Video	SVGA	SVGA
Operating system	Windows for Workgroups 3.11, Windows 95, Windows NT Workstation	Windows NT Server
Printer	optional (HP DeskJet)	Mandatory (HP LaserJet) or set up a separate print server

By the time you read this book, this profile probably will be out of date (minimum specifications change *this* fast), so adjust accordingly. See Chapter 3, "The Application Development Environment," for more information on client/server hardware requirements.

V

Upgrading the Application

Why Scale Up?

There are many reasons why you want to scale up your database environment, and we start with the following:

- Improved performance
- Enhanced security
- The protection of transaction logging
- Seven by twenty-four availability
- Extensibility, support for larger and more complex applications
- Flexibility in choice of database servers

Improved Performance

Although Access 95 has a multithreading engine, as you saw previously in this chapter, there is a difference, for example, between the approach used by Access and Microsoft SQL Server. The single-process multithreading approach of Microsoft SQL Server is far more efficient and uses far more resources than the single-process-per-user model of Access 95.

Many of the server database management systems have been optimized for high-volume transaction processing, which, due to its file/server nature, Access 95 cannot support. The client/server model splits the load, with each end doing some of the work and the server portion coordinating both transaction and lock management, and controlling concurrent users. Access 95 does all data processing, presentation, transaction management, and lock management from the various client ends, requesting only that the file management system on the server end store the data.

In the area of distributed database and distributed processing, Access 95 is out of the league. Although it supports "replication," the technique Access 95 uses is extremely limited and unsuitable for enterprise (or even departmental) data distribution. Chapter 20, "Replication with Access 95," discusses replication in the Access 95 environment.

Enhanced Security

Although the security model of Access 95 is quite good, it doesn't stand up to the scrutiny of C2 requirements. If your company is under contract to an agency of the government, for example, you probably will have to provide *at least* C2-level security protection for your computing and database environment.

Chapter 12, "Securing the Access 95 Application," covered the Access security model in some depth. The Access security model, like C2, is discretionary in that individual users—either by themselves or by virtue of their participation in a workgroup—can be granted permission to access or modify various objects in the database. However, C2 requirements are more extensive. To qualify as a C2-compliant computing environment, you must provide the following:

- **Authentication**—Requires a *mandatory* logon and authentication by the operating system/environment.

- **Discretionary access control**—Restricts modification of database objects to certain individuals with appropriate security clearance and monitors access to these objects.

- **Object reuse protection**—Protects areas of memory from being reopened by unauthorized users after having been shut down and protects deleted records from being accessed, either on the hard disk or in memory.

- **Auditing**—Provides for tracking of user activities in the system.

Access 95 cannot provide any of the preceding features. Even operating under the control of Windows NT, the Access database environment doesn't qualify as C2. However, any database management system that is tightly coupled to Windows NT can, and does, meet C2 standards.

Microsoft SQL Server V6.x is a database management system that meets C2 standards. It uses the native services of Windows NT for many of its database functions, including thread scheduling, file management, user authentication, and security.

Transaction Logging

Access doesn't support *transaction logging*, although it does support transaction processing. From Chapter 11, "Managing Transactions," a transaction is defined as a logical unit of work, a set of statements or commands that will succeed or fail as a group. Transaction logging, as you will see in Chapter 19, "System Administration," is a record of all the transactions that have happened against the database since the last full backup was taken. Transaction logging is absolutely vital to ensure full data integrity in a multiuser environment.

A fact of life: occasionally, *your database will fail*. For a myriad of reasons, specific to each vendor's implementation and the operational environment, your database will come down. The vendor's job is to design subsequent versions of the product that are more robust and extend the mean time between failure. Your job, to have a plan in place that you can execute when the database fails.

If the database suffers a *soft crash*, meaning no hardware failure was involved, that all disk volumes are intact and fully operational, you need only—in most cases—restart the database (check your vendor's instructions first). The transaction log contains the transactions that were executing at the time of failure. It rolls back any incomplete transactions that may have been recorded to the physical database, and it ensures that any completed transactions that may have been in memory at the time of system failure are written to the physical database.

In the event of disk failure and a *hard crash* of the database, the database can be rebuilt by restoring from the most current database backup, and then regenerating the post-backup updates from the copies of the transaction log. Without this protection scheme known as transaction logging, when your hard disk fails, you can count on losing data. Server backups and regenerating the database are discussed in greater detail in Chapter 19.

V

Upgrading the Application

Seven by Twenty-Four Availability

More and more companies are demanding that their databases stay online at all times; thus, the *seven by twenty-four model* of computing. Access 95 was never meant for this operational paradigm, and you will encounter serious problems if it is not occasionally cycled.

One of these problem areas that you encounter is query execution. The *cost-based statistical model* used by Access to build plans for efficient query execution is based on the database statistics contained in the Access data dictionary. As is the usual process with cost-based systems, these statistics are calculated from the following:

■ The cardinality, or number of rows, in each table involved in the query

■ The indexes that are built on a table

■ The number of hard disk pages (blocks) used to store the data in a table or index

■ The location of the table or index, local or remote (ODBC)

■ The data variance, or the variation in the set of data values contained by a column of a table or index (also known as selectivity)

■ The presence (or absence) of NULLs in an index(es)

Every modification to the data, every index built or dropped, affects the statistics. Over a period of time, the statistics stored in the Access 95 data dictionary will cease to reflect the reality of the database, and query execution will suffer.

Access 95 doesn't dynamically update its statistics. To see a clear and current picture of the statistics, you have to periodically compact the database. To compact the database, you have to take it off-line, which makes it unavailable to your user community.

Server database management systems are built to handle changing internal conditions while operational. In a server database environment, data dictionary statistics are either updated dynamically (when the query is compiled) or they can be updated by running a system procedure. For example, with Microsoft SQL Server, simply run the stored procedure, **UpdateStatistics**:

```
UPDATE STATISTICS ([database_name.owner_name.]table_name [index_name])
```

If *index_name* isn't included, all indexes attached to the table are automatically included in the statistical update.

The other main problem area you will encounter with Access and seven-by-twenty-four operation is database backups. Although there are some third-party vendor packages that claim to do *on-line database backups* for Access, they need to be evaluated carefully. A successful database or table backup allows you to restore the data so that you do not compromise data integrity, even to the point of supporting multi-table updates. The only way you can do this successfully in the on-line environment is to dump the data out of the tables(s), and dump the transaction log to capture any updates that were made during the initial database dump. Chapter 19, "System Administration," discusses on-line backups and how they are handled in a representative server database environment.

Access 95 doesn't have a transaction log to dump. Therefore, the only way to ensure a fully successful backup of the database is to take it off-line, again making it unavailable to your user community.

Extensibility

After your custom database application is installed and in use, if it is of any value, it will grow. New features, new functionality, new users, more data, more operations, connect to legacy data stores, move from an operational paradigm (OLTP) to a decision support system (DSS/OLAP)—this is the nature of database systems in today's business environment. By being able to detach the Access 95 back end (the data.MDB portion) and replace it with one or more robust, powerful client/server database management systems, you can meet these ever-changing and ever-challenging requirements with (generally) minimal disruption to operations.

Extensibility isn't restricted to only the back end, it's also possible to implement on the front, or client, end. As the requirements grow on the back end, don't forget the options you have on the front end. Any ODBC client can be used to access the ODBC data, so your user community is not restricted to retrieving data through your custom front-end application. By using the query function of Microsoft Word and Microsoft Excel, for example, your user community can query and retrieve data from the database, to format as needed in Word or Excel. Refer to Chapter 14, "Communicating with Other Applications," for more information on how to do this.

> **Note**
>
> There are some misnamed third-party "query" tools that allow not only data retrieval but also data update from outside the database environment. As long as you use this kind of software to retrieve data from the database you are not compromising data integrity. However, when you attempt to update data without letting the database management system control the transactions and possible concurrent access to the same data by multiple users, you are putting the integrity, or accuracy, of the data at risk.

Flexibility

All the topics discussed in this section have set the stage for flexibility, the need to be able to choose the server database or databases that best fit the situation. It is common for an Access application to grow beyond the file/server stage, to upsize to one or more client/server database management systems on the back end, and even to connect to existing nonrelational legacy systems to provide support at the enterprise level. As a database or systems administrator, you need to have these options available, whether or not you choose to execute them.

Target Database Management Systems

Any relational database management system that supports the Open Database Connectivity (ODBC) Standard is a candidate for a server. Realistically, with the demands of a growing database environment, you will want to choose one that offers transaction logging for quick and sure recoverability. If your organization is going to require more than one copy of the database be available to the user community, you may need to limit your options to database management systems that support distribution via a transaction manager and the two-phase commit model. If your company is under contract to an organization that mandates a certain level of security or accountability—or both—your options are limited even further.

The Open Database Connectivity (ODBC) Standard was developed by a consortium of database vendors lead by Microsoft Corporation. Briefly, the two applications that want to talk to each other each must be equipped with an ODBC driver. The client application (the client can be Access, Visual Basic, Microsoft Word, Microsoft Excel, or any other ODBC-compliant front end) initiates a call to its own ODBC driver, which then talks to the target (server) ODBC driver, which in turn talks to the server application (usually a database management system).

ODBC provides a consistent way to access data stored in a multitude of database environments, heralding the beginnings of the *Intergalactic Network Model* (see the *Essential Client/Server Survival Guide* by Orfali, Harkey, and Edwards, Van Nostrand Reinhold, 1994, for further explanations of intergalactic computing). With continuing work on and the continued effort from the participating database vendors on implementation of standards development and adoption, the time is fast approaching when data is universally accessible—no matter where it is stored or how it is retrieved.

> **Tip**
>
> For an excellent discussion on ODBC the authors direct you to *Inside ODBC* by Kyle Geiger, Microsoft Press, 1995.

The following database management systems are only some of many that support ODBC. If you plan to upsize to a back-end database management system that isn't on this list, you may want to get in touch with the vendor to confirm an ODBC driver is available.

- ADABAS SQL Server, Software AG of North America
- Btrieve
- CA-IDMS, Computer Associates
- CA-Ingres, Computer Associates
- CA-Datacom, Computer Associates
- CA-DB, Computer Associates
- CA-RDB, Computer Associates
- DAL
- dBASE
- DEC-RMS, Digital Equipment Company

- Focus
- SQL Anywhere (formerly Gupta SQLBase)
- HP ALLBASE/SQL
- HP IMAGE/SQL
- IBI EDA/SQL
- IBM DB2, IBM Corporation
- IBM DB2/2, IBM Corporation
- IBM DB2/6000, IBM Corporation
- IBM SQL/400, IBM Corporation
- IBM SQL/DS, IBM Corporation
- Informix, Informix Corporation
- Integra SQL
- Interbase
- Microsoft Access
- Microsoft Excel
- Microsoft FoxPro
- Microsoft Visual Basic and Visual Basic for Applications
- Model 204
- NetWareSQL
- Nomad Gateway
- Oracle, Oracle Corporation
- Paradox, Borland Corporation
- PICK
- Progress, Progress Software Corporation
- Quadbase
- Raima
- R:BASE
- Siemens/Nixdorf SESAM
- Siemens/Nixdorf UDSD
- Microsoft SQL Server
- SupraServer
- Systems 2000
- Tandem NonStop SQL
- Teradata
- UNIFY
- Watcom SQL for Windows

V

Upgrading the Application

■ White Cross 9000

■ XDB

How and When to Make the Transition

When you decide to upgrade depends on the circumstances surrounding your situation, but "how" needs to be carefully thought out. You should have the following at your disposal:

■ Time

■ Tools

■ Target database management system knowledge

Time

The old saying in the world of carpentry, "Measure three times, cut once," also holds true for upsizing your Access 95 database. You need to plan, plan, and plan some more, and for this planning, you need time. Upsizing, although it normally brings with it significant performance increases and other enhancements, also has headaches attached.

The authors have put together the following short checklist for upsizing:

1. **Prepare the client application**. In the next chapter, "Upsizing Techniques," you will find a checklist of things to look for in the Access 95 client application that should be modified before upsizing.

2. **Upgrade the documentation**. Both user and system documentation, printed and on-line, need to be synchronized with the planned changes. Coordinate the user-documentation upgrade so that it will be ready when the new client/server application is introduced. Upgrade the system documentation while the changes are being made.

3. **Evaluate and select a server database management system**. This is no trivial task. The choice is immensely simpler if a corporate standard is in place that says you must use either Oracle, Informix, Microsoft SQL Server, or Sybase System 10. If no corporate standard is in place and you must make the decision yourself, allow plenty of time to review and evaluate. Set up a scenario that is representative of the requirements of your future environment to use as a baseline for judging. You may want to bring onboard a business systems consultant and/or a database consultant to assist with the evaluation. So many good server database management systems exist—each with its own strengths and failings—that making a choice is a tough task, and you should allow enough time to do a reasonably thorough job.

4. **Get familiar with the new database management system**. After you make your choice and install the new database manager, you either must have time to get familiar with it or you have to bring onboard a consultant who is

willing to work with you while you learn. This is in addition to any new database administration, network administration, and/or systems administration staff you may have to add.

5. **Do the conversion**. On a test copy of the database, make the first attempt at conversion. Using one or more of the techniques covered in the following chapter, you will get your feet wet.

6. **Debug the conversion**. Of course it's not going to go smoothly! In the following chapter, you will find a section that explains what to do when—following the conversion—your application simply no longer works!

Tools

You need to have at your disposal some help for upsizing all but the tiniest databases. These tools vary from the Export facility of Access 95 to the Upsizing Tools distributed by Microsoft Corporation.

A rather unconventional upsizing tool, if you have a working familiarity with it, is a CASE (Computer-Assisted Software Engineering) program. Most CASE tools can build scripts that will create a database environment on any of a rather sizable group of database management systems, from desktop to mainframe. The following chapter shows how to use these CASE tools to move a database from one system platform to another.

Target DBMS Knowledge

With the introduction of a new database management system into your working environment, you may find yourself interviewing for someone with the appropriate skills to help you in the administration and feeding of the new beast. The file/server model of database management system is only a little removed from the word processors and spreadsheets; management is no big deal. The server database management system, however, is another story. This system is an operating environment of its own and is capable of managing and manipulating all the corporate data.

Whether or not you are adding staff to manage the server database, you do need to expand your own skill set. As a database developer, you cannot ignore the new database environment; you need to know enough about it to be highly dangerous.

Besides the new people and new skills you may be inheriting in the near future, you probably need to upgrade some of your hardware to accommodate the new server database management system.

From Here...

In this chapter, we discussed reasons for moving beyond the file/server architecture into a client/server paradigm. We talked about scalability, what it is and the benefits of designing and developing in a scaleable environment. We looked at candidate ODBC servers, and then listed the general steps involved in making the move to a client/server system.

From here, jump to the following chapters for more information on:

- Chapter 3, "The Application Development Environment," discusses client/server hardware requirements.
- Chapter 11, "Managing Transactions," reviews transaction processing.
- Chapter 18, "Upsizing Techniques," shows how to plan and execute your upsizing operation.
- Chapter 19, "System Administration," discusses how to manage the newer and larger database environment.
- Chapter 20, "Replication with Access 95," gives information on Access replication versus full Microsoft SQL Server distribution.
- Chapter 21, "Client/Server Performance and Tuning," gives tips on how to keep the new environment running smoothly.
- Chapter 22, "The Human Factor," discusses the human side of your brave new world.

CHAPTER 18

Upsizing Techniques

In the preceding chapter we discussed some issues surrounding the decision to upsize—migrating the Access data.MDB to a full server environment—and why you would want or need to do so. In this chapter we cover some of the techniques used to upsize. This is not meant to be an exhaustive treatise on the subject, but merely an overview of several of the most-used methods to make the conversion from an Access data.MDB to a server database management system environment.

The source databases that will be converted are Access 2 and Access 95. The target ODBC databases used throughout this chapter are Microsoft SQL Server versions 4.2 and 6.5 (at the time of writing, 6.5 was still in beta). The concepts and principles used in the different upsizing schemes can be applied to any target database management system, with the lone exception of the Microsoft Upsizing Tools, which are meant to target only Microsoft SQL Server.

The authors must beg your patience because it seems that we will have to demonstrate most of the upsizing techniques on old technology (Access 2 and Microsoft SQL Server 4.2). None of the CASE vendors to which we talked have their tools ready to read in from or export schema to either Access 95 or Microsoft SQL Server 6.x. Microsoft currently is working on an Upsizing Tool for Access 95 but at the time of writing, it wasn't even ready for beta. The good news is, the export facility of Access 95 to Microsoft SQL Server 6.x works just fine.

In this chapter we will discuss the following:

- How to prepare your Access 95 (or Access 2.x) application for upsizing
- How to use the Access Export facility to build tables in Microsoft SQL Server
- How to use the Microsoft Upsizing Tools
- How to use CASE software to upsize
- Testing and debugging the upsized application

Preparation for Upsizing

Sometimes, it helps to get the overview of a procedure before delving into the details. From the 40,000-foot level—upsizing, or migrating—Access tables from a file/server environment to a client/server environment involves the following steps:

1. Check through the Access tables and client application to remove anomalies that may prevent a successful upsize experience. Always make sure that you have adequate backups before beginning any procedure that involves modification to your database or the application.

2. Create and configure the ODBC database, if it doesn't already exist.

3. Confirm that you have security authorization to create table, create view, create *trigger*, plus everything else you need to do in the ODBC environment.

   A triggered event, or trigger, is a code snippet that executes in response to an update, delete, or insert command at the table level or any of a collection of other commands at the form level. Not supported by Access, triggers usually are found in the server database management systems.

4. Export the Access tables to the ODBC database, using one of several techniques we discuss in following sections of this chapter.

5. Add indexes to the ODBC server tables, as necessary.

6. Add ODBC server integrity rules, default values, and everything else the server can support that is as nearly equivalent as possible to the Access table/column properties.

7. Disconnect the Access tables from your client application, and reattach to the ODBC server tables.

8. Debug and optimize the Access client application to run in a client/server environment.

Before taking steps to re-create your Access database in any server environment, there are some tasks that you have to attend to beforehand, as in the following steps:

1. Check the client-side database for design anomalies that will hinder performance or operation in a server environment.

2. Create the ODBC data source.

3. Set up and configure the ODBC data source.

4. Confirm that you have security access to the ODBC data source.

The following sections cover all these topics.

Client Side Checks

As mentioned in Chapter 17, "Transitioning to Another Back-End DBMS," when upsizing you should have time, tools, and target database knowledge at your disposal. The time is needed mainly for evaluating the current Access database, developing an upsizing plan, and debugging the upsized application.

The following short sections provide some tips for your client application, so that it performs best in the soon-to-be client/server environment.

Don't Load Data on Opening Data Entry Forms. Design data entry forms so that they do not load data on opening, which generates an immense amount of network traffic. In form design mode, on the Data Tab, use the following settings (see fig. 18.1):

- Allow Edits = Yes
- Allow Deletions = Yes
- Allow Additions = Yes
- Data Entry = Yes
- Recordset Type = Dynaset
- Record Locks = EditedRecord

Add a command button for editing data, which then populates the form from the ODBC tables.

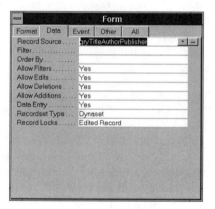

Fig. 18.1

Setting up a form so that it opens in data entry mode.

Use Snapshot Recordsets for Viewing Data. When using forms for viewing data (no updating of ODBC tables is required) use snapshot recordsets. In form design mode, on the Data Tab, use the following settings:

- Allow Edits = No
- Allow Deletions = No
- Allow Additions = No
- Data Entry = No
- Recordset Type = Snapshot
- Record Locks = NoLocks

Add a command button for editing data, which should reset the Data Tab parameters to allow for data edits, and then reload the form.

V

Upgrading the Application

Copy Reference Tables to the Clients. If the lists that populate combo boxes are fairly static, place a copy of these "reference tables" on each local client computer, and index appropriately. Retrieve snapshots, not dynasets, into the combo box. If you have given the user the ability to dynamically update the reference lists from the combo box on the form, remove it, and then replace it with a maintenance menu for updating the ODBC server copy of these reference lists.

Refresh Reference Tables at Startup. In conjunction with the previous point, code a procedure for the clients that, at application startup, causes a refresh of all the client copies of the reference tables from the ODBC server copy. You may want to extend this refresh capability to the client maintenance menu and give users a means of refreshing their copy of a newly updated reference table. If your ODBC data source supports cross-platform replication, make the client reference tables replicates, and refreshing (updating) the client copies of the reference tables can be done on a timed schedule.

Create Temporary Tables to Store Data. If the application is a decision support system that compares multiple sets of the same data, create a set of local "temporary" tables to store the data returned by the server. Data compare and contrast then can be done quickly with far less load on the network. Give users the ability to "Read New"— to read a fresh copy of data from the server. Your code should first check for the existence of the primary key value being returned; if present in the local "temp" table, then SQL update, otherwise SQL insert.

Follow ODBC Naming Rules. Check for conformance to ODBC object naming rules. Depending on which ODBC target you are migrating to, your table and column names may be restricted to as few as 12 alphanumeric characters. Special characters usually are not allowed. For user objects (tables, views, columns, and so on), the first character usually must be a letter or number—system object naming conventions vary with each ODBC target, so check your systems manual. Some ODBC targets allow a few special characters, such as the underscore character (_), the pound sign (#), and the dollar sign ($) but again, check your target environment rules. Spaces are not allowed in almost any ODBC environment.

Case Consistency. Check for inconsistencies in use of uppercase and lowercase when naming database objects in the Access environment. Although Access is not case-sensitive, your target ODBC server may be.

Object Names that Will Not Convert. Scan all Access objects for violations of the ODBC server naming conventions. Use *SPEED* Ferret (evaluation copy included on this book's companion CD-ROM) to find and replace instances of object names that will not convert, both on the data.MDB and on the client.MDB. Alternatively, you can build alias queries to map the new table and column names to the old, supposedly (according to Microsoft technical support) without encountering additional overhead or performance degradation. Following corrections, test thoroughly in the Access environment before converting the data.MDB.

> **Note**
>
> The authors simply don't see how you can add an additional layer of operation (the translation of the name), and not suffer some degradation, however slight. It takes extra machine cycles to translate from the alias name to the real name. Microsoft tends to brush these kinds of "crumbs" under the rug. I suspect that there is a minor performance hit, maybe not enough to even notice, possibly tied to how many name translations you have to do in an application. When the authors (Mount Vernon Data Systems) do conversions, our Access naming conventions map directly to the target environment, or we make the changes by using *SPEED* Ferret, so that we don't have to alias.

Find Access Items that Do Not Convert to the ODBC Environment. There are many objects, methods, and techniques used in Access with no counterpart in an ODBC environment. The following short list is based on previous versions of Access and Microsoft SQL Server. Check the documentation that will accompany the Upsizing Tools for Access 95; you may find more idiosyncratic and proprietary things that do not convert. Additionally, know your target ODBC database, what it supports, and what it doesn't.

- The following Access data access objects are not supported by Microsoft SQL Server:

    Container

    Document

    Index

    QueryDef

    Relation

- The following Access methods are not supported by Microsoft SQL Server:

CompactDatabase	ListTables
CreateDatabase	OpenQueryDef
CreateField	OpenTable
CreateQueryDef	RepairDatabase
DeleteQueryDef	Seek
ListParameters	SetDefaultWorkspace

- Nested transactions are not supported by the majority of ODBC environments, even though the technique is used within the Access 95 environment. If your Access objects contain code with nested transactions, only the outermost transaction is sent to the server. The inner transactions are ignored, and no error message will be returned to Access.

> **Caution**
>
> This situation can endanger data integrity in that some updates (the ones associated with the outer transaction) will be made while other, related updates (associated with the inner transaction(s)) will never execute. With no error message to warn of this problem, this situation could go undetected for some time.

■ Code that uses nested transactions needs to be revised to "flatten" the operation.

■ Default and counter value behavior may change after the client application is connected to the ODBC data source. In a homogeneous Access environment, default and counter values appear as soon as you begin to edit a new record. Microsoft SQL Server defaults and counter values generated by insert triggers appear only after a record is inserted. Other ODBC environments may behave in either way; you need to check to ensure which behavior to expect. Any situation that depends on having default or counter values before the record is committed must be revised for conversion to Microsoft SQL Server.

■ Validation rules attached to Access columns are checked when the user tabs out of a text box on a form. When the same form is attached to some ODBC data sources, the triggers and rules will not fire until the user tries to leave the record. Modifications may be needed.

Avoid Direct Server Access. Don't use "direct" server access (opening remote data sources and directly executing queries against them). Rather, attach the tables (Access will build local indexes on attached ODBC for faster query resolution), or use SQL pass-through queries.

Check Record Locks Property. Record locking on ODBC tables is handled by the ODBC data source. Scan through your application, make sure that all instances of the RecordLocks property are set to either NoLocks or EditedRecord. When accessing ODBC data sources, EditedRecord is treated as NoLocks. The setting AllRecords, which will open a dynaset in exclusive mode, is illegal in an ODBC environment and generates an error message.

Use Filters or Queries Rather Than *Find* Method. Be cautious on how you use the **Find** method against very large ODBC tables. It was optimized to work well against local (Access) tables of any size and against ODBC datasets of limited size. When operating against ODBC tables of many thousands of records you can get better performance by using a filter or query rather than the **Find** method.

Process Queries at the ODBC Server. Make sure that queries are sent to the ODBC server for processing. The Access Jet will try to send an entire query to the server for remote processing, but if clauses or expressions in the query are not consistent with the ODBC server's brand of SQL, at least part of the query will have to be evaluated locally. Some of the statements, functions, and techniques that are not universally supported outside of Access are as follows:

■ Operations that cannot be expressed in a single remote server SQL statement. If you have an Access 95 query that uses another query as input or if a Totals query or Distinct query is embedded in the FROM clause, the query will be processed locally. Try rewriting your query to calculate totals or find distinct instances after all other operations.

■ Jet-specific extensions to the SQL language are not *remoteable*—they are not recognized by other database SQL dialects, and therefore must be processed locally. Crosstab query operations, TOP queries, and reports with multiple levels of grouping and totals may cause the ODBC server to ship data to the local node for processing.

■ The financial functions and statistical aggregations of Access have no server equivalents.

■ User-defined Visual Basic functions that use remote column values as arguments are processed locally.

■ Access has tremendous flexibility with data types, allowing violation of the concept of *union-compatibility* (see Chapter 4, "Getting By in SQL '92—Structured Query Language"), which is adhered to by most, if not all, ODBC servers. Access, for example, allows mixing of data types when two columns are unioned together. Use explicit conversion functions when mixing text and number data types in Access operators or UNION queries if data type leniency isn't a feature of the ODBC server environment.

When a DBMS does allow dynamic casting of data types, the performance is terrible. It's good practice to explicitly control this situation.

■ *Heterogeneous joins* between local tables and remote tables (also known as *cross-database joins*) may be resolved locally, causing the entire remote table to be shipped across the wire to the local node.

■ *Non-remoteable expressions* will cause local query resolution. A non-remoteable expression cannot be resolved by your ODBC server. Unsupported output expressions in the Access SQL SELECT clause will not force local evaluation unless these expressions occur in a Totals query, a Distinct query, or a Union query. Non-remoteable or unsupported expressions in other clauses of the Access SQL statement—the WHERE clause, the ORDER BY clause, the GROUP BY or HAVING clauses—forces at least partial local query evaluation.

■ *Outer joins*, or certain types of outer joins supported by Access SQL, may not be valid in your ODBC server environment, and thus would be processed locally. The Jet will not send multiple outer joins to a server.

■ Certain numeric, string, and date-time functions (Log, Mid$, and DatePart, respectively) are not remoteable and cause at least part of the query to be processed locally.

■ Conversion functions such as CInt, CStr, and CVDate are not remoteable and cause at least part of a query to be processed locally.

Back Up the Database. Make a backup of the Access database that you are planning to upsize and store it in a safe place!

Creating and Configuring the ODBC Database

Unless you have an ODBC database administrator on staff, you have to assume the tasks of creating and configuring an ODBC database. Fortunately, with either Microsoft SQL Server 4.2 or 6.5, the initial creation of a database is not difficult.

The authors are creating two Microsoft SQL Server databases here. The first database is Advisor42; it is a SQL Server version 4.2 database. The second is Advisor65, a SQL Server version 6.5 database. They both will be used as target servers for the conversions that we will be doing throughout this chapter.

For Microsoft SQL Server 4.2, take these steps:

1. Start the SQL Server database (SQL Service Manager, Start, Continue).

2. Open SQL Administrator. From the top menu, select Manage, Database, and finally Create Database.

3. Give the database a name, select the device (Master by default, and which we chose to use for the tiny example conversion), select the log device (also Master by default). Set the maximum size for the database and the log file (see fig. 18.2). Click OK. See server side suggestions in a following section of this chapter for more information on how to accurately size a conversion.

4. When the SQL Administrator asks for verification to create a database, click OK (see fig. 18.3).

Fig. 18.2

SQL Administrator 4.2, showing the Create Database dialog box.

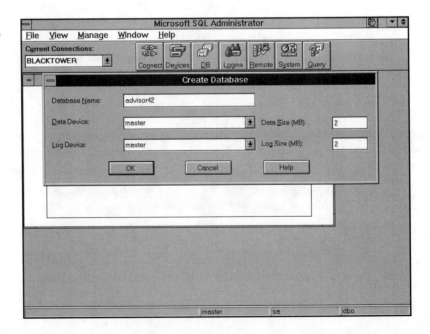

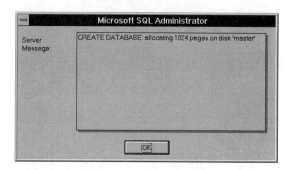

Fig. 18.3

SQL Administrator 4.2, creating database Advisor42.

For Microsoft SQL Server 6.5:

1. Start SQL Server 6.5.

2. Open the SQL Enterprise Manager, select Manage, Databases from the top menu to open the Manage Databases window.

3. Create a new database by clicking the leftmost icon in the upper left corner of the window (see fig. 18.4). When the New Database dialog box appears, fill in the new database Name and both Data and Log Devices (see fig. 18.5). Size it accordingly, as described in the following section.

4. Click Create Now. The new database appears in the list of databases in the Manage Databases window (see fig. 18.6).

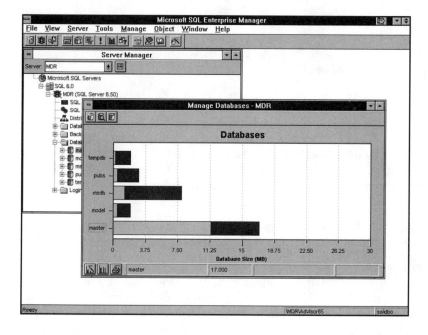

Fig. 18.4

Microsoft SQL Server 6.5 Manage Databases dialog box.

V

Upgrading the Application

Fig. 18.5

SQL Server 6.5, creating the new Advisor65 database.

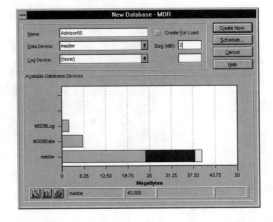

Fig. 18.6

The SQL Server 6.5 Advisor65 database.

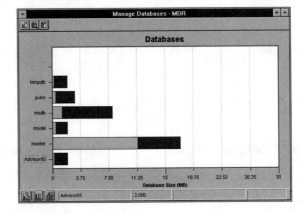

How to Size Your ODBC Database

Each ODBC server will have a different method of configuring itself physically, but the general rule is, for each megabyte of Access database you are migrating, reserve 2 megabytes of space for the ODBC database. Access stores all rules and assertions at the engine level, as properties of the table or column objects. Almost all ODBC databases store rules and assertions as programmed procedures or triggers that are bound to a table or column.

By preallocating twice the space taken for an Access database on the ODBC server, you should have plenty of room for the upgrade and for future growth.

In the Microsoft SQL Server world, there are databases and there are devices. A SQL device contains SQL Server databases and log files. At the lowest level, a device is a physical file that is created by SQL Server for future use—preallocating space on the hard disk. The SQL Server 4.2 device cannot be increased without a total rebuild; the SQL Server 6.x device can be increased simply by resizing it, either through the graphical SQL Server Manager, Edit Database Devices screen, or by using the following DISK RESIZE command:

```
DISK RESIZE
NAME = 'Logical_Device_Name'
SIZE = device_final_size
```

The caveat is that the physical hard drive(s) the device resides on must have enough free space to accommodate the requested increase, or the operation returns an error message. Device size is specified in 2K pages, regardless of the page size of the operating system.

A SQL Server database lives in a SQL Server device, and this database should be twice the size of the Access database, at least for the test phase of the upgrade. If you expect a great deal of growth in your database (a lot of records added in the near future), allocate three to four times the ODBC space as was the original size of the Access database.

For more information on SQL Server Administration, consult one of the two following references:

- *The Guide to SQL Server, Second Edition: Version 4.2 and SQL Server NT*, Aloke Nath, Addison-Wesley, 1995, ISBN 0-201-62631-4.
- *Microsoft SQL Server DBA Survival Guide*, Orryn Sledge & Mark Spenik, Sams Publishing, 1996, ISBN 0-672-30797-9.

Register Your New ODBC Data Source

It isn't enough to simply create a database to receive the tables from Access, you also have to register it as an ODBC data source. Registering is not done in the Microsoft SQL Server environment, this process is handled through the Windows NT Control Panel, ODBC icon.

If you are simply testing the migration procedure and will be adding some tables to an established database, such as SQL Server Master or Pubs, when you open the ODBC drivers dialog box, they may already be listed. The Microsoft SQL Server installation inserts the standard databases provided with its installation into the NT Control Panel as ODBC data sources.

To make sure that the ODBC data source you want to use is registered, follow these steps:

1. Open the Windows NT Control Panel and double-click the ODBC icon to bring up the list of ODBC drivers (Data Sources).

2. If the ODBC data source (the new SQL Server database that you just created) isn't in the list of drivers, click Add.

3. From the Add Data Source dialog box, in the list of Installed ODBC Drivers, highlight SQL Server and click OK.

4. In the ODBC SQL Server Setup dialog box, enter the Data Source <u>N</u>ame (the name of the new database you just created), a <u>D</u>escription (free-form commentary), select a <u>S</u>erver, enter a Network <u>A</u>ddress and Network <u>L</u>ibrary if appropriate, and click the <u>O</u>ptions button to add Login information (see fig. 18.7). Click OK.

The new database Advisor42 is now registered as an ODBC data source (see fig. 18.8).

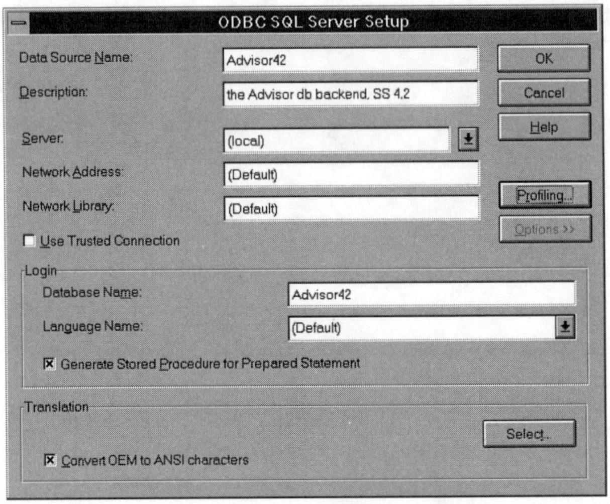

Fig. 18.7

The ODBC SQL Server setup dialog box, registering Advisor42 as an ODBC data source.

Fig. 18.8

Advisor42 in the list of ODBC Data Sources.

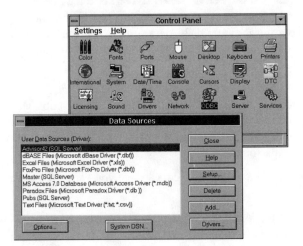

Confirm Security Access to the ODBC Database

You need to ensure that you have adequate permissions on the ODBC server that you are targeting. You need the ability to create tables and indexes, perhaps to create views (depending on your application), and create triggers, assertions, rules, or anything else your ODBC server uses to support referential and business integrity as defined by Access.

Chapter 19, "System Administration," contains a thorough discussion on setting up security in the operating system and the database environments, specifically security in Microsoft SQL Server 6.5. The instructions for SQL Server 6.5 essentially are those for preceding versions of SQL Server (4.2).

Access Export Facility

At the time of this writing, neither the Upsizing Tools for Access 95 nor the individual CASE tool vendors were ready for market with support for Access 95. If you are faced with the prospect of migrating an Access 95 application to an ODBC server, you have to use the Access Export facility (unless your ODBC server has other migration tools specific to its environment).

The argument in favor of using Export is that it works on any version of Access, and exports table structure and data to any ODBC server. Remember, you must have purchased a license for the target ODBC driver if the driver didn't come as part of the database package, and have loaded it as an ODBC data source in the Windows NT environment.

The argument(s) against using the Export facility is that indexes, referential and business integrity rules, and default values are not exported with the table, and will need to be re-created on the ODBC server. If permissions vary for different users of the Access database, these permissions also must be reestablished on the ODBC server. Finally, when using Export only one table at a time can be processed, which—with a large database—may mean a lengthy procedure to convert the entire database.

Besides making a backup of the Access database before beginning migration, you may want to print out a full, comprehensive report from the Access Database Documentor, just so you don't forget anything in the conversion. Plus, it makes a reasonably good checklist during the migration process.

We chose to illustrate the process of exporting a table from Access 95 to Microsoft SQL Server 4.2 by using a small Access 95 database, AdvData7.MDB, which is the data.MDB portion of a small database named Advisor7. This database is used to record the location of articles from periodicals. Both AdvData7.MDB and Advisor7.MDB are included on the companion CD-ROM, so you can follow along with this procedure.

To export a table from Access 95 to Microsoft SQL Server 4.2, follow these steps:

1. Open the Access database from which you want to export tables (AdvData7.MDB).

2. Make sure that you're in the table container, and then highlight the table you want to export (`tblMyRefs`).

3. From the top menu select <u>F</u>ile and Save <u>A</u>s/Export.

   4. In the Save As dialog box, make sure that you Save Table **tblMyRefs** To an <u>e</u>xter-
   nal File or Database, click OK (see fig. 18.9).

Fig. 18.9

*Access 95 database
Advisor7, exporting
tblMyRefs and saving it to
an external database.*

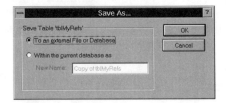

   5. In the Save Table "tblMyRefs" In... dialog box, from the bottom combo box
   (Save as Type) select ODBC Database( ).

   6. From the Export dialog box, Export "tblMyRefs" to **tblMyRefs** in the ODBC
   database, press OK (see fig. 18.10). Keep the same table name in the ODBC database as you had in the Access database.

Fig. 18.10

*Access 95 tblMyRefs, the
Export dialog box, saving
the table in an ODBC
database.*

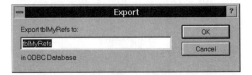

   7. From the SQL Data Sources dialog box, highlight the target ODBC database (use
   either Advisor42 or Advisor65, depending on your circumstances), and then
   press OK (see fig. 18.11).

Fig. 18.11

*The SQL Data Sources for
export, Advisor42 is the
target ODBC database.*

   8. At this point, if you have to log on to your ODBC server, you are prompted to
   do so. After you are authenticated on the ODBC server, the export will execute.

   9. After the export is finished, you can check the results one of two ways—from
   the ODBC server's interactive SQL prompt (ISQL in Microsoft SQL Server, see
   fig. 18.12) or by linking to the ODBC server and tblMyRefs from Access.

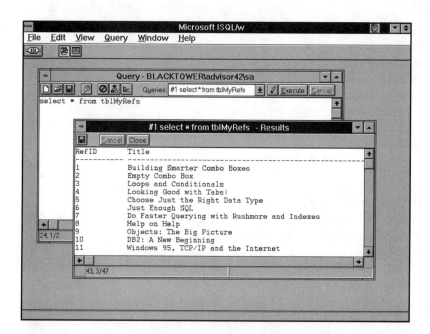

Fig. 18.12

*SQL Server ISQL 4.2, select
* from tblMyRefs.*

V

Upgrading the Application

Tip

If you followed the steps to export a table to Microsoft SQL Server and the table exported, but to a database different from the one you indicated, make sure that you are exporting to the default database.

In the SQL Server 4.2 Administrator (the SQL Enterprise Manager for 6.5), select Manage, Logins or, if you don't have authority to do so, have your database administrator do it for you. For your login, set the default database to the target database you are exporting to.

Adding Server-Based Integrity Constraints

The Access Database Documentor report that you generated previously now will come in handy for re-creating the multiple types of integrity rules that you established with your Access application.

From the inception of Access 2.0, there has been support for declarative referential integrity, which is built into the Jet engine, using SQL-92 reserved words such as PRIMARY KEY, FOREIGN KEY, CONSTRAINT, and REFERENCES to enforce the various integrities. Prior to 2.0, you would have had to create macros or write code in Access Basic to enforce referential integrity (cascade update and cascade delete, for example).

In a relational database management system environment, integrity rules (primary, domain, referential, and business or user) should be enforced by the database (at the engine or table level), not by application code. Chapter 6, "Establishing the Ground Rules," discusses this theme at length.

Client/server relational database management systems that do not support integrity enforcement at the engine level require coding of triggers to provide integrity features. A *trigger* is a rule, an assertion, a snippet of code, which is bound or attached to a table or a column of a table, and is activated or "triggered" as a result of some action (update, insert, delete) taken against the table or column. The general syntax of a trigger in the Microsoft SQL Server dialect is as follows:

```
CREATE TRIGGER [owner.]trigger_name
    ON [owner.]table_name
    [FOR {INSERT ¦ UPDATE ¦ DELETE }] AS
    sql statement
```

Enforcing Primary Integrity

Primary integrity enforcement is made possible in any relational database environment through the implementation of a primary key (see Chapter 6). In the ODBC environment primary keys can be established in one of (at least) two ways—by assigning one column of a table the PRIMARY KEY property at **create table** or **alter table** time or by creating a unique clustered index.

Later in this chapter, the section on Upsizing, Primary Key, and Index Migration explains how the Microsoft Upsizing Tool carries forward primary keys from Access into the Microsoft SQL Server 4.2 environment. Generally, for any target server environment you need to add all indexes to the server tables, using the attributes (Primary Key, No Duplicates, No Nulls) identical to those listed in the Access data dictionary report.

The counter data type in Access doesn't map directly to most server databases, in that few remote database management systems have an automatically incrementing counter that assigns unique values to the primary key column. This functionality can be emulated by triggers or other mechanisms (a special counter table). In the Microsoft SQL Server 4.2 environment, the Transact-SQL code to create an equivalent to the Access counter looks like the following:

```
CREATE TRIGGER Itrig_add_RefID ON dbo.tblMyRefs
FOR INSERT AS
UPDATE dbo.tblMyRefs
SET inserted.RefID = (SELECT MAX(RefID) from dbo.tblMyRefs) + 1
WHERE dbo.tblMyRefs.RefID IS NULL
```

The behavior of a server-generated "counter" will be unlike the Access counter field. Where in Access the counter field value appears at the start of a record edit, the server-generated counter value does not appear until after the new record is saved to the database. You may have to modify your client-side application to accommodate this change.

Enforcing Domain and Referential Integrity

Domain integrity enforcement is done through the export facility of Access, in that Access will try to map its data types to the data types of the target server. You must know the target server data types and be prepared to intervene if the export facility does not get it quite right.

Referential integrity enforcement will be done through declarative constraints, triggers, or a combination of the two techniques. You must understand the target server environment to know how it will handle referential integrity. In this chapter the section on Upsizing, Relationship Migration, explains how the Microsoft Upsizing Tool carries forward relationships from Access into the Microsoft SQL Server 4.2 environment. Generally, for any target server environment, you need to be prepared to intervene with triggers and stored procedures to emulate the full functionality provided by Access, especially the cascade update and cascade delete operations. The client-side Jet will not be aware of any of the server-stored procedures, but if the client application violates any rules, an error message is returned from the server.

Default Values, the Required Property

Most remote server environments support a default constraint so that you can set a default value for a column. The following default constraint adds a default value of (000) 000-0000 for each new author's phone number in the Microsoft SQL Server Pubs database:

```
ALTER TABLE authors
    ADD DEFAULT '(000) 000-0000' FOR phone
```

If your target environment doesn't, you need to write triggers to emulate the Access functionality.

All relational database management systems support the concept of NULL. NULL can be used to emulate the Required property of Access:

```
CREATE TABLE refKeyword
    (Keyword      varchar(30) NOT NULL)
```

If your target database management system isn't relational and doesn't support NULL, you will have to write stored procedures that take into account the various conditions and situations, and then handle them accordingly. The authors suggest that it isn't realistic to port an Access data.MDB to a non-relational server.

Attaching to the Server Tables

When the server tables are ready, or at least ready to be tested, you can *attach* the tables to your Access client application. Attaching, or linking a table, creates a reference to the remote table and saves it within the client Jet. The reference is a record of the remote table structure, and greatly enhances performance between the Access client and the remote server. Additionally, a database designer can build queries, forms, and reports from Access as if the attached tables were Access tables.

Following the attachment, relationships between tables need to be reestablished by using the Relationships Window.

Attached server tables can be accessed through Access table design mode in the same manner that attached Access tables can be accessed. In design mode, the **Format**, **InputMask**, and **Caption** properties can be modified. All other properties are read-only.

Upsizing Tools

Microsoft has provided developers with an Upsizing Tool for converting Access 2 databases to Microsoft SQL Server 4.2. At the time of writing, Microsoft was in the process of developing a similar tool for the Access 95 to Microsoft SQL Server 6 migration. According to sources at Microsoft, however, these are the only tools they intend to provide.

If you will be migrating from Access 2 to Microsoft SQL Server 6, you may want to first convert the Access 2 database to an Access 95 database, debug it in this environment, and then use the new Upsizing Tool (when it is available) to convert the Access 95 database to Microsoft SQL Server 6. If you will migrate Access 95 to Microsoft SQL Server 4.2, you may want to investigate using some CASE assist (see the following section).

If you are working in the environment supported by the currently available Microsoft Upsizing Tools, you can save yourself a lot of time and headache by taking advantage of them. These tools generally are available through one of the developer distribution channels, either the TechNet or the DevNet CD-ROM. Check with your local Microsoft office for more information on current availability.

Using the Upsizing Wizard

You can quickly walk through upsizing an Access 2 copy of the Advisor database to Microsoft SQL Server 4.2, the only environment set that the current Upsizing Tool supports. You start the upsizing process by taking the following steps:

1. Open the Access database that contains the tables you want to upsize. If your Access application is in two parts, the data.MDB and the client.MDB, then open the data.MDB for upsizing.

2. From the top menu, select File, Add-Ins, Upsizing Wizard (see fig. 18.13).

3. Choose to upsize to an existing database, or take this opportunity to create a new target database for the upsize (see fig. 18.14).

   While Microsoft SQL Server does allow you to create devices and databases on multiple disks, the Upsizing Wizard will create them on only one physical disk—only on the disk on which the Master database device resides. The primary rule of good database administration is that you always place the physical database and the transaction log file on separate physical devices. So, you may want to first build your devices and databases, and then start the Upsizing Wizard.

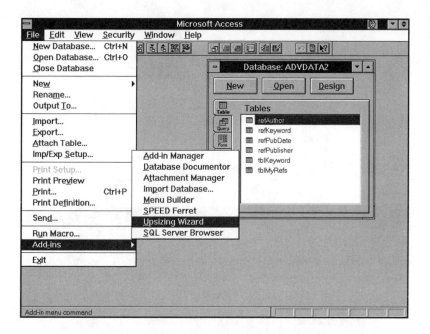

Fig. 18.13

From the File and Add-In menus, select the Upsizing Wizard to begin the upsizing process.

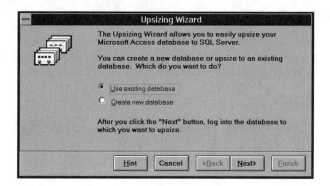

Fig. 18.14

Use an existing database or create a new database as the target for the upsize process.

4. If you choose to upsize to an existing database, select the database name from the list of SQL Data Sources presented (see fig. 18.15), and log in on the next screen.

Fig. 18.15

*Pick an existing SQL Data
Source as the target
database.*

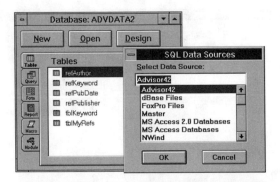

> ### Tip
>
> If the target database that you want to upsize to doesn't appear in the SQL Data Sources
> list, and *it is present* in the Control Panel list of ODBC sources, then check one other
> place. In the Access 2 program group, there should be an icon for ODBC Administrator,
> which points to an executable in the Windows library, named ODBCADM.EXE. This
> second list of SQL Data Sources, apparently, is the one used by Access, so you also
> should add the target database to this list.
>
> It doesn't appear that Access 95 has a second ODBC Data Source listing, which is sepa-
> rate and distinct from the listing on Control Panel, so you shouldn't have this problem
> when the Upsizing Tool for Access 95 is released.

5. Using standard Access Wizard dialog box methodology, select table or tables
that you want to upsize (see fig. 18.16).

Fig. 18.16

*Select which tables from
the Access database to
upsize.*

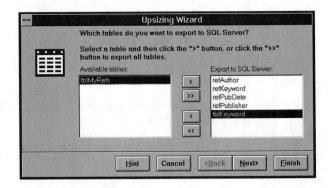

6. Select the desired upsizing options from the Wizard's dialog box (see fig. 18.17).
The options are described in the following sections.

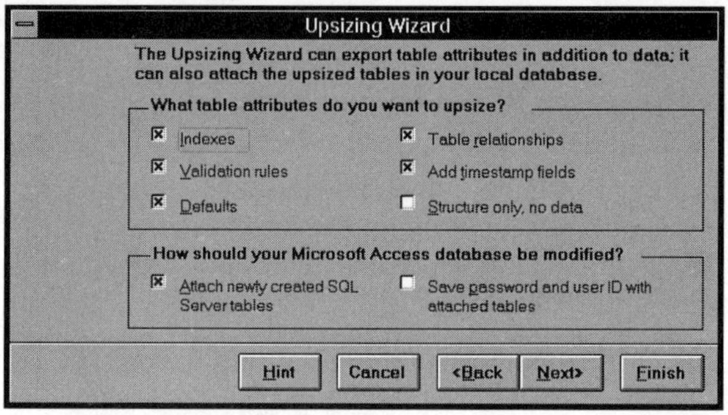

Fig. 18.17

Select the export and upsizing options from the Upsizing Wizard dialog box.

Choosing Upsizing Options. You can choose from the following options in the Upsizing Wizard dialog box:

- The attributes Indexes, Validation Rules, Defaults, and Table Relationship are all turned on and by default are included in the upsize operation. The authors suggest you go with the defaults, at least for the first upsize operation. We discuss each more fully a bit later in this chapter.

- By default the Add Timestamp Fields will be checked. The Upsizing Wizard adds a new column with a SQL Server timestamp data type to each Access export table that contains either single, double, memo, or OLE data types. Microsoft SQL Server uses this timestamp column as a write timestamp for updated rows in the SQL Server table. Access then can check the value of the write timestamp when determining if a remote row needs to be updated. In the absence of the timestamp column Access must do a record scan and compare to make the determination whether or not to update, causing a significant negative impact on performance.

- By default, the Attach Newly Created SQL Server Tables option will be turned on. This feature is very nice if your Access application is an all-in-one, with both data and client application bundled together. However, if you are upsizing a data.MDB, then take the following steps:

  1. Upsize the data.MDB as instructed, using the Attach Newly Created SQL Server Tables option.

  2. After upsizing is complete, open the client.MDB in Access.

  3. From the table container, delete any attachments to the back-end data.MDB file.

  4. Select File, Add-Ins, Import Database.

5. From the File Open dialog box, select the data.MDB you just upsized, click OK. This action imports everything, including the attached SQL Server tables, the local Access table, and any alias queries that were built during the upsize process.

6. Delete from the client.MDB file all extraneous objects that aren't needed. To delete the local tables (duplicates of the upsized Access tables from the data.MDB file), you may have to go into the relationship editor and delete the relationships from the client.MDB.

■ Alias queries handle the inconsistencies in naming conventions between Access and Microsoft SQL Server. The Upsizing Wizard automatically replaces spaces and illegal characters in a table or a column name with an underscore (_). If a name was changed when the table was exported, the attached SQL Server table gets the name *tablename_remote*, and then creates an alias query that has the original *tablename*. Access tables are not deleted following export, they are simply renamed, *tablename_local*. According to Microsoft technical support, there is little if any performance penalty when using an alias query.

■ By default, the Save Password and User ID with Attached Tables is turned off, and the authors recommend that you follow the default suggestion. If this option is checked for the upsizing process, users can store their passwords locally, eliminating the need to log on to Microsoft SQL Server, but also leaving access to the server database wide open from any unattended client application.

Completing the Upsizing Process. Have the Upsizing Wizard generate an upsizing report (see fig. 18.18). This is excellent documentation for what will happen during the process.

Preview the Upsizing Report after the upsize process is complete (see fig. 18.19). All modifications that need to be made will have to be made to the copy of the tables that now resides on the remote server.

Fig. 18.18

Generate the upsize report as documentation of what happened during the upsizing process.

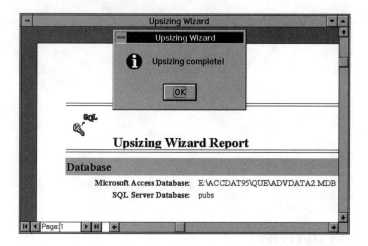

Fig. 18.19

Finished, and the upsize report waits for preview!

View the table container (see fig. 18.20). The original Access tables were renamed *tablename*_local, and an attachment was established from the native Access tables to the remote Microsoft SQL Server tables.

All tables that have invalid column names or, for any other reason cannot be named the same as the original Access table, will have a corresponding alias query, which remaps valid column and table names to the invalid ones (see fig. 18.21).

Fig. 18.20

The Access table container, with local tables renamed and the remote server tables attached.

Fig. 18.21

The alias query, which maps illegal column and table names to names that are valid for the remote server.

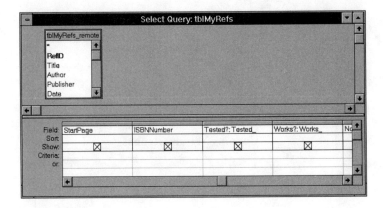

Object Mapping Overview

When the Upsizing Wizard migrates an Access database to Microsoft SQL Server, it creates SQL Server objects that, as much as possible, do everything that the Access source objects did. However, the differences between Access and Microsoft SQL Server make a completely 1:1 mapping unrealistic.

Access databases, tables, columns, default values, and indexes will map 1:1 to Microsoft SQL Server databases, tables, columns, default values, and indexes.

Access validation rules and referential integrity are part of the data dictionary and are enforced at the engine level. Microsoft SQL Server 4.2 validation rules and referential integrity aren't part of the data dictionary and are enforced through code bound to a table. Beginning with SQL Server 6.0, referential integrity is enforced through the use of the REFERENCE constraint, from the engine level. The authors can only make the assumption that the new Upsizing Tool for Access 95 will be able to map referential integrity between Access 95 and SQL Server 6.x in a 1:1 configuration.

Some of the Access data dictionary cannot be directly converted to SQL Server data dictionary entries and must, therefore, be enabled through the use of triggers. We discuss triggers in a few pages.

Database and Table Migration

An Access .MDB file maps directly to a Microsoft SQL Server database. An Access table, without part of its data dictionary content (depending on which version of Microsoft SQL Server you are migrating to), will map to a SQL Server table.

If an Access database or table object uses a SQL Server-reserved word, the Upsizing Wizard will supplement the object name with an underscore (_), so that GROUP becomes GROUP_. The Wizard then creates an alias query in Access to accommodate the naming inconsistencies.

If you selected the Attach Newly Created SQL Server Tables option when upsizing, according to the documentation, columns in the remote tables should inherit the following properties from the original Access columns:

- The description (the authors found that this attribute does not carry across)
- The caption (for labeling on forms and reports—the authors have found that this attribute does not carry across)
- The format
- Any input mask built for the Access column
- The number of decimal places indicated for a number field

Primary Key and Index Migration

An Access index is very similar to a Microsoft SQL Server index. The Upsizing Wizard will convert Access primary keys to SQL Server 4.2 and build clustered, unique indexes that are always named *aaaaa_PrimaryKey*.

When Access attaches a remote table, it looks for the first in an alphabetized list of available indexes from the attached table and assumes that is the primary key. By giving the primary key index such a strange name, the Upsizing Wizard assures that Access chooses the right index. All other Access indexes retain their original name on migration, except where an illegal character is converted to an underscore (_).

Starting with version 6.0, Microsoft SQL Server has introduced the PRIMARY KEY constraint, which you can define at the table level and is enforced by the SQL Server data dictionary. At the time of table creation in SQL Server, a column can be declared PRIMARY KEY. The set of data values contained within the column must be unique, and no NULL is allowed. The Upsizing Wizard for Access 95 probably will take advantage of the PRIMARY KEY constraint, which automatically causes the creation of a system-level, system-administered, unique, clustered index. The naming convention for the PRIMARY KEY constraint, however, may make it necessary for the Access 95 Upsizing Wizard to build its own primary key index.

Relationship Migration

When two Access tables are joined in a relationship, Access automatically creates an index on the foreign key column in the table of the many, and names the index, Reference. Subsequent foreign key indexes built on the same table are named Reference1, Reference2, and so on. These system-generated indexes cannot be accessed by the Access index editor.

As a responsible database designer, you also may have created indexes on the foreign key columns in these same tables, thereby creating a duplicate index within Access. The Upsizing Wizard exports all indexes, user and system-generated, when the Indexes option is selected.

Simply by checking through the Upsizing Report, you can find the duplicate indexes and delete one of the two. Remember, for an OLTP database you want to index wisely but create indexes only where you need them, to minimize multiple update/insert operations for each update/insert command.

With the advent of Microsoft SQL Server 6.0, there is a new constraint named FOREIGN KEY which, like the PRIMARY KEY constraint, is declared at table creation time.

Unlike the PRIMARY KEY constraint, the FOREIGN KEY constraint doesn't automatically cause the creation of a SQL Server index. The presumption is that the Upsizing Wizard for Access 95 will continue to export the Access "Reference" indexes.

Column Migration

Column names and data types are automatically translated from Access into Microsoft SQL Server by the Upsizing Wizard, as shown in Table 18.1.

Table 18.1 Data Type Equivalents for Access 95 and Microsoft SQL Server 6.5	
Access 95 Data Type	**Microsoft SQL Server Data Type**
Yes/No	bit
Number (Byte)	smallint
Number (Integer)	smallint
Number (Long Integer)	int
Number (Single)	real
Number (Double)	float
Currency	money
Date/Time	datetime
AutoNumber	int (4.2), identity (6.x)
Text (n)	varchar(n)
Memo	text
OLE	image

Default Value Migration

Access and Microsoft SQL Server handle default values a little differently, especially in SQL Server 4.2. A SQL Server 4.2 default value is independent of any column in a table. After a default value is created, it can be bound to any number of columns in any number of tables. The Upsizing Wizard tries to create a SQL Server 4.2 default, based on the expression of the default property of the Access column.

SQL Server 4.2 defaults are named according to the table to which they are bound, with a number portion to the name that represents the position of the column in the table. If two or more columns of a table have the same non-zero default value, the Upsizing Wizard creates two defaults that are functionally the same, with different names. All zero default values are defined by the SQL Server 4.2 default named UW_ZeroDefault.

When migrating to SQL Server 4.2, if any exported tables contain counter fields, the UW_ZeroDefault is created by default and is bound to each counter field, whether or not you selected Defaults during the upsize process.

All Access Yes/No data types that do not have a default designated will automatically have a "no" default bound to them, which makes interaction between Access and Microsoft SQL Server much smoother.

If the Access default property contains an Access Basic or Visual Basic for Applications expression or function, the Upsizing Wizard tries to convert the code into Transact-SQL. The Upsizing Report will indicate whether or not the Wizard is successful.

SQL Server 6.x contains a DEFAULT constraint, which allows a default value to be specified for a column at table creation time. The DEFAULT constraint can be created at the column level and is by default bound to the column, not to the data type. One DEFAULT constraint can be specified per column, and a default cannot be specified for an identity data type. The DEFAULT constraint also can be declared at the table level, if a default value for multiple columns is required. System values can be input by using the DEFAULT constraint, values such as USER, CURRENT_USER, SESSION_USER, SYSTEM_USER, and CURRENT_TIMESTAMP.

AutoNumber Data Type Migration

Access counter data types were not supported in SQL Server 4.2, but they do have an equivalent in SQL Server 6.x.—the identity data type.

Counter fields that are upsized to SQL Server 4.2 are converted to SQL Server integer data types, and the Upsizing Wizard creates an INSERT trigger on the column to retain equivalent functionality. The format of the INSERT trigger looks like the following:

```
CREATE TRIGGER Itrig_add_RefID ON dbo.tblMyRefs
FOR INSERT AS
UPDATE dbo.tblMyRefs
SET inserted.RefID = (SELECT MAX(RefID) from dbo.tblMyRefs) + 1
WHERE dbo.tblMyRefs.RefID IS NULL
```

Counter fields that are upsized to SQL Server 6.x probably will be converted to an identity data type, which has built-in functionality equivalent to the Access counter data type.

Validation Rule Migration

Access validation rules map to Microsoft SQL Server through the use of triggers. A trigger is a sequence of Transact-SQL statements, which is bound to a specific table or column and is set off when one of three actions happens: the insert of a row in a table, the update of a row in a table, or the delete of a row in a table.

When upsizing to SQL Server 4.2, the Upsizing Wizard creates triggers for Access validation rules, table relationships, or counter fields. Validation rules and table relationships do not map directly to a single trigger, but each may become part of several triggers, and a single trigger can contain code to emulate the functionality of several validation and referential integrity rules.

Table 18.2 describes the types of triggers created by the Upsizing Wizard. Any trigger may contain code to emulate some or all of the Access functions listed.

V

Upgrading the Application

Table 18.2 SQL Server Triggers and How They Are Implemented in Access 95

Trigger Type	Access Functionality
UPDATE	Validation rules (on column or row, or Required property=Yes), referential integrity enforced
INSERT	Validation rules (on column or row, or Required property=Yes), referential integrity enforced (child table triggers)
DELETE	Referential integrity enforced (parent table triggers)

With the advent of Microsoft SQL Server 6.0, there are new constraints that, when used in conjunction with each other, can support counter fields (see the previous section, "Counter Data Type Migration") and referential integrity. The REFERENCE constraint is used to enforce referential integrity when used in conjunction with the PRIMARY KEY and FOREIGN KEY constraints (see previous section on Relationship Migration). However, cascade update and cascade delete must still be defined by triggers. The assumption is that the Upsizing Wizard for Access 95 will avail itself of these new constraints and the associated interactions to build an emulation of the Access 95 validation rules.

Required Property Migration

The Access column property Required, when set to Yes, does not allow a user to leave the field blank (or NULL) when entering data, if no default value was specified for that column. The Upsizing Wizard generates SQL Server 4.2 code to emulate this functionality.

Rather than use the SQL Server NULL property—which is enforced by the engine—the Wizard builds an UPDATE trigger. You then can allow or disallow NULL by changing the trigger, as in the following code:

```
CREATE TRIGGER tblMyRefs_UTrig ON tblMyRefs FOR UPDATE AS
/* VALIDATION RULE FOR FIELD 'Title' */
IF (SELECT Count(*) FROM inserted WHERE NOT (Title Is Not Null)) > 0
    BEGIN
        RAISERROR 44444 "Please enter a title - required field."
        ROLLBACK TRANSACTION
    END
```

Finishing Up

There are a few things you need to do to ensure that your client/server application runs as planned. The following sections provide a short checklist.

Unique Indexes for Updatability. Any attached table must have a unique index to be updatable from the Access client. Although the Upsizing Wizard will export an existing unique index, it cannot create one. Make sure that all attached tables that your application needs to update have a unique index.

Upsizing Security. The Upsizing Wizard to Microsoft SQL Server 4.2 will not export users, groups, or permissions from the Access security file. You have to reestablish security in the SQL Server environment. See Chapter 19, "System Administration," for a discussion on the SQL Server security model.

Database Logon Permission. If you created a new SQL Server database for the upsizing, this database will be accessible only to system administrators and the database owner. Use the SQL Security Manager to establish new users and groups, or use the SQL system procedures **sp_adduser** and **sp_addgroup** from the ISQL prompt.

Object Permission. All objects upsized by the Upsizing Wizard will be accessible only to the system administrators and the database owner. This limitation is true whether you created a new database for the upsize procedure or exported to an existing database. If you overwrote existing objects, you also overwrote the object permissions. Use the SQL Security Manager to grant permissions on tables and views, or use the SQL commands **GRANT** and **REVOKE** from the ISQL prompt.

Synchronizing Security. Even though Access is not aware of Microsoft SQL Server security, it cannot violate it. If a user tries to insert a record in a SQL Server table for which he or she lacks permission, the insert action will fail and the server returns an error message to the user. Every effort should be made to establish corresponding security profiles on both platforms, to minimize user (and Information Systems group) distress.

If the local user permissions and password match the remote permissions and password, Access to Microsoft SQL Server uses a pass-through security. If the permissions/password are not synchronized, Access prompts the user for a SQL Server logon the first time the user accesses the remote server.

Planning for Success. Make sure that your new server database is fully recoverable. Establish the transaction log on a separate device, on a separate physical hard drive, away from the location of the physical database. Schedule regular backups of both the upsized database and the Master database, to make sure that the new system records that were written during upsizing were captured. Consider and implement fault-tolerant schemes (see Chapter 19, "System Administration") for extra reliability and non-stop availability of your data.

Case Assist

If you used a CASE (Computer-Assisted Software Engineering) tool to assist through the conceptual and logical phases of the database design, your CASE software also may be able to help with the physical implementation.

Many CASE tools have facilities to implement the logical schema (the logical design that should include your table layout—base, reference, and associative tables—and at least primary and foreign key designations). Some CASE tools can reverse-engineer your Access data.MDB into an entity model/logical model, and from there, export the logical scheme to another database platform.

To demonstrate how this works, we use ERwin/ERX, from Logic Works (the ERwin/ERX Quickstart demo is included on this book's companion CD-ROM), and quickly walk through the reverse engineering of the Advisor database. The Advisor database is in its original form, Access 2, and ERwin will generate a SQL script intended for use on Microsoft SQL Server 4.2. At the time of this writing, Logic Works did not have a version available that could accommodate either Access 95 or Microsoft SQL Server 6.x.

The steps to convert an Access database to some other server platform are as follows:

1. Start the CASE software—in this example, ERwin/ERX, and select a new diagram.
2. Select a target server database management system, the one from which you will read in the database for reverse engineering.
3. Synchronize ERwin with the selected database management system. This starts the reverse engineering process (see fig. 18.22).
4. Select a database to read into ERwin for analysis (see fig. 18.23).

Fig. 18.22

Synchronizing ERwin with an Access database in preparation for reverse engineering.

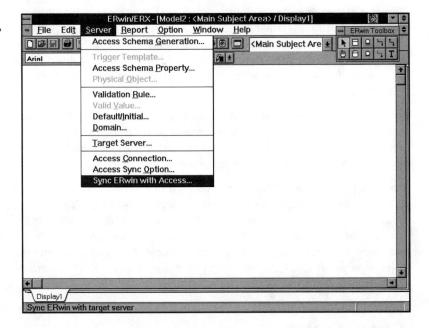

5. Import the table objects from the Access database that will be reverse engineered by the CASE software (see fig. 18.24).
6. Generate an ERM (entity-relationship model) based on the Access tables (see fig. 18.25). At this point in the migration, you can study the prototype (Access) database design and modify it, if appropriate, before exporting to another database platform. You even can use the CASE software to read in the layout of an existing database, edit and correct the design, and then generate a schema to the same platform—using the CASE software to assist on the iterations of the design phase during prototype development.

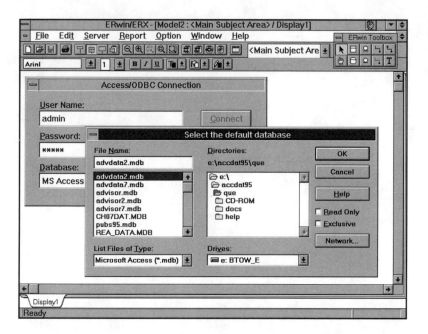

Fig. 18.23

Select an Access database to read into the CASE environment.

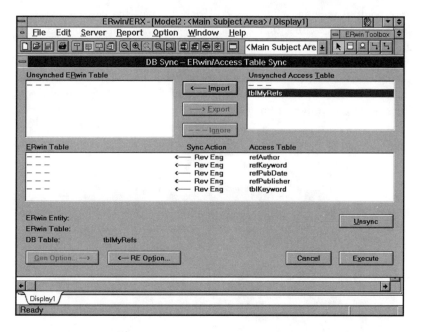

Fig. 18.24

Select the Access table object for import into ERwin.

7. After the ERM is acceptable, again select a target server database management system—only this time, it is one to which you will migrate the original Access database. In this example, we selected Microsoft SQL Server (see fig. 18.26).

Fig. 18.25

The entity-relationship model, created through the reverse engineering process.

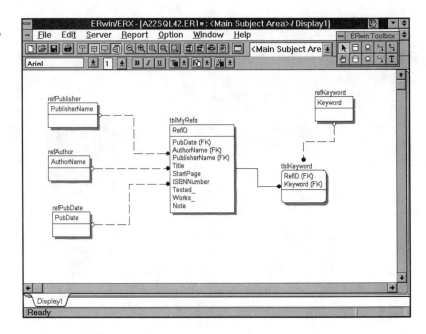

8. Generate the output schema (see fig. 18.27). Each database management system has properties that are peculiar to it, so each schema generation dialog box varies, according to the server selected. Choose the options that will be implemented when the database is built. Then, either generate the schema directly into the recipient database management system or generate a report (paper or electronic) of the SQL script that can later be edited, if necessary, and executed to build the server environment.

Fig. 18.26

Select a target server database environment for schema export.

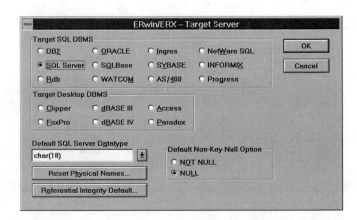

ERwin generated the following code, shown in Listing 18.1, to rebuild the Advisor database in Microsoft SQL Server 4.2. The online version, 18code01.txt, is available on the companion CD-ROM.

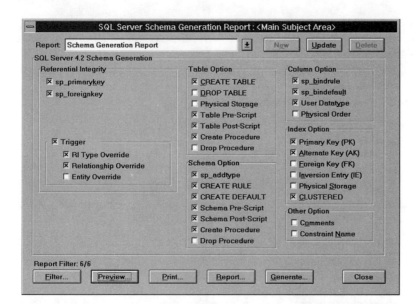

Fig. 18.27

Customize the target environment prior to output, and then generate the schema or print the SQL script for later generation.

Listing 18.1   18code01.txt—Code Generated by ERwin to Build the Advisor Database in a Microsoft SQL Server 4.2 Environment

```
/* the script created by ERWin to convert the Access 2      */
/* data.MDB to a Microsoft SQL Server 4.2 database          */

CREATE TABLE refAuthor
     (AuthorName      varchar(80) NOT NULL)
go

CREATE UNIQUE INDEX PrimaryKey
 ON refAuthor (AuthorName)
go

exec sp_primarykey refAuthor, AuthorName
go

CREATE TABLE refKeyword
     (Keyword      varchar(50) NOT NULL)
go

CREATE UNIQUE INDEX PrimaryKey
 ON refKeyword (Keyword)
go

exec sp_primarykey refKeyword, Keyword
go

CREATE TABLE refPubDate
     (PubDate      datetime NOT NULL)
go
```

(continues)

Listing 18.1 Continued

```
CREATE UNIQUE CLUSTERED INDEX XPKrefPubDate
 ON refPubDate (PubDate)
go

exec sp_primarykey refPubDate, PubDate
go

CREATE TABLE refPublisher
     (PublisherName      varchar(80) NOT NULL)
go

CREATE UNIQUE INDEX PrimaryKey
 ON refPublisher (PublisherName)
go

exec sp_primarykey refPublisher, PublisherName
go

CREATE TABLE tblKeyword
 (RefID          int NOT NULL,
 Keyword varchar(50) NOT NULL)
go

CREATE UNIQUE INDEX PrimaryKey
 ON tblKeyword (RefID, Keyword)
go

exec sp_primarykey tblKeyword, RefID, Keyword
go

CREATE TABLE tblMyRefs
 (RefID int NOT NULL,
 PubDate datetime NULL,
 AuthorName varchar(80) NULL,
 PublisherName varchar(80) NULL,
 Title varchar(80) NOT NULL,
 StartPage varchar(10) NULL,
 ISBNNumber varchar(50) NULL,
 Tested_ bit NOT NULL,
 Works_ bit NOT NULL,
 Note text NULL)
go

CREATE UNIQUE INDEX PrimaryKey
 ON tblMyRefs (RefID)
go

CREATE UNIQUE INDEX Title
 ON tblMyRefs (Title)
go

exec sp_primarykey tblMyRefs, RefID
go

exec sp_foreignkey tblKeyword, refKeyword, Keyword
go
```

```
exec sp_foreignkey tblKeyword, tblMyRefs, RefID
go

exec sp_foreignkey tblMyRefs, refPubDate, PubDate
go

exec sp_foreignkey tblMyRefs, refAuthor, AuthorName
go

exec sp_foreignkey tblMyRefs, refPublisher, PublisherName
go

create trigger tI_tblKeyword on tblKeyword for INSERT as
/* ERwin Builtin Sat Mar 09 14:04:23 1996 */
/* INSERT trigger on tblKeyword */
begin
 declare @numrows int,
 @nullcnt int,
 @validcnt int,
 @errno int,
 @errmsg varchar(255)

 select @numrows = @@rowcount
 /* ERwin Builtin Sat Mar 09 14:04:22 1996 */
 /* refKeyword R/2 tblKeyword ON CHILD INSERT SET NULL */
 if
 /* %ChildFK(" or",update) */
 update(Keyword)
 begin
 update tblKeyword
 set
 /* %SetFK(tblKeyword,NULL) */
 tblKeyword.Keyword = NULL
 from tblKeyword,inserted
 where
 /* %JoinPKPK(tblKeyword,inserted," = "," and") */
 tblKeyword.RefID = inserted.RefID and
 tblKeyword.Keyword = inserted.Keyword and
 not exists (
 select * from refKeyword
 where
 /* %JoinFKPK(inserted,refKeyword," = "," and") */
 inserted.Keyword = refKeyword.Keyword
 )
 end
 /* ERwin Builtin Sat Mar 09 14:04:23 1996 */
 return
error:
 raiserror @errno @errmsg
 rollback transaction
end
go

create trigger tU_tblKeyword on tblKeyword for UPDATE as
/* ERwin Builtin Sat Mar 09 14:04:23 1996 */
/* UPDATE trigger on tblKeyword */
```

(continues)

V

Upgrading the Application

Listing 18.1 Continued

```
begin
 declare @numrows int,
 @nullcnt int,
 @validcnt int,
 @insRefID int,
 @insKeyword varchar(50),
 @errno int,
 @errmsg varchar(255)

 select @numrows = @@rowcount
 /* ERwin Builtin Sat Mar 09 14:04:23 1996 */
 /* refKeyword R/2 tblKeyword ON CHILD UPDATE SET NULL */
 if
 /* %ChildFK(" or",update) */
 update(Keyword)
 begin
 update tblKeyword
 set
 /* %SetFK(tblKeyword,NULL) */
 tblKeyword.Keyword = NULL
 from tblKeyword,inserted
 where
 /* %JoinPKPK(tblKeyword,inserted," = "," and") */
 tblKeyword.RefID = inserted.RefID and
 tblKeyword.Keyword = inserted.Keyword and
 not exists (
 select * from refKeyword
 where
 /* %JoinFKPK(inserted,refKeyword," = "," and") */
 inserted.Keyword = refKeyword.Keyword
 )
 end
 /* ERwin Builtin Sat Mar 09 14:04:23 1996 */
 return
error:
 raiserror @errno @errmsg
 rollback transaction
end
go

create trigger tD_tblMyRefs on tblMyRefs for DELETE as
/* ERwin Builtin Sat Mar 09 14:04:23 1996 */
/* DELETE trigger on tblMyRefs */
begin
 declare @errno int,
 @errmsg varchar(255)
 /* ERwin Builtin Sat Mar 09 14:04:23 1996 */
 /* tblMyRefs R/1 tblKeyword ON PARENT DELETE CASCADE */
 delete tblKeyword
 from tblKeyword,deleted
 where
 /* %JoinFKPK(tblKeyword,deleted," = "," and") */
 tblKeyword.RefID = deleted.RefID
 /* ERwin Builtin Sat Mar 09 14:04:23 1996 */
```

```
 return
error:
 raiserror @errno @errmsg
 rollback transaction
end
go

create trigger tI_tblMyRefs on tblMyRefs for INSERT as
/* ERwin Builtin Sat Mar 09 14:04:24 1996 */
/* INSERT trigger on tblMyRefs */
begin
 declare @numrows int,
 @nullcnt int,
 @validcnt int,
 @errno int,
 @errmsg varchar(255)

 select @numrows = @@rowcount
 /* ERwin Builtin Sat Mar 09 14:04:23 1996 */
 /* refPubDate R/6 tblMyRefs ON CHILD INSERT SET NULL */
 if
 /* %ChildFK(" or",update) */
 update(PubDate)
 begin
 update tblMyRefs
 set
 /* %SetFK(tblMyRefs,NULL) */
 tblMyRefs.PubDate = NULL
 from tblMyRefs,inserted
 where
 /* %JoinPKPK(tblMyRefs,inserted," = "," and") */
 tblMyRefs.RefID = inserted.RefID and
 not exists (
 select * from refPubDate
 where
 /* %JoinFKPK(inserted,refPubDate," = "," and") */
 inserted.PubDate = refPubDate.PubDate
 )
 end
 /* ERwin Builtin Sat Mar 09 14:04:23 1996 */
 /* refAuthor R/4 tblMyRefs ON CHILD INSERT SET NULL */
 if
 /* %ChildFK(" or",update) */
 update(AuthorName)
 begin
 update tblMyRefs
 set
 /* %SetFK(tblMyRefs,NULL) */
 tblMyRefs.AuthorName = NULL
 from tblMyRefs,inserted
 where
 /* %JoinPKPK(tblMyRefs,inserted," = "," and") */
 tblMyRefs.RefID = inserted.RefID and
 not exists (
 select * from refAuthor
 where
```

(continues)

V

Upgrading the Application

Listing 18.1   Continued

```
/* %JoinFKPK(inserted,refAuthor," = "," and") */
inserted.AuthorName = refAuthor.AuthorName
)
end
/* ERwin Builtin Sat Mar 09 14:04:23 1996 */
/* refPublisher R/3 tblMyRefs ON CHILD INSERT SET NULL */
if
/* %ChildFK(" or",update) */
update(PublisherName)
begin
update tblMyRefs
set
/* %SetFK(tblMyRefs,NULL) */
tblMyRefs.PublisherName = NULL
from tblMyRefs,inserted
where
/* %JoinPKPK(tblMyRefs,inserted," = "," and") */
tblMyRefs.RefID = inserted.RefID and
not exists (
select * from refPublisher
where
/* %JoinFKPK(inserted,refPublisher," = "," and") */
inserted.PublisherName = refPublisher.PublisherName
)
end
/* ERwin Builtin Sat Mar 09 14:04:24 1996 */
return
error:
raiserror @errno @errmsg
rollback transaction
end
go

create trigger tU_tblMyRefs on tblMyRefs for UPDATE as
/* ERwin Builtin Sat Mar 09 14:04:24 1996 */
/* UPDATE trigger on tblMyRefs */
begin
declare @numrows int,
@nullcnt int,
@validcnt int,
@insRefID int,
@errno int,
@errmsg varchar(255)

select @numrows = @@rowcount
/* ERwin Builtin Sat Mar 09 14:04:24 1996 */
/* tblMyRefs R/1 tblKeyword ON PARENT UPDATE CASCADE */
if
/* %ParentPK(" or",update) */
update(RefID)
begin
if @numrows = 1
begin
select @insRefID = inserted.RefID
```

```
from inserted
update tblKeyword
set
/* %JoinFKPK(tblKeyword,@ins," = ",",") */
tblKeyword.RefID = @insRefID
from tblKeyword,inserted,deleted
where
/* %JoinFKPK(tblKeyword,deleted," = "," and") */
tblKeyword.RefID = deleted.RefID
end
else
begin
select @errno = 30006,
@errmsg = 'Cannot cascade "tblMyRefs" UPDATE because
➥more than one row has been affected.'
raiserror @errno @errmsg
end
end
/* ERwin Builtin Sat Mar 09 14:04:24 1996 */
/* refPubDate R/6 tblMyRefs ON CHILD UPDATE SET NULL */
if
/* %ChildFK(" or",update) */
update(PubDate)
begin
update tblMyRefs
set
/* %SetFK(tblMyRefs,NULL) */
tblMyRefs.PubDate = NULL
from tblMyRefs,inserted
where
/* %JoinPKPK(tblMyRefs,inserted," = "," and") */
tblMyRefs.RefID = inserted.RefID and
not exists (
select * from refPubDate
where
/* %JoinFKPK(inserted,refPubDate," = "," and") */
inserted.PubDate = refPubDate.PubDate
)
end
/* ERwin Builtin Sat Mar 09 14:04:24 1996 */
/* refAuthor R/4 tblMyRefs ON CHILD UPDATE SET NULL */
if
/* %ChildFK(" or",update) */
update(AuthorName)
begin
update tblMyRefs
set
/* %SetFK(tblMyRefs,NULL) */
tblMyRefs.AuthorName = NULL
from tblMyRefs,inserted
where
/* %JoinPKPK(tblMyRefs,inserted," = "," and") */
tblMyRefs.RefID = inserted.RefID and
not exists (
select * from refAuthor
where
```

V

Upgrading the Application

(continues)

Listing 18.1 Continued

```
/* %JoinFKPK(inserted,refAuthor," = "," and") */
inserted.AuthorName = refAuthor.AuthorName
)
end
/* ERwin Builtin Sat Mar 09 14:04:24 1996 */
/* refPublisher R/3 tblMyRefs ON CHILD UPDATE SET NULL */
if
/* %ChildFK(" or",update) */
update(PublisherName)
begin
update tblMyRefs
set
/* %SetFK(tblMyRefs,NULL) */
tblMyRefs.PublisherName = NULL
from tblMyRefs,inserted
where
/* %JoinPKPK(tblMyRefs,inserted," = "," and") */
tblMyRefs.RefID = inserted.RefID and
not exists (
select * from refPublisher
where
/* %JoinFKPK(inserted,refPublisher," = "," and") */
inserted.PublisherName = refPublisher.PublisherName
)
end
/* ERwin Builtin Sat Mar 09 14:04:24 1996 */
return
error:
raiserror @errno @errmsg
rollback transaction
end
go
```

Other CASE tools have similar capabilities, and although the keystrokes differ in each tool, the general principles remain the same. The CASE software that can reverse engineer a database from Access should be able to output to a variety of target server database management systems.

Although the CASE assist may not be quite as complete as the specific Upsizing Tools, they have the following advantages:

- CASE software is dual purpose. Not only can you use this software to upsize an Access database, you can use it to check your design logic while developing the Access prototype.

- The CASE software you select may not be version- and vendor-restrictive, like the Upsizing Tools are. If the CASE software supports schema analysis and generation for all the versions of all the database platforms in which you are interested, it will be able to convert from any vendor/version to any vendor/version.

From Here...

In this chapter we looked at three ways to upsize your Access 95 database to a server database management system. We chose two targets for our case studies—Microsoft SQL Server version 4.2 and Microsoft SQL Server version 6.5. We used the Access export facility, the Access Upsizing Wizard, and a third-party desktop CASE software, Logic Works ERWin.

From here, jump to these chapters to find out more about the following:

■ Chapter 4, "Getting By in SQL '92—Structured Query Language," presents more discussion on data typing in SQL unions.

■ Chapter 6, "Establishing the Ground Rules," discusses the four relational database integrities.

■ Chapter 17, "Transitioning to Another Back-End DBMS," discusses why you may want to upsize.

■ Chapter 19, "System Administration," presents a discussion on setting up security in Windows NT, Windows 95, and Microsoft SQL Server 6.5.

V

Upgrading the Application

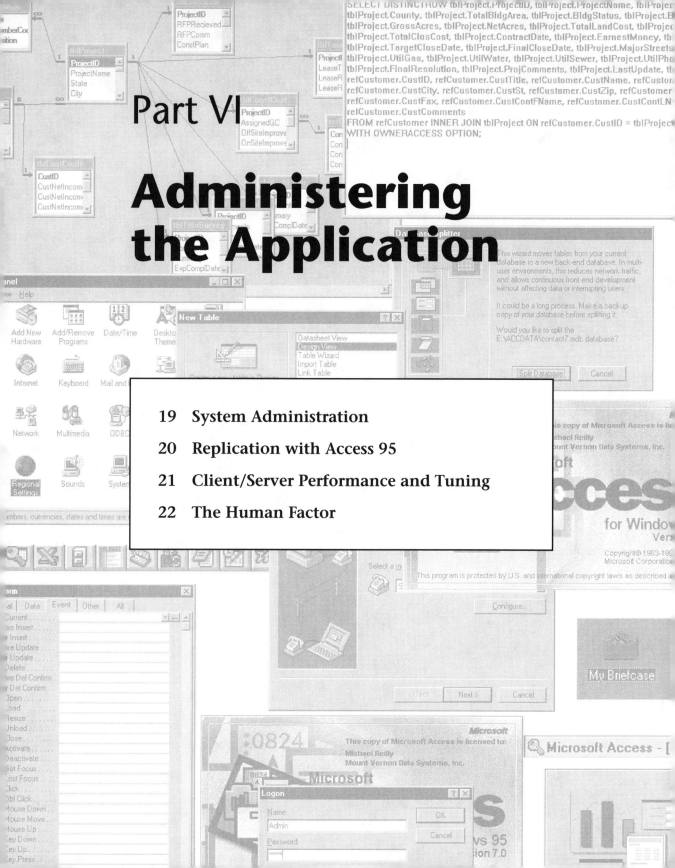

Part VI

Administering
the Application

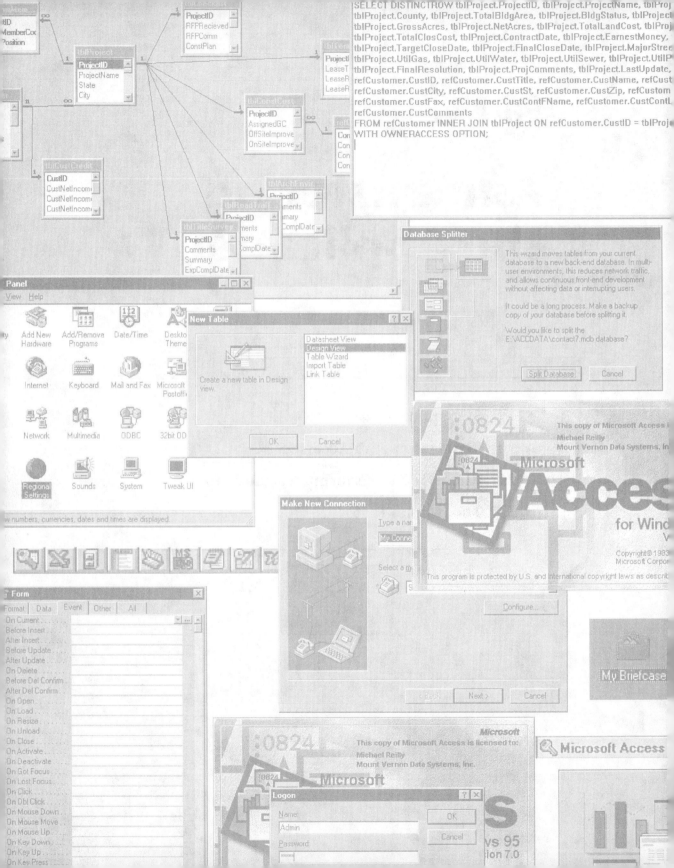

System Administration

Even if it isn't the job of the database developer to administer the network or the database, it pays to understand the work involved in these tasks. Some aspects of the database design can be changed to make the job of the administrator easier, and usually there are features and peculiarities of the physical environment that, as a database designer, you can exploit with your database layout.

For the purposes of this discussion, we refer to the system administrator, the network administrator, and the database administrator as if they are the same person. More than likely, these three positions will not be one person but through this chapter, it should be fairly obvious how the job duties are divided. Where there may be doubt, we try to indicate who is responsible because of the potential for conflict or for borderline responsibilities falling through the cracks.

In this chapter we cover the following:

- Software licensing policies and procedures
- User account creation and management
- Backup strategies for the operating system and the database management system
- Database recovery
- Remote administration of the database
- Fail-safe technology—hardware and software solutions

Licensing

Licensing software, and managing the licenses, is a concept more familiar to mainframe and mid-range computer users than to personal-computer users. Before networking, the personal-computer user bought a shrink-wrapped box of software, installed it from floppy disks, and then used it with no further concern over who owned the software. With networking came network server licenses, and over-the-network software installation. Now, the personal-computer user can connect to mainframe databases—and although the physical and programming connections usually concern the developer, licensing issues cannot be overlooked.

The cost of software development with tools such as Access is far less now than in past years, when teams of programmers wrote COBOL code to run on the mainframe. An application can be put together at a reasonable cost to the client, while still providing a good return or decent salary to the developer. If the application, however, connects to a large industrial-strength database, running on a server computer, the server license costs can be substantial. The costs associated with connecting to the server can make a difference on whether or not the application is a sound investment for the company. These costs can even stop a project in its tracks. These costs need to be calculated up-front, which will avoid an awkward situation later in the development cycle.

If you are an independent developer, understanding how your client plans to license the server connections is important to you. When you submit a proposal to the client, the deciding factor is what the project will do to improve profits or lower costs. Unless you know the total cost of implementing and using the application, all you can provide is an incomplete picture, showing only the initial costs of development. You are in a much better position if you can show the total life-cycle costs of the application, and the costs of the alternatives.

Licensing Models

There is a range of *licensing models*, and it helps to know the terminology. Here are some of the more popular models (sometimes, these are used in combination).

- **Floating license**—A license that may be used by anyone on the network (one floating license needed per floating user). The license is available to any user who wants to run the software.

- **Concurrent license**—The number of licenses needed is determined by the maximum number of users who will be running the software at any one time. License cost is determined by maximum actual use, not potential use.

- **Personal license**—A license allocated to a specific computer, usually to a specific user. This license may be combined with other schemes when selected users must be able to run the software at any time.

- **Restricted or Reserved licensing**—An extension of the personal license, in which the use of a certain number of instances of the software is set aside for a specific group.

- **Metered licensing**—Like a postage meter, the cost of this license is based on the number of times it is used, starting with some preset value that decrements with each use. No further use is allowed when zero count is reached until the meter is "reset" by purchasing more licenses. Used for employee-skill testing, for example, the number of tests purchased can be varied, according to projected needs.

- **Held** or **check-out licensing**—This scheme is used for portable and home-based computers to allow them to "check out" a license like a library book, for some period, without being connected to the server that is running the licensing management software.

- **Component-based licensing**—This licensing scheme allows the customer to install a minimal feature set at lower cost, and then add features later (usually by paying for and receiving a code that unlocks the extra features).

- **Value-based licensing**—This scheme bases licenses on the hardware platform. The faster the speed of the computer, the higher the cost of the license.

There are several *license management software packages* available, which can be integrated into your application. An alternative, which provides good security, is the *hardware key* (or "*dongle*," as it is known in Great Britain) that connects to the computer, often via the parallel port. Keys now are available that can be programmed to monitor and limit the number of concurrent users connected to an application. These keys offer no usage reporting, and many users consider them a nuisance. When they break, they take down the entire application. The system stays down until a new key is shipped out to the client. Still, if your application is going places that are known for buying only one copy of any software package, hardware keys are worth consideration.

Possibly the most troublesome metering schemes are used by Novell NetWare networks. Most of these packages work by allocating a copy of the software to each user, up to a preset limit. Because NetWare has been an application/server model of computing, not a client/server, the metering software doesn't send a license token, which permits the use of a local copy of the software. Rather, it sends a copy of the application file, thereby increasing network traffic. This approach can be especially troublesome to client database applications. Even using a run-time version of a client application build on Access 95, there are many individual programs needed for the application to run, such as the Access run-time executable, the application .MDB, and a bunch of DLLs (Dynamic Link Libraries). All these programs are continually called and released, called and released, creating a huge amount of network traffic when using the Novell application/server model. Unlike simpler programs (such as Word and Excel), there is no single "application file" that can be sent to the client once.

Compounding this problem is the Windows programming model, which uses DLLs to provide optimized code that can be shared by multiple applications. For the sharing to work, these DLLs should be in the SYSTEM folder, under each individual Windows 95 directory. The application looks for the DLLs in this folder, and of course cannot find them because, in the Novell application/server model, the application is never installed on the client computer. It is installed on the server, the only place where the DLLs are located.

This model may work if nothing was installed on the client computers beyond what is needed to boot them, with even Windows run from the application server. The network traffic at the start of the workday, as everyone downloaded copies of Windows, Word, Excel, Access, e-mail software, and so on, would be enormous. Frankly, in the opinion of the authors, we have been describing an out-of-date computing model. Network bandwidth should be used for moving data, not copies of applications.

One positive point about the Novell application/server model is the ease of application maintenance and upgrade. If only one copy of every application package is installed on the server, software upgrades are a trivial task. With today's network management tools and across-the-network installations, however, there is less reason to have to go to each client machine for software maintenance and upgrades. With a network administration package such as Microsoft's Systems Management Server, no reason remains to keep the software restricted to one location. Distribution and updates for the entire network can be handled automatically from one computer.

Licensing Access 95

Most Microsoft desktop products, including Access 95, use personal licensing. The server products offer a choice between personal and concurrent licensing, which we discuss in following sections of this chapter. Of course, everyone using a full development copy of Access must have a license to install it on their computers.

Software Licenses

A person can be licensed to use a copy of Access 95 in one of the following ways:

- Purchase a full copy of Access 95
- Purchase an upgrade from a legal previous version
- Purchase a copy of Microsoft Office Professional for Windows 95

> **Note**
>
> Only the Professional version of Microsoft Office includes Access 95, so do not assume that you can install Access on computers that are running the standard version of Office.

- Upgrade from a legal copy of a previous version of Microsoft Office Professional
- Purchase a license for Access 95, using the Microsoft multi-license pack

Multi-License Packs

Many companies are opting for the *multi-license pack*. To get the exact details, contact Microsoft or your reseller. Now that more companies install over the network from one physical copy of the software, it's no longer necessary or advisable to distribute floppy disks or even CD-ROMs to every employee. So, a company really needs only the license that permits a multiple-user network installation of the software. Obviously, the cost savings is substantial because the media costs—for production and distribution—are approaching zero.

The 80-20 Rule

Microsoft also applies an *80-20 rule*, which is great for employees who want to take work home and finish it on their own personal computer. Essentially, the rule states that the employee is allowed to load the application on a second computer, presumably at home, provided that the software is used at home less than 20 percent of the time, and at the office 80 percent of the time. Presumably, these numbers can be switched for a home-based employee who comes in to the office one day each week. Also, the employee is not supposed to run this software at home for personal use.

Run-Time Licensing

As we discussed in Chapter 13, "Building the Run-Time Application," you can use the Access Developer's Toolkit to build run-time versions of the client application. You then can distribute the application without royalties to Microsoft. In effect, Microsoft is giving out the *run-time license* for the price of the ADT. You can place your own licensing arrangements on your custom-developed application. If, for example, you developed the application as a consultant, and the customer agrees to pay for each unit installed, you can write a separate licensing agreement between you and your client. If the ADT is owned by a corporation and you work for the corporation, the application probably will be installed company-wide, without further discussion (unless the IS department does internal billing to other departments, which we will not go into here). As we said in Chapter 13, the run-time licensing is an attractive option because there is no need to install a full development copy of Access 95 on each user's computer.

Client Access Licenses

It is obvious that each user must have a license, also known as a *client access license*, for the copy of the operating system on his or her personal desktop computer. What is not as obvious is that he or she also needs a license to connect to the server operating system. If the server is running Windows NT Server, there are two possible ways to purchase the licenses, which are discussed shortly. If the server is running on Novell, Banyan Vines, or Open VMS, client licenses to connect to the server still are required. There is no software that comes with these licenses: they are simply permission to connect users to the server. The following discussion refers to Windows NT but also applies to SQL Server. Other software vendors have similar licensing schemes. The authors suggest you contact your vendor for specific licensing information.

Per-Server or Per-Seat Licensing. Although the Microsoft *per-server licensing or per-seat licensing* model may at first seem confusing, it was developed in an attempt to satisfy customers from both large and small companies. It also takes into account how the server is used. Microsoft has tried to propose a licensing scheme that is fair and that provides a reasonable return to Microsoft, without being too complex to administer. Figure 19.1 shows the Choose Licensing mode dialog box, which you encounter when installing Microsoft BackOffice software.

Fig. 19.1

Selecting the licensing model for Windows NT, either the Per Server mode or the Per Seat mode.

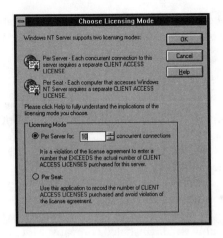

The per-server licensing is the simplest scheme, and is the best starting point for a small organization. A license is purchased for the server software, and then additional client access licenses are purchased, up to the maximum number of simultaneous connections that are expected at the server. When the Windows NT Server software is installed, you are asked what type of licensing you prefer. When you choose the per-server mode, you then have to input the number of client access licenses. This number is not checked for the number of concurrent connections: the licensing model from Microsoft is based on the honor system (at present, anyway). You can exceed this number of connections without the users being denied access. There is a way to audit license use so that you can tell if the number of users is exceeding the number of licenses purchased. You can always add more licenses on an as-needed basis.

This approach to licensing works well when not all users in your organization are connected to the server at the same time. For example, if you have 500 users, but you know that no more than 50 of them will be connected to the server at any one time, you can purchase one server license and 50 client access licenses.

Note

If for some reason you choose to put a database on Windows NT Workstation and connect to it in a peer-to-peer network, be aware that it has a limit of ten incoming user connections. This is a software-imposed limit and has nothing to do with licensing.

This model starts to become more expensive when you supplement the system with a second server. The original per server licenses apply to the first server. You have to purchase an additional server license for the second server, and you have to estimate how many users are connected to each server at any time because you also will need to purchase additional client access licenses. Some users may need to connect to both the servers, sometimes simultaneously, thereby using up two of the client access licenses. The per-server license model also becomes expensive as more users connect to the servers. Suppose that you have 500 users, and 200 of them connect to one server, and 200 to the other server. Then an additional 100 people who are connected to both servers. You need a total of 600 client access licenses.

In this scenario, you may want to consider the per-seat license. The per-seat license applies to the client, not the server. With that license, the client can connect to any of the servers, or even multiple servers at the same time. In our example, you need 500 client access licenses for anyone to connect anywhere at any time. When you add another server, you need only the additional server software license. You do not need additional client access licenses when adding a server using the per-seat model. For any organization with several servers, where the majority of the users are connected to one or more servers most of the time, the per-seat license is the best way to go.

Converting Licenses. Recognizing that companies may start with, and then add to, a small Windows NT installation, Microsoft allows a one-time conversion from the per-server to the per-seat licensing scheme. You cannot reverse the conversion, however. You can find the icon to perform the conversion in the Control Panel folder, under the Main program group (see fig. 19.2).

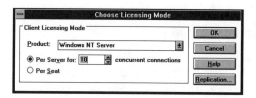

Fig. 19.2

Changing the licensing model through the Control Panel.

Monitoring License Usage. Using the License Manager built into Windows NT Server, you can monitor the number of client licenses in use and see if this number exceeds the number purchased (see fig. 19.3). The License Manager also handles the licensing for other Microsoft BackOffice products (see fig. 19.4). You use the License Manager to add new licenses as they are purchased (see fig. 19.5).

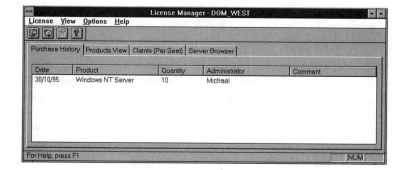

Fig. 19.3

The License Manager, through which you can add licenses as you purchase them and monitor their use.

VI

Administering the App

Fig. 19.4

Licenses for BackOffice products, showing a 10-seat license for the Windows NT Server product.

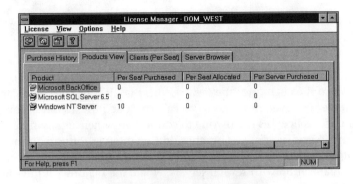

Fig. 19.5

Adding two new client access licenses for Microsoft BackOffice.

Local Administration

Part of the duties of the administrator includes adding user accounts to both the client and the server applications. The client application is relatively simple, and Chapter 12, "Securing the Access 95 Application," showed how to add new users to the Access security list. We discussed how to add a user from any workstation by logging on as the administrator. We also added a utility to our custom REA application that allows a user—from the user's own client station—to change his/her own password.

Adding User Accounts: Server Operating System

The users who connect to a server database management system also need to have accounts established for them, and also on the server operating system. To add a user account on a Windows NT Server, open the User Manager for Domains (an icon in the Administrative Tools group), as shown in figure 19.6. Select the User, New User menu item, and add the new user account, with the appropriate settings (see fig. 19.7).

If you expect to add a number of users with the same permissions and rights, then you may want to set up a user template, and copy this template each time you add a new person to the user roster. Using the Windows NT Server Domain model, it's a good idea to define a global user group with a name, such as **AccessSQL**. A discussion of the Domain model is beyond the scope of this book. The authors suggest that you consult a text, such as Que's *Special Edition Using Windows NT Workstation 3.51*, for a more in-depth discussion of domains. Briefly, all the necessary permissions will, from here on, be assigned to the group AccessSQL (see fig. 19.8). Permissions will not be assigned to individuals. The employee will inherit rights and permissions by being a member of the group. If an employee leaves or is transferred to another group, the administrator only has to remove the employee's name from the group and, if this is a transfer, add it to the new group. One action is sufficient to remove all the rights and permissions assigned to this employee through the group AccessSQL.

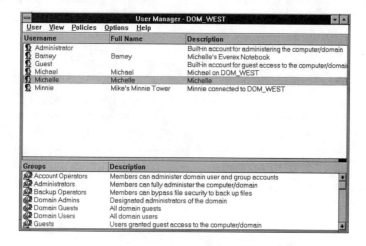

Fig. 19.6

Windows NT Server User Manager for Domains, from which you can manage user accounts.

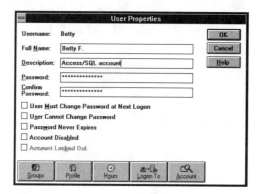

Fig. 19.7

Adding a new user account for Betty F., setting up the logon and initial password.

Fig. 19.8

Adding the global group AccessSQL in Windows NT Server, and adding members to the global group.

VI

Administering the App

To follow the Windows NT domain model for the examples shown here, we created a global group, named AccessSQL. Then we created a local group in this domain, named LocalAccessSQL. The last step is to make the global group a member of the local group. If this sounds too complex, then either leave this process to the system administrator, or refer to the previously mentioned book, *Special Edition Using Windows NT Server 3.51.*

Note

Even when you have set up an account on the operating system and assign file access and system management privileges through groups, you still have to set up an account for this user in SQL Server or Oracle, or the database management system currently in use on the server.

When your users are logging on from Windows NT workstations, rather than Windows 95 computers, these user workstations should be added to the list of workstations that participate in the Windows NT security model (see fig. 19.9).

Fig. 19.9

Adding the workstation Barney to the Windows NT security model.

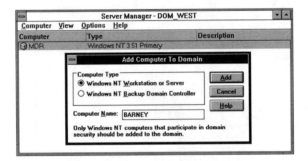

You need to go through similar steps to add user accounts on NetWare or UNIX servers when the server database management system is located on one of these operating systems.

Make sure that your users set up Windows 95 to log on to the Windows NT Server domain, if you want to use the domain security model—or set it up for them. Either you or they need to take the following steps:

1. Using Control Panel, open the Network Configuration options box (see fig. 19.10).
2. Select Client for Microsoft Networks, and then click Properties to display the properties sheet (see fig. 19.11).
3. Select the Log On to Windows NT Domain option.
4. Type the name of the domain to which this user should connect.

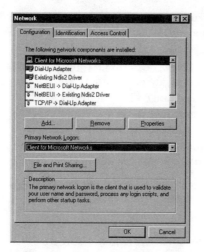

Fig. 19.10

Windows 95 Network Configuration options box, from which you can administer the Windows NT network connections.

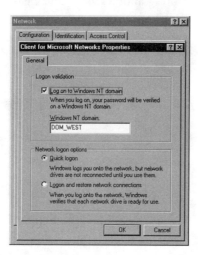

Fig. 19.11

The Client for Microsoft Networks Properties dialog box, which is the Windows 95 network client management interface.

5. Choose the Network logon option you prefer, either Quick Logon (which connects to network drives as you use them) or Logon and Restore Network Connections (which connects to network drives immediately). To minimize network traffic at startup, select the first option.

6. Click OK two times to return to the desktop.

Adding User Accounts: DBMS

Although the users in your client/server application already have accounts at the client end, you do need to set up accounts for them at the server DBMS also. Obviously, the specifics vary from one package to another. The examples shown here use SQL Server.

Adding User Accounts in Microsoft SQL Server. Because Microsoft SQL Server is part of Microsoft's BackOffice, as is Windows NT Server, some of the database security is integrated with the Windows NT security model. For example, the user can have the same user name and password for both Windows NT and Microsoft SQL Server. The user no longer must remember a separate password for the database, and when it is changed in Windows NT, it also is changed for Microsoft SQL Server. Of course, this means SQL Server can benefit from the features of Windows NT security such as password aging and auditing, and also automatic lockout if someone tries to hack in. To use integrated security, you must check a few things. If you are the database administrator, you have to work with the system administrator on this.

First, SQL Server must be running a network protocol that supports trusted connections. In version 4.2, you are limited to using named pipes. In version 6.0 and above, you can use named pipes and multi-protocol.

Next, SQL Server must be installed and configured. Using the Microsoft SQL Server Security Options tab in the Server Configuration Options dialog box, you can turn on integrated security (see fig. 19.12).

Fig. 19.12

Configuring SQL Server security options; NT integrated security causes the user to be authenticated by the OS, and authentication then is passed through to MS SQL Server when the user seeks access to the DBMS.

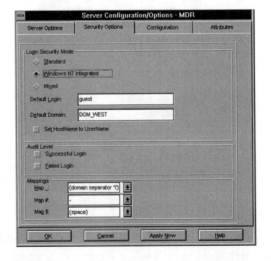

Then, you can add the users and groups in Windows NT, with the User Manager (refer to figs. 19.6, 19.7, and 19.8). Finally, you add the new Windows NT users and groups to SQL Server, using the SQL Server Security Manager. Keep in mind that the Windows NT groups are not the same animal as SQL Server groups. However, the Security Manager can create a SQL Server group from a Windows NT group. In fact, you cannot select individual Windows NT users from within Security Manager—but you can select a group. This limiting is consistent with the Domain model, where only groups are assigned permissions.

> **Note**
>
> By default, all members of the Windows NT Admin group have *sa* (system administrator) privileges on SQL Server when using integrated security.

To add a group using the SQL Security manager, take these steps:

1. Open the Security Manager (see fig. 19.13) and from the menu, select <u>V</u>iew.

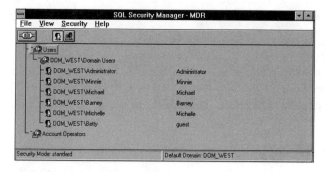

Fig. 19.13

The SQL Server Security Manager, from which you can manage SQL Server users.

2. Select <u>U</u>ser Privilege.

3. Select <u>S</u>ecurity, and then select <u>G</u>rant New to open the Grant User Privilege dialog box (see fig. 19.14).

Fig. 19.14

The Grant User Privilege dialog box, from which you can grant logon IDs to group members or add users to a database.

4. Select the group that you want added from the Grant Privilege list. Note that the groups shown by default are the local groups. You also can select (global) groups from the domain.

5. Check the Add Login ID for group members box. This action ensures that a login ID is created for each member of the group.

6. Check the add users to database option, and select a default database for these users.

7. Click the Grant button to create SQL login IDs for the users in the selected group.

To remove a user, repeat the above process but select the Revoke option instead of the Grant option at the security menu.

After the users have a valid login ID, you can grant the login ID access to the different databases, by creating a user for the database that corresponds to the login ID. This process must be repeated for each database to which the user needs to connect. Now, the Access clients have the privileges that they need to connect to the SQL database tables.

Note

It isn't the intent of this book to provide an introduction to Microsoft SQL Server or any other server database management system. If you want to learn more about Microsoft SQL Server, look for *Special Edition Using Microsoft SQL Server 6.5*, published by Que. For the Oracle RDBMS, the authors suggest *The Oracle DBA Survival Guide*, by Joe Greene, by Sams.

Backup Strategy

All client/server applications contain data that is important to the organization and, possibly, critical to the survival of the company. Statistics show that companies that lose their data due to a catastrophe, such as by fire, are almost certain to be out of business within a year. The question is not whether you should back up your data. The question is how often you must make backups and which method you will use. One of the most important tasks of any database or system administrator is making absolutely certain that it is possible to recover from a system failure.

System Backup

A full *system backup* of the server should be performed at least once a week, with additional backups daily to capture files that changed since the last full backup. The two methods for backing up changed files are *incremental backup* and *differential backup*.

Incremental Backup. The incremental backup will back up files that changed since the previous backup. Each time an incremental backup is run, changed files are marked as having been backed up. Suppose that the system backup is run on Sunday. The first incremental backup tape contains files changed on Monday, the second contains files changed on Tuesday, and so on until Saturday, when the cycle starts again with a new full system backup. This method requires seven tapes per week, unless you append each day's backup to the same tape as the previous day's—which risks losing the data if the tape is damaged. Restoring the data requires the full backup taken on Sunday and each one of the daily backup tapes, restored in the proper order. If one tape cannot be read, the entire restore process beyond this point is invalid.

Differential Backup. A differential backup will back up files that were changed since the last *full* backup. Each time a differential backup is run, changed files are *not* marked as having been backed up. So the Monday tape contains files changed on Monday, the Tuesday tape contains files changed on Monday and Tuesday, and so on through the week. If you want, you can recycle Monday's tape and use it again on Wednesday or Thursday, because you know that you have the data on a more recent tape. The differential method does not necessarily use fewer tapes and may take more time because, by Friday, you are backing up all the files that changed during the week. On the plus side, to restore the data, you need only the full backup and the most recent tape from the differential set. The differential method works well if you have large database files that change every day.

Off-Site Backup. Although everyone knows that they should perform regular back-ups, many companies overlook the need to keep a copy of the backup tapes off-site. If the server is destroyed in a fire, there is not much hope for backup tapes stored in the same room, or possibly even in the same building. When you have a replicated data-base in another building, you do have some security from physical disasters, as you can use the replicated database to rebuild the master. More on this shortly.

Testing the Backup. *Testing the backup tapes* was mentioned in Chapter 3, "The Ap-plication Development Environment," but it's worth repeating because it is a poten-tially dangerous trap. From time to time, you should restore some files from a backup set, just to make sure that the tape drive(s) and the tape media are working as ex-pected. If they are not, better you should know under controlled conditions than when you are trying to restore after a severe system crash.

The other point to check is that the backup media—whether it is tape, optical disk, or removable cartridges—can be read by a drive other than the drive that created them. If your server primary tape backup unit has misaligned heads, you may be in for a rude surprise and because so many backup units are electro-mechanical devices with exposed read/write heads, this happens with disturbing frequency. You may be able to read the tapes on the drive on which the backup was created, but if the server and drive unit are destroyed, can you restore this data to another server from a different drive? Remember, the job of the DBA or system administrator is not to make backups; it is to ensure that recovery is possible when things go wrong, and having a set of useable backup data is the first step in the recovery process.

Real-Time Backup. *Real-time backup* is achieved by always having more than one copy of the database updated by the transactions. Real-time backup can be handled in one of several ways. One method is to use full database replication, so that all transactions are written to both databases at the same time. If either update fails, the other is rolled back or cached for subsequent update, so that the databases are always synchronized with the same information. SQL Server 6.0 offers enhanced replication, and both SQL Server 6.5 and Oracle can replicate data to heterogeneous databases. The plus here is that if one server is unavailable, the client applications still can access data from the second server. Response time may suffer, but the users still can get to the data.

Another option is to employ real-time data protection. We discuss this approach later, in the section "Fail-Safe Technology."

Database Backup

A *system backup* may be effective for most data files from word-processing programs and spreadsheets, but may not be an effective backup tool for a database. Depending on your operating system and database management system, it may not be possible or advisable to back up a file while it is open. There may be transactions in progress at any time, and the data probably will change even during the time it takes to perform the backup. So the system administrator may want to shut down the database to back it up. However, if your corporate mandate is a seven-by-twenty-four operation and your users must always have access to the data, you can't do this. You have to use a database management system that supports *on-line backups*.

This is why many industrial-strength server database management system software packages have built-in, on-line, backup capability. When the on-line backup is handled under the control of the database management system, there is no risk—in theory—of incomplete or partial transactions being backed up. If a record is locked by a user for update, the DBMS can move on to the other records, and then back up the locked record after the lock is released.

Access 95 doesn't have a built in database backup capability, which is not surprising because it is actually a desktop database environment. There are ways to code a scheduled table export, and you may be able to come up with other schemes to make regular copies of the data. But the first step in a table export is to lock the table, making it unavailable to the users. So, why not just shut down the database at some time when the users will not be inconvenienced, and then make a tape backup or use Briefcase replication (discussed in Chapter 20, "Replication with Access 95") or the Replication Manager (also in Chapter 20) to make a backup copy of the database?

One point in favor of Access—when you back up the .MDB file, you have a complete backup of the data, indexing, and all objects such as tables, queries, forms, and so on that are resident in the .MDB. The only other file that you need to back up is the SYSTEM.MDW file, which contains the security account information. Of course, the client.MDB file also should be backed up, but this can be handled on a less-frequent schedule than the data.MDB because it changes less frequently. There is no need to back up copies of the client application on everyone's desktop because they all should be the same and can be restored by an over-the-network installation faster than they can be retrieved from tape.

Backups on Microsoft SQL Server. When Microsoft SQL Server (and this also applies to other DBMS software) does a database backup, it copies all the data, system tables, and user-defined objects such as data tables, forms, and queries, to a backup device. It also copies the transaction log. The backup device, often referred to as a *dump device*, can be a file, another hard drive, or a tape drive. SQL Server 6.0 and above can use dump devices defined on a Novell server, and can perform *striped backups* to multiple backup devices. Refer to Chapters 1 and 3, "Client/Server, What Is It?" and "The Application Development Environment," for more information on striping.

So how does Microsoft SQL Server perform a backup while the database is running? Briefly, when SQL Server receives the DUMP command, it writes all the completed transactions to disk, and then begins the process of copying the database to the dump device. It doesn't back up any transactions that were incomplete when the backup started, nor does it back up any transactions that are completed after the dump process is started. To back up these transactions, you also must dump the transaction log after the backup is complete.

A *transaction log* is a record of all of the transactions that have happened on the database since the last backup. Consider the database dump as a full backup, and the transaction log as an incremental backup.

> ### Tip
>
> If the database disk fails, you need the last backup and the current transaction log to re-create the database on a new disk. To be safe, never position the physical database and the transaction log on the same physical disk.
>
> If you ignore this tip and keep the database and transaction log on the same disk device, you will not be able to back up the transaction log.

A transaction log dump does more than just provide an incremental backup of database transactions. Dumping the transaction log also clears out the inactive part of the transaction log. The inactive part of the transaction log is defined as the completed transactions in the log, preceding, but not on the same page, as the earliest outstanding (incomplete) transaction.

The full database dump doesn't clear out the transaction log. So, although you may be performing database dumps on a regular basis, the transaction log will continue to fill up, and eventually will exceed the available disk space. At this point, no more transactions will be allowed until the transaction log is emptied, and no more transaction logging means no more updates to the database. Making transaction log dumps a normal part of your database backup avoids the problem of your database coming to a screeching halt.

VI

Administering the App

> **Note**
>
> Not all database management systems follow this approach. For example, Software AG's ADABAS has a transaction log that fills up and then starts over, writing over the beginning of the log. It has an automatic mechanism for making transaction log dumps so that a log file of completed transactions is always available for a restore. The transaction log is essentially always full, and the DBA doesn't have to worry about manually cleaning out the transaction log.

There is a new feature, added in SQL Server 6.0, that works with Windows NT to prevent the transaction log from filling up. Using what is known as a *threshold dump*, the transaction log is dumped automatically when the space available drops to a user-defined level. This process requires the SQL Executive, the Performance Monitor, and the Messenger Service to be running on the NT Server. So ideally, these processes should be set to start automatically when Windows NT starts.

The actual backup is performed in SQL Server 6.0 and above through the SQL Server Enterprise Manager. (Up to version 4.2, backups were run through the SQL Administrator). Figure 19.15 shows the SQL Enterprise Manager.

Fig. 19.15

The SQL Enterprise Manager, new to version 6, allows you to manage nearly every function within the SQL Server environment.

Use the Tools, Database Backup/Restore menu option to bring up the SQL Server Backup options dialog box (see fig. 19.16). Select the database, select the backup device, and set the expiration date of the backup. Then you can run the backup. For a more detailed description of the various options, consult the SQL Server documentation or one of the previously mentioned SQL Server books.

Backups can be scheduled through the SQL Server Backup dialog box, using the Schedule button (see fig. 19.17). This schedule will initiate an unattended backup weekly, every Sunday, starting at midnight. Backup scheduling is much improved over SQL Server version 4.2, so there is no longer any need to use the Windows NT **AT** command.

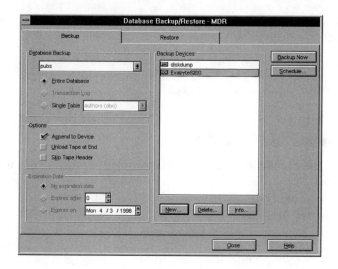

Fig. 19.16

The SQL Server Backup/ Restore dialog box, which allows you to set up and schedule backups and restores of previously completed backups.

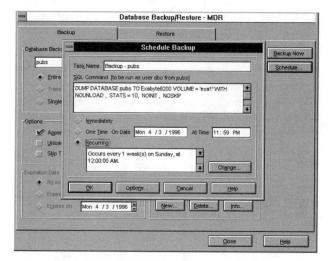

Fig. 19.17

The SQL Server Schedule Backup dialog box allows you to schedule regular "unattended" backups.

Restore/Recovery

As before, the description here applies to Microsoft SQL Server, but the principles are the same for any server database. If a problem arises with the database, if the disk is corrupted so that data cannot be read, your first response should be to dump the transaction log with the NO_TRUNCATE option (this action dumps all transactions, completed or not, since the last transaction log dump). Then, you must drop and re-create the corrupted database. To recover the data, restore from the most recent full backup. Next, apply the transaction logs, *in order*, to recover the data up to the point where the system crashed. Then restart the database management system. On database restart, SQL Server will roll back any incomplete transactions from the end of the transaction log.

Restore/recovery is a simple and straightforward (although lengthy) process, if you have a good set of backups.

If your server database is Access, then you can recover by restoring from the most recent backup of the data.MDB file. Because Access doesn't support transaction logging, all changes made since the last backup are lost.

Remote Administration

Remote management of the client computers should be handled as much as possible by the systems/database administrator. From the client (user) perspective, the level of administration required should be fairly small. The user accounts must be set up and the software made available over the network or as floppy disks. From this point on, the main administrative task is distributing the software upgrades, which easily can be done over the network. In its simplest form, you can upgrade the distribution disk images on the network server, and then send a broadcast e-mail message, requesting that the users upgrade their software. Using a package such as Systems Management Server, the entire upgrade process can be made automatic. All the hardware and software configurations can be determined from the server, and software changes can be made under the control of the administrator.

Remote management of a server is a little more complex. If your operating system is Windows NT Server, keep in mind that you do not have to be sitting in front of the server to manage it. In fact, if you download the Network management client software, you can administer the network (including managing across domains) from a Windows NT Workstation computer, or even from a Windows for Workgroups or Windows 95 computer. However, these tools are limited to Windows NT management, and not to Microsoft SQL Server or other database administration. The Microsoft SQL server, SQL Executive, for example, must reside on the NT Server. So, if you are the database administrator, count on doing most of your administration from a system running Windows NT Server and Microsoft SQL Server, or the database management system that you currently are running.

It is possible, by using a combination of the features of SQL Server and Windows NT, to set up alerts that will page or e-mail the database administrator when certain events occur. For example, if the disk space is running low and the database is in danger of running out of space or if a table becomes corrupted, an alert can be sent to the database administrator. The examples shown here are for the SQL Server alert menus (see fig. 19.18 and fig. 19.19).

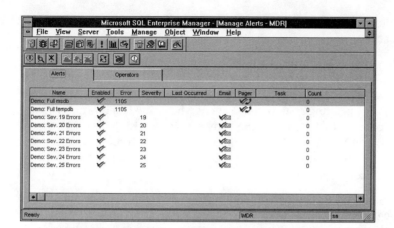

Fig. 19.18

The SQL Server Alert menu, showing alerts that have occurred and the subsequent action taken as a result.

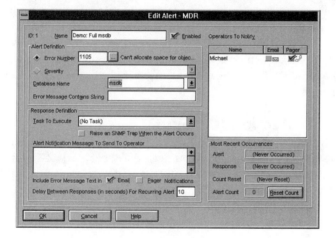

Fig. 19.19

Editing a SQL Server Alert, where you assign an action to a specific error message. In this instance, if the database runs out of space (error 1105), Michael is paged.

Fail-Safe Technology

Another responsibility of the system administrator is to protect the data from corruption caused by hardware problems, and ensure that it is available to the users when they need it. There are some hardware and software choices that can help achieve this objective.

Disk Arrays

We discussed RAID systems in Chapter 3, "The Application Development Environment," where we pointed out the benefits of redundant disk arrays. The system administrator and the database administrator have to cooperate to ensure that sufficient disk space is available for the server database. In the event of a physical disk failure, the system administrator is responsible for replacing the disk, and for restoring the redundancy to the system in case a second disk fails. In some cases, fixing the disk problem may necessitate shutting down the database for a few minutes. In this case,

VI

Administering the App

the database administrator should be involved so that all the users can be notified (usually by broadcast message), can log off, and the database quiesced.

One feature of Windows NT is the capability to extend volume sets. If your database is on drive E, and the disk is almost full, you can add another disk, and allocate the space on the new disk to the E drive. Now, the database thinks it has a much larger disk to use, and the operating system takes care of where the data is actually written. The clients still connect to drive E, avoiding any problems arising from moving the database to another drive. Extending volumes works only with the NTFS file system. Unlike striping, the data is written to the first disk until it is full, and then writing continues to the second disk.

The authors suggest that extending volumes be done as a stopgap measure until the database can be backed up, a bigger drive installed, and the database restored. If either disk goes down, it may be impossible to recover the data, especially if a large database file is spread across two physical disks. An alternative to backing up and restoring is to add a large physical disk to the server, copy the database to it, and then remove the extended volume set. You then can make the new large drive use the same drive letter as the database previously used (which is easier with the NTFS file system, where drive letter assignments are more flexible). The database needs to be down only for a short time to make this change.

Real-Time Data Protection (Octopus)

One of the more innovative approaches to data recovery is a product called *Octopus*, which provides a *software fail-safe solution*. If you need 7-day per week, 24-hour per day availability of your data, and can afford absolutely no downtime, check out this product. You can start by investigating the demo version on this book's companion CD-ROM. Octopus was originally developed for Windows NT but a Windows 95 version will be available by the time this book is published.

Octopus operates at the system level. It mirrors user-specified files by capturing the changes as they are saved on the source machine, and then forwarding the changes across the network to the target machine. The bandwidth required is minimized because only changes are forwarded, rather than copying entire files. Any type of file can be protected, not just database files. The servers involved in the Octopus protection scheme do not need to be identical—they can be Intel-based or they can be DEC Alpha, MIPS, or Power PC servers, in any combination. Mirroring can be set up as one-to-one, one-to-many, or many-to-many so, for example, one master server can be mirrored in multiple backup locations. The memory-resident Octopus code requires less than 500 Kbytes of RAM, and so can be run on a Windows NT Server, usually without requiring a memory upgrade.

The benefits of Octopus over replication is that the Octopus code is truly real-time, extends beyond database files, and doesn't have to be scheduled. It just runs quietly in the background. If the main server goes down unexpectedly, you can repair or replace it and copy the files back from the target machine. An even more rapid recovery can be achieved if the target server is configured to look like the primary server.

All you have to do is switch the backup server to the primary server, and data access is immediately cut over.

Administration of the Octopus servers is handled from a single computer, following the Windows NT centralized administration model. The Octopus Automatic Switch Over facility eliminates the need for manual switching of control from a failed primary server to a backup server dedicated to the support of that primary server. Octopus installation takes only a few minutes, and setup is straightforward.

Octopus Technologies has announced a new product, Octopus WinStation for Windows 95, which will provide all the Octopus functionality for Windows NT, but on the Windows 95 platform. This new product is interoperable with the Octopus products for Windows NT—Windows 95 systems can act as repositories for Windows NT data, and it offers desktop systems running Windows 95 the fail-safe protection of the Octopus utility. This sheds a whole new light on using Access 95 as a server or as a replicated data access source, because of the additional fault-tolerance provided by Octopus.

For more information, contact:

Octopus Technologies, Inc.
Department WJW
301 Oxford Valley Road, Suite 102A
Yardley, PA 19067

(215) 321-8750

From Here...

In this chapter, we discussed the responsibilities of the system, network, and database administrators. We looked at how to administer the server to allow users to connect from the client applications, and discussed how to protect data to ensure the constant availability of the server database. From here, jump to one of the following:

- Chapter 1, "Client/Server, What Is It?" gives information on hardware requirements, RAID, striped volumes, and so on.
- Chapter 3, "The Application Development Environment," gives information on hardware requirements, RAID, and so on.
- Chapter 12, "Securing the Access 95 Application," discusses Access security, user accounts, and permissions.
- Chapter 13, "Building the Run-Time Application," covers more about building, distributing, and installing run-time client applications
- Chapter 20, "Replication with Access 95," for more information on Briefcase and Replication Manager.

VI

Administering the App

CHAPTER 20

Replication with Access 95

In the real world, we cannot assume that a client/server setup will remain neat and tidy. If all the clients were connected to a single server—or even multiple servers—all the time, the job of the system administrator would be much simpler than it truly is. Unfortunately, in today's world, with more "road warriors" armed with laptop computers and with more employees telecommuting, the task of servicing becomes increasingly complex. These mobile workers want to connect to their data, and when they cannot connect easily, they want to take a copy of the data with them. This pressure to make the data always available presents several challenges to the database designer and the database systems administrator. In this chapter, we look at these challenges and consider how they may be addressed.

In this chapter we cover the following:

- *Database replication*, what it is, and how to synchronize replicas and reconcile differences
- The various updating schemes used by mainframe servers
- Replication within Windows 95 and how it works, and the Windows 95 Briefcase and how to copy it to other systems
- How to reconcile differences in Briefcase replication
- Converting your Access 95 database, and the implications therein
- How to synchronize replica sets and how to synchronize from within an application
- The Replication Manager, and how to configure it
- How to convert your Access 95 database by using Replication Manager
- How to build replicas and synchronize by using Replication Manager
- How to *schedule synchronization*, how to *resolve conflicts* by using Replication Manager, and using replication as a backup scheme
- DAO programming for replication and the SQL Server tie-in to replication

The Need for Distributed Data

One design goal of a client/server application, and one of its main benefits, is the capability to make one set of data available to everyone in the company by using one server database with multiple clients. There are cases, however, when a single server database will not meet your needs. These cases include, but are not limited to, the following:

- The data must be available in geographically distant locations.
- You must allow clients to connect to one of several servers for load balancing.
- A backup database must be available in case the main server fails.
- An employee must take a copy of the data on a portable computer out to the field.
- An employee needs to connect to the data from a remote location.

The last item in the list can be handled with relative ease if the user has *dial-in access* to the server. The Windows 95 Dial-Up Networking, or *RAS* (*Remote Access Service*), lets users connect to the server just as if they were on the network, but with the lower bandwidth provided by the telephone lines.

When the situation requires multiple copies of a database, you can simply put up copies at various locations. But any time that you have more than one copy of the same database, you immediately have a problem with data synchronization. If users are allowed to make changes to more than the master copy of the database, how do you reconcile the changes between copies? Part of the answer is *replication*, which uses features that are part of the database software or the operating system to maintain synchronized copies of the database.

Examples of databases that might be replicated include the following:

- The corporate telephone directory
- A sales contact database shared among the sales staff
- A list of products, specifications, and so on
- A catalog of products
- Knowledge bases

Synchronizing Replicas

After the database is replicated and you have multiple copies of it placed here and there, the other part of the equation to consider is *synchronization*. This is the process that ensures that the various copies of the database all contain the same information. Synchronization may be done in real time, so that all copies of the database remain identical at all times, or it may be done on a scheduled basis, so that a delay occurs between updates. The scheduling is under the control of the system administrator or database administrator. Finally, there is a form of synchronization that can be done when client machines connect to the server following a period when they are detached. This is the case of the traveling sales personnel with the laptop, for example.

Reconciling Differences

Reconciliation of differences in data is a third part of this complex equation. You have multiple copies of the database, and the potential for users to make updates to any one of the copies. How will your software handle changes made by different users to the same record but on different copies of the database? If your users frequently update existing records on the database, there will be a significant potential for conflict. If most changes to the database are appended records, the conflict potential is significantly reduced.

The "right" answer to reconciling differences of opinion depends on many factors, two of which are the size of the database and how the client connects to the server. Look at some of the possible scenarios to see how each factor might be handled. We start with corporate data on a legacy system, connected to Access 95 clients on personal computers.

Mainframe Servers, Simultaneous Updates

Assume that the server database is large and is stored on a mainframe or a powerful microcomputer. The database may range up to the multi-gigabyte range or even beyond in size. In some ways, this is a simple case for replication. The full database can be replicated only to another machine of equal or similar capacity and power. It may make sense for the corporation to have the same data available in different locations, especially for geographically separate and distant locations. Replication (or distribution, as it is more accurately called in this case) is handled by the server DBMS. A copy of the database is installed at a remote location, and the two copies can be kept synchronized by the distribution manager of the database management system. If true *distributed processing* is implemented, then two-phase commits ensure that either the changes within a transaction are executed on both machines, or the transaction is rolled back on both machines. This concept can be extended to multiple servers as needed. The question of a master database is moot because changes must be made on all copies of the database or not at all. Modern DBMSs such as Oracle and SQL Server have the capability to delay transactions and updates, so that the synchronization doesn't happen in real time. The benefit with this "in time enough" scheme is that it is not absolutely necessary that the servers be linked continuously.

Although the servers must be linked, the traffic over the link represents the transactions being processed. In other words, only changes to the data are being sent between the servers. This makes for far less network traffic than having several hundred users at the remote location all connecting to one server in the main office. Less network traffic means that it is feasible to keep the databases synchronized over a lower bandwidth, lower-speed line (Wide Area Network, or WAN). The net result is a faster response to the users who obtain their data from a local server.

Mainframe Servers, Regular Updates

In this scenario, you have a server that is recording updates on a frequent basis—for example, sales of items to customers. So that orders can be promptly packed and shipped, inventory updated as it is being diminished, and so on, this server will be designated the master Order Placement server, and will be used by all the employees involved in order processing. The database may then be replicated to another server, possibly at a different location, for use by the accounting and purchasing staff. In fact, if several Order Placement servers existed at different locations, the updates can be "rolled up" to a single Purchasing/Accounting server so that the purchasing department could reorder from suppliers on behalf of all the various retail locations.

In this kind of scenario, updating the Purchasing/Accounting server might happen only once or twice a day, perhaps at the open and close of business. Note that the situation we describe here is one-way. It can easily be made to work in both directions. As purchasing places a resupply order, the individual retail-center database associated with the resupply order is advised that the items are on the way and can be expected by a certain date. Again, this update from the Purchasing/Accounting server to the Order Placement server and the synchronization of data can happen on a daily basis.

Mainframe Servers, No Updates

If your application is intended for *data warehousing* or *data mining* (although the authors question whether Access is the best choice here, for all its capability), then replication becomes a relatively simple task because data warehouses should have limited updatability. The main data warehouse server is being updated—most likely in batch operations—with data from the OLTP (On-Line Transaction Processing) database(s). Because this data is now historical and may be aggregated and/or de-normalized, it should not be updated any other way. When an executive wants to know the total number of blue widgets the company sold in North Dakota in April of last year, the answer can be retrieved from the data warehouse.

If there is a requirement for the data to be replicated to another data warehouse server, you can do so without fear of losing synchronization between the servers. The batch update "refresh" programs can be applied to both copies of the data warehouse, to keep them in sync, or if there are many copies of the data warehouse, you can use the built-in synchronization tools of the distributed database management system to make the necessary changes and keep the remote servers synchronized with your master database.

Mainframe Servers, Update Subset

With a large database, there is no question of putting a copy on a portable computer, or even a desktop system—it simply cannot be done. However, users may request a subset of the data, as it relates to their project. From the database administrator and designer's point of view, this probably is the worst-case scenario. The client application is, of course, written in Access 95, so there is no problem about loading this subset on the personal computer. But when the server database is running on SQL Server or Oracle or Ingres, how do you split off a piece and give it to the user to place on his or her computer? One solution is to simply state that this will not happen.

When you are overruled and told to, "Make it happen," what do you do? One possible option is to write a query in the Access client application that will extract and download the required subset of the data from the server into a set of Access tables on the client side. You have to provide code so that, when the users are not connected to the server, they can connect to their local copy of the data that lives on an MDB file. This approach works, if you built your client/server application to attach to the remote server tables, and then work with them as if they were native Access tables. This setup breaks down if you use remote procedure calls, for example, or open server tables directly through Visual Basic code.

If your users community has the need, you may want to provide a customized version of the client application that has less functionality than the regular version, but avoids any direct calls to server tables. The example that comes to mind is the traveling sales force, where each salesperson wants only the data from her or his own territory. Making a virtue out of necessity, you agree to produce an "REA Light" application, with one-third less bulk. The users are grateful because they get the functionality they need, and now the application is smaller and runs better on their laptop computers.

Updates remain a problem in this scenario. Potential updates fall into the following categories:

- Data copied from the server is changed
- Data copied from the server is deleted
- Data is added to that which was copied from the server

If data copied from the server is changed or deleted, the problem is how to get the changes back into the server database. With this change goes the question of what happens if someone else changed the data on the server while the copy was checked out. Now, you are dealing with corporate policy and people issues as much as you are dealing with technical considerations. You could mandate that no changes will be allowed—the copy of the server data is considered read-only. If so, why not just remove the capability to make changes in this data from your on-the-road version of the software (set the flag to open the laptop copy of the database as read-only)? The users cannot make changes to their copy that will be lost, and so they will not be upset at you for this reason.

You can allow data changes to be added back to the server, if the computing model supports this activity. Our example of the sales staff that take data only from their territory is a good example. No one else should be modifying that data, so why not allow the salesperson to update it? Unfortunately, it isn't quite so easy to go back from Access tables to a server because Access doesn't have the level of replication and *conflict resolution* that distributed database management systems offer. Perhaps, if your database management system will support it, you can load the Access data into temporary tables on the server, and then reconcile the data in the temporary tables with the data in the base tables.

A common situation is that of new data, over and above what was copied from the server. For example, an existing customer may place a new order with the field sales-person. You could add this order to the tables in the MDB file on the salesperson's laptop computer, but then the problem is reconciling these new rows with older order data. An alternative scheme worth considering is to have a second table named NewOrders, either in the data.MDB file or even in the customized client application. New orders could be stored in this NewOrders table, separate from existing orders. Now, when the itinerant salesperson visits the office or even dials in via modem, your code can update the server tables from the NewOrders table, append the NewOrders data into the existing order table on the laptop, and, as a final step, delete the new orders from the NewOrders table. Tomorrow, the salesperson can go out and start filling the NewOrders table all over again.

> **Tip**
>
> Don't overlook the possibility of writing copies of the data MDB file on CD-ROM, if appropriate. Sales staff, for example, can carry a large database of product specifications, diagrams, pictures, and so on, assuming that they have laptop computers that contain CD-ROM drives. The benefit of this approach is that the CD-ROM data cannot be changed, so you don't have to worry about updates.

Replication in Windows 95

Now, take a look at the scenario where your server database is an Access .MDB file, and you are of course connecting to it with an Access client. You can use the features of Windows 95 to handle replication.

The Briefcase

Access 95 added a replication capability that works together with the replication in Windows 95, known as the Briefcase (see fig. 20.1). It also works under Windows NT 3.51, if you install the *Replication Manager* that comes with the Access Distribution Kit (discussed in Chapter 13). Windows NT 4.0 has the Windows 95 interface but at the time of writing, it is not clear whether the *Briefcase* feature will be included in this release. Be aware, however, if you are familiar with replication (distribution) in high-end databases, the Briefcase is not the same function. Still, it's a useful tool, as long as you understand how it operates and what it can and cannot do.

Fig. 20.1

The Windows 95 Briefcase icon.

If you don't see the briefcase icon on the Windows 95 desktop, you used the standard installation method, where Briefcase is not installed or, if you used the Custom installation but did not elect to install the Briefcase, it will not appear on the desktop. The Briefcase is installed as part of the Portable installation option because it's assumed that portable computer users will want to connect to a desktop system and synchronize files from time to time. If you do not see this icon, you can install Briefcase by using the Windows 95 Control Panel's Add/Remove Programs function. You need your original Windows 95 CD-ROM or disks to load this software.

Replica Sets

Before you can use the replication capability, you must build what is known as a *replica set*. Synchronization of changes can take place only within a replica set. A replica set consists of a *Design Master* and one or more replicas. The Design Master is a copy of your data MDB file that was converted by using a process that we discuss shortly. The *Design Master—Replica model* is hierarchical in nature—changes flow from the top down. You can make design changes to the structure of the Design Master, but the only way to change the structure of the associated replicas is to replicate through the Design Master. Because the data MDB file contains mostly tables, all changes made are to the table structure and, therefore, should be performed with care.

> **Tip**
>
> You can use Briefcase replication to distribute updates to your client software also, if the client.MDB is configured to participate in the replication process.

When *Briefcase replication* is installed in Access 95, it's entered into the Windows 95 registry. Briefcase is a class ID (CLSID) for Jet 3.0 MDB files. Then, when a file with an MDB extension is dragged into the briefcase, the Briefcase calls its reconciler code to convert the database to a format that can be replicated. After the conversion is complete, the Design Master is left at the original location, and a replica of the MDB file is placed in the Briefcase. (You can select to reverse the locations.) Then you can begin to update data in one or both copies of the replica set.

When you use the Briefcase menu to update the replica set, Briefcase invokes the *Merge Reconciler* (also registered at setup), to merge the changes. The update happens only between the replica selected and the Design Master, and only when you tell Briefcase to perform the update.

A replica set in Access 95 has a unique identifier, known as a *Globally Unique ID (GUID)*, which is automatically generated at the time of creation. A GUID is a 128-bit hex data value, which means that the probability it will be duplicated is extremely small. Each replica set, therefore, is handled as a separate entity within the Briefcase.

The Briefcase replication built into Windows 95 works with many other applications, not just with Access. For example, Word or Excel files can use the Briefcase replication, provided that they were written by the Windows 95 versions of these programs. The mechanism used for replication relies on OLE (Object Linking and Embedding), version 2.1, which is new with Windows 95. Only data files generated from an OLE 2.1 application can participate in the Briefcase replication and synchronization. Version 2.1 adds several new features to OLE, including identifying the data in the briefcase and using the GUIDs referred to in the preceding sentences. It also handles reconciling the replica files in the Briefcase with the Design Master and with each other.

Converting Your Database

A word of caution before you begin. If you plan to use replication to distribute changes to your application .MDB, because this converted database is the Design Master, you may want to use a copy of your development database file as the Design Master. As suggested in Chapter 13, "Building the Run-Time Application," when preparing an application for distribution, the authors recommended removing comments and test routines from a copy of the original and using this copy as the distribution copy. Your Design Master also should follow these guidelines. Otherwise, the first time you replicate the application MDB file, all the comments that you carefully removed will reappear on all the client versions.

The conversion is performed by taking the following steps:

1. First, build the replica set. Open the Windows 95 Explorer, and then drag and drop the database icon onto the Briefcase icon. You may need to rearrange the screen display so that you can see both the Explorer folders and the Briefcase. You see a message that informs you that the file will be converted into a member of a replica set (see fig. 20.2). Choose <u>Y</u>es to continue.

Fig. 20.2

Preparing to create a replicated database by using the Briefcase; here the dialog box requests confirmation to convert the database file to a replicatable format.

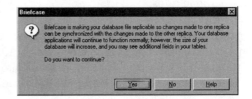

2. Briefcase offers to create a backup copy of your database. If you haven't already made a backup, accept the offer because the conversion process adds tables, fields, and properties that configure the database as a Design Master. These added tables will not necessarily be visible in the database window. Choose <u>Y</u>es to continue.

3. Briefcase then asks where you plan to make changes to the design of your database (see fig. 20.3). The answer is in the original file, not in the Briefcase replica. You do not want users to be able to make changes to the structure, only to the data.

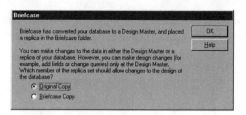

Fig. 20.3

Briefcase asks which copy of the replicated database will be the Design Master, the original copy or the briefcase copy.

4. Minimize Explorer and start My Briefcase. You see the replica in the Briefcase list. At this point, it is synchronized with the original.

5. Right-click the name of the replica database in the Briefcase, and then open the Properties dialog box. Select the Update Status tab. The two databases show as synchronized (see fig. 20.4). Close this dialog box.

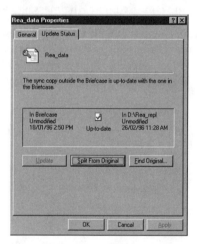

Fig. 20.4

The Update Status dialog box, which shows that the two members of the replica set are synchronized.

Now, you have both the Design Master and a replica database. Because you nominated the original as the database where changes can be made, the replica is read-only in design mode. To demonstrate this, double-click the name of the replica MDB file in the Briefcase list. Access opens, and you will see that the database window shows this to be a replica (notice the title bar in fig. 20.5).

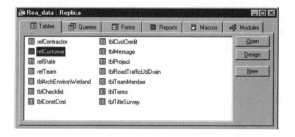

Fig. 20.5

The replica member of the replica set, with the "Replica" designation in the title bar of the database window.

Try opening a table in design mode—you can do so, but you are limited to opening it in read-only mode. Access informs you that you can make changes only to the Design Master (see the message in fig. 20.6).

Fig. 20.6
_____

*When you try to make
design changes to the
Replica member of the
replica set, you see a
warning that this database
is read-only.*

When you do open the table in design mode, Access shows that this is a replicated table. There is little excuse for getting confused here, the messages are clear.

Close the copy of the database from the Briefcase. If you again open the Properties dialog box, you should find that the Briefcase copy shows as modified because Access always updates the date stamp when you open and close an MDB file, not because you made changes (see fig. 20.7). Do not synchronize the two copies just yet.

Fig. 20.7
_____

*The Update Status dialog
box shows that the
Briefcase copy of the replica
set was most recently
updated, and that you need
to synchronize it with the
original copy.*

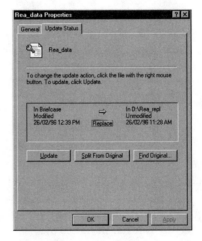

Synchronizing the Replica Set

To examine how the replication works for design changes, close this database, go to your original .MDB file, and make a small change, such as adding a new field to a table. Notice that as you do so, the database window denotes this .MDB file as a Design Master, and the table is shown as a replicated table (see fig. 20.8).

Fig. 20.8

The original database is now the Design Master, and the table refCustomer is now designated as a Replicated Table.

While you are here, look at the system tables used for replication management. Use the menu choice Tools, Options, and then click the View tab. Check the boxes for System Objects and Hidden Objects, and then close the Options box. You see replication tables, which include *MSysReplicas*, *MSysRepinfo*, *MSysRepLock*, and the oddly named *MSysTombstone* (see fig. 20.9). Look at MSysReplicas, and you see the original file and the copy in the Briefcase listed there. To avoid confusion in the future, turn off the display of the system and hidden tables before you close this database.

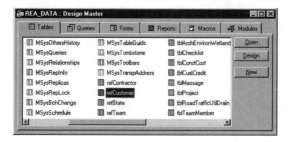

Fig. 20.9

The Hidden System tables that are used by Access 95 for Replication are designated by the prefix Msys, and are shown at the beginning of this list of tables in the database container.

Return to the Briefcase, open the list, and open the Properties dialog box for the replicated database. Now the original should be the most recent version. (If you look at the Properties box for the original, it will not show the status box—this shows only for the copy in the Briefcase.) However, changes have been made (or at least the time stamp updated) in both locations, so the Briefcase indicates that the files should be merged, as shown in figure 20.10.

VI

Administering the App

Fig. 20.10

Both copies of the replica set have changes that need to be merged with each other, as recommended by the Briefcase Properties dialog box.

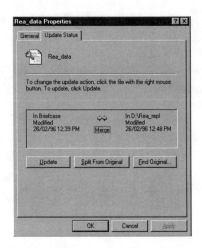

You can update here, but in practice, you update from the Briefcase menus. Select Briefcase, Update All, to perform the synchronization between the two .MDB files. Then sit back and watch as Windows 95 shows the little pieces of paper flying between the Briefcase icon and the file folder icon.

We used a change to the database structure in this example, to make the point about the replica being read-only in design mode. In practice, the data in the replica—and possibly in the original—would change, and so the update would exchange data values rather than design information. The synchronization works by exchanging only the data values that changed, which reduces network traffic significantly. Exchanging only the updated information also makes possible the synchronization of a remote computer over a telephone connection.

Copying the Briefcase to Other Systems

Until now, you have only synchronized a replica on your computer, which has questionable meaning and value. Now you need to get this replica to another system where it can be updated. There are several approaches, and none are described very well in the Window 95 books currently available on the market.

First, consider the situation where you need to work on the files on another computer (as may be the case when you take your development database home or on a business trip). You only have to *move* the briefcase to the other system. We assume here that you have a network connection or at least a Direct Connect link to the target computer. In the following examples, we use two computers, to which we have assigned the names Barney and Minnie.

Moving the Briefcase. Use the Explorer or open a folder that shows the drives on the other computer. Drag the Briefcase and drop it on the appropriate drive. In this scenario, the briefcase should exist in one place—on one computer or the other. If you don't change the name of the Briefcase before you move it, you are asked if you mean to write over the Briefcase on the target computer. You can update the original data-base, or the file in the briefcase on the remote computer. Then you can synchronize the two files over the network the next time you connect.

To move the briefcase, follow these steps:

1. Open Explorer and locate the target computer in your list of networked drives, or in the Network Neighborhood.

2. Locate the target disk drive on the remote computer—where the copy of the Briefcase will be placed.

3. Drag the Briefcase from your desktop on the originating computer, and drop it on the target drive.

4. You can now open the Briefcase on the target computer. It is another folder on the target drive (see fig. 20.11).

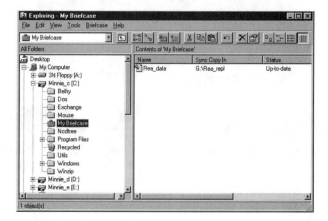

Fig. 20.11

The Briefcase and its contents on the target computer: note the Briefcase option on the top menu line.

5. If you want, drag the Briefcase from the target drive and drop it on the desktop on your target computer.

To confirm that the replication is working, make changes on one computer, then on the other, and finally on both. For each set of changes, check the status at each end of the connection, and then synchronize the copies.

Copying the Briefcase to Multiple Systems. Now suppose that you want to make copies for several computers and tie them back to the original Design Master. You do this by taking the following steps:

1. Make the Briefcase copy as described previously.

2. Copy and paste the Briefcase to your desktop as many times as you have target computers. The copies will be labeled Copy(*n*) of My Briefcase but you can re-name them to more easily keep track of what's going on (see fig. 20.12). Perhaps you could name each copy after the target computers for which the copy is bound.

Fig. 20.12

After creating multiple copies of the Briefcase, you are now ready to move each copy to a different target computer.

3. Drag and drop each briefcase onto the appropriate target computer desktop.

Now when you open one of these Briefcase folders on any of the remote computers, you can check the status and, if necessary, update the copy. If either the local copy or the Design Master has changed, the status in the Briefcase will indicate that the replica set needs updating (see fig. 20.13).

Fig. 20.13

The Briefcase Status shows that one of the replicas was updated and that the databases need to be synchronized.

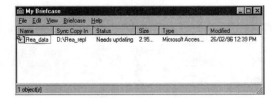

> **Tip**
>
> Make sure that the time clocks are synchronized on the various computers, so that when you look at the update information, you are not confused about which file is the most recent.

By default, when you use the Briefcase, Update All menu item to drop down the Update My Briefcase dialog box, the update shows the direction in which the synchronization will take place (see fig. 20.14). If one file was modified and the other was not, the update is essentially a replacement of one file by the other.

Fig. 20.14

The Update My Briefcase dialog box: the file on the right, the replica, was changed; the master file on the left now needs updating, and the scheme suggested is a Replace operation.

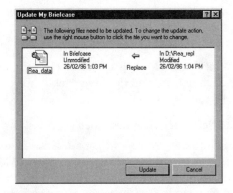

Notice that you can change the default operation. By clicking with the secondary mouse button on one of the files, you can swap the direction of the Replace operation. If both files were changed, the default operation is a merge (see fig. 20.15).

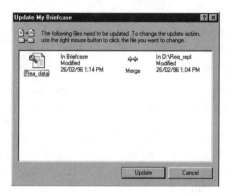

Fig. 20.15

The Update My Briefcase dialog box: both copies were modified; therefore, both files need updating. The changes will be merged.

As before, you can change the operation from a merge to a replace in one direction or the other, choosing one version of the replica set to write over the other.

Reconciling Differences in Briefcase Replication

> **Caution**
>
> The Briefcase replication is really intended for a user to transfer files to a laptop computer, modify these files, and then restore them to the desktop computer. The synchronization is designed to keep the user's two computers synchronized. Briefcase wasn't intended as a heavy-duty distribution or replication manager of the type found in an enterprise DBMS. The capabilities of Briefcase replication are somewhat limited. The authors do not recommend relying on the Briefcase replication to keep a large number of copies of data synchronized. All critical corporate data should use a more robust replication or distribution method, such as the method found in Microsoft SQL Server.

The biggest problem with any replication scheme is in deducing a method to handle *conflicting updates*. The simplest case of conflicting updates is when the same data was changed by two or more people. Then, it is a question of which change or set of changes takes precedence because only one value can be correct. (If this is not the case, you have a flaw in the database design or a hole in your business logic.)

Suppose that one salesperson changed a customer's telephone number, and another changed the name of the contact person. Are both changes valid? The truth may be that there are two contacts at that company but the phone number and the name were mismatched. If you accept both changes, the name and number still will be mismatched. If you leave the name and change the number, the number will be correct for the named contact. Then, you have to add the other contact person and phone number as a new record.

Fortunately, Briefcase includes a method for resolving conflicts. When Briefcase replication finds two records that both were changed but the changes are different, it uses the following logic:

- Compare the two records for change status.
- Whichever record was changed the most times becomes the master record and is used to update all the other records.
- Changes from the other records are placed in a log file for conflict resolution.

Each record has a version number, stored in the hidden s_Lineage field for the table. When the data in a record is changed, the version number is incremented by one. An unchanged record has a version number of 0. Changing the data increments the version number to 1. A second change to the same data, or a change to different data in the record, increments the version number to 2. If the record at one replica was changed once and the same record at the second replica was changed three times, the record at the second replica has a higher version number than the record at the first replica. The Jet Engine compares the version numbers for the same record, and assumes that the version that changed the most is the more correct of the two versions. If both records have the same version number, Microsoft Jet examines the ReplicaID and selects the replica set member with the lowest ReplicaID.

The method of taking the record that changed the most is intended to reduce the number of entries in the error file. If user A changed the record four times and user B only once, then it is better to resolve the conflict on the one change from user B.

The conflict may not necessarily show up at the Design Master, which is where the Database Manager is most likely located. The conflict shows up at whichever copy has the record in conflict. This method is not really an ideal way of handling conflicts; it puts the problem back on the originating user. Ideally, the DBA (the assumed owner of the Design Master) should be involved in this conflict resolution. At least, there should be some way of sending a message about conflicts to the Design Master, even if the conflict shows up only in the replica. Even if the DBA uses the Tools, Replication, Resolve Conflicts menu option, she or he will see no conflicts. Conflicts are visible only at the copy that has the conflicting data. A dialog box appears as this database is opened, stating that conflicting records exist (see fig. 20.16).

Fig. 20.16

The replica set is unsynchronized. When this happens, the copy originating the resolution is notified of the conflict.

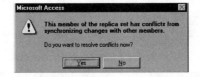

You can then go to the *Resolve Replication Conflicts* dialog box, which shows the table with the conflicting records (see fig. 20.17). The record is shown with the table fields side-by-side.

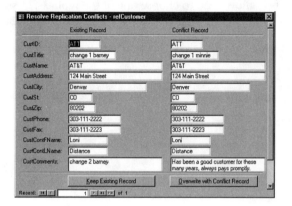

Fig. 20.17

The Resolve Replication Conflicts dialog box, showing the two records that are in conflict with one another. This gives a user the chance to view the differences and select the "correct" version.

You have the option of specifying which set of changes to accept—the set that was accepted or the conflicting data. You can accept either set, and it will write to your local database as a change. When you accept one set or the other, you should replicate this change by running the briefcase replication again. Here, a danger lies....

As we mentioned, the conflicts can appear at the user replica database. The changes were already written at the Design Master. Now the user decides that his or her changes were correct and resolves the conflict by selecting the changes again, overriding what was sent from the Design Master. This change is written at the user's local replica. When the user does a synchronization again, the user's database shows changes since the last synchronization. The Master Design database shows no changes. Therefore, the synchronization assumes that the user's changes should be accepted, and this time, they overwrite the data with which they were in conflict.

For this reason alone, many DBAs do not want to use the Briefcase replication. It leaves too much control in the hands of the user, especially in the area of conflict resolution. Briefcase replication works best between two computers used only by the same person. It's also suitable for providing current copies of read-only information to multiple users. It works reasonably well for a shared database, where each person updates a subset of the data and no overlap exists between subsets. It starts to fall apart when multiple users make changes to the same records, and it's totally unsuited for any kind of heavy transaction processing.

Synchronization from Within the Application

You can synchronize the replicas from within Access, rather than using the Briefcase replication. Open the database and use the Tools, Replication, Synchronize Now menu option. The dialog box allows you to choose one of the replicas, as shown in figure 20.18 (assuming that you are running this from the Design Master database). No option is available to choose all of them and synchronize the entire replica set at the same time.

Fig. 20.18

The Synchronize Database dialog box for replica synchronization from within Access; choosing a replica to synchronize with the Design Master.

When you make a selection, the synchronization happens. You will not see the options that show which copy is the most recent or be able to select which way to perform a replace. After the replication is complete, you are prompted to allow Access to close and reopen the database.

Notes on Replication

Certain sources state that you cannot use *password protection* on .MDB files that you want to replicate with the Briefcase, but this opinion runs counter to the authors' findings. The authors have used Briefcase replication on secured databases with no problem. The literature states that the change reconciliation uses the Jet database engine to open Access, but it runs in background and doesn't actually launch Access. It also states that if you have password-protected the database, you need to open Access to read the files. The authors have found that this is not true in the operational environment in which they are working.

Because the background operation opens the Access MDB file, it changes the time stamp. Therefore, the replicas always seem to be in need of updating. You can synchronize one replica, then a second, and the first will indicate that it is in need of updating, even if no changes were made. This is just a side effect of the way in which Access always updates the time stamp when the database is opened and closed again, even when no changes were made.

Using the Replication Manager

The Briefcase replication works as long as your clients are running Access 95 and Windows 95. But if you are running Windows NT 3.51, Server or Workstation, you still can take advantage of the benefits of replication. To do so, you need to install the *Replication Manager* from the Access Developers Toolkit (which we discussed in Chapter 13). The Replication Manager works a little differently from the Briefcase, so we will now look at these differences and how they affect applications. The major differences are that the Replication Manager offers the capability to schedule updates and to update multiple replicas.

The main features offered by the Replication Manager are the following:

- Management of a large number of replicas
- Capability to replicate more than one database at the same time
- Scheduler with graphical user interface for setting update schedule (but still allows on-demand updates)
- Capability to configure updates to send or receive data or both
- Support for laptop users with network "drop boxes," where synchronization information is deposited for later retrieval
- Runs under either Windows NT 3.51 or Windows 95
- Can be distributed royalty-free to clients

If you installed the Access Developer's Toolkit on Windows 95, the Replication Manager was installed in the ADT folder. However, you can install it separately, if you want.

Installing and Configuring the Replication Manager

To install the Replication Manager, begin with the installation of the Access Developer's Toolkit. Select the Custom install option, and choose only the Replication manager. You see a message when you opt not to install the ADT core software, but Replication Manager doesn't seem to need any other boxes checked to install successfully. Follow the directions on-screen to complete the installation (see fig. 20.19).

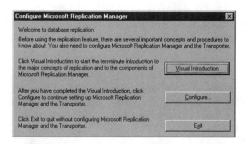

Fig. 20.19

Configuring the Replication Manager is handled through a sequence of dialog boxes, much like an Access Wizard; this is the Replication Manager introduction screen.

VI

Administering the App

When you first open Replication Manager, you are offered the opportunity to look at a short visual introduction (see fig. 20.20). If you are new to replication, or at least to Microsoft's version of replication, this introduction is worth the few minutes of study. It defines the terminology used in the configuration of the Replication Manager. You then must configure the Replication Manager before you can use it (see fig. 20.21).

Fig. 20.20

Replication Manager has a Visual Introduction, an on-line walk-through of Microsoft's implementation of replication, which helps you get acquainted with the concept and how Microsoft implements it.

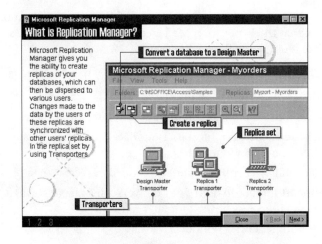

Fig. 20.21

Configuring The Replication Manager: The Configuration Wizard opening dialog box.

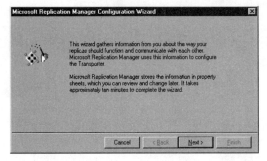

The first item of business in the configuration is specifying the folder in which your Design Master database file is located. The folder is added to the list of managed folders (see fig. 20.22). Folder location is how Replication Manager distinguishes between replicas.

Fig. 20.22

You must specify and add to the list of Managed Folders the folder in which your Design Master database file is located.

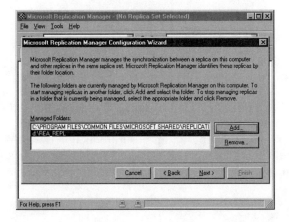

Add to this list your folder that contains the copy of the database that you want to make the Design Master. Then proceed to the next step, specifying a shared network folder (see fig. 20.23). Replication manager needs to have available a temporary storage area for the Transporter to keep the changes during synchronization. (The *Transporter* is the mechanism that performs the actual synchronization between replicas.) If no shared folder is available on your computer, you can create a share or you can specify a path to a shared folder on the network server.

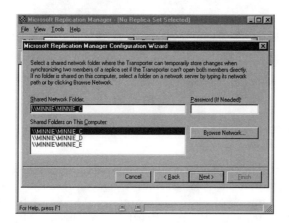

Fig. 20.23

You also need to Specify a shared network folder for the Transporter to use during synchronization.

The Replication Manager and the Transporter keep a *Transporter Log* (which sounds like something out of *Star Trek*), and ask for a file location for this log. The default location is the folder that contains the Design Master. The Configuration Wizard also requests a name for the icon used for the Transporter for these replicas.

At this point, configuration is complete. The Wizard finishes its work and starts up the Replication Manager.

Converting Your Database with Replication Manager

After the Replication Manager is configured, it opens a screen that offers to either convert a database to a Design Master or create a replica (see fig. 20.24).

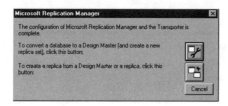

Fig. 20.24

Configuration Complete; now you can create the Design Master.

VI

Administering the App

The *Conversion Wizard* opens at the folder that you added to the list of *managed folders*, and allows you to select the .MDB file for conversion. When you do, the Wizard requests a description for the entire replica set, which presently contains only one member, the Design Master (see fig. 20.25).

Fig. 20.25

The Convert Database to Design Master Wizard: providing a description for the replica set.

The next screen asks you to specify in which managed folder to place the Design Master, although it doesn't default to the location from which you read the .MDB file (see fig. 20.26). It also offers the option of adding a new managed folder for the Design Master. Notice that, like Briefcase, the Wizard offers to make a backup of your database before conversion.

Fig. 20.26

The Convert Database to Design Master Wizard: indicating in which managed folder the Design Master will be located.

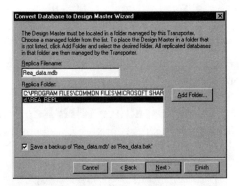

The Replication Manager can configure the database replicas either to be read-only or to allow the user to make changes to the replicas. On the next screen, you specify the alternative you want (see fig. 20.27).

A major difference between Briefcase and Replication Manager is the capability to limit which objects are available to the replication set (see fig. 20.28). Replicated objects are available to the entire replica set and take part in the synchronization. Local objects remain where they were created and do not take part in replication.

Fig. 20.27

The Convert Database to Design Master Wizard: indicating whether the replicas will be read-only or updatable.

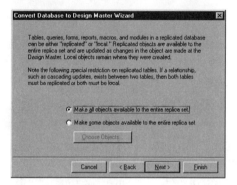

Fig. 20.28

The Convert Database to Design Master Wizard: indicating that all database objects will be available to the replica set.

If you elect to make only some objects available to the replica set, the Wizard lets you specify which objects by checking or unchecking items in a list of objects—which looks just like the old familiar Access database window, but with the addition of check boxes for the objects (see fig. 20.29).

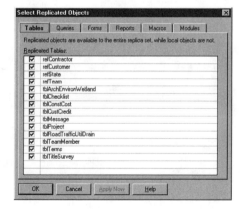

Fig. 20.29

If only some of the database objects will be available for replication, you must select which of the objects will be replicatable.

Finally, you are asked to provide a description for the Design Master, and then the Wizard completes the conversion process. The Replication Manager window opens, showing your Design Master (see fig. 20.30).

Fig. 20.30

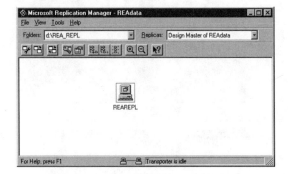

At the very end of the conversion process, the Replication Manager window will open, and it will contain the newly created Design Master.

Building Replicas with Replication Manager

Now that the Design Master is in place, you can begin building replicas on other computers on the network. You do this by taking the following steps:

1. Use the File, Create Replica menu option to open a list of database files. The Create Replica Of window opens.

2. Select the Design Master and open it. You have the opportunity again here to specify if this replica will be updatable or read-only.

3. Place the replica in a folder on the target computer. To do so, you need to add the name of a managed folder on the target computer, as illustrated by figure 20.31. (You cannot create a new folder from this dialog box; you must add the name of an existing folder.)

Fig. 20.31

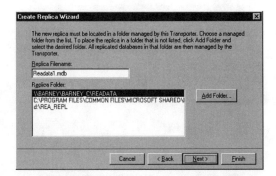

The Create Replica Wizard, which helps you build a replica of the Design Master. You must designate a managed folder in which the replica will reside.

4. After specifying the folder and a file name for the replica, you are prompted for a description of the replica, and then the Wizard takes over and creates the replica. Notice that now, your Replication Manager window shows that you have two managed replicas, the Design Master and the replica that you just created.

5. Repeat the process to create replicas on the other computers on your network.

Synchronization with Replication Manager

You can force a synchronization with Replication Manager, using the Synchronize Now icon or the Tools, Synchronize Now menu item. You can send and receive changes (the equivalent of the Briefcase merge option). You also can limit the replication to just receiving or just sending the changes, which corresponds to the direction of replacement in the Briefcase synchronization (see fig. 20.32). Watch the bar between the transporters change as the data is transferred.

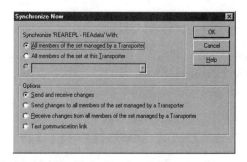

Fig. 20.32

Using the Replication Manager to force a synchronization of all copies within the replica set.

Remember that Replication Manager synchronizes all the replicas, not just one replica, as Briefcase does. If a replica isn't connected to the network, the changes are stored in the temporary folder by the transporter and applied the first time the user connects again.

Scheduling Synchronization

To modify the default schedule, right-click the replica icon and select the Edit Default Schedule option. You see a graphical representation of times during the week when synchronization is turned on or turned off, and you can modify the schedule by clicking in the time slots (see fig. 20.33).

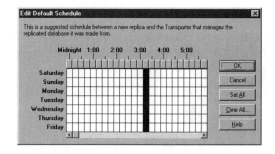

Fig. 20.33

Scheduling a synchronization through the Replication Manager is as easy as editing the Synchronization Schedule.

Replication from Within Access 95

Although you used the Replication Manager to build the replicas, you still can perform on-demand synchronization from within Access. To do so, start Access, and open the database. Use the Tools, Replication, Create Replica command from the menus in Access to perform the conversion.

Resolving Conflicts in Replication Manager

Conflicts are resolved in just the same way as when using Briefcase. The replica with the conflict receives the message and has to make a choice to resolve the conflict.

Replication as a Backup

It is possible to use the Briefcase replication to make a *backup* of the Access database. If this backup is written to a different disk, or even a different computer, it can be used to rebuild the server MDB file if the server crashes. The advantage to this backup method is that only changes are transferred, which means less disk I/O than making a regular copy of a large MDB file, and less network traffic when using another computer to store the reserve copy. Of course, there is no substitute for an offsite tape or optical backup when performed on a regular schedule.

DAO Programming of Replication

If you do not want to give control of replication to the user, you can program replication into your application by using the standard DAO (Data Access Object) interface. Using DAO, you can implement several of the features offered by Briefcase replication, including the following:

- Converting a database to a Design Master
- Making replicas from the Design Master
- Synchronizing replicas

When should you use *DAO programming*? DAO may be the best approach when you need to synchronize replicas on an irregular schedule or have a requirement to trigger a synchronization when a certain event happens. For example, you can trigger a synchronization when a tax rate changes to make sure that all invoices are generated with the new rate.

You also may want to program your synchronization and replication when your user community has limited familiarity with computers. You can provide a simplified replication interface, or you can even hide it entirely.

The SQL Server Tie-In

Microsoft SQL Server 6.5 has added more capability in its replication (actually, distribution) feature. It now supports replication to Access databases. You can use this feature, for example, to push data from SQL Server out to an Access database, which can then be distributed to the traveling sales force. Unfortunately, because Access doesn't support replication at the same level as SQL Server, it isn't a two-way process. If any changes are made to the copies, they are lost when the next replication happens.

There is always the option, as discussed previously in this chapter, of using a separate set of temporary tables in the Access application, and then writing all updates back to the SQL database.

For a discussion of how replication is handled in SQL Server, the authors suggest *The Microsoft SQL Server DBA Survival Guide*, by Mark Spenik and Orryn Sledge, Sams Publishing, Indianapolis, IN, 1995, $49.99.

From Here...

In this chapter we covered how to set up replication within Access to keep multiple copies of a database synchronized. We looked at Briefcase replication, new in Windows 95. We discussed the Replication Manager, which runs under Windows 95 and Windows NT 3.51. From here, jump to the following chapters:

- Chapter 13, "Building the Run-Time Application," discusses the Access Developers Toolkit.
- Chapter 22, "The Human Factor," covers the human factors to consider when distributing and replicating databases.

VI

Administering the App

CHAPTER 21

Client/Server Performance and Tuning

Tuning a client/server application requires a truly broad knowledge of the client software, the server database management system, the client and server operating systems, the network, and—oh yes—the hardware. It also requires an understanding of the needs of the user community. Performance tuning is more an art than it is a science, although a great deal of science does go into *performance monitoring*. This chapter looks at some of the factors that can make a difference to the overall performance of the client/server application. In this chapter, we discuss the following areas:

- The goals of performance monitoring and tuning
- Defining, managing, and meeting user expectations
- Factors that affect performance
- How the network affects the application
- How to identify bottlenecks
- Capacity planning
- Enhancements and changes you can make to up performance

An important item to remember: no amount of tuning and tweaking makes up for bad design. If the design is sound and the programming efficient, tuning just adds a little extra to the package. With an unsound design, tuning may just be a waste of time and effort.

Goals of Performance Monitoring and Tuning

There can be several reasons which are the driving forces behind performance monitoring and tuning the client/server application, but it really comes down to the need to provide a responsive, secure, and robust database application to the end users. Some specific goals for performance tuning might include the following:

- Maximize throughput for all requests from the user community
- Provide acceptable response time to queries

- Keep the overall server performance optimized
- Track down and eliminate bottlenecks

How do you measure performance in a client/server environment? There are many criteria, including the amount of I/O per transaction, the load on the CPU, the throughput in transactions per second, or the time a query takes to show an answer on the user's screen. But even with all these measurements, who designates "acceptable" performance, and how is it defined?

Managing and Meeting User Expectations

Meeting user expectations can be one of the most frustrating experiences for a developer. Your application gathers information that would take the user all day to round up in the old paper-based system, and then places it on-screen in a nice, organized, and sensible fashion. The users then complain because it takes more than five seconds to return the information for a specific record. How can you overcome this perception that the system is slow?

During the design phase, set some target expectations. First, explain what the database will do behind the scenes. Clearly state that the data isn't in memory on the desktop, and that it has to be retrieved from many server data sources. Most users are accustomed to applications such as word processors or spreadsheets, where the entire file is loaded into memory, and they can move from one place to another quickly within the text file or spreadsheet. Point out that they can do this as long as they are the only person working on that document or spreadsheet. Ask them to imagine how different it would be if everyone were working on the same document or file at the same time.

Survey the users for input on how long they think the response time should be, and try to get some realistic estimates. It's an interesting exercise to also ask users to estimate how long the current process takes, whether it be manual or computerized. When the users request a new feature, point out the impact that feature may have on performance, and what it adds to the application's functionality. The users may be willing to accept a short delay in displaying a record if they also see additional data or some new calculated fields that make their job easier.

In the final analysis, it doesn't matter how many benchmarks or tests you run, or what numbers show up in the Performance Monitor readings on the server. The only significant measure is whether or not the users are satisfied with the performance of the application—to be more accurate, whether or not the users are satisfied with the perceived performance, which may not be the same thing. For this reason, Access displays the first record of a data set even while it is retrieving more data. It is the reason for making forms seem more efficient by displaying a splash screen while the application is loading, and other "tricks" that make the application appear more responsive than it may be. The perceived performance usually is referred to by the response time. Actual performance is measured in throughput, the number of queries handled by the server in a given time.

You cannot assume that because two groups of users get the same performance and one group is happy, that the second group is unreasonable when it complains. Its demands on the system may be greater, or it may need to access the data in a different way, and it really does need faster response. The most obvious symptom of unacceptable performance is when the system administrator's phone rings off the desk. A little checking with the users, and staying sensitive to their needs, even involving them in the design and development of the application, will hopefully head off the next step, which is your boss's phone ringing off the desk.

Chapter 22, "The Human Factor," discusses some of the reasons why users are resistant to the introduction of new software. For now, you can conclude that keeping the user expectations within realistic limits is as much a part of the development process as optimizing queries or normalizing tables. Unfortunately, so much misinformation is floating around about client/server applications that the users may be expecting miracles. Unless you can deliver miracles on a regular and repeatable basis, user education and distributing information may be a better technique with more dependable results.

Factors That Affect Performance

Many factors can affect database performance. Some of them are within your control, and some you may have no control over but must still take into account. The main areas that affect performance are the following:

The design:

- The specifications, requirements, and expectations for the application
- The design of the server component
- The design of the client component, including the user interface
- The efficiency with which the application design was implemented

The hardware:

- The speed of the CPU
- The number of CPUs
- The amount of RAM (memory)
- The speed of the hard disk subsystem
- The efficiency of the network

The software:

- Query optimization
- Locking mechanisms
- Data distribution across devices
- Transaction logging

Database functions:

- Bulk data loading
- On-line backup
- Replication to other databases
- Maintaining statistics

We previously discussed the design of both the client and the server components, and we looked at how prototyping in Access can help shake out the design before the server component is upsized. We also looked at the hardware, for both client and server portions of the application. A few additional considerations to get the best possible performance are worth investigating when running the application over the corporate network.

Network Traffic Considerations

Network tuning can be conveniently split into two areas: reducing the amount of *network traffic*, and speeding up the traffic that must flow across the network. We have talked in other chapters about various methods to reduce traffic. Now let's look at some ways in which we might speed up the essential traffic.

Use a Fast Network Card

The *network card* in the server should be running on the PCI bus and, ideally, should be a 100 Mbps card. Of course, to keep pace, the cards in the client workstations also should have similar qualifications. It's easy to overlook or cut corners on the network card, especially when a company orders a large number of computers and looks for good price savings. If your server is running Windows NT, the authors advise to stay with a card that is on the NT Hardware Compatibility List. Avoid CheaperNet cards in plain white boxes. Windows NT supports more than one network card, and some of the documentation suggests that you may want to run one card per protocol. However, recent testing indicates that, because of the way in which Windows NT handles interrupts, you can get better throughput for all protocols with just one fast card.

> **Tip**
>
> For a complete treatment of networking in the Windows NT environment, the authors recommend the *Windows NT Networking Guide,* Volume 2 of the Windows NT Resource Kit, Microsoft Press.

As was mentioned in Chapter 3, "The Application Development Environment," if you can afford optical fiber networks, buy them. If you want a truly secure network, optical fiber is far better than wire carrying, and radiating, electrical signals. Also, because optical cabling is unaffected by electromagnetic interference, the number of errors and re-sent packets are dramatically reduced.

Watch Your Interrupts

You also should avoid network cards that limit your choice of *interrupts* to those normally used for other devices. Some network cards have a bad habit of defaulting to interrupt 3, which means they will conflict with the second serial port. You can get away with this on Windows for Workgroups, but Windows 95 reports the conflict, and Windows NT doesn't allow shared interrupts at all, so the network card does not work until you change the interrupt.

Remove Protocols That Are Not in Use

It's possible, especially in an environment that began as peer-to-peer and evolved into enterprise computing, that you have multiple *protocols* installed. Some of these protocols may no longer be used. Perhaps you started with NWLINK and now use TCP/IP. You can remove the protocols that you no longer use to avoid confusion and reduce the number of decisions the software must make when sending network traffic. Just use care with what you remove. The Browser service in Windows NT, for example, which provides the lists of available resources, depends on NetBIOS. The protocol may still be in use, although you don't think you are actively making use of it.

Check Your Bindings

If you are a skier, you probably will agree that checking your bindings is a good idea. Actually, we are referring to *network bindings*. In Windows NT, using the Network icon in Control Panel, you can check the bindings, which simply means how the various software components are connected to each other and to the hardware. Rather than removing a protocol, you can disable the binding. You also can change the order of the bindings, so that the most-frequently used protocol is listed first. If you are unfamiliar with bindings, ask your network administrator to give you a hand.

Use the Latest Drivers

First skiing, and now golf? No, here we mean *network drivers*. If your client application is Windows 95, your clients should be using NDIS 3.0 network card drivers. These drivers offer benefits over the older NDIS 2.0 drivers; for example, they load into extended memory. If a 3.0 driver is not available for your network card, it's probably because the card is an inexpensive, no-name network card, and/or the manufacturer has gone out of business. Windows NT requires NDIS 3.0 drivers. The latest drivers can be obtained from the manufacturer of the card, or may be found on the manufacturer's bulletin board or web site, or on Microsoft's Download Service Bulletin board. Today, most new drivers can be found on the Internet. If you prefer to get the drivers on CD-ROM, every third month, Microsoft's TechNet CD-ROM includes all the latest drivers.

Using Performance Monitor

The *Performance Monitor* is available only on Windows NT, not on Windows 95. Although it would be nice to have the capability of monitoring the desktop systems, the server database management system will be running on a platform such as Windows NT, and this is where you really need performance monitoring. NT Performance Monitor can be configured to show any combination of several hundred parameters, or performance counters. Each group of performance counters allows you to monitor a performance object.

Access 95 and Performance Monitor

Because Access 95 is a 32-bit application, it shows in the Performance Monitor as a process that can be tracked. Start Performance Monitor and select the Process object, and the Access instance. (An *instance* is just a list of the available items within an object: for example, a two-CPU computer will show two instances for the processor, labeled, in true programmer fashion, 0 and 1). You then can select from the various counters for this process, as shown in figure 21.1.

Fig. 21.1

Monitoring Access 95 with NT Performance Monitor: adding the Percent Processor Time counter to the output display.

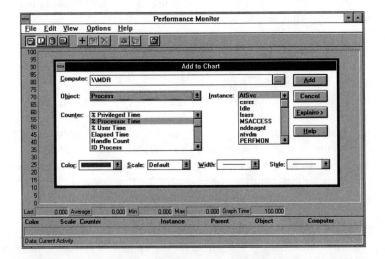

> **Tip**
>
> When you start Performance Monitor, the default object is Processor—the CPU. Do not confuse this with Process, which is easy to do!

In the example shown in figure 21.2, the counters for processor time and the number of Access 95 threads were selected and are being tracked.

The number of threads remains constant at six. The percent of processor time varies, depending on what Access 95 is doing at a given moment. If you select the Threads object and the Percent Process Time (see fig. 21.3), you see the six threads listed, and you can even track them, as shown in figure 21.4. One thread dominates, virtually overlaying the overall CPU usage for the Access process.

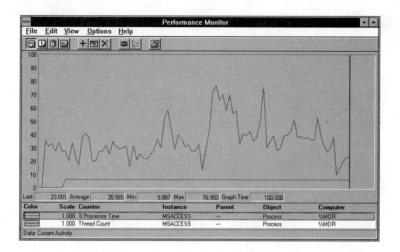

Fig. 21.2

Using NT Performance Monitor to record Access 95 behavior; both Percent Processor Time and Thread Count are being monitored.

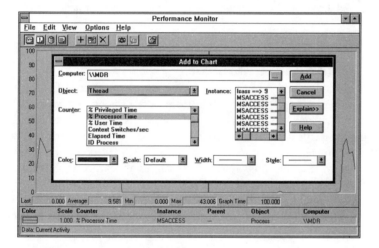

Fig. 21.3

Monitoring Access 95 with NT Performance Monitor: selecting the Threads object and the Percent Processor Time for display.

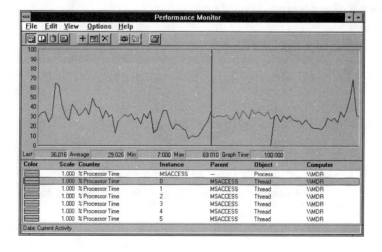

Fig. 21.4

Monitoring Access 95 with NT Performance Monitor: tracking the Access 95 Threads, Percent Processor Time.

VI

Administering the App

Unfortunately, no description is available of what each thread represents. In fact, no way exists to track individual parameters or counters *within* Access 95, as you can with Microsoft SQL Server or some other server database management system.

Incidentally, if you use Performance Monitor to track a 16-bit version of Access, you will not find it listed as a process. It is running in a *Windows-on-Windows* 16-bit session in a *Virtual DOS Machine* (*VDM*). You can monitor the VDM, and if you set up Access to run in its own memory space, you know that only Access is being monitored, and not another Windows 3.1 application.

Besides monitoring the Access process, you can add other system counters, such as the processor time, disk usage, and so on.

> **Note**
>
> If you want to measure disk parameters in Windows NT, you must go to a command prompt, type **diskperf -y**, and then reboot the computer to turn on the gathering of statistics on the disks.

Interpreting Performance Monitor

The horizontal axis of the Performance Monitor screen is time; the vertical axis is the values of the counters being monitored. At the bottom of the screen, you see a list of the counters. As each *counter* is added, a different color is assigned to the added counter for graphing, and this color also is shown next to the counter in the list. By highlighting any one counter, you can look at the statistics for the counter, including the minimum, maximum, and average values. These values appear in small windows above the list and below the chart. You also can build a log file in Performance Monitor and store it for future reference and comparison, or you can generate a report rather than a chart. For more information about Performance Monitor, consult the Windows NT Resource Kit.

SQL Server and Performance Monitor

You can monitor many more parameters in the industrial-strength back-end databases than you can in Access 95. Some of these databases, such as Microsoft SQL Server, add their own performance counters to the Windows NT Performance Monitor, as shown in figure 21.5, rather than having a dedicated performance monitor. This idea is neat because it allows you to monitor system counters and database counters at the same time, on the same screen. An icon in the SQL program group brings up the Performance Monitor, with the SQL Server default items selected.

> **Note**
>
> Other software packages can add their own performance counters to the Performance Monitor. IBM's new DB2 for Windows NT, for example, adds about 130 different counters.

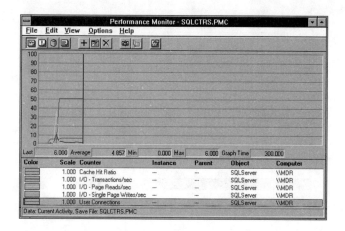

Fig. 21.5

Microsoft SQL Server performance counters, displayed by the NT Performance Monitor.

Using Microsoft SQL Server as an example, the counters that appear by default in the performance monitor include the following:

- **Cache Hit Ratio**—The percentage of time that a request is handled from the database cache, rather than being read from the hard disk.

- **I/O Transactions/second**—The count of Transact-SQL command batches executed per second.

- **I/O Page Reads/second**—The number of physical page reads per second.

- **I/O Single Page Writes/second**—The number of single page writes per second including logging and cache flushes.

- **User Connections**—The count of current user connections.

The *Cache Hit Ratio* shows how often SQL Server needs to read from the physical disk in order to service a request. If the ratio remains high, most requests are being handled from the database cache and not from the disk drive. If the ratio is consistently low, you may need to add more memory for use as cache.

The *User Connections* value can show periods of heavy or light traffic and also can show when you may be close to the number of user connections or client access licenses allocated. You may want to set up an alert on this value to avoid users being denied access during times when many users are connecting to the server.

From here, if you want to add counters, you will find that all the standard Performance Monitor counters are available, and about 40 SQL Server counters, as shown in figures 21.6 and 21.7.

Each of these objects contains multiple counters. A few of the counters for the SQL Server object are shown in figure 21.7.

VI

Administering the App

Fig. 21.6

Choosing additional SQL Server objects for display, using NT Performance Monitor.

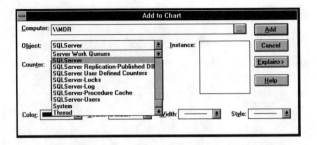

Fig. 21.7

Each SQL Server object is composed of multiple counters, which are displayed in the NT Performance Monitor graph.

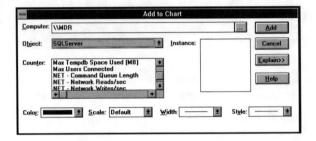

These examples apply to most server database management systems running on Windows NT. There are a few performance counters that are especially useful and that you may want to monitor for awhile at system installation, to provide a baseline for later measurements. These counters include the following:

■ **Log Space Used** (%)—This counter ensures that the transaction log has enough space to write in and that the database doesn't lock up just because the log is full.

■ **Processor - % Processor time**—If this counter is running constantly at or above the 90 percent level, you need either an additional processor or a faster processor.

■ **Network Reads/Second**—If the Network Reads value is high, and the transaction counters are low, you can deduce that you are running long transactions, and each transaction moves large amounts of data across the network. If the data is truly needed, you have to deal with the network traffic. But if each user requires only a small portion of the data being transferred, a design problem exists. In this case, look at using stored procedures on the server to return just the data that the users need.

Identifying Bottlenecks

In a client/server environment, tracking the bottlenecks can be a time-consuming process. The problem can be at the client, at the server, or in the network.

For performance tuning and detecting bottlenecks in the Windows NT environment, the best reference is Volume 4 of the Windows NT Resource Kit. The author is Russ Blake, who designed the Windows NT Performance Monitor. The book, at 650 pages, is the definitive reference on the Performance Monitor. It also contains three floppy disks (which are duplicated on the CD-ROM that comes with the Resource Kit), which include tuning tools and a "synthetic load generator" that helps check your system. Unfortunately, this book is available only as part of the whole Resource Kit. It is worth studying, especially for the "ten rules of bottleneck detection." If you want to add performance counters to your application, this book explains how. Counters must be built into the program code; no quick way exists to add a few counters to an existing application, in case you were wondering.

No matter what your choice of server database management system, certain counters can be useful in tuning the application. The first step is to make an educated guess as to which counters to check first. These counters fall into one of the following five categories:

- Processor
- Memory
- Disk
- Locks
- User Connections

Bottleneck: the Processor

We previously mentioned the processor and the options of increasing the processor speed or adding another processor if the percentage of Processor Time is consistently running in the 85-90 percent range or higher. You should measure this value while the application is running, not as it is first starting up. Spikes reaching 100% are OK, but a steady high level indicates a bottleneck. Some database management systems are better than others for scalability, and the manufacturer's claims are sometimes best-case scenarios. Actually, all vendor's claims are based on best-case scenarios, so look for benchmark tests run by independent organizations. SQL Server 6.0 is definitely better than version 4.2 at scaling to multiple processors because it scales in a relatively linear manner up to four processors. Version 6.5 is rumored to do better, but at the time of writing, only beta copies were available for testing. Oracle offers parallel querying and parallel recovery on SMP computers, and from version 7.0 on has written code to take advantage of multiple processors running in one computer.

Bottleneck: Memory

Every server database management system consumes memory in large quantities. You almost always can increase performance by adding memory, given the self-tuning capabilities of modern operating systems and DBMS software. However, physical and financial limits exist on just how much memory you have available, and in any case it makes sense to optimize the use of the memory currently installed. Some of the counters that you can look at include the following:

- DBMS: Cache Hit Ratio
- DBMS: I/O Lazy Writes
- Memory: Page Faults/Second

Notice that two of these are not counters for the Memory object; they belong to the database management system. We previously discussed the Cache Hit Ratio, which can indicate a need for more memory if it drops below the 80 percent level. You always prefer to read data from the cache rather than from disk because it's orders of magnitude faster. However, before assuming that a low value indicates a problem, consider what the database does while you take the measurements. In a transaction processing environment, you hope to get a high hit ratio. But if the database is measured while running a series of batch jobs and performing bulk-load operations, then you expect the cache hits to be quite low.

The I/O Lazy Writes (the name used by SQL Server; other DBMSs use a similar name) tracks the number of flushed pages per second. A number consistently greater than 0 means that the Lazy Writer is working continuously, flushing buffers to disk, which indicates that the database cache size is too small, implying that system memory is insufficient.

The Page Faults per second shows the number of times per second that a virtual page had to be retrieved from the disk because it wasn't found in memory. After the database management system has started and is allowed to stabilize, this value should be close to zero. If not, it's possible that too much memory was allocated to, or claimed by, the database management system, and not enough memory is available for the operating system to use as cache.

Bottleneck: Disk

In an ideal DBMS, disk I/O is kept to an absolute minimum. Compared to operations performed in memory, disk activity is extremely slow, even with today's fast hard disks. Remember to turn on disk monitoring with the *diskperf* command. On 80386 CPU-based computers, disk activity monitoring can account for a 2-3 percent drop in performance, which is why disk monitoring is turned off by default. This may change in newer versions of Windows NT, which no one would run on a 386 (would they?). The counters that you can check include the following:

- PhysicalDisk: % Disk Time
- PhysicalDisk: Disk Queue Length

The first counter simply measures the percentage of time that your disk is busy with read/write operations. If this value is always high, then a bottleneck may exist at the disk. Of course, you also should consider, as you did with network traffic, whether far more data is being read than is actually needed. The Disk Queue Length, if greater than 3, may show a bottleneck. It measures the number of outstanding requests on a disk at any time, and should be low for all disks. If it's high for one disk and low for the other disks, you may be able to eliminate or reduce the bottleneck by redistributing data.

Bottleneck: Locks

When your application was in the prototype stage with few users, locking of records was unlikely and, therefore, not a potential bottleneck. But after it's in use in a production environment, you may see more contention. Locks are necessary in a multi-user client/server situation, and no way exists to avoid them entirely. The problem is the blocking locks, which force a process to wait until another process is finished. To see if this type of lock is affecting your application, use the SQL Server-Locks, Total Blocking Locks. Figure 21.8 shows just a few of the locks that have associated counters.

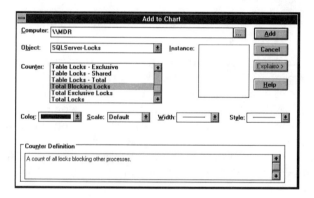

Fig. 21.8

There are multiple types of SQL Server locks that can be displayed by NT Performance Monitor.

Expect to see a few blocking locks, but the counter normally should be at or close to zero. If not, there are several possible causes. Poor table or query design may be the root of the problem, if a major glitch exists in the transaction processing. It's possible that inefficient hardware is just not allowing transactions to complete and release locks fast enough, but this degree of hardware inefficiency should be obvious. If it's a software problem, it's time to head back to the drawing board.

Bottleneck: User Connections

As we previously stated, without users, the system administrator's life would lack challenge and be very dull indeed. There are times when the system works just fine, like 3:00 a.m. on Sunday. Then, there are times when it crawls, as on Monday morning at 8:30 a.m. Creative solutions include flex-time and telecommuting. There is no software around, however, that works faster as you add more users, so to survive in the real world, you may want to monitor DBMS: User connections.

We previously mentioned User Connections as one of the default values in the SQL Server Performance Monitor. If you can determine at what level the performance starts to spiral downward, you have some hard evidence to support plans for remedial action. If everything is cool and there is no performance drop with your current user community, you still may want to monitor this value. If you never see the total number of concurrent users reach the allowed number of connections, you can consider reducing the number of available connections. Each connection you drop recovers 37K of memory, which may improve performance for the users who are connected.

In SQL Server, and in other database management systems, it is possible to monitor the individual user. Using the Current Activity option in the Enterprise Manager, you can go into great detail about any process. This goes beyond the scope of this book, but if you want to learn more, consult the *Microsoft SQL Server DBA Survival Guide* by Mark Spenik and Orryn Sledge, Sams Publishing, Indianapolis 1996. If your server runs Oracle, look for the *Oracle DBA Survival Guide*, by Joe Greene, Sams Publishing, Indianapolis 1996. There also is a *Sybase DBA Survival Guide,* Sams Publishing, Indianapolis 1996.

Capacity Planning

Up to a certain point, *capacity planning* can be handled from a theoretical perspective. You know how many users you have and how many records will be in the database. The load on the network can be estimated. When you present a plan for increasing capacity, however, it's more likely to be approved if you can show numbers or—even better—some graphs from a tool such as Performance Monitor. If you collect data from the installation of the system through to the present day, you can estimate when you need to add another server or increase the network bandwidth. Management doesn't like surprises, so the further ahead you can predict the need for additional capacity, the better.

As mentioned previously, you can set alerts in the Performance Monitor on your server, so that you are notified when certain values approach critical levels. Examples include the number of user connections: if you set an alert and are notified when the number of connections is within 10 users of the total allowed, you can plan to add more client-access licenses and, possibly, more network bandwidth. Another useful alert is when free space on a disk falls below a safe margin.

Ask yourself the following few questions as a starting point when doing your capacity planning for your database:

- How much data will be in the database initially? You can estimate this from the maximum record length (calculated by adding the length of the data types in each field), and the estimated number of records. Don't forget that each index you define (or the system defines for you) requires additional space. Add a percentage (20 percent) for the data dictionary, especially if your database management system supports declarative integrity.

- How will the database grow? The previous experience of the corporation may be an indicator, or there may be a projected growth factor in the initial design, based on plans for increased database use.

- Is there a seasonal factor to the size of the database? For example, if you are booking ski vacations, the database grows during the winter, but some of this data can be archived by early summer.

- When can the data be archived? And how much? In the ski vacation example, you need to retain some data for making plans for the upcoming year, but perhaps not every item. Do you retain the data in the operational (OLTP) database, or do you port it to the OLAP/decision support system and aggregate it into the historical information stored there?

There also is the *transaction log*, which must have space allocated, preferably on a different physical drive. Perhaps, only experience will show what size this log file needs to be, but as a starting point, consider the following questions:

- How many transactions are made between transaction log dumps?

- How big are the transaction log entries?

- How long between transaction log dumps?

The last question is related partly to how long of a time span you can allow during which you may lose data. If the system is backed up at night, and the log dumped every hour, then in the worst case, you lose only one hour of data entry and changes. If the log is backed up only at the close of business each day, you risk losing an entire day's work. So, a bigger transaction log doesn't necessarily mean better. It depends on how your business operates.

To some extent, the availability of relatively inexpensive hardware makes capacity planning less critical than it once was. Many of us who remember mainframes with 512K of memory and 30M hard disks the size of washing machines probably are more likely to worry about capacity planning. Now that a 2G (Gigabyte) disk costs about $500, which is less than the cost of determining whether or not we need another disk, capacity planning is no longer expensive.

The rule in Microsoft SQL Server is a transaction log which is 20 percent the size of the allocated database size.

Enhancements and Changes for Performance

You can use a variety of other ideas to improve the overall performance of your application. The following sections offer a few suggestions.

Turn Off Auditing

Operating systems such as Windows NT offer extensive *auditing* capabilities. Unlike mainframe charge-back auditing, modern operating systems concern themselves more with security auditing. Many different objects and processes can be audited, down to the level of who is accessing individual files, and how often. It's reasonable to turn on auditing when the system is first installed, to gather reference data in case changes happen later that require a baseline. (The same applies to Performance Monitor logs.) Then after a few days, turn off auditing unless it's needed for security reasons. Any auditing imposes a performance penalty. To put it another way, turning off auditing increases performance. (Not that you would take credit for "tuning" the system by turning off auditing, and not telling anyone how you boosted system responsiveness, of course. Your boss may have read this book, too.)

Configure the Server as a Server

If your network operating system is Windows NT Server, if possible, don't put SQL Server on the *Primary Domain Controller*. If you have multiple servers, configure the SQL Server machine as just a Server, not a Primary or even a Backup Domain Controller. When you configure a computer as a Domain Controller, the software installed differs from the standard server installation. The PDC and BDC spend considerable CPU cycles in administrative chores, such as validating users, maintaining browse lists of available resources, and so on. They are optimized for these tasks and ideally, should not also be used as database or file and print servers. But if you have only one Windows NT Server, and want to use the domain model, you have to make it both the Domain Controller and the database server.

Minimize Open Applications

On the desktop computers running the client applications, encourage the users to avoid having multiple applications open at the same time. We have seen offices where everyone has Word, Excel, a scheduler, and an e-mail package in their Windows startup group, and then they wonder why the client/server application seems slow. The computers with 8M of memory are especially slow, which is not surprising. Even with 16M, response is not great. In one case, the reason the users worked this way was simply that the Windows-based applications were stored on a Novell server, which meant that they had to be downloaded over the network every time they were opened. (We talked about why this isn't a good idea in Chapter 13, "Building the Run-Time Application"). They would turn on their computers in the morning, and then go for a cup of coffee and do other tasks while the computer was coming up and moving the applications across the network. The alternative—opening the application each time it was needed—was unacceptably slow.

When the applications are stored locally, users may be more willing to close down the applications that they aren't running. Starting the application again doesn't take much longer than swapping it back into memory from the page file on the disk. Educating the user community to the reasons why applications take so long to start up, what impact it has on their computer when too many programs are running concurrently, and how they can minimize the load on the system may result in some changes in use patterns. Windows 3.1 was notorious for running out of system resources long before it ran out of memory. Windows 95 is considerably better than Windows 3.1 at managing resources, and Windows NT doesn't run into the resource heap limits at all, but all three still have to swap applications in and out of memory.

Create Temporary Tables in RAM

SQL Server uses a temporary database, *tempdb*, for sorting or creating temporary tables used in certain query join operations. It's possible to create this *tempdb* in RAM, which significantly increases the speed of these operations. The temporary file is just a scratch area that goes away every time the database is shut down, so having it in RAM isn't a risk, but it takes away from the amount of RAM available for the data cache, so think carefully before implementing this or similar schemes. It works best in situations where the Cache Hit Ratio is low and a large number of operations are performed that need the *tempdb* storage area.

From Here...

In this chapter, you looked at some of the factors involved in tuning the client/server application as a whole, and attempted to give the art of performance tuning some scientific foundation. From here, you can jump to the following chapters to find out more about these related subjects:

- Chapter 3, "The Application Development Environment," gives more information on hardware requirements, RAID, and so on.

- Chapter 5, "Client/Server Database Application Design Fundamentals," discusses how to design your application to avoid problems later.

- Chapter 10, "Making the Right Connections," shows how to design the client/server application for optimum performance on a network.

- Chapter 11, "Managing Transactions," discusses locking.

- Chapter 16, "Tuning the Access 95 Application," gives ideas on how to make the client application more efficient.

- Chapter 19, "System Administration," discusses setting up security in Windows NT, Windows 95, and Microsoft SQL Server 6.5.

- Chapter 22, "The Human Factor," discusses the human element in the client/server environment.

VI

Administering the App

The Human Factor

Industry analysts estimate that $140 billion a year is spent on developing software that either is never used or falls far short of expectations and needs. This number is astounding, and it suggests that a lot of bad software is being written. But is it really "bad," or is the problem that the software doesn't match the needs of the user? How can you avoid having your projects fall into the category of "It may be what I asked for, but it is not what I wanted," or even when it is exactly what the managers wanted, why does it not gain acceptance from the user community? In this chapter we discuss some issues that we as developers need to understand to make our applications successful.

First, we look at how an application fits into the daily routine of the people for whom we designed it. The driving force behind client/server technology is to make the same data in the server database available to everyone who is working on a project, or whose work depends on the input of others. Then we look at how the technology enables the telecommuter and the road warrior to be part of the team.

One key to success is how the application is introduced. Just as with a person, a bad first impression is hard to overcome. The technology is only one of the factors that you must consider when introducing new software. If you understand a little about people and how they react to change, our chances for a successful product rollout are greatly enhanced.

Finally, we take a closer look at the ideas introduced in the first chapter, where client/server computing was shown to be an integral part of business process reengineering.

In this chapter, we discuss the following concerns:

- Workgroup computing, from three different viewpoints
- Telecommuting and the needs of the road warrior
- Change management, and how change affects the user community
- Rollout of an application and how to handle it

Workgroup Computing

Several factors affect whether or not the application takes its place in the daily routine of the intended users. One of these factors is whether or not it supports workgroup computing. It must facilitate not only the work of the individuals, but also the flow of work within the group or project team. The handoff from one person to the next should be smooth. The necessary data must be in place so that a team member doesn't have to back up and repeat steps in the process. The importance of how the work flows is the reason for the growth of products such as Lotus Notes, Microsoft Exchange, and a multitude of document management/workflow software packages.

There are various types of workflow as defined by current management theories. Some of these types fit better than others with the client/server model. Take a look at some of the possibilities, and consider how to design a client/server application to fit.

Transaction or Production Workflow

Transaction or *production workflow* involves the computerization of a complex set of procedures. The procedures are defined by strict corporate business rules and policies, which have evolved over considerable time. The processes and procedures are the business—they are what the company does. The various processes are completed every business day in the same way, with no room for change or flexibility. The corporate structure exists to carry out these processes and make sure that errors do not occur. Because transaction workflow usually involves some financial exposure, an audit trail must exist to track a project through each step in the process. This is especially true when many of the transactions are handled by clerical employees.

Examples of transaction workflow include mortgage-application processing, insurance-claim resolution, and loan approvals. If anything goes wrong in any step of the process, the corporation may not only lose the deal, it may be held liable for consequences of the error.

A client/server application for this type of corporation includes the following features:

- A centralized repository of data accessible to everyone involved in the process from start to finish
- A messaging scheme or even better, automatic notification, as the project is passed from one worker to the next
- A system of alerts before critical dates are reached or missed
- Checking of data to make sure that all values entered are within limits and do not contradict each other
- A management-overview screen display that shows the status of all current projects, with notification of trouble spots and the ability to drill down and investigate potential problems
- The ability to incorporate document imaging into the workflow

Because of the requirements for data integrity, security, and an audit trail, the back-end database management system must be a true server, rather than a file/server system such as Access. It would run on an operating system such as Windows NT, which also meets these requirements. The client application will offer very little flexibility to the user. Using code behind the forms, data entries must be checked for validity. The controls placed on the user—and the algorithms that drive the administrative alerts on the overview screen—are business rules that must be converted to Visual Basic for Applications code. Each algorithm, each piece of code must be thoroughly tested to ensure that it follows the business rules precisely.

Security concerns mandate that the users log on to the Access client application, and that the user ID is used in the audit trail. All auditing, whether in the application or at the operating system level, represents overhead and should be kept to the minimum required to comply with corporate requirements.

There is an example of the management-overview screen on the CD-ROM that accompanies this book. Our fictional REA real estate company is an example of a process that must be followed, with considerable financial exposure if things go wrong. The management-overview screen (see fig. 22.1) clearly shows whether a project is on track or is running into trouble. When a problem occurs, as shown by the red light, the manager can drill down to the exact cause of the problem.

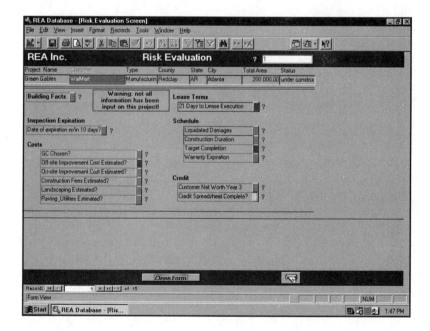

Fig. 22.1

The management-overview screen, which gives at a single glance an overview of a project and the risks associated with it.

Although this kind of screen is intended for the managers, it also should be available to the data entry staff. They need to learn how to use it to avoid causing problems that will trigger an alert. It almost becomes a game—don't let the managers see red.

One enterprising user we know would set his system clock a day ahead, to make sure that he was alerted to time-sensitive problems a day before his boss. Making this screen available to the users defuses any allegations that you are building "employee monitoring" into the application.

Administrative Workflow

Administrative workflow is based more on e-mail systems than on databases, but still may offer some opportunities for client/server solutions. Typical examples of this kind of workflow include the processing of expense accounts, purchase orders for incidental items, or scheduling vacations.

Some of these examples may lend themselves to a client/server application, even using Access to service the data files. A simple application such as scheduling vacations may require that the vacation schedule be kept in one place; there are probably business rules about not allowing too many employees to be gone at the same time. Some of these rules are probably unwritten, so as a database designer, you have to ferret them out. It may be understood that a deputy department head may not be on vacation at the same time as his or her boss, but it's unlikely that the rule is written anywhere.

This point brings up an interesting aside about the way companies are heading, with reengineering and reshaping themselves. Many companies are tossing out the volumes of rules, in some cases literally thousands of pages, and replacing them with a one page statement of the company's values. This may be great for the customer, who is now the focus of attention. Unfortunately, no way exists to tell an Access program that "Put the customer first" means scheduling more employees to be on duty around noon when a rush of customers occurs. The programs that run the company's operations still require the business rules to be translated into "if...then.." statements. The opportunity for the database designer is to shape the application to reflect the corporate values.

The challenge in this kind of workflow application is to make it interactive—so that an employee can look at the vacation schedules for the department, and then request specific dates from within the application. The request would trigger a message to the manager, who then can approve the request from within the application. Such an application would rapidly expand because it makes sense to tie the vacation schedule into the payroll data, thereby tracking how much vacation the employee can claim. Because the employee's position and length of service also determine the vacation entitlement, your application needs to read data from the personnel department. So the application grows and takes on more functionality as it expands. Keep in mind that this application may be configured with read-only access to data from the personnel and payroll databases, and that these other databases might be completely separate entities. What seemed like a simple request to track vacation schedules turns into a client/server application with multiple back-end databases! Such is the life of the developer.

Ad Hoc Workflow

Ad hoc workflow is the opposite of transaction workflow. There is no rigidly defined structure, and the end result rarely is the same twice. Examples include activities such as designing a new product, planning the rollout of a new customer service, or setting up a branch office. Where in transaction workflow the database defines the process and incorporates the rules, in ad hoc workflow the database plays only a supporting role. Some projects, such as building a new store, are better handled by project management software. Others, such as planning the company picnic, can be handled quite well with a spreadsheet and a word-processing package.

Even in a supporting role, a place still exists for client/server applications. The engineers designing a new product may want to examine the service records of the old product that is being phased out. Identifying the weak points of the old product can make a big difference to the reliability of the new one. It's unlikely that the engineers will want to pore over thousands of service records. However, if these records exist in a database, you can provide a client application that allows the engineers to analyze the data in various ways.

Obviously, this is an application that may be prototyped and in use in a matter of days or weeks. This example may live on as a tool to measure the reliability of the new widget. Other applications may be used and discarded. There is neither the time nor the need to build a robust, user-proof application with sophisticated error trapping and complex screen layouts.

Consideration of the workflow and how your application fits will help in determining the complexity, cost, and timeline for your development project.

Telecommuting

Client/server technology fits well with the idea of telecommuting. When using the term "telecommuting," we refer to the employee who connects in to the office server from a computer at home rather than the itinerant employee who may be calling from a hotel or airport lounge. The home-based worker has a computer, on which there is a copy of the client application. Using the Windows 95 Dial-up networking or the Windows NT Remote Access Services, connections are easily made to the database server. As long as the connection is reasonably fast and the application was tuned for remote access, the telecommuter can take part in the workflow as effectively as the person at the office.

The needs of the telecommuter differ somewhat from the needs of the road warrior, and your database design should reflect these differences. The traveling sales staff work mainly off-line. They may only need to check in once a day, exchange information, and log off. They are used to being out on their own, scheduling their own activities and reporting in only from time to time. On the other hand, the telecommuter expects to stay connected for longer periods of time, and expects to work on-line a least some of the time. This means that the application must offer fast response, and cannot be expected to transfer large volumes of data over telephone lines. Strategies that help achieve this goal include the use of remote procedure calls, keeping lookup tables local, and retrieving memo fields only when called for.

Internal Messaging

Not only is the remote connection a link to the server, it's a link to the office and to the rest of the group. One problem of telecommuting is a feeling of isolation, of not being part of the group. By sharing data on the server, the home-based worker may feel a heightened sense of participation. We like to include internal messaging in our applications, separate from the e-mail system. It allows users to leave notes for each other about specific data items—an electronic version of the yellow sticky notes that you sometimes use when passing paper documents to a colleague. As soon as the user connects to the server, he or she checks the message box, and then can deal with any outstanding issues promptly. As an example, our simple messaging system is in the final REA database on the CD-ROM (see fig. 22.2).

Fig. 22.2

The internal messaging system: the main menu screen, from which you can send messages, pick up your messages, and review messages that you sent.

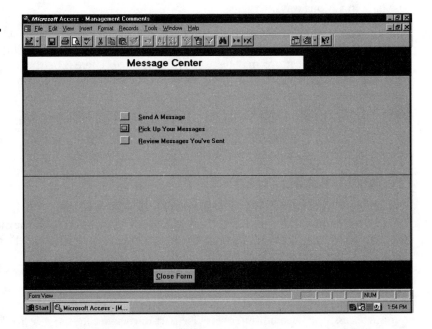

A message should include, at least, the following information:

- The name of the sender
- The project to which the message refers
- The name of the form or report that contains the data in question
- The time at which the message was sent

Figure 22.3 shows the main screen of the internal messaging system included in the REA application.

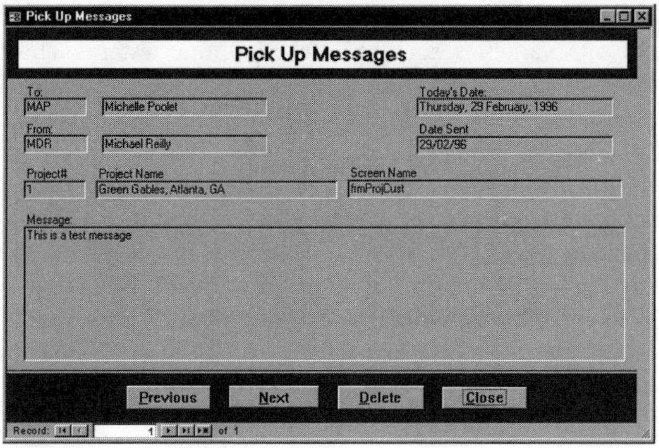

Fig. 22.3

The Internal Message screen, which you can use to manage your own messages.

Because we use the logon ID to identify the user, anyone can check messages that they sent or messages that they received, but not messages to or from other people. You can expand this concept to allow an assistant to pick up messages for the boss or have employees cover for someone who is out of town or on vacation.

The messaging application as shown is just an outline. You will want to add features, such as the capability to jump directly to the form listed in the message, and open the form at the appropriate project. The capability to reply directly to the sender also would be a useful addition.

If you want, the internal messaging scheme can be expanded to merge with the company e-mail and beyond into the Internet. In today's marketplace, Internet service providers can facilitate telecommunications and extend the reach of even the most modestly financed organization. This expansion adds an additional layer of complexity and removes the capability to go directly to the problem data and investigate. However, it does mean that the users don't have to get into the application to see that they have messages because most e-mail systems notify you when a message comes in.

If your telecommuter has two phone lines, a client/server application allows them to pull up on-screen the same data as a coworker and discuss this data over the second phone connection. (Although to do this in a reasonable time frame may require an ISDN connection, especially if the company runs on a fast server. Currently, POTS lines are very slow, and you have to be careful about heavy graphical displays. WAN connections, on the other hand, are supposedly getting better, cheaper, faster, and less restricted to ISDN.)

The Road Warrior

We briefly discussed the needs of the road warrior in previous chapters. There are two special situations for the mobile worker. One situation is the need to dial in and update data. The other is to be able to come into the office and connect to the server for one or two days.

Unlike the home-based worker, the mobile worker must dial in from a variety of locations and must contend with variables, such as hotel telephone systems. The chances are high that they need to run the client application on a portable computer that is less powerful than the desktop computers in the office. For this reason, we suggest a "light" version of the application, one that looks and feels like its office counterpart. This mobile-specific version can connect to only the server tables that it requires, and omit tables that refer to parts of the process not handled by the mobile employees. Consider using a mechanism such as the Briefcase, discussed in Chapter 20, "Replication with Access 95," to update the remote copies of the database. Even if your server is a DBMS such as SQL Server, you can write procedures that replicate a subset of the server data to an Access database in a Briefcase folder, which becomes the back-end database for the mobile clients.

Preparing the Users for Change

You involved the users in the design of the application, and they reviewed the forms, the reports, and even the data fields in each table. A few users beta tested the application, and everyone is excited because this new client/server application will make their job much easier. Then the application is installed, and nobody uses it. Eventually, it just fades away and joins all the other applications that never quite made it. What happened?

Change Management

If this application is the first client/server application to be introduced in a company, the extent of the change will be far more than just loading a new piece of software. Any client/server application changes the way people work, and it may change the nature of the work that they do. The application may cut across traditional department boundaries. It may require the cooperation of people who aren't used to working together. The concept of sharing data may not sit well with those who view information as power and try to hoard it.

The art (and science) of convincing people to embrace change is called *change management*. A principle of modern management theories is that people resist change. Even a change that the majority perceive as good may be resisted. In fact, it isn't that people resist change, it just takes some action to persuade them to change direction. When you are driving down the road and see a sign that shows the road going off to the right or left, you do not expect your car to change direction simply because of the sign. You have to turn the steering wheel, and the resulting forces acting on the car cause it to change direction and, therefore, stay on the road. In the same way, telling people that a new application is being introduced does not cause them to use it. You need to take action to move them in the desired direction, perhaps to elicit an enthusiastic champion or two within the user community. Otherwise, they simply continue doing what they always did.

Management Support

The single most-critical factor in introducing any change is that management must be behind it, and their support must be visible and consistent. As a developer, you do not have enough influence over the users to overcome their inertia. If management sends conflicting signals, your clients will play it safe and not adopt the new technology.

There are many books on handling change, and if you want your application to be accepted, a couple of them may be worth further study. These books don't talk about software; they explain in broader terms how to handle change. After you understand why it takes so long and takes so much effort to change the way people work, you will realize that they aren't rejecting your software. They are only reluctant to leave a comfortable and secure place and to move ahead. Rather than taking it personally, you can respond to their concerns, and even anticipate many of them.

One book that the authors like is *Managing at the Speed of Change*, by Daryl Conner. The author talks about the different stages of the change process, and the way in which people react to change. There are stages in the change process, and remember that change is a process that happens over time. The first phase is the present state, the *status quo*. This is an equilibrium state that continues until some force disrupts the status quo and initiates a change. The second stage is the *transition state*, which is characterized by a feeling of uncertainty and discomfort. During this stage, we must let go of the old ways of doing things and make the switch to the new way. Eventually, we reach the third stage, the desired outcome of the change. In reality, today's business environment is imposing a rate of change such that we rarely get settled into the third stage when a new wave of change happens. In companies that espouse the "management philosophy *du jour*," the rate of change may be so great that employees never get out of the uncomfortable transition stage. In this situation, introducing new software is never a simple or straightforward task.

You can take steps to prepare the users for the change. Some of these steps must involve corporate management. They need to explain to the employees the reasons for the change, how the change fits with the company's values, and how the change will affect both the company and the employees. Management should point out that change is stressful for everyone, and it is normal to feel uncomfortable when change takes place. It's quite proper for the managers to admit that they feel concern, but they intend to make sure that the change works as planned.

Introducing the Application

The application should not just show up unannounced on the corporate computing scene. The user community should be told that it is coming, what it will do for them, and what it means to the corporate bottom line. From the developer's viewpoint, the best technique is to have a senior member of management explain how your application fits with the overall corporate direction and, possibly, with other changes currently taking place. This support gives the application a credibility, and a seal of approval, from the top down. If a member of the management team takes "owner-ship" of the application, even better! The authors remember one presentation to a group of users, where the manager explained how the application would help every-one be more efficient and productive. As we were about to begin demonstrating the application, he said, "Here, let me drive," and he took over the computer. To us, this was gratifying because he had truly "bought in" to the application.

As we watched him show off the application, we saw that he emphasized parts of the application that we took for granted—he didn't even mention some of the neat fea-tures that we liked. What appeals to a user doesn't always excite a developer, and vice versa. When you must demonstrate your own application, try to look at it from the perspective of the users. What will it do for them? How will it make them more pro-ductive? Will the error trapping stop them from making errors?

A common pitfall among developers is to show off the parts of the application that took the most effort and, in particular, the results of the sudden insights or flashes of inspiration that we all get from time to time. Unfortunately, the average user really doesn't care about how difficult something was to program or how many late nights the application demanded of the developer. On the other hand, users often get ex-cited about some little additional feature that took all of ten minutes to add. There is absolutely no correlation between how long something took to develop and its impor-tance to the end user.

The Rollout

The people at Microsoft Consulting Services recommend an official *rollout* of an appli-cation. Make it a celebration, marking the end of the development phase and the beginning of the useful life of the application. Sort of a graduation ceremony, if you like. Bring in pizza, or cake and soft drinks. (But no breaking champagne bottles across the departmental server, claiming the application is being "launched.") The important point is to acknowledge the contribution of the corporate sponsor, and the users who assisted in the development and testing.

As a developer, acknowledgments may not be the *most* important point. The critical item on the agenda is not the chocolate-chip cookies. It's the recognition that the "%#!*#!@#" project is finally finished. Anything else is add-ons, enhancements, and modifications. Take a stack of Change/Enhancement request forms to the party, and hand them out. Make it clear that the project has reached a new stage in the develop-ment cycle. There should be a clear time (4:00 p.m. on July 22nd in the 4th floor conference room) when the application changed ownership from developer to user.

If not, the door is open for creeping incremental changes and modifications, and the project will never be finished. This situation is bad for several reasons. If you are a contract developer, payment may be delayed until the project is officially finished. If you are an internal developer, you may be scheduled to move to another project, and unless the product is officially released, the users may be hesitant to begin using it, thinking that it is incomplete. The worst situation is where the number of beta testers grows, because people see the application and decide they need it. Before you know it, everyone is using it but they all want more features added before they will admit that the product is completed.

To remove any doubt about whether the project is finished, you should of course have some benchmarks or deliverables agreed upon at the start of the project. A formal acceptance test also works well to ensure that the application meets the requirements as defined. Then, the official rollout can be scheduled for a few days after completion of the acceptance test.

Training the Users

No matter how intuitive the application is, *schedule training for the users*. The training acts as a reinforcement of the rollout, showing that the application is ready for everyone to use. Allocating employee time for training also is a commitment by management to the success of the application. The training is part of the change management process because it assists the users in overcoming any uncertainties about the new software.

Deploying the Application

If you use software such as Systems Management Server, the deployment is much easier, as we mentioned in the discussion in Chapter 19, "System Administration." The users can simply download the software when convenient, or you can "push" the software out to their computers. If you aren't using SMS or an equivalent software tool, the easiest method is a user-initiated, over-the-network installation, again described in previous chapters.

We suggest that you not schedule everyone for installation on Monday morning at 8:30. Actually, Monday may be a bad day for introducing new software, depending on the corporate culture. Many companies have meetings on Monday morning, and many people have a routine they follow to get back "in the groove" after the weekend. Friday afternoon may not work too well either—thoughts are more on getting out of the office than on learning new software. This still leaves four days (Monday afternoon through Friday morning) when the software can be deployed without causing too much anxiety and stress.

For the home-based user or the road warriors, you may have to make floppy-disk installation sets. In this case it's worth spending a few minutes with a word-processing program, to produce some neat, informative disk labels on a laser printer. After all the effort you put into developing the application, it pays to present it well. Don't pass out a set of mismatched disks with handwritten labels. You also want to put the version number and the date of the release on the disk labels.

Gaining User Support

Even though your application has management support, it is not automatic that it immediately will be accepted by the users. It helps if the users understand how it will make their jobs more productive. If management expects everyone to get more done in a shorter time as a result of this new application, there may be some resistance among the employees.

One very real stumbling block that you may encounter is an overload of work brought about by the transition to a new system. At the point at which the users change to the new application, a backlog of years of paper data may need to be converted to electronic format. Data that was already computerized in one form or another may need to be converted and/or updated to meet the new format. What users see coming with the new system is a loss of weeks or months in getting up to speed. This is a very real reason why new programs or systems are allowed to fail.

A typical user thought is: "We're trying to make money, we're already under too much pressure, we need to get things done, we know the current system and can make it work. Why should we change our method, when this one works?" If the users are not made to see that the tradeoff of time invested in getting up to speed on the new system is at least balanced by its efficiencies and power, they will believe that the transition isn't worth their effort. This is particularly true when the system planning has involved only management-level staff and not the real users, who believe that management has no idea how anything gets done and refuse to believe that the new system can meet their needs, unless they were part of its creation.

This resistance may be expressed as a dislike for the application, which brought with it these extra demands. One way to head off this hostility is to work out a plan with the managers, so that time is allowed for a learning curve. In other words, productivity is not expected to jump on the day the application is installed. After a few weeks or months, when everyone is accustomed to the application, then some gains in productivity should be measurable.

The users should have been included in the development process, even if it was just a representative team that provided input and participated in the beta testing. It helps if these employees can be enlisted as informal, first-line support for the quick questions that everyone will have during the first few days. It isn't so much that this reduces the load on the technical support staff, but rather that many employees would rather ask a coworker than calling technical support and feeling foolish when the answer is quite simple or obvious.

The work of the developer isn't done after the application is installed. There is a temptation, especially after working overtime to meet the installation date, to sit back for a few days and catch your breath. In practice, spending some time with the users during the deployment of the application, and for the few days immediately following, will help to overcome some of the initial resistance to the application. Then you can collapse, go sailing, or whatever.

Among the first people whose support you must have—even if you don't count them as users—are the network administrators. After all, you are putting your application on their server, and using their network to run it. Without their support, the application will be in trouble from the start.

Handling Changing Requirements

One of the benefits to the developer of RAD (Rapid Application Development) techniques is that the product can be ready and functional before the customer changes his or her mind too much. The longer the development process, the more the tendency for changes to creep in (this phenomenon is known as "feature creep"). You expect, and indeed encourage, some changes during the development process. When the customer sees the first prototype, changes are inevitable. But you must be careful to distinguish between changes that help to define, and even narrow, the scope of the project, and changes that enlarge the scope. Most problematic are those that change the direction of the project, thereby wasting what has already been done.

During the project definition phase, before coding has been done, any number of changes can be made with no negative consequences. It is really critical that everyone spend the time necessary to properly define the project. Sometimes, the customer (using this term to include your internal, corporate customers where appropriate) becomes impatient at the amount of time spent on this phase. Meeting after meeting takes place and no code has been written. The authors often will build forms with nothing behind them (not even tables), to illustrate what the application will look like.

It is common to find members of the customer team arguing among themselves about the business rules and procedures that they want you to formulate and embody in the code. To avoid being caught in the middle, ask the customer to meet outside of the design meetings, and come up with a consensus, in writing. This approach keeps your design meetings focused, and shorter, and puts the responsibility of defining the business rules back where it belongs—on the customer.

After the design meetings define the application adequately, and the definition is in writing, have the customer sign the design specification and give him or her copies. Then you can begin building prototypes. Part of the objective of the prototype is to stimulate discussion and put some "life" into the design as soon as possible. Of course, this initiates more requests for change. After the modifications to the prototype are agreed upon, get the changes in writing and signed again. From this point on, all changes to the design require that a Change/Enhancement Request form be completed, reviewed by the company representative, and submitted.

Ideally, there should be no further changes to the application after the prototype is reviewed and the changes agreed upon. In reality, there will be some changes. Minor changes can be incorporated, as long as you are sure that they are minor. Major changes require a decision. As any project manager will tell you, when the scope of a project changes, something has to give. Either the cost increases—because more people have to be assigned to the project or because the project will take longer with the same resources. The only other alternative is that the project risk increases, meaning that on-time and within-budget completion with the original feature set is now unlikely. If the changed scope is agreed upon as necessary, the cost of the project must be reevaluated. Don't fall for the line, "This should have been included in the design from the start." Perhaps it should, but it was up to the customer to ensure that the specification was complete.

One of the most dangerous customers—especially if you are a consultant—is the one who demands a major change, and insists that the whole project is worthless without this change. The threat of course is that they will not pay for a worthless project, and all your work so far will be wasted. At this point, you have to produce the signed specifications and ask why the requested changes were not included in the original design. Offer the client an option: either you will quote an additional cost for the requested changes or they cancel the project at this point and pay for the work already done. Hopefully, you have been paid for the design and prototyping phases already. (Although the authors wonder why major corporations think a mission-critical database can be developed in less time than it takes them to pay a single invoice, usually 90 days.) If you have a signed contract for the full implementation of the design, letting the customer back out with no further costs is generous.

Don't be intimidated into giving in and making a major design change at no cost to the customer. It was our experience that when they get away with this, there will be several more major components, any one of which would render the entire application useless if not included. Each change moves the application further from the original concept, and soon serious problems begin to surface because an overall design plan no longer exists.

From the beginning, spell out the requirements and expected working relationship between the development team and the customer at the very start of the project. Then, always refer to this document when discussing changes, modifications, and responsibilities.

Starting Over Again

As the computer industry approaches the year 2000, we hear a lot about 30-year-old COBOL programs that break down as their calendar model fails. When these programs were written, no one expected them to be around for more than a few years. Their replacements almost certainly will not last as long. The modern programmer is under even more pressure to write code that does the job now, and not worry about future expansion. This is not to say that you can cut corners on your database design. If the design is sound and extensible and can be expanded as the need arises, the database itself and the data it contains may be around for many years.

What *will* change is the user interface. As the business processes change and the business rules evolve, the client application may be modified or even rewritten to accommodate the new ways of doing business. A major change in the operating system, such as the introduction of Windows 95 or the upcoming Cairo release of Windows NT, may require more sophisticated client applications. New operating system features, such as Briefcase, offer functionality that can be incorporated in a new version of the client software.

The original user application can be expanded with change requests and minor revisions for awhile. You may want to consider a major reworking of the application when either the client or the server software changes radically. For example, Access 2.0 offered improvements over version 1.1 but was quite similar in most respects. Access version 7.0, however, is considerably different and, when taken with the changes in Windows 95, offers features and capabilities that weren't previously available to the developer. This is especially true in the areas of connectivity and support for mobile employees. Although it's possible to simply convert the Access 2.0 application, this would be a good time to return to the original design, see how new features will fit in, and produce a new client application.

Given the rapid pace of development and the major shifts in how businesses operate, expect to start over on your applications every few years. Looking on the bright side, there should be no shortage of work for client/server developers for a long time!

Business Process Reengineering

As we said at the start of this book, Client/server technology is tightly coupled with the idea of business process reengineering. The concept was introduced in 1993 by Michael Hammer and James Champy, in their best-selling book, *Reengineering the Corporation*. Hammer and Champy advocated a radical reinvention of how American businesses operate. The old Adam Smith theories of multiple levels of management supervising workers in tightly controlled jobs is out. Instead, the successful companies are looking at each *process*, not at each job function.

For example, consider how customer returns are handled in a mail-order company. The customer calls and is given a return authorization. The item arrives at receiving, which regards its job as unloading trucks, not handling individual packages. So, it ends up in shipping, which regards its job as sending out orders, not taking them back. The package is finally accepted, and sent to the warehouse where it is checked and, possibly, entered back into inventory. At some point, accounting may be notified that the item came in. It must cross-reference the item with the return authorization and issue a refund. But it isn't its job to tell the customer that the refund was issued. The key point: nobody in the company is responsible for the overall process of taking care of the customer. The poor customer is calling to find out where the refund is, and cannot get an answer. All the customer gets is the runaround—does this sound familiar?

When the company reengineers, this process is defined—as are many others—as being the way the company does business. It's important to note that the process usually cuts straight across traditional department lines. More responsibility, and more decision-making power, is handed to the employees. No longer will the phrase, "It's not my job," be heard because taking care of the customer is everybody's job. One of the winners in an effective reengineering is the company, the employees who now have more responsibility, more authority to make decisions, and more job satisfaction. The other winner is the customer. Businesses with a customer-satisfaction orientation tend to be more pleasant to deal with—and also deliver better product and service—than those to whom the customer is irrelevant. The losers in reengineering tend to be the middle-level managers, who are no longer needed to make decisions for the employees or to protect their departmental turf.

In our example, handling returns is just one part of the whole client/server application that handles customer orders. More employees will have access to the system and to the data. When customers call, they may not talk with the same sales representative each time. Nor is it necessary that they do so because any representative can pull up data that shows when the item was received, whether the credit was issued, and if so, when. For this to happen, each person in the process must update his or her component of the process. In some cases, messages may be generated to notify another person of the status of the process.

Business process reengineering involves starting over and examining what the company actually does, or what it wants to do. Often, the first step is to write down a set of company values, and a "mission statement." This is the point at which, as we mentioned previously, the old rules are tossed out. It's also the point at which the client/server solution may become the obvious choice, which offers both a major challenge and a great opportunity to the developer. Even when the server is a legacy system, the client application can start from a clean sheet of paper. The client/server application will not just follow the business process, it helps define the process and makes it possible. Each business rule implemented by your application must be examined for relevance—tradition is not a good enough reason to include a rule.

A company that is truly reengineering does not start by asking how to improve the handling of customer returns. Instead, the question would be, "Why do we have returns at all?" "How can we eliminate them?" Or at least, "How can we reduce them to a fraction of the former level?" (This may be a good place for a quick database application to analyze the reason for returns.) True reengineering is not reducing returns by 10 percent. It is reducing returns to 10 percent or less of the former level. Reengineering isn't about incremental improvements, it is about order of magnitude improvements.

Client/server technology is based on sharing data across the company, from one department to another. It enables workflow between departments, and not just handing off work to the next person—it allows cooperation between departments. It emphasizes business processes, not job functions. The application computerizes a process, not an employee's job. Many of these ideas run counter to business practices in many companies. For this reason, implementing client/server applications means breaking down these barriers and adopting a new business model. The decision to go with client/server computing implies a decision to reengineer. If your customers do not realize and accept this, walk away. They cannot just implement a client/server solution in a traditional, hierarchical corporate culture.

It's also true that any company serious about reengineering will find itself looking at client/server technology. It's the computing model that best fits the concept of processes that cut across the company, rather than job functions that split the company vertically. It may be possible to reengineer a company without going to a client/server model—but not if the company uses computers.

This topic, and the topic of change management, may seem out of place in a computer book, but the authors hope that the readers of this book will develop successful client/server applications, which deliver real, measurable benefits to their clients. To do so, it helps to know a little about the company and its business philosophy. To ensure the success of the application, it helps to know some psychology, and the basics of change management, to ensure a satisfied user community. We hardly scratched the surface on these topics here, so we attached a suggested reading list at the end of this chapter.

Good luck with your client/server development projects!

From Here...

From here, the authors suggest the following:

On workgroup computing:

- *Introduction to Groupware, Workflow and Workgroup Computing,* Setrag Khoshafian & Marek Buckiewicz, Wiley, New York, 1995, $34.95.
- *Computer Support for Cooperative Work,* editors: Spurr, Layzell, Jennsion & Richards, Wiley, New York, 1994.
- *Groupware, Technology & Applications,* editors Coleman & Khanna, Prentice Hall, New Jersey, 1995.

On change management:

- *Managing At The Speed of Change,* Daryl R. Conner, Villard Books, New York, 1992.
- *Managing Transitions,* William Bridges, Addison-Wesley, Reading MA, 1991, $16.95.
- *Break-Point and Beyond,* George Land & Beth Jarman, Harper Business, New York, 1992, $20.00.

On business process reengineering:

- *Reengineering the Corporation,* Michael Hammer & James Champy, Harper Business, New York, 1993, $13.00.
- *The Reengineering Revolution,* Michael Hammer & Steven A. Stanton, Harper Business, New York, 1995, $15.00.
- *Reengineering Management,* James Champy, Harper Business, New York, 1995, $25.00.

VI

Administering the App

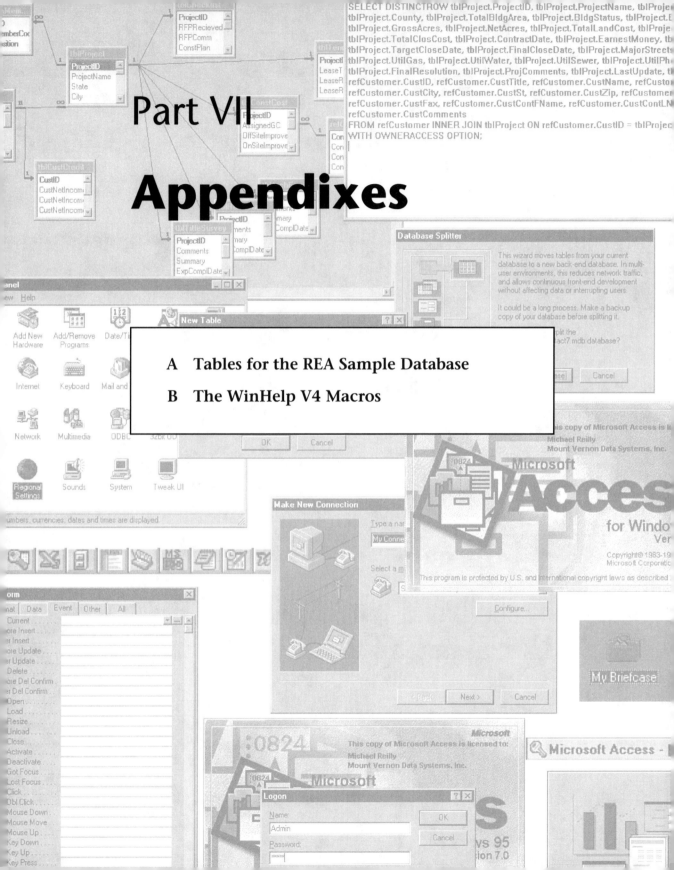

Part VII

Appendixes

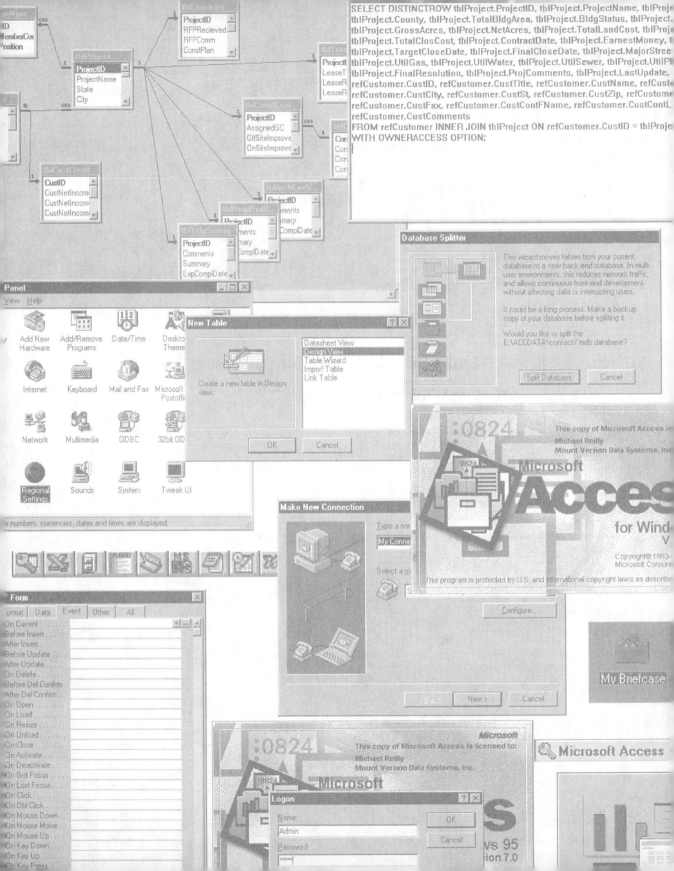

Tables for the REA Sample Database

This appendix contains the layouts for all the tables in the REA database. If you do not have a CD-ROM unit in your computer and therefore, cannot copy over the REA database that is included on it, you can reconstruct the database by using this information.

For ease of data entry when constructing the columns of each table, the field length is included with the data type in the following tables. Also, the entries in the field properties column are those where the value varies from the Access 95 default. So, unless the data contained here indicates otherwise, accept all default values assigned when a column is created.

The Project Table

The Project table (see Table A.1) is the main table of the REA database. It contains information about each building project undertaken by REA.

Table A.1   tblProject

Field Name	Data Type	Description	Field Properties	Lookup
ProjectID	AutoNumber (long integer)	Primary key, unique identifier for each project	NewValues= Increment Caption= Project# Indexed= Yes (No Duplicates)	
ProjectName	Text(50)	Name of the project and/or development	Caption= Project Name Required= Yes Indexed= Yes (Duplicates OK)	

(continues)

Table A.1 Continued

Field Name	Data Type	Description	Field Properties	Lookup
State	Text(2)	State code in which this project is located		Display Control= Combo Box Row Source Type= Table/Query Row Source= refStates Bound Column=1 Column Count=2 Limit To List=yes
City	Text(30)	City in which this project is located	Field Size= 30	
County	Text(30)	County in which this project is located	Field Size= 30	
TotalBldgArea	Number (Single)	Approximate total square feet of finished building	Field Size= Single Caption= Total Square Footage	
BldgStatus	Text(20)	The status of this project	Field Size= 20 Caption= Building Status	Display Control= Combo Box Row Source Type= Value List Row Source=; planning stage; under construction; construction complete; closed Limit To List= Yes
BldgType	Text(30)	The kind of building	Caption= Building Type	Display Control= Combo Box Row Source Type= Value List Row Source=; single-family home; multi-family home; retail bldg; office bldg; warehouse Limit To List=No

Field Name	Data Type	Description	Field Properties	Lookup
CustID	Text(12)	The customer for this project	Indexed=Yes (Duplicates OK)	Display Control= Combo Box Row Source Type= Table/Query Row Source= refCustomer Bound Column=1 Column Count=2 Limit To List=Yes
GrossAcres	Number (Single)	The total gross acreage involved in this project	Caption= Gross Acres	
NetAcres	Number (Single)	Total net developed acreage involved in this project	Caption= Net Acres	
TotalLandCost	Number (Single)	Base price paid for the land	Format= Currency Decimal Places =2 Caption= Total Land Costs	
Acquisition Cost	Number (Single)	Total acquisition costs other than base land and closing costs	Format= Currency Decimal Places =2 Caption= Acquisition Costs	
TotalClosCost	Number (Single)	Total closing costs for the sale to the new owner	Format= Currency Decimal Places =2 Caption= Total Closing Costs	
ContractDate	Date/Time	Date the contract was signed	Format= Short Date Caption= Contract Date	

(continues)

Table A.1 Continued

Field Name	Data Type	Description	Field Properties	Lookup
EarnestMoney	Number (Single)	The amount of earnest money put down on this project	Format= Currency Decimal Places =2 Caption= Earnest Money	
InspectExpire	Date/Time	Expiration date of the inspection period	Format= Caption= Short Date Inspection Expiration Date	
TargetClose Date	Date/Time	Target closing date	Format= Short Date Caption= Target Closing Date	
FinalCloseDate	Date/Time	Final closing date, the date the purchase is completed or the project is finished	Format= Short Date Caption= Final Closing Date	
MajorStreets	Text(60)	Major cross streets closest to the project	Caption=Major Cross Streets	
UtilElectric	Text(60)	Electric company servicing the project	Caption= Electric Company	
UtilGas	Text(60)	Gas company servicing the project	Caption= Gas Company	
UtilWater	Text(60)	Water company servicing the project	Caption=Water Company	

Field Name	Data Type	Description	Field Properties	Lookup
UtilSewer	Text(60)	Sewer company servicing the project	Caption=Sewer Company	
UtilPhone	Text(60)	Phone company servicing the project	Caption=Phone Company	
Final Resolution	Text(60)	Final outcome of this project	Caption= Final Resolution	
ProjComments	Memo	Additional comments or notes regarding this project	Caption= Comments	
LastUpdate	Date/Time	Last date change was made to this record (takes the timestamp from the system clock)	Format= general date Default= date( ) Caption= Last Update	
ByWhom	Text(12)	Last user to change this record (Logon id of person who made the change)	Form Property Default= currentuser( ) Caption= By Whom	

The Construction Costs Table

The Construction Costs table (see Table A.2) contains cost information for the general construction sections of a project. The Construction Costs are dependent for its existence on an associated Project—without a project, there can be no construction costs—and it is related to the Project table in a 1:1 relationship. In the Relationships window, these two tables are connected as 1:1, Enforce Referential Integrity on, Cascade Update and Cascade Delete on, Join type 2 (left outer).

Table A.2   tblConstCost

Field Name	Data Type	Description	Field Properties	Lookup
ProjectID	Number (long integer)	Primary key, links back to tblProject	Caption= Project# Required= Yes Indexed=Yes (No Duplicates)	
AssignedGC	Text(12)	General contractor assigned to this project	Caption= General Contractor	Display Control= Combo Box Row Source Type= Table/Query Row Source= refContractor Bound Column=1 Column Count=3 Limit To List=Yes
OffSiteImprove	Currency	Cost for off-site improve-ments, total cost and calculated per square foot	Decimal Places=2 Caption= Off-Site Improvement Costs	
OnSiteImprove	Currency	Cost for on-site improve-ments, total cost and calculated per square foot	Decimal Places=2 Caption= On-Site Improvement Costs	
ConstFees	Currency	All construc-tion and development fees and licenses, total and calculated per square foot	Decimal Places=2 Caption= Construction & License Fees	
Landscape	Currency	All landscaping costs, total and calculated per square foot	Decimal Places=2 Caption= Landscaping Costs	

Field Name	Data Type	Description	Field Properties	Lookup
PaveUtil	Currency	All paving and utility costs, total and calculated per square foot	Decimal Places=2 Caption= Paving & Utility Costs	
SoftCost	Currency	All soft costs, total and calculated per square foot	Decimal Places=2 Caption= Soft Costs	
ConstCost Comments	Memo	Comments and notes on this project	Caption= Comments	

The Terms and Assumptions Table

The Terms and Assumptions table (see Table A.3) contains information regarding the terms and lease/purchase assumptions that are made on a project between REA, Inc. and its customer. Terms and Assumptions are dependent for their existence on an associated Project and are related to the Project table in a 1:1 relationship. In the Relationships window, these two tables are connected as 1:1, Enforce Referential Integrity on, Cascade Update and Cascade Delete on, Join type 2 (left outer).

Table A.3   tblTerms

Field Name	Data Type	Description	Field Properties	Lookup
ProjectID	Number (long integer)	Primary key, links back to tblProject.	Caption= Project# Required= Yes Indexed= Yes (No Duplicates)	
LeaseTerm	Number (long integer)	Length of the lease, in months.	Format= Standard Caption= Lease in Months	

(continues)

Table A.3 Continued

Field Name	Data Type	Description	Field Properties	Lookup
LeaseRate	Currency	Lease rate per square foot per month.	Decimal Places=2 Caption= Lease Rate PSF/Month	
LeaseRenewal	Yes/No	Renewal option; can customer renew the lease?	Caption= Lease Renewal Option?	
LeasePurchase	Yes/No	Purchase option; can the customer purchase this property at end of lease?	Caption= Lease Purchase Option?	
LeaseCancel	Yes/No	Cancel-lation option; can the customer cancel lease before end of term?	Caption= Lease Cancel Option?	
EstLeaseExDate	Date/Time	Estimated lease execution date. Use mm/dd/yy format for this field.	Format= ShortDate Caption= Estimated Lease Execution Date	
ReqOccDate	Date/Time	Requested occupancy date. Use mm/dd/yy format for this field.	Format= ShortDate Caption= Requested Occupancy Date	
ProjOccDate	Date/Time	Projected occupancy date. Use mm/dd/yy format for this field.	Format=ShortDate Caption= Projected Occupancy Date	
TargOccDate	Date/Time	Target occupancy date. Use mm/dd/yy format for this field.	Format=ShortDate Caption= Target Occupancy Date	

Field Name	Data Type	Description	Field Properties	Lookup
LeaseLiqDamDay	Currency	Liquidated damages expressed in lease in dollars per day.	Caption=Lease Liquidated Damages/Day	
GCLiqDamDay	Currency	Liquidated damages agreed to by general contractor, in dollars per day.	Caption=GC Liquidated Damages/Day	
TargetConstComm	Date/Time	Target construction commencement date. Use mm/dd/yy format for this field.	Format=ShortDate Caption= Target Construction Commencement Date	
GCTargetSubCompl	Date/Time	Target substantial completion date, estimated by general contractor. Use the mm/dd/yy format for this field.	Format=ShortDate Caption=GC Target Substantial Completion	
LeaseTarget SubCompl	Date/Time	Target substantial completion date, required by lease or purchase contract. Use the mm/dd/yy format for this field.	Format=ShortDate Caption=Lease Target Substantial Completion	
GCExpirWarranty	Date/Time	Expiration date of the general contractor's warranty. Use the mm/dd/yy format for this field.	Format=ShortDate Caption=GC Warranty Expiration Date	

(continues)

VII

Appendixes

Table A.3   Continued

Field Name	Data Type	Description	Field Properties	Lookup
LeaseExpir Warranty	Date/Time	Expiration date of the lease warranty. Use the mm/dd/yy format for this field.	Format= ShortDate Caption=Lease Warranty Expiration Date	

The Checklist Table

The Checklist table is a checklist for a project (see Table A.4). Checklist contains information that is time-related and order-sensitive. The Checklist is dependent on an associated Project for its existence and is related to the Project table in a 1:1 relationship. In the Relationships window, these two tables are connected as 1:1, Enforce Referential Integrity on, Cascade Update and Cascade Delete on, Join type 2 (left outer).

Table A.4   tblChecklist

Field Name	Data Type	Description	Field Properties	Lookup
ProjectID	Number (long integer)	Primary key, links back to tblProject.	Caption=Project# Required=Yes Indexed=Yes (No Duplicates)	
RFPReceived	Date/Time	Date request for proposal was received back from general contractor. Use mm/dd/yy format for this field.	Format=ShortDate Caption=Date RFP Received	
RFPComm	Memo	Comments on request for proposal.	Caption=Comments on RFP	
ConstPlan	Yes/No	Are the construction plans done?	Caption= Construction Plans Done?	
ConstEst	Yes/No	Is construction estimate done?	Caption=Construction Estimate Done?	

Field Name	Data Type	Description	Field Properties	Lookup
ConstComm	Memo	Comments or notes on construction plans or construction.	Caption=Comments	
FinAnal	Date/Time	Date financial analysis was done. Use mm/dd/yy format for this field.	Format=ShortDate Caption=Date Financial Analysis Done	
FinAnalComm	Memo	Comments on financial analysis.	Caption=Comments	
FactSheetAppr	Yes/No	Was fact sheet approved?	Caption=Fact Sheet Approved?	
CredAnal	Date/Time	Date credit analysis was completed. Use mm/dd/yy format for this field.	Format=ShortDate Caption=Date of Credit Analysis	
CredAnalComm	Memo	Comments on credit analysis.	Caption=Comments	

The Messages Table

The Messages table is a set of slots where users can leave messages for each other (see Table A.5). In this application it isn't tied into the corporate mail system. The Messages table doesn't appear in the Relationships window.

Table A.5   tblMessages

Field Name	Data Type	Description	Field Properties	Lookup
MessageNo	AutoNumber	Primary key, unique identifier for each message.	Indexed=Yes (No Duplicates) Caption= Message#	
ProjectID	Number (long integer)	Foreign key, links back to tblProject.	Caption=Project# Required=No Indexed=Yes (Duplicates OK)	

(continues)

Table A.5 Continued

Field Name	Data Type	Description	Field Properties	Lookup
ScreenName	Text(30)	Which screen in the application did this message come from?	Caption=Screen Name	
ToWhom	Text(12)	Who is this message meant for? Select from the TeamMember list.	Caption=To	Display Control =Combo Box Row Source Type =Table/Query RowSource= refTeam Bound Column=1 Column Count=4 Limit To List=No
Message	Memo	Body of the message, comments and notes.		
DateStamp	Date/Time	Date and time message was created, automatically filled in from the system.	Format=General Date Caption=Date Sent Default=Date( )	
FromWhom	Text(12)	Who created this message, automatically filled in from the system.	Caption=From	

The Customer Table

The Customer table is a reference table, a list of customers and information about each (see Table A.6). The Customer table has a 1:M relationship with the Project table, which means that a customer can be involved in one or more projects. This relationship is independent—both the Customer records and the Project records can exist without each other. In the Relationships window, these two tables are connected as 1:M, refCustomer to tblProject, Enforce Referential Integrity on, Cascade Update on, Cascade Delete off, Join type 1 (equijoin).

Table A.6   refCustomer

Field Name	Data Type	Description	Field Properties	Lookup
CustID	Text(12)	Primary key, code value that uniquely identifies this customer.	Format=> Caption=CustomerID Required=Yes Indexed=Yes (No Duplicates)	
CustTitle	Text(18)	Title to use in letter salutations, (Mr., Ms., Professor).	Caption=Title	Display Control =Combo Box Row Source Type= Value List Row Source=; Mr.; Mrs.; Ms.; Professor; Reverend Bound Column=1 Column Count=1 Limit To List=No
CustName	Text(50)	Customer (company) name.	Caption=Company Indexed=Yes (Duplicates OK)	
CustAddress	Text(60)	St. address.	Caption=Street Address	
CustCity	Text(30)	Customer (company) city.	Caption=City	
CustSt	Text(2)	Customer (company) state code, select from drop-down list.	Format=> Caption=State Indexed=Yes (Duplicates OK)	Display Control= Combo Box Row Source Type= Table/Query Row Source= refStates Bound Column=1 Column Count=2 Limit To List=Yes
CustZip	Text(10)	Customer (company) postal code.	Caption=Postal Code Indexed=Yes (Duplicates OK)	
CustPhone	Text(20)	Customer (company) voice phone number, enter area code first.	Caption=Phone Input Mask= !\(999") "000\-0000;0;_	
CustFax	Text(20)	Customer (company) fax phone number, enter area code first.	Caption=Fax Input Mask= !\(999") "000\-0000;0;_	

(continues)

Table A.6 Continued

Field Name	Data Type	Description	Field Properties	Lookup
CustContFName	Text(15)	Customer contact's first name.	Caption=Contact First Name	
CustContLName	Text(15)	Customer contact's last name.	Caption=Contact Last Name	
CustComments	MEMO	Additional notes or comments about this customer.		

The Customer Credit Table

The Customer Credit table (see Table A.7) contains sensitive information regarding the credit history of a specific customer. Between Customer and Customer Credit, a dependent relationship exists—without a customer, there would be no customer credit report—and in this application, there is a 1:1 relationship between the Customer table and the Customer Credit table. In the Relationships window, these two tables are connected as 1:1, Enforce Referential Integrity on, Cascade Update on, Cascade Delete on, Join type 2 (left outer).

Table A.7 tblCustCredit

Field Name	Data Type	Description	Field Properties	Lookup
CustID	Text(12)	Primary key, links back to Customer table.	Format=> Caption=CustomerID Required=Yes Indexed=Yes (No duplicates)	
CustNetIncomeYr1	Currency	Customer net income for year 1.	Decimal Places=2 Caption=Net Income Year 1	
CustNetIncomeYr2	Currency	Customer net income for year 2.	Decimal Places=2 Caption=Net Income Year 2	
CustNetIncomeYr3	Currency	Customer net income for year 3.	Decimal Places=2 Caption=Net Income Year 3	
CustNetWorthYr1	Currency	Customer net worth for year 1.	Decimal Places=2 Caption=Net Worth Year 1	

Field Name	Data Type	Description	Field Properties	Lookup
CustNetWorthYr2	Currency	Customer net worth for year 2.	Decimal Places=2 Caption=Net Worth Year 2	
CustNetWorthYr3	Currency	Customer net worth for year 3.	Decimal Places=2 Caption=Net Worth Year 3	
CustCredComments	Memo	Comments and notes on this customer's credit report.	Caption=Comments	

The Contractor Table

The Contractor table (see Table A.8) is a reference table, a list of contractors (general contractor, roofing contractor, architectural contractor, and so on) and information about each contractor. The Contractor table has a 1:M relationship with the Construction Costs table, which means that a contractor can be involved in one or more projects. This relationship is independent—both the Contractor records and the Construction Costs records can exist without each other. In the Relationships window, these two tables are connected as 1:M, refContractor to tblConstCost, Enforce Referential Integrity on, Cascade Update on, Cascade Delete off, Join type 1 (equijoin).

Table A.8 refContractor

Field Name	Data Type	Description	Field Properties	Lookup
ContractorID	Text(12)	Primary key, uniquely identifies each contractor.	Format=> Caption=Contractor ID Required=Yes Indexed=Yes (No duplicates)	
ContractorType	Text(30)	What kind of contractor is this? Select from list (not restrictive).	Caption=Type of Contractor	Display Control= Combo Box Row Source Type=Value lLst Row Source=; General Contractor; Architect; Civil Engineer; Environmental Consultant;

(continues)

Table A.8 Continued

Field Name	Data Type	Description	Field Properties	Lookup
				Field Consultant; Geotechnical Consultant; Landscape Architect; Roofing Engineer; Survey Company; Title Company; Wetlands Consultant Bound Column=1 Column Count=3 Limit To List= No
ContractorName	Text(30)	Name of contractor (company name).	Caption=Company Name Indexed=Yes (Duplicates OK)	
Contractor Address	Text(50)	Contractor (company) street address.	Caption=Street Address	
ContractorCity	Text(30)	Contractor (company) city.	Caption=City	
ContractorSt	Text(2)	Contractor (company) state code, select from drop-down list.	Format=> Caption= State Code Indexed= Yes (Duplicates OK)	Display Control= Combo Box Row Source Type= Table/Query Row Source= refState Bound Column=1 Column Count=2 Limit To List=Yes
ContractorZip	Text(10)	Contractor (company) postal code.	Caption= Postal Code Indexed=Yes (Duplicates OK)	

Field Name	Data Type	Description	Field Properties	Lookup
Contractor Phone	Text(20)	Contractor (company) voice phone number, enter area code first.	Input Mask=!\(999") "000\-0000;0;_ Caption=Phone	
ContractorFax	Text(20)	Contractor (company) fax phone number, enter area code first.	Input Mask=!\(999") "000\-0000;0;_ Caption=Fax	
Contractor CFName	Text(15)	Contractor contact's 1st name.	Caption=Contact First Name	
Contractor CLName	Text(15)	Contractor contact's last name.	Caption=Contact Last Name	
Comments	Memo	Comments or notes on this contractor.		

The States Table

The States table (see Table A.9) is a reference table, a list of state codes and corresponding state names. The States table has an implied 1:M relationship with any table that contains an address (city, state, zip) or otherwise needs to decode the state code. The States table doesn't appear in the Relationships window.

Table A.9   refState

Field Name	Data Type	Description	Field Properties	Lookup
StateCode	Text(2)	Two-letter code for each state.	Format=> Caption=State Code Required=Yes Indexed=Yes (No Duplicates)	
StateName	Text(50)	Long name for each state.	Caption=State Long Name	

The Team Table

The Team table (see Table A.10) is a reference table, a list of team members and phone numbers. Team members, in this context, are defined as employees of REA. This reference list is a list of all employees who can be assigned to a project team. In the conceptual model the Team table has a 1:M relationship with the Team Member table, which means that a person in the Team list can be involved in one or more project teams. However, due to operational constraints inherent with many-to-many relationships, as in the following example:

```
(refTeam ------>>  tblTeamMember <<----- tblProject)
```

The Team table will not appear in the Relationships window.

Table A.10	refTeam			
Field Name	**Data Type**	**Description**	**Field Properties**	**Lookup**
TMbrCode	Text(12)	Pkey, code assigned to each person who may be a team member.	Caption=Team Member Code Required=Yes Indexed=Yes (No Duplicates)	
TMbrFName	Text(15)	Team member first name.	Caption=Team Member First Name	
TMbrLName	Text(15)	Team member last name.	Caption=Team Member Last Name	
TMbrOfficePhone	Text(20)	Team member office phone number.	Input Mask=!\(999") "000\-0000;0;_ Caption=Office Phone	
Comments	Memo	Comments or notes about this team member.		

The Team Member Table

The Team Member table (see Table A.11) contains information about the people who are assigned to a project team, occupying positions such as project manager, land agent, attorney, and so on. The Team Member table has an M:1 relationship with the Project table, which means that one or more team members exist for each project. This relationship is dependent—the Team Member records cannot exist without an associated Project record. In the Relationships window, these two tables are connected as 1:M, tblProject to tblTeamMember, Enforce Referential Integrity on, Cascade Update on, Cascade Delete on, Join type 2 (left outer).

Table A.11   tblTeamMember

Field Name	Data Type	Description	Field Properties	Lookup
ProjectID	Number (long integer)	Part of primary key, links this team member to a project.	Caption= Project# Required=Yes Indexed=Yes (No Duplicates)	
TeamMemberCode	Text(12)	Part of primary key, code (usually logon ID) assigned to each.	Caption= Member Code Required=Yes Indexed=Yes (No Duplicates)	Display Control=Combo Box Row Source Type =Table/Query Row Source =refTeam Bound Column=1 Column Count=4 Limit To List=No
TeamPosition	Text(30)	Position this team member holds on the team. Select from list.	Caption= Position Required=Yes Indexed=Yes (No Duplicates)	Display Control =Combo Box Row Source Type =Value List Row Source=; Project Manager; Assistant Project Manager; Land Agent; Attorney; Real Estate Attorney; Environmental Attorney Bound Column=1 Column Count=1 Limit To List=No

The Archaeology, Environmental, and Wetlands Table

This table is a place to record issues regarding archaeological findings, environmental issues, wetlands penetration, and even endangered species threats for each project (see Table A.12). There is a 1:1 relationship between the Archaeology, Environment, and Wetlands table and the Project table. The rows in this table are dependent for their existence on an associated Project—without a project there would be no issues about archaeology, environment, or wetlands—and is related to the Project table in a 1:1 relationship. In the Relationships window, these two tables are connected as 1:1, Enforce Referential Integrity on, Cascade Update and Cascade Delete on, Join type 2 (left outer).

Table A.12   tblArchEnvironWetland

Field Name	Data Type	Description	Field Properties	Lookup
ProjectID	Number (long integer)	Primary key, links back to tblProject.	Caption= Project# Required=Yes Indexed=Yes (No Duplicates)	
Comments	Memo	Comment field, free-form text, Shift+Enter to start new line.		
Summary	Memo	Summary field, free-form text, Shift+Enter to start new line.	Caption= Summary/ Status	
ExpComplDate	Date/Time	Expected completion date. Use mm/dd/yy format for this field.	Format=Short Date Input Mask= 99/99/00;0;_ Caption=Expected Completion Date	
DateCompleted	Date/Time	Date this task was completed. Use mm/dd/yy format for this field.	Format=Short Date Input Mask= 99/99/00;0;_ Caption=Date Completed	
LastUpdate	Date/Time	Timestamp of last change made to this record in this table. Use mm/dd/yy format for this field.	Format=General Date Caption= Last Update	
ByWhom	Text(12)	Who made the change?	Caption=By Whom	

The Road & Traffic, Utilities, and Drainage Table

In this table, you record information about roads and traffic patterns, utilities, and drainage issues for each project (see Table A.13). A 1:1 relationship exists between the

Road & Traffic, Utilities, and Drainage table and the Project table. The rows in this table are dependent for their existence on an associated Project—without a project, there can be no issues about roads and traffic or utilities and drainage—and is related to the Project table in a 1:1 relationship. In the Relationships window, these two tables are connected as 1:1, Enforce Referential Integrity on, Cascade Update and Cascade Delete on, Join type 2 (left outer).

Table A.13   tblRoadTrafficUtilDrain

Field Name	Data Type	Description	Field Properties	Lookup
ProjectID	Number (long integer)	Primary key, links back to tblProject.	Caption= Project# Required=Yes Indexed=Yes (No Duplicates)	
Comments	Memo	Comment field, free-form text, Shift+Enter to start new line.		
Summary	Memo	Summary field, free-form text, Shift+Enter to start new line.	Caption= Summary/ Status	
ExpComplDate	Date/Time	Expected completion date. Use mm/dd/yy format for this field.	Format=Short Date Input Mask= 99/99/00;0;_ Caption=Expected Completion Date	
DateCompleted	Date/Time	Date this task was completed. Use mm/dd/yy format for this field.	Format=Short Date Input Mask= 99/99/00;0;_ Caption=Date Completed	
LastUpdate	Date/Time	Timestamp of last change made to this record in this table. Use mm/dd/yy format for this field.	Format=General Date Caption= Last Update	
ByWhom	Text(12)	Who made the change?	Caption=By Whom	

The Title and Survey Table

This table is a place to record information regarding the title and survey for each project (see Table A.14). A 1:1 relationship exists between the Title and Survey table and the Project table. The rows in this table are dependent on an associated Project for their existence—without a project there can be no issues about title and survey—and is related to the Project table in a 1:1 relationship. In the Relationships window, these two tables are connected as 1:1, Enforce Referential Integrity on, Cascade Update and Cascade Delete on, Join type 2 (left outer).

Table A.14   tblTitleSurvey

Field Name	Data Type	Description	Field Properties	Lookup
ProjectID	Number (long integer)	Primary key, links back to tblProject.	Caption= Project# Required=Yes Indexed=Yes (No Duplicates)	
Comments	Memo	Comment field, free-form text, Shift+Enter to start new line.		
Summary	Memo	Summary field, free-form text, Shift+Enter to start new line.	Caption= Summary/ Status	
ExpComplDate	Date/Time	Expected completion date. Use mm/dd/yy format for this field.	Format=Short Date Input Mask= 99/99/00;0;_ Caption=Expected Completion Date	
DateCompleted	Date/Time	Date this task was completed. Use mm/dd/yy format for this field.	Format=Short Date Input Mask= 99/99/00;0;_ Caption=Date Completed	
LastUpdate	Date/Time	Timestamp of last change made to this record in this table. Use mm/dd/yy format for this field.	Format=General Date Caption= Last Update	
ByWhom	Text(12)	Who made the change?	Caption=By Whom	

The WinHelp V4 Macros

WinHelp provides the Windows Help programmer with a set of macros that enable him or her to control and customize the functionality of the on-line Help systems. WinHelp V4, the new 32-bit compiler/Help Workshop combination that coordinates with Windows 95 and Windows NT 3.51, has enhanced the suite of macros by adding 26 new ones to the family.

The macros are broken down by the following types:

- Button
- Menu
- Linking
- Window
- Functionality (keyboard and auxiliary)
- Text-marker

Macro Syntax

Macro syntax is fairly straightforward. Macros are composed of two parts—the macro name and the arguments, or parameters, which are enclosed in parentheses, as in the following example:

```
MacroName([argument_1, argument_2, ..., argument_n])
```

Here, the *MacroName* is not case-sensitive, and arguments must be separated by commas.

Arguments can be text strings or numbers. If the value of the final argument(s) is 0 or " ", this argument can be omitted.

Even if a macro has no arguments, you still must include the parentheses.

If you create a custom macro, the naming convention dictates that it begin with an alpha character, followed by any combination of alpha characters, numbers, or the underscore (_).

You can build macro strings, separating macros with either a colon (:) or a semicolon (;). WinHelp runs the macros in sequence.

The backslash (\) is the macro escape character, which allows you to use quotes, for example, as part of a macro argument. If you need to use a literal backslash, as in a path statement, you must double the backslash (\\) for every level of macro nesting. You can instead use the forward slash (/) to indicate path specifications.

Implementing Macros

You can implement your macros in the following ways:

- Place them in the Project (.HPJ) file so that when the user opens Help, they are automatically executed
- Place them in the topic footnote so that they run when the user displays the topic
- Place them in the Contents (.CNT) file so they are run when the user clicks the page icon
- Place them behind menu items or buttons on the menu bar
- Place them behind topic hotspots
- Call them from an external program

A brief description of each of the macros is presented here, grouped by category. You can find enhanced documentation and a full description of each macro in the on-line Help file for the Microsoft Help Workshop, HCW.HLP.

> **Tip**
>
> If you are running Windows NT 3.51 and cannot directly run HCW.HLP, then access it through the Help Workshop. Double-click HCW.EXE in File Manager and go to the on-line Help in the application itself.

Button Macros

Button macros enable the WinHelp programmer to access, create, or modify buttons, as described in the following table:

Macro Name	Description
Back	Displays the previous topic in the Back list
BrowseButtons	Adds the Browse Buttons to the Help Button Bar
ChangeButtonBinding	Changes the assigned function of a Help button
ChangeEnable	Assigns a macro to a navigation button bar and enables that button (equivalent to calling both ChangeButtonBinding and EnableButton)

VII

Macro Name	Description
Contents	Displays the Contents tab or "home" topic of the current Help file
CreateButton	Creates a new button and adds it to the Button Bar
DestroyButton	Removes a button from the Button Bar
DisableButton	Disables a button on the Button Bar
EnableButton	Enables a disabled button on the Button Bar
EndMPrint	Dismisses the printing message box and ends the printing of multiple topics
Finder	Displays the Help Topics dialog box, in its last state
History	Displays the history list
InitMPrint	Begins printing multiple topics by presenting the Print dialog box
Menu	Displays the Context menu usually accessed by the right mouse button
Next	Displays the next topic in a browse sequence
Prev	Displays the previous topic in a browse sequence
Search	Displays the Search Index
SetContents	Designates a specific topic as the Contents topic

Menu Macros

Menu macros enable the WinHelp programmer to access, create, or modify menus and menu items, as described in the following table:

Macro Name	Description
About	Displays the About dialog box
Annotate	Displays the Annotate dialog box
AppendItem	Appends a menu item to the end of a custom menu
BookmarkDefine	Displays the Bookmark Define dialog box
BookmarkMore	Displays the Bookmark dialog box
ChangeItemBinding	Changes the assigned function of a menu item
CheckItem	Displays a check mark next to a menu item
CopyTopic	Copies the current topic to the Clipboard
DeleteItem	Removes a menu item from a menu
DisableItem	Disables a menu item
EnableItem	Enables a disabled menu item
Exit	Exits the WinHelp program

(continues)

(continued)

Macro Name	Description
ExtAbleItem	Enables a custom menu item that was added with the ExtInsertItem macro
ExtInsertItem	Inserts a menu item at a given position on a menu, in a given state
ExtInsertMenu	Inserts a new menu to the WinHelp menu bar, in a given state
FileOpen	Displays the Open dialog box
FloatingMenu	Displays a floating menu with author-specified items at the current mouse position
HelpOn	Displays the How to Use Help file
InsertItem	Inserts a menu item at a given position within a menu
InsertMenu	Adds a new menu to the WinHelp menu bar
Print	Sends the current topic to the default printer
ResetMenu	Resets the WinHelp menu bar and menus to their default states
UncheckItem	Removes a check mark from a menu item

Linking Macros

Linking macros define hypertext links. See the following table for details:

Macro Name	Description
Alink	Jumps to the topics that contain the specified A-keywords
JumpContents	Jumps to the contents topic of a specific WinHelp file
JunpContext	Jumps to the topic with a specific context number
JumpHash	Jumps to the topic with a specific hash number
JumpHelpOn	Jumps to the contents topic of the How to Use Help file
JumpID	Jumps to the topic with a specific topic ID
JumpKeyword	Jumps to the topic that contains a specified K-keyword
Klink	Jumps to the topics that contain the specified K-keywords
PopupContext	Displays the topic with a specific context number in a pop-up window
PopupHash	Displays the topic with a specific hash code in a pop-up window
PopupId	Displays the topic with a specific topic ID in a pop-up window
UpdateWindow	Jumps to the specified topic in the specified window, and then returns the focus to the window that called the macro

Window Macros

Window macros enable the WinHelp programmer to control and modify the WinHelp windows. The following table describes these macros:

Macro Name	Description
CloseSecondarys	Closes all but the current secondary WinHelp windows
CloseWindow	Closes the main or secondary WinHelp window
FocusWindow	Changes the focus to a specific WinHelp window
Generate	Sends a message to the currently active WinHelp window
WinHelpOnTop	Places all WinHelp windows on top of other windows
NoShow	Prevents the WinHelp window from appearing
PositionWindow	Sets the size and position of a WinHelp window
SetPopupColor	Sets the background color of pop-up windows

Functionality Macros

Functionality macros add functionality to your WinHelp files. For details on these macros, see the following table:

Macro Name	Description
AddAccelerator	Assigns an accelerator key to a WinHelp macro
Compare	Runs a second instance of WinHelp next to the first
ControlPanel	Opens a specific tab on a dialog box in the Control Panel program
ExecFile	Opens a file and runs the program associated with the file
ExecProgram	Starts a program
FileExist	Checks to see whether a specified file exists on a user's computer
Flush	Forces WinHelp to process all pending messages, including previously called macros
IsBook	Determines if WinHelp is being run as a stand-alone system (as a book), or if it is being run from a program
MPrintHash	Prints a topic, identified by a specific hash number
MPrintID	Prints a topic, identified by a specific topic ID
RegisterRoutine	Registers a function within a DLL as a WinHelp macro
RemoveAccelerator	Removes an accelerator key from a WinHelp macro
ShellExecute	Opens or prints the specified file

(continues)

(continued)

Macro Name	Description
ShortCut	Runs a program if it isn't already running, and sends it a WM_COMMAND message with the specified wParam and lParam values
Tcard	Sends a message to the program that is invoking WinHelp as a training card
Test	Enables an author or a program to test a WinHelp file
TestALink	Tests whether an ALink macro has an effective link to at least one topic
TestKLink	Tests whether a KLink macro has an effective link to at least one topic

Text-Marker Macros

Text-marker macros enable the WinHelp programmer to set and manage placeholder and navigation markers within a WinHelp file. These macros are described in the following table.

Macro Name	Description
DeleteMark	Removes a marker added by SaveMark
GotoMark	Jumps to a marker set by SaveMark
IfThen	Runs a Help macro if a given marker exists
IfThenElse	Runs one of two macros if a given marker exists
IsMark	Tests whether a marker set by SaveMark exists
IsNotMark	Tests to see if a marker set by SaveMark does not exist
Not	Reserves the result returned by IsMark
SaveMark	Saves a marker for the current topic and WinHelp file

Index

Symbols

A

Complete and Return this Card
for a *FREE* Computer Book Catalog

Thank you for purchasing this book! You have purchased a superior computer book written expressly for your needs. To continue to provide the kind of up-to-date, pertinent coverage you've come to expect from us, we need to hear from you. Please take a minute to complete and return this self-addressed, postage-paid form. In return, we'll send you a free catalog of all our computer books on topics ranging from word processing to programming and the internet.

Mr. ☐   Mrs. ☐   Ms. ☐   Dr. ☐

Name (first) ☐☐☐☐☐☐☐☐☐☐   (M.I.) ☐   (last) ☐☐☐☐☐☐☐☐☐☐☐☐☐☐☐

Address ☐☐☐☐☐☐☐☐☐☐☐☐☐☐☐☐☐☐☐☐☐☐☐☐☐☐☐☐☐

☐☐☐☐☐☐☐☐☐☐☐☐☐☐☐☐☐☐☐☐☐☐☐☐☐☐☐☐☐

City ☐☐☐☐☐☐☐☐☐☐☐☐   State ☐☐   Zip ☐☐☐☐☐ ☐☐☐☐

Phone ☐☐☐ ☐☐☐ ☐☐☐☐   Fax ☐☐☐ ☐☐☐ ☐☐☐☐

Company Name ☐☐☐☐☐☐☐☐☐☐☐☐☐☐☐☐☐☐☐☐☐☐☐☐☐☐

E-mail address ☐☐☐☐☐☐☐☐☐☐☐☐☐☐☐☐☐☐☐☐☐☐☐☐☐☐

1. Please check at least (3) influencing factors for purchasing this book.

Front or back cover information on book .... ☐
Special approach to the content .... ☐
Completeness of content .... ☐
Author's reputation .... ☐
Publisher's reputation .... ☐
Book cover design or layout .... ☐
Index or table of contents of book .... ☐
Price of book .... ☐
Special effects, graphics, illustrations .... ☐
Other (Please specify): _____ ☐

2. How did you first learn about this book?

Saw in Macmillan Computer Publishing catalog .... ☐
Recommended by store personnel .... ☐
Saw the book on bookshelf at store .... ☐
Recommended by a friend .... ☐
Received advertisement in the mail .... ☐
Saw an advertisement in: _____ ☐
Read book review in: _____ ☐
Other (Please specify): _____ ☐

3. How many computer books have you purchased in the last six months?

This book only .... ☐   3 to 5 books .... ☐
2 books .... ☐   More than 5 .... ☐

4. Where did you purchase this book?

Bookstore .... ☐
Computer Store .... ☐
Consumer Electronics Store .... ☐
Department Store .... ☐
Office Club .... ☐
Warehouse Club .... ☐
Mail Order .... ☐
Direct from Publisher .... ☐
Internet site .... ☐
Other (Please specify): _____ ☐

5. How long have you been using a computer?

☐ Less than 6 months   ☐ 6 months to a year
☐ 1 to 3 years   ☐ More than 3 years

6. What is your level of experience with personal computers and with the subject of this book?

	With PCs	With subject of book
New	☐	☐
Casual	☐	☐
Accomplished	☐	☐
Expert	☐	☐

Source Code ISBN: 0-7897-0366-1

7. Which of the following best describes your job title?

Administrative Assistant ☐
Coordinator ☐
Manager/Supervisor ☐
Director ☐
Vice President ☐
President/CEO/COO ☐
Lawyer/Doctor/Medical Professional ☐
Teacher/Educator/Trainer ☐
Engineer/Technician ☐
Consultant ☐
Not employed/Student/Retired ☐
Other (Please specify): _____ ☐

8. Which of the following best describes the area of the company your job title falls under?

Accounting ☐
Engineering ☐
Manufacturing ☐
Operations ☐
Marketing ☐
Sales ☐
Other (Please specify): _____ ☐

9. What is your age?

Under 20 ☐
21-29 ☐
30-39 ☐
40-49 ☐
50-59 ☐
60-over ☐

10. Are you:

Male ☐
Female ☐

11. Which computer publications do you read regularly? (Please list)

_____
_____
_____
_____
_____
_____
_____
_____
_____
_____

Comments: _____
_____
_____

Fold here and scotch-tape to mail.

A VIACOM SERVICE

The Information SuperLibrary™

Bookstore

Search

What's New

Reference

Software

Newsletter

Company Overviews

Yellow Pages

Internet Starter Kit

HTML Workshop

Win a Free T-Shirt!

Macmillan Computer Publishing

Site Map

Talk to Us

CHECK OUT THE BOOKS IN THIS LIBRARY.

You'll find thousands of shareware files and over 1600 computer books designed for both technowizards and technophobes. You can browse through 700 sample chapters, get the latest news on the Net, and find just about anything using our massive search directories.

All Macmillan Computer Publishing books are available at your local bookstore.

We're open 24-hours a day, 365 days a year.

You don't need a card.

We don't charge fines.

And you can be as **LOUD** as you want.

The Information SuperLibrary
http://www.mcp.com/mcp/ ftp.mcp.com

Licensing Agreement

By opening this package, you are agreeing to be bound by the following: